THE ANNALS
OF
AMERICA

THE ANNALS OF AMERICA

Volume 2

1755 - 1783

Resistance and Revolution

ENCYCLOPÆDIA BRITANNICA, INC.

Chicago London New Delhi Paris Sydney Taipei Tokyo Seoul

The editors wish to express their gratitude for permission to reprint
material from the following sources:

The Arthur H. Clark Company for Selection 9 from *A
Documentary History of American Industrial Society*, ed.
by John R. Commons *et al.*

Harvard University Press for Selection 89, from *Adams Family Correspondence*, ed. by Lyman H. Butterfield *et al.*, Cambridge, Mass.: The Belknap Press of
Harvard University Press, Copyright 1963 by Massachusetts Historical Society.

Princeton University Press and the American Philosophical Society for Selections 40 and 116, from *Letters of Benjamin Rush*, ed. by I. H. Butterfield, Vol. I,
Copyright 1951 by the American Philosophical Society.

University of North Carolina and The Institute of Early American History and Culture for Selection 39,
from *The Carolina Back-country on the Eve of the Revolution: The Journal and Other Writings of Charles
Woodmason, Anglican Itinerant*, ed. by Richard J.
Hooker.

Yale University Press for Selections 41, 45, 46, 53,
from *The Correspondence of General Thomas Gage with
the Secretaries of State 1763-1775*, ed. by Clarence Ed-
win Carter, Vol. I.

CODED SOURCES IN THIS VOLUME

Archives	*American Archives: Fourth Series Containing a Documentary History of the English Colonies in North America from the King's Message to Parliament of March 7, 1774, to the Declaration of Independence by the United States.* Edited by Peter Force. In 6 vols. Washington, 1837-1846. The six series of this collection contain documents dating from *circa* 1600 to 1787.
Butterfield	*Letters of Benjamin Rush.* Edited by L. H. Butterfield. In 2 vols. covering the years 1761-1813. Princeton, 1951.
Carter	*The Correspondence of General Thomas Gage with the Secretaries of State 1763-1775.* Edited by Clarence E. Carter. In 2 vols. New Haven, 1931-1933.
C. F. Adams	*The Works of John Adams, Second President of the United States, with a Life of the Author.* Edited by Charles Francis Adams. In 10 vols. Boston, 1850-1856.
Commons	*A Documentary History of American Industrial Society.* Edited by John R. Commons *et al.* In 10 vols. Cleveland, 1910-1911.
Ford	*The Writings of Thomas Jefferson.* Edited by Paul L. Ford. In 10 vols. New York and London, 1892-1899.
H. A. Washington	*The Writings of Thomas Jefferson: Being his Autobiography, Correspondence, Reports, Messages, Addresses and Other Writings, Official and Private.* Edited by H. A. Washington. In 9 vols. Washington, 1853-1854. Vol. 8, Philadelphia, 1871.
J. C. Hamilton	*The Works of Alexander Hamilton, etc., etc.* Edited by John C. Hamilton. In 7 vols. New York, 1850-1851.
Johnston	*The Correspondence and Public Papers of John Jay.* Edited by Henry P. Johnston. In 4 vols. New York, 1890-1893.
Journals	*Journals of the American Congress: from 1774 to 1788.* In 4 vols. Washington, 1823.
MHSC	*Collections, Massachusetts Historical Society.* Cambridge and Boston, 1795 *et seq.*
MHSP	*Proceedings of the Massachusetts Historical Society.* Boston, 1791 *et seq.*

Niles	*Principles and Acts of the Revolution in America.* Edited by Hezekiah Niles. Centennial edition, New York, 1876 (first published Baltimore, 1822).
OSL	*Old South Leaflets.* Published by the Directors of the Old South Work, Old South Meeting House. In 8 vols. (Documents 1-200). Boston, n.d.
Pickering	*The Statutes at Large* [of Great Britain]. Volumes 1-46 edited by Danby Pickering. Cambridge (England), various dates.
Poore	*The Federal and State Constitutions, Colonial Charters, and Other Organic Laws of the United States.* Edited by B. P. Poore. In 2 vols. Washington, 1877.
Sparks	*The Works of Benjamin Franklin, etc., etc.* Edited by Jared Sparks. In 10 vols. Boston, 1836-1840.
Thorpe	*The Federal and State Constitutions, Colonial Charters, and Other Organic Laws of the States, Territories, and Colonies now or Heretofore Forming the United States of America.* Edited by Francis N. Thorpe. In 7 vols. Washington, 1909.
Works [of Benjamin Franklin]	*The Complete Works in Philosophy, Politics, and Morals of the Late Dr. Benjamin Franklin, now First collected and Arranged, with Memoirs of his Early Life, written by Himself.* 2nd edition in 3 vols. London, n.d.

Contents

1775

1776

1782

1783

RESISTANCE AND REVOLUTION

In Pictures

As British and French settlements expanded, conflict was inevitable,
particularly in frontier areas. This, combined with the international
rivalry of the two empires, led to the outbreak of hostilities in America.

The Indians had been on the whole loyal to the French, and after the
English victory in the war came the task of winning them over
to make the lands between the Appalachians and the
Mississippi safe for English settlement.

The work of professional artists gained an increasing colonial
market as the caliber of the painters improved and daily life adopted
more of the old world refinements. Two major painters,
Benjamin West and John Singleton Copley, achieved recognition
in America and later moved to England.

Rule and Rebellion 227-239

Neglected for almost a century by the British government, the
colonies were "rediscovered" when it was necessary to raise money
to pay for the war with France. This sudden pressure on
the colonies was met by strong resistance.

The Revolutionary War 463-481

Failing to gain sympathy in Parliament for their position
regarding colonial taxation, leaders in America began to organize for
independence. After a few early victories came a series of setbacks,
but able military leaders and French support combined to turn the tide.

The Ingredients for a New Nation 513-529

The physical separation of America from Europe gave impetus to
the growth of a unique culture. The colonies did not lack for
raw materials or ingenuity when the need for local manufactures arose.
Before long the rustic character of the cities was replaced by a look of
permanence and taste. Inherited values resulted in emphasis
on education, both in schools and in the home.

Colonial Architecture 593-597

Surviving buildings from the colonial period reflect the influence
of all the European countries that established colonies in
America, even though many of these were short lived. The buildings
help point out the differences in ways of living in the different colonies.

1755

1.

George Washington: On Braddock's Defeat

The French and Indian War, as the Americans called it, was a phase, and perhaps the most important one, of a global conflict (called by some historians the Seven Years' War, by others the Great War for the Empire) between France and Britain, fought over the issue of which empire would control the future of the North American continent. In the American colonies, the war broke out in the Pennsylvania wilderness on May 28, 1754, when George Washington, aged twenty-two, attacked a small French force at Great Meadows. Washington was forced to surrender on July 3, but this was only a minor skirmish; the war began in earnest the following year, when General Edward Braddock attempted to capture Fort Duquesne, which the French had recently built on the site of what is now Pittsburgh. Braddock's regulars — Colonel Washington was a member of the general's staff — had chopped their way westward for over a month through dense forest. On July 9, 1755, they were surprised by a small force (mostly Indians) seven miles from the fort that was their objective. The ensuing Battle of the Monongahela ended in a complete rout of the British; Braddock was killed, and Colonel Thomas Dunbar, the new commander, led the survivors — only about 1,500 out of an original 2,500 — back to Philadelphia. Despite Braddock's crushing defeat, the bravery of the "Virginia blues" was caught up in the postwar myth of the vast superiority of the quick-witted American farmer-soldier over the British regular. In the following letter, written by Washington to his mother on July 18, Washington described the battle, and told her of his near escape from death.

Source: *The Writings of George Washington*, John C. Fitzpatrick, ed., Vol. I, Washington, 1931, pp. 150-152.

Honored Madam:

As I doubt not but you have heard of our defeat, and perhaps have it represented in a worse light (if possible) than it deserves, I have taken this earliest opportunity to give you some account of the engagement as it happened, within seven miles of the French fort, on Wednesday, the 9th inst.

We marched on to that place without any considerable loss, having only now and then a straggler picked up by the Indian scouts of the French. When we came there, we were attacked by a body of French and Indians, whose number (I am certain) did not exceed 300 men. Ours consisted of about 1,300 well-armed troops, chiefly of the English soldiers, who were struck with such a panic that they behaved with more cowardice than it is possible to conceive. The officers behaved gallantly in order to encourage their men, for which they suffered greatly, there being near 60 killed and wounded — a large proportion out of the number we had!

The Virginia troops showed a good deal of bravery, and were near all killed; for I believe out of three companies that were there, there are scarce 30 men left alive. Captain Peyrouny and all his officers, down to a corporal, were killed; Captain Polson shared near as hard a fate, for only one of his was left. In short, the dastardly behavior of those they call regulars exposed all others that were inclined to do their duty to almost certain death; and, at last, in despite of all the efforts of the officers to the contrary, they broke and ran as sheep pursued by dogs; and it was impossible to rally them.

The general was wounded; of which he died three days after. Sir Peter Halket was killed in the field, where died many other brave officers. I luckily escaped without a wound, though I had four bullets through my coat, and two horses shot under me. Captains Orme and Morris, two of the general's aides de camp, were wounded early in the engagement, which rendered the duty hard upon me, as I was the only person then left to distribute the general's orders; which I was scarcely able to do as I was not half recovered from a violent illness that confined me to my bed and a wagon for above ten days.

I am still in a weak and feeble condition; which induces me to halt here two or three days in hopes of recovering a little strength to enable me to proceed homeward; from whence I fear I shall not be able to stir till toward September, so that I shall not have the pleasure of seeing you till then, unless it be in Fairfax. . . .

P.S. We had about 300 men killed and as many, and more, wounded.

COUPE ET PLAN D'UN FORT

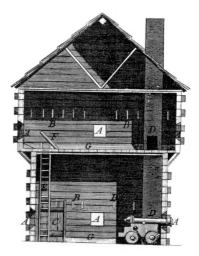

Renvois

A Embrasures
B Meurtrières
C Porte
D Cheminées
E { Echelle de Communication à l'Etage Supérieure
F Trappe
G { Platte forme qui sert de Parapet et sur laquelle dorment les Soldats

1756

2.

GOTTLIEB MITTELBERGER: Journey to Pennsylvania

African slaves were not the only bound servants brought to the American colonies. It has been estimated that at least half of the immigrants who arrived during the colonial period were contract laborers — obligated to an employer for a term of years in return for the cost of their transportation. Nor did all of them have even the security, such as it was, of a contract, or "indenture." German immigrants of the middle of the eighteenth century were known simply as "redemptioners." Collected by emigrant agents from among the poor of Baden, Württemberg, and the Palatinate, they were herded aboard ship through promises, threats, and trickery of various kinds, to be sold off to colonial purchasers on whatever terms could be got. They went chiefly to Pennsylvania, Maryland, Virginia, and South Carolina, where eventually they joined the ranks of small back country farmers, westward-wandering pioneers, and other marginalized groups. The sufferings of these people, who on the whole were mercilessly exploited, were recounted by Gottlieb Mittelberger, a native of Württemberg, who arrived in Philadelphia in 1750 and returned to his homeland four years later. There, in 1756, he published an indictment of the redemption system, part of which, dealing with the transportation and sale of his countrymen, is reprinted here.

Source: *Journey to Pennsylvania in the Year 1750 and Return to Germany in the Year 1754, etc., etc.,* Philadelphia, 1898, pp. 24-32.

AT LENGTH, when, after a long and tedious voyage, the ships come in sight of land, so that the promontories can be seen, which the people were so eager and anxious to see, all creep from below on deck to see the land from afar, and they weep for joy, and pray and sing, thanking and praising God. The sight of the land makes the people on board the ship, especially the sick and the half-dead, alive again, so that their hearts leap within them; they shout and rejoice and are content to bear their misery in patience, in the hope that they may soon reach the land in safety. But alas!

When the ships have landed at Philadelphia after their long voyage, no one is permitted to leave them except those who pay for their passage or can give good security;

the others, who cannot pay, must remain on board the ships till they are purchased and are released from the ships by their purchasers. The sick always fare the worst, for the healthy are naturally preferred and purchased first; and so the sick and wretched must often remain on board in front of the city for two or three weeks and frequently die, whereas many a one, if he could pay his debt and were permitted to leave the ship immediately, might recover and remain alive.

Before I describe how this traffic in human flesh is conducted, I must mention how much the journey to Philadelphia or Pennsylvania costs.

A person over ten years pays for the passage from Rotterdam to Philadelphia £ 10, or 60 florins. Children from five to ten years pay half-price, £ 5 or 30 florins. All children under five years are free. For these prices the passengers are conveyed to Philadelphia and, as long as they are at sea, provided with food, though with very poor. . . .

But this is only the sea passage; the other costs on land, from home to Rotterdam, including the passage on the Rhine, are at least 40 florins, no matter how economically one may live. No account is here taken of extraordinary contingencies. I may safely assert that, with the greatest economy, many passengers have spent 200 florins from home to Philadelphia.

The sale of human beings in the market on board the ship is carried on thus: Every day Englishmen, Dutchmen, and High-German people come from the city of Philadelphia and other places, in part from a great distance, say twenty, thirty, or forty hours away, and go on board the newly arrived ship that has brought and offers for sale passengers from Europe, and select among the healthy persons such as they deem suitable for their business, and bargain with them how long they will serve for their passage money, which most of them

are still in debt for. When they have come to an agreement, it happens that adult persons bind themselves in writing to serve three, four, five, or six years for the amount due by them, according to their age and strength. But very young people, from ten to fifteen years, must serve till they are twenty-one years old.

Many parents must sell and trade away their children like so many head of cattle, for if their children take the debt upon themselves, the parents can leave the ship free and unrestrained; but as the parents often do not know where and to what people their children are going, it often happens that such parents and children, after leaving the ship, do not see each other again for many years, perhaps no more in all their lives.

When people arrive who cannot make themselves free but have children under five years, the parents cannot free themselves by them; for such children must be given to somebody, without compensation, to be brought up, and they must serve for their bringing up till they are twenty-one years old. Children from five to ten years, who pay half-price for their passage, viz., 30 florins, must likewise serve for it till they are twenty-one years of age. They cannot, therefore, redeem their parents by taking the debt of the latter upon themselves. But children above ten years can take part of their parents' debt upon themselves.

A woman must stand for her husband if he arrives sick, and, in like manner, a man for his sick wife, and take the debt upon herself or himself, and thus serve five to six years, not alone for his or her own debt but also for that of the sick husband or wife. But if both are sick, such persons are sent from the ship to the sick-house [hospital], but not until it appears probable that they will find no purchasers. As soon as they are well again they must serve for their passage or pay if they have means.

It often happens that whole families —

husband, wife, and children — are separated by being sold to different purchasers, especially when they have not paid any part of their passage money.

When a husband or wife has died at sea, when the ship has made more than half of her trip, the survivor must pay or serve, not only for himself or herself but also for the deceased.

When both parents have died over halfway at sea, their children, especially when they are young and have nothing to pawn or to pay, must stand for their own and their parents' passage, and serve till they are twenty-one years old. When one has served his or her term, he or she is entitled to a new suit of clothes at parting; and if it has been so stipulated, a man gets, in addition, a horse; a woman, a cow.

When a serf has an opportunity to marry in this country, he or she must pay for each year which he or she would have yet to serve, £5 to £6. But many a one who has thus purchased and paid for his bride has subsequently repented his bargain, so that he would gladly have returned his exorbitantly dear ware and lost the money besides.

If someone in this country runs away from his master who has treated him harshly, he cannot get far. Good provision has been made for such cases, so that a runaway is soon recovered. He who detains or returns a deserter receives a good reward.

If such a runaway has been away from his master one day, he must serve for it as a punishment a week, for a week a month, and for a month half a year. But if the master will not keep the runaway after he has got him back, he may sell him for so many years as he would have to serve him yet.

Work and labor in this new and wild land are very hard and manifold, and many a one who came there in his old age must work very hard to his end for his bread. I will not speak of young people. Work mostly consists in cutting wood, felling oak

trees, rooting out, or, as they say there, clearing large tracts of forest. Such forests, being cleared, are then laid out for fields and meadows. From the best hewn wood, fences are made around the new fields; for, there, all meadows, orchards, and fruit fields, are surrounded and fenced in with planks made of thickly split wood, laid one above the other, as in zigzag lines; and, within such enclosures, horses, cattle, and sheep are permitted to graze.

Our Europeans, who are purchased, must always work hard, for new fields are constantly laid out; and so they learn that stumps of oak trees are in America certainly as hard as in Germany. In this hot land they fully experience in their own persons what God has imposed on man for his sin and disobedience; for in Genesis we read the words: "In the sweat of thy brow shalt thou eat bread." Who, therefore, wishes to earn his bread in a Christian and honest way, and cannot earn it in his fatherland otherwise than by the work of his hands, let him do so in his own country, and not in America; for he will not fare better in America. However hard he may be compelled to work in his fatherland, he will surely find it quite as hard, if not harder, in the new country.

Besides, there is not only the long and arduous journey lasting half a year, during which he has to suffer more than with the hardest work; he has also spent about 200 florins which no one will refund to him. If he has so much money, it will slip out of his hands; if he has it not, he must work his debt off as a slave and poor serf. Therefore, let everyone stay in his own country and support himself and his family honestly. Besides, I say that those who suffer themselves to be persuaded and enticed away by the man-thieves are very foolish if they believe that roasted pigeons will fly into their mouths in America or Pennsylvania without their working for them.

How miserably and wretchedly so many

thousand German families have fared since they lost all their cash means in consequence of the long and tedious journey; because many of them died miserably and were thrown into the water; because, on account of their great poverty, most of these families after reaching the land are separated from each other and sold far away from each other, the young and the old. And the saddest of all this is that parents must generally give away their minor children without receiving a compensation for them; inasmuch as such children never see or meet their fathers, mothers, brothers, or sisters again, and as many of them are not raised in any Christian faith by the people to whom they are given; for there are many doctrines of faith and sects in Pennsylvania which cannot all be enumerated, because many a one will not confess to what faith he belongs.

Besides, there are many hundreds of adult persons who have not been and do not even wish to be baptized. There are many who think nothing of the sacraments and the Holy Bible, nor even of God and His word. Many do not even believe that there is a true God and devil, a heaven and a hell, salvation and damnation, a resurrection of the dead, a judgment and an eternal life; they believe that all one can see is natural; for in Pennsylvania everyone may not only believe what he will but he may even say it freely and openly.

Consequently, when young persons, not yet grounded in religion, come to serve for many years with such free thinkers and infidels and are not sent to any church or school by such people, especially when they live far from any school or church — thus it happens that such innocent souls come to no true divine recognition and grow up like heathens and Indians.

1756 - 1758

3.

JOHN WOOLMAN: Journal Entries on Slavery, Taxation, and the Military

John Woolman was the most influential American Quaker of his day. A tailor by trade, and always prosperous in his affairs, he cared little for business but devoted the better portion of his life to social and moral causes. For thirty years he traveled from his native New Jersey throughout the colonies, writing and talking against the slave trade, protesting unjust treatment of the Indians, and arguing against war. The Journal *by which he is best known is often compared to Jonathan Edwards'* Personal Narrative, *of which it is the equal in religious devotion, and which reports a similar youthful conversion. Woolman lacked both the brilliance and the passion of Edwards, but he possessed an unfailingly generous and gentle temper and a quiet radiance of spirit. Woolman's sincere, often eloquent, espousal of Quaker doctrine is particularly evident in the following entries from his* Journal. *They were written between 1756 and 1758.*

Source: *The Journal of John Woolman*, Boston, 1871, pp. 86-138.

SCRUPLING TO DO WRITINGS relative to keeping slaves has been a means of sundry small trials to me, in which I have so evidently felt my own will set aside that I think it good to mention a few of them. Tradesmen and retailers of goods, who depend on their business for a living, are naturally inclined to keep the goodwill of their customers; nor is it a pleasant thing for young men to be under any necessity to question the judgment or honesty of elderly men, and more especially of such as have a fair reputation. Deep-rooted customs, though wrong, are not easily altered; but it is the duty of all to be firm in that which they certainly know is right for them. A charitable, benevolent man, well-acquainted with a Negro, may, I believe, under some circumstances, keep him in his family as a servant on no other motives than the Negro's good; but man, as man, knows not what shall be after him, nor hath he any assurance that his children will attain to that perfection in wisdom and goodness necessary rightly to exercise such power; hence it is clear to me that I ought not to be the scribe where wills are drawn in which some children are made ales masters over others during life.

About this time an ancient man of good esteem in the neighborhood came to my house to get his will written. He had young Negroes, and I asked him privately how he purposed to dispose of them. He told me; I then said, "I cannot write thy will without breaking my own peace," and respectfully gave him my reasons for it. He signified that he had a choice that I should have written it, but as I could not, consistently with my conscience, he did not desire it, and so he got it written by some other person. A few years after, there being great alterations in his family, he came again to get me to write his will. His Negroes were yet young, and his son, to whom he intended to give them, was, since he first spoke to me, from a libertine become a sober young man, and he supposed that I would have been free on that account to write it. We had much friendly talk on the subject, and then deferred it. A few days after he came again and directed their freedom, and I then wrote his will.

Near the time that the last-mentioned Friend first spoke to me, a neighbor received a bad bruise in his body and sent for me to bleed him, which having done, he desired me to write his will. I took notes, and amongst other things he told me to which of his children he gave his young Negro. I considered the pain and distress he was in, and knew not how it would end, so I wrote his will, save only that part concerning his slave, and carrying it to his bedside read it to him. I then told him in a friendly way that I could not write any instruments by which my fellow creatures were made slaves without bringing trouble on my own mind. I let him know that I charged nothing for what I had done, and desired to be excused from doing the other part in the way he proposed. We then had a serious conference on the subject; at length, he agreeing to set her free, I finished his will.

Having found drawings in my mind to visit Friends on Long Island, after obtaining a certificate from our Monthly Meeting, I set off May 12, 1756. . . . My mind was deeply engaged in this visit, both in public and private, and at several places where I

was, on observing that they had slaves, I found myself under a necessity, in a friendly way, to labor with them on that subject; expressing, as way opened, the inconsistency of that practice with the purity of the Christian religion, and the ill effects of it manifested amongst us. . . .

Until this year, 1756, I continued to retail goods, besides following my trade as a tailor; about which time I grew uneasy on account of my business growing too cumbersome. I had begun with selling trimmings for garments and from thence proceeded to sell cloths and linens. And, at length, having got a considerable shop of goods, my trade increased every year, and the way to large business appeared open, but I felt a stop in my mind.

Through the mercies of the Almighty, I had, in a good degree, learned to be content with a plain way of living. I had but a small family; and, on serious consideration, believed truth did not require me to engage much in cumbering affairs. It had been my general practice to buy and sell things really useful. Things that served chiefly to please the vain mind in people, I was not easy to trade in; seldom did it; and whenever I did I found it weaken me as a Christian.

The increase of business became my burden; for though my natural inclination was toward merchandise, yet I believed truth required me to live more free from outward cumbers; and there was now a strife in my mind between the two. In this exercise, my prayers were put up to the Lord, who graciously heard me and gave me a heart resigned to His holy will. Then I lessened my outward business, and, as I had opportunity, told my customers of my intentions that they might consider what shop to turn to; and in a while I wholly laid down merchandise and followed my trade as a tailor by myself, having no apprentice. I also had a nursery of apple trees, in which I employed some of my time in hoeing, grafting, trimming, and inoculating. In merchandise it is the custom where I lived to sell chiefly on credit, and poor people often get in debt; when payment is expected, not having wherewith to pay, their creditors often sue for it at law. Having frequently observed occurrences of this kind, I found it good for me to advise poor people to take such goods as were most useful and not costly.

In the time of trading I had an opportunity of seeing that the too liberal use of spirituous liquors and the custom of wearing too costly apparel led some people into great inconveniences; and that these two things appear to be often connected with each other. By not attending to that use of things which is consistent with universal righteousness, there is an increase of labor which extends beyond what our Heavenly Father intends for us. And by great labor, and often by much sweating, there is even among such as are not drunkards a craving of liquors to revive the spirits; that partly by the luxurious drinking of some, and partly by the drinking of others (led to it through immoderate labor), very great quantities of rum are every year expended in our colonies; the greater part of which we should have no need of did we steadily attend to pure wisdom.

When men take pleasure in feeling their minds elevated with strong drink, and so indulge their appetite as to disorder their understandings, neglect their duty as members of a family or civil society, and cast off all regard to religion, their case is much to be pitied. And where those whose lives are for the most part regular, and whose examples have a strong influence on the minds of others, adhere to some customs which powerfully draw to the use of more strong liquor than pure wisdom allows, it hinders the spreading of the spirit of meekness and strengthens the hands of the more excessive drinkers. This is a case to be lamented.

Every degree of luxury hath some connection with evil; and if those who profess to be disciples of Christ, and are looked upon as leaders of the people, have that mind in them which was also in Christ, and

so stand separate from every wrong way, it is a means of help to the weaker. As I have sometimes been much spent in the heat and have taken spirits to revive me, I have found by experience that in such circumstances the mind is not so calm, nor so fitly disposed for divine meditation, as when all such extremes are avoided. I have felt an increasing care to attend to that Holy Spirit which sets right bounds to our desires and leads those who faithfully follow it to apply all the gifts of Divine Providence to the purposes for which they were intended. Did those who have the care of great estates attend with singleness of heart to this heavenly Instructor, which so opens and enlarges the mind as to cause men to love their neighbors as themselves, they would have wisdom given them to manage their concerns, without employing some people in providing the luxuries of life, or others in laboring too hard; but for want of steadily regarding this principle of divine love, a selfish spirit takes place in the minds of people, which is attended with darkness and manifold confusions in the world.

Though trading in things useful is an honest employ, yet through the great number of superfluities which are bought and sold, and through the corruption of the times, they who apply to merchandise for a living have great need to be well experienced in that precept which the prophet Jeremiah laid down for his scribe: "Seekest thou great things for thyself? seek them not."

In the winter this year I was engaged with Friends in visiting families, and through the goodness of the Lord we oftentimes experienced his heart-tendering presence amongst us. . . .

Feeling the exercise in relation to a visit to the Southern provinces to increase upon me, I acquainted our Monthly Meeting therewith and obtained their certificate. Expecting to go alone, one of my brothers who lived in Philadelphia, having some business in North Carolina, proposed going with me part of the way; but as he had a view of some outward affairs, to accept of him as a companion was some difficulty with me, whereupon I had conversation with him at sundry times. At length feeling easy in my mind, I had conversation with several elderly Friends of Philadelphia on the subject, and he obtaining a certificate suitable to the occasion, we set off in May 1757. . . .

Soon after I entered this province, a deep and painful exercise came upon me, which I often had some feeling of, since my mind was drawn toward these parts, and with which I had acquainted my brother before we agreed to join as companions. As the people in this and the Southern provinces live much on the labor of slaves, many of whom are used hardly, my concern was that I might attend with singleness of heart to the voice of the true Shepherd, and be so supported as to remain unmoved at the faces of men.

As it is common for Friends on such a visit to have entertainment free of cost, a difficulty arose in my mind with respect to saving my money by kindness received from what appeared to me to be the gain of oppression. Receiving a gift, considered as a gift brings the receiver under obligations to the benefactor, and has a natural tendency to draw the obliged into a party with the giver. To prevent difficulties of this kind, and to preserve the minds of judges from any bias, was that divine prohibition: "Thou shalt not receive any gift; for a gift blindeth the wise, and perverteth the words of the righteous" (Ex. 23:8). As the disciples were sent forth without any provision for their journey, and our Lord said the workman is worthy of his meat, their labor in the gospel was considered as a reward for their entertainment, and therefore not received as a gift; yet, in regard to my present journey, I could not see my way clear in that respect. The difference appeared thus: the entertainment the disciples met with was from them whose hearts God

had opened to receive them, from a love to them and the truth they published; but we, considered as members of the same religious society, look upon it as a piece of civility to receive each other in such visits; and such reception, at times, is partly in regard to reputation and not from an inward unity of heart and spirit. Conduct is more convincing than language, and where people, by their actions, manifest that the slave trade is not so disagreeable to their principles but that it may be encouraged, there is not a sound uniting with some Friends who visit them.

The prospect of so weighty a work, and of being so distinguished from many whom I esteemed before myself, brought me very low, and such were the conflicts of my soul that I had a near sympathy with the prophet, in the time of his weakness, when he said: "If thou deal thus with me, kill me, I pray thee, if I have found favor in thy sight" (Num. 11:15). But I soon saw that this proceeded from the want of a full resignation to the divine will. Many were the afflictions which attended me, and in great abasement, with many tears, my cries were to the Almighty for His gracious and fatherly assistance, and after a time of deep trial I was favored to understand the state mentioned by the Psalmist more clearly than ever I had done before, to wit: "My soul is even as a weaned child" (Ps. 131:2). Being thus helped to sink down into resignation, I felt a deliverance from that tempest in which I had been sorely exercised, and in calmness of mind went forward, trusting that the Lord Jesus Christ, as I faithfully attended to him, would be a counselor to me in all difficulties, and that by his strength I should be enabled even to leave money with the members of society where I had entertainment, when I found that omitting it would obstruct that work to which I believed He had called me.

As I copy this after my return, I may here add that oftentimes I did so under a sense of duty. The way in which I did it was thus: When I expected soon to leave a Friend's house where I had entertainment, if I believed that I should not keep clear from the gain of oppression without leaving money, I spoke to one of the heads of the family privately, and desired them to accept of those pieces of silver and give them to such of their Negroes as they believed would make the best use of them; and at other times I gave them to the Negroes myself, as the way looked clearest to me. Before I came out, I had provided a large number of small pieces for this purpose, and thus offering them to some who appeared to be wealthy people was a trial both to me and them. But the fear of the Lord so covered me at times that my way was made easier than I expected; and few, if any, manifested any resentment at the offer, and most of them, after some conversation, accepted of them.

May 9. A Friend at whose house we breakfasted setting us a little on our way, I had conversation with him, in the fear of the Lord, concerning his slaves, in which my heart was tender. I used much plainness of speech with him, and he appeared to take it kindly. We pursued our journey without appointing meetings, being pressed in my mind to be at the Yearly Meeting in Virginia. In my traveling on the road, I often felt a cry rise from the center of my mind, thus: "O Lord, I am a stranger on the earth, hide not Thy face from me." On the 11th, we crossed the rivers Patowmack [Potomac] and Rapahannock and lodged at Port Royal. On the way we had the company of a colonel of the militia, who appeared to be a thoughtful man. I took occasion to remark on the difference in general between a people used to labor moderately for their living, training up their children in frugality and business, and those who live on the labor of slaves; the former, in my view, being the most happy life. He concurred in the remark, and mentioned the trouble arising from the untoward, slothful disposition of the Negroes, adding that one

of our laborers would do as much in a day as two of their slaves. I replied that free men, whose minds were properly on their business, found a satisfaction in improving, cultivating, and providing for their families; but Negroes, laboring to support others who claim them as their property, and expecting nothing but slavery during life, had not the like inducement to be industrious.

After some further conversation, I said that men having power too often misapplied it; that though we made slaves of the Negroes, and the Turks made slaves of the Christians, I believed that liberty was the natural right of all men equally. This he did not deny, but said the lives of the Negroes were so wretched in their own country that many of them lived better here than there. I replied, "There is great odds in regard to us on what principle we act"; and so the conversation on that subject ended.

I may here add that another person, some time afterward, mentioned the wretchedness of the Negroes, occasioned by their intestine wars, as an argument in favor of our fetching them away for slaves. To which I replied, if compassion for the Africans, on account of their domestic troubles, was the real motive of our purchasing them, that spirit of tenderness being attended to would incite us to use them kindly that, as strangers brought out of affliction, their lives might be happy among us. And as they are human creatures, whose souls are as precious as ours, and who may receive the same help and comfort from the Holy Scriptures as we do, we could not omit suitable endeavors to instruct them therein; but that while we manifest by our conduct that our views in purchasing them are to advance ourselves, and while our buying captives taken in war animates those parties to push on the war and increase desolation amongst them, to say they live unhappily in Africa is far from being an argument in our favor. I further said the present circumstances of these provinces to me appear difficult; the slaves look like a burdensome stone to such as burden themselves with them; and that if the white people retain a resolution to prefer their outward prospects of gain to all other considerations and do not act conscientiously toward them as fellow creatures, I believe that burden will grow heavier and heavier, until times change in a way disagreeable to us. The person appeared very serious, and owned that in considering their condition and the manner of their treatment in these provinces, he had sometimes thought it might be just in the Almighty so to order it.

Having traveled through Maryland, we came amongst Friends at Cedar Creek in Virginia, on the 12th; and the next day rode, in company with several of them, a day's journey to Camp Creek. As I was riding along in the morning, my mind was deeply affected in a sense I had of the need of divine aid to support me in the various difficulties which attended me, and in uncommon distress of mind I cried in secret to the Most High, "O Lord be merciful, I beseech Thee, to Thy poor afflicted creature!" After some time, I felt inward relief, and, soon after, a Friend in company began to talk in support of the slave trade, and said the Negroes were understood to be the offspring of Cain, their blackness being the mark which God set upon him after he murdered Abel his brother; that it was the design of Providence they should be slaves as a condition proper to the race of so wicked a man as Cain was. Then another spoke in support of what had been said.

To all which I replied in substance as follows: That Noah and his family were all who survived the flood, according to Scripture; and as Noah was of Seth's race, the family of Cain was wholly destroyed. One of them said that after the flood Ham went to the land of Nod and took a wife; that Nod was a land far distant, inhabited by Cain's race, and that the flood did not reach it; and as Ham was sentenced to be a servant of servants to his brethren, these two families, being thus joined, were undoubted-

ly fit only for slaves. I replied the flood was a judgment upon the world for their abominations, and it was granted that Cain's stock was the most wicked, and therefore unreasonable to suppose that they were spared. As to Ham's going to the land of Nod for a wife, no time being fixed, Nod might be inhabited by some of Noah's family before Ham married a second time; moreover the text saith "That all flesh died that moved upon the earth" (Gen. 7:21).

I further reminded them how the prophets repeatedly declare "that the son shall not suffer for the iniquity of the father, but everyone be answerable for his own sins." I was troubled to perceive the darkness of their imaginations, and in some pressure of spirit said, "The love of ease and gain are the motives in general of keeping slaves, and men are wont to take hold of weak arguments to support a cause which is unreasonable. I have no interest on either side, save only the interest which I desire to have in the truth. I believe liberty is their right, and as I see they are not only deprived of it but treated in other respects with inhumanity in many places, I believe He who is a refuge for the oppressed will, in His own time, plead their cause, and happy will it be for such as walk in uprightness before Him." And thus our conversation ended.

May 14. I was this day at Camp Creek Monthly Meeting and then rode to the mountains up James River and had a meeting at a Friend's house, in both which I felt sorrow of heart, and my tears were poured out before the Lord, who was pleased to afford a degree of strength by which way was opened to clear my mind amongst Friends in those places. . . .

The sense I had of the state of the churches brought a weight of distress upon me. The gold to me appeared dim, and the fine gold changed, and though this is the case too generally, yet the sense of it in these parts hath in a particular manner borne heavy upon me. It appeared to me that through the prevailing of the spirit of this world the minds of many were brought to an inward desolation, and instead of the spirit of meekness, gentleness, and heavenly wisdom, which are the necessary companions of the true sheep of Christ, a spirit of fierceness and the love of dominion too generally prevailed. From small beginnings in error great buildings by degrees are raised, and from one age to another are more and more strengthened by the general concurrence of the people; and as men obtain reputation by their profession of the truth, their virtues are mentioned as arguments in favor of general error; and those of less note, to justify themselves, say, such and such good men did the like. By what other steps could the people of Judah arise to that height in wickedness as to give just ground for the prophet Isaiah to declare, in the name of the Lord, "that none calleth for justice, nor any pleadeth for truth" (Isa. 59:4), or for the Almighty to call upon the great city of Jerusalem just before the Babylonish captivity, "If ye can find a man, if there be any who executeth judgment, that seeketh the truth, and I will pardon it" (Jer. 5:1).

The prospect of a way being open to the same degeneracy in some parts of this newly settled land of America in respect to our conduct toward the Negroes hath deeply bowed my mind in this journey, and though briefly to relate how these people are treated is no agreeable work; yet, after often reading over the notes I made as I traveled, I find my mind engaged to preserve them. Many of the white people in those provinces take little or no care of Negro marriages; and when Negroes marry after their own way, some make so little account of those marriages that with views of outward interest they often part men from their wives by selling them far asunder, which is common when estates are sold by executors at vendue. Many whose labor is heavy being followed at their business in the field by a man with a whip, hired for that purpose, have in common little else allowed but one peck of Indian corn and some salt, for one week, with a few potatoes; the potatoes they commonly raise by their labor on the first day of the week. The correction ensuing on their disobedience to overseers, or slothfulness in business, is often very severe and sometimes desperate.

Men and women have many times scarcely clothes sufficient to hide their nakedness, and boys and girls ten and twelve years old are often quite naked amongst their master's children. Some of our Society, and some of the society called Newlights, use some endeavors to instruct those they have in reading; but in common this is not only neglected but disapproved. These are the people by whose labor the other inhabitants are in a great measure supported, and many of them in the luxuries of life. These are the people who have made no agreement to serve us, and who have not forfeited their liberty that we know of. These are the souls for whom Christ died, and for our conduct toward them we must answer before Him who is no respecter of persons. They who know the only true God, and Jesus Christ whom He hath sent, and are thus acquainted with the merciful, benevolent, gospel spirit, will therein perceive that the indignation of God is kindled against oppression and cruelty, and in beholding the great distress of so numerous a people will find cause for mourning.

From my lodgings I went to Burleigh Meeting. . . . The next meeting we had was at Black-Water, and from thence went to the Yearly Meeting at the Western Branch. When business began, some queries were introduced by some of their members for consideration, and, if approved, they were to be answered hereafter by their respective Monthly Meetings. They were the Pennsylvania queries, which had been examined by a committee of Virginia Yearly Meeting appointed the last year, who made some alterations in them, one of which alterations was made in favor of a custom which troubled me. The query was, "Are there any concerned in the importation of Negroes, or in buying them after imported?" which was thus altered, "Are there any concerned in the importation of Negroes, or buying them to trade in?" As one query admitted with unanimity was, "Are any concerned in buying or vending goods unlawfully imported, or prize goods?" I found my mind engaged to say that as we profess the truth and were there assembled to support the testimony of it, it was necessary for us to dwell deep and act in that wisdom which is pure, or otherwise we could not prosper. I then mentioned their alteration, and, referring to the last-mentioned query, added that as purchasing any merchandise taken by the sword was always allowed to be inconsistent with our principles, so Negroes being captives of war, or taken by stealth, it was inconsistent with our testimony to buy them; and their being our fellow creatures and sold as slaves added greatly to the iniquity. Friends appeared attentive to what was said; some expressed a care and concern about their Negroes; none made any objection, by way of reply to what I said, but the query was admitted as they had altered it.

As some of their members have heretofore traded in Negroes, as in other merchandise, this query being admitted will be one step further than they have hitherto gone, and I did not see it my duty to press for an alteration, but felt easy to leave it all to Him who alone is able to turn the hearts of the mighty and make way for the spreading of truth on the earth, by means agreeable to His infinite wisdom. In regard to those they already had, I felt my mind engaged to labor with them and said that as we believe the Scriptures were given forth by holy men, as they were moved by the Holy Ghost, and many of us know by experience that they are often helpful and comfortable, and believe ourselves bound in duty to teach our children to read them, I believed that if we were divested of all self-ish views, the same good spirit that gave them forth would engage us to teach the Negroes to read that they might have the benefit of them. Some present manifested a concern to take more care in the education of their Negroes.

May 29. At the house where I lodged was a meeting of ministers and elders. I found an engagement to speak freely and plainly to them concerning their slaves; mentioning how they, as the first rank in the Society, whose conduct in that case was much noticed by others, were under the stronger obligations to look carefully to themselves. Expressing how needful it was for them in that situation to be thoroughly divested of all selfish views; that living in the pure truth and acting conscientiously toward those people in their education and otherwise, they might be instrumental in helping forward a work so exceedingly necessary, and so much neglected amongst them. . . .

A FEW YEARS PAST, money being made current in our province for carrying on wars, and to be called in again by taxes laid on the inhabitants, my mind was often affected with the thoughts of paying such taxes; and I believe it right for me to preserve a memorandum concerning it. I was told that Friends in England frequently paid taxes when the money was applied to such purposes. I had conversation with several noted Friends on the subject, who all favored the payment of such taxes; some of them I preferred before myself, and this made me easier for a time; yet there was in the depth of my mind a scruple which I never could get over; and at certain times I was greatly distressed on that account.

I believed that there were some upright-hearted men who paid such taxes, yet could not see that their example was a sufficient reason for me to do so, while I believe that the spirit of truth required of me, as an individual, to suffer patiently the distress of goods rather than pay actively.

To refuse the active payment of a tax which our Society generally paid was exceedingly disagreeable; but to do a thing contrary to my conscience appeared yet more dreadful. When this exercise came upon me, I knew of none under the like difficulty; and in my distress I besought the Lord to enable me to give up all, that so I might follow Him wheresoever He was pleased to lead me. Under this exercise I went to our Yearly Meeting at Philadelphia, in the year 1755, at which a committee was appointed of some from each Quarterly Meeting to correspond with the meeting for sufferings in London, and another to visit our Monthly and Quarterly Meetings. After their appointment, before the last adjournment of the meeting, it was agreed that these two committees should meet together in Friends' schoolhouse in the city to consider some things in which the cause of truth was concerned. They accordingly had a weighty conference in the fear of the Lord; at which time I perceived there were many Friends under a scruple like that before mentioned.

As scrupling to pay a tax on account of the application hath seldom been heard of heretofore, even amongst men of integrity who have steadily borne their testimony against outward wars in their time, I may therefore note some things which have occurred to my mind, as I have been inwardly exercised on that account. From the steady opposition which faithful Friends in early times made to wrong things then approved, they were hated and persecuted by men living in the spirit of this world, and, suffering with firmness, they were made a blessing to the church, and the work prospered. It equally concerns men in every age to take heed to their own spirits; and in comparing their situation with ours, to me it appears that there was less danger of their being infected with the spirit of this world, in paying such taxes, than is the case with us now. They had little or no share in civil government, and many of them declared that they were, through the power of God, separated from the spirit in which wars were, and being afflicted by the rulers on account of their testimony, there was less likelihood of their uniting in spirit with them in things inconsistent with the purity of truth.

We, from the first settlement of this land, have known little or no troubles of that sort. The profession of our predecessors was for a time accounted reproachful, but at length their uprightness being understood by the rulers, and their innocent sufferings moving them, our way of worship was tolerated, and many of our members in these colonies became active in civil government. Being thus tried with favor and prosperity, this world appeared inviting; our minds have been turned to the improvement of our country, to merchandise and the sciences, amongst which are many things useful, if followed in pure wisdom; but in our present condition I believe it will not be denied that a carnal mind is gaining upon us. Some of our members, who are officers in civil government, are, in one case or other, called upon in their respective stations to assist in things relative to the wars; but being in doubt whether to act or to crave to be excused from their office, if they see their brethren united in the payment of a tax to carry on the said wars, may think their case not much different, and so might quench the tender movings of the Holy Spirit in their minds. Thus, by small degrees, we might approach so near to fighting that the distinction would be little else than the name of a peaceable people.

It requires great self-denial and resignation of ourselves to God to attain that state wherein we can freely cease from fighting when wrongfully invaded if, by our fighting, there were a probability of overcoming the invaders. Whoever rightly attains to it does in some degree feel that spirit in which our Redeemer gave His life for us; and, through divine goodness, many of our predecessors, and many now living, have learned this blessed lesson; but many others, having their religion chiefly by education and not being enough acquainted with that cross which crucifies to the world, do manifest a temper distinguishable from that of an entire trust in God. In calmly considering these things, it hath not appeared strange to me that an exercise hath now fallen upon some, which, with respect to the outward means, is different from what was known to many of those who went before us.

Some time after the Yearly Meeting, the said committees met at Philadelphia, and, by adjournments, continued sitting several days. The calamities of war were now increasing; the frontier inhabitants of Pennsylvania were frequently surprised; some were slain, and many taken captive by the Indians; and while these committees sat, the corpse of one so slain was brought in a wagon and taken through the streets of the city in his bloody garments, to alarm the people and rouse them to war.

Friends thus met were not all of one mind in relation to the tax, which, to those who scrupled it, made the way more difficult. To refuse an active payment at such a time might be construed into an act of disloyalty, and appeared likely to displease the rulers, not only here but in England; still there was a scruple so fixed on the minds of many Friends that nothing moved it. It was a conference the most weighty that ever I was at, and the hearts of many were bowed in reverence before the Most High. Some Friends of the said committees who appeared easy to pay the tax, after several adjournments, withdrew; others of them continued till the last. At length an epistle of tender love and caution to Friends in Pennsylvania was drawn up, and being read several times and corrected, was signed by such as were free to sign it, and afterward sent to the Monthly and Quarterly Meetings.

August 9, 1757. Orders came at night to the military officers in our county (Burlington) directing them to draft the militia and prepare a number of men to go off as soldiers, to the relief of the English at Fort William Henry, in New York government; a few days after which there was a general review of the militia at Mount Holly, and a number of men were chosen and sent off under some officers. Shortly after, there came orders to draft three times as many, who were to hold themselves in readiness to march when fresh orders came. On the 17th there was a meeting of the military officers at Mount Holly, who agreed on draft. Orders were sent to the men so chosen to meet their respective captains at set times and places, those in our township to meet at Mount Holly, amongst whom were a considerable number of our Society. My mind being affected herewith, I had fresh opportunity to see and consider the advantage of living in the real substance of religion, where practice doth harmonize with principle. Amongst the officers are men of understanding, who have some regard to sincerity where they see it; and when such in the execution of their office have men to deal with whom they believe to be upright-hearted, it is a painful task to put them to trouble on account of scruples of conscience, and they will be likely to avoid it as much as easily may be. But where men profess to be so meek and heavenly minded, and to have their trust so firmly settled in God that they cannot join in wars, and yet by their spirit and conduct in common life manifest a contrary disposition, their difficulties are great at such a time.

When officers who are anxiously endeavoring to get troops to answer the demands of their superiors see men who are insincere pretend scruple of conscience in hopes of being excused from a dangerous employment, it is likely they will be roughly handled. In this time of commotion some of our young men left these parts and tarried abroad till it was over; some came and proposed to go as soldiers; others appeared to have a real tender scruple in their minds against joining in wars and were much humbled under the apprehension of a trial so near. I had conversation with several of them to my satisfaction. When the captain came to town, some of the last-mentioned went and told him in substance as follows: That they could not bear arms for conscience' sake; nor could they hire any to go in their places, being resigned as to the event. At length the captain acquainted them all that they might return home for the present, but he required them to provide themselves as soldiers, and be in readiness to march when called upon. This was such a time as I had not seen before; and yet I may say, with thankfulness to the Lord, that I believed the trial was intended for our good; and I was favored with resignation to him. The French Army having taken the fort they were besieging, destroyed it and went away; the company of men who were first drafted, after some days' march, had orders to return home, and those on the second draft were no more called upon on that occasion.

April 4, 1758. Orders came to some officers in Mount Holly to prepare quarters for a short time for about one hundred soldiers An officer and two other men, all inhabitants of our town, came to my house. The officer told me that he came to desire me to provide lodging and entertainment for two soldiers, and that 6s. a week per man would be allowed as pay for it. The case being new and unexpected I made no answer suddenly but sat a time silent, my mind being inward. I was fully convinced that the proceedings in wars are inconsistent with the purity of the Christian religion; and to be hired to entertain men, who were then under pay as soldiers, was a difficulty with me. I expected they had legal authority for what they did; and after a short time I said to the officer, if the men are sent here for entertainment I believe I shall not refuse to admit them into my house, but the nature of the case is such that I expect I cannot keep them on hire. One of the men intimated that he thought I might do it consistently with my religious principles. To

which I made no reply, believing silence at that time best for me. Though they spoke of two, there came only one, who tarried at my house about two weeks and behaved himself civilly. When the officer came to pay me, I told him I could not take pay, having admitted him into my house in a passive obedience to authority. I was on horseback when he spoke to me, and as I turned from him, he said he was obliged to me; to which I said nothing; but, thinking on the expression, I grew uneasy; and afterward, being near where he lived, I went and told him on what grounds I refused taking pay for keeping the soldier. . . .

The Monthly Meeting of Philadelphia having been under a concern on account of some Friends, who this summer (1758) had bought Negro slaves, proposed to their Quarterly Meeting to have the minute reconsidered in the Yearly Meeting, which was made last on that subject, and the said Quarterly Meeting appointed a committee to consider it and to report to their next. This committee having met once and adjourned, and I, going to Philadelphia to meet a committee of the Yearly Meeting, was in town the evening on which the Quarterly Meeting's committee met the second time; and finding an inclination to sit with them, I, with some others, was admitted, and Friends had a weighty conference on the subject. Soon after their next Quarterly Meeting I heard that the case was coming to our Yearly Meeting. This brought a weighty exercise upon me, and under a sense of my own infirmities, and the great danger I felt of turning aside from perfect purity, my mind was often drawn to retire alone and put up my prayers to the Lord that He would be graciously pleased to strengthen me; that setting aside all views of self-interest and the friendship of this world, I might stand fully resigned to His holy will.

In this Yearly Meeting several weighty matters were considered, and, toward the last, that in relation to dealing with persons who purchase slaves. During the several sittings of the said meeting, my mind was frequently covered with inward prayer, and I could say with David "that tears were my meat day and night." The case of slave-keeping lay heavy upon me, nor did I find any engagement to speak directly to any other matter before the meeting.

Now, when this case was opened, several faithful Friends spoke weightily thereto, with which I was comforted; and feeling a concern to cast in my mite, I said in substance as follows: "In the difficulties attending us in this life, nothing is more precious than the mind of truth inwardly manifested; and it is my earnest desire that in this weighty matter we may be so truly humbled as to be favored with a clear understanding of the mind of truth, and follow it; this would be of more advantage to the Society than any medium not in the clearness of divine wisdom. The case is difficult to some who have slaves, but if such set aside all self-interest and come to be weaned from the desire of getting estates, or even from holding them together, when truth requires the contrary, I believe way will so open that they will know how to steer through those difficulties."

Many Friends appeared to be deeply bowed under the weight of the work and manifested much firmness in their love to the cause of truth and universal righteousness on the earth. And though none did openly justify the practice of slave-keeping in general, yet some appeared concerned lest the meeting should go into such measures as might give uneasiness to many brethren, alleging that if Friends patiently continued under the exercise, the Lord, in His time, might open a way for the deliverance of these people. Finding an engagement to speak, I said, "My mind is often led to consider the purity of the Divine Being and the justice of His judgments; and

herein my soul is covered with awfulness. I cannot omit to hint of some cases where people have not been treated with the purity of justice, and the event hath been lamentable. Many slaves on this continent are oppressed, and their cries have reached the ears of the Most High. Such are the purity and certainty of His judgments that He cannot be partial in our favor. In infinite love and goodness He hath opened our understanding from one time to another concerning our duty toward this people, and it is not a time for delay. Should we now be sensible of what He requires of us, and through a respect to the private interest of some persons, or through a regard to some friendships which do not stand on an immutable foundation, neglect to do our duty in firmness and constancy, still waiting for some extraordinary means to bring about their deliverance, God may by terrible things in righteousness answer us in this matter."

Many faithful brethren labored with great firmness, and the love of truth in a good degree prevailed. Several who had Negroes expressed their desire that a rule might be made to deal with such Friends as offenders who bought slaves in future. To this it was answered that the root of this evil would never be effectually struck at until a thorough search was made in the circumstances of such Friends as kept Negroes, with respect to the righteousness of their motives in keeping them, that impartial justice might be administered throughout. Several Friends expressed their desire that a visit might be made to such Friends as kept slaves, and many others said that they believed liberty was the Negro's right; to which, at length, no opposition was publicly made. A minute was made more full on that subject than any heretofore; and the names of several Friends entered who were free to join in a visit to such as kept slaves.

1757

4.

Peter Fontaine: A Defense of Slavery in Virginia

By the middle of the eighteenth century, slaves had become an indispensable commodity on the tobacco, indigo, and rice plantations of Maryland, Virginia, and South Carolina. Not yet established as a social institution — many slaveholders deplored the ethics of the practice — the use of slave labor was defended as an economic necessity by such respected leaders as the Reverend Peter Fontaine of Westover, Virginia, who discussed the subject in the following letter of March 30, 1757, to his brother Moses.

Source: *Memoirs of a Huguenot Family*, Ann Maury, ed., New York, 1853, pp. 348-353.

Now, to answer your first query — whether by our breach of treaties we have not justly exasperated the bordering nations of Indians against us, and drawn upon ourselves the barbarous usage we meet with from them and the French? To answer this fully would take up much time. I shall only hint at some things which we ought to have done, and which we did not do at our first settlement among them, and which we might have learned long since from the practice of our enemies the French.

I am persuaded we were not deficient in the observation of treaties, but, as we got the land by concession and not by conquest, we ought to have intermarried with them, which would have incorporated us with them effectually, and made of them staunch friends, and, which is of still more consequence, made many of them good Christians. But this our wise politicians at home put an effectual stop to at the beginning of our settlement here, for, when they heard that Rolfe had married Pocahontas, it was deliberated in Council whether he had not committed high treason by so doing, that is, marrying an Indian Princess. And had not some troubles intervened which put a stop to the inquiry, the poor man might have been hanged up for doing the most just, the most natural, the most generous and politic action that ever was done this side of the water. This put an effectual stop to all intermarriages afterward.

Our Indian traders have indeed their squaws, alias whores, at the Indian towns where they trade, but leave their offspring like bulls or boars to be provided for at random by their mothers. As might be expected, some of these bastards have been the leading men or war captains that have done us so much mischief. This ill treatment was sufficient to create jealousy in the natural man's breast, and made the Indians look upon us as false and deceitful friends, and cause all our endeavors to convert them to be ineffectual. But here, methinks, I can hear you observe — What! Englishmen intermarry with Indians? But I can convince you that they are guilty of much more heinous practices, more unjustifiable in the sight of God and man (if that, indeed, may be called a bad practice), for many base wretches among us take up with Negro women, by which means the country swarms with mulatto bastards, and these mulattoes, if but three generations removed from the black father or mother, may, by the indulgence of the laws of the country, intermarry with the white people, and actually do every day so marry.

Now, if, instead of this abominable practice which has polluted the blood of many among us, we had taken Indian wives in the first place, it would have made them some compensation for their lands. They are a free people, and the offspring would not be born in a state of slavery. We should become rightful heirs to their lands and should not have smutted our blood; for the Indian children when born are as white as Spaniards or Portuguese, and were it not for the practice of going naked in the summer and besmearing themselves with bears' grease, etc., they would continue white. And had we thought fit to make them our wives, they would readily have complied with our fashion of wearing clothes all the year round; and, by doing justice to these poor, benighted heathen, we should have introduced Christianity among them.

Your own reflections upon these hints will be a sufficient answer to your first query. I shall only add that General Johnson's success was owing, under God, to his fidelity to the Indians and his generous conduct to his Indian wife, by whom he has several hopeful sons, who are all war captains, the bulwarks with him of the Five Nations, and

loyal subjects to their mother country.

As to your second query, if enslaving our fellow creatures be a practice agreeable to Christianity, it is answered in a great measure in many treatises at home, to which I refer you. I shall only mention something of our present state here.

Like Adam, we are all apt to shift off the blame from ourselves and lay it upon others, how justly in our case you may judge. The Negroes are enslaved by the Negroes themselves before they are purchased by the masters of the ships who bring them here. It is, to be sure, at our choice whether we buy them or not, so this then is our crime, folly, or whatever you will please to call it.

But our Assembly, foreseeing the ill consequences of importing such numbers among us, has often attempted to lay a duty upon them which would amount to a prohibition, such as £10 or £20 a head; but no governor dare pass such a law, having instructions to the contrary from the Board of Trade at home. By this means they are forced upon us, whether we will or will not. This plainly shows the African Company has the advantage of the colonies, and may do as it pleases with the Ministry.

Indeed, since we have been exhausted of our little stock of cash by the war, the importation has stopped; our poverty then is our best security. There is no more picking for their ravenous jaws upon bare bones; but should we begin to thrive, they will be at the same again. All our taxes are now laid upon slaves and on shippers of tobacco, which they wink at while we are in danger of being torn from them, but we dare not do it in time of peace, it being looked upon as the highest presumption to lay any burden upon trade. This is our part of the grievance, but to live in Virginia without slaves is morally impossible.

Before our troubles, you could not hire a servant or slave for love or money, so that, unless robust enough to cut wood, to go to mill, to work at the hoe, etc., you must starve or board in some family where they both fleece and half starve you. There is no set price upon corn, wheat, and provisions; so they take advantage of the necessities of strangers, who are thus obliged to purchase some slaves and land. This, of course, draws us all into the original sin and curse of the country of purchasing slaves, and this is the reason we have no merchants, traders, or

artificers of any sort but what become planters in a short time.

A common laborer, white or black, if you can be so much favored as to hire one, is 1s. sterling or 15d. currency per day; a bungling carpenter, 2s. or 2s. 6d. per day; besides diet and lodging. That is, for a lazy fellow to get wood and water, £19 16s. 3d. current per annum; add to this £7 or £8 more and you have a slave for life.

5.

Joseph Noyes: Academic Freedom at Yale College

By the middle of the eighteenth century, Yale College was beginning to show the effects of the religious toleration that was gaining ground everywhere in the colonies. When President Thomas Clap, moved by his ideal of a sectarian institution, tried to expel the Reverend Joseph Noyes from the Yale corporation, he was met by vigorous and unprecedented opposition both from Noyes himself and from other spokesmen of an opposing Congregationalist faction. Noyes, whom Clap suspected of having fallen from the faith, was asked to submit to an examination by other members of the corporation. His letter "absolutely" refusing this request was dated September 14, 1757.

Source: *Extracts from the Itineraries and Other Miscellanies of Ezra Stiles, etc., etc.,* Franklin B. Dexter, ed., New Haven, 1916, pp. 4-5.

My absolute refusal to submit to an examination in pursuance to the resolve of the Corporation at their last meeting, in consequence of a resolve of the Corporation made Nov. 21, 1751, wherein it was provided, "That when it is suspected by any of the Corporation that either the president, or any fellow or professor of divinity, etc., has fallen from the profession of his faith, etc., he shall be examined by the Corporation," is, I think, fully warranted by the following reasons:

1. I have once qualified myself to serve as a member of the Corporation and have good right to be esteemed and treated as a member in good standing, until I am proved to be disqualified.

2. The law or resolve upon which my examination is founded is arbitrary; for a man to be subjected to an examination, on suspicion only, is contrary to all reason.

3. Said law or resolve is manifestly unjust, as it subjects a man, though innocent, to suffer in his character and influence, and leaves him without remedy.

4. Said law or resolve is singular and unprecedented, there having never been hereto any law or rule of the like nature in this Corporation, or any other Christian community, except the Courts of Inquisition and Star Chamber.

5. Said law or resolve is inconsistent with the ecclesiastical constitution of this colony. As I am a minister of the Gospel under the constitution, I am accountable to the consociation to which I belong, touching my principles, and not to this board.

6. Said law or resolve is contrary to the rules of the common law. All legal processes, according to the common law, must be built upon some express accusation or charge, to be supported by proper and sufficient evidence; but suspicion and surmise are always discountenanced.

7. The Corporation have no right or power to make such a law or rule, nor to act upon it. Whatever power the Corporation have, as legislators, they are invested with by charter, and hence, therefore, just so much power as the charter gives them and no more, which in general is only to make laws respecting the well ordering and governing the college, but have no right or power to make any law respecting the removal of a member of the Corporation, this matter being specially provided for by the charter itself; and a member must be removed for reasons assigned in the charter, or not removed at all, which are unfaithfulness, default, or incapacity only.

8. I have taken the oaths and subscribed the declaration, etc., as required by the charter (and is the only thing required therein), and have thereby given as great security, as either the King of any of his subjects, or this government of any of its members do require to their sustaining any office, for which they are otherwise fit and appointed to serve.

9. I do not esteem this Corporation so important and singular, or the ends to be promoted by it to be of so extraordinary and peculiar a nature, but that these securities, usually given to other corporations, may be sufficient for this.

1758

6.

SAMUEL DAVIES: The Curse of Cowardice

Samuel Davies, a noted Presbyterian educator in Virginia, early acquired a reputation as one of the greatest orators of his generation. After Braddock's defeat at the hands of the French and Indians at Fort Duquesne in 1755, the Virginia frontier was exposed to a series of devastating Indian attacks. The Virginia militia was in dire need of volunteers when, on May 8, 1758, Davies delivered the following sermon on a Christian's duty to defend his country. The fervor of Davies' appeal, a portion of which follows, stimulated such a rush of recruits that some had to be turned away.

Source: *The Curse of Cowardice: A Sermon Preached to the Militia of Hanover County, in Virginia, etc., etc.,* London, 1758.

Cursed be he that doth the Work of the Lord deceitfully; and cursed be he that keepeth back his Sword from Blood. Jer. 48:10

NOTHING CAN BE MORE AGREEABLE to the God of Peace than to see universal harmony and benevolence prevail among His creatures; and He has laid them under the strongest obligations to cultivate a pacific temper toward one another, both as individuals and as nations. "Follow peace with all men," is one of the principal precepts of our holy religion. And the great Prince of Peace has solemnly pronounced, "Blessed are the peacemakers."

But when, in this corrupt, disordered state of things, where the lusts of men are perpetually embroiling the world with wars and fightings and throwing all into confusion; when ambition and avarice would rob us of our property, for which we have toiled and on which we subsist; when they would enslave the freeborn mind and compel us meanly to cringe to usurpation and arbitrary power; when they would tear from our eager grasp the most valuable blessing of Heaven, I mean our *religion;* when they invade our country, formerly the region of tranquillity, ravage our frontiers, butcher our fellow subjects, or confine them in a barbarous captivity in the dens of savages; when our earthly all is ready to be seized by rapacious hands, and even our eternal all is in danger by the loss of our religion; when this is the case, what is then the will of God?

Must peace then be maintained? Maintained with our perfidious and cruel invaders? Maintained at the expense of property, liberty, life, and everything dear and valuable? Maintained, when it is in our power to vindicate our right and do ourselves justice? Is the work of peace then our only business? No; in such a time even the God of Peace proclaims by His providence, "To arms!"

Then the sword is, as it were, consecrated to God; and the art of war becomes a part of our religion. Then happy is he that shall reward our enemies, as they have served us. Blessed is the brave soldier; blessed is the defender of his country and the destroyer of its enemies. Blessed are they who offer themselves willingly in this service, and who faithfully discharge it. But, on the other hand, "Cursed is he that doth the work of the Lord deceitfully; and cursed is he that keepeth back his sword from blood." . . .

"Cursed be he that keepeth back his sword from blood." This denunciation, like the artillery of heaven, is leveled against the mean, sneaking coward who, when God, in the course of His providence, calls him to arms, refuses to obey and consults his own ease and safety more than his duty to God and his country.

"Cursed be he that doth the work of the Lord deceitfully." This seems to be leveled against another species of cowards — sly, hypocritical cowards who undertake the work of the Lord, that is, take up arms; but they do the work of the Lord *deceitfully*, that is, they do not faithfully use their arms for the purposes they were taken. They commence soldiers, not that they may serve their country and do their duty to God but that they may live in ease, idleness, and pleasure, and enrich themselves at the public expense. "Cursed is he that doth the work of the Lord deceitfully," and serves himself under pretense of serving his country. . . .

Need I inform you what barbarities and depredations a mongrel race of Indian savages and French Papists have perpetrated upon our frontiers? How many deserted or demolished houses and plantations! How wide an extent of country abandoned! How many poor families obliged to fly in consternation and leave their all behind them! What breaches and separations between the nearest relations! What painful ruptures of heart from heart! What shocking dispersions of those once united by the strongest and most endearing ties!

Some lie dead, mangled with savage wounds, consumed to ashes with outrageous flames, or torn and devoured by the beasts of the wilderness, while their bones lie whitening in the sun and serve as tragical memorials of the fatal spot where they fell. Others have been dragged away captives and made the slaves of imperious and cruel savages. Others have made their escape and live to lament their butchered or captivated friends and relations. In short, our frontiers have been drenched with the blood of our fellow subjects, through the length of a thousand miles; and new wounds are still opening.

We, in these inland parts of the country, are as yet unmolested, through the unmerited mercy of Heaven. But let us glance a thought to the western extremities of our body politic; and what melancholy scenes open to our view! Now, perhaps, while I am speaking; now, while you are secure and unmolested, our fellow subjects there may be feeling the Calamities I am describing. Now, perhaps, the savage shouts and whoops of Indians, and the screams and groans of some butchered family, may be mingling their horrors and circulating their horrendous echoes through the wilderness of rocks and mountains. Now, perhaps, some tender, delicate creature may be suffering an involuntary prostitution to savage lust; and perhaps debauched and murdered by the same hand. Now, perhaps, some miserable Briton or Virginian may be passing through a tedious process of experiments in the infernal art of torture. Now, some helpless children may be torn from the arms of their murdered parents and dragged away weeping and wringing their hands, to receive their education among barbarians and to be formed upon the model of a ferocious Indian soul.

And will these violences cease without a vigorous and timely resistance from us? Can Indian revenge and thirst for blood be glutted? Or can French ambition and avarice be satisfied? No, we have no method left but to repel force with force, and to give them blood to drink in their turn who have drunk ours. If we sit still and do nothing, or content ourselves, as alas we have hitherto, with feeble, dilatory efforts, we may expect these barbarities will not only continue but that the Indians, headed by the French, those eternal enemies of peace, liberty, and Britons, will carry their inroads still farther into the country and reach even to us.

By the desertion of our remote settlements, the frontiers are approaching every day nearer and nearer to us; and if we can not stand our ground now, when we have above 100 miles of a thick-settled country between us and the enemy, much less shall we be able when our strength is weakened by so vast a loss of men, arms, and riches, and we lie exposed to their immediate incursions. Some cry, "Let the enemy come down to us, and then we will fight them." But this is the trifling excuse of cowardice or security, and not the language of prudence and fortitude. Those who make this plea, if the enemy should take them at their word and make them so near a visit, would be as forward in flight as they are now backward to take up arms.

Such, my brethren, such, alas! is the present state of our country. It bleeds in a thousand veins; and, without a timely remedy, and the wound will prove mortal. And, in such circumstances, is it not our duty, in the sight of God, is it not a work to which the Lord loudly calls us, to take up arms for the defense of our country? . . .

Our countrymen, in general, have acted as if beings of their importance and merit might certainly rest in the quiet, unmolested possession of their liberty and property without anyone daring to disturb them, and without their doing anything for their own defense; or as if neither God nor man could strip them of their enjoyments. What vain, self-confident presumption, what intolerable insolence is this, in a sinful nation, a people laden with iniquity, who have forfeited every blessing, even the ground they tread upon and the air they breathe in, and who live merely by the unmerited grace and bounty of God?

Is not cowardice and security, or an unwillingness to engage with all our might in the defense of our country, in such a situation an enormous wickedness in the sight of God and worthy of His curse, as well as a scandalous, dastardly meanness in the sight of men, and worthy of public shame and indignation? Is it not fit that those who so contemptuously depreciate the rich and undeserved bounties of Heaven, and who swell so insolently with a vain conceit of their own importance and worth, should be punished with the loss of these blessings? . . .

Ye young and hardy men, whose very faces seem to speak that God and nature formed you for soldiers, who are free from the encumbrance of families depending upon you for subsistence, and who are perhaps but of little service to society while at home, may I not speak for you and declare as your mouth, "Here we are, all ready to abandon our ease and rush into the glorious dangers of the field, in defense of our country?" Ye that love your country, enlist; for honor will follow you in life or death in such a cause. You that love your religion, enlist; for your religion is in danger. Can Protestant Christianity expect quarters from heathen savages and French Papists? Sure in such an alliance, the powers of hell make a third party. Ye that love your friends and relations, enlist; lest ye see them enslaved or butchered before your eyes. Ye that would catch at money, here is a proper bait for you — £10 for a few months' service, besides the usual pay of soldiers.

I seriously make the proposal to you, not only as a subject of the best of kings and a friend to your country but as a servant of the most high God; for I am fully persuaded what I am recommending is His will; and disobedience to it may expose you to His curse.

This proposal is not liable to the objections that have been urged against former measures for raising men. You can no longer object "that you are dragged away like slaves against your wills, while others are without reason exempted"; for now it is left to your own honor, and you may act as free men. Nor can you object "that you are arbitrarily thrust under the command of foreign, unknown, or disagreeable officers"; for the gentleman that has the immediate command of this company and his subordinate officers are of yourselves, your neighbors' children, and, perhaps, your old companions.

And I hope, I may add, you need not object that you shall be badly used, for, Gentlemen Officers, may I not promise for you that not one man in your company shall be treated with cruelty or injustice as far as your authority or influence can prevent? May I not be your security that none but the guilty shall be punished, and they only according to the nature of the offense?

Perhaps some may object that should they enter the army their morals would be in danger of infection, and their virtue would be perpetually shocked with horrid scenes of vice. This may also be a discouragement to parents to consent to their children's engaging in so good a cause. I am glad to hear this objection, when it is sincere and not an empty excuse. And I wish I could remove it by giving you a universal assurance that the army is a school of religion and that soldiers, as they are more exposed to death than other men, are proportionably better prepared for it than others. But, alas! the reverse of this is too true; and the contagion of vice and irreligion is perhaps nowhere stronger than in the army;

where, one would think, the Supreme Tribunal should be always in view, and it should be their chief care to prepare for eternity, on the slippery brink of which they stand every moment.

But, Gentlemen Officers, I must again appeal to you that, as for this company, you will not willingly allow any form of vice to be practised in it with impunity, but will always endeavor to recommend and enforce religion and good morals by your example and authority and to suppress the contrary. May I not give the public the satisfaction of such an assurance concerning you, that, whatever others do, as for you and your company you will serve the Lord? Do you not own yourselves bound to this in honor and duty? Such a conduct, I can assure you, will render you popular among the wise and good; though perhaps it may expose you to the senseless contempt of fools who *make a mock of sin*, and who esteem it bravery to insult that God in whose hand their breath is and whose are all their ways. Such a conduct will afford you pleasure in the review, when the terrors of the bloody field are spread round you and death starts up before you in a thousand shocking forms. Such a conduct will be a source of true courage and render you nobly indifferent about life or death in a good cause. And let me honestly warn you that, if you do not maintain such a conduct, you will bitterly repent it, either in time or eternity. . . .

Everyone can complain of the bad management of our public undertakings, and lament the general security and inactivity that prevails. Everyone can wish that something were effectually done and that this and that person would enlist. Everyone can tell what great achievements he *would* perform were it not for this and that and a hundred obstructions in his way. But this idle complaining, wishing, and lamenting, and boasting will answer no end. SOMETHING MUST BE DONE! must be done BY YOU! Therefore, instead of assuming the state of patriots and heroes at home, To ARMS! and away to the field and prove your pretensions sincere. Let the thunder of this imprecation rouse you out of your ease and security — "Cursed be he that doth the work of the Lord deceitfully; and cursed be he that keepeth back his sword from blood." . . .

Thus far have I addressed you as soldiers, or at least as persons concerned in your stations to do all in your power to save your country. But we must not part thus. It is possible we may never meet more till we mingle with the assembled universe before the Supreme Tribunal. Therefore, before I dismiss you, I must address myself to you as sinners and as candidates for eternity. You are concerned to save your souls as well as your country; and should you save or gain a kingdom, or even the whole world, and lose your souls, your loss will be irreparable.

None of you, I hope, will reply, "I am now a soldier and have nothing more to do with religion." What! Has a soldier nothing to do with religion? Is a soldier under no obligations to the God that made him and that furnishes him with every blessing? Is not a soldier as much exposed to death as other men? May not a soldier be damned for sin as well as other sinners? And will he be able to dwell with devouring fire and everlasting burnings? Are these things so? Can any of you be so stupid as to think them so? If not, you must own that even a soldier has as much concern with religion as another. Therefore, hear me seriously upon this head.

You are about entering into the school of vice; for such the army has generally been. And are any of you already initiated into any of the mysteries of iniquity there practised? Must I so much as suppose that some of you, who have bravely espoused the cause of your country, are addicted to drunkenness, swearing, whoredom, or any gross vice? I cannot now take time to reason with you for your conviction; it may suffice to appeal to your own reason and conscience. Do you do well in indulging

these vices? Will you approve of it in the honest hour of death? Will this conduct prove a source of courage to you, when the arrows of death are flying thick around you and scores are falling on every side? No, you are self-condemned; and may I not reasonably hope you will endeavor to reform what you cannot but condemn?

Soldiers, indeed, are too commonly addicted to such immoralities; but are they the better soldiers on that account? Can an oath or a debauch inspire them with a rational fortitude against the fears of death? Would not prayer and a life of holiness better answer this purpose? Their courage, if they have any, must be the effect, not of thought but of the want of thought; it must be a brutal stupidity or ferocity, but not the rational courage of a man or a Christian.

Some of you, I doubt not, are happily free from these gross vices; and long may you continue so! But I must tell you, this negative goodness is not enough to prepare you for death, or to constitute you true Christians. The temper of your minds must be changed by the power of divine grace; and you must be turned from the love and practice of all sin to the love and practice of universal holiness. You must become humble, brokenhearted penitents and true believers in Jesus Christ. You must be enabled to live righteously, soberly, and godly in this present evil world.

This is religion; this is religion, that will keep you uncorrupted in the midst of vice and debauchery; this is religion, that will befriend you when cannons roar and swords gleam around you, and you are every moment expecting the deadly wound; this is religion, that will support you in the agonies of death and assure you of a happy immortality. . . .

Here I thought to have concluded; but I must take up a few minutes more to ask this crowd — Is there nothing to be done by us who stay at home toward the defense of our country and to promote the success of the expedition now in hand? Shall we sin on still impenitent and incorrigible? Shall we live as if we and our country were *self-dependent* and had nothing to do with the Supreme Ruler of the universe? Can an army of saints or of heroes defend an obnoxious people, ripe for destruction, from the righteous judgment of God?

The cause in which these brave men, and our army in general, are engaged is not so much their own as *ours.* Divine Providence considers them not so much in their private, personal character as in their public character as the representatives and guardians of their country; and, therefore, they will stand or fall, not so much according to their own personal character as according to the public character of the people whose cause they have undertaken. Be it known to you, then, their success depends upon *us* even more than upon themselves. . . .

Ye that complain of the burden of our public taxes; ye that love ease and shrink from the dangers of war; ye that wish to see peace restored once more; ye that would be happy beyond the grave and live forever — attend to my proposal. It is this: A THOROUGH NATIONAL REFORMATION. This will do what millions of money and thousands of men, with guns and swords and all the dreadful artillery of death, could not do — it will procure us peace again, a lasting, well-established peace.

7.

NATHANIEL AMES: The Future State of North America

Though Benjamin Franklin's Poor Richard *is now the best known almanac of the eighteenth century, Nathaniel Ames's annual publication, the* Astronomical Diary and Almanack, *which he issued from 1726 to his death in 1764, was almost equally popular at the time. In the 1750s and 1760s, when America's population was only a little more than a million, the* Almanack *reached a yearly circulation of 60,000, making Ames's name a household word. One of the most versatile almanacs of the period, it offered astronomical observations, extracts from the English poets, such as Milton and Pope, and pithy and witty maxims. A selection from the 1758 edition of the* Almanack *is reprinted below.*

Source: *The Essays, Humor, and Poems of Nathaniel Ames,* Sam. Briggs, ed., Cleveland, 1891, pp. 284-286.

AMERICA IS A SUBJECT which daily becomes more and more interesting. I shall therefore fill these pages with a word upon its past, present, and future state.

First of its past state. Time has cast a shade upon this scene. Since the creation, innumerable accidents have happened here, the bare mention of which would create wonder and surprise; but they are all lost in oblivion. The ignorant natives, for want of letters, have forgot their stock; and know not from whence they came, or how, or when they arrived here, or what has happened since. Who can tell what wonderful changes have happened by the mighty operations of nature, such as deluges, volcanoes, earthquakes, etc.! Or whether great tracts of land were not absorbed into those vast lakes or inland seas which occupy so much space to the west of us.

But to leave the natural, and come to the political state: We know how the French have erected a line of forts from the Ohio to Nova Scotia, including all the inestimable country to the west of us, into their exorbitant claim. This, with infinite justice, the English resented; and in this cause our blood has been spilled. Which brings to our consideration:

Second, the present state of North America. A writer upon this present time says, "The parts of North America which may be claimed by Great Britain or France are of as much worth as either kingdom. That fertile country to the west of the Appalachian Mountains (a string of 800 or 900 miles in length), between Canada and the Mississippi, is of larger extent than all France, Germany, and Poland; and all well provided with rivers, a very fine, wholesome air, a rich soil, capable of producing food and physic and all things necessary for the conveniency and delight of life. In fine, the "Garden of the World!"

Time was we might have been possessed of it. At this time, two mighty kings contend for this inestimable prize. Their respective claims are to be measured by the length of their swords. The poet says, the gods and opportunity ride post; that you must take her by the forelock, being bald behind. Have we not too fondly depended upon our numbers? Sir Francis Bacon says, "The wolf careth not how many the sheep be." But numbers, well spirited, with the blessing of Heaven, will do wonders when, by military skill and discipline, the commanders can actuate (as by one soul) the most numerous bodies of armed people.

Our numbers will not avail till the colonies are united; for while divided, the strength of the inhabitants is broken like the petty kingdoms in Africa. If we do not join heart and hand in the common cause against our exulting foes but fall to disputing among ourselves, it may really happen as the governor of Pennsylvania told his Assembly, "We shall have no privilege to dispute about, nor country to dispute in."

Third, of the future state of North America. Here we find a vast stock of proper materials for the art and ingenuity of man to work upon — treasures of immense worth, concealed from the poor, ignorant aboriginal natives! The curious have observed that the progress of humane literature (like the sun) is from the east to the west; thus has it traveled through Asia and Europe and now is arrived at the eastern shore of America.

As the celestial light of the Gospel was directed here by the finger of God, it will doubtless finally drive the long, long night of heathenish darkness from America; so arts and sciences will change the face of nature in their tour from hence over the Appalachian Mountains to the western ocean. And as they march through the vast desert, the residence of wild beasts will be broken up, and their obscene howl cease forever. Instead of which, the stones and trees will dance together at the music of *Orpheus*; the rocks will disclose their hidden gems; and the inestimable treasures of gold and silver be broken up. Huge mountains of iron ore are already discovered, and vast stores are reserved for future generations. This metal, more useful than gold and silver, will employ millions of hands, not only to form the martial sword and peaceful share, alternately, but an infinity of utensils improved in the exercise of art and handcrafted among men.

Nature, through all her works, has stamped authority on this law, namely, "That all fit matter shall be improved to its best purposes." Shall not then those vast quarries that teem with mechanic stone — those for structure be piled into great cities; and those for sculpture into statues to perpetuate the honor of renowned heroes, even those who shall *now* save their country. O! ye unborn inhabitants of America! Should this page escape its destined conflagration at the year's end, and these alphabetical letters remain legible, when your eyes behold the sun after he has rolled the seasons round for two or three centuries more, you will know that in Anno Domini 1758, we dreamed of your times.

8.

BENJAMIN FRANKLIN: The Way to Wealth

The Way to Wealth (1758) is, apart from the Autobiography, *Franklin's best-known piece of writing. In fact, it is a sort of anthology of the maxims which for twenty-five years he had placed here and there in his yearly* Poor Richard's Almanac. *Most of these maxims were not original with him, having been borrowed from Dryden, Pope, Prior, Gay, Swift, Bacon, La Rochefoucauld, Rabelais, and other masters of the epigram; many were simply popular sayings, immemorially old. But Franklin altered their phraseology as he pleased, showing himself to be a master of proverbs in his own right. The Way to Wealth was not entirely representative of Franklin, since it revealed only the prudential side of his nature. Omitted from it were many of the lighter, wittier sayings that helped make* Poor Richard *delightful as well as instructive reading. Wit, perhaps, was to Franklin not so clearly the way to worldly success as were industry and frugality.*

Source: *Works*, III, pp. 453-463.

Courteous Reader,

I have heard that nothing gives an author so great pleasure as to find his works respectfully quoted by others. Judge, then, how much I must have been gratified by an incident I am going to relate to you. I stopped my horse lately where a great number of people were collected at an auction of merchants goods. The hour of the sale not being come, they were conversing on the badness of the times; and one of the company called to a plain, clean old man, with white locks, "Pray, Father Abraham, what think you of the times? Will not those heavy taxes quite ruin the country? How shall we ever be able to pay them? What would you advise us to?" Father Abraham stood up, and replied, "If you would have my advice, I will give it you in short, 'for a word to the wise is enough,' as Poor Richard says." They joined in desiring him to speak his mind and gathering round him, he proceeded as follows:

"Friends," says he, "the taxes are, indeed, very heavy, and, if those laid on by the government were the only ones he had to pay, we might more easily discharge them; but we have many others, and much more grievous to some of us. We are taxed twice as much by our idleness, three times as much by our pride, and four times as much by our folly; and from these taxes the commissioners cannot ease or deliver us by allowing an abatement. However, let us hearken to good advice, and something may be done for us; 'God helps them that help themselves,' as Poor Richard says.

"It would be thought a hard government that should tax its people one-tenth part of their time, to be employed in its service; but idleness taxes many of us much more; sloth, by bringing on diseases, absolutely shortens life. 'Sloth, like rust, consumes faster than labor wears, while the used key is always bright,' as Poor Richard says. 'But dost thou love life, then do not squander time, for that is the stuff life is made of,' as Poor Richard says. How much more than is necessary do we spend in sleep, forgetting that 'the sleeping fox catches no poultry, and that there will be sleeping enough in the grave,' as Poor Richard says.

" 'If time be of all things the most precious, wasting time must be,' as Poor Richard says, 'the greatest prodigality,' since, as he elsewhere tells us, 'lost time is never found again; and what we call time enough always proves little enough.' Let us then up and be doing, and doing to the purpose, so by diligence shall we do more with less perplexity. 'Sloth makes all things difficult, but industry all easy; and he that riseth late must trot all day and shall scarce overtake his business at night; while laziness travels so slowly that poverty soon overtakes him. Drive thy business, let not that drive thee; and early to bed and early to rise, makes a man healthy, wealthy, and wise,' as Poor Richard says.

"So what signifies wishing and hoping for better times? We may make these times better if we bestir ourselves. 'Industry need not wish, and he that lives upon hope will die fasting. There are no gains without pains; then help hands for I have no lands.' Or, if I have, they are smartly taxed. 'He that hath a trade, hath an estate; and he that hath a calling, hath an office of profit and honor,' as Poor Richard says. But then the trade must be worked at, and the calling well followed, or neither the estate nor the office will enable us to pay our taxes. If we are industrious, we shall never starve; for, 'at the workingman's house, hunger looks in but dares not enter.' Nor will the bailiff or the constable enter, for 'industry pays debts, while despair increaseth them.'

"What though you have found no treasure, nor has any rich relation left you a legacy, 'diligence is the mother of good luck, and God gives all things to industry. Then plow deep, while sluggards sleep, and you shall have corn to sell and to keep.' Work while it is called today, for you know not how much you may be hindered tomorrow. 'One today is worth two tomorrows,' as Poor Richard says; and further,

'never leave that till tomorrow which you can do today.'

"If you were a servant, would you not be ashamed that a good master should catch you idle? Are you then your own master? Be ashamed to catch yourself idle when there is so much to be done for yourself, your family, your country, and your king. Handle your tools without mittens; remember that 'the cat in gloves catches no mice,' as Poor Richard says. It is true, there is much to be done, and perhaps you are weakhanded; but stick to it steadily, and you will see great effects, for 'constant dropping wears away stones; and by diligence and patience the mouse ate in two the cable; and little strokes fell great oaks.'

"Methinks I hear some of you say, 'must a man afford himself no leisure?' I will tell thee, my friend, what Poor Richard says: 'Employ thy time well, if thou meanest to gain leisure; and since thou art not sure of a minute, throw not away an hour.' Leisure is time for doing something useful; this leisure the diligent man will obtain, but the lazy man never; for 'a life of leisure and a life of laziness are two things. Many, without labor, would live by their wits only, but they break for want of stock'; whereas industry gives comfort and plenty and respect. 'Fly pleasures, and they will follow you. The diligent spinner has a large shift; and now I have a sheep and a cow, everybody bids me goodmorrow.'

"But with our industry we must likewise be steady, settled, and careful, and oversee our own affairs with our own eyes, and not trust too much to others; for, as Poor Richard says,

I never saw an oft-removed tree.
Nor yet an oft-removed family,
That throve so well as those that
    settled be.

"And again, 'Three removes is as bad as a fire'; and again, 'Keep thy shop, and thy shop will keep thee'; and again, 'If you would have your business done, go, if not, send'; and again,

He that by the plough would thrive,
Himself must either hold or drive.

"And again, 'The eye of a master will do more work than both his hands'; and again, 'Want of care does us more damage than want of knowledge'; and again, 'Not to oversee workmen is to leave them your purse open.' Trusting too much to others' care is the ruin of many; for, 'in the affairs of this world, men are saved, not by faith but by the want of it.' But a man's own care is profitable, for, 'if you would have a faithful servant, and one that you like, serve yourself. A little neglect may breed great mischief; for want of a nail the shoe was lost, and for want of a shoe the horse was lost, and for want of a horse the rider was lost,' being overtaken and slain by the enemy; all for want of a little care about a horseshoe nail.

"So much for industry, my friends, and attention to one's own business; but to these we must add frugality, if we would make our industry more certainly successful. A man may, if he knows not how to save as he gets, 'keep his nose all his life to the grindstone and die not worth a groat at last. A fat kitchen makes a lean will'; and

Many estates are spent in the getting,
Since women for tea forsook spinning
    and knitting,
And men for punch forsook hewing
    and splitting.

"If you would be wealthy, think of saving as well as of getting. The Indies have not made Spain rich, because her outgoes are greater than her incomes.

"Away, then, with your expensive follies, and you will not then have so much cause to complain of hard times, heavy taxes, and chargeable families; for,

Women and wine, game and deceit,
Make the wealth small, and the want
    great.

"And further, 'What maintains one vice, would bring up two children.' You may think, perhaps, that a little tea, or a little punch now and then, diet a little more costly, clothes a little finer, and a little entertainment now and then can be no great matter; but remember, 'Many a little makes a mickle.' Beware of little expenses; 'A small leak will sink a great ship,' as Poor Richard says; and again, 'Who dainties love shall beggars prove'; and moreover, 'Fools make feasts, and wise men eat them.'

"Here you are all got together to this sale of fineries and knickknacks. You call them *goods,* but if you do not take care, they will prove *evils* to some of you. You expect they will be sold cheap, and perhaps they may, for less than they cost; but, if you have no occasion for them, they must be dear to you. Remember what Poor Richard says, 'Buy what thou hast no need of, and ere long thou shalt sell thy necessaries.' And again, 'At a great pennyworth pause a while.' He means that perhaps the cheapness is apparent only, and not real; or the bargain, by straitening thee in thy business, may do thee more harm than good. For in another place he says, 'Many have been ruined by buying good pennyworths.' Again, 'It is foolish to lay out money in a purchase of repentance'; and yet this folly is practised every day at auctions, for want of minding the *Almanac.*

"Many a one, for the sake of finery on the back, have gone with a hungry belly, and half-starved their families; 'Silks and satins, scarlet and velvets, put out the kitchen fire,' as Poor Richard says. These are not the necessaries of life, they can scarcely be called the conveniences; and yet, only because they look pretty, how many want to have them? By these and other extravagancies, the genteel are reduced to poverty, and forced to borrow of those whom they formerly despised, but who, through industry and frugality, have maintained their standing; in which case it appears plainly, that 'a ploughman on his legs is higher than a gentleman on his knees,' as Poor Richard says.

Perhaps they have had a small estate left them, which they knew not the getting of; they think 'it is day and will never be night'; that a little to be spent out of so much is not worth minding; but 'always taking out of the meal tub, and never putting in, soon comes to the bottom,' as Poor Richard says; and then, when the well is dry, they know the worth of water. But this they might have known before, if they had taken his advice: 'If you would know the value of money go and try to borrow some; for he that goes a-borrowing goes a-sorrowing,' as Poor Richard says; and, indeed, so does he that lends to such people, when he goes to get it in again. Poor Dick further advises and says,

Fond pride of dress is sure a very curse,
Ere fancy you consult, consult your purse.

"And again, 'Pride is as loud a beggar as want, and a great deal more saucy.' When you have bought one fine thing, you must buy ten more that your appearance may be all of a piece; but Poor Dick says, 'It is easier to suppress the first desire than to satisfy all that follow it'; and it is as truly folly for the poor to ape the rich as for the frog to swell in order to equal the ox.

Vessels large may venture more,
But little boats should keep near shore.

"It is, however, a folly soon punished; for, as Poor Richard says, 'Pride that dines on vanity, sups on contempt; pride breakfasted with plenty, dined with poverty, and supped with infamy.' And, after all, of what use is this pride of appearance, for which so much is risked, so much is suffered? It cannot promote health, nor ease pain; it makes no increase of merit in the person; it creates envy; it hastens misfortune.

"But what madness must it be to *run in debt* for these superfluities! We are offered, by the terms of this sale, six-months credit; and that, perhaps, has induced some of us to attend it, because we cannot spare the ready money and hope now to be fine without it. But, ah! think what you do when you run in debt; you give to another power over your liberty. If you cannot pay at the time, you will be ashamed to see your creditor; you will be in fear when you speak to him; you will make poor pitiful sneaking excuses and, by degrees, come to lose your veracity and sink into base, downright lying; for, 'the second vice is lying, the *first* is running in debt,' as Poor Richard says; and again, to the same purpose, 'lying rides upon debt's back'; whereas a freeborn Englishman ought not to be ashamed nor afraid to see or speak to any man living. But poverty often deprives a man of all spirit and virtue. 'It is hard for an empty bag to stand upright.'

"What would you think of that prince, or of that government, who should issue an edict forbidding you to dress like a gentleman or gentlewoman, on pain of imprisonment or servitude? Would you not say that you were free, have a right to dress as you please, and that such an edict would be a breach of your privileges, and such a government tyrannical? And yet you are about to put yourself under that tyranny, when you run in debt for such dress! Your creditor has authority, at his pleasure, to deprive you of your liberty by confining you in gaol for life, or by selling you for a servant, if you should not be able to pay him.

"When you have got your bargain, you may, perhaps, think little of payment; but, as Poor Richard says, 'Creditors have better memories than debtors; creditors are a superstitious sect, great observers of set days and times.' The day comes round before you are aware, and the demand is made before you are prepared to satisfy it; or, if you bear your debt in mind, the term, which at first seemed so long, will, as it lessens, appear extremely short — time will seem to have added wings to his heels as well as his shoulders. 'Those have a short Lent who owe money to be paid at Easter.' At present, perhaps, you may think yourselves in thriving circumstances, and that you can bear a little extravagance without injury; but

For age and want save while you may,
No morning sun lasts a whole day.

"Gain may be temporary and uncertain, but ever, while you live, expense is constant and certain; and, 'it is easier to build two chimneys than to keep one in fuel,' as Poor Richard says; so 'rather go to bed supperless than rise in debt.'

Get what you can, and what you
    get hold,
'Tis the stone that will turn all your lead
    into gold.

"And when you have got the philosopher's stone, sure you will no longer complain of bad times, or the difficulty of paying taxes.

"This doctrine, my friends, is reason and wisdom; but, after all, do not depend too much upon your own industry and frugality and prudence, though excellent things; for they may all be blasted, without the bless-

ing of heaven. And, therefore, ask that blessing humbly, and be not uncharitable to those that at present seem to want it, but comfort and help them. Remember Job suffered and was afterward prosperous.

"And now, to conclude, 'experience keeps a dear school, but fools will learn in no other,' as Poor Richard says, and scarce in that; for, it is true, 'We may give advice, but we cannot give conduct'; however, remember this, 'They that will not be counseled cannot be helped'; and further, that 'if you will not hear reason she will surely rap your knuckles,' as Poor Richard says."

Thus the old gentleman ended his harangue. The people heard it and approved the doctrine and immediately practised the contrary, just as if it had been a common sermon; for the auction opened and they began to buy extravagantly.

I found the good man had thoroughly studied my almanacs and digested all I had dropped on those topics during the course of twenty-five years. The frequent mention he made of me must have tired anyone else; but my vanity was wonderfully delighted with it, though I was conscious that not a tenth part of the wisdom was my own, which he ascribed to me but rather the gleanings that I had made of the sense of all ages and nations. However, I resolved to be the better for the echo of it; and, though I had at first determined to buy stuff for a new coat, I went away, resolved to wear my old one a little longer. Reader, if thou wilt do the same, thy profit will be as great as mine.

FRENCH AND INDIAN WAR

The French and Indian War was the culmination of over a century of Anglo-French colonial rivalry in America. By 1755 the British colonies had far outstripped the French in population and prosperity. Traders and settlers from Virginia and Pennsylvania were beginning to trickle across the Allegheny Mountains into areas of French claim in the Ohio Valley. Indians attempting to resist this encroachment allied themselves with France. By 1755, when the first major engagements between British and French forces took place, conflict along the frontier was almost continuous. In spite of the growing intensity of the fighting war was not declared until fighting broke out in 1756 among the rival European alliances. The war in America, now a portion of a general European war, progressed inconclusively until the fall of Louisbourg in 1758. The surrender of Quebec in the following year and the eventual surrender of French control throughout Canada signaled the end of her colonial venture in America. However, in doubling the size of her American possessions, Britain unwittingly took on military and financial burdens that would eventually cost her the original colonies. Revenue policies, intended to place more of the costs of colonial administration on the colonies themselves, touched off the chain of circumstances that ended in revolution.

George Washington, was Braddock's aide and later commanded Virginia militia

Gen. Edward Braddock, commander of "All His Majesty's Forces in America"

Preliminary Battles

This three-part woodcut shows two phases of the battle of Lake George and a map of the area

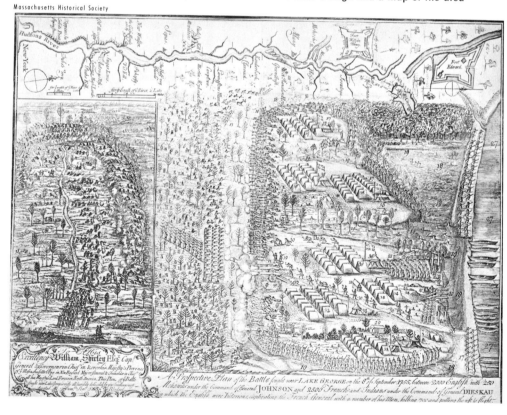

Sir William Johnson, commander of British forces at Lake George

"A Perspective View of Lake George," looking south from a small fort erected to guard a landing place for supplies

By the time England declared war on France in May of 1756, several battles had already been fought in America and the British were on the defensive. In particular, the defeat of General Braddock in western Pennsylvania severely weakened British strength west of the Allegheny Mountains for the duration of the war. Thousands of settlers had to return East or face French and Indian attacks. The French forces were defeated at Lake George in upper New York in 1755, but the victory proved to be of minor importance as the British were unable to follow up on it for several years.

Fanciful version of Braddock's defeat at Great Meadows depicts the general's death in battle

Earl of Loudoun, British commander

Marquis de Montcalm

French Victories

Taking the initiative under the leadership of Montcalm, the French captured the fort at Oswego, N.Y., in 1756 and controlled Lake Ontario. In the following year Montcalm demolished Ft. William Henry near Ticonderoga. A planned British expedition against Louisbourg was abandoned and the English commander, Loudoun, was replaced. Fighting in 1758 began with the defeat of a British attack on Ticonderoga, but this was the last French success of the war.

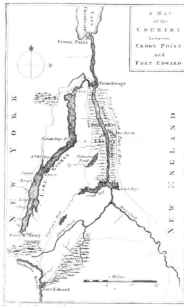

View of the fort at Oswego on Lake Ontario at the mouth of the Onondago River, New York

In a battle near Ft. Ticonderoga Montcalm's 3,000 men routed a much larger British force

Ticonderoga, on Lake Champlain, guarded the main route between Canada and the colonies

PLAN
OF THE FORT
at
TIENDEROGA
at
the HEAD of
Lake Champlain;
1759.

PART

Road from the Saw Mill

OF

Garden

LAKE

A. The Fort.........
B. Stone work......
C. Earth work......
D. Wharf..........
E. Store house for
  the Naval Stores
F. The Redoubt...
G. Lower Battery
  for 2 Guns.
H. Store houses
  for Provisions.

I. 9 Ovens
K. Brick Kiln
L. Lime Kilns
M. Old French Batt.?
N. The French Lines
O. Batterys thereon
P. Abbatis of branches
  of Trees before ÿ Lines
a. Wharf & Harbour for
  ÿ Vessels of War stockaded
  round to prevent the Ene
  my destroying them

CHAMPLAIN

Scale 400 Feet to an Inch.

The Turning Point

The campaign of 1758, which began badly at Ticonderoga, ended well for the British. Louisbourg, guarding the waters off Nova Scotia, had been returned to France after King George's War in 1748. The fortress was attacked again in July 1758 and taken permanently out of French hands. This success and the victories in 1759 were due in large part to the military reorganization of the new prime minister, William Pitt.

Lord Jeffrey Amherst was made commander in chief of British forces after leading the successful attack on Louisbourg

This 1755 English engraving exults prematurely over the blockade of Louisbourg

A general view of the siege of Louisbourg shows the British fleet blocking the French

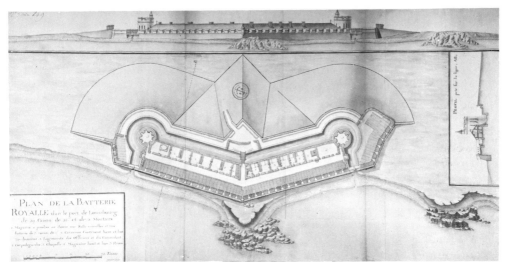

In spite of elaborate fortifications Louisbourg never successfully resisted attack

A French attempt to break the siege in 1758 forestalled a planned British attack

The naval blockade of Louisbourg was repeatedly challenged by the French fleet until Amherst's victory

William Pitt, first earl of Chatham, (1708-1778), became prime minister in July 1757

The Fall of Quebec

Gen. James Wolfe, commander of the attacking British forces at Quebec

British troops landed upstream from Quebec and defeated the defenders on the Plains of Abraham

Before a landing could be made the British had to run past massed batteries lining the waterfront

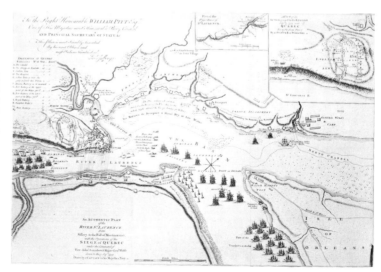

The bombardments of the long siege left much of Quebec in ruins

The most important engagement of the French and Indian War, and the largest, was the siege of Quebec in 1759. Both General Wolfe, the British commander, and Montcalm were killed before the seemingly impregnable city surrendered. This proved to be the decisive battle of the war in America. After a century of conflict Canada was effectively controlled by the British. Several years of fighting in Europe culminated in the Treaty of Paris, 1763, which formalized the end of the French colonial presence in America. England's next war in America would be with her own colonies.

The conclusion of the peace treaty was celebrated in a formal dinner at Versailles

1759

9.

RICHARD CORBIN: The Management of Plantations

Virginia owed its early prosperity to the cultivation of tobacco. By the 1750s, although many planters were beginning to substitute wheat for tobacco, the latter crop still dominated the economy. The following letter of January 1, 1759, from Richard Corbin to his overseer carefully outlined management policies for his Virginia plantation. As the letter shows, slave labor was by now an important element in the colony's agriculture.

Source: Commons, I, pp. 109-112.

As IT WILL BE NECESSARY to say something to you and to suggest to you my thoughts upon the business you have undertaken, I shall endeavor to be particular and circumstantial.

The care of Negroes is the first thing to be recommended that you give me timely notice of their wants that they may be provided with all necessaries. The breeding wenches more particularly you must instruct the overseers to be kind and indulgent to and not force them, when with child, upon any service or hardship that will be injurious to them; and that they have every necessary when in that condition that is needful for them; and the children to be well looked after; and to give them every spring and fall the Jerusalem oak seed for a week together; and that none of them suffer in time of sickness for want of proper care.

Observe a prudent and watchful conduct over the overseers that they attend their business with diligence, keep the Negroes in good order, and enforce obedience by the example of their own industry, which is a more effectual method in every respect of succeeding and making good crops than hurry and severity. The ways of industry are constant and regular; not to be in a hurry at one time and do nothing at another but to be always usefully and steadily employed. A man who carries on business in this manner will be prepared for every incident that happens. He will see what work may be proper at the distance of some time and be gradually and leisurely providing for it. By this foresight he will never be in confusion himself and his business instead of a labor will be a pleasure to him.

Next to the care of Negroes is the care of stock, and, supposing the necessary care taken, I shall only here mention the use to be made of them for the improvement of the tobo [tobacco] grounds. Let them be constantly and regularly penned. Let the size of the pens be 1,000 tobo hills for 100 cattle, and so in proportion for a greater or less quantity, and the pens moved once a week. By this practice, steadily pursued, a convenient quantity of land may be provided at Moss's Neck without clearing; and as I intend this seat of land to be a settlement for one of my sons, I would be very sparing of the woods, and that piece of woods that lies on the left hand of the Ferry Road must not be cut down on any account. A proper use of the cattle will answer every purpose of making tobo without the disturbance too commonly made of the timber land; as you will see this estate once a fortnight, you may easily discover if they have been neglectful of penning the cattle and moving the cowpens.

Take an exact account of all the Negroes and stocks at each plantation and send to me. And though once a year may be sufficient to take this account, yet it will be advisable to see them once a month at least; as such, an inspection will fix more closely the overseers' attentions to these points.

As complaints have been made by the Negroes in respect to their provision of corn, I must desire you to put that matter under such a regulation as your own prudence will dictate to you. The allowance to be sure is plentiful, and they ought to have their belly full, but care must be taken with this plenty that no waste is committed. You must let Hampton know that the care of the Negroes' corn, sending it to mill, always to be provided with meal that everyone may have enough, and that regularly and at stated times, this is a duty as much incumbent upon him as any other.

As the corn at Moss's Neck is always ready money, it will not be advisable to be at much expense in raising hogs. The shattered corn will probably be enough for this purpose. When I receive your account of the spare corn at Moss's Neck and Richland, which I hope will be from King and Queen Court, I shall give orders to Colonel Tucker to send for it.

Let me be acquainted with every incident that happens, and let me have timely notice of everything that is wanted, that it may be provided. To employ the fall and winter well is the foundation of a successful crop in the summer. You will therefore animate the overseers to great diligence that their work may be in proper forwardness and not have that to do in the spring that ought to be done in the winter. There is business sufficient for every season of the year, and to prevent the work of one season from interfering with the work of another depends upon the care of the overseer.

The time of sowing tobo seed, the order the plant patch ought to be in, and the use of the wheat straw I have not touched upon, it being too obvious to be overlooked.

Supposing the corn new laid and the tobo ripe for housing — to cut the corn tops and gather the blades in proper time is included under the care of cattle, their preservation in the winter depending upon good fodder — I shall therefore confine myself to tobo. Tobo hogsheads should always be provided the first week in September; every morning of the month is fit for striking and stripping; every morning, therefore, of this month they should strike as much tobo as they can strip while the dew is upon the ground, and what they strip in the morning must be stemmed in the evening. This method constantly practised, the tobacco will be all priced before Christmas, weigh well, and at least one hogshead in ten gained by finishing the tobo thus early. You shall never want either for my advice or assistance. These instructions will hold good for Poplar Neck and Portobacco, and perhaps Spotsylvania, too.

I now send my two carpenters, Mack and Abram, to Moss's Neck to build a good barn, mend up the quarters, and get as many staves and heading as will be sufficient for next year's tobo hogsheads. I expect they will complete the whole that is necessary upon that estate by the last of March.

10.

FRANCIS ALISON: A Plea for Uniform Education in the Colonies

The eighteenth-century colleges (the present Princeton, Brown, Rutgers, Dartmouth, and the University of Pennsylvania) that were a direct result of the Great Awakening considered themselves, as had their seventeenth-century predecessors, as centers for the education of ministers. Although there were small variations in curriculum, for the most part the colleges were content to retain the traditional course of study — the Latin and Greek classics, mathematics, and religion. It is not surprising, therefore, considering this unity of purpose, to find Thomas Clap, the president of Yale, proposing a uniform plan of education for all the colonial colleges. The following letter of May 27, 1759, from Francis Alison of the College of Philadelphia (University of Pennsylvania), was an attempt, among other things, to arouse support for the plan. The letter was sent to Ezra Stiles, student (1742-1746), tutor (1749-1755), and later president (1778-1795) of Yale College.

Source: *Extracts from the Itineraries and Other Miscellanies of Ezra Stiles, etc., etc.,* Franklin B. Dexter, ed., New Haven, 1916, pp. 422-424.

I WAS FAVORED with yours by Mr. Solomon Southwick and am highly pleased that you continue so unwearied in the pursuit of knowledge. I pray God that He may long spare you and make you a blessing to His church, and a useful instrument to promote knowledge and learning.

I am sorry that I am able to give you so little satisfaction concerning the comet; when it first appeared, Mr. Grew, our professor of mathematics, could see it but twice, the weather was so hazy. I got up about three one morning to observe it with him, but the sky was clouded, and the morning was so raw, that I almost lost my health by it, which brought me to a resolution that effectually destroyed my stargazing. When it appeared again, we conjectured that it was another comet and were in great doubts whether either of them was

the one so eagerly expected last year. Mr. Grew made some observations, but on my application to him to communicate them, I find that he either has not obtained the satisfaction he desired, or that he is more reserved than usual.

It appears to me to be no easy matter to calculate their periods from the short visits which they pay us, notwithstanding that some have made great pretensions this way. As I hope with more certainty and less trouble to acquire this kind of knowledge in the next stage of my existence, if it be necessary, I have determined to give myself no further trouble till I be allowed to converse with Newton, Halley, Whiston, and Flamstead, and some others of the same complexion, if these great names be allowed to shine in one constellation in heaven. Yet I am far from blaming you for your careful and accurate researches; it may make you more useful here and form your taste to examine the works of God with a higher satisfaction in the coming world.

I have seen proposals to unite the several colleges on this continent, as near as might be, in the same plan of education, to govern them nearly by the same laws, and to admit none in one college that were expelled or denied admittance in another, without previously consulting the heads of the college from whence the student was expelled, etc. This proposal was made by Mr. President Clap, and deserves a serious consideration. I think that there ought to be more care taken to prepare boys for the college than is now used. Certainly the design of the founders is not complied with by preparing boys to recite Virgil, Tully, and the Greek Testament, as it were by rote, without sufficiently understanding the Latin and Greek grammars, and being able to write Latin and English at least grammatically, if not elegantly.

Euclid's elements and algebra, at least so much as might enable them to solve quadratic equations, should be taught the classes statedly and carefully, and moral philosophy should be a business of greater care and closer application than is now the common practice; without this branch of knowledge, we shall be ill able to defend our holy Christian religion; to understand the rights of mankind; or to explain and enforce the duties which we owe to God, our neighbors, and ourselves. I would, as a friend to learning, recommend it to you to engage gentlemen and gospel ministers of the first rank, and of more enlarged views to engage in this reformation.

It is a shame that almost everywhere learning dwindles in colleges and universities; and that the loudest complaints cannot awaken them from their lethargy. I will count it a favor to receive, and will punctually answer your letters, especially while you are active in promoting the . . . cause of liberty, virtue, or learning.

———◆———

Since in a bed a man and maid
May bundle and be chaste,
It doth no good to burn up wood;
It is a needless waste.

New England Broadside in Defense of Bundling

11.

Defense of the Virginia Paper Currency

Throughout the period of economic growth of the first half of the eighteenth century, England maintained a tight control over the colonial money supply. As most of the business of the colonies was based on trade, the economy could and did function on an extensive credit system, without suffering much from the lack of a medium of exchange. Occasionally, in order, say, to pay soldiers in time of war, the colonies did issue paper money, but British merchants, who stood to lose if the currency depreciated, were always quick to complain about the practice. At the outbreak of the Seven Years' War in Europe, Britain looked to the colonies for support and, as an incentive, relaxed her restrictions on paper currency. The colonies then circulated increasing amounts of paper money, only to be reprimanded at the end of the war. Virginia's House of Burgesses, having issued paper currency for the first time during this period, responded to the complaints of English merchants with a defense of the colony's actions. The Committee of Correspondence sent the following letter of instructions to the Virginia agent in London. The letter is dated December 12, 1759.

Source: *Virginia Magazine of History and Biography,* XI, July, 1903, pp. 1-5.

WE ARE INFORMED that the merchants of Great Britain are much alarmed at our Assembly's passing some acts for emitting large quantities of paper money, which is made a legal tender for all debts (the King's quitrents excepted), and they are very apprehensive that they may be great sufferers thereby in collecting their debts due here.

These apprehensions of the merchants proceed from a mistaken notion of our having a law in force for paying off sterling debts in current money at 25 percent exchange.

No loss can arise to the merchants from making this paper money a legal tender for sterling debts as the law now stands, and they are in a much better condition and less liable to losses in collecting their debts than

if nothing but sterling or lawful money of Great Britain were held a tender for such debts, as the Act of the 6th of Queen Anne, which they so much rely on to be a good precedent in such case.

If this can be shown, it is to be hoped the gentlemen in the trade will be satisfied that there is no necessity to solicit their memorial so far as to procure an instruction about this matter.

True it is that before this war, and when exchange was rarely above 25 percent, we had a law to settle the payment of judgments for sterling debts at that rate, and it was passed to prevent disputes about the exchange, and as a direction to the sheriffs in levying executions on these judgments. There was likewise a further view: to prevent creditors from taking an unreasonable advantage of the necessity of the debtor for his forbearing to execute the judgment perhaps 10 or 15 percent above the then current exchange, which, as it was a kind of traffic about bills of exchange, did not come under the penalties of our laws against usury, or at least was hard to be come at and punished by them.

But when, at the breaking out of the present war, exchange began to rise, or rather it was foreseen that it would do so, and it was found that injustice would be done to many, especially the merchants in Great Britain, if that law remained in force, it was repealed by an Act of the 28th George II, entitled "An Act to amend an Act entitled 'An Act declaring the law concerning executions, and for the relief of insolvent debtors and for other purposes therein mentioned.'" The preamble of which shows its intention to take care of the merchants' interest, and the principal enacting clause is, "That in any action which has been or shall be commenced, and is or shall be depending for the recovery of any sterling money, in any court of record within this dominion, wherein the plaintiff or plaintiffs shall recover, such court shall have power, and are hereby directed by rule to be entered at the foot of their judgment in such action, to order such judgment to be discharged or levied in current money, at such a difference of exchange as they shall think just, any law, usage, or custom to the contrary thereof in anywise notwithstanding."

And what rate of exchange can a court under the direction of this act think just but that which is current at the time of entering the judgment, or such a one that the merchant may have his whole debt remitted to him without those losses they so much apprehend?

If our notable agent, at the other end of the town, had known and stated these things to the merchants, they would hardly have thought it necessary to present any memorial about it. And this it was his duty to have known and done, as he has an allowance of £200 per annum to negotiate the affairs of the country; and these acts above mentioned are regularly transmitted, as he knows, to the board of trade, and were remaining in that office at the very time the memorial was presented.

But it may be thought that the greatest difficulty is yet to come, viz., to obviate the heavy complaint, and that which seems to carry weight at first view, that the Assembly have passed a law, *ex post facto*, to declare paper bills of credit a good tender even for sterling debts contracted before the passing such law; whereas the merchants think that nothing less than sterling or lawful money of Great Britain should be allowed to be a good tender, agreeable to the Act of the 6th of Queen Anne, especially for such precontracted debts. This is to be done, and at the same time it is to be shown, that the merchants are in a better condition and less liable to losses in receiving their sterling debts under our laws than they would be if nothing but sterling or lawful money of Great Britain were held a tender.

For this purpose let us suppose that a merchant in London obtains a judgment here for £100 sterling; the debtor is obliged by the 6th of Queen Anne and therefore procures £100 sterling, or lawful money of Great Britain, and pays this debt. Now, this sum being only of equal value to £125 current money, and exchange being now at 35 percent (and in wartime it is rarely lower), the agent here must in that case give £10 current money more to purchase a bill of exchange to remit this debt to his principal, which £10 is so much real loss to the merchant; whereas, by the provision of our law, no such loss is incurred, but the creditor has his whole £135 decreed to him, with which a bill is bought and the full debt remitted.

Thus it is hoped the proposition is proved, and that our legislature have conceived just apprehensions of the interest of the merchants, and all other creditors for sterling debts, and have made a proper provision for their security.

But to set this matter still in a stronger light: The merchants in their memorial quote the provisions in the Act of the 6th of Queen Anne, that even foreign gold and silver coin, made current by that act, was not to be held a legal tender for sterling debts, much less ought paper bills of credit, which are, they say, of a local, uncertain, and fluctuating value. But give us leave to tell them that if they had no better dependence than that act affords for collecting their sterling debts, they might be great sufferers indeed; for though that act, when it was made and for many years after, was a good provision for them in that respect (nothing but sterling or lawful British money being a legal tender for sterling debts), inasmuch as the exchange then current here was under the rate settled by that act, viz., 25 percent, or 1s. passed for 1s. 3d., but since exchange has been higher than that,

which is always the case in time of war, a tender exactly agreeable to that act would occasion a loss to the merchants of so much as 25 percent falls short of the highest exchange, viz., 10, 15, or perhaps 20 percent.

Let it be observed that, however contemptibly the merchants look upon this paper money as of a local, uncertain, and fluctuating value, yet it is emitted on such funds that everyone is glad to receive it in any kind of payment; and exchange is now 10 percent lower than it was last war, when we had nothing current but gold and silver coin, a circumstance very favorable to the credit of our paper.

And although the King's quitrents, as the merchants rightly observe, are not payable in paper by that act, that was done because His Majesty had, by instruction to the governor and officers of his revenue, directed them to be received only in sterling, or gold and silver coin, at a certain rate, which instruction the governor dared not contravene by including them in the act; yet the receiver general never refuses paper money for the quitrents, because he can readily procure bills of exchange for it.

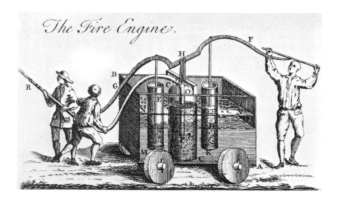

The Fire Engine.

1760

12.

Benjamin Franklin: Great Britain's Interest in Her Colonies

During the French and Indian War, some farsighted Americans tried to persuade Britain that the acquisition of Canada would not only effectively aid the defense of the colonies but also assure England's status as a great nation. In the early years of the war, Britain was reluctant to seize French colonial lands, believing that the protection of New England's commercial and other interests was not sufficient cause. Franklin was one of the colonists who foresaw the advantages in British control of Canada and the Mississippi Valley, and, with Richard Jackson, he wrote a pamphlet entitled The Interest of Great Britain Considered, with Regard to her Colonies, etc. *The pamphlet, portions of which follow, appeared in London in April or May of 1760 and is said to have had a great deal of influence on future British policy. The whole of Canada, which was surrendered by France after the British victory at Montreal in September 1760, was retained by England in the peace treaty of 1763.*

Source: *Works*, III, pp. 89-143.

I HAVE PERUSED with no small pleasure the Letter addressed to Two Great Men[1] and the Remarks on that letter. It is not merely from the beauty, the force, and perspicuity of expression, or the general elegance of manner conspicuous in both pamphlets that my pleasure chiefly arises; it is rather from this, that I have lived to see subjects of the greatest importance to this nation publicly discussed without party views or party heat, with decency and politeness, and with no other warmth than what a zeal for the honor and happiness of our king and country may inspire; and this by writers whose understanding (however they may differ from each other) appears not unequal to their candor and the uprightness of their intention.

1. In the year 1760, upon the prospect of a peace with France, the late earl of Bath addressed a Letter to Two Great Men (Mr. Pitt and the duke of New-castle) on the terms necessary to be insisted upon in the negotiation. He preferred the acquisitions in the West Indies. In the same year there appeared Remarks on the Letter addressed to Two Great Men, containing opposite opinions on this and other subjects.

But, as great abilities have not always the best information, there are, I apprehend, in the Remarks, some opinions not well-founded, and some mistakes of so important a nature as to render a few observations of them necessary for the better information of the public. . . .

1. *The security of a dominion, a justifiable and prudent ground upon which to demand cessions from an enemy.*

Whether we are to confine ourselves to those possessions only that were "the objects for which we began the war." This the Remarker seems to think right, when the question relates to "Canada, properly so called; it having never been mentioned as one of those objects in any of our memorials or declarations, or in any national or public act whatsoever." But the gentleman himself will probably agree that if the cession of Canada would be a real advantage to us, we may demand it under his second head, as an "indemnification for the charges incurred" in recovering our just rights; otherwise, according to his own principles, the demand of Guadaloupe can have no foundation. That "our claims before the war were large enough for possession and for security too," though it seems a clear point with the ingenious Remarker, is, I own, not so with me. I am rather of the contrary opinion. . . .

First, let me observe that we did not make those claims because they were large enough for security but because we could rightfully claim no more. Advantages gained in the course of this war may increase the extent of our rights. Our claims before the war contained *some* security; but that is no reason why we should neglect acquiring *more* when the demand of more is become reasonable. It may be reasonable in the case of America to ask for the security recommended by the author of the Letter, though

it would be preposterous to do it in many other cases. His proposed demand is founded on the little value of Canada to the French; the right we have to ask, and the power we may have to insist on an indemnification for our expenses; the difficulty the French themselves will be under of restraining their restless subjects in America from encroaching on our limits and disturbing our trade; and the difficulty on our parts of preventing encroachments that may possibly exist many years without coming to our knowledge.

But the Remarker "does not see why the arguments employed concerning a security for a peaceable behavior in Canada would not be equally cogent for calling for the same security in Europe." On a little further reflection, he must, I think, be sensible that the circumstances of the two cases are widely different. *Here* we are separated by the best and clearest of boundaries, the ocean, and we have people in or near every part of our territory. Any attempt to encroach upon us by building a fort even in the obscurest corner of these islands must, therefore, be known and prevented immediately. The aggressors also must be known, and the nation they belong to would be accountable for their aggression.

In America it is quite otherwise. A vast wilderness, thinly or scarce at all peopled, conceals with ease the march of troops and workmen. Important passes may be seized within our limits, and forts built in a month, at a small expense, that may cost us an age and a million to remove. Dear experience has taught this. But what is still *worse*, the wide, extended forests between our settlements and theirs are inhabited by barbarous tribes of savages that delight in war and take pride in murder; subjects properly neither of the French nor English, but strongly attached to the former by the art and indefatigable industry of priests, similarity of superstitions, and frequent family alliances. These are easily, and have been continually, instigated to fall upon and massacre our planters, even in times of full peace between the two Crowns; to the certain diminution of our people and the contraction of our settlements. And though it is known they are supplied by the French and carry their prisoners to them, we can, by complaining, obtain no redress; as the governors of Canada have a ready excuse, that the Indians are an independent people, over whom they have no power and for whose actions they are therefore not accountable. Surely circumstances so widely different may reasonably authorize different demands of security in America from such as are usual or necessary in Europe. . . .

Canada, in the hands of Britain, will endanger the kingdom of France as little as any other cession; and from its situation and circumstances cannot be hurtful to any other state. Rather, if peace be an advantage, this cession may be such to all Europe. The present war teaches us that disputes arising in America may be an occasion of embroiling nations who have no concerns there. If the French remain in Canada and Louisiana, fix the boundaries as you will between us and them, we must border on each other for more than 1,500 miles. The people that inhabit the frontiers are generally the refuse of both nations, often of the worst morals and the least discretion; remote from the eye, the prudence, and the restraint of government. Injuries are therefore frequently, in some part or other of so long a frontier, committed on both sides, resentment provoked, the colonies first engaged, and then the mother countries. . . . The flames of war, once kindled, often spread far and wide, and the mischief is infinite.

Happy it proved to both nations that the Dutch were prevailed on finally to cede the New Netherlands (now the province of New York) to us at the peace of 1674; a peace that has ever since continued between us, but must have been frequently disturbed if they had retained the possession of that country, bordering several hundred miles on our colonies of Pennsylvania westward, Connecticut and the Massachusetts eastward. Nor is it to be wondered at that people of different language, religion, and manners should in those remote parts engage in frequent quarrels; when we find that even the people of our *own colonies* have frequently been so exasperated against *each other* in their disputes about boundaries as to proceed to open violence and bloodshed.

2. *Erecting forts in the back settlements, almost in no instance a sufficient security against the Indians and the French; but the possession of Canada implies every security, and ought to be had, while in our power.*

But the Remarker thinks we shall be sufficiently secure in America if we "raise English forts at such passes as may at once make us respectable to the French and to the Indian nations." The security desirable in America may be considered as of three kinds. (1) A security of possession that the French shall not drive us out of the country. (2) A security of our planters from the inroads of savages, and the murders committed by them. (3) A security that the British nation shall not be obliged, on every new war, to repeat the immense expense occasioned by this to defend its possessions in America.

Forts, in the most important passes, may, I acknowledge, be of use to obtain the first kind of security; but as those situations are far advanced beyond the inhabitants, the expense of maintaining and supplying the garrisons will be very great even in time of full peace and immense on every interruption of it; as it is easy for skulking parties of the enemy, in such long roads through the woods, to intercept and cut off our convoys, unless guarded continually by great bodies of men.

The second kind of security will not be obtained by such forts, unless they were connected by a wall like that of China, from one end of our settlements to the other. If the Indians, when at war, marched like the Europeans, with great armies, heavy cannon, baggage, and carriages, the passes through which alone such armies could penetrate our country, or receive their supplies, being secured, all might be sufficiently secure; but the case is widely different. They go to war, as they call it, in small parties — from fifty men down to five. Their hunting life has made them acquainted with the whole country, and scarce any part of it is impracticable to such a party. They can travel through the woods even by night, and know how to conceal their tracks. They pass easily between your forts undiscovered; and privately approach the settlements of your frontier inhabitants. They need no convoys of provisions to follow them; for whether they are shifting from place to place in the woods, or lying in wait for an opportunity to strike a blow, every thicket and every stream furnishes so small a number with sufficient subsistence. When they have surprised separately, and murdered and scalped a dozen families, they are gone with inconceivable expedition through unknown ways; and it is very rare that pursuers have any chance of coming up with them. In short, long experience has taught our planters that they cannot rely upon forts as a security against Indians. The inhabitants of Hackney might as well rely upon the Tower of London to secure them against highwaymen and housebreakers.

As to the third kind of security, that we shall not, in a few years, have all we have now done to do over again in America and be obliged to employ the same number of troops and ships at the same immense expense to defend our possessions there, while we are in proportion weakened here. Such forts, I think, cannot prevent this. During a peace, it is not to be doubted the French, who are adroit at fortifying, will likewise erect forts in the most advantageous places of the country we leave them; which will make it more difficult than ever to be reduced in case of another war. We know by the experience of this war how extremely difficult it is to march an army through the American woods, with its necessary cannon and stores, sufficient to reduce a very slight fort. The accounts at the Treasury will tell you what amazing sums we have necessarily spent in the expeditions against two very trifling forts, Duquesne and Crown Point.

While the French retain their influence over the Indians, they can easily keep our long extended frontier in continual alarm by a very few of those people; and with a small number of regulars and militia, in such a country, we find they can keep an army of ours in full employ for several years. We therefore shall not need to be told by our colonies that if we leave Canada, however circumscribed, to the French, "we have done nothing", we shall soon be made sensible *ourselves* of this truth, and to our cost.

I would not be understood to deny that even if we subdue and retain Canada, some *few forts* may be of use to secure the goods of the traders and protect the commerce in case of any sudden misunderstanding with any tribe of Indians; but these forts will be best under the care of the colonies interested in the Indian trade and garrisoned by their provincial forces and at their own expense. Their own interest will then induce the American governments to take care of such forts in proportion to their importance and see that the officers keep their corps full and mind their duty. But any troops of ours placed there, and accountable here, would, in such remote and obscure places and at so great a distance from the eye and inspection of superiors, soon become of little consequence, even though the French were left in possession of Canada.

If the four independent companies maintained by the Crown in New York more than forty years, at a great expense, consisted, for most part of the time, of faggots chiefly; if their officers enjoyed their places as sinecures and were only, as a writer of that country styles them, a kind of military monks; if this was the state of troops posted in a populous country, where the imposition could not be so well concealed, what may we expect will be the case of those that shall be posted 200, 300, or 400 miles from the inhabitants in such obscure and remote places as Crown Point, Oswego, Duquesne, or Niagara? They would scarce be even faggots; they would dwindle to mere names upon paper and appear nowhere but upon the muster rolls.

Now, *all the kinds* of security we have mentioned are obtained by subduing and *retaining* Canada. Our present possessions in America are secured; our planters will no longer be massacred by the Indians, who, depending absolutely on us for what are now become the necessaries of life to them (guns, powder, hatchets, knives, and clothing) and having no other Europeans near that can either supply them or instigate them against us, there is no doubt of their being always disposed, if we treat them with common justice, to live in perpetual peace with us. And with regard to France, she cannot, in case of another war, put us to the immense expense of defending that long extended frontier; we shall then, as it were, have our backs against a wall in America; the seacoast will be easily protected by our superior naval power; and here "our own watchfulness and our own strength" will be properly, and cannot but be successfully, employed. In this situation, the force now employed in that part of the world may be spared for any other service here or elsewhere; so that both the offensive and defensive strength of the British Empire, on the whole, will be greatly increased.

But to leave the French in possession of Canada, when it is in our power to remove them and depend (as the Remarker proposes) on our own "strength and watchfulness"

to prevent the mischiefs that may attend it, seems neither safe nor prudent. Happy as we now are, under the best of kings and in the prospect of a succession promising every felicity a nation was ever blessed with; happy too in the wisdom and vigor of every part of the administration, we cannot, we ought not to, promise ourselves the uninterrupted continuance of those blessings. The safety of a considerable part of the state, and the interest of the whole, are not to be trusted to the wisdom and vigor of *future administrations*, when a security is to be had more effectual, more constant, and much less expensive.

They, who can be moved by the apprehension of dangers so remote as that of the future independence of our colonies, . . . seem scarcely consistent with themselves when they suppose we may rely on the wisdom and vigor of an administration for their safety. I should indeed think it less material whether Canada were ceded to us or not if I had in view only the security of *possession* in our colonies. I entirely agree with the Remarker that we are in North America "a far greater continental as well as naval power"; and that only cowardice or ignorance can subject our colonies there to a French conquest. But for the same reason I disagree with him widely upon another point.

3. *The blood and treasure spent in the American wars, not spent in the cause of the colonies alone.*

I do not think that our "blood and treasure has been expended," as he intimates, *"in the cause of the colonies,"* and that we are "making conquests for *them*," yet I believe this is too common an error. I do not say they are altogether unconcerned in the event. The inhabitants of them are, in common with the other subjects of Great Britain, anxious for the glory of her Crown, the extent of her power and commerce, the welfare and future repose of the whole British people. They could not therefore but take a large share in the affronts offered to Britain; and have been animated with a truly British spirit to exert themselves beyond their strength, and against their evident interest. Yet, so unfortunate have they been that their virtue has made against them; for upon no better foundation than this have they been supposed the authors of a war carried on for their advantage only.

It is a great mistake to imagine that the American country in question between Great Britain and France is claimed as the property of any *individuals or public body in America*; or that the possession of it by Great Britain is likely, in any lucrative view, to redound at all to the advantage of any person there. On the other hand, the bulk of the inhabitants of North America are *landowners*, whose lands are inferior in value to those of Britain, only by the want of an equal number of people. It is true, the accession of the large territory claimed before the war began (especially if that be secured by the possession of Canada) will tend to the increase of the British subjects faster than if they had been confined within the mountains; yet the increase within the mountains only would evidently make the comparative population equal to that of Great Britain much sooner than it can be expected, when our people are spread over a country six times as large. I think this is the only point of light in which this question is to be viewed, and is the only one in which any of the colonies are concerned.

No colony, no possessor of lands in any colony, therefore, wishes for conquests, or can be benefited by them, otherwise than as they may be a means of *securing peace on their borders*. No considerable advantage has resulted to the colonies by the conquests of this war, or can result from confirming them by the peace, but what they must enjoy in common with the rest of the British people; with this evident drawback from their share of these advantages, that they will necessarily lessen, or at least prevent

the increase of, the value of what makes the principal part of their private property [their land].

A people, spread through the whole tract of country on this side the Mississippi, and secured by Canada in our hands, would probably for some centuries find employment in agriculture, and thereby free us at home effectually from our fears of American manufactures. Unprejudiced men well know that all the penal and prohibitory laws that ever were thought on will not be sufficient to prevent manufactures in a country whose inhabitants surpass the number that can subsist by the husbandry of it. That this will be the case in America soon, if our people remain confined within the mountains, and almost as soon should it be unsafe for them to live beyond, though the country be ceded to us, no man acquainted with political and commercial history can doubt.

Manufactures are founded in poverty; it is the multitude of poor without land in a country, and who must work for others at low wages or starve, that enables undertakers to carry on a manufacture, and afford it cheap enough to prevent the importation of the same kind from abroad, and to bear the expense of its own exportation. But no man who can have a piece of land of his own, sufficient by his labor to subsist his family in plenty, is poor enough to be a manufacturer and work for a master. Hence, while there is land enough in America for our people, there can never be manufactures to any amount or value.

It is a striking observation of a very able pen that the natural livelihood of the thin inhabitants of a forest country is hunting; that of a greater number, pasturage; that of a middling population, agriculture; and that of the greatest, manufactures; which last must subsist the bulk of the people in a full country, or they must be subsisted by charity, or perish. The extended population, therefore, that is most advantageous to Great Britain, will be best effected, because only effectually secured, by our possession of Canada.

So far as the *being* of our present colonies in North America is concerned, I think indeed with the Remarker that the French there are not "an enemy to be apprehended" — but the expression. is too vague to be applicable to the present, or indeed to any other case. Algiers, Tunis, and Tripoli, unequal as they are to this nation in power and numbers of people, are enemies to be still apprehended; and the Highlanders of Scotland have been so for many ages, by the greatest princes of Scotland and Britain. The wild Irish were able to give a great deal of disturbance even to Queen Elizabeth and cost her more blood and treasure than her war with Spain.

Canada, in the hands of France, has always stinted the growth of our colonies in the course of this war; and indeed, before it, has disturbed and vexed even the best and strongest of them; has found means to murder thousands of their people and unsettle a great part of their country. Much more able will it be to starve the growth of an infant settlement. Canada has also found means to make this nation spend two or three millions a year in America; and a people, how small soever, that in their present situation can do this as often as we have a war with them, is, methinks, "an enemy to be apprehended."

Our North American colonies are to be considered as the *frontier of the British Empire* on that side. The frontier of any dominion being attacked, it becomes not merely "the cause" of the people immediately attacked (the inhabitants of that frontier) but properly "the cause" of the whole body. Where the frontier people owe and pay obedience, there they have a right to look for protection; no political proposition is better established than this. It is therefore invidious to represent the "blood and treasure" spent in this war as spent in "the cause of the colonies" only; and that they are "absurd and ungrateful" if they think

we have done nothing, unless we "make conquests for them" and reduce Canada to gratify their "vain ambition," etc. It will not be a conquest for *them*, nor gratify any vain ambition of theirs. It will be a conquest for the *whole*; and all our people will, in the increase of trade, and the case of taxes, find the advantage of it.

Should we be obliged at any time to make a war for the protection of our commerce, and to secure the exportation of our manufactures, would it be fair to represent such a war merely as blood and treasure spent in the cause of the weavers of Yorkshire, Norwich, or the West, the cutlers of Sheffield, or the buttonmakers of Birmingham? I hope it will appear before I end these sheets that, if ever there was a national war, this is truly such a one: a war in which the interest of the whole nation is directly and fundamentally concerned. Those who would be thought deeply skilled in human nature affect to discover self-interested views everywhere at the bottom of the fairest, the most generous conduct. Suspicions and charges of this kind meet with ready reception and belief in the minds even of the multitude, and therefore less acuteness and address than the Remarker is possessed of would be sufficient to persuade the nation generally that all the zeal and spirit manifested and exerted by the colonies in this war was only in "their own cause" to "make conquests for themselves," to engage us to make more for them, to gratify their own "vain ambition."

But should they now humbly address the mother country in the terms and the sentiments of the Remarker; return her their grateful acknowledgments for the blood and treasure she had spent in "their cause"; confess that enough had not been done "for them"; allow that "English forts, raised in proper passes, will, with the wisdom and vigor of her administration," be a sufficient future protection; express their desires that their people may be confined within the mountains, lest [if] they are suffered to spread and extend themselves in the fertile and pleasant country on the other side, they should "increase infinitely from all causes," "live wholly on their own labor" and become independent; beg therefore that the French may be suffered to remain in possession of Canada, as their neighborhood may be useful to prevent our increase, and the removing them may "in its consequences be even dangerous."

I say, should such an address from the colonies make its appearance here (though, according to the Remarker, it would be a most just and reasonable one) would it not, might it not with more justice be answered: We understand you, gentlemen, perfectly well; you have only your own interest in view; you want to have the people confined within your present limits that in a few years the lands you are possessed of may increase tenfold in value! You want to reduce the price of labor by increasing numbers on the same territory that you may be able to set up manufactures and vie with your mother country! You would have your people kept in a body that you may be more able to dispute the commands of the Crown and obtain an independency. You would have the French left in Canada to exercise your military virtue, and make you a warlike people, that you may have more confidence to embark in schemes of disobedience and greater ability to support them! You have tasted, too, the sweets of TWO OR THREE MILLIONS sterling per annum spent among you by our fleets and forces, and you are unwilling to be without a pretense for kindling up another war, and thereby occasioning a repetition of the same delightful doses!

But, gentlemen, allow us to understand *our* interest a little likewise. We shall remove the French from Canada that you may live in peace, and we be no more drained by your quarrels. You shall have land enough to cultivate that you may have neither necessity nor inclination to go into

manufactures; and we will manufacture for you and govern you.

A reader of the Remarks may be apt to say, if this writer would have us restore Canada, on principles of moderation, how can we, consistent with those principles, retain Guadaloupe, which he represents of so much greater value! I will endeavor to explain this, because by doing it I shall have an opportunity of showing the truth and good sense of the answer to the interested application I have just supposed. The author then is only apparently and not really inconsistent with himself. If we can obtain the credit of moderation by restoring Canada, it is well; but we should, however, restore it at all *events;* because it would not only be of no use to us but "the possession of it (in his opinion) may in its consequences be dangerous."

As how? Why, plainly (at length it comes out), if the French are not left there to check the growth of our colonies, "they will extend themselves almost without bounds into the inland parts, and increase infinitely from all causes; becoming a numerous, hardy, independent people; possessed of a strong country, communicating little or not at all with England, living wholly on their own labor, and in process of time knowing little and inquiring little about the mother country." In short, according to this writer, our present colonies are large enough and numerous enough; and the French ought to be left in North America to prevent their increase, lest they become not only useless but dangerous to Britain.

I agree with the gentleman that, with Canada in our possession, our people in America will increase amazingly. I know that their common rate of increase, where they are not molested by the enemy, is doubling their numbers every twenty-five years, by natural generation only — exclusive of the accession of foreigners. I think this increase continuing would probably, in a century more, make the number of British subjects on that side the water more numerous than they now are on this. . . .

4. *Not necessary that the American colonies should cease being useful to the mother country. Their preference over the West Indian colonies stated.*

I am far from entertaining on that account any fears of their becoming either useless or dangerous to us; and I look on those fears to be merely imaginary, and without any probable foundation. The Remarker is reserved in giving his reasons, as in his opinion this "is not a fit subject for discussion." I shall give mine, because I conceive it a subject necessary to be discussed; and the rather, as those fears, how groundless and chimerical soever, may, by possessing the multitude, possibly induce the ablest ministry to conform to them against their own judgment, and thereby prevent the assuring to the British name and nation a stability and permanency that no man acquainted with history dared have hoped for, till our American possessions opened the pleasing prospect.

The Remarker thinks that our people in America, "finding no check from Canada, would extend themselves almost without bounds into the inland parts, and increase infinitely from all causes." The very reason he assigns for their so extending, and which is indeed the true one (their being "invited to it by the pleasantness, fertility, and plenty of the country") may satisfy us that this extension will continue to proceed as long as there remains any pleasant fertile country within their reach. And if we even suppose them confined by the waters of the Mississippi westward, and by those of St. Lawrence and the lakes to the northward, yet still we shall leave them room enough to increase, even in the manner of settling now practised there, till they amount to perhaps 100,000,000 souls.

This must take some centuries to fulfill;

and in the meantime, this nation must necessarily supply them with the manufactures they consume; because the new settlers will be employed in agriculture; and the new settlements will so continually draw off the spare hands from the old that our present colonies will not, during the period we have mentioned, find themselves in a condition to manufacture, even for their own inhabitants, to any considerable degree, much less for those who are settling behind them.

Thus our trade must, till that country becomes as fully peopled as England (that is for centuries to come) be continually increasing, and with it our naval power; because the ocean is between us and them, and our ships and seamen must increase as that trade increases. . . .

But, say the objectors, "there is a *certain distance from the sea* in America, beyond which the expense of carriage will put a stop to the sale and consumption of your manufactures; and this, with the difficulty of making returns for them, will oblige the inhabitants to manufacture for themselves. Of course, if you suffer your people to extend their settlements beyond that distance your people become useless to you." And this distance is limited by some to 200 miles, by others to the Appalachian Mountains. . . .

Our trade at the West India islands is undoubtedly a valuable one; but whatever is the amount of it, it has long been at a stand. Limited as our sugar planters are by the scantiness of territory, they cannot increase much beyond their present number; and this is an evil . . . that will be little helped by our keeping Guadaloupe. The trade to our northern colonies is not only greater but yearly increasing with the increase of people; and even in greater proportion as the people increase in wealth and the ability of spending, as well as in numbers. . . . Our people in the northern colonies double in about twenty-five years, exclusive of the accession of strangers. . . .

In fact, the occasion for English goods in North America, and the inclination to have and use them, is, and must be for ages to come, much greater than the ability of the people to pay for them; they must, therefore, as they now do, deny themselves many things they would otherwise choose to have, or increase their industry to obtain them. And thus, if they should at any time manufacture some coarse article which, on account of its bulk or some other circumstance, cannot so well be brought to them from Britain, it only enables them the better to pay for finer goods that *otherwise* they could not indulge themselves in; so that the exports thither are not diminished by such manufacture but rather increased. . . .

5. *The American colonies not dangerous in their nature to Great Britain.*

Thus much to the apprehension of our colonies becoming useless to us. I shall next consider the other supposition, that their growth may render them *dangerous*. Of this, I own, I have not the least conception, when I consider that we have already *fourteen separate governments* on the maritime coast of the continent; and, if we extend our settlements, shall probably have as many more behind them on the inland side. Those we now have are not only under different governors but have different forms of government, different laws, different interests, and some of them different religious persuasions and different manners. Their jealousy of each other is so great that, however necessary a union of the colonies has long been for their common defense and security against their enemies, and how sensible soever each colony has been of that necessity, yet they have never been able to effect such a union among themselves; nor even to agree in requesting the mother country to establish it for them. Nothing but the immediate command of the Crown has been able to produce even the imperfect union, but lately seen there, of the forces of some colonies.

If they could not agree to unite for their defense against the French and Indians, who were perpetually harassing their settlements, burning their villages, and murdering their people, can it reasonably be supposed there is any danger of their uniting against their own nation, which protects and encourages them, with which they have so many connections and ties of blood, interest, and affection, and which, it is well known, they all love much more than they love one another?

In short, there are so many causes that must operate to prevent it that I will venture to say a union among them for such a purpose is not merely improbable, it is impossible. And if the union of the whole is impossible, the attempt of a part must be madness, as those colonies that did not join the rebellion would join the mother country in suppressing it. When I say such a union is impossible, I mean, without the most grievous tyranny and oppression. People who have property in a country which they may lose, and privileges which they may endanger, are generally disposed to be quiet, and even to bear much, rather than hazard all. While the government is mild and just, while important civil and religious rights are secure, such subjects will be dutiful and obedient. The waves do not rise but when the winds blow. . . .

But what is the prudent policy inculcated by the Remarker to obtain this end — security of dominion over our colonies? It is to leave the French in Canada, to "check" their growth; for otherwise, our people may "increase infinitely from all causes." We have already seen in what manner the French and their Indians check the growth of our colonies. It is a modest word, this "check," for massacring men, women, and children. The writer would, if he could, hide from himself as well as from the public the horror arising from such a proposal by couching it in general terms. It is no wonder he thought it a "subject not fit for discussion" in his letter, though he recommends it as "a point that should be the constant object of the minister's attention!"

But if Canada is restored on this principle, will not Britain be guilty of all the blood to be shed, all the murders to be committed, in order to check this dreaded growth of our own people? Will not this be telling the French in plain terms that the horrid barbarities they perpetrate with their Indians in our colonies are agreeable to us; and that they need not apprehend the resentment of a government with whose views they so happily concur? Will not the colonies view it in this light? Will they have reason to consider themselves any longer as subjects and children when they find their cruel enemies hallooed upon them by the country from whence they sprung; the government that owes them protection, as it requires their obedience? Is not this the most likely means of driving them into the arms of the French, who can invite them by an offer of that security their own government chooses not to afford them? . . .

But all this debate about the propriety or impropriety of keeping or restoring Canada is possibly too early. We have taken the capital, indeed, but the country is yet far from being in our possession; and perhaps never will be; for if our m ——— rs are persuaded by such counselors as the Remarker, that the French there are "not the worst of neighbors," and that if we had conquered Canada, we ought, for our own sakes, to restore it, as a check to the growth of our colonies, I am then afraid we shall never take it. For there are many ways of avoiding the completion of the conquest that will be less exceptionable and less odious than the giving it up.

7. *Canada easily peopled, without draining Great Britain of any its inhabitants.*

The objection I have often heard, that if we had Canada we could not people it

without draining Britain of its inhabitants, is founded on ignorance of the nature of population in new countries. When we first began to colonize in America, it was necessary to send people and to send seed corn; but it is not now necessary that we should furnish, for a new colony, either one or the other. The annual increment alone of our present colonies, without diminishing their numbers, or requiring a man from hence, is sufficient in ten years to fill Canada with double the number of English that it now has of French inhabitants. Those who are Protestants among the French will probably choose to remain under the English government; many will choose to remove, if they can be allowed to sell their lands, improvements, and effects; the rest in that thin-settled country will in less than half a century, from the crowds of English settling round and among them, be blended and incorporated with our people both in language and manners. . . .

I do not deny the utility of the conquest, or even of our future possession of Guadaloupe, if not bought too dear. The trade of the West Indies is one of our most valuable trades. Our possessions there deserve our greatest care and attention. So do those of North America. I shall not enter into the invidious task of comparing their due estimation. It would be a very long and a very disagreeable one to run through everything material on this head. It is enough to our present point, if I have shown that the value of North America is capable of an immense increase, by an acquisition and measures that must necessarily have an effect the direct contrary of what we have been industriously taught to fear; and that Guadaloupe is, in point of advantage, but a very small addition to our West India possessions; rendered many ways less valuable to us than it is to the French, who will probably set more value upon it, than upon a country [Canada] that is much more valuable to us than to them.

62

13.

Joseph Galloway: Importance of an Independent Judiciary

Even though judicial salaries were paid by the colonial assemblies, the tenure of judges in most of the colonies was at the pleasure of the Crown. In practice, this meant the judiciary could thwart the will of the royal governor only on pain of dismissal. On September 29, 1759, the Pennsylvania Assembly passed a law granting the judges life tenure, quamdiu se bene gesserint *("as long as they conduct themselves properly"). The Crown, realizing that the judiciary would thus become an effective political weapon, immediately disallowed the law. The following pamphlet, entitled* A Letter to the People of Pennsylvania *(1760), was written in defense of the law. Joseph Galloway, to whom the pamphlet is attributed, argued that the King was violating British constitutional tradition in denying the colonists a right enjoyed by all other Englishmen. The lack of an independent judiciary remained a colonial grievance up to the time of the Revolution.*

Source: *A Letter to the People of Pennsylvania, etc., etc.,* Philadelphia, 1760.

Whoever has made himself acquainted with ancient history and looked into the original design of government will find that one of its chief and principal ends was to secure the persons and properties of mankind from private injuries and domestic oppression.

In forming a plan of government completely to answer these excellent purposes, the fundamental laws and rules of the constitution, which ought never to be infringed, should be made alike distributive of justice and equity, and equally calculated to preserve the sovereign's prerogative and the people's liberties. But power and liberty ever being *opponents,* should the work stop here, the constitution would bear a near analogy to a ship without rudder, rigging, or sails, utterly incapable of answering the end of its construction. For though the wisest and best laws were enacted to fix the bounds of power and liberty, yet, without a due care in constituting persons impartially to execute them, the former by its influence

and encroachments on liberty would soon become tyranny, and the latter by the like extent of its limits might possibly degenerate into licentiousness. In both cases, the condition of mankind would be little mended, scarcely better than in their original state of nature and confusion, before any civil polity was agreed upon.

The men, therefore, who are to settle the contests between prerogative and liberty, who are to ascertain the bounds of sovereign power and to determine the rights of the subject, ought certainly to be perfectly free from the influence of either. But more especially of the former, as history plainly evinces that it is but too apt to prevail over the ministers of justice by its natural weight and authority, notwithstanding the wisest precautions have been used to prevent it.

The necessity of this independent state of justice is rendered apparent by the slightest consideration of human frailty. Consider men as they really are, attended with innumerable foibles and imperfections, ever liable to err, and you will find but very few who are so obstinately just as to be proof against the enticing baits of honor and interest. The love of promotion and private advantage are passions almost universal and admit of the most dangerous extremes. The one in excess generally produces the most servile obedience; the other, intolerable avarice and a base dereliction of virtue. That which we love and engages our attention we are ever ready to purchase at any *price*.

Thus, an inordinate lover of promotion, sooner than part with it would surrender up his regard for justice, his duty to his country and to his God for its preservation. And the avaricious man, sooner than lose his pelf [riches], would part with his honor, his reputation, I had almost said his life. And such is the influence of this dread of parting with that which we esteem, whatever it be, that it so effectually chains down the powers of the human soul that it cannot be said to enjoy freedom of judgment, scarcely freedom of thought.

Of this truth the abject promises and servile conduct of the great Lord Bacon exhibit an irrefragable proof. It was but rational to think that a man of his extensive abilities and capacious soul, that could comprehend all the beauties of rectitude and justice at a view, would at least preserve in his public station an independent and unperverted judgment. And yet his virtue fell a victim to his love of promotion. He begged for preferment with the same low servility that the necessitous pauper would beg for daily bread. His promise to the King in order to obtain the chancellor's place was, "That when a direction was once given, it should be pursued and performed." And when he succeeded in his wishes, his conduct with respect to the Court and its arbitrary measures showed that he strictly fulfilled his engagement.

Whoever has read the form of a commission *during pleasure* and considered its limitations must certainly be surprised that a generous mind would accept of a tenure so servile and so incompatible with the very nature of justice. He can be but a *tenant at will* of a g[overno]r at best, and for the most part of an at[torne]y g[enera]l, or perhaps some other favorite in the several counties. The terms of tenure are *until our further will and pleasure shall be made known,* which, by a natural construction, if we may call reason and experience to our aid, is no longer than you gratify us, our favorites and creatures, in your determinations, let our *will and pleasure* therein be ever so illegal, ever so partial and unjust.

That some men of independent circumstances, happy in the possession of virtue, have accepted of those commissions and acted uprightly I will not pretend to dispute. They are remarkable instances of public integrity and merit the highest commendation. They are among mankind as a comet among the stars, rarely to be seen. But generally to look for strict impartiality and a pure administration of justice, to expect that power should be confined within its legal limits, and right and justice done to the subject by men who are dependent is to ridicule all laws against bribery and corruption, and to say that human nature is insensible of the love or above the lure of honor, interest, or promotion.

With what freedom and justness do the modern writers of a certain great nation complain against the multiplicity of ministerial officers who hold their commissions *during pleasure;* and what renders that freedom so justifiable and those complaints so just but the misfortunes the nation has suffered by the weight these *creatures* have thrown into the scale of power by paying an implicit obedience to its commands and a devoted adherence to its measures? If, then, such are the dangerous effects of a dependency in the ministerial officers whose conduct is circumscribed by positive laws and checked by the superior courts of justice, how much more so must a dependency of the judicial officers be where everything is left in the power and to the discretion of the judge on whose breath the security of all property and the liberty of the people depend? Must it not produce more dangerous consequences? Will it not bring on inevitable ruin?

But further to illustrate the necessity of an independent state of justice in every community, where the security of property and the happiness of mankind is the object of its *polity,* numerous instances might be adduced from the histories of Europe, in which it has been the principal policy of the most arbitrary princes who have conceived a design of quelling the spirit of liberty and enslaving their subjects to their *will and pleasure* to draw over to their party the ministers of the law. By this means, having effectually superseded the execution of the laws and subdued the power which alone could check a tyrannical exercise of prerogative, they have let loose every instrument of oppression and left nothing in the community able to oppose the torrent. Attempts of this kind have frequently succeeded, and sometimes in reigns when the judges have been as independent as the law could make them. If so, how much more easily is this policy pursued and executed when the judges hold their offices on the servile tenure of *during pleasure. . . .*

Here it is worthy your information, first, that the rights and liberties claimed and declared by the Bill of Rights, that second Magna Carta, and the Act of Settlement created no innovation of the ancient constitution. The Parliament had no design to change but only to restore the ancient laws and customs of the Realm, which were the true and indubitable rights and liberties of the people of England. This appears as well from the Bill of Rights and the resolves which preceded the Act of Settlement as from the act itself. From whence it follows that this right of the people to have their judges indifferent men and independent of the Crown is not of a late date but part of the ancient constitution of your government and inseparably inherent in the persons of every freeborn Englishman; and that the granting commissions to the judges *during pleasure* was then esteemed by the Parliament and truly *was* an arbitrary and illegal violation of the people's ancient liberties.

Second, that those excellent laws were *intended* to extend, and actually do extend, to all the King's subjects in America. That their faith and allegiance are bound by them to the present most excellent royal family, and of course that they are entitled to the rights and liberties therein claimed, asserted, and confirmed. And yet your former g[overno]rs, as if they had been determined to revive and pursue the wicked policy of those arbitrary reigns I have mentioned and to throw aside the worthy example of His present Most Gracious Majesty, have acted as if those excellent laws were not to be executed, and the example of their sovereign unworthy of influencing their conduct. They have granted all the commissions of the judges *during their will and pleasure,* and, like Charles and James, have occasionally removed such as dared oppose their arbitrary designs, and filled up their places with others who would ratify and support their measures, however unjust and illegal.

This being the case, what censure and blame would your representatives have merited had they not seized the first opportunity of rendering your *courts and judges independent.* An opportunity offered, they passed a law limiting the number of judges, which before was unlimited, and left it in the power of a bad g[overno]r to create as many dependents as his measures should call for. It directs that the judges of the Supreme Court and Common Pleas shall hereafter hold their commissions *during their good behavior;* which before have often depended on the nod of a g[overno]r or an at[torne]y g[enera]l. And it ordains that the judges of the Common Pleas shall hold the Orphans Court; that in no instance your properties exceeding the value of £5 should be determined by men *dependent* on power or its advocates; and the ministers of justice, who ought to be the ministers of your protection, may not be prevailed on either to pervert your laws or to give up your rights.

A law so full of advantages to the people one would imagine could not have an enemy; and yet we find there is nothing so virtuous but the enemies of virtue will decry. The principal objection against this law is that "It brings a great expense on the counties without any benefit accruing from it." Let us inquire what mighty burden will attend it in the county of Philadelphia, where the expense will be greatest. The judges have never sat above five days in the quarter at most, which, at 20s. per day will amount to £100 per annum. One hundred pounds divided among 7,000 taxables, which this county contains, will not make it 3½d. per man. Is an expense so trifling equal to the advantages to be derived from such a law? Is that expense unnecessary which procures safety to your property and protection to your persons? Is an impartial administration of justice of so little moment to the people? For what purpose were the courts of judicature established? Was it that judgment should be given according to the nod and direction of a p[roprietar]y, g[overno]r, or att[orne]y g[enera]l, or as the last shall happen to be employed? Or was it that they should be free from all fear, favor, or affection whatsoever? That their determinations might flow from an honest conscience, from an impartial and unbiased mind?

The enemies to this law, like all other persons who do not act upon principle, manifestly contradict their own constant practice. What man among them, who has a controversy with his neighbor, would not choose to have it determined by arbitrators at least as independent of his opponent as himself? I think I am safe in asserting that no man of common sense would submit his cause to the judgment of arbitrators who are the *tenants at will* or debtors of his antagonist, or to persons who are connected with him by blood or affinity or by obligations and favors conferred.

Is it not a common objection at our courts of justice in the election of referees that the person named is of the same religious persuasion with the other party? Whence arises the objection but from a well-grounded suspicion that in some men even similitude of sentiments may create undue favor and attachment to the interest of one side and bias the private judgment and be the cause of injustice.

If this be the case between neighbor and neighbor, how does it stand between the proprietaries and the people of this province? Every freeholder is by contract their debtor, and therefore every one of them may, and many often will, have disputes and lawsuits with them respecting the many covenants contained in their grants and the quitrents. Does not the same reason which declares the use of indifferent arbitrators in the case of private persons loudly proclaim the necessity of independent men to settle the differences between power and property, between the proprietaries and the people? Have not men who are clothed with immense property and extensive power by the weight of these alone too great an opportunity of influencing the courts of justice without this unnatural and unreasonable dependency of the judges *on their pleasure?*

I have shown you in the reigns of Charles and James that men of fortune and the most extensive abilities have sacrificed their honor, their oaths, and their consciences on the altar of court influence; that they have violated the sacred office and trust of a judge, which were committed to them for the welfare of the people. Do you think it would be a difficult task to produce you examples of the like immolations in your own government? Have some of your past administrations been less oppressive and arbitrary than those of Charles and James? Have not the royal grant and proprietary charter, the foundations of your constitution, been dispensed with and superseded by arbitrary p[roprietar]y edicts? Have not those edicts, which like the laws of the Medes and Persians were to alter not, chained down the judgments of your rulers and deprived them of their discretion in matters of legislation?

Have you known a scheme of power to deprive you of your properties in which your m—g—st—es [magistrates] have not been concerned? Have you forgot the attempt to destroy the freedom of your elections, abetted and supported by the men who ought to have suppressed it? Have not your servants, as much your property as the money in your purses, been illegally enlisted by a former g[overno]r, and scarcely any could be found who dared to execute the laws made for its safety? What part did they act in preventing your houses (which by law are to every man a place of refuge and safety) from being made barracks for the soldiery? Did they execute the penal statute of our mother country against it, or did not some of them act a *shameful* neutrality while others united with power and in its very council abetted the illegal attempt? How *manfully* and *conscientiously* did they exert themselves in suppressing the rioters, those instruments of power, who were collected to frighten the representatives to surrender up your sacred rights, or were not some of them mixed with the mob, promoting and abetting their wicked design?

Where then is the difference? If Charles and James dispensed with penal statutes in order to introduce *popery*, your former g[overno]rs have dispensed with the laws and fundamentals of your liberties and priv-

ileges in order to introduce *slavery*. If the former influenced the determinations of the judges and thereby perverted the laws of the country, your p[roprieta]ries by severe penalties have deprived the head of the executive as well as legislative authority of his discretion and reason. And your g[overno]rs have so influenced the courts of justice to justify and support their despotic designs that you and your predecessors from the like dangerous policy have suffered equal mischief and the like misfortunes.

Should, then, the same illegal and arbitrary measures hereafter be pursued by some future son of oppression, should a design be formed of dispensing with your laws and of imposing unnecessary taxes and burdens *heavy to be borne* without the assent of your representatives, and the ministers of justice be thought the proper instruments of effecting these horrid purposes, how certain the success! how easy the task! while your judges are dependent on the *will of the oppressor*. Can you doubt that human nature, wearing the yoke engraved with the motto "During Pleasure," will not hold and practise the doctrine of *passive obedience* and *nonresistance* with respect to the destruction of your rights and privileges? If it should retain virtue enough not to be active in their ruin, will not the same cause ever produce the same effect? Will that which was once destructive now change its nature and become harmless and innocent? Has the poison of the asp ever lost its virulent quality? Will you then surrender up your sacred rights into the hands of power for protection? Will you suffer the safety of your persons, which is still more precious, to depend on the humor and caprice of your rulers and their favorites?

Consider, my countrymen, further, are the Pennsylvanians men of more independent fortunes or of greater abilities? Do they inherit a greater share of inflexible virtue? And are they less liable to influence and corruption than the people of England?

Has not fatal experience evidently demonstrated that the private property of your p[roprieta]ries and their favorites will daily clash more and more with yours, more frequently and in a much greater degree than the private *interest* of your sovereign possibly can with that of his subjects? And yet has not the wise example and policy of a British Parliament thought it indispensably necessary, even there, that the judges should hold their commissions *during good behavior*, as independent of the Crown as of the nation?

If those things be so, can the least spark of reason be offered why a British subject in America shall not enjoy the like safety, the same protection against domestic oppression? Is it because you have left your native land at the risk of your lives and fortunes to toil for your mother country, to load her with wealth, that you are to be rewarded with a loss of your privileges? Are you not of the same stock? Was the blood of your ancestors polluted by a change of soil? Were they freemen in England and did they become slaves by a six-weeks' voyage to America? Does not the sun shine as bright, our blood run as warm? Is not our honor and virtue as pure, our liberty as valuable, our property as dear, our lives as precious here as in England? Are we not subjects of the same King, and bound by the same laws and have we not the same God for our protector?

What, then, can you think of those abject Americans, those slaves by principle, those traitors to their own and posterity's happiness, who, plunging the dagger into the vitals of their own liberty, do not blush at declaring that you are not *entitled to the same security of property, the same rights and privileges of the freeborn subjects of England?* Let me ask those enemies to your welfare how much thereof are you entitled to? Who will measure out and distribute your poor pittance, your short allowance? Is a tenth, a hundredth, or a thousandth part to

be the portion of your liberty? Abject, detestable thought! The poor African who is taken captive in war and dragged an involuntary slave to Jamaica calls for your humanity and compassion; but the voluntary wretch that works out his own and posterity's slavish condition for the sake of a little present lucre, promotion, or power is an object deserving your deepest resentment, your highest indignation.

Ye who are not willfully blind to the advantages of this beneficial law, who for want of a little reflection have spoken derogatorily of its merits, let me rouse you from your lethargy and prevail on you to see through the perspective of truth your and your posterity's danger and approaching misery. What will avail the laws which are and shall be made for your protection if they are not impartially executed? What will avail the virtuous struggles, the noble victories of your representatives over the attempts of your intestine enemies? What will avail the heavy taxes you labor under? the thousands you have exhausted? the blood and treasure you have expended to protect your persons and properties from foreign invaders, if they are not safe from the insidious designs of ambition and power, their ever vigilant and active foes, nor even from the artful attempts of a litigious neighbor who is in favor with the *great* or can first employ a favorite attorney?

Whatever, then, be the fate of the law which has occasioned this address to you, let me entreat you to insist on the enjoyment of this your native, your ancient, and indubitable right. 'Tis yours by the usage and custom of ages; 'tis yours by the rules of reason; 'tis yours by covenant with the first founder of your government; 'tis yours by the united consent of King, Lords, and Commons; 'tis yours by birthright and as Englishmen. Complain, and remonstrate to your representatives incessantly, until they shall, like the great and good Alfred, make a restitution of this your most important and essential right, the first and principal object of their concern; until they prevail on your g[overno]rs to grant the judges commissions to the people of Pennsylvania in the same free and constitutional manner as your sovereign grants them to his subjects in England.

Be assured, if a privilege thus justly founded, so often ratified and confirmed, if an impartial and independent administration of justice is once wrested from your hands, neither the money in your pockets, nor the clothes on your backs, nor your inheritances, nor even your persons can remain long safe from violation. You will become slaves indeed, in no respect different from the sooty Africans, whose persons and properties are subject to the disposal of their tyrannical masters.

14.

John Galt: An American Painter in Rome

John Galt's Life and Studies of Benjamin West, *while not wholly accurate as biography, contains colorful accounts of West's experiences as a young American painter in Rome. Galt used West's introduction to Cardinal Albani in 1760 to symbolize the meeting of American innocence and European sophistication. West subsequently attained eminence in the art world as president of the Royal Academy of London, in which position he sought to encourage many talented young American artists, among them John Singleton Copley.*

Source: *The Life and Studies of Benjamin West, etc., etc.,* London, 1816, pp. 95-112.

DURING THE PONTIFICATE of Pope Rezzonico, the society of Rome had attained a pitch of elegance and a liberality of sentiment superior to that of any other city of Christendom. The theocratic nature of the government induced an exterior decorum in the public form of politeness, which, to strangers who took no interest in the abuses of the state, was so highly agreeable that it tended even to appease their indignation against the laxity of private morals. If the traveler would forget that the name of Christianity was employed in supporting a baneful administration to the vices, or could withdraw his thoughts from the penury and suffering which such an administration necessarily entailed on the people, he had opportunities of access at Rome to the most various and delightful exercises of the faculties of memory, taste, and judgment, in the company of persons distinguished for their knowledge and genius. For, with all the social intercourse for which Paris was celebrated in the reign of Louis XV, the local objects at Rome gave a higher and richer tone to conversation there; even the living vices were there less offensive than at Paris, the rumors of them being almost lost in the remembrance of departed virtue, constantly kept awake by the sight of its monuments and vouchers.

Tyranny in Rome was exercised more intellectually than in the French capital. Injustice and oppression were used more in the form of persuasion; and though the crosier was not less pernicious than the bayonet, it inflicted a less irritating injury. The virtuous endured with patience the wrongs that their misguided judgment led them to believe were salutary to their eternal welfare. But it ought to be observed that the immorality of the Romans was greatly exaggerated. Individuals redeemed by their merits the reproach of universal profligacy; and strangers, by being on their guard against the moral contagion, suffered a less dangerous taint than in the atheistical coteries of Paris. Many, in consequence, who came prepared to be disgusted with the degenerated Romans, often bade them adieu with sentiments of respect, and remembered their urbanity and accomplishments with delightful satisfaction.

It was not, however, the native inhabitants of Rome who constituted the chief attractions of society there but the number of accomplished strangers of all countries and religions, who, in constant succession, came in pilgrimage to the shrine of antiquity; and who, by the contemplation of the merits and glories of departed worth, often felt themselves, as it were, miraculously endowed with new qualities. The collision of minds fraught with learning, in that high state of excitement which the genius of the place produced on the coldest imaginations, together with those innumerable brilliant and transitory topics which were never elicited in any other city, made the Roman conversations a continual exercise of the understanding. The details of political intrigue and the follies of individuals excited but little interest among the strangers in Rome.

It seemed as if, by a universal tacit resolution, national and personal peculiarities and prejudices were forgotten, and that all strangers simultaneously turned their attention to the transactions and affairs of former ages, and of statesmen and authors now no

more. Their mornings were spent in surveying the monuments raised to public virtue and in giving local features in their minds to the knowledge which they had acquired by the perusal of those works that have perpetuated the dignity of the Roman character. Their evenings were often allotted to the comparison of their respective conjectures, and to ascertain the authenticity and history of the relics which they had collected of ancient art. Sometimes the day was consumed in the study of those inestimable ornaments of religion by which the fraudulent disposition of the priesthood had, in the decay of its power, rendered itself venerable to the most enlightened minds; and the night was devoted to the consideration of the causes which contribute to the development of genius, or of the events which tend to stifle and overwhelm its powers. Every recreation of the stranger in Rome was an effort of the memory, of abstraction, and of fancy.

Society, in this elevated state of enjoyment, surrounded by the greatest works of human creation and placed amidst the monuments of the most illustrious of mankind, and that of the Quakers of Pennsylvania, employed in the mechanical industry of felling timber, and amid the sobriety of rural and commercial economy, were like the extremes of a long series of events, in which, though the former is the necessary consequence of the latter, no resemblance can be traced in their respective characteristics. In America all was young, vigorous, and growing — the spring of a nation, frugal, active, and simple. In Rome all was old, infirm, and decaying — the autumn of a people who had gathered their glory, and were sinking into sleep under the disgraceful excesses of the vintage.

On the most inert mind, passing from the one continent to the other, the contrast was sufficient to excite great emotion. On such a character as that of Mr. West, who was naturally disposed to the contemplation of the sublime and beautiful, both as to their moral and visible effect, it made a deep and indelible impression. It confirmed him in the wisdom of those strict religious principles which denied the utility of art when solely employed as the medium of amusement; and impelled him to attempt what could be done to approximate the uses of the pencil to those of the pen, in order to render painting, indeed, the sister of eloquence and poetry.

BUT THE COURSE OF STUDY in the Roman schools was not calculated to enable him to carry this grand purpose into effect; for the principles by which Michelangelo and Raphael had attained their excellence were no longer regarded. The study of nature was deserted for that of the antique; and pictures were composed according to rules derived from other paintings, without respect to what the subject required, or what the circumstances of the scene probably appeared to be. It was, therefore, not one of the least happy occurrences in his life that he went to Rome when society was not only in the most favorable state for the improvement of his mind, and for convincing him of the deleterious influence of the arts when employed as the embellishments of voluptuousness and luxury, but also when the state of the arts was so mean that the full effect of studying the antique only, and of grouping characters by academical rules, should appear so striking as to satisfy him that he could never hope for any eminence if he did not attend more to the phenomena of Nature than to the productions of the greatest genius. The perusal of the works of other painters, he was sensible, would improve his taste; but he was convinced that the design which he had formed for establishing his own fame could not be realized if, for a single moment, he forgot that their works, however exquisite, were but the imitations and forms of those eternal models to which he had been instinctively directed.

IT WAS ON THE 10TH of July, 1760, that he arrived at Rome. The French courier conducted him to a hotel, and having mentioned in the house that he was an American, and a Quaker, come to study the fine arts, the circumstance seemed so extraordinary that it reached the ears of Mr. Robinson, afterward Lord Grantham, who immediately found himself possessed by an irresistible desire to see him; and who, before he had time to dress or refresh himself, paid him a visit and insisted that he should dine with him.

In the course of dinner, that gentleman inquired what letters of introduction the artist had brought with him; and West having informed him, he observed it was somewhat remarkable that the whole of them should be addressed to his most particular friends, adding that, as he was engaged to meet them at a party in the evening, he expected West would accompany him. This attention and frankness was acknowledged as it deserved to be, and is remembered by the artist among those fortunate incidents which have rendered the recollection of his past life so pleasant, as scarcely to leave a wish for any part of it to have been spent otherwise than it was. At the hour appointed, Mr. Robinson conducted him to the house of Mr. Crispigné, an English gentleman who had long resided at Rome, where the evening party was held.

AMONG THE DISTINGUISHED PERSONS whom Mr. West found in the company was the celebrated Cardinal Albani. His Eminence, although quite blind, had acquired, by the exquisite delicacy of his touch and the combining powers of his mind, such a sense of ancient beauty that he excelled all the virtuosi then in Rome, in the correctness of his knowledge of the verity and peculiarities of the smallest medals and intaglios. Mr. Robinson conducted the artist to the inner apartment, where the Cardinal was sitting, and said, "I have the honor to present a young American who has a letter of introduction to Your Eminence, and who has come to Italy for the purpose of studying the fine arts." The Cardinal, fancying that the American must be an Indian, exclaimed, "Is he black or white?" and on being told that he was very fair, "What, as fair as I am?" cried the Cardinal still more surprised.

This latter expression excited a good deal of mirth at the Cardinal's expense, for his complexion was of the darkest Italian olive, and West's was even of more than the usual degree of English fairness. For some time after, if it be not still in use, the expression of "as fair as the Cardinal" acquired proverbial currency in the Roman conversations, applied to persons who had any inordinate conceit of their own beauty.

THE CARDINAL, after some other short questions, invited West to come near him, and running his hands over his features, still more attracted the attention of the company to the stranger by the admiration which he expressed at the form of his head. This occasioned inquiries respecting the youth; and the Italians, concluding that, as he was an American, he must, of course, have received the education of a savage, became curious to witness the effect which the works of art in the Belvedere and Vatican would produce on him. The whole company, which consisted of the principal Roman nobility and strangers of distinction then in Rome, were interested in the event; and it was arranged in the course of the evening that on the following morning they should accompany Mr. Robinson and his protégé to the palaces.

AT THE HOUR APPOINTED, the company assembled; and a procession, consisting of upward of thirty of the most magnificent equipages in the capital of Christendom and filled with some of the most erudite charac-

ters in Europe, conducted the young Quaker to view the masterpieces of art. It was agreed that the Apollo should be first submitted to his view, because it was the most perfect work among all the ornaments of Rome, and, consequently, the best calculated to produce that effect which the company were anxious to witness.

The statue then stood in a case, enclosed with doors, which could be so opened as to disclose it at once to full view. West was placed in the situation where it was seen to the most advantage, and the spectators arranged themselves on each side. When the keeper threw open the doors, the artist felt himself surprised with a sudden recollection altogether different from the gratification which he had expected; and without being aware of the force of what he said, exclaimed, "My God, how like it is to a young Mohawk warrior!" The Italians, observing his surprise and hearing the exclamation, requested Mr. Robinson to translate to them what he said; and they were excessively mortified to find that the god of their idolatry was compared to a savage.

Mr. Robinson mentioned to West their chagrin and asked him to give some more distinct explanation by informing him what sort of people the Mohawk Indians were. He described to him their education; their dexterity with the bow and arrow; the admirable elasticity of their limbs; and how much their active life expands the chest, while the quick breathing of their speed in the chase dilates the nostrils with that apparent consciousness of vigor which is so nobly depicted in the Apollo. "I have seen them often," added he, "standing in that very attitude, and pursuing, with an intense eye, the arrow which they had just discharged from the bow." This descriptive explanation did not lose by Mr. Robinson's translation. The Italians were delighted, and allowed that a better criticism had rarely been pronounced on the merits of the statue.

The view of the other great works did not awaken the same vivid feelings. Those of Raphael, in the Vatican, did not at first particularly interest him; nor was it until he had often visited them alone, and studied them by himself, that he could appreciate the fullness of their excellence. His first view of the works of Michelangelo was still less satisfactory. Indeed, he continued always to think that, with the single exception of the Moses, that artist had not succeeded in giving a probable character to any of his subjects, notwithstanding the masterly hand and mind which pervade the weakest of his productions.

AMONG THE FIRST OBJECTS which particularly interested Mr. West, and which he never ceased to revisit day after day with increasing pleasure, were the celebrated statues ascribed to Phidias, on the Monte Cavallo. The action of the human figure appeared to him so majestic that it seemed to throw, as it were, a visible kind of awe into the very atmosphere and over all the surrounding buildings. But the smallness of the horse struck him as exceedingly preposterous. He had often examined it before the idea occurred to him that it was probably reduced according to some unknown principle of ancient art; and in this notion he was confirmed, by observing something of the same kind in the relative proportion of human figures and animals on the different gems and bas-reliefs to which his attention was subsequently directed. The ancient sculptors uniformly seemed to consider the human figure as the chief object and sacrificed, to give it effect, the proportions of inferior parts. The author of the group on the Monte Cavallo, in the opinion of Mr. West, represented the horse smaller than the natural size in order to augment the grandeur of the man.

How far this notion, as the principle of a rule, may be sound, it would be unnecessary, perhaps impertinent, to inquire here; but its justness as applicable to the sculp-

tures of antiquity is abundantly verified by the bas-reliefs brought from the Parthenon of Athens. It is, indeed, so admitted a feature of ancient art as to be regarded by some critics as having for its object the same effect in sculpture which is attained by light and shadow in painting. In a picture, the artist, by a judicious obscurity, so veils the magnitude of the car in which he places a victor, that, notwithstanding its size, it may not appear the principal object; but this artifice is denied to the sculptor, who is necessitated to diminish the size of those things which are of least importance in order to give dignity to the dominant figures.

Raphael, in making the boat so small in the miraculous draft of fishes, is thought to have injudiciously applied this rule of ancient sculpture; for he ought to have accomplished, by foreshortening, the same effect which he meant to produce by diminishing the size. It should, however, be observed that great doubts are entertained if the statues on the Monte Cavallo were originally integral parts of the same group; but although this doubt may be well founded, it will not invalidate the supposed general principle of the ancient sculptors, corroborated as it is by innumerable examples.

IN THE EVENING, after visiting the palaces, Mr. Robinson carried Mr. West to see a grand religious ceremony in one of the churches. Hitherto he was acquainted only with the simple worship of the Quakers. The pomp of the papal ceremonies was as much beyond his comprehension as the overpowering excellence of the music surpassed his utmost expectations. Undoubtedly, in all the spectacles and amusements of Rome, he possessed a keener sense of enjoyment, arising from the simplicity of his education, than most other travelers. That same sensibility to the beauty of forms and colors which had awakened his genius for painting was, probably, accompanied with a general superior susceptibility of the other organs as well as the sight; for it is observed that a taste for any one of the fine arts is connected with a general predilection for them all.

But neither the Apollo, the Vatican, nor the pomp of the Catholic ritual excited his feelings to so great a degree as the spectacle which presented itself to his view around the portico of the church. Bred in the universal prosperity of Pennsylvania, where the benevolence of the human bosom was only employed in acts of hospitality and mutual kindness, he had never witnessed any spectacle of beggary, nor had he ever heard the name of God uttered to second an entreaty for alms. Here, however, all the lazars and the wretched in Rome were collected together; hundreds of young and old in that extreme of squalor, nakedness, and disease which affrights the English traveler in Italy were seen on all sides; and their importunities and cries, for the love of God and the mercy of Christ to relieve them, thrilled in his ears, and smote upon his heart to such a degree that his joints became as it were loosened, and his legs scarcely able to support him. Many of the beggars knew Mr. Robinson, and seeing him accompanied by a stranger, an Englishman, as they concluded the artist to be from his appearance, surrounded them with confidence and clamors.

As they returned from the church, a woman somewhat advanced in life, and of a better appearance than the generality of the beggars, followed them, and Mr. West gave her a small piece of copper money, the first Roman coin which he had received in change, the relative value of which to the other coins of the country was unknown to him. Shortly afterward they were joined by some of the Italians, whom they had seen in the morning, and while they were conversing together, he felt some one pull his coat, and turned round. It was the poor woman to whom he had given the piece of copper money. She held out in her hand several smaller pieces, and as he did not understand her language, he concluded that she was chiding him for having given her such a trifle, and colored deeply with the idea.

His English friend, observing his confusion, inquired what he had given her, and he answered that he did not know, but it was a piece of money which he had received in change. Robinson, after a short conversation with the beggar, told Mr. West that she had asked him to give her a farthing. "But as you gave her a two-penny-piece," said he, "she has brought you the change." This instance of humble honesty, contrasted with the awful mass of misery with which it was united, gave him a favorable idea of the latent sentiments of the Italians. How much, indeed, is the character of that people traduced by the rest of Europe! How often is the traveler in Italy, when he dreads the approach of robbers and prepares against murder, surprised at the bountiful disposition of the common Italians and made to blush at having applied the charges against a few criminals to the character of a whole people — without reflecting that the nation is only weak because it is subdivided.

1761

15.

James Otis: Against Writs of Assistance

The Navigation Acts and the Writs of Assistance that accompanied them empowered customs officers with general search privileges, and resulted in a series of court cases, the most famous of which was tried in February 1761. In the following speech, James Otis, a Massachusetts lawyer, argued before the Superior Court of Massachusetts that the writs were unconstitutional. This "master of the laws of nature and nations," as John Adams called him, based his case on the theory of political and social rights that he found in English common law. His open opposition to the power of Parliament marked the beginning of Otis' prominence as a popular agitator against the Crown.

Source: *Modern Eloquence*, Thomas B. Reed, ed., Philadelphia, 1901, Vol. XIV, pp. 1526-1531.

I WAS DESIRED by one of the Court to look into the books and consider the question now before them concerning "Writs of Assistance." I have accordingly considered it, and now appear not only in obedience to your order but likewise in behalf of the inhabitants of this town who have presented another petition, and out of regard to the liberties of the subject. And I take this opportunity to declare that whether under a fee or not (for in such a cause as this I despise a fee), I will to my dying day oppose with all the powers and faculties God has given me all such instruments of slavery on the one hand and villainy on the other as this Writ of Assistance is.

It appears to me the worst instrument of arbitrary power, the most destructive of English liberty and the fundamental principles of law, that ever was found in an English lawbook. I must therefore beg Your Honors' patience and attention to the whole range of an argument that may perhaps appear uncommon in many things, as well as to points of learning that are more remote and unusual, that the whole tendency of my design may the more easily be perceived, the conclusions better descend, and the force of them be better felt. I shall not think much of my pains in this cause, as I engaged in it from principle.

I was solicited to argue this cause as advocate general, and because I would not, I have been charged with desertion from my office. To this charge I can give a very sufficient answer. I renounced that office, and I argue this cause from the same principle; and I argue it with the greater pleasure, as it is in favor of British liberty, at a time when we hear the greatest monarch upon earth declaring from his throne that he glories in the name of Britain, and that the privileges of his people are dearer to him than the most valuable prerogatives of his Crown, and as it is in opposition to a kind of power, the exercise of which, in former periods of history, cost one king of England his head and another his throne. I have taken more pains in this cause than I ever will take again, although my engaging in this and another popular cause has raised much resentment. But I think I can sincerely declare that I cheerfully submit myself to every odious name for conscience's sake, and from my soul I despise all those whose guilt, malice, or folly has made them my foes. Let the consequences be what they will, I am determined to proceed. The only principles of public conduct that are worthy of a gentleman or a man are to sacrifice estate, ease, health, and applause, and even life, to the sacred calls of his country.

These manly sentiments in private life make the good citizen; in public life, the patriot and the hero. I do not say that when brought to the test I shall be invincible. I pray God I may never be brought to the melancholy trial, but if ever I should, it will be then known how far I can reduce to practice principles which I know to be founded in truth. In the meantime I will proceed to the subject of this writ.

Your Honors will find in the old books concerning the office of a justice of the peace precedents of general warrants to search suspected houses. But in more modern books you will find only special warrants to search such and such houses, specially named, in which the complainant has before sworn that he suspects his goods are concealed, and will find it adjudged that special warrants only are legal. In the same manner, I rely on it that the writ prayed for in this petition, being general, is illegal. It is a power that places the liberty of every man in the hands of every petty officer. I say I admit that special writs of assistance, to search special places, may be granted to certain persons on oath; but I deny that the writ now prayed for can be granted, for I beg leave to make some observations on the writ itself before I proceed to other acts of Parliament.

In the first place, the writ is universal, being directed "to all and singular justices, sheriffs, constables, and all other officers and subjects"; so that, in short, it is directed to every subject in the King's dominions. Everyone, with this writ, may be a tyrant; if this commission be legal, a tyrant in a legal manner, also, may control, imprison, or murder anyone within the Realm. In the next place, it is perpetual, there is no return. A man is accountable to no person for his doings. Every man may reign secure in his petty tyranny and spread terror and desolation around him, until the trump of the archangel shall excite different emotions in his soul. In the third place, a person with this writ, in the daytime, may enter all houses or shops, at will, and command all to assist him. Fourth, by this writ, not only deputies but even their menial servants are allowed to lord it over us. What is this but to have the curse of Canaan with a witness on us; to be the servant of servants, the most despicable of God's creation?

Now, one of the most essential branches of English liberty is the freedom of one's house. A man's house is his castle; and while he is quiet, he is as well guarded as a prince in his castle. This writ, if it should be declared legal, would totally annihilate this privilege. Customhouse officers may enter our houses when they please; we are commanded to permit their entry. Their menial servants may enter, may break locks, bars, and everything in their way; and whether they break through malice or revenge, no man, no court can inquire. Bare suspicion without oath is sufficient.

This wanton exercise of this power is not chimerical suggestion of a heated brain. I will mention some facts. Mr. Pew had one of these writs, and when Mr. Ware succeeded him, he endorsed this writ over to Mr. Ware, so that these writs are negotiable from one officer to another; and so Your

Honors have no opportunity of judging the persons to whom this vast power is delegated. Another instance is this: Mr. Justice Walley had called this same Mr. Ware before him, by a constable, to answer for a breach of the Sabbath-Day acts, or that of profane swearing. As soon as he had finished, Mr. Ware asked him if he had done. He replied, "Yes." "Well, then," said Mr. Ware, "I will show you a little of my power. I command you to permit me to search your house for uncustomed goods"; and went on to search the house from the garret to the cellar; and then served the constable in the same manner!

But to show another absurdity in this writ, if it should be established, I insist upon it every person — by the 14th Charles II — has this power as well as the customhouse officers. The words are, "It shall be lawful for any person or persons authorized. . . ." What a scene does this open! Every man prompted by revenge, ill humor, or wantonness to inspect the inside of his neighbor's house, may get a writ of assistance. Others will ask it from self-defense; one arbitrary exertion will provoke another, until society be involved in tumult and in blood. [The rest of the speech exists only in a summary by John Adams.]

A DISSERTATION ON THE RIGHTS of man in a state of nature. He asserted that every man, merely natural, was an independent sovereign, subject to no law but the law written on his heart and revealed to him by his Maker, in the constitution of his nature and the inspiration of his understanding and his conscience. His right to his life, his liberty, no created being could rightfully contest. Nor was his right to his property less incontestable. The club that he had snapped from a tree, for a staff or for defense, was his own. His bow and arrow were his own; if by a pebble he had killed a partridge or a squirrel, it was his own. No creature, man or beast, had a right to take it from him. If

he had taken an eel or a smelt or a sculpin, it was his property. In short, he sported upon this topic with so much wit and humor, and at the same time with so much indisputable truth and reason, that he was not less entertaining than instructive.

He asserted that these rights were inherent and inalienable. That they never could be surrendered or alienated but by idiots or madmen and all the acts of idiots and lunatics were void and not obligatory, by all the laws of God and man. Nor were the poor Negroes forgotten. Not a Quaker in Philadelphia or Mr. Jefferson in Virginia ever asserted the rights of Negroes in stronger terms. Young as I was and ignorant as I was, I shuddered at the doctrine he taught; and I have all my life shuddered, and still shudder, at the consequences that may be drawn from such premises. Shall we say that the rights of masters and servants clash and can be decided only by force? I adore the idea of gradual abolitions! but who shall decide how fast or how slowly these abolitions shall be made?

From individual independence he proceeded to association. If it was inconsistent with the dignity of human nature to say that men were gregarious animals, like wild geese, it surely could offend no delicacy to say they were social animals by nature, that there were natural sympathies, and, above all, the sweet attraction of the sexes, which must soon draw them together in little groups, and by degrees in larger congregations, for mutual assistance and defense And this must have happened before any formal covenant, by express words or signs, was concluded.

When general councils and deliberations commenced, the objects could be no other than the mutual defense and security of every individual for his life, his liberty, and his property. To suppose them to have surrendered these in any other way than by equal rules and general consent was to suppose them idiots or madmen whose acts

James Otis, Jr., portrait by J. Blackburn

were never binding. To suppose them surprised by fraud or compelled by force into any other compact, such fraud and such force could confer no obligation. Every man had a right to trample it underfoot whenever he pleased. In short, he asserted these rights to be derived only from nature and the Author of nature; that they were inherent, inalienable, and indefeasible by any laws, pacts, contracts, covenants, or stipulations which man could devise. These principles and these rights were wrought into the English constitution as fundamental laws. And under this head he went back to the old Saxon laws and to Magna Carta and the fifty confirmations of it in Parliament and the executions ordained against the violators of it and the national vengeance which had been taken on them from time to time, down to the Jameses and Charleses, and to the position of rights and the Bill of Rights and the revolution.

He asserted that the security of these rights to life, liberty, and property had been the object of all those struggles against arbitrary power, temporal and spiritual, civil and political, military and ecclesiastical, in every age. He asserted that our ancestors, as British subjects, and we their descendants, as British subjects, were entitled to all those rights by the British constitution as well as by the law of nature and our provincial character as much as any inhabitant of London or Bristol or any part of England, and were not to be cheated out of them by any phantom of "virtual representation" or any other fiction of law or politics or any monkish trick of deceit and hypocrisy.

He then examined the Acts of Trade, one by one, and demonstrated that, if they were considered as revenue laws, they destroyed all our security of property, liberty, and life, every right of nature and the English constitution and the charter of the province. Here he considered the distinction between "external and internal taxes," at that time a popular and commonplace distinction. But he asserted that there was no such distinction in theory or upon any principle but "necessity." The necessity that the commerce of the Empire should be under one direction was obvious. The Americans had been so sensible of this necessity that they had connived at the distinction between external and internal taxes, and had submitted to the Acts of Trade as regulations of commerce but never as taxations or revenue laws. Nor had the British government till now ever dared to attempt to enforce them as taxations or revenue laws.

The Navigation Act he allowed to be binding upon us because we had consented to it by our own legislature. Here he gave a history of the Navigation Act of the first of Charles II, a plagiarism from Oliver Cromwell. In 1675, after repeated letters and orders from the King, Governor Leverett very candidly informs His Majesty that the law had not been executed because it was thought unconstitutional, Parliament not having authority over us.

1763

16.

John Woolman: A Plea for the Poor

The Quaker John Woolman, who as a young man responded to a "call" to the ministry, spent the rest of his life urging social reforms in behalf of the deprived and downtrodden. Nor was he without effect, at least in later times and especially in England, where he died of smallpox while laboring among the poor. He became one of the prophets both of the antislavery movement and eventually of English socialism. A Plea for the Poor, part of which appears here, was written in 1763. It was reissued in London by the Fabian Society in 1897.

Source: *The Journal of John Woolman,* Boston, 1871, Appendix: "A Word of Remembrance and Caution to the Rich."

SECTION I

WEALTH DESIRED for its own sake obstructs the increase of virtue, and large possessions in the hands of selfish men have a bad tendency, for, by their means, too small a number of people are employed in useful things, and some of them are necessitated to labor too hard, while others would want business to earn their bread, were not employments invented which, having no real usefulness, serve only to please the vain mind.

Rents on lands are often so high that persons of but small substance are straitened in taking farms, and while tenants are healthy and prosperous in business, they often find occasion to labor harder than was intended by our gracious Creator. Oxen and horses are often seen at work when, through heat and too much labor, their eyes and the motions of their bodies manifest that they are oppressed. Their loads in wagons are frequently so heavy that, when weary with hauling them far, their drivers find occasion, in going up hills or through mire, to get them forward by whipping. Many poor people are so thronged in their business that it is difficult for them to provide shelter for their cattle against the storms. These things are common when in health, but through sickness and inability to labor, through loss of cattle, and miscarriage in business, many are so straitened that much of their increase goes to pay rent, and they have not wherewith to buy what they require.

Hence, one poor woman, in providing for her family and attending the sick, does as much business as would for the time be suitable employment for two or three; and honest persons are often straitened to give their children suitable learning. The money which the wealthy receive from the poor, who do more than a proper share of business in raising it, is frequently paid to other poor people for doing business which is foreign to the true use of things. Men who have large estates and live in the spirit of charity; who carefully inspect the circumstances of those who occupy their estates and, regardless of the customs of the times, regulate their demands agreeably to universal love, being righteous on principle, do good to the poor without placing it to an act of bounty. Their example in avoiding superfluities tends to excite moderation in others; their uprightness in not exacting what the laws and customs would support them in tends to open the channel to moderate labor in useful affairs and to discourage those branches of business which have not their foundation in true wisdom.

To be busied in that which is but vanity and serves only to please the insatiable mind, tends to an alliance with those who promote that vanity and is a snare in which many poor tradesmen are entangled. To be employed in things connected with virtue is most agreeable with the character and inclinations of an honest man. While industrious, frugal people are borne down with poverty and oppressed with too much labor in useful things, the way to apply money without promoting pride and vanity remains open to such as truly sympathize with them in their various difficulties.

SECTION II

THE CREATOR OF THE EARTH is the owner of it. He gave us being thereon, and our nature requires nourishment from the produce of it. He is kind and merciful to His creatures; and while they live answerably to the design of their creation, they are so far entitled to convenient subsistence that we may not justly deprive them of it. By the agreements and contracts of our predecessors, and by our own doings, some enjoy a much greater share of this world than others; and while those possessions are faithfully improved for the good of the whole, it agrees with equity. But he who, with a view to self-exaltation, causes some to labor immoderately, and with the profits arising therefrom employs others in the luxuries of life, acts contrary to the gracious designs of Him who is the owner of the earth; nor can any possessions, either acquired or derived from ancestors, justify such conduct. Goodness remains to be goodness, and the direction of pure wisdom is obligatory on all reasonable creatures.

Though the poor occupy our estates by a bargain to which they in their poor circumstances agree, and we may ask even less than a punctual fulfilling of their agreement, yet if our views are to lay up riches or to live in conformity to customs which have not their foundation in the truth, and our demands are such as require from them greater toil or application to business than is consistent with pure love, we invade their rights as inhabitants of a world of which a good and gracious God is the proprietor, and under whom we are tenants.

Were all superfluities and the desire of outward greatness laid aside, and the right use of things universally attended to, such a number of people might be employed in things useful as that moderate labor with the blessing of Heaven would answer all good purposes, and a sufficient number would have time to attend to the proper affairs of civil society.

SECTION III

WHILE OUR SPIRITS ARE LIVELY, we go cheerfully through business; either too much or too little action is tiresome, but a right portion is healthful to the body and agreeable to an honest mind.

Men who have great estates stand in a

place of trust; and to have it in their power to live without difficulty in that manner which occasions much labor, and at the same time to confine themselves to that use of things prescribed by our Redeemer and confirmed by His example and the examples of many who lived in the early age of the Christian Church, that they may more extensively relieve objects of charity, requires close attention to divine love.

Our gracious Creator cares and provides for all His creatures. His tender mercies are over all His works, and so far as true love influences our minds, so far we become interested in His workmanship and feel a desire to make use of every opportunity to lessen the distresses of the afflicted and to increase the happiness of the creation. Here we have a prospect of one common interest from which our own is inseparable, so that to turn all we possess into the channel of universal love becomes the business of our lives.

Men of large estates whose hearts are thus enlarged are like fathers to the poor; and in looking over their brethren in distressed circumstances and considering their own more easy condition, they find a field for humble meditation and feel the strength of the obligations they are under to be kind and tenderhearted toward them. Poor men, eased of their burdens and released from too close an application to business, are enabled to hire assistance, to provide well for their cattle, and to find time to perform those duties among their neighbors which belong to a well-guided social life. When the latter reflect on the opportunity such had to oppress them and consider the goodness of their conduct, they behold it lovely and consistent with brotherhood; and as the man whose mind is conformed to universal love has his trust settled in God and finds a firm foundation in any changes or revolutions that happen among men, so also the goodness of his conduct tends to spread a kind, benevolent disposition in the world. . . .

SECTION VI

IF MORE MEN WERE USEFULLY EMPLOYED, and fewer ate bread as a reward for doing that which is not useful, food and raiment would on a reasonable estimate be more in proportion to labor than they are at present; for if four men working eight hours per day can do a portion of labor in a certain number of days, then five men equally capable may do the same business in the same time by working only six hours and twenty-four minutes per day. In proceeding agreeably to sound wisdom, a small portion of daily labor might suffice to keep a proper stream gently circulating through all the channels of society; and this portion of labor might be so divided and taken in the most advantageous parts of the day that people would not have that plea for the use of strong liquors which they have at present. The quantity of spirituous liquors imported and made in our country is great; nor can so many thousand hogsheads of it be drunk every year without having a powerful effect on our habits and morals.

People spent with much labor often take strong liquor to revive them. The portion of the necessaries of life is such that those who support their families by day labor find occasion to labor hard, and many of them think strong drink a necessary part of their entertainment.

When people are spent with action and take these liquors, not only as a refreshment from past labors but also to enable them to go on without giving sufficient time to recruit by resting, it gradually turns them from that calmness of thought which attends those who apply their hearts to true wisdom. That the spirits being scattered by too much bodily motion and again revived by strong drink makes a person unfit for divine meditation I suppose will not be denied; and as multitudes of people are in this practice who do not take so much as to hinder them from managing their affairs, this custom is strongly supported; but as through divine goodness I have found that there is a more quiet, calm, and happy way intended for us to walk in, I am engaged to express what I feel in my heart concerning it.

As cherishing the spirit of love and meekness belongs to the family of Jesus Christ, so to avoid those things which are known to work against it is an indispensable duty. Every degree of luxury of what kind soever, and every demand for money inconsistent with divine order, has some connection with unnecessary labor. By too much labor the spirits are exhausted, and nature craves help from strong drink; and the frequent use of strong drink works in opposition to the celestial influence on the mind. There is in the nature of people some degree of likeness with that food and air to which they have been accustomed from their youth; this frequently appears in those who, by a separation from their native air and usual diet, grow weak and unhealthy for want of them; nor is it reasonable to suppose that so many thousand hogsheads of fiery liquor can be drunk every year and the practice continued from age to age without altering in some degree the natures of men and rendering their minds less apt to receive the pure truth in the love of it.

As many who manifest some regard to piety in degree conform to those ways of living and of collecting wealth which increase labor beyond the bounds fixed by divine wisdom; my desire is that they may so consider the connection of things as to take heed lest by exacting of poor men more than is consistent with universal righteousness they promote that by their conduct which in word they speak against. To treasure up wealth for another generation by means of the immoderate labor of those who in some measure depend upon us is doing evil at present without knowing that wealth thus gathered may not be applied to evil purposes when we are gone. To labor hard or cause others to do so that we may live conformably to customs, which Christ

our Redeemer discountenanced by His example in the days of His flesh and which are contrary to divine order, is to manure a soil for propagating an evil seed in the earth.

They who enter deeply into these considerations and live under the weight of them will feel these things so heavy and their ill effects so extensive that the necessity of attending singly to divine wisdom will be evident; and will thereby be directed in the right use of things in opposition to the customs of the times; and will be supported to bear patiently the reproaches attending singularity. To conform a little strengthens the hands of those who carry wrong customs to their utmost extent; and the more a person appears to be virtuous and heavenly minded, the more powerfully does his conformity operate in favor of evildoers. Lay aside the profession of a pious life, and people expect little or no instruction from the example; but while we profess in all cases to live in constant opposition to that which is contrary to universal righteousness, what expressions are equal to the subject, or what language is sufficient to set forth the strength of the obligations we are under to beware lest by our example we lead others astray! . . .

SECTION IX

THE WAY OF CARRYING ON WARS common in the world is so far distinguishable from the purity of Christ's religion that many scruple to join in them. Those who are so redeemed from the love of the world as to possess nothing in a selfish spirit have their "life hid with Christ in God," and He preserves them in resignedness, even in times of commotion.

As they possess nothing but what pertains to His family, anxious thoughts about wealth or dominion have little or nothing in them on which to work; and they learn contentment in being disposed of according to His will who, being omnipotent and always mindful of His children, causes all things to work for their good. But when that spirit works which loves riches, and in its working gathers wealth and cleaves to customs which have their root in self-pleasing, whatever name it has, it still desires to defend the treasures thus gotten. This is like a chain in which the end of one link encloses the end of another. The rising up of a desire to obtain wealth is the beginning; this desire being cherished, moves to action; and riches thus gotten please self; and while self has a life in them it desires to have them defended.

Wealth is attended with power, by which bargains and proceedings contrary to universal righteousness are supported; and hence oppression, carried on with worldly policy and order, clothes itself with the name of justice and becomes like a seed of discord in the soul. And as a spirit which wanders from the pure habitation prevails, so the seeds of war swell and sprout and grow and become strong until much fruit is ripened. Then comes the harvest spoken of by the prophet, which "is a heap in the day of grief and desperate sorrows." O, that we who declare against wars and acknowledge our trust to be in God only may walk in the light and therein examine our foundation and motives in holding great estates! May we look upon our treasures, the furniture of our houses, and our garments, and try whether the seeds of war have nourishment in these our possessions. Holding treasures in the self-pleasing spirit is a strong plant, the fruit whereof ripens fast. A day of outward distress is coming, and divine love calls to prepare against it. . . .

SECTION XII

WHILE OUR MINDS ARE PREPOSSESSED in favor of customs distinguishable from perfect purity, we are in danger of not attending with singleness to that light which opens to our view the nature of universal righteousness.

In the affairs of a thickly settled country are variety of useful employments besides tilling the earth; so that for some men to have more land than is necessary to build upon and to answer the occasions of their families may consist with brotherhood; and from the various gifts which God has bestowed on those employed in husbandry, for some to possess and occupy much more than others may likewise so consist. But when any, on the strength of their possessions, demand such rent or interest as necessitates their tenants to a closer application to business than our merciful Father designed for us, it puts the wheels of perfect brotherhood out of order and leads to employments, the promoting of which belongs not to the family of Christ, whose example in all points being a pattern of wisdom, the plainness and simplicity of His outward appearance may well make us ashamed to adorn our bodies with costly array or treasure up wealth by the least oppression.

Though by claims grounded on prior possession great inequality appears among men, yet the instructions of the Great Proprietor of the earth are necessary to be attended to in all our proceedings as possessors or claimers of the soil. "The steps of a good man are ordered of the Lord," and those who are thus guided and whose hearts are enlarged in His love give directions concerning their possessions agreeably thereto; and that claim which stands on universal righteousness is a good right; but the continuance of that right depends on properly applying the profits thereof.

The word "right" commonly relates to our possessions. We say, a right of propriety to such a division of a province, or a clear, indisputable right to the land within certain bounds. Thus this word is continued as a remembrancer of the original intent of dividing the land by boundaries and implies that it was equitably or rightly divided, that is, divided according to righteousness. In this — that is, in equity and righteousness

— consists the strength of our claim. If we trace an unrighteous claim and find gifts or grants proved by sufficient seals and witnesses, it gives not the claimant a right. . . .

Suppose twenty free men, professed followers of Christ, discovered an island, and that they with their wives, independent of all others, took possession of it, and, dividing it equally, made improvements and multiplied. Suppose these first possessors, being generally influenced by true love, did with paternal regard look over the increasing condition of the inhabitants, and, near the end of their lives, gave such directions concerning their respective possessions as best suited the convenience of the whole and tended to preserve love and harmony. And that their successors, in the continued increase of people, generally followed their pious example and pursued means the most effectual to keep oppression out of their island; but that one of these first settlers, from a fond attachment to one of his numerous sons, no more deserving than the rest, gives the chief of his lands to him, and by an instrument sufficiently witnessed strongly expressed his mind and will.

Suppose this son, being landlord to his brethren and nephews, demands such a portion of the fruits of the earth as may supply himself, his family, and some others; and that these others, thus supplied out of his store, are employed in adorning his building with curious engravings and paintings, preparing carriages to ride in, vessels for his house, delicious meats, fine-wrought apparel and furniture, all suiting that distinction lately arisen between him and the other inhabitants; and that, having the absolute disposal of these numerous improvements, his power so increases that, in all conferences relative to the public affairs of the island, these plain, honest men, who are zealous for equitable establishments, find great difficulty in proceeding agreeably to their righteous inclinations. Suppose this son, from a fondness to one of his children, joined with a desire to continue this grandeur under his

own name, confirms the chief of his possessions to him, and thus for many ages there is one great landlord over near a twentieth part of this island, and the rest are poor oppressed people, to some of whom, from the manner of their education, joined with a notion of the greatness of their predecessors, labor is disagreeable; who, therefore, by artful applications to the weakness, unguardedness, and corruptions of others in striving to get a living out of them, increase the difficulties among them, while the inhabitants of other parts, who guard against oppression and with one consent train up their children in frugality and useful labor, live more harmoniously.

If we trace the claims of the ninth or tenth of these great landlords down to the first possessor and find the claim supported throughout by instruments strongly drawn and witnessed, after all we could not admit a belief into our hearts that he had a right to so great a portion of land after such a numerous increase of inhabitants.

The first possessor of that twentieth part held no more, we suppose, than an equitable portion; but when the Lord, who first gave these twenty men possession of this island unknown to all others, gave being to numerous people who inhabited the twentieth part, whose natures required the fruits thereof for their sustenance, this great claimer of the soil could not have a right to the whole to dispose of it in gratifying his irregular desires. But they, as creatures of the Most High God, Possessor of heaven and earth, had a right to part of what this great claimer held, though they had no instruments to confirm their right. Thus oppression in the extreme appears terrible; but oppression in more refined appearances remains to be oppression, and when the smallest degree of it is cherished it grows stronger and more extensive.

To labor for a perfect redemption from this spirit of oppression is the great business of the whole family of Christ Jesus in this world.

17.

Proclamation of 1763

The Treaty of Paris, ending the Franco-British War in 1763, left Britain the most powerful empire in the world. In America, her victory meant the acquisition of all French territory east of the Mississippi. However, difficulties with Indians in this area, especially Pontiac's Rebellion, led the Privy Council to decide to discourage immediate settlement. Hoping to eliminate tensions with the Indians, at least for the time being, and unwilling to have settlers occupy lands where English rule could not yet be enforced, the Crown issued the Proclamation of (October 7) 1763. Specifically, the Proclamation prohibited settlement beyond the Appalachian crest, and instead called for the development of the new colonies of East and West Florida and Nova Scotia. Though the measure was designed to be temporary, it seemed to the colonial governments to deprive them of lands that had been given to them as part of their original charters, and, although private speculation was lessened, English colonists continued to press westward. Looking back, it is evident that their disobedience was but one more indication of the growing opposition to British colonial policy that soon would lead to open rebellion.

Source: *The Annual Register . . . for the Year 1763*, London, 1768, pp. 208-213.

Whereas we have taken into our royal consideration the extensive and valuable acquisitions in America, secured to our Crown by the late definitive treaty of peace concluded at Paris the 10th day of February last; and being desirous that all our loving subjects, as well of our Kingdom as of our colonies in America, may avail themselves, with all convenient speed, of the great benefits and advantages which must accrue therefrom to their commerce, manufactures, and navigation; we have thought fit, with the advice of our Privy Council, to issue this our Royal Proclamation, hereby to publish and declare to all our loving subjects that we have, with the advice of our said Privy Council, granted our letters patent under our great seal of Great Britain, to erect within the countries and islands ceded and confirmed to us by the said treaty, four distinct and separate governments, styled and called by the names of Quebec, East Florida, West Florida, and Grenada. . . .

And to the end that the open and free fishery of our subjects may be extended to and carried on upon the coast of Labrador and the adjacent islands, we have thought fit . . . to put all that coast, from the river St. John's to Hudson's Straits, together with the islands of Anticosti and Madelaine, and all other smaller islands lying upon the said coast, under the care and inspection of our governor of Newfoundland.

We have also . . . thought fit to annex the islands of St. John and Cape Breton, or Isle Royale, with the lesser islands adjacent thereto, to our government of Nova Scotia.

We have also . . . annexed to our province of Georgia all the lands lying between the rivers Altamaha and St. Mary's.

And . . . so soon as the state and circumstances of the said colonies will admit thereof, they shall, with the advice and consent of the members of our Council, summon and call general assemblies within the said governments respectively, in such manner and form as is used and directed in those colonies and provinces in America, which are under our immediate government. And we have also given power to the said governors, with the consent of our said councils and the representatives of the people, so to be summoned as aforesaid, to make, constitute, and ordain laws, statutes, and ordinances for the public peace, welfare, and good government of our said colonies, and of the people and inhabitants thereof, as near as may be agreeable to the laws of England, and under such regulations and restrictions as are used in other colonies.

And, in the meantime and until such assemblies can be called as aforesaid, all persons inhabiting in, or resorting to, our said colonies may confide in our royal protection for the enjoyment of the benefit of the laws of our Realm of England. . . .

We have also thought fit . . . to give unto the governors and councils of our said three new colonies upon the continent full power and authority to settle and agree with the inhabitants of our said new colonies, or to any other person who shall resort thereto, for such lands, tenements, and hereditaments as are now, or hereafter shall be, in our power to dispose of; and . . . to grant to any such person or persons upon such terms and under such moderate quitrents, services, and acknowledgments as have been appointed and settled in other colonies, and under such other conditions as shall appear to us to be necessary and expedient for the advantage of the grantees and the improvement and settlement of our said colonies.

And whereas we are desirous, upon all occasions, to testify our . . . approbation of the conduct and bravery of the officers and soldiers of our armies, and to reward the same, we do hereby command and empower our governors of our said three new colonies and other our governors of our several provinces on the continent of North America to grant, without fee or reward, to such reduced officers as have served in North America during the late war, and are actually residing there, and shall personally apply for the same . . . quantities of land subject, at the expiration of ten years, to the same quitrents as other lands are subject to in the province within which they are granted, as also subject to the same conditions of cultivation and improvement. . . .

And whereas it is just and reasonable and essential to our interest and the security of our colonies that the several nations or tribes of Indians with whom we are connected, and who live under our protection, should not be molested or disturbed in the possession of such parts of our dominions and territories as, not having been ceded to or purchased by us, are reserved to them, or any of them, as their hunting grounds; we do therefore, with the advice of our Privy Council, declare it to be our royal will and pleasure that no governor or commander in chief, in any of our colonies of Quebec, East Florida, or West Florida, do presume, upon any pretense whatever, to grant warrants of survey or pass any patents for lands beyond the bounds of their respective governments, as described in their commissions; as also that no governor or commander in chief of our other colonies or plantations in America do presume for the present, and until our further pleasure be known, to grant warrants of survey or pass patents for any lands beyond the heads or sources of any of the rivers which fall into the Atlantic Ocean from the west or northwest; or upon any lands whatever which, not having been ceded to or purchased by us, as aforesaid, are reserved to the said Indians or any of them.

And we do further declare it to be our royal will and pleasure, for the present as aforesaid, to reserve under our sovereignty, protection, and dominion, for the use of the said Indians, all the land and territories not included within the limits of our said three new governments, or within the limits of the territory granted to the Hudson's Bay Company; as also all the land and territories lying to the westward of the sources of the rivers which fall into the sea from the west and northwest as aforesaid. And we do hereby strictly forbid, on pain of our displeasure, all our loving subjects from making any purchases or settlements whatever, or taking possession of any of the lands above reserved, without our special leave and license for that purpose first obtained.

And we do further strictly enjoin and require all persons whatever who have either willfully or inadvertently seated themselves upon any lands within the countries above described, or upon any other lands which, not having been ceded to or purchased by us, are still reserved to the said Indians as aforesaid, forthwith to remove themselves from such settlements.

And whereas great frauds and abuses have been committed in the purchasing lands of the Indians, to the great prejudice of our interests and to the great dissatisfaction of the said Indians; in order, therefore, to prevent such irregularities for the future, and to the end that the Indians may be convinced of our justice and determined resolution to remove all reasonable cause of discontent, we do, with the advice of our Privy Council, strictly enjoin and require that no private person do presume to make any purchase from the said Indians of any lands reserved to the said Indians within those parts of our colonies where we have thought proper to allow settlement; but that if at any time any of the said Indians should be

inclined to dispose of the said lands, the same shall be purchased only for us, in our name, at some public meeting or assembly of the said Indians, to be held for that purpose by the governor or commander in chief of our colony, respectively, within which they shall lie. And in case they shall lie within the limits of any proprietary government, they shall be purchased only for the use and in the name of such proprietaries, conformable to such directions and instructions as we or they shall think proper to give for that purpose.

And we do, by the advice of our Privy Council, declare and enjoin that the trade with the said Indians shall be free and open to all our subjects whatever, provided that every person who may incline to trade with the said Indians do take out a license for carrying on such trade, from the governor or commander in chief of any of our colonies, respectively, where such person shall reside, and also give security to observe such regulations as we shall at any time think fit, by ourselves or commissaries to be appointed for this purpose, to direct and appoint for the benefit of the said trade. And we do hereby authorize, enjoin, and require the governors and commanders in chief of all our colonies, respectively, as well those under our immediate government as those under the government and direction of proprietaries, to grant such licenses without fee or reward, taking special care to insert therein a condition that such license shall be void and the security forfeited in case the person to whom the same is granted shall refuse or neglect to observe such regulations as we shall think proper to prescribe as aforesaid.

1764

18.

THOMAS FITCH *et al.*: On the Right to Raise Revenue

The American phase of the Seven Years' War — it was known here as the French and Indian War — had been costly for Britain; her national debt had doubled and the expense of protecting her colonies, which now included lands newly won from France, had quadrupled. George Grenville, head of the British Ministry, suggested a tax on commercial transactions — a stamp tax — as a means of helping to defray the increased cost of colonial administration. Stamp taxes were not new, nor are they unfamiliar today, but the colonists of the 1760s reacted violently to Grenville's proposal. The Connecticut Assembly requested Governor Thomas Fitch and others to draw up its objections to the tax. Fitch was unsympathetic to the tax as proposed, but in his report of 1764, part of which is reprinted here, he at least implicitly conceded Parliament's right to raise monies in America. His moderate views created a furor in England, but in fact others of his countrymen soon went far beyond him, questioning the legality of any British taxation of her colonies whatever. Thus, even though Fitch had the support of conservatives, he was defeated for reelection in 1766; paradoxically, by this time the British would have been glad to accept his limited criticism of their tax policies.

Source: *Reasons Why the British Colonies, in America Should Not be Charged with Internal Taxes, etc., etc.*, New Haven, 1764 [*The Public Records of the Colony of Connecticut*, Hartford, 1881].

BY THE CONSTITUTION, government, and laws of Great Britain, the English are a free people. Their freedom consists principally if not wholly in this general privilege, that "No laws can be made or abrogated without their consent by their representatives in Parliament."

By the common law of England, every commoner has a right not to be subjected to laws made without his consent, and because such consent (by reason of the great inconvenience and confusion attending

numbers in such transactions) cannot be given by every individual man in person, therefore is the power of rendering such consent lodged in the hands of representatives by them elected and chosen for that purpose. Their subjection, then, to their laws is not forced but voluntary.

As the chief excellency of the British constitution consists in the subjects' being bound only by such laws to which they themselves consent, as aforesaid, and as, in order to their enjoying that right, they are (agreeable to the constitution) necessarily vested with the power of electing their representatives, so this right or power is a fundamental privilege and so essential a part of the constitution that without it the subject cannot be said to be free. Therefore, if he be hindered from voting in such election or obstructed in the lawful use of that real right or privilege, a suit will lie for him at common law.

None of the privileges included in those general rights (which in a special manner denominate the British subjects a free people) is maintained with greater care and circumspection, and of which they are more jealous, than this particular, known, approved, and fixed one, that no tax, loan, or benevolence can be imposed on them but with their own consent by their representatives in Parliament. This privilege is of ancient date, and whenever it has been encroached upon has been claimed, struggled for, and recovered as being essential for the preservation of the liberty, property, and freedom of the subject. For if the privilege of not being taxed without their consent be once taken from them, liberty and freedom are certainly gone with it. That power which can tax as it shall think proper may govern as it pleases; and those subjected to such taxations and government must be far, very far from being a free people. They cannot, indeed, be said to enjoy even so much as the shadow of English liberties.

Upon these general and fundamental principles, it is conceived that the Parliament (although it has a general authority, a supreme jurisdiction over all His Majesty's subjects, yet as it is also the high and safe guardian of their liberties) does not extend its taxations to such parts of the British dominions as are not represented in that grand legislature of the nation; nor is it to be presumed that this wise and vigilant body will permit such an essential right, which is as the very basis of the constitution, in any instance ever to be violated. And upon the same principles (as is apprehended) those subordinate jurisdictions or governments which by distance are so separated from Great Britain that they are not and cannot be represented in Parliament have always been permitted to have and enjoy privileges similar to those of their fellow subjects in the mother country, that is, of being subjected only to taxations laid by the particular legislatures wherein they are or may be represented by persons by them elected for that purpose, and consequently of not being taxed without their consent. Thus, in Ireland taxes are laid by the Parliament of that kingdom; and in the colonies or plantations in America by the several assemblies or legislatures therein.

These being the essential rights and privileges of the British constitution, founded on the principles of the common law, though in diverse respects particularly regulated by sundry statutes, the King's subjects in the plantations claim a general right to the substance and constitutional part of them as their birthright and inheritance. This claim is founded on such considerations as follow, viz.:

First, the people in the colonies and plantations in America are really, truly, and in every respect as much the King's subjects as those born and living in Great Britain are. "All persons born in any part of the King's dominions and within his protection are his subjects, as all those born in Ireland. Scotland, Wales, the King's plantations, or on the English seas, who by their birth owe such an inseparable allegiance to the King that they cannot by any act of theirs renounce or transfer their subjection to any foreign prince."

Second, all the King's subjects, both in Great Britain and in the colonies and plantations in America, have right to the same general and essential privileges of the British constitution, or those privileges which denominate them to be a free people.

As protection necessarily demands and

binds to subjection and obedience to that authority and those laws whereby a people are protected, so subjection and obedience as necessarily and justly entitle to protection; these mutually imply, require, and support each other. The King, as political head of his subjects, stands equally related to them in that capacity, and is as really obligated to protect one subject as well as another; and as he has an interest in all his subjects, so they have an interest in him, regulated according to the political constitution. Though the particular and formal parts of the governments of the colonies may be various one from another and diverse from that of Great Britain, and such diversity of forms or establishments necessarily arise from their different situations and circumstances, yet both law and equity agree in this general principle, that all the King's subjects ought to be supported and protected in their rights and liberties, and especially in such as are fundamental and essential to their freedom. The subjects in Great Britain are under no greater or stronger obligations of submission and obedience to the Crown than those in the colonies are; and surely, if the colonists are under the same obligations to submission and obedience with other their fellow subjects, it will not be easy to show that they have not the same right to be protected and secured in the enjoyment of every just and legal privilege.

Though the subjects in the colonies are situated at a great distance from their mother country, and for that reason cannot participate in the general legislature of the nation nor enjoy some particular formal immunities possessed by those at home, yet as they settled at this distance by royal license and under national encouragements and thereby enlarged the British dominions and commerce, which add riches and strength to the nation, and as they brought with them and constantly claimed the general principles, those fundamental principles which contain the essence and spirit of the common law of the nation, it may not be justly said they have lost their birthright by such their removal into America; for to suppose that those settlements, that the performance of such important and public services, should be prejudicial to the claim of the colonies to the general privileges of British subjects would be inconsistent both with law and reason, would naturally lead to unjust and absurd conclusions, inasmuch as those public national advantages would not have been promoted unless some of the King's subjects had planted, settled, and dwelt in his colonies abroad, and yet that such planting, settling, and living should subject the inhabitants to the loss of their essential rights as Englishmen would be to reward great, public and meritorious services with great and unspeakable losses and disadvantages.

And how inconsistent such measures and principles are with the honor and justice of the British Crown and government may well deserve consideration. It therefore seems apparent that the King's subjects in the plantations have a right, and that it is for the honor of the Crown and law that they should have a right, to the general and essential privileges of the British constitution, as well as the rest of their fellow subjects. And with regard to the colony of Connecticut in particular, there can be no question of its having such right, as these general privileges and immunities are fully and explicitly granted and declared to belong to them by the royal charter of incorporation given to the said colony by King Charles II in the fourteenth year of his reign, in which is contained this paragraph, viz.:

> And further Our will and pleasure is, and we do for Us, Our Heirs, and Successors, ordain, declare, and grant unto the said Governor and Company and their Successors that all and every the subjects of Us, Our Heirs, or Successors,

which shall go to inhabit within the said colony, and every of their children which shall happen to be born there, or on the seas in going thither or returning from thence, shall have and enjoy all liberties and immunities of free and natural subjects within any of the dominions of Us, Our Heirs, or Successors, to all intents, constructions, and purposes whatsoever, as if they, and every of them, were born within the Realm of England.

Now, whether these words are to be understood only as declarative of the principles of the ancient common law of England and of the common rights of Englishmen settled by royal license and under the protection of the Crown in a colony or plantation abroad and so evidential of the rights and immunities belonging to all the King's subjects in America, or whether they are to be considered as a grant and confirmation of such privileges and immunities to His Majesty's subjects of the colony of Connecticut in particular, they equally evince (as far as a royal declaration and grant can operate to that purpose) the truth of what is here pleaded for so far as respects the people of the said colony. Indeed, these words (on the general principles of the common law) ought (as is apprehended) to be construed as containing a full declaration of the rights of the subject, and in order to remove all doubts about the same, a confirmation of them is annexed to or joined therewith.

It may also be further observed that by this paragraph cannot be meant or intended that the King's subjects within all his dominions should have or be governed by the same particular and formal laws or regulations, because their situations are in distant parts of the world, and their circumstances are so widely different that the same particular establishments and formal regulations which in one place might be good and wholesome for the people, in another would be unwholesome, prejudicial, and by no means answer the end of laws. But this

declaration and confirmation denotes and imports (as is conceived) that all those general and essential rights which the free and natural subjects in the mother country are possessed of and vested with by virtue of the main, leading, and fundamental principles of the common law or constitution of the Realm, the King's subjects in the said colony of Connecticut shall have and enjoy to all intents, constructions, and purposes whatsoever, that is, in such plenitude as always to be, and ever to be treated as, free and natural subjects.

Third, in order that the King's subjects in the colonies and plantations in America might have and enjoy the like liberties and immunities as other their fellow subjects are favored with, it was and is necessary the colonies should be vested with the authority and power of legislation; and this they have accordingly assumed and exercised from their first regular settlement down to this time, and have been constantly owned and acknowledged therein, treated as having such authority, and protected in the same by the Crown and the supreme legislature of the nation. Those corporations which by their situation and circumstances are privileged with the right of electing their representatives to bear a proportionable part in the general legislature of the nation, although they may be vested with authority to make bylaws and regulations within their own jurisdictions agreeable to the bounds and limits of the charters which institute and give them existence, indeed are, and ought to be, immediately subject to the laws, orders, and taxes of such general legislature, as well as others, and that even without being expressly named, for this obvious and solid reason: because they are legally represented therein.

But with regard to those corporations or governments which by their distance and situation have no possible opportunity of such a representation, the case is far otherwise. Whenever, therefore, acts are formed by the supreme legislature that are, in any respect, to extend to the governments abroad, they are made to be so extended by express words; and even such as are so extended to subjects who are not admitted a representation, or to bear a part in the legislation, may not improperly be said to be sovereign acts, or acts supported by the sovereign dominion of the makers of them. And as the exercise of such sovereign authority may be said (as is humbly conceived) to be in some measure an exception from the general rule by which British subjects (according to the constitution) are governed, it is most justly to be presumed and relied upon that the supreme guardians of the liberties of the subjects will never extend that authority further than may be done without depriving any of the King's subjects of those privileges which are essential to their liberty and freedom or leave them in possession of such rights and liberties.

It is a clear point that the colonies may not, they cannot, be represented in Parliament; and if they are not vested with legislative authority within themselves where they may be represented by persons of their own electing, it is plain they will not be represented in any legislature at all, and, consequently, if they are subjected to any laws it must be to such as they have never consented to either by themselves or any representatives, which will be directly contrary to that before-mentioned fundamental principle of the British constitution that "No law can be made or abrogated without the consent of the people by their representatives."

It therefore appears that for the Crown to govern the colonies and plantations abroad by and with the consent of the people represented in assemblies or legislative bodies is properly and truly to govern them agreeable to the British constitution of government; and although this may not in every form and manner be exactly similar to the government at home, yet as near as the different situation and circumstances admit will it agree with the fundamental principles thereof. That the colony of Connecticut (agreeable to these general principles) is vested with such a legislative authority appears by their charter full to that effect. By this charter the colony are empowered to meet in a General Assembly, consisting of a governor or deputy governor, assistants, and deputies, annually to be chosen by the freemen; and such assembly is vested with authority from time to time to make, ordain, and establish all manner of wholesome and reasonable laws, statutes, and ordinances, directions, and instructions not contrary to the laws of the Realm of England; and every officer appointed for putting such laws, ordinances, etc., from time to time into due execution is sufficiently warranted and discharged against the King's Majesty, His Heirs, and Successors, by a special clause in the same charter express to that purpose.

By this royal patent it is therefore evident that a full power of legislation is granted to the colony, limited with a restriction that they conform or are not to act contrary to the general principles of the laws of the nation; and consequently, as when they exceed the bounds and limits prescribed in the charter, their acts will be void, so when they conform and regulate their acts agreeable to the intent and meaning of it their acts may properly be said to have the royal approbation and assent. And these powers, rights, and privileges the colony has been in possession of for more than a century past. This power of legislation necessarily includes in it an authority to impose taxes or duties upon the people for the support of government and for the protection and defense of the inhabitants, as, without such authority, the general rights of legislation would be of no avail to them.

These privileges and immunities, these powers and authorities, the colony claims not only in virtue of their right to the general principles of the British constitution and by force of the royal declaration and grant in their favor, but also as having been in the possession, enjoyment, and exercise of them for so long a time, and constantly owned, acknowledged, and allowed to be just in the claim and use thereof by the Crown, the Ministry, and the Parliament, as may evidently be shown by royal instructions, many letters and acts of Parliament, all supposing and being predicated upon the colony's having and justly exercising these privileges, powers, and authorities; and what better foundation for, or greater evidence of, such rights can be demanded or produced is certainly difficult to be imagined.

These points being thus rendered so clear and evident, may it not thence be very justly inferred,

Fourth, that charging stamp duties or other internal taxes on the colonies in America by parliamentary authority will be an infringement of the aforementioned rights and privileges, and deprive the colonists of their freedom and inheritance so far as such taxations extend? The charging a tax on any particular part of the subject's estates in the plantations by authority of Parliament will doubtless be found nothing less than taking from them a part of their estates on the sole consideration of their being able to bear it, or of having a sufficiency left notwithstanding. It must certainly be admitted that the people thus charged do not consent, nor have any opportunity so to do. An express consent, either by themselves or representatives, can by no means be pretended; neither can their consent be argued from implication, as their subjection and allegiance to the Crown are supposed to be according to the tenor of the laws of the nation, for although the King is styled the head of the commonwealth, supreme governor, *parens patriae*, etc., yet he is still to make the law of the land the rule of his government, that being the measure as well of his power as of the subject's obedience; for as the law asserts, maintains, and provides for the safety of the King's royal person, crown, and dignity, and all his just rights, revenues, powers, and prerogatives, so it likewise declares and asserts the rights and liberties of the subject.

Therefore, in this case, as there can be no other implied consent than what the general principles of the law or constitution imply or what is included in the obligations to submission and obedience to laws, and as the general, fundamental principles of the British constitution or laws, which the Americans claim the privilege of, are quite the reverse of such implications and really imply and suppose the contrary, it follows that charging such taxes will be to take part of their estates from the people without their consent, either expressed or implied. It cannot be said such charging would be founded on contract, as it might be where the subjects are represented in the legislature; neither may it be founded on a forfeiture, as there is no pretense of that kind in these cases; surely, then, there can be no right either to demand or receive a man's estate where both these are wanting.

If these internal taxations take place, and the principles upon which they must be founded are adopted and carried into execution, the colonies will have no more than a show of legislation left, nor the King's subjects in them any more than the shadow of true English liberty; for the same principles which will justify such a tax of a penny will warrant a tax of a pound, a hundred, or a thousand pounds, and so on without limitation; and if they will warrant a tax on one article, they will support one on as many particulars as shall be thought necessary to raise any sum proposed. And all such subjections, burdens, and deprivations, if they take place with respect to the King's subjects abroad, will be without their consent, without their having opportunity to be represented or to show their ability, disability, or circumstances. They will no longer enjoy that fundamental privilege of Englishmen whereby, in special, they are denominated a free people. The legislative authority of the colonies will in part actually be cut off; a part of the same will be taken out of their own assemblies, even such part as they have enjoyed so long and esteem most dear.

Nay, may it not be truly said in this case that the assemblies in the colonies will have left no other power or authority, and the people no other freedom, estates, or privileges than what may be called a tenancy at will; that they have exchanged, or rather lost, those privileges and rights which, according to the national constitution, were their birthright and inheritance, for such a disagreeable tenancy? Will not such determinations amount to plain declarations to the colonies that although they have enjoyed those immunities and privileges heretofore, and been acknowledged and encouraged in the possession and use of them, yet now they must expect, for reasons of state, for some public utility, to part with them, and be brought under a kind of subjection not far from the very reverse of that freedom they justly claim and so highly value? May it not be inquired what reasons are or may be assigned for so different treatment of the subjects of the same most gracious King, of the same general state or community? May it not, upon the whole, be concluded that charging stamp duties or other internal duties by authority of Parliament, as has been mentioned, will be such an infringement of the rights, privileges, and authorities of the colonies that it may be humbly and firmly trusted and even relied upon that the supreme guardians of the liberties of the subject will not suffer the same to be done, and will not only protect them in the enjoyment of their just rights but treat them with great tenderness, indulgence, and favor?

Objection — Perhaps it may be here objected that these principles, if allowed, will prove too much, as the Parliament by its supreme dominion has a superintendency over all the colonies and plantations abroad, and right to govern and control them as shall be thought best and most conducive to the general good of the whole, and accordingly has passed diverse acts for regulating their trade and navigation and in other respects directed their conduct, limited the exercise of their authorities, etc.

Answer — To objections and observations of this kind it may be answered that as the Parliament of Great Britain is most certainly vested with the supreme authority of the nation, and its jurisdiction and power most capacious and transcendent, the colonies will be far, very far from urging or even attempting anything in derogation of the power or authority of that august assembly, or pretending to prescribe bounds or limits to the exercise of their dominion; nothing in the foregoing observations, be sure, is intended by way of objection but that the Crown by its prerogative or the Parliament by its supreme and general jurisdiction may justly order and do some things which may affect the property of the American subjects in a way which, in some sense, may be said to be independent upon or without the will or consent of the people, as by regulations of trade and commerce and the like, and by general orders relative to and restrictions of their conduct for the good of the whole.

For as the colonies are so many governments independent on each other, or not subjected the one to the other, they can only establish regulations within and for themselves respectively; and as they are all subordinate to and dependent upon the mother country, and propriety, convenience, and even necessity require that they should be subject to some general superintendency and control in order that the general course of their trade and business should be so uniform as to center in some general national interest, it becomes plainly expedient that there should be some supreme director over all His Majesty's dominions; and this character and authority all men must acknowledge and allow properly belong to the British Parliament.

Against the exercise of such general jurisdiction for the common interest and advantage of the mother country and of the plantations, collectively taken, the before-mentioned observations are in no measure intended; for it is humbly conceived that the subjects in the colonies may enjoy their rights, privileges, and properties as Englishmen, and yet, for political reasons, be restrained from some particular correspondence or branches of trade and commerce, or may be subjected therein to such duties, charges, and regulations as the supreme power may judge proper to establish as so many conditions of enjoying such trade. Reasons of state may render it expedient to prohibit some branches of trade and to burden others as aforesaid. And as such regulations will doubtless appear, upon examination, rather to be a preventing the subject from acquiring property than taking it from him after it is legally become his own, the objections relative to such establishment ought to be only against those that may be supposed unequal, unprofitable, or not expedient, the determination of which must nevertheless be left to the supreme authority of the nation.

What therefore is designed to be urged from these general principles of the British constitution is that the legislatures of the colonies ought to be left entire, and that His Majesty's good subjects in them should be permitted the continued enjoyment of their essential rights, immunities, and privileges, which will not, as is supposed, by any means be the case if the internal taxations before-mentioned should take place. But if restrictions on navigation, commerce, or other external regulations only are established, the internal government, powers of

taxing for its support, an exemption from being taxed without consent, and other immunities which legally belong to the subjects of each colony agreeable to their own particular constitutions will be and continue in the substance of them whole and entire; life, liberty, and property, in the true use of the terms, will then remain secure and untouched.

Objection — On this distinction it may perhaps be further said, by way of objection, that a stamp duty differs from a tax as it will oblige the subjects only to pay for paper, parchment, etc., which they are at liberty to use or not to use at pleasure; and so, if they choose to make use of it they voluntarily submit to the charge, and can't be said to be taxed without their consent.

Answer — This by no means will obviate the arguments; for a regulation which necessarily obliges a man to part with any certain portion of his estate amounts to the same thing as the actual taking such portion from him. It must be supposed that the people in America will buy and sell their lands, nay, in a multitude of instances they would not know how to subsist without such dispositions. They will also be necessitated to give and take obligations, and to use paper for various other purposes, or there will be of course so great a stagnation of business as almost to bring on a dissolution of their civil and political existence. These things will be found as necessary as the use of agriculture itself. They will therefore be as certainly taxed by a duty charged on the transfer of their lands as by a tax laid directly on the land itself. If lands were to be taxed it might as well be said people are not obliged to have lands (and indeed some have none), so that such as do acquire them voluntarily submit to the charge — which is really saying nothing to the purpose, for the use and improvement of lands, barter, and transmutation of property are as necessary in civilized countries as food and raiment are to the body natural. Indeed, the supposition of the necessity and certain use of the articles to be charged can be the only foundation to render a revenue arising therefrom worthy of notice, as otherwise the effect would be altogether precarious.

Fifth, another reason offered as an objection against charging stamp duties, etc., in the colonies may be drawn from the consequence of such a measure, as it is most probable, if not certain, it will, in the event, prove prejudicial to Great Britain itself. The colonies and plantations in America are indeed of great importance to their mother country and an interest worthy of her most tender regard. The more they prosper and increase in number, riches, and commerce the greater will be the advantage not only to them but also to the nation at home. In the colonies there is a vent for and a consumption of almost all sorts of British manufactures, and of many and various kinds of goods of the produce of other countries first imported into Britain and from thence brought into the plantations, whereby the revenue of the Crown and wealth of the nation are much increased at the expense of the colonies; for these goods the colonies make remittances with what monies they are able to collect in a variety of their own produce, and by circular trade; and taking the whole trade together, it amounts to a very great sum, the profits of which in general center in Great Britain. If the plantations are encouraged and prosper, this will be an increasing interest and become more and more of importance; but if measures should be taken which, in regard to them, would have a natural tendency to abate their vigor, spirit, and industry, or to turn them into some other channel to supply the necessaries of life, what can be expected but a decrease of the colonies' wealth and prosperity, and consequently a decay of an important national interest?

And as, on the one hand, depriving the colonies of part of their powers and privileges and rendering the tenures of them and of their liberties and properties precarious, as by charging stamp duties or other internal taxes upon them by act of Parliament, etc., will naturally produce that unhappy effect of causing the colonies to languish and decrease, so, on the other hand, upholding and continuing the freedom of their governments, maintaining their authority, their laws, securing their properties, considering and treating their privileges and immunities as matters too sacred to be violated will naturally tend to invigorate, enliven, and encourage the people and keep up in them a spirit of industry in all kinds of dealing and business, and of emulation in the service of their mother country, whereby they will become more able and zealous to promote the national interest. This will doubtless be found almost universally to be the case of a people where they enjoy liberty, and their lives, properties, and privileges are secure, and the reverse of it as generally to be the consequence of a contrary treatment; for what encouragement has the merchant to expose his interest to chances and dangers, the farmer, the mechanic, and the common laborer to weary themselves in their fatiguing toilsome employments, if, after all, part of their estates (and how great a part is to them altogether uncertain) may be taken from them, and in such ways and manner as they have heretofore been led to think are inconsistent with their essential rights and liberties?

Surely, then, if subjecting the colonies to burdens which will discourage and abate their industry will eventually prove disadvantageous to the mother country, and the charging of stamp duties or other internal taxes on them will, in the end, have that effect (as has been endeavored to be shown and evinced), the taking such a measure must be inconsistent with good policy and the true interest of the nation.

Sixth, furthermore to enforce the objections against stamp duties or other internal taxations, it is conceived that a summary representation of the settlement, special services, and circumstances of the colony of Connecticut may be here with great propriety adduced, from whence very cogent reasons may be drawn in their favor. . . .

Objection — Perhaps, after all that has been offered, it will be objected by some that America ought, and is able, to bear a just proportion of the American expense, and that as the duty already charged will, they suppose, not be sufficient to defray that expense, it becomes necessary to make additions to the duties already laid.

Answer — First, in order to obviate and answer this objection it may be necessary to enter a little into a consideration of the occasion and nature of those charges which by some are denominated American expenses. That expense which is occasioned merely for the defense and protection of the new governments and acquisitions, it is conceived, ought not to be charged upon the colonies in general, as it is truly no other than a national interest, or an interest of the particular new governments or acquisitions, and consequently ought, where it is not purely national, to be laid on those whose immediate profit is advanced thereby. The old colonies, especially New England, were at the sole charge of settling and defending themselves, and that they should now be compelled to contribute toward settling others under much better advantages in that regard than they were, will not fail of being esteemed hard and injurious. If the expense arises in defending and securing the fur trade and the outposts requisite for carrying on the same, to oblige these colonies which receive no immediate advantage by it to bear a proportionable part of the burden will also be hard and unequal, and especially if that trade is sufficiently profitable to support itself; if otherwise, why is there so much care and mighty attention constantly exercised toward it? If the expense occurs in holding and protecting the new and large acquisitions, wherefore should the colonies

bear that when they have no interest in them? They do indeed properly belong to the Crown, and will finally be disposed of and settled for the benefit of the Crown and the nation in general, and not for the advantage of the colonies in particular. . . .

Second, what America's proportionable part in the American expense will be is somewhat uncertain and difficult to determine. And in order to form any tolerable judgment in the case; it will be necessary to consider the wealth of the colonies compared with the mother country; their number of inhabitants compared with the extent of their own country; the nature of their climates, in some of which the cold seasons are of such long continuance as to occasion a consumption of the greatest part of their produce; their trade and commerce, the profits of which in general center in Great Britain; their business, advantages and disadvantages and other circumstances, such as their being, in a general way, obliged to spend so great a proportion of their labor in clearing, fencing, and preparing their lands for improvement; and that the surplus of their labor in many instances is but very little and in some nothing at all. The clear profits, therefore, to the colonies being so very inconsiderable, it must surely be found, on a just and reasonable computation, that their proportion of any general national expense, if anything, will be very small. . . .

Third, if notwithstanding, it shall be judged necessary (which is even a difficult supposition) to make an addition to the charges on America, yet is it humbly conceived, for the reasons already offered, it will not by any means ever be thought proper or just, in order to effect that purpose, it should be done in a way that shall be an infringement on the constitutions of the colonies or that will deprive the subjects in them of some of those important liberties and privileges which, as Englishmen and freemen, they so justly value, and have a legal and equitable right to, as well as the rest of their fellow subjects. Revenues are never raised in Great Britain by a violation of the constitution or any part of it, but the liberties and privileges of the subjects are always saved and maintained in those cases. And why the Americans should not value their privileges at as high a rate as their fellow subjects in Great Britain do theirs, and wherefore the same justice is not due to the one as to the other, what sufficient reasons can possibly be assigned?

Therefore, whatever may be done in this matter it is humbly trusted will surely be effected in such manner as to leave the legislatures of the colonies entire, and the people in the full possession and enjoyment of their just rights and immunities. This, it is conceived, might be effected by a duty (if thought necessary and proper) on the importation of Negroes and on the fur trade, etc.; for although that on slaves may and doubtless will fall with most weight where the greatest numbers are imported, yet will none be charged thereby but such as voluntarily submit to it; and was such importation lessened, which might indeed be some disadvantage to a few individuals, yet probably it would be attended with many salutary effects both with respect to Great Britain and her colonies in general. And as a principal article of the expense in America must be for protecting and securing the fur trade, what good reasons can be adduced wherefore that trade should not be so charged as to support itself? For (as has been already hinted) if it will not bear this charge, why is it still held and maintained at such great expense?

Having thus shown that the English are a free people; that their freedom consists in these general privileges, that no laws can be made or abrogated without their consent by representatives, and for that purpose have right to elect their representatives; that the American colonists are as really the King's

subjects, as loyal, and have as much right to the general and fundamental privileges of the British constitution and to protection in the enjoyment thereof as the rest of their fellow subjects in the mother country; that, in consequence hereof, the colonies and plantations in America, according to the general principles of the national constitution, are vested with authority of legislation and have right to be represented in their assemblies, in whom that authority is lodged, and with whose consent they are to be governed by the Crown; that for the Crown to govern these colonies and plantations by and with the consent of the people in such legislative assemblies is properly and truly to govern them agreeable to the national constitution, or that it is as conformable to the fundamental principles of the British government that the subjects in the colonies should be represented in assemblies or legislative bodies as that the subjects in Great Britain should be represented in Parliament or the supreme legislature of the nation, and that the government of the subjects, with the consent of their respective representatives, is founded on the same general and essential principles of liberty; that charging stamp duties, or internal taxes on the colony, by authority of Parliament, will be inconsistent with those authorities and privileges which the colonies and the people in them legally enjoy, and have, with the approbation of the supreme power of the nation, been in the use and possession of for a long course of years; as also the probability that such measures will, in the event, prove prejudicial to the national interest as well as hurtful to the colonies; together with some matters and circumstances more directly and peculiarly in favor of the colony of Connecticut, and the special public and benevolent services performed by it on many occasions, which may justly merit some favorable considerations; and answered such objections as might probably be made against the tenor of the reasonings and representations herein offered and laid down, it is now concluded that on . . . account of these and such other weighty reasons as may occur, a British Parliament, whose design is to keep up that constitution, support the honor and prerogative of the Crown, and maintain the privileges of the people, will have a tender regard for the rights and immunities of the King's subjects in the American colonies and charge no internal taxations upon them without their consent.

19.

Thomas Pownall: The King and the Colonies

British imperial policy faced serious new problems in the 1760s. Thomas Pownall, former governor of Massachusetts, wrote an account of the problems of colonial government which appeared anonymously in 1764, entitled The Administration of the Colonies. *In it he outlined ideas for imperial reform which, if successful, would provide a sound economic justification for binding the colonies to Great Britain permanently.*

Source: *The Administration of the Colonies*, London, 1768, pp. 67-80.

How FAR THE POWER of King and Parliament, the whole imperium of Great Britain, may go in conjunction with right is matter of more difficulty to ascertain, and of more danger to decide. If the provinces have any rights, however much subordinate, even this imperium must be bounded by them. However, I have formed my opinion on this subject, and I will speak it out; if I am in an error, even error may give occasion to the rise of truth. But this is not the place. . . .

It is right, perhaps necessary, to say, I am sure it may be said with the utmost precision and conviction, that the King must retain in himself, and in his deputy set over them in his government of them, all those same preeminences, royal rights, powers, and prerogatives which are vested in the Crown, as part of the government of England. And that whenever the people, or their representatives in the colonies, act toward his royal person, or toward his representative, in derogation of these rights and powers, they can neither be justified by right, or the constitution, or even good policy toward themselves, whatever specious temporary reasons they may assign for it; for this mode of conduct will be permitted to a certain degree only, and for a certain time; but will always in the end, as it always has in fact done, call forth some remedy, so far as relates to the colonists' ideas, worse than the disease. I will instance in one case only — the constant refusal of the assemblies to fix permanent salaries for the civil establishment of government.

The above is the actual and rightful relation between the King and the American colonies; and, by the rule of this relation, we ought to review and decide those several points wherein the Crown, or its governors acting under its commission and instruction, differ with the people.

Upon such review it will appear, under this first general head, in various instances, that the two great points which the colonists labor to establish are the exercise of their several rights and privileges, as founded in the rights of an Englishman; and second, as what they suppose to be a necessary measure in a subordinate government, the keeping in their own hands the command of the revenue and the pay of the officers of government, as a security for the conduct of those officers toward them.

Under the first head come all the disputes about the King's instructions and the governor's power as founded on them.

The King's commission to his governor, which grants the power of government, and directs the calling of a legislature, and the establishing courts, at the same time that it fixes the governor's power, according to the several powers and directions granted and appointed by the commission and instructions, adds "and by such further powers, instructions, and authorities, as shall, at any time hereafter, be granted or appointed you, under our signet or sign manual, or by our order in our Privy Council." It should here seem that the same power which framed the commission, with this clause in it, could also issue its future orders and instructions in consequence thereof. But the people of the colonies say that the inhabitants of the colonies are entitled to all the privileges of Englishmen; that they have a right to participate in the legislative power; and that no commands of the Crown, by orders in Council, instructions, or letters from secretaries of state, are binding upon them further than they please to acquiesce under such, and conform their own actions thereto. . . .

They [say that they] hold this right of legislature, not derived from the grace and will of the Crown and depending on the commission which continues at the will of the Crown; that this right is inherent and essential to the community, as a community of Englishmen; and that therefore they must have all the rights, privileges, and full and free exercise of their own will and liberty in making laws which are necessary to that act of legislation, uncontrolled by any power of the Crown or of the governor, preventing or suspending that act. [They say] the clause in the commission, directing the governor to call together a legislature by his writs, is declarative and not creative; and therefore he is directed to act conformably to a right actually already existing in the people, etc. Therefore such clause ought not to be in the commission, or to be understood as being of no effect, so far as concerns the colonists.

When I speak of full, uncontrolled, independent powers of debate and result, so far as relates to the framing bills and passing them into laws, uncontrolled by any power of the Crown or of the governor, as an essential property of a free legislature, I find some persons in the colonies imagine that I represent the colonies as claiming a power of legislature independent of the King's or governor's negative. These gentlemen, knowing that it is not my intention to do injustice to the colonies, wish me so to explain this matter that it may not bear even the interpretation of such a charge. I do therefore here desire that the reader will give his attention to distinguish a full, free, uncontrolled, independent power in the act of legislation from a full, free, uncontrolled, independent power of carrying the results of that legislation into effect, independent either of the governor's or King's negative.

The first right is that which I represent the colonists claiming as a right essential to the very existence of the legislature. The second is what is also essential to the nature of a subordinate legislature, and what the colonists never call in question. That, therefore, the point here meant to be stated as in debate is whether a subordinate legislature can be instructed, restricted, and controlled in the very act of legislation; whether the King's instructions or letters from secretaries of state, and such like significations of His Majesty's will and pleasure, are a due and constitutional application of the governor's or of the royal negative. The colonists constantly deny it, and the Ministry . . . constantly maintain it.

After experience of the confusion and obstruction which this dubitable point has occasioned to business, it is time surely that it were some way or other determined. Or whether in fact or deed the people of the colonies, having every right to the full powers of government and to a whole legislative power, are not under this claim entitled in the powers of legislature and the administration of government, to use and exercise in conformity to the laws of Great Britain, the same full, free, independent, unrestrained power and legislative will in their several corporations, and under the King's commission and their respective charters, as the government and legislature of Great Britain holds by its constitution, and under the Great Charter.

Every subject born within the Realm, under the freedom of the government of Great Britain or by adoption admitted to the same, has an essential indefeasible right to be governed under such a mode of government as has the unrestrained exercise of all those powers which form the freedom and rights of the constitution. . . . Therefore, "the Crown cannot establish any colony upon — or contract it within a narrower scale than the subject is entitled to, by the Great Charter of England." The government of each colony must have the same powers and the same extent of powers that the government of Great Britain has, and must have, while it does not act contrary to the laws of Great Britain, the same freedom and independence of legislature as the Parliament of Great Britain has. This right (say they) is founded not only in the general

principles of the rights of a British subject, but is actually declared, confirmed, or granted to them in the commissions and charters which gave the particular frame of their respective constitutions.

If, therefore, in the first original establishment, like the original contract, they could not be established upon any scale short of the full and complete scale of the powers of the British government, nor the legislature be established on anything less than the whole legislative power, much less can this power of government and legislature, thus established, be governed, directed, restrained, or restricted by any posterior instructions or commands by the letters of secretaries of state. But upon the supposition that a kind of general indetermined power in the Crown, to superadd instructions to the commissions and charter be admitted, where the colonists do not make a question of the case wherein it is exerted, yet there are particular cases wherein both directive and restrictive instructions are given, and avowedly not admitted by the colonists.

It is a standing instruction as a security of the dependence of the government of the colonies on the mother country, that no acts wherein the King's rights or the rights of the mother country or of private persons can be affected shall be enacted into a law without a clause suspending the effect thereof till His Majesty's pleasure shall be known. This suspending clause is universally rejected on the principles above because such suspension disfranchises the inherent full power of legislature, which they claim by their rights to the British liberties, and by the special declarations of such in their charters. It does not remove this difficulty by saying that the Crown has already in its hands the power of fixing this point by the effect of its negative given to its governor. It is said that if the Crown should withdraw that instruction which allows certain bills to be passed into laws with a sus-

Gov. Thomas Pownall, 18th-century portrait attributed to Daniel Gardner

pending clause, which instruction is not meant as a restriction upon but an indulgence to the legislature; that if the Crown should withdraw this instruction and peremptorily restrain its governor from enacting laws, under such circumstances as the wisdom of government cannot admit of, that then these points are actually fixed by the true constitutional power. But wherever it is so said, I must repeat my idea that this does not remove the difficulty. For waiving the doubt which the colonists might raise, especially in the charter colonies, how far the governor ought, or ought not, to be restricted from giving his assent in cases contrary only to instructions and not to the laws of Great Britain; waiving this point, let administration consider the effects of this measure.

In cases where the bills offered by the two branches are for providing laws absolutely necessary to the continuance, support, and exercise of government, and where yet the orders of the Crown and the sense of the people are so widely different as to the mode that no agreement can ever be come to in these points — is the government and administration of the government of the colonies to be suspended? [Is] the interest, perhaps the being of the plantations, to be hazarded by this obstinate variance, and can the exercise of the Crown's negative, in such emergencies and with such effect, ever be taken up as a measure of administration? And when everything is thrown into confusion, and abandoned even to ruin by such measure, will administration justify itself by saying that it is the fault of the colonists? On the contrary, this very state of the case shows the necessity of some other remedy.

In the course of examining these matters will arise to consideration the following very material point: As a principal tie of the subordination of the legislatures of the colonies on the government of the mother country, they are bound by their constitutions and charters to send all their acts of legislature to England to be confirmed or abrogated by the Crown. But if any of the legislatures should be found to do almost every act of legislature by votes or orders, even to the repealing the effects of acts, suspending establishments of pay, paying services, doing chancery and other judicatory business; if matters of this sort, done by these votes and orders, never reduced into the form of an act, have their effect without ever being sent home as acts of legislature, or submitted to the allowance or disallowance of the Crown; if it should be found that many or any of the legislatures of the colonies carry the powers of legislature into execution independent of the Crown by this device, it will be a point to be determined how far, in such cases, the subordination of the legislatures of the colonies to the government of the mother country is maintained or suspended. Or if, from emergencies arising in these governments, this device is to be admitted, the point, how far such is to be admitted, ought to be determined; and the validity of these votes and orders, these *senatus consulta* so far declared. For a point of such great importance in the subordination of the colony legislatures, and of so questionable a cast in the valid exercise of this legislative power, ought no longer to remain in question.

The next general point yet undetermined, the determination of which very essentially imports the subordination and dependence of the colony governments on the government of the mother country, is the manner of providing for the support of government, and for all the executive officers of the Crown. The freedom and right efficiency of the constitution require that the executive and judicial officers of government should be independent of the legislative; and more especially in popular governments where the legislature itself is so much influenced by the humors and passions of the people; for if they do not, there will be neither justice nor equity in any of the courts of law, nor any efficient execution of the laws and orders of government in the magistracy. According, therefore, to the constitution of Great Britain, the Crown has the appointment and payment of the several executive and judicial officers, and the legislature settles a permanent and fixed appointment for the support of government and the civil list in general. The Crown therefore has, *a fortiori*, a right to require of the colonies, to whom, by its commission or charter, it gives the power of government, such permanent support, appropriated to the offices, not the officers, of government, that they may not depend upon the temporary and arbitrary will of the legislature.

The Crown does, by its instructions to its governors; order them to require of the legislature a permanent support. This order of the Crown is generally, if not universally, rejected by the legislatures of the colonies. The assemblies quote the precedents of the British constitution, and found all the rights and privileges which they claim on the principles thereof. They allow the truth and fitness of this principle in the British constitu-

tion where the executive power of the Crown is immediately administered by the King's Majesty; yet say, under the circumstances in which they find themselves, that there is no other measure left to them to prevent the misapplications of public money than by an annual voting and appropriation of the salaries of the governor and other civil officers, issuing from moneys lodged in the hands of a provincial treasurer appointed by the assemblies. For in these subordinate governments, remote from His Majesty's immediate influence, administered oftentimes by necessitous and rapacious governors who have no natural, although they have a political, connection with the country, experience has shown that such governors have misapplied the moneys raised for the support of government, so that the civil officers have been left unpaid, even after having been provided for by the Assembly.

The point then of this very important question comes to this issue: whether the inconveniences arising and experienced by some instances of misapplications of appropriations (for which, however, there are in the King's courts of law due and sufficient remedies against the offender) are a sufficient reason and ground for establishing a measure so directly contrary to the British constitution; and whether the inconveniences to be traced in the history of the colonies through the votes and journals of their legislatures, in which the support of governors, judges, and officers of the Crown will be found to have been withheld or reduced on occasions where the assemblies have supposed that they have had reason to disapprove the nomination, or the person, or his conduct; whether, I say, these inconveniences have not been more detrimental and injurious to government; and whether, instead of these colonies being dependent on, and governed under, the officers of the Crown, the scepter is not reversed, and the officers of the Crown dependent on and governed by the assemblies, as the colonists themselves allow that this measure "renders the governor, and all the other servants of the Crown, dependent on the Assembly."

But the operation of this measure does not end here; it extends to the assuming by the assemblies the actual executive part of the government in the case of the revenue, than which nothing is more clearly and unquestionably settled in the Crown. In the colonies the treasurer is solely and entirely a servant of the Assembly or General Court; and although the moneys granted and appropriated be, or ought to be, granted to the Crown on such appropriations, the treasurer is neither named by the Crown, nor its governor, nor gives security to the Crown or to the lord high treasurer (which seems the most proper), nor in many of the colonies, is to obey the governor's warrant in the issue, nor accounts in the auditor's office, nor in any one colony is it admitted that he is liable to such account. In consequence of this supposed necessity, for the Assembly's taking upon them the administration of the treasury and revenue, the governor and servants of the Crown, in the ordinary revenue of government, are not only held dependent on the Assembly, but all services where special appropriations are made for the extraordinaries which such services require are actually executed and done by commissioners appointed by the Assembly, to whose disposition such appropriations are made liable.

It would be perhaps invidious, and might tend to prejudging on points which ought very seriously and dispassionately to be examined, if I were here to point out in the several instances of the actual execution of this assumed power, how almost every executive power of the Crown lodged in its governor, is, where money is necessary, thus exercised by the Assembly and its commissioners. I therefore rest the matter here.

20.

James Otis: Rights of the British Colonies

The Revenue Act of 1764 was meant to replace the Sugar Act of 1733. Its purpose was to raise money for defense and improve the tax collecting system. To counteract this new act of Parliament, James Otis, a political leader of Massachusetts Bay, published in the same year The Rights of the British Colonies Asserted and Proved. *Otis discussed the constitutional position of the colonies in the Commonwealth which he believed the British empire to be. In the* Rights, *Otis developed principles he had earlier stated in 1761 in his argument against the writs of assistance.*

Source: *The Rights of the British Colonies Asserted and Proved*, 3rd edition, London, 1766, pp. 17-22, 52-65, 70-77, 95-99.

Government having been proved to be necessary by the law of nature, it makes no difference in the thing to call it, from a certain period, *civil*. This term can only relate to form, to additions to or deviations from the substance of government: this being founded in nature, the superstructures and the whole administration should be conformed to the law of universal reason. A supreme legislative and a supreme executive power must be placed *somewhere* in every commonwealth. Where there is no other positive provision or compact to the contrary, those powers remain in the *whole body of the people.* It is also evident there can be but *one* best way of depositing those powers; but what that way is, mankind have been disputing in peace and in war more than 5,000 years. If we could suppose the individuals of a community met to deliberate whether it were best to keep those powers in their own hands or dispose of them in trust, the following questions would occur: Whether those two great powers of *legislation* and *execution* should remain united? If so, whether in the hands of the many or jointly or severally in the hands of a few, or jointly in some one individual?

If both those powers are retained in the hands of the many, where nature seems to have placed them originally, the government is a simple *democracy* or a government of all over all. This can be administered only by establishing it as a first principle that the votes of the majority shall be taken as the voice of the whole. If those powers are lodged in the hands of a few, the government is an *aristocracy* or *oligarchy.* Here too the first principle of a practicable administration is that the majority rules the whole. If those great powers are both lodged in the hands of one man, the government is a *simple monarchy,* commonly though falsely called *absolute* if by that term is meant a right to do as one pleases. *Sic volo, sic jubeo, stet pro ratione voluntas* [Thus I will it, thus I command it, let my desire serve for reason] belongs not of right to any mortal man.

The same law of nature and of reason is equally obligatory on a *democracy,* an *aristocracy,* and a *monarchy:* whenever the administrators in any of those forms deviate from truth, justice, and equity, they verge toward tyranny, and are to be opposed; and if they prove incorrigible they will be deposed by the people, if the people are not rendered too abject. Deposing the administrators of a simple democracy may sound odd, but it is done every day and in almost every vote. A, B, and C, for example, make a democracy. Today A and B are for so vile a measure as a standing army. Tomorrow B and C vote it out. This is as really deposing the former administrators as setting up and making a new king is deposing the old one. Democracy in the one case and monarchy in the other still remain; all that is done is to change the administration.

The first principle and great end of government being to provide for the best good of all the people, this can be done only by a supreme legislative and executive ultimately in the people or whole community where God has placed it; but the inconveniences, not to say impossibility, attending the consultations and operations of a large body of people have made it necessary to transfer the power of the whole to a *few.* This necessity gave rise to deputation, proxy, or a right of representation.

A power of legislation without a power of execution in the same or other hands would be futile and vain. On the other hand, a power of execution, supreme or subordinate, without an independent legislature would be perfect despotism.

The difficulties attending a universal congress, especially when society became large, have brought men to consent to a delegation of the power of all: the weak and the wicked have too often been found in the same interest, and in most nations have not only brought these powers jointly into the hands of one or some few of their number but made them hereditary in the families of despotic nobles and princes.

The wiser and more virtuous states have always provided that the representation of the people should be numerous. Nothing but life and liberty are *naturally* hereditable; this has never been considered by those who have tamely given up both into the hands of a tyrannical oligarchy or despotic monarchy.

The analogy between the natural, or material, as it is called, and the moral world is very obvious; God himself appears to us at some times to cause the intervention or

combination of a number of simple principles, though never when one will answer
the end; gravitation and attraction have
place in the revolution of the planets, because the one would fix them to a center
and the other would carry them off indefinitely; so in the moral world the first simple principle is equality and the power of
the whole. This will answer in small numbers; so will a tolerably virtuous oligarchy
or a monarchy. But when the society grows
in bulk, none of them will answer well singly, and none worse than absolute monarchy. It becomes necessary, therefore, as
numbers increase, to have those several
powers properly combined, so as from the
whole to produce that harmony of government so often talked of and wished for but
too seldom found in ancient or modern
states.

The grand political problem in all ages
has been to invent the best combination or
distribution of the supreme powers of legislation and execution. Those states have ever
made the greatest figure, and have been
most durable, in which those powers have
not only been separated from each other
but placed each in more hands than one or
a few. The Romans are the most shining
example, but they never had a balance between the Senate and the people, and the
want of this is generally agreed by the few
who know anything of the matter to have
been the cause of their fall. The British
constitution in theory and in the present administration of it in general comes nearest
the idea of perfection of any that has been
reduced to practice; and if the principles of
it are adhered to it will, according to the
infallible prediction of Harrington, always
keep the Britons uppermost in Europe till
their only rival nation shall either embrace
that perfect model of a commonwealth giv-
en us by that author or come as near it as
Great Britain is. Then indeed, and not till
then, will that rival and our nation either be
eternal confederates or contend in greater

earnest than they have ever yet done, till
one of them shall sink under the power of
the other and rise no more.

Great Britain has at present most evidently the advantage and such opportunities
of honest wealth and grandeur as perhaps
no state ever had before, at least not since
the days of Julius Caesar, the destroyer of
the Roman glory and grandeur, at a time
when, but for him and his adherents, both
might have been rendered immortal.

We have said that the form and mode of
government is to be settled by compact, as
it was rightfully done by the Convention after the abdication of James II, and assented
to by the first representative of the nation
chosen afterward, and by every Parliament
and by almost every man ever since but the
bigots to the indefeasible power of tyrants,
civil and ecclesiastic. There was neither time
for nor occasion to call the whole people
together. If they had not liked the proceedings it was in their power to control them,
as it would be should the supreme legislative or executive powers ever again attempt
to enslave them. The people will bear a
great deal before they will even murmur
against their rulers; but when once they are
thoroughly roused and in earnest against
those who would be glad to enslave them
their power is irresistible. . . .

Every British subject born on the continent of America or in any other of the British dominions is by the law of God and
nature, by the common law, and by act of
Parliament (exclusive of all charters from
the Crown) entitled to all the natural, essential, inherent, and inseparable rights of
our fellow subjects in Great Britain. Among
those rights are the following, which it is
humbly conceived no man or body of men,
not excepting the Parliament, justly, equitably, and consistently with their own rights
and the constitution can take away.

First, that the supreme and subordinate
powers of legislation should be free and sacred in the hands where the community
have once rightfully placed them.

Second, the supreme national legislative cannot be altered justly till the Commonwealth is dissolved, nor a subordinate legislative taken away without forfeiture or other good cause. Nor then can the subjects in the subordinate government be reduced to a state of slavery and subject to the despotic rule of others. A state has no right to make slaves of the conquered. Even when the subordinate right of legislature is forfeited and so declared, this cannot affect the natural persons either of those who were invested with it or the inhabitants so far as to deprive them of the rights of subjects and of men. The colonists will have an equitable right, notwithstanding any such forfeiture of charter, to be represented in Parliament or to have some new subordinate legislature among themselves. It would be best if they had both.

Deprived, however, of their common rights as subjects they cannot lawfully be while they remain such. A representation in Parliament from the several colonies — since they are become so large and numerous as to be called on not to maintain provincial government, civil and military among themselves (for this they have cheerfully done) but to contribute toward the support of a national standing army, by reason of the heavy national debt, when they themselves owe a large one contracted in the common cause — can't be thought an unreasonable thing, nor if asked could it be called an immodest request. *Qui sentit commodum sentire debet et onus* [He who derives the advantage ought to sustain the burden] has been thought a maxim of equity. But that a man should bear a burden for other people as well as himself without a return never long found a place in any lawbook or decrees but those of the most despotic princes. Besides the equity of an American representation in Parliament, a thousand advantages would result from it. It would be the most effectual means of giving those of both countries a thorough knowledge of each other's interests, as well as that of the whole, which are inseparable.

Were this representation allowed, instead of the scandalous memorials and depositions that have been sometimes, in days of old, privately cooked up in an inquisitorial manner by persons of bad minds and wicked views and sent from America to the several boards, persons of the first reputation among their countrymen might be on the spot from the several colonies truly to represent them. Future ministers need not, like some of their predecessors, have recourse for information in American affairs to every vagabond stroller that has run or rid post through America from his creditors, or to people of no kind of reputation from the colonies, some of whom, at the time of administering their sage advice, have been as ignorant of the state of this country as of the regions in Jupiter and Saturn.

No representation of the colonies in Parliament alone would, however, be equivalent to a subordinate legislative among themselves, nor so well answer the ends of increasing their prosperity and the commerce of Great Britain. It would be impossible for the Parliament to judge so well of their abilities to bear taxes, impositions on trade, and other duties and burdens, or of the local laws that might be really needful, as a legislative here.

Third, no legislative, supreme or subordinate, has a right to make itself arbitrary. It would be a most manifest contradiction for a free legislative, like that of Great Britain, to make itself arbitrary.

Fourth, the supreme legislative cannot justly assume a power of ruling by extempore arbitrary decrees, but is bound to dispense justice by known settled rules and by duly authorized independent judges.

Fifth, the supreme power cannot take from any man any part of his property, without his consent in person or by representation.

Sixth, the legislature cannot transfer the power of making laws to any other hands.

These are their bounds, which by God and nature are fixed; hitherto have they a right to come, and no further.

1. To govern by stated laws.

2. Those laws should have no other end ultimately but the good of the people.

3. Taxes are not to be laid on the people but by their consent in person or by deputation.

4. Their whole power is not transferable.

These are the first principles of law and justice, and the great barriers of a free state and of the British constitution in particular. I ask, I want, no more. Now let it be shown how 'tis reconcilable with these principles, or to many other fundamental maxims of the British constitution, as well as the natural and civil rights which by the laws of their country all British subjects are entitled to as their best inheritance and birthright, that all the northern colonies, who are without one representative in the House of Commons, should be taxed by the British Parliament.

That the colonists, black and white, born here are freeborn British subjects and entitled to all the essential civil rights of such, is a truth not only manifest from the provincial charters, from the principles of the common law, and acts of Parliament, but from the British constitution, which was re-established at the Revolution with a professed design to secure the liberties of all the subjects to all generations.

In the 12 and 13 of William . . . the liberties of the subject are spoken of as their best birthrights. No one ever dreamed, surely, that these liberties were confined to the Realm. At that rate no British subjects in the dominions could, without a manifest contradiction, be declared entitled to all the privileges of subjects born within the Realm to all intents and purposes which are rightly given foreigners by Parliament after residing seven years. These expressions of Parliament as well as of the charters must be vain and empty sounds unless we are allowed the essential rights of our fellow subjects in Great Britain.

Now; can there be any liberty where property is taken away without consent? Can it with any color of truth, justice, or equity be affirmed that the northern colonies are represented in Parliament? Has this whole continent of near three thousand miles in length, and in which and his other American dominions His Majesty has or very soon will have some millions of as good, loyal, and useful subjects, white and black, as any in the three kingdoms, the election of one member of the House of Commons?

Is there the least difference as to the consent of the colonists whether taxes and impositions are laid on their trade and other property by the Crown alone or by the Parliament? As it is agreed on all hands the Crown alone cannot impose them, we should be justifiable in refusing to pay them, but must and ought to yield obedience to an act of Parliament, though erroneous, till repealed.

I can see no reason to doubt but that the imposition of taxes, whether on trade, or on land, or houses, or ships, on real or personal, fixed or floating property, in the colonies is absolutely irreconcilable with the rights of the colonists as British subjects and as men. I say men, for in a state of nature no man can take my property from me without my consent; if he does, he deprives me of my liberty and makes me a slave. If such a proceeding is a breach of the law of nature, no law of society can make it just. The very act of taxing exercised over those who are not represented appears to me to be depriving them of one of their most essential rights as freemen, and if continued seems to be in effect an entire disfranchisement of every civil right. For what one civil right is worth a rush after a man's property is subject to be taken from him at pleasure without his consent? If a man is not his own assessor in person or by deputy, his liberty is gone or lies entirely at the mercy of others.

I think I have heard it said that when the Dutch are asked why they enslave their colonies, their answer is that the liberty of Dutchmen is confined to Holland, and that it was never intended for provincials in America or anywhere else. A sentiment, this, very worthy of modern Dutchmen; but if their brave and worthy ancestors had entertained such narrow ideas of liberty, seven poor and distressed provinces would never have asserted their rights against the whole Spanish monarchy, of which the present is but a shadow. It is to be hoped none of our fellow subjects of Britain, great or small, have borrowed this Dutch maxim of plantation politics; if they have, they had better return it from whence it came; indeed they had. Modern Dutch or French maxims of state never will suit with a British constitution.

It is a maxim that the King can do no wrong; and every good subject is bound to believe his King is not inclined to do any. We are blessed with a prince who has given abundant demonstrations that in all his actions he studies the good of his people and the true glory of his Crown, which are inseparable. It would therefore be the highest degree of impudence and disloyalty to imagine that the King, at the head of his Parliament, could have any but the most pure and perfect intentions of justice, goodness, and truth that human nature is capable of.

All this I say and believe of the King and Parliament in all their acts, even in that which so nearly affects the interest of the colonists, and that a most perfect and ready obedience is to be yielded to it while it remains in force. I will go further, and readily admit that the intention of the Ministry was not only to promote the public good by this act, but that Mr. Chancellor of the Exchequer had therein a particular view to the "ease, the quiet, and the good will of the colonies," he having made this declaration more than once. Yet I hold that 'tis possible he may have erred in his kind intentions toward the colonies, and taken away our fish and given us a stone.

With regard to the Parliament, as infallibility belongs not to mortals, 'tis possible *they* may have been misinformed and deceived. The power of Parliament is uncontrollable but by themselves, and we must obey. They only can repeal their own acts. There would be an end of all government if one or a number of subjects or subordinate provinces should take upon them so far to judge of the justice of an act of Parliament as to refuse obedience to it. If there was nothing else to restrain such a step, prudence ought to do it, for forcibly resisting the Parliament and the King's laws is high treason. Therefore let the Parliament lay what burdens they please on us, we must, it is our duty to submit and patiently bear them till they will be pleased to relieve us. And 'tis to be presumed the wisdom and justice of that august assembly always will afford us relief by repealing such acts as through mistake or other human infirmities have been suffered to pass, if they can be convinced that their proceedings are not constitutional or not for the common good.

The Parliament may be deceived, they may have been misinformed of facts, and the colonies may in many respects be misrepresented to the King, his Parliament, and his Ministry. In some instances, I am well assured the colonies have been very strangely misrepresented in England. I have now before me a pamphlet called the *Administration of the Colonies*, said to be written by a gentleman who formerly commanded in chief in one of them. I suppose this book was designed for public information and use. There are in it many good regulations proposed which no power can enforce but the Parliament. From all which I infer that if our hands are tied by the passing of an act of Parliament, our mouths are not stopped, provided we speak of that transcendent body with decency, as I have endeavored always to do; and should anything have escaped me or hereafter fall from my pen that bears the least aspect but that of obedience, duty, and loyalty to the King and Parliament, and the highest respect for the Ministry, the candid will impute it to the agony of my heart rather than to the pravity of my will.

If I have one ambitious wish, 'tis to see Great Britain at the head of the world, and to see my King, under God, the father of mankind. I pretend neither to the spirit of prophecy nor any uncommon skill in predicting a crisis, much less to tell when it begins to be "nascent" or is fairly midwived into the world. But if I were to fix a meaning to the two first paragraphs of the *Administration of the Colonies*, though I do not collect it from them, I should say the world was at the eve of the highest scene of earthly power and grandeur that has been ever yet displayed to the view of mankind. The cards are shuffling fast through all Europe. Who will win the prize is with God. This however I know, *detur digniori*. [Let it be given to the more worthy.]

The next universal monarchy will be favorable to the human race, for it must be founded on the principles of equity, moderation, and justice. No country has been more distinguished for these principles than Great Britain, since the Revolution. I take it every subject has a right to give his sentiments to the public, of the utility or inutility of any act whatsoever, even after it is passed, as well as while it is pending. The equity and justice of a bill may be questioned with perfect submission to the legislature. Reasons may be given why an act ought to be repealed, and yet obedience must be yielded to it till that repeal takes place. If the reasons that can be given against an act are such as plainly demonstrate that it is against *natural* equity, the executive courts will adjudge such act void. It may be questioned by some, though I make no doubt of it, whether they are not obliged by their oaths to adjudge such act void. If there is not a right of private judgment to be exercised, so far at least as to petition for a repeal or to determine the expediency of risking a trial at law, the Parliament might make itself arbitrary, which it is conceived it cannot by the constitution.

I think every man has a right to examine as freely into the origin, spring, and foundation of every power and measure in a commonwealth as into a piece of curious machinery or a remarkable phenomenon in nature, and that it ought to give no more offense to say the Parliament have erred or are mistaken in a matter of fact or of right than to say it of a private man, if it is true of both. If the assertion can be proved with regard to either, it is a kindness done them to show them the truth. With regard to the public, it is the duty of every good citizen to point out what he thinks erroneous in the Commonwealth.

I have waited years in hopes to see some one friend of the colonies pleading in public for them. I have waited in vain. One privilege is taken away after another, and where we shall be landed God knows, and I trust will protect and provide for us even should we be driven and persecuted into a more western wilderness on the score of liberty, civil and religious, as many of our ancestors were to these once inhospitable shores of America. I have formed great expectations from a gentleman who published his first volume in quarto on the rights of the colonies two years since; but, as he foresaw, the state of his health and affairs has prevented his further progress.

The misfortune is, gentlemen in America, the best qualified in every respect to state the rights of the colonists, have reasons that prevent them from engaging. Some of them have good ones. There are many infinitely better able to serve this cause than I pretend to be; but from indolence, from timidity, or by necessary engagements they are prevented. There has been a most profound and I think shameful silence, till it seems almost too late to assert our indisputable rights as men and as citizens. What must posterity think of us? The trade of the whole continent taxed by Parliament, stamps and other internal duties and taxes as they are called, talked of, and not one petition to the King and Parliament for relief.

I cannot but observe here that if the Parliament have an equitable right to tax our trade, 'tis indisputable that they have as good a one to tax the lands and everything else. The taxing trade furnishes one reason why the other should be taxed, or else the burdens of the province will be unequally borne, upon a supposition that a tax on trade is not a tax on the whole. But take it either way, there is no foundation for the distinction some make in England between an internal and an external tax on the colonies. By the first is meant a tax on trade, by the latter a tax on land and the things on it.

A tax on trade is either a tax of every man in the province, or 'tis not. If 'tis not a tax on the whole, 'tis unequal and unjust that a heavy burden should be laid on the trade of the colonies to maintain an army of soldiers, customhouse officers, and fleets of guardships, all which the incomes of both trade and land would not furnish means to support so lately as the last war, when all was at stake, and the colonies were reimbursed in part by Parliament. How can it be supposed that all of a sudden the trade of the colonies alone can bear all this terrible burden? The late acquisitions in America, as glorious as they have been and as beneficial as they are to Great Britain, are only a security to these colonies against the ravages of the French and Indians. Our trade upon the whole is not, I believe, benefited by them one groat.

All the time the French islands were in our hands, the fine sugars, etc., were all shipped home. None as I have been informed were allowed to be brought to the colonies. They were too delicious a morsel for a North American palate. If it be said that a tax on the trade of the colonies is an equal and just tax on the whole of the inhabitants, what then becomes of the notable distinction between external and internal taxes? Why may not the Parliament lay stamps, land taxes, establish tithes to the Church of England, and so indefinitely? I know of no bounds. I do not mention the tithes out of any disrespect to the Church of England, which I esteem by far the best *national* church and to have had as ornaments of it many of the greatest and best men in the world. But to those colonies who in general dissent from a principle of conscience it would seem a little hard to pay toward the support of a worship whose modes they cannot conform to.

If an army must be kept up in America at the expense of the colonies, it would not seem quite so hard if after the Parliament had determined the sum to be raised, and apportioned it, to have allowed each colony to assess its quota and raise it as easily to themselves as might be. But to have the whole levied and collected without our consent is extraordinary. 'Tis allowed even to *tributaries* and those laid under *military* contribution to assess and collect the sums demanded. The case of the provinces is certainly likely to be the hardest that can be instanced in story. Will it not equal anything but downright military execution? Was there ever a tribute imposed even on the conquered? A fleet, an army of soldiers, and another of tax gatherers kept up, and not a single office either for securing or collecting the duty in the gift of the tributary state. . . .

To say the Parliament is absolute and arbitrary is a contradiction. The Parliament cannot make 2 and 2, 5: omnipotency cannot do it. The supreme power in a state is *jus dicere* [to declare the law] only: *jus dare* [to give the law], strictly speaking, belongs alone to God. Parliaments are in all cases to declare what is for the good of the whole; but it is not the declaration of Parliament that makes it so. There must be in every instance a higher authority, viz., God. Should an act of Parliament be against any of His natural laws, which are immutably true, their declaration would be contrary to eternal truth, equity, and justice, and consequently void; and so it would be adjudged by the Parliament itself when convinced of their mistake. Upon this great principle, parliaments repeal such acts as soon as they find they have been mistaken in having declared them to be for the public good when in fact they were not so. When such mistake is evident and palpable, as in the instances in the appendix, the judges of the executive courts have declared the act "of a whole Parliament void." See here the grandeur of the British constitution! See the wisdom of our ancestors!

The supreme legislative and the supreme executive are a perpetual check and balance to each other. If the supreme executive errs it is informed by the supreme legislative in Parliament. If the supreme legislative errs it is informed by the supreme executive in the King's courts of law. Here the King appears, as represented by his judges, in the highest luster and majesty, as supreme executor of the Commonwealth; and he never shines brighter but on his throne, at the head of the supreme legislative. This is government! This is a constitution! to preserve which, either from foreign or domestic foes, has cost oceans of blood and treasure in every age; and the blood and the treasure have upon the whole been well spent.

British America has been bleeding in this cause from its settlement. We have spent all we could raise, and more; for, notwithstanding the parliamentary reimbursements of part, we still remain much in debt. The province of the Massachusetts, I believe, has expended more men and money in war since the year 1620, when a few families first landed at Plymouth, in proportion to their ability than the three kingdoms together. The same, I believe, may be truly affirmed of many of the other colonies; though the Massachusetts has undoubtedly had the heaviest burden. This may be thought incredible, but materials are collecting; and though some are lost, enough may remain to demonstrate it to the world. I have reason to hope at least that the public will soon see such proofs exhibited as will show that I do not speak quite at random.

Why then is it thought so heinous by the author of the *Administration of the Colonies,* and others, that the colonists should aspire after "a one whole legislative power" not independent of but subordinate to the laws and Parliament of Great Britain? It is a mistake in this author to bring so heavy a charge as high treason against some of the colonists, which he does in effect in this place by representing them as "claiming in fact or in deed the same full, free, independent, unrestrained power and legislative will in their several corporations, and under the King's commission and their respective charters, as the government and legislature of Great Britain holds by its constitution and under the great charter." No such claim was ever thought of by any of the colonists. They are all better men and better subjects; and many of them too well versed in the laws of nature and nations and the law and constitution of Great Britain to think they have a right to more than a *provincial subordinate legislative.*

All power is of God. Next and only subordinate to Him in the present state of the well-formed, beautifully constructed British monarchy, standing where I hope it ever will stand, for the pillars are fixed in judgment, righteousness, and truth, is the King and Parliament. Under these, it seems easy to conceive subordinate powers in gradation, till we descend to the legislative of a town council or even a private social club. These have each "a one whole legislative" subordinate, which, when it doesn't counteract the laws of any of its superiors, is to be indulged. Even when the laws of subordination are transgressed, the superior does not destroy the subordinate, but will negative its acts, as it may in all cases when disapproved.

This right of negative is essential, and may be enforced. But in no case are the essential rights of the subjects inhabiting the subordinate dominions to be destroyed. This would put it in the power of the superior to reduce the inferior to a state of slavery; which cannot be rightfully done even with conquered enemies and rebels. After satisfaction and security is obtained of the former and examples are made of so many of the latter as the ends of government require, the rest are to be restored to all the essential rights of men and citizens. This is the great law of nature; and agreeable to this law is the constant practice of all good and mild governments. This lenity and humanity has nowhere been carried further than in Great Britain. The colonies have been so remarkable for loyalty that there never has been any instance of rebellion or treason in them. This loyalty is in very handsome terms acknowledged by the author of the *Administration of the Colonies:*

> It has been often suggested that care should be taken in the administration of the plantations lest, in some future time, these colonies should become independent of the mother country. But perhaps it may be proper on this occasion, nay, it is justice to say it, that if by becoming independent is meant a revolt, nothing is further from their nature, their interest, their thoughts. If a defection from the alliance of the mother country be suggested, it ought to be and can be truly said that their spirit abhors the sense of such; their attachment to the Protestant succession of the House of Hanover will

ever stand unshaken; and nothing can eradicate from their hearts their natural and almost mechanical affection to Great Britain, which they conceive under no other sense nor call by any other name than that of home. Any such suggestion, therefore, is a false and unjust aspersion on their principles and affections, and can arise from nothing but an entire ignorance of their circumstances.

After all this loyalty, it is a little hard to be charged with claiming, and represented as aspiring after, independency. The inconsistency of this I leave. We have said that the loyalty of the colonies has never been suspected; this must be restricted to a just suspicion. For it seems there have long been groundless suspicions of us in the minds of individuals. And there have always been those who have endeavored to magnify these chimerical fears. I find Mr. Dummer complaining of this many years since. "There is," says he, "one thing more I have heard often urged against the charter colonies, and indeed 'tis what one meets with from people of all conditions and qualities, though with due respect to their better judgments, I can see neither reason nor color for it. 'Tis said that their increasing numbers and wealth, joined to their great distance from Britain, will give them an opportunity, in the course of some years, to throw off their dependence on the nation and declare themselves a free state if not curbed in time by being made entirely subject to the Crown."

This jealousy has been so long talked of that many seem to believe it really well grounded. Not that there is danger of a "revolt," even in the opinion of the author of the *Administration*, but that the colonists will by fraud or force avail themselves, in "fact or in deed," of an independent legislature. This, I think, would be a revolting with a vengeance. What higher revolt can there be than for a province to assume the right of an independent legislative or state? I must therefore think this a greater aspersion on the colonists than to charge them with a design to revolt in the sense in which the gentleman allows they have been abused: it is a more artful and dangerous way of attacking our liberties than to charge us with being in open rebellion. That could be confuted instantly; but this seeming indirect way of charging the colonies with a desire of throwing off their dependency requires more pains to confute it than the other; therefore it has been recurred to.

The truth is, gentlemen have had departments in America the functions of which they have not been fortunate in executing. The people have by these means been rendered uneasy at bad provincial measures. They have been represented as factious, seditious, and inclined to democracy whenever they have refused passive obedience to provincial mandates as arbitrary as those of a Turkish bashaw: I say provincial mandates, for to the King and Parliament they have been ever submissive and obedient.

These representations of us many of the good people of England swallow with as much ease as they would a bottle bubble or any other story of a cock and a bull; and the worst of it is, among some of the most credulous have been found stars and garters. However, they may all rest assured, the colonists, who do not pretend to understand themselves so well as the people of England, though the author of the *Administration* makes them the fine compliment to say they "know their business much better," yet will never think of independency. Were they inclined to it, they know the blood and the treasure it would cost, if ever effected; and when done, it would be a thousand to one if their liberties did not fall a sacrifice to the victor.

We all think ourselves happy under Great Britain. We love, esteem, and reverence our mother country, and adore our King. And could the choice of independency be offered the colonies or subjection to Great Britain upon any terms above absolute slavery, I am convinced they would accept the latter. The Ministry in all future generations may rely on it that British America will never prove undutiful till driven to it as the last fatal resort against ministerial oppression, which will make the wisest mad, and the weakest strong. . . .

Sometimes we have been considered only as the corporations in England; and it may be urged that it is no harder upon us to be taxed by Parliament for the general cause than for them, who besides are at the expense of their corporate subordinate government. I answer: 1. Those corporations are represented in Parliament. 2. The colonies are and have been at great expense in raising men, building forts, and supporting the King's civil government here. Now I read of no governors and other officers of His Majesty's nomination that the City of London taxes its inhabitants to support; I know of no forts and garrisons that the City of London has lately built at its own expense, or of any annual levies that they have raised for the King's service and the common cause. These are things very fitting and proper to be done by a subordinate dominion, and 'tis their duty to do all they are able; but it seems but equal they should be allowed to assess the charges of it themselves. The rules of equity and the principles of the constitution seem to require this. Those who judge of the reciprocal rights that subsist between a supreme and subordinate state or dominion by no higher rules than are applied to a corporation of button-makers will never have a very comprehensive view of them.

Yet sorry am I to say it, many elaborate writers on the administration of the colonies seem to me never to rise higher in their notions than what might be expected from a secretary to one of the quorum. If I should be ranked among this number I shall have this consolation, that I have fallen into what is called very good company and among some who have seen very high life below stairs. I agree with the Administrator that of whatever revenues raised in the colonies, if they must be raised without our consent, "the first and special appropriation of them ought to be the paying the governors and all the other Crown officers," for it would be hard for the colonists to be obliged to pay them after this. It was on this principle that at the last Assembly of this province I moved to stop every grant to the officers of the Crown, more especially as I know some who have built very much upon the fine salaries they shall receive from the plantation branch of the revenue. Nor can I think it "injustice to the frame of human nature" to suppose, if I did not know it, that with similar views several officers of the Crown in some of the colonies have been pushing for such an act for many years. They have obtained their wish, and much good it will do them. But I would not give much for all that will center net in the exchequer after deducting the costs attending the execution of it and the appropriations to the several officers proposed by the Administrator.

What will be the unavoidable consequence of all this, suppose another war should happen and it should be necessary to employ as many provincials in America as in the last? Would it be possible for the colonies, after being burdened in their trade, perhaps after it is ruined, to raise men? Is it probable that they would have spirit enough to exert themselves? If 'tis said the French will never try for America, or if they should, regular troops are only to be employed, I grant our regular troops are the best in the world, and that the experience of the present officers shows that they are capable of every species of American service; yet we should guard against the worst. If another trial for Canada should take place, which from the known temper of France we may judge she will bring on the first fair opportunity, it might require 30,000 or 40,000 regulars to secure His Majesty's just rights.

If it should be said that other American duties must then be levied, besides the impossibility of our being able to pay them, the danger recurs of a large standing army so remote from home; whereas a good provincial militia, with such occasional succors from the mother country as exigencies may require, never was and never will be attended with hazard. The experience of past times will show that an army of 20,000 or 30,000 veterans, half 3,000 miles from Rome, were very apt to proclaim Caesars. The first of the name, the assassin of his country, owed his false glory to stealing the affections of an army from the commonwealth.

I hope these hints will not be taken amiss; they seem to occur from the nature of the subject I am upon; they are delivered in pure affection to my King and country, and amount to no reflection on any man. The best army and the best men we may hereafter have may be led into temptation, all I think is that a prevention of evil is much easier than a deliverance from it.

The sum of my argument is: that civil government is of God; that the administrators of it were originally the whole people; that they might have devolved it on whom they pleased; that this devolution is fiduciary, for the good of the whole; that by the British constitution this devolution is on the King, Lords, and Commons, the supreme, sacred, and uncontrollable legislative power not only in the Realm but through the dominions; that by the abdication, the original compact was broken to pieces; that by the Revolution it was renewed and more firmly established, and the rights and liberties of the subject in all parts of the dominions more fully explained and confirmed.

That in consequence of this establishment and the acts of succession and union, His Majesty George III is rightful King and sovereign, and, with his Parliament, the supreme legislative of Great Britain, France, and Ireland, and the dominions thereto belonging; that this constitution is the most free one and by far the best now existing on earth; that by this constitution every man in the dominions is a free man; that no parts of His Majesty's dominions can be taxed without their consent; that every part has a right to be represented in the supreme or some subordinate legislature; that the refusal of this would seem to be a contradiction in practice to the theory of the constitution; that the colonies are subordinate dominions and are now in such a state as to make it best for the good of the whole that they should not only be continued in the enjoyment of subordinate legislation but be also represented in some proportion to their number and estates in the grand legislature of the nation; that this would firmly unite all parts of the British empire in the greatest peace and prosperity, and render it invulnerable and perpetual.

21.

Charter of Rhode Island College

In 1763, Ezra Stiles supported a project to establish a Baptist institution of learning in New England. The work of drawing up the charter for Rhode Island College (now Brown University) was given to Stiles, a Congregationalist, because he was regarded by the Baptists as better fitted for the task than any of their own sect. However, the first draft of the charter in 1764 was objected to by the Providence Baptists in the Rhode Island Assembly on the grounds that it gave the Congregationalists too much power in the college administration. Stiles was accused of playing a trick on the Baptists by giving administrative control of the college to members of his own denomination. In fact, the Baptists still had the final decision in any matter. Before the charter was granted by the Assembly, it was changed in order to insure that the Baptists would be in a majority.

Source: Reuben A. Guild, *Early History of Brown University,* Providence, 1897, Appendix.

Whereas institutions for liberal education are highly beneficial to society, by forming the rising generation to virtue, knowledge, and useful literature; and thus preserving in the community a succession of men duly qualified for discharging the offices of life with usefulness and reputation; they have therefore justly merited and received the attention and encouragement of every wise and well-regulated state. And whereas a public school or seminary, erected for that purpose within this colony, to which the youth may freely resort for education in the vernacular and learned languages, and in the liberal arts and sciences, would be for the general advantage and honor of the government . . . and thereupon a petition has been preferred to this Assembly, praying that full liberty and power may be granted . . . to found, endow, order, and govern a college or university within this colony; and that, for the more effectual execution of this design, they may be incorporated into one body politic, to be known in the law, with the powers, privileges, and franchises necessary for the purposes aforesaid. . . .

And furthermore, by the authority aforesaid, it is hereby enacted, ordained, and declared that it is now, and at all times hereafter shall continue to be, the unalterable constitution of this college, or university, that the corporation thereof shall consist of two branches, to wit: That of the trustees, and that of the fellowship, with distinct, separate, and respective powers. And that the number of the trustees shall, and may be thirty-six; of which twenty-two shall forever be elected of the denomination called Baptists, or Antipedobaptists; five shall forever be elected of the denomination called Friends, or Quakers; four shall forever be elected of the denomination called Congregationalists; and five shall forever be elected of the denomination called Episcopalians. And that the succession in this branch shall be forever chosen and filled up from the respective denominations in this proportion, and according to these numbers, which are hereby fixed, and shall remain to perpetuity immutably the same. . . .

And that the number of the fellows, inclusive of the president (who shall always be a fellow), shall and may be twelve; of which, eight shall be forever elected of the denomination called Baptists, or Antipedobaptists; and the rest indifferently of any or all denominations . . . to whom the president, when hereafter elected (who shall forever be of the denomination called Baptists, or Antipedobaptists), shall be joined to complete the number.

And, furthermore, it is declared and ordained that the succession in both branches shall at all times hereafter be filled up and supplied according to these numbers, and this established and invariable proportion from the respective denominations by the separate election of both branches of this corporation, which shall at all times sit and act by separate and distinct powers; and, in general, in order to the validity and con-summation of all acts, there shall be in the exercise of their respective, separate, and distinct powers, the joint concurrence of the trustees and fellows, by their respective majorities, except in adjudging and conferring the academical degrees, which shall forever belong, exclusively, to the fellowship as a learned faculty.

And, furthermore, it is constituted that the instruction and immediate government of the college shall forever be, and rest in, the president and fellows, or fellowship. . . .

And, in case any president, trustee, or fellow shall see cause to change his religious denomination, the corporation is hereby empowered to declare his or their place or places vacant, and may proceed to fill up it or them accordingly, as before directed, otherwise each trustee and fellow, not an officer of instruction, shall continue in his office during life or until resignation. And, further, in case either of the religious denominations should decline taking a part in this catholic, comprehensive, and liberal institution, the trustees and fellows shall and may complete their number by electing from their respective denominations, always preserving their respective proportions herein before prescribed and determined; and all elections shall be by ballot, or written suffrage. And that a quorum of four trustees and three fellows may transact any business, excepting placing the college edifice, election of trustees, president, fellows, and professors, that is to say, so that their act shall be of force and validity until the next annual meeting, and no longer. . . .

And, furthermore, it is hereby enacted and declared that into this liberal and catholic institution shall never be admitted any religious tests; but, on the contrary, all the members hereof shall forever enjoy full, free, absolute, and uninterrupted liberty of conscience. And that the places of professors, tutors, and all other officers, the president alone excepted, shall be free and open for all denominations of Protestants. And that youth of all religious denominations shall and may be freely admitted to the equal advantages, emoluments, and honors of the college or university; and shall receive a like fair, generous, and equal treatment during their residence therein, they conducting themselves peaceably, and conforming to the laws and statutes thereof. And that the public teaching shall, in general, respect the sciences. And that the sectarian differences of opinions shall not make any part of the public and classical instruction; although all religious controversies may be studied freely, examined, and explained by the president, professors, and tutors, in a personal, separate, and distinct manner, to the youth of any or each denomination; and, above all, a constant regard be paid to, and effectual care taken of, the morals of the college. . . .

And, furthermore, for establishing the perpetuity of this corporation, and in case that at anytime hereafter, through oversight, or otherwise through misapprehensions and mistaken constructions of the powers, liberties, and franchises herein contained, any laws should be enacted, or any matters done and transacted by this corporation contrary to the tenor of this charter, it is hereby enacted, ordained, and declared that all such laws, acts, and doings shall be, in themselves, null and void. Yet, nevertheless, the same shall not, in any courts of law, or by the General Assembly, be deemed, taken, interpreted, or adjudged into an avoidance, defeasance, or forfeiture of this charter; but that the same shall be, and remain, unhurt, inviolate, and entire unto the said corporation, in perpetual succession; which corporation may, at all times, and forever hereafter, proceed, and continue to act. And all their acts conformable to the powers, tenor, true intent, and meaning of the charter, shall be and remain in full force and validity; the nullity and avoidance of any such illegal acts to the contrary in anywise notwithstanding.

22.

A Remonstrance of Distressed and Bleeding Frontier Inhabitants

The great majority of back-country farmers had little direct political influence in the colonial legislatures in 1763. During the French and Indian War, the Pennsylvania Assembly, composed largely of eastern seaboard Quakers, had refused to vote financial aid for protection of the outlying settlements. Throughout the course of the war, the frontier was repeatedly raided. A group of frontiersmen, calling themselves the Paxton Boys, marched to Philadelphia to state their grievances to the officials of the colony. On February 13, 1764, they presented the following remonstrance to the Provincial Council of Pennsylvania.

Source: *Minutes of the Provincial Council of Pennsylvania*, Vol. IX, Harrisburg, 1852.

WE, MATTHEW SMITH AND JAMES GIBSON, in behalf of ourselves and His Majesty's faithful and loyal subjects, the inhabitants of the frontier counties of Lancaster, York, Cumberland, Berks, and Northampton, humbly beg leave to remonstrate and to lay before you the following grievances, which we submit to your wisdom for redress.

First, we apprehend that as freemen and English subjects, we have an indisputable title to the same privileges and immunities with His Majesty's other subjects who reside in the interior counties of Philadelphia, Chester, and Bucks, and therefore ought not to be excluded from an equal share with them in the very important privilege of legislation. Nevertheless, contrary to the proprietor's charter and the acknowledged principles of common justice and equity, our five counties are restrained from electing more than ten representatives, viz.: four for Lancaster, two for York, two for Cumberland, one for Berks, and one for Northampton; while the three counties and city of Philadelphia, Chester, and Bucks elect twenty-six. This we humbly conceive is oppressive, unequal, and unjust, the cause of many of our grievances, and an infringement of our natural privileges of freedom and equality. Wherefore we humbly pray that we may be no longer deprived of an equal number with the three aforesaid counties, to represent us in Assembly.

Second, we understand that a bill is now before the House of Assembly wherein it is provided that such persons as shall be charged with killing any Indians in Lancaster County shall not be tried in the county where the fact was committed, but in the counties of Philadelphia, Chester, or Bucks. This is manifestly to deprive British subjects of their known privileges to cast an eternal reproach upon whole counties, as if they were unfit to serve their country in the quality of jurymen, and to contradict the well-known laws of the British nation in a point whereon life, liberty, and security essentially depend, namely, that of being tried by their equals in the neighborhood where their own, their accusers', and the witnesses' character and credit, with the circumstances of the fact, are best known, and instead thereof putting their lives in the hands of strangers who may as justly be suspected of partiality to, as the frontier counties can be of prejudices against, Indians; and this, too, in favor of Indians only, against His Majesty's faithful and loyal subjects. . . .

Third, during the late and present Indian war, the frontiers of this province have been repeatedly attacked and ravaged by skulking parties of the Indians, who have with the most savage cruelty murdered men, women, and children without distinction, and have reduced near a thousand families to the most extreme distress. It grieves us to the very heart to see such of our frontier inhabitants as have escaped savage fury with the loss of their parents, their children, their wives or relatives, left destitute by the public, and exposed to the most cruel poverty and wretchedness while upward of 120 of these savages, who are with great reason suspected of being guilty of these horrid barbarities under the mask of friendship, have procured themselves to be taken under the protection of the government, with a view to elude the fury of the brave relatives of the murdered, and are now maintained at the public expense.

Some of these Indians now in the barracks of Philadelphia are confessedly a part of the Wyalusing Indians, which tribe is now at war with us, and the others are the Moravian Indians, who, living amongst us under the cloak of friendship, carried on a correspondence with our known enemies on the Great Island. We cannot but observe with sorrow and indignation that some persons in this province are at pains to extenuate the barbarous cruelties practised by these savages on our murdered brethren and relatives, which are shocking to human nature, and must pierce every heart but that of the hardened perpetrators or their abettors. Nor is it less distressing to hear others pleading that although the Wyalusing tribe is at war with us, yet that part of it which is under the protection of the government may be friendly to the English and innocent.

In what nation under the sun was it ever the custom that when a neighboring nation took up arms, not an individual should be touched but only the persons that offered hostilities? Who ever proclaimed war with a part of a nation, and not with the whole? Had these Indians disapproved of the perfidy of their tribe, and been willing to cultivate and preserve friendship with us, why did they not give notice of the war before it happened, as it is known to be the result of long deliberations, and a preconcerted combination amongst them? Why did they not leave their tribe immediately, and come amongst us before there was ground to suspect them, or war was actually waged with their tribe? No, they stayed amongst them, were privy to their murders and ravages, until we had destroyed their provisions; and when they could no longer subsist at home, they come not as deserters but as friends to be maintained through the winter, that they may be able to scalp and butcher us in the spring.

And as to the Moravian Indians, there are strong grounds at least to suspect their friendship, as it is known they carried on a correspondence with our enemies on the Great Island. We killed three Indians going from Bethlehem to the Great Island with blankets, ammunition, and provisions, which is an undeniable proof that the Moravian Indians were in confederacy with our open enemies; and we cannot but be filled with indignation to hear this action of ours painted in the most odious and detestable colors, as if we had inhumanly murdered our guides who preserved us from perishing in the woods, when we only killed three of our known enemies, who attempted to shoot us when we surprised them.

And besides all this, we understand that one of these very Indians is proved by the oath of Stinton's widow to be the very person that murdered her husband. How then comes it to pass that he alone, of all the Moravian Indians, should join with the enemy to murder that family? Or can it be supposed that any enemy Indians, contrary to their known custom of making war, should penetrate into the heart of a settled country to burn, plunder, and murder the inhabitants, and not molest any houses in their return, or ever be seen or heard of? Or how can we account for it, that no ravages have been committed in Northampton County, since the removal of the Moravian Indians, when the Great Cove has been struck since? These things put it beyond doubt with us that the Indians now at Philadelphia are His Majesty's perfidious enemies and therefore to protect and maintain them at the public expense, while our suffering brethren on the frontiers are almost destitute of the necessaries of life and are neglected by the public, is sufficient to make us mad with rage, and tempt us to do what nothing but the most violent necessity can vindicate. We humbly and earnestly pray, therefore, that those enemies of His Majesty may be removed as soon as possible out of the province.

Fourth, we humbly conceive that it is contrary to the maxims of good policy, and extremely dangerous to our frontiers, to suffer any Indians of what tribe soever to live within the inhabited parts of this province while we are engaged in an Indian war, as experience has taught us that they are all perfidious, and their claim to freedom and independency puts it in their power to act as spies, to entertain and give intelligence to our enemies, and to furnish them with provisions and warlike stores. To this fatal intercourse between our pretended friends and open enemies, we must ascribe the greatest of the ravages and murders that have been committed in the course of this

and the last Indian war. We therefore pray that this grievance be taken under consideration and remedied.

Fifth, we cannot help lamenting that no provision has been hitherto made, that such of our frontier inhabitants as have been wounded in defense of the province, their lives and liberties, may be taken care of and cured of their wounds at the public expense. We therefore pray that this grievance may be redressed.

Sixth, in the late Indian war, this province, with others of His Majesty's colonies, gave rewards for Indian scalps, to encourage the seeking them in their own country, as the most likely means of destroying or reducing them to reason; but no such encouragement has been given in this war, which has damped the spirits of many brave men who are willing to venture their lives in parties against the enemy. We therefore pray that public rewards may be proposed for Indian scalps, which may be adequate to the dangers attending enterprises of this nature.

Seventh, we daily lament that numbers of our nearest and dearest relatives are still in captivity among the savage heathen, to be trained up in all their ignorance and barbarity, or to be tortured to death with all the contrivances of Indian cruelty, for attempting to make their escape from bondage; and we see they pay no regard to the many solemn promises which they have made to restore our friends who are in bondage amongst them. We therefore earnestly pray that no trade may hereafter be permitted to be carried on with them until our brethren and relatives are brought home to us.

Eighth, we complain that a certain society of people in this province, in the late Indian war, and at several treaties held by the King's representatives, openly loaded the Indians with presents, and that J. P., a leader of the said society, in defiance of all government, not only abetted our Indian enemies, but kept up a private intelligence with them, and publicly received from them a belt of wampum, as if he had been our governor or authorized by the King to treat with his enemies. By this means the Indians have been taught to despise us as a weak and disunited people, and from this fatal source have arisen many of our calamities under which we groan. We humbly pray therefore that this grievance may be redressed, and that no private subject be hereafter permitted to treat with, or carry on, a correspondence with our enemies.

Ninth, we cannot but observe with sorrow that Fort Augusta, which has been very expensive to this province, has afforded us but little assistance during this or the last war. The men that were stationed at that place neither helped our distressed inhabitants to save their crops, nor did they attack our enemies in their towns, or patrol on our frontiers. We humbly request that proper measures may be taken to make that garrison more serviceable to us in our distress, if it can be done.

N.B. We are far from intending any reflection against the commanding officer stationed at Augusta, as we presume his conduct was always directed by those from whom he received his orders.

Signed on behalf of ourselves, and by appointment of a great number of the frontier inhabitants.

———————◆———————

Who Is There to Mourn for Logan?
Inscription on an obelisk erected to the memory of Tahgahjute, or Logan, Chief of the Cayugas, in Fort Hill Cemetery, Auburn, New York. The monument of the chief, whose entire family was murdered by white men, surmounts a mound which is said to be an ancient Indian altar.

23.

BENJAMIN FRANKLIN: Concerning a Massacre of Friendly Indians

The Conestoga Massacre of 1763 occurred in Lancaster County, Pennsylvania. Conestoga Indians, long regarded as friendly to the settlers, were suspected of connivance with other Indians who had been pillaging and scalping. A group of Pennsylvania settlers, known as the Paxton Boys, seized the Conestogas and murdered the entire community, men, women, and children. Benjamin Franklin's description of the massacre, written in 1764, follows.

Source: Sparks, IV: "A Narrative of the Late Massacres, in Lancaster County, etc., etc."

THESE INDIANS WERE THE REMAINS of a tribe of the Six Nations, settled at Conestoga, and thence called Conestoga Indians. On the first arrival of the English in Pennsylvania, messengers from this tribe came to welcome them with presents of venison, corn, and skins; and the whole tribe entered into a treaty of friendship with the first proprietor, William Penn, which was to last "as long as the sun should shine, or the waters run in the rivers."

This treaty has been since frequently renewed, and the chain brightened, as they express it, from time to time. It has never been violated, on their part or ours, till now. As their lands by degrees were mostly purchased, and the settlements of the white people began to surround them, the proprietor assigned them lands on the manor of Conestoga, which they might not part with; there they have lived many years in friendship with their white neighbors, who loved them for their peaceable, inoffensive behavior.

It has always been observed that Indians settled in the neighborhood of white people do not increase but diminish continually. This tribe accordingly went on diminishing till there remained in their town on the manor but twenty persons, viz., seven men, five women, and eight children, boys and girls.

Of these, Shehaes was a very old man, having assisted at the second treaty held with them by Mr. Penn in 1701, and ever since continued a faithful and affectionate friend to the English. He is said to have been an exceeding good man, considering his education, being naturally of a most kind, benevolent temper.

Peggy was Shehaes' daughter; she worked for her aged father, continuing to live with him, though married, and attended him with filial duty and tenderness.

John was another good old man; his son Harry helped to support him.

George and Will Soc were two brothers, both young men.

John Smith, a valuable young man of the Cayuga nation, who became acquainted with Peggy, Shehaes' daughter, some few years since, married her, and settled in that family. They had one child, about three years old.

Betty, a harmless old woman, and her son Peter, a likely young lad.

Sally, whose Indian name was Wyanjoy, a woman much esteemed by all that knew her for her prudent and good behavior in some very trying situations of life. She was a truly good and an amiable woman, had no children of her own, but, a distant relation dying, she had taken a child of that relation's to bring up as her own, and performed toward it all the duties of an affectionate parent.

The reader will observe that many of their names are English. It is common with the Indians that have an affection for the English to give themselves and their children the names of such English persons as they particularly esteem.

This little society continued the custom they had begun when more numerous of addressing every new governor, and every descendant of the first proprietor, welcoming him to the province, assuring him of their fidelity, and praying a continuance of that favor and protection they had hitherto experienced. They had accordingly sent up an address of this kind to our present governor on his arrival; but the same was scarce delivered, when the unfortunate catastrophe happened, which we are about to relate.

On Wednesday, the 14th of December, 1763, fifty-seven men from some of our frontier townships who had projected the destruction of this little commonwealth came, all well mounted and armed with firelocks, hangers, and hatchets, having traveled through the country in the night, to Conestoga manor. There they surrounded the small village of Indian huts, and just at break of day broke into them all at once. Only three men, two women, and a young boy were found at home, the rest being out among the neighboring white people, some to sell the baskets, brooms, and bowls they

manufactured, and others on other occasions. These poor defenseless creatures were immediately fired upon, stabbed, and hatcheted to death! The good Shehaes, among the rest, cut to pieces in his bed. All of them were scalped and otherwise horribly mangled. Then their huts were set on fire, and most of them burned down. Then the troop, pleased with their own conduct and bravery, but enraged that any of the poor Indians had escaped the massacre, rode off, and in small parties, by different roads, went home.

The universal concern of the neighboring white people on hearing of this event, and the lamentations of the younger Indians when they returned and saw the desolation and the butchered, half-burned bodies of their murdered parents and other relations cannot well be expressed.

The magistrates of Lancaster, sent out to collect the remaining Indians, brought them into the town for their better security against any farther attempt; and it is said condoled with them on the misfortune that had happened, took them by the hand, comforted and promised them protection. They were all put into the workhouse, a strong building, as the place of greatest safety.

When the shocking news arrived in town, a proclamation was issued by the governor, in the following terms, viz.:

Whereas I have received information that on Wednesday, the 14th day of this month, a number of people, armed and mounted on horseback, unlawfully assembled together and went to the Indian town in the Conestoga manor, in Lancaster County, and without the least reason or provocation, in cool blood, barbarously killed six of the Indians settled there, and burned and destroyed all their houses and effects.

And whereas so cruel and inhuman an act, committed in the heart of this province on the said Indians, who have lived peaceably and inoffensively among us during all our late troubles and for many years before, and were justly considered as under the protection of this government and its laws, calls loudly for the vigorous exertion of the civil authority to detect the offenders, and bring them to condign punishment; I have, therefore, by and with the advice and consent of the Council, thought fit to issue this proclamation, and do hereby strictly charge and enjoin all judges, justices, sheriffs, constables, officers, civil and military, and all other His Majesty's liege subjects within this province to make diligent search and inquiry after the authors and perpetrators of the said crime, their abettors and accomplices, and to use all possible means to apprehend and secure them in some of the public jails of this province, that they may be brought to their trials, and be proceeded against according to law.

And whereas a number of other Indians, who lately lived on or near the frontiers of this province, being willing and desirous to preserve and continue the ancient friendship which heretofore subsisted between them and the good people of this province, have, at their own earnest request, been removed from their habitations and brought into the county of Philadelphia and seated for the present for their better security on the province island, and in other places in the neighborhood of the city of Philadelphia, where provision is made for them at the public expense; I do, therefore, hereby strictly forbid all persons whatsoever to molest or injure any of the said Indians, as they will answer the contrary at their peril.

Given under my hand, and the Great Seal of the said province, at Philadelphia, the 22nd day of December, Anno Domini 1763, and in the fourth year of His Majesty's reign.

JOHN PENN

By His Honor's Command,

JOSEPH SHIPPEN, Jun., Secretary.

God Save the King.

Notwithstanding this proclamation, those cruel men again assembled themselves, and hearing that the remaining fourteen Indians were in the workhouse at Lancaster, they suddenly appeared in that town on the 27th of December. Fifty of them, armed as before, dismounting, went directly to the workhouse, and by violence broke open the door, and entered with the utmost fury in their countenances. When the poor wretches saw they had no protection nigh, nor could possibly escape, and being without the least weapon for defense, they divided into their little families, the children clinging to the parents; they fell on their knees, protested their innocence, declared their love to the English, and that in their whole lives they had never done them injury; and in this posture they all received the hatchet! Men, women, and little children were every one inhumanly murdered in cold blood!

The barbarous men who committed the atrocious fact in defiance of government, of all laws human and divine, and to the eternal disgrace of their country and color then mounted their horses, huzza'd in triumph, as if they had gained a victory, and rode off — unmolested!

The bodies of the murdered were then brought out and exposed in the street, till a hole could be made in the earth to receive and cover them.

But the wickedness cannot be covered, the guilt will lie on the whole land, till justice is done on the murderers. The blood of the innocent will cry to heaven for vengeance.

It is said that Shehaes, being before told that it was to be feared some English might come from the frontier into the country and murder him and his people, replied: "It is impossible. There are Indians, indeed, in the woods, who would kill me and mine, if they could get at us, for my friendship to the English; but the English will wrap me in their matchcoat, and secure me from all danger." How unfortunately was he mistaken!

Another proclamation has been issued, offering a great reward for apprehending the murderers, in the following terms, viz.:

Whereas on the 22nd day of December last, I issued a proclamation for the apprehending and bringing to justice a number of persons who, in violation of the public faith and in defiance of all law, had inhumanly killed six of the Indians who had lived in Conestoga manor for the course of many years, peaceably and inoffensively, under the protection of this government, on lands assigned to them for their habitation.

Notwithstanding which, I have received information, that on the 27th of the same month, a large party of armed men again assembled and met together in a riotous and tumultous manner, in the county of Lancaster, and proceeded to the town of Lancaster, where they violently broke open the workhouse, and butchered and put to death fourteen of the said Conestoga Indians, men, women, and children, who had been taken under the immediate care and protection of the magistrates of the said county, and lodged for their better security in the said workhouse, till they should be more effectually provided for by order of the government.

And whereas common justice loudly demands, and the laws of the land (upon the preservation of which not only the liberty and security of every individual, but the being of the government itself depend) require, that the above offenders should be brought to condign punishment.

I have, therefore, by and with the advice of the Council, published this proclamation, and do hereby strictly charge and command all judges, justices, sheriffs, constables, officers, civil and military, and all other His Majesty's faithful and liege subjects within this province to make diligent search and inquiry after the authors and perpetrators of the said last-mentioned offense, their abettors and accomplices, and that they use all possible means to apprehend and secure them in some of the public jails of this province, to be dealt with according to law.

And I do hereby further promise and engage that any person or persons who shall apprehend and secure or cause to be apprehended and secured any three of the ringleaders of the said party, and prosecute them to conviction, shall have and receive for each the public reward of £200; and any accomplice, not concerned in the immediate shedding the blood of the said Indians, who shall make discovery of any or either of the said ringleaders, and apprehend and prosecute them to conviction, shall, over and above the said reward, have all the weight and influence of the government, for obtaining His Majesty's pardon for his offense.

Given under my hand and the Great Seal of the said province, at Philadelphia, the 2nd day of January, in the fourth year of His Majesty's reign, and in the year of our Lord 1764.

JOHN PENN

By His Honor's Command,
JOSEPH SHIPPEN, Jun., Secretary.
God Save the King.

These proclamations have as yet produced no discovery, the murderers having given out such threatenings against those that disapprove their proceedings that the whole country seems to be in terror, and no one dares speak what he knows; even the letters from thence are unsigned in which any dislike is expressed of the rioters.

There are some (I am ashamed to hear it) who would extenuate the enormous wickedness of these actions by saying: "The inhabitants of the frontiers are exasperated with the murder of their relations by the enemy Indians in the present war." It is possible; but though this might justify their going out into the woods to seek for those enemies and avenge upon them those murders, it can never justify their turning into the heart of the country, to murder their friends.

If an Indian injures me, does it follow that I may revenge that injury on all Indians? It is well known that Indians are of different tribes, nations, and languages as well as the white people. In Europe, if the French, who are white people, should injure the Dutch, are they to revenge it on the English, because they too are white people?

The only crime of these poor wretches seems to have been that they had a reddish-brown skin and black hair; and some people of that sort, it seems, had murdered some of our relations. If it be right to kill men for such a reason, then should any man with a freckled face and red hair kill a wife or child of mine, it would be right for me to revenge it by killing all the freckled, red-haired men, women, and children I could afterward anywhere meet with.

But it seems these people think they have a better justification; nothing less than the word of God. With the Scriptures in their hands and mouths, they can set at nought that express command, Thou shalt do no murder, and justify their wickedness by the command given Joshua to destroy the heathen. Horrid perversion of Scripture and of religion! To father the worst of crimes on the God of peace and love! Even the Jews, to whom that particular commission was directed, spared the Gibeonites, on account of their faith once given. The faith of this government has been frequently given to those Indians; but that did not avail them with people who despise government. . . .

I will not dissemble that numberless stories have been raised and spread abroad against not only the poor wretches that are murdered but also against the 140 Christianized Indians still threatened to be murdered; all which stories are well known, by those who know the Indians best, to be pure inventions, contrived by bad people, either to excite each other to join in the murder, or since it was committed, to justify it; and believed only by the weak and credulous. I call thus publicly on the makers and venders of these accusations to produce their evidence. Let them satisfy the public that even Will Soc, the most obnoxious of all that tribe, was really guilty of those offenses against us which they lay to his charge. But if he was, ought he not to have been fairly tried? He lived under our laws, and was subject to them; he was in our hands, and might easily have been prosecuted; was it English justice to condemn and execute him unheard? Conscious of his own innocence, he did not endeavor to hide himself when the door of the workhouse, his sanctuary, was breaking open. "I will meet them," says he, "for they are my brothers." These brothers of his shot him down at the door, while the word "brothers" was between his teeth.

But if Will Soc was a bad man, what had poor old Shehaes done? What could he or the other poor old men and women do? What had little boys and girls done? What could children of a year old, babes at the breast, what could they do, that they too must be shot and hatcheted? Horrid to relate! And in their parents' arms! This is done by no civilized nation in Europe. Do we come to America to learn and practise the manners of barbarians? But this, barbarians as they are, they practise against their enemies only, not against their friends.

These poor people have been always our friends. Their fathers received ours, when strangers here, with kindness and hospitality. Behold the return we have made them! When we grew more numerous and powerful, they put themselves under our protection. See, in the mangled corpses of the last remains of the tribe, how effectually we have afforded it to them!

Unhappy people! to have lived in such times, and by such neighbors! We have seen that they would have been safer among the ancient heathens with whom the rites of hospitality were sacred. They would have been considered as guests of the public, and the religion of the country would have operated in their favor. But our frontier people call themselves Christians! They would have been safer if they had submitted to the Turks; for ever since Mahomet's reproof to Khaled, even the cruel Turks never kill prisoners in cold blood. These were not even prisoners. But what is the example of Turks to Scripture Christians?

They would have been safer, though they had been taken in actual war against the Saracens, if they had once drank water with them. These were not taken in war against us, and have drank with us, and we with them, for fourscore years. But shall we compare Saracens to Christians?

They would have been safer among the Moors in Spain, though they had been murderers of sons, if faith had once been pledged to them, and a promise of protection given. But these have had the faith of the English given to them many times by the government, and in reliance on that faith they lived among us and gave us the opportunity of murdering them. However, what was honorable in Moors, may not be a rule to us; for we are Christians! They would have been safer it seems among popish Spaniards, even if enemies, and delivered into their hands by a tempest. These were not enemies; they were born among us, and yet we have killed them all. But shall we imitate idolatrous Papists, we that are enlightened Protestants? They would have even been safer among the Negroes of Africa, where at least one manly soul would have been found with sense, spirit, and humanity enough to stand in their defense. But shall white men and Christians act like a pagan Negro? In short, it appears that they would have been safe in any part of the known world except in the neighborhood of the Christian white savages of Peckstang and Donegall!

O, ye unhappy perpetrators of this horrid wickedness! Reflect a moment on the mischief ye have done, the disgrace ye have brought on your country, on your religion, and your Bible, on your families and children! Think on the destruction of your captivated country folks (now among the wild Indians) which probably may follow in resentment of your barbarity! Think on the wrath of the united Five Nations, hitherto our friends, but now provoked by your murdering one of their tribes, in danger of

becoming our bitter enemies. Think of the mild and good government you have so audaciously insulted; the laws of your King, your country, and your God, that you have broken; the infamous death that hangs over your heads; for justice, though slow, will come at last. All good people everywhere detest your actions. You have imbrued your hands in innocent blood; how will you make them clean? The dying shrieks and groans of the murdered will often sound in your ears. Their specters will sometimes attend you, and affright even your innocent children! Fly where you will, your consciences will go with you. Talking in your sleep shall betray you, in the delirium of a fever you yourselves shall make your own wickedness known.

One hundred and forty peaceable Indians yet remain in this government. They have, by Christian missionaries, been brought over to a liking, at least, of our religion; some of them lately left their nation which is now at war with us because they did not choose to join with them in their depredations, and to show their confidence in us, and to give us an equal confidence in them, they have brought and put into our hands their wives and children. Others have lived long among us in Northampton County, and most of their children have been born there. These are all now trembling for their lives. They have been hurried from place to place for safety, now concealed in corners, then sent out of the province, refused a passage through a neighboring colony, and returned, not unkindly perhaps, but disgracefully, on our hands. O Pennsylvania! Once renowned for kindness to strangers, shall the clamors of a few mean niggards about the expense of this public hospitality, an expense that will not cost the noisy wretches sixpence a piece (and what is the expense of the poor maintenance we afford them compared to the expense they might occasion if in arms against us).

Shall so senseless a clamor, I say, force

you to turn out of your own doors these unhappy guests who have offended their own country folks by their affection for you, who, confiding in your goodness, have put themselves under your protection? Those whom you have disarmed to satisfy groundless suspicions, will you leave them exposed to the armed madmen of your country? Unmanly men! who are not ashamed to come with weapons against the unarmed, to use the sword against women, and the bayonet against young children; and who have already given such bloody proofs of their inhumanity and cruelty!

Let us rouse ourselves, for shame, and redeem the honor of our province from the contempt of its neighbors; let all good men join heartily and unanimously in support of the laws, and in strengthening the hands of government; that justice may be done, the wicked punished, and the innocent protected; otherwise we can, as a people, expect no blessing from Heaven; there will be no security for our persons or properties; anarchy and confusion will prevail over all; and violence without judgement dispose of everything.

When I mention the baseness of the murderers in the use they made of arms, I cannot, I ought not to forget the very different behavior of brave men and true soldiers, of which this melancholy occasion has afforded us fresh instances. The Royal Highlanders have, in the course of this war, suffered as much as any other corps, and have frequently had their ranks thinned by an Indian enemy; yet they did not for this retain a brutal undistinguishing resentment against all Indians, friends as well as foes. But a company of them happening to be here, when the 140 poor Indians above mentioned were thought in too much danger to stay longer in the province, cheerfully undertook to protect and escort them to New York, which they executed (as far as that government would permit the Indians to come) with fidelity and honor; and their Captain Robinson is justly applauded and honored by all sensible and good people for the care, tenderness, and humanity with which he treated those unhappy fugitives during their march in this severe season.

General Gage, too, has approved of his officer's conduct, and, as I hear, ordered him to remain with the Indians at Amboy and continue his protection to them till another body of the King's forces could be sent to relieve his company and escort their charge back in safety to Philadelphia, where His Excellency has had the goodness to direct those forces to remain for some time, under the orders of our governor, for the security of the Indians — the troops of this province being at present necessarily posted on the frontier. Such just and generous actions endear the military to the civil power, and impress the minds of all the discerning with a still greater respect for our national government. I shall conclude with observing that cowards can handle arms, can strike where they are sure to meet with no return, can wound, mangle, and murder; but it belongs to brave men to spare and to protect; for, as the poet says,

Mercy still sways the brave.

THE OHIO FRONTIER: EXPANSION AND CONFLICT

In the mid-18th century, multiple claims to land caused hostilities among Indian tribes as well as between the Indians and the settlers. With loyalties shifting back and forth, warfare broke out frequently in the frontier regions on either side of the Appalachians.

Clashes between Indians and settlers took the form of Indian raids on villages in which whites were massacred or taken prisoner. After several such raids in Pennsylvania, the settlers retaliated by attacking Indian villages, including those of the peaceful Conestoga tribe. When the Moravian Indians who had taken refuge in Philadelphia were similarly threatened, Quaker leaders in that city used their influence to end the colonial attacks.

The Indians who suffered most in Pennsylvania were the Delawares. Victimized by the whites in unjust land-transfer agreements and defeated by the Iroquois in the Susquehanna Valley, they migrated into the Ohio region. The Iroquois had previously granted this land to the English, who organized land companies to promote settlement, which created conflict with the French and Indian interests.

During the French and Indian War, Pontiac, the Ottawa chief, organized various tribes in the Ohio region in a short-lived stand that terrorized colonists and impeded settlement of the area for several years.

When the English took control of the region, Guy Johnson was appointed the chief Indian agent. His skill, combined with the Proclamation of 1763 which restricted settlement in this territory, brought peace until the Revolution.

(Above) Cartoon depicting the alarm in Philadelphia caused by the threatened attack by the "Paxton Boys"; (center) two proclamations issued in an attempt to ease tension between whites and Indians on the frontier; (bottom) plan of a newly cleared farm

BY THE HONOURABLE

JOHN PENN, Esq;

Lieutenant-Governor and Commander in Chief of the Province of *Pennsylvania*,
and Counties of *New-Castle, Kent* and *Sussex,* on *Delaware,*

A PROCLAMATION.

WHEREAS I have received Information, That on *Wednesday,* the Fourteenth Day of this Month, a Number of People, armed, and mounted on Horseback, unlawfully assembled together, and went to the *Indian* Town in the *Conestogoe* Manor, in *Lancaster* County, and without the least Reason or Provocation, in cool Blood, barbarously killed six of the *Indians* settled there, and burnt and destroyed all their Houses and Effects: AND WHEREAS so cruel and inhuman an Act, committed in the Heart of this Province on the said *Indians,* who have lived peaceably and inoffensively among us, during all our late Troubles, and for many Years before, and were justly considered as under the Protection of this Government and its Laws, calls loudly for the vigorous Exertion of the civil Authority, to detect the Offenders, and bring them to condign Punishment; I HAVE THEREFORE, by and with the Advice and Consent of the Council, thought fit to issue this Proclamation, and do hereby strictly charge and enjoin all Judges, Justices, Sheriffs, Constables, Officers Civil and Military, and all other His Majesty's liege Subjects within this Province, to make diligent Search and Enquiry after the Authors and Perpetrators of the said Crime, their Abettors and Accomplices, and to use all possible Means to apprehend and secure them in some of the public Goals of this Province, that they may be brought to their Trials, and be proceeded against according to Law.

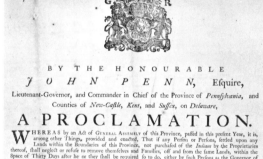

BY THE HONOURABLE

JOHN PENN, Esquire,

Lieutenant-Governor, and Commander in Chief of the Province of *Pennsylvania,* and
Counties of *New-Castle, Kent,* and *Sussex,* on *Delaware,*

A PROCLAMATION.

WHEREAS by an Act of GENERAL ASSEMBLY of this Province, passed in this present Year, it is, among other Things, provided and enacted, That if any Person or Persons, settled upon any Lands within the Boundaries of this Province, not purchased of the *Indians* by the Proprietaries thereof, shall neglect or refuse to remove themselves and Families, off and from the same Lands, within the Space of Thirty Days after he or they shall be required so to do, either by such Persons as the Governor of this Province shall appoint for that Purpose, or by his Proclamations, to be set up in the most public Places of the Settlements on such unpurchased Lands ; or if any Person or Persons, being so removed, shall afterwards return to his or their Settlement, or the Settlement of any other Person, with his or their Family, or without any Family, to remain and settle on such Lands ; or if any Person shall, after the said Notice to be given as aforesaid, reside and settle on such Lands, every such Person and Persons, so neglecting or refusing to remove, with his or their Family, or returning to settle as aforesaid, or that shall settle on any such Lands, after the Requisition or Notice aforesaid, being thereof legally convicted, by their own Con-

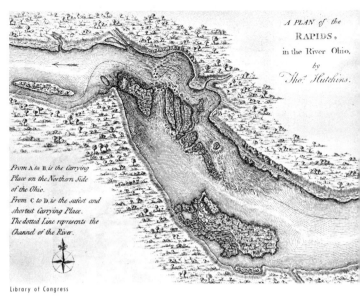

Map of the falls of the Ohio River, site of Louisville, Ky.

Settlement of St. Louis

Following peace with France in 1763, England controlled all land east of the Mississippi River. French fur traders now moved farther west, outside the British domain. Auguste Chouteau, when only 14 years old, was a leader of the group that established the first permanent settlement at St. Louis in 1764. Although this area was under the Spanish after the war, fur-trading interests preserved the predominantly French culture.

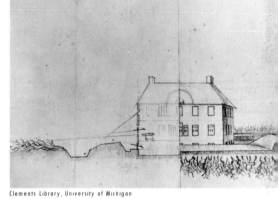

Plan of a two-story building converted into a strong point for defense against Indians

(Below) Auguste Chouteau; (right) first home built by Chouteau in St. Louis

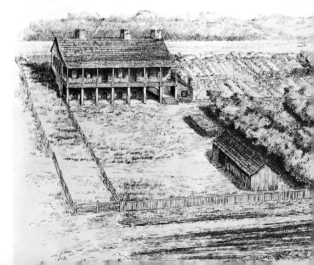

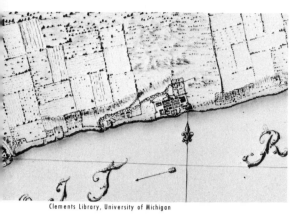

Pacifying the Indians

With the fall of New France came the task of pacifying the western Indians. In 1763 scattered tribes, led by Pontiac, attacked British forts on the frontier. Pontiac besieged Detroit for almost a year before his defeat in 1764. Meanwhile, Colonel Bouquet led an expedition into the Ohio territory subduing the Indians and recovering white captives.

(Above left) Plan of Detroit and its environs at time of Pontiac's siege; (left) Pontiac and his embassy meeting with Major Rogers at the end of Pontiac's War; (below) map of Bouquet's march through the Ohio territory

(Left and below) Bouquet frees white captives from the Indians; engravings after sketches by Benjamin West

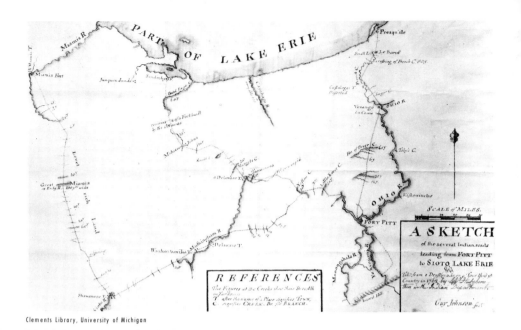

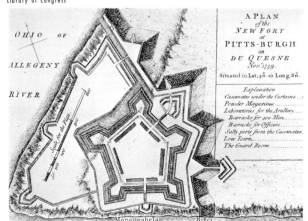

Colonel Guy Johnson, portrait by Benjamin West

1765

24.

GEORGE CROGHAN: Early Exploration of the Ohio Valley

George Croghan spent most of his adult life as a frontiersman. His ability to negotiate with Native Americans and his knowledge of their various languages earned him, in 1756, the position of deputy superintendent of Indian Affairs. Following the French and Indian War, General Thomas Gage gave Colonel Croghan the assignment of opening up the Illinois Territory, which was still largely under French domination. His diary for 1765, portions of which are reprinted here, tells of these explorations.

Source: Mann Butler, *A History of the Commonwealth of Kentucky,* Louisville, 1834, Appendix: "The Journal of Colonal Croghan."

May 15, 1765. I set off from Fort Pitt with two batteaux [boats] and encamped at Chartier's Island, in the Ohio, three miles below Fort Pitt.

16th. Being joined by the deputies of the Seneca, Shawnesse [Shawnee], and Delawares that were to accompany me, we set off at 7 o'clock in the morning, and at 10 o'clock arrived at the Log's Town, an old settlement of the Shawnesse, about seventeen miles from Fort Pitt, where we put ashore, and viewed the remains of that village, which was situated on a high bank, on the south side of the Ohio River, a fine fertile country around it. At 11 o'clock we re-embarked and proceeded down the Ohio to the mouth of Big Beaver Creek, about ten miles below the Log's Town. This creek

empties itself between two fine rich bottoms, a mile wide on each side from the banks of the river to the highlands. About a mile below the mouth of Beaver Creek we passed an old settlement of the Delawares, where the French, in 1756, built a town for that nation. On the north side of the river some of the stone chimneys are yet remaining; here the highlands come close to the banks and continue so for about five miles. After which we passed several spacious bottoms on each side of the river, and came to Little Beaver Creek, about fifteen miles below Big Beaver Creek. A number of small rivulets fall into the river on each side. From thence we sailed to Yellow Creek, being about fifteen miles from the last mentioned creek; here and there the hills come close to the banks of the river on each side, but where there are bottoms, they are very large, and well watered; numbers of small rivulets running through them, falling into the Ohio on both sides. We encamped on the river bank, and find a great part of the trees in the bottom are covered with grape vines. This day we passed by eleven islands, one of which being about seven miles long. For the most part of the way we made this day, the banks of the river are high and steep. The course of the Ohio from Fort Pitt to the mouth of Beaver Creek inclines to the northwest; from thence to the two creeks partly due west.

17th. At 6 o'clock in the morning we embarked, and were delighted with the prospect of a fine open country on each side of the river as we passed down. We came to a place called the Two Creeks, about fifteen miles from Yellow Creek, where we put to shore; here the Seneca have a village on a high bank, on the north side of the river; the chief of this village offered me his service to go with me to the Illinois, which I could not refuse for fear of giving him offense, although I had a sufficient number of deputies with me already. From thence we proceeded down the river, passed many large, rich, and fine bottoms; the highlands being at a considerable distance from the river banks, till we came to the Buffalo Creek, being about ten miles below the Seneca village; and from Buffalo Creek, we proceeded down the river to Fat Meat Creek, about thirty miles. The face of the country appears much like what we met with before; large, rich, and well-watered bottoms, then succeeded by the hills pinching close on the river; these bottoms, on the north side, appear rather low, and consequently subject to inundations, in the spring of the year, when there never fails to be high freshets in the Ohio, owing to the melting of the snows. This day we passed by ten fine islands, though the greatest part of them are small. They lay much higher

out of the water than the main land, and of course less subject to be flooded by the freshets. At night we encamped near an Indian village. The general course of the river from the Two Creeks to Fat Meat Creek inclines to the southwest.

18th. At 6 a.m. we set off in our batteaux; the country on both sides of the river appears delightful; the hills are several miles from the river banks, and consequently the bottoms large; the soil, timber, and banks of the river much like those we have before described. About fifty miles below the Fat Meat Creek, we enter the long reach, where the river runs a straight course for twenty miles, and makes a delightful prospect; the banks continue high; the country on both sides, level, rich, and well watered. At the lower end of the reach we encamped. This day we passed nine islands, some of which are large, and lay high out of the water.

19th. We decamped at 6 in the morning, and sailed to a place called the Three Islands, being about fifteen miles from our last encampment; here the highlands come close to the river banks, and the bottoms for the most part — till we come to the Muskingum (or Elk) River — are but narrow. This river empties itself into the Ohio about fifteen miles below the Three Islands; the banks of the river continue steep, and the country is level for several miles back from the river. The course of the river from Fat Meat Creek to Elk River is about southwest and by south. We proceeded down the river about fifteen miles to the mouth of Little Conhawa [Kanawha] River with little or no alteration in the face of the country; here we encamped in a fine rich bottom, after having passed fourteen islands, some of them large, and mostly lying high out of the water. Here buffaloes, bears, turkeys, with all other kinds of wild game are extremely plenty. A good hunter, without much fatigue to himself, could here supply daily one hundred men with meat. The course of the Ohio, from Elk River to Little

Conhawa, is about south.

20th. At 6 in the morning we embarked in our boats, and proceeded down to the mouth of Hochocken or Bottle River, where we were obliged to encamp, having a strong head wind against us. We made but twenty miles this day, and passed by five very fine islands; the country the whole way being rich and level, with high and steep banks to the rivers. From here I dispatched an Indian to the Plains of Scioto with a letter to the French traders from the Illinois residing there, amongst the Shawnesse, requiring them to come and join me at the mouth of Scioto, in order to proceed with me to their own country, and take the oaths of allegiance to His Britannic Majesty, as they were now become his subjects, and had no right to trade there without license. At the same time I sent messages to the Shawnesse Indians to oblige the French to come to me in case of refusal.

21st. We embarked at half past 8 o'clock in the morning, and sailed to a place called the Big Bend, about thirty-five miles below Bottle River. The course of the Ohio, from Little Conhawa River to Big Bend, is about southwest by south. The country hereabouts abounds with buffalo, bears, deer, and all sorts of wild game in such plenty that we killed out of our boats as much as we wanted. We proceeded down the river to the Buffalo Bottom, about ten miles from the beginning of the Big Bend, where we encamped. The country on both sides of the river, much the same as we passed the day before. This day we passed nine islands, all lying high out of the water.

22nd. At half an hour past 5 o'clock, set off and sailed to a place called Alum Hill, so called from the great quantity of that mineral found there by the Indians; this place lies about ten miles from Buffalo Bottom; thence we sailed to the mouth of Great Conhawa River, being ten miles from the Alum Hill. The course of the river from the Great Bend to this place is mostly west;

from hence we proceeded down to Little Guyondott River, where we encamped, about thirty miles from Great Conhawa; the country still fine and level; the bank of the river high, with abundance of creeks and rivulets falling into it. This day we passed six fine islands. In the evening one of our Indians discovered three Cherokee near our encampment, which obliged our Indians to keep out a good guard the first part of the night. Our party being pretty strong, I imagine the Cherokee were afraid to attack us, and so ran off.

23rd. Decamped about 5 in the morning, and arrived at Big Guyondott, twenty miles from our last encampment; the country as of yesterday; from hence we proceeded down to Sandy River, being twenty miles farther; thence to the mouth of Scioto, about forty miles from the last-mentioned river. The general course of the river from Great Conhawa to this place inclines to the southwest; the soil rich, the country level, and the banks of the river high. The soil on the banks of Scioto, for a vast distance up the country, is prodigious rich, the bottoms very wide, and in the spring of the year, many of them are flooded, so that the river appears to be two or three miles wide. Bears, deer, turkeys, and most sorts of wild game are very plent[iful] on the banks of this river.

On the Ohio, just below the mouth of Scioto, on a high bank, near forty feet, formerly stood the Shawnesse town called the Lower Town, which was all carried away, except three or four houses, by a great flood in the Scioto. I was in the town at the time, though the banks of the Ohio were so high the water was nine feet on the top, which obliged the whole town to take to their canoes and move with their effects to the hills. The Shawnesse afterward built their town on the opposite side of the river, which, during the French war, they abandoned, for fear of the Virginians, and removed to the plains on Scioto. The Ohio is about one hundred yards wider here than at Fort Pitt, which is but a small augmentation, considering the great number of rivers and creeks that fall into it during the course of 420 miles; and as it deepens but very little, I imagine the water sinks, though there is no visible appearance of it. In general all the lands on the Scioto River, as well as the bottoms on Ohio, are too rich for anything but hemp, flax, or Indian corn.

24th, 25th, and *26th.* Stayed at the mouth of Scioto, waiting for the Shawnesse and French traders, who arrived here on the evening of the 26th, in consequence of the message I sent them from Hochocken, or Bottle Creek.

27th. The Indians requested me to stay this day, which I could not refuse.

28th. We set off, passing down the Ohio, the country on both sides the river level; the banks continue high. This day we came sixty miles; passed no islands. The river being wider and deeper, we drove all night.

29th. We came to the Little Miami River, having proceeded sixty miles last night.

30th. We passed the Great Miami River, about thirty miles from the little river of that name, and in the evening arrived at the place where the elephant's bones are found, where we encamped, intending to take a view of the place next morning. This day we came about seventy miles. The country on both sides level, and rich bottoms well watered.

31st. Early in the morning we went to the great Lick, where those bones are only found, about four miles from the river, on the southeast side. In our way we passed through a fine timbered clear wood; we came into a large road which the buffaloes have beaten, spacious enough for two wagons to go abreast, and leading straight into the Lick. It appears that there are vast quantities of these bones lying five or six feet underground, which we discovered in the bank, at the edge of the Lick. We found here two tusks above six feet long; we car-

ried one, with some other bones, to our boats, and set off. This day we proceeded down the river about eighty miles, through a country much the same as already described, since we passed the Scioto. In this day's journey we passed the mouth of the Kentucky River, or Holsten's River.

June 1. We arrived within a mile of the falls of Ohio, where we encamped, after coming about fifty miles this day.

2nd. Early in the morning we embarked, and passed the falls. The river being very low we were obliged to lighten our boats, and pass on the north side of a little island, which lays in the middle of the river. In general, what is called the Fall here, is no more than rapids; and in the least freshet, a batteau of any size may come and go on each side without any risk. This day we proceeded sixty miles, in the course of which we passed Pidgeon River. The country pretty high on each side of the Ohio River.

3rd. In the forepart of this day's course, we passed high lands; about midday we came to a fine, flat, and level country, called by the Indians the Low Lands; no hills to be seen. We came about eighty miles this day, and encamped.

4th. We came to a place called the Five Islands; these islands are very long, and succeed one another in a chain; the country still flat and level, the soil exceedingly rich and well watered. The highlands are at least fifty miles from the banks of the Ohio. In this day's course we passed about ninety miles, the current being very strong.

5th. Having passed the Five Islands, we came to a place called the Owl River. Came about forty miles this day. The country the same as yesterday.

6th. We arrived at the mouth of the Ouabache [Wabash], where we found a breastwork erected, supposed to be done by the Indians. The mouth of this river is about two hundred yards wide, and in its course runs through one of the finest countries in the world, the lands being exceedingly rich, and well watered; here hemp might be raised in immense quantities. All the bottoms, and almost the whole country abounds with great plenty of the white and red mulberry tree. These trees are to be found in great plenty, in all places between the mouth of Scioto and the Ouabache: the soil of the latter affords this tree in plenty as far as Ouicatonon, and some few on the Miami River. Several large fine islands lie in the Ohio, opposite the mouth of the Ouabache, the banks of which are high, and consequently free from inundations; hence we proceeded down the river about six miles to encamp, as I judged some Indians were sent to waylay us, and came to a place called the Old Shawnesse Village, some of that nation having formerly lived there. In this day's proceedings we came about seventy-six miles. The general course of the river, from Scioto to this place, is southwest.

7th. We stayed here, and dispatched two Indians to the Illinois by land, with letters to Lord Frazer, an English officer, who had been sent there from Fort Pitt, and Monsieur St. Ange, the French commanding officer at Fort Chartres, and some speeches to the Indians there, letting them know of my arrival here; that peace was made between us and the Six Nations, Delawares, and Shawnesse, and of my having a number of deputies of those nations along with me, to conclude matters with them also on my arrival there. This day one of my men went into the woods and lost himself.

8th. At daybreak we were attacked by a party of Indians, consisting of eighty warriors of the Kiccapoos [Kickapoo] and Musquattimes, who killed two of my men and three Indians, wounded myself and all the rest of my party, except two white men and one Indian; then made myself and all the white men prisoners, plundering us of everything we had. A deputy of the Shawnesse who was shot through the thigh, hav-

ing concealed himself in the woods for a few minutes after he was wounded — not knowing but they were southern Indians, who are always at war with the northward Indians — after discovering what nation they were, came up to them and made a very bold speech, telling them that the whole northward Indians would join in taking revenge for the insult and murder of their people; this alarmed those savages very much, who began excusing themselves, saying their fathers, the French, had spirited them up, telling them that the Indians were coming with a body of southern Indians to take their country from them, and enslave them; that it was this that induced them to commit this outrage. After dividing the plunder, (they left great part of the heaviest effects behind, not being able to carry them) they set off with us to their village at Ouattonon, in a great hurry, being in dread of a pursuit from a large party of Indians they suspected were coming after me. Our course was through a thick woody country, crossing a great many swamps, morasses, and beaver ponds. We traveled this day about forty-two miles.

9th. An hour before day we set out on our march; passed through thick woods, some highlands, and small savannas, badly watered. Traveled this day about thirty miles.

10th. We set out very early in the morning, and marched through a high country, extremely well timbered, for three hours; then came to a branch of the Ouabache, which we crossed. The remainder of this day we traveled through fine rich bottoms, overgrown with reeds, which make the best pasture in the world, the young reeds being preferable to sheaf oats. Here is great plenty of wild game of all kinds. Came this day about twenty-eight, or thirty miles.

11th. At daybreak we set off, making our way through a thin woodland, interspersed with savannas. I suffered extremely by reason of the excessive heat of the weather, and scarcity of water; the little springs and runs being dried up. Traveled this day about thirty miles.

12th. We passed through some large savannas, and clear woods; in the afternoon we came to the Ouabache; then marched along it through a prodigious rich bottom, overgrown with reeds and wild hemp; all this bottom is well watered, and an exceeding fine hunting ground. Came this day about thirty miles.

13th. About an hour before day we set out; traveled through such bottoms as of yesterday, and through some large meadows, where no trees, for several miles together, are to be seen. Buffaloes, deer, and bears are here in great plenty. We traveled about twenty-six miles this day.

14th. The country we traveled through this day appears the same as described yesterday, excepting this afternoon's journey through woodland, to cut off a bend of the river. Came about twenty-seven miles this day.

15th. We set out very early, and about 1 o'clock came to the Ouabache, within six or seven miles of Port Vincent [Vincennes]. On my arrival there, I found a village of about eighty or ninety French families settled on the east side of this river, being one of the finest situations that can be found. The country is level and clear, and the soil very rich, producing wheat and tobacco. I think the latter preferable to that of Maryland or Virginia. The French inhabitants hereabouts are an idle, lazy people, a parcel of renegades from Canada, and are much worse than the Indians. They took a secret pleasure at our misfortunes, and the moment we arrived, they came to the Indians, exchanging trifles for their valuable plunder. As the savages took from me a considerable quantity of gold and silver in specie, the French traders extorted ten half johannes from them for one pound of vermilion. Here is likewise an Indian village of the Pyankeshaws [Piankashaw], who were

much displeased with the party that took me, telling them that "our and your chiefs are gone to make peace, and you have begun a war, for which our women and children will have reason to cry."

From this post the Indians permitted me to write to the commander at Fort Chartres, but would not suffer me to write to anybody else (this I apprehend was a precaution of the French, lest their villainy should be perceived too soon), although the Indians had given me permission to write to Sir William Johnson and Fort Pitt on our march, before we arrived at this place. But immediately after our arrival they had a private council with the French, in which the Indians urged (as they afterward informed me) that, as the French had engaged them in so bad an affair, which was likely to bring a war on their nation, they now expected a proof of their promise and assistance. Then delivered the French a scalp and part of the plunder, and wanted to deliver some presents to the Pyankeshaws, but they refused to accept of any, and declared they would not be concerned in the affair. This last information I got from the Pyankeshaws, as I had been well acquainted with them several years before this time.

Port Vincent is a place of great consequence for trade, being a fine hunting country all along the Ouabache, and too far for the Indians, which reside hereabouts, to go either to the Illinois, or elsewhere, to fetch their necessaries.

16th. We were obliged to stay here to get some little apparel made up for us, and to buy some horses for our journey to Ouicatonon, promising payment at Detroit, for we could not procure horses from the French for hire; though we were greatly fatigued, and our spirits much exhausted in our late march, they would lend us no assistance.

17th. At midday we set out; traveling the first five miles through a fine thick wood.

We traveled eighteen miles this day, and encamped in a large, beautiful, well-watered meadow.

18th and *19th*. We traveled through a prodigious large meadow, called the Pyankeshaw's Hunting Ground; here is no wood to be seen, and the country appears like an ocean; the ground is exceedingly rich, and partly overgrown with wild hemp; the land, well watered, and full of buffalo, deer, bears, and all kinds of wild game.

20th and *21st*. We passed through some very large meadows, part of which belong to the Pyankeshaws on Vermilion River; the country and soil much the same as that we traveled over for these three days past, wild hemp grows here in abundance; the game very plenty: at any time, in half an hour, we could kill as much as we wanted.

22nd. We passed through part of the same meadow as mentioned yesterday; then came to a high woodland, and arrived at Vermilion River, so called from a fine red earth found here by the Indians, with which they paint themselves. About half a mile from the place where we crossed this river, there is a village of Pyankeshaws, distinguished by the addition of the name of the river. We then traveled about three hours, through a clear high woody country, but a deep and rich soil; then came to a meadow, where we encamped.

23rd. Early in the morning we set out through a fine meadow, then some clear woods; in the afternoon came into a very large bottom on the Ouabache, within six miles of Ouicatonon; here I met several chiefs of the Kiccapoos and Musquattimes, who spoke to their young men who had taken us, and reprimanded them severely for what they had done to me, after which they returned with us to their village, and delivered us all to their chiefs.

The distance from Port Vincent to Ouicatonon is 210 miles. This place is situated on the Ouabache. About fourteen French families are living in the fort, which stands on the north side of the river. The Kiccapoos and Musquattimes, whose warriors had taken us, live nigh the fort, on the same side of the river, where they have two villages; and the Ouicatonons have a village on the south side of the river. At our arrival at this post, several of the Wawcottonans (or Ouicatonons), with whom I had been formerly acquainted, came to visit me, and seemed greatly concerned at what had happened. They went immediately to the Kiccapoos and Musquattimes, and charged them to take the greatest care of us, till their chiefs should arrive from the Illinois, where they were gone to meet me some time ago, and who were entirely ignorant of this affair, and said the French had spirited up this party to go and strike us.

The French have a great influence over these Indians, and never fail in telling them many lies to the prejudice of His Majesty's interest, by making the English nation odious and hateful to them. I had the greatest difficulties in removing these prejudices. As these Indians are a weak, foolish, and credulous people, they are easily imposed on by a designing people, who have led them hitherto as they pleased. The French told them that as the southern Indians had for two years past made war on them, it must have been at the instigation of the English, who are a bad people. However, I have been fortunate enough to remove their prejudice, and, in a great measure, their suspicions against the English. The country hereabouts is exceedingly pleasant, being open and clear for many miles; the soil very rich and well watered; all plants have a quick vegetation, and the climate very temperate through the winter. This post has always been a very considerable trading place. The great plenty of furs taken in this country induced the French to establish this post, which was the first on the Ouabache, and by a very advantageous trade they have been richly recompensed for their labor.

On the south side of the Ouabache runs a

big bank, in which are several fine coal mines, and behind this bank is a very large meadow, clear for several miles. It is surprising what false information we have had respecting this country; some mention these spacious and beautiful meadows as large and barren savannas. I apprehend it has been the artifice of the French to keep us ignorant of the country. These meadows bear fine wild grass, and wild hemp ten or twelve feet high, which, if properly manufactured, would prove as good, and answer all the purposes of the hemp we cultivate.

July 25. We set out from this place (after settling all matters happily with the natives) for the Miami, and traveled the whole way through a fine rich bottom, overgrown with wild hemp, alongside the Ouabache, till we came to Eel River, where we arrived the 27th. About six miles up this river is a small village of the Twightwee, situated on a very delightful spot of ground on the bank of the river. The Eel River heads near St. Joseph's, and runs nearly parallel to the Miami, and at some few miles distance from it, through a fine, pleasant country, and after a course of about 180 miles empties itself into the Ouabache.

28th, 29th, 30th, and 31st. We traveled still alongside the Eel River, passing through fine clear woods, and some good meadows, though not so large as those we passed some days before. The country is more overgrown with woods, the soil is sufficiently rich, and well watered with springs.

August 1. We arrived at the carrying place between the Miami River and Ouabache, which is about nine miles long in dry seasons, but not above half that length in freshets. The head of the Ouabache is about 40 miles from this place, and after a course of about 760 miles from the head spring, through one of the finest countries in the world, it empties itself into the Ohio. The navigation from hence to Ouicatonon, is very difficult in low water, on account of

many rapids and rifts; but in freshets, which generally happen in the spring and fall, batteaux or canoes will pass, without difficulty, from here to Ouicatonon in three days, which is about 240 miles, and by land about 210 miles. From Ouicatonon to Port Vincent, and thence to the Ohio, batteaux and canoes may go at any season of the year. Throughout the whole course of the Ouabache the banks are pretty high, and in the river are a great many islands. Many shrubs and trees are found here unknown to us.

Within a mile of the Twightwee village, I was met by the chiefs of that nation, who received us very kindly. The most part of these Indians knew me, and conducted me to their village, where they immediately hoisted an English flag that I had formerly given them at Fort Pitt. The next day they held a council, after which they gave me up all the English prisoners they had, then made several speeches, in all which they expressed the great pleasure it gave them, to see the unhappy differences which embroiled the several nations in a war with their brethren, the English, were now so near a happy conclusion, and that peace was established in their country.

The Twightwee village is situated on both sides of a river called St. Joseph. This river, where it falls into the Miami River, about a quarter of a mile from this place, is one hundred yards wide, on the east side of which stands a stockade fort, somewhat ruinous.

The Indian village consists of about forty or fifty cabins, besides nine or ten French houses — a runaway colony from Detroit during the late Indian war; they were concerned in it, and being afraid of punishment, came to this post, where ever since they have spirited up the Indians against the English. All the French residing here are a lazy, indolent people, fond of breeding mischief, and spiriting up the Indians against the English, and should by no means be suffered to remain here. The country is pleasant, the soil rich and well watered. After several conferences with these Indians, [they delivered to me] all the English prisoners they had.

On the 6th of August we set out for Detroit, down the Miami River in a canoe. This river heads about ten miles from hence. The river is not navigable till you come to the place where the St. Joseph River joins it, and makes a considerably large stream. Nevertheless we found a great deal of difficulty in getting our canoe over shoals, as the waters at this season were very low. The banks of the river are high, and the country overgrown with lofty timber of various kinds; the land is level, and the woods clear. About ninety miles from the Miami or Twightwee, we came to where a large river, that heads in a large lick, falls into the Miami River; this they call the Forks. The Ottawa claim this country, and hunt here, where game is very plenty. From hence we proceeded to the Ottawa village. This nation formerly lived at Detroit, but is now settled here, on account of the richness of the country, where game is always to be found in plenty.

Here we were obliged to get out of our canoes, and drag them eighteen miles, on account of the rifts which interrupt the navigation. At the end of these rifts, we came to a village of the Wyondotts [Wyandotte], who received us very kindly, and from thence we proceeded to the mouth of this river, where it falls into Lake Erie. From the Miami to the lake is computed 180 miles, and from the entrance of the river into the lake to Detroit, is 60 miles; that is, 42 miles upon the lake, and 18 miles up the Detroit River to the garrison of that name. The land on the lake side is low and flat. We passed several large rivers and bays, and on the 16th of August, in the afternoon, we arrived at Detroit River. The country here is much higher than on the lake side; the river is about 900 yards wide, and the current runs very strong. There are several fine and large islands in this river, one of which is nine miles long; its banks high, and the soil very good.

17th. In the morning we arrived at the fort, which is a large stockade enclosing about eighty houses; it stands close on the north side of the river, on a high bank, commands a very pleasant prospect for nine miles above and nine miles below the fort; the country is thick settled with French; their plantations are generally laid out about three or four acres in breadth on the river, and eighty acres in depth; the soil is good, producing plenty of grain. All the people here are generally poor wretches, and consist of three or four hundred French families, a lazy, idle people, depending chiefly on the savages for their subsistence; though the land, with little labor, produces plenty of grain, they scarcely raise as much as will supply their wants, in imitation of the Indians, whose manners and customs they have entirely adopted, and cannot subsist without them. The men, women, and children speak the Indian tongue perfectly well.

In the last Indian war the most part of the French were concerned in it (although the whole settlement had taken the oath of allegiance to His Britannic Majesty); they have, therefore, great reason to be thankful to the English clemency in not bringing them to deserved punishment. Before the late Indian war there resided three nations of Indians at this place: the Putawatimes [Potawatomi], whose village was on the west side of the river, about one mile below the fort; the Ottawa, on the east side, about three miles above the fort; and the Wyondotts, whose village lies on the east side, about two miles below the fort. The former two nations have removed to a considerable distance, and the latter still remain where they were, and are remarkable for their good sense and hospitality. They have a particular attachment to the Roman Catholic religion, the French, by their priests, having taken uncommon pains to instruct them.

During my stay here, I held frequent conferences with the different nations of Indians assembled at this place, with whom I settled matters to their general satisfaction.

September 26. Set out from Detroit for Niagara; passed Lake Erie along the north shore in a birch canoe, and arrived the 8th of October at Niagara. The navigation of the lake is dangerous for batteaux or canoes, by reason the lake is very shallow for a considerable distance from the shore. The bank, for several miles, high and steep, and affords a harbor for a single batteau. The lands in general, between Detroit and Niagara, are high, and the soil good, with several fine rivers falling into the lake. The distance from Detroit to Niagara is computed 300 miles.

25.

The Stamp Act

The Stamp Act that was passed in Parliament on March 22, 1765, seriously preempted the colonial governments' power of the purse. The act imposed taxes and required the affixing of stamps as evidence of payment on all documents, newspapers, etc., issued in the American colonies. The stamps ranged in cost from a halfpenny to ten pounds. Although all the colonies protested the proposed stamp tax, they could not or would not suggest another method of raising the needed revenue. John Adams called the Stamp Act "that enormous engine fabricated by the British Parliament, for battering down all the rights and liberties of America." The colonial response to the Stamp Act initiated the revolutionary activity that eventually led to the separation from England.

Source: Pickering, XXVI.

An act for granting and applying certain stamp duties, and other duties, in the British colonies and plantations in America, toward further defraying the expenses of defending, protecting, and securing the same; and for amending such parts of the several acts of Parliament relating to the trade and revenues of the said colonies and plantations, as direct the manner of determining and recovering the penalties and forfeitures therein mentioned.

Whereas, by an act made in the last session of Parliament, several duties were granted, continued, and appropriated toward defraying the expenses of defending, protecting, and securing the British colonies and plantations in America: *And whereas* it is just and necessary that provision be made for raising a further revenue within Your Majesty's dominions in America toward defraying the said expenses: We, Your Majesty's most dutiful and loyal subjects, the Commons of Great Britain in Parliament assembled, have therefore resolved to give and grant unto Your Majesty the several rates and duties hereinafter mentioned; and do most humbly beseech Your Majesty that it may be enacted, and be it enacted by the King's most excellent majesty, by and with the advice and consent of the Lords spiritual and temporal, and Commons, in this present Parliament assembled, and by the authority of the same, that from and after the 1st day of November, 1765, there shall be raised, levied, collected, and paid unto His Majesty, His Heirs, and Successors, throughout the colonies and plantations in America which now are, or hereafter may be, under the dominion of His Majesty, His Heirs, and Successors.

For every skin or piece of vellum or parchment, or sheet or piece of paper, on which shall be engrossed, written, or printed any declaration, plea, replication, rejoinder, demurrer, or other pleading, or any copy thereof, in any court of law within the British colonies and plantations in America, a stamp duty of 3d.

For every skin . . . on which shall be engrossed, written, or printed any special bail and appearance upon such bail in any such court, a stamp duty of 2s.

For every skin . . . on which shall be engrossed, written, or printed any petition, bill, answer, claim, plea, replication, rejoinder, demurrer, or other pleading in any Court of Chancery or Equity within the said colonies and plantations, a stamp duty of 1s. 6d.

For every skin . . . on which shall be engrossed, written, or printed any copy of any petition, bill, answer, claim, plea, replication, rejoinder, demurrer, .or other pleading in any such court, a stamp duty of 3d. . . .

For every skin . . . on which shall be engrossed, written, or printed any license, appointment, or admission of any counselor, solicitor, attorney, advocate, or proctor to practise in any court, or of any notary within the said colonies and plantations, a stamp duty of £10.

For every skin . . . on which shall be en-

grossed, written, or printed any note or bill of lading which shall be signed for any kind of goods, wares, or merchandise to be exported from, or any cocket or clearance granted within, the said colonies and plantations, a stamp duty of 4d.

For every skin . . . on which shall be engrossed, written, or printed letters of mart, or commission for private ships of war, within the said colonies and plantations, a stamp duty of 20s.

For every skin . . . on which shall be engrossed, written, or printed any grant, appointment, or admission of or to any public beneficial office or employment, for the space of one year, or any lesser time, of or above the value of £20 per annum sterling money, in salary, fees, and perquisites, within the said colonies and plantations (except commissions and appointments of officers of the Army, Navy, Ordnance, or Militia, of judges, and of justices of the peace), a stamp duty of 10s.

For every skin . . . on which any grant of any liberty, privilege, or franchise, under the seal of any of the said colonies or plantations, or under the seal or sign manual of any governor, proprietor, or public officer alone, or in conjunction with any other person or persons, or with any council, or any council and assembly, or any exemplification of the same, shall be engrossed, written, or printed, within the said colonies and plantations, a stamp duty of £6.

For every skin . . . on which shall be engrossed, written, or printed any license for retailing of spirituous liquors, to be granted to any person who shall take out the same, within the said colonies and plantations, a stamp duty of 20s. . . .

For every skin . . . on which shall be engrossed, written, or printed any probate of a will, letters of administration, or of guardianship for any estate above the value of £20 sterling money, within the British colonies and plantations upon the continent of America, the islands belonging thereto, and the Bermuda and Bahama islands, a stamp duty of 5s. . . .

For every skin . . . on which shall be engrossed, written, or printed any such order or warrant for surveying or setting out any quantity of land above 200 and not exceeding 320 acres, and in proportion for every such order or warrant for surveying or setting out every other 320 acres, within the said colonies and plantations, a stamp duty of 1s. 6d. . . .

For every skin . . . on which shall be engrossed, written, or printed any grant, appointment, or admission of or to any public beneficial office or employment, not hereinbefore charged, above the value of £ 20 per annum sterling money in salary, fees, and perquisites, or any exemplification of the same, within the British colonies and plantations upon the continent of America, the islands belonging thereto, and the Bermuda and Bahama islands (except commissions of officers of the Army, Navy, Ordnance, or Militia, and of justices of the peace), a stamp duty of £4. . . .

For every skin . . . on which shall be engrossed, written, or printed any register, entry, or enrollment of any grant, deed, or other instrument whatsoever hereinbefore charged, within the said colonies and plantations, a stamp duty of 3d. . . .

And for and upon every pack of playing cards, and all dice, which shall be sold or used within the said colonies and plantations, the several stamp duties following (that is to say):

For every pack of such cards, the sum of 1s.

And for every pair of such dice, the sum of 10s.

And for and upon every paper, commonly called a pamphlet, and upon every newspaper containing public news, intelligence, or occurrences, which shall be printed, dispersed, and made public within any of the said colonies and plantations, and for and upon such advertisements as are hereinafter mentioned, the respective duties following (that is to say):

For every such pamphlet and paper contained in half a sheet, or any lesser piece of paper which shall be so printed, a stamp duty of one halfpenny for every printed copy thereof.

For every such pamphlet and paper (being larger than half a sheet, and not exceeding one whole sheet) which shall be so printed, a stamp duty of one penny for every printed copy thereof.

For every pamphlet and paper being larger than one whole sheet, and not exceeding six sheets in octavo, or in a lesser page, or not exceeding twelve sheets in quarto, or twenty sheets in folio which shall be so printed, a duty after the rate of 1s. for every sheet of any kind of paper which shall be contained in one printed copy thereof.

For every advertisement to be contained in any gazette, newspaper, or other paper, or any pamphlet which shall be so printed, a duty of 2s.

For every almanac or calendar for any one particular year, or for any time less than a year, which shall be written or printed on one side only of any one sheet, skin, or piece of paper, parchment, or vellum, within the said colonies and plantations, a stamp duty of 2d.

For every other almanac or calendar for any one particular year, which shall be written or printed within the said colonies and plantations, a stamp duty of 4d.

And for every almanac or calendar, written or printed within the said colonies and plantations, to serve for several years, duties to the same amount respectively shall be paid for every such year.

For every skin . . . on which any instrument, proceeding, or other matter or thing aforesaid shall be engrossed, written, or printed, within the said colonies and plantations, in any other than the English language, a stamp duty of double the amount of the respective duties before charged thereon.

And there shall be also paid in the said colonies and plantations, a duty of 6d. for every 20s., in any sum not exceeding £50 sterling money, which shall be given, paid, contracted, or agreed for, with or in relation to any clerk or apprentice, which shall be put or placed to or with any master or mistress to learn any profession, trade, or employment.

And also a duty of 1s. for every 20s. in any sum exceeding £50, which shall be given, paid, contracted, or agreed for, with or in relation to any such clerk or apprentice. . . .

And be it further enacted by the authority aforesaid that every deed, instrument, note, memorandum, letter, or other minument or writing between the captain or master or owner of any ship or vessel and any merchant, trader, or other person, in respect to the freight or conveyance of any money, goods, wares, merchandises, or effects, laden or to be laden on board of any such ship or vessel, shall be deemed and adjudged to be a charter party within the meaning of this act.

And be it further enacted by the authority aforesaid that all books and pamphlets serving chiefly for the purpose of an almanac, by whatsoever name or names entitled or described, are and shall be charged with the duty imposed by this act on almanacs, but not with any of the duties charged by this act on pamphlets, or other printed papers anything herein contained to the contrary notwithstanding.

Provided always that this act shall not extend to charge any bills of exchange, accompts, bills of parcels, bills of fees, or any bills or notes not sealed for payment of money at sight, or upon demand, or at the end of certain days of payment. . . .

And be it further enacted by the authority aforesaid that the said several duties shall be under the management of the commission-

ers, for the time being, of the duties charged on stamped vellum, parchment, and paper, in Great Britain; and the said commissioners are hereby empowered and required to employ such officers under them, for that purpose, as they shall think proper; and to use such stamps and marks to denote the stamp duties hereby charged as they shall think fit; and to repair, renew, or alter the same, from time to time, as there shall be occasion; and to do all other acts, matters, and things necessary to be done for putting this act in execution with relation to the duties hereby charged. . . .

And every commissioner and other officer, before he proceeds to the execution of any part of this act, shall take an oath in the words, or to the effect following (that is to say):

I . . . do swear that I will faithfully execute the trust reposed in me, pursuant to an act of Parliament made in the fifth year of the reign of His Majesty King George the Third, for granting certain stamp duties, and other duties, in the British colonies and plantations in America, without fraud or concealment; and will from time to time true account make of my doing therein, and deliver the same to such person or persons as His Majesty, His Heirs, or Successors shall appoint to receive such account; and will take no fee, reward, or profit for the execution or performance of the said trust, or the business relating thereto, from any person or persons, other than such as shall be allowed by His Majesty, His Heirs, and Successors, or by some other person or persons under him or them to that purpose authorized. . . .

And be it further enacted by the authority aforesaid that, if any person or persons shall sign . . . in any of the said colonies or plantations, or in any other part of His Majesty's dominions, any matter or thing for which the vellum, parchment, or paper is hereby charged to pay any duty, before the same shall be marked or stamped with the marks or stamps to be provided as aforesaid, or upon which there shall not be some stamp or mark resembling the same; or shall sign . . . any matter or thing upon any vellum, parchment, or paper that shall be marked or stamped for any lower duty than the duty by this act made payable in respect thereof; every such person so offending shall, for every such offense, forfeit the sum of £ 10. . . .

And be it further enacted by the authority aforesaid that if any person shall forge, counterfeit, erase, or alter any such certificate, every such person so offending shall be guilty of felony, and shall suffer death as in cases of felony without the benefit of clergy. . . .

And be it further enacted by the authority aforesaid that all the monies which shall arise by the several rates and duties hereby granted (except the necessary charges of raising, collecting, recovering, answering, paying, and accounting for the same, and the necessary charges from time to time incurred in relation to this act and the execution thereof) shall be paid into the receipt of His Majesty's Exchequer, and shall be entered separate and apart from all other monies, and shall be there reserved to be, from time to time, disposed of by Parliament, toward further defraying the necessary expenses of defending, protecting, and securing the said colonies and plantations. . . .

And it is hereby further enacted and declared that all the powers and authorities by this act granted to the commissioners for managing the duties upon stamped vellum, parchment, and paper shall and may be fully and effectually carried into execution by any three or more of the said commissioners; anything hereinbefore contained to the contrary notwithstanding.

And be it further enacted by the authority aforesaid that all forfeitures and penalties incurred after the 29th day of September, 1765, for offenses committed against an act passed in the fourth year of the reign of His present Majesty, entitled "An act for granting certain duties in the British colonies and plantations in America . . ." and for offenses committed against any other act or acts of Parliament relating to the trade or revenues of the said colonies or plantations, shall and may be prosecuted, sued for, and recovered in any court of record, or in any Court of Admiralty, in the respective colony or plantation where the offense shall be committed, or in any Court of Vice-Admiralty appointed or to be appointed, and which shall have jurisdiction within such colony, plantation, or place (which Courts of Admiralty or Vice-Admiralty are hereby respectively authorized and required to proceed, hear, and determine the same) at the election of the informer or prosecutor. . . .

And be it further enacted by the authority aforesaid that all the offenses which are by this act made felony, and shall be committed within any part of His Majesty's dominions, shall and may be heard, tried, and determined before any court of law within the respective kingdom, territory, colony, or plantation where the offense shall be committed, in such and the same manner as all other felonies can or may be heard, tried, and determined in such court.

Taxation without representation is tyranny.
JAMES OTIS, 1765

26.

Virginia Stamp Act Resolutions

Patrick Henry, at a meeting of the Virginia House of Burgesses, proposed seven resolutions against the Stamp Act. While only four were adopted, on May 30, 1765, all seven proposed Virginia resolves were printed in the newspapers of many of the colonies, providing a basis for popular opposition to the Stamp Act.

Source: *Journals of the House of Burgesses of Virginia 1761-1765,*
John Pendleton Kennedy, ed., Richmond, 1907.

Resolved, that the first adventurers and settlers of this His Majesty's colony and dominion of Virginia brought with them and transmitted to their posterity, and all other His Majesty's subjects since inhabiting in this His Majesty's said colony, all the liberties, privileges, franchises, and immunities that have at any time been held, enjoyed, and possessed by the people of Great Britain.

Resolved, that by two royal charters, granted by King James I, the colonists aforesaid are declared entitled to all liberties, privileges, and immunities of denizens and natural subjects to all intents and purposes as if they had been abiding and born within the Realm of England.

Resolved, that the taxation of the people by themselves, or by persons chosen by themselves to represent them, who can only know what taxes the people are able to bear, or the easiest method of raising them, and must themselves be affected by every tax laid on the people, is the only security against a burdensome taxation, and the distinguishing characteristic of British freedom, without which the ancient constitution cannot exist.

Resolved, that His Majesty's liege people of this his most ancient and loyal colony have without interruption enjoyed the inestimable right of being governed by such laws, respecting their internal polity and taxation, as are derived from their own consent, with the approbation of their sovereign, or his substitute; and that the same has never been forfeited or yielded up, but has been constantly recognized by the kings and people of Great Britain.

Caesar had his Brutus, Charles the First had his Cromwell, and George the Third ["*Treason!*" *cried the Speaker*] — *may profit by their example. If this be treason, make the most of it.*

PATRICK HENRY, speech in the House of Burgesses, Williamsburg, Virginia, May 29, 1765

27.

Francis Bernard: Boston Stamp Act Riots

Colonial resistance to the new British imperial policies was directed particularly toward the Stamp Act. The reaction of the colonies to its passage was vehement. In Boston, a radical group called the Sons of Liberty destroyed the stamps wherever they found them, tarred and feathered the stamp agents, and sacked the homes and warehouses of the rich, who could be presumed to be favorites of the royal governors. The following account of the riots by Francis Bernard, governor of Massachusetts, was prepared for the Earl of Halifax on August 31, 1765.

Source: *British Public Record Office, C.O. 5/755.*

It is with the utmost concern that I am obliged to continue the subject of my last letters of the 15th and 16th and of the 22nd instant; the disorders of the town having been carried to much greater lengths than what I have before informed Your Lordship of.

After the demolition of Mr. Oliver's house was found so practicable and easy that the government was obliged to look on without being able to take any one step to prevent it, and the principal people of the town publicly avowed and justified the act, the mob, both great and small, became highly elated, and all kinds of ill humors were set on float. Everything that for years past had been the cause of any popular discontent was revived and private resentments against persons in office worked themselves in and endeavored to execute themselves under the mask of the public cause. Among others the affairs of the attack upon the Admiralty and Custom House above four years ago (which after a contestation of a year by the steadiness and resolution of myself I may truly say, and the other officers of the Crown, ended entirely in conclusions on the side of the Crown) was brought up again and became as fresh as if it had been a business of yesterday. One B—— H—— of this town, who was in London about two years ago, had got a sight of the depositions which were sent home on the behalf of the Crown. Upon his return to Boston he took upon him to report the substance of these with additions of his own, and concluded with an assertion that the whole body of merchants had been represented as smugglers. This occasioned some murmuring at that time but it soon passed over.

All this story has been now revived with fresh circumstances of acrimony and inflammation, and a diligent pointing out the persons who in the former contest had acted on the side of the Crown, and H——, instead of telling his story verbally, reduced it into writing, which was handed about the town. This occasioned much clamor among some of the merchants who were told, without the least foundation in truth, that they were represented at home by name; and the clamor, as usual, soon descended from the top to the bottom of the town, and several persons' houses began to be threatened. This was truly the principal if not the sole cause of the second insurrection, which has had such shocking effects.

On Monday, August 26, there was some small rumor that mischief would be done that night, but it was in general disregarded. Toward evening some boys began to light a bonfire before the Town House, which is a usual signal for a mob. Before it was quite dark a great company of people gathered together crying liberty and property, which is the usual notice of their intention to plunder and pull down a house. They first went to Mr. Paxton's house (who is marshal of the Court of Admiralty and surveyor of the port), and finding before it the owner of the house (Mr. Paxton being only a tenant), he assured them that Mr. Paxton had quitted the house with his best effects; that the house was his; that he had never injured them, and finally invited them to go to the tavern and drink a barrel of punch. The offer was accepted and so that house was saved. As soon as they had drunk the punch, they went to the house of Mr. Story, registrar deputed of the Admiralty, broke into it and tore it all to pieces; and took out all the books and papers, among which were all the records of the Court of Admiralty, and carried them to the bonfire and there burned them. They also looked about for him with an intention to kill him. From thence they went to Mr. Hallowell's, comptroller of the customs, broke into his house and destroyed and carried off everything of value, with about £30 sterling in cash. This house was lately built by himself and fitted and furnished with great elegance. But the grand mischief of all was to come.

The lieutenant governor had been apprised that there was an evil spirit gone forth against him, but being conscious that he had not in the least deserved to be made a party in regard to the Stamp Act or the Custom House, he rested in full security that the mob would not attack him, and he was at supper with his family when he received advice that the mob were coming to him. He immediately sent away his children and determined to stay in the house himself, but happily his eldest daughter returned and declared she would not stir from the house unless he went with her; by which means she got him away, which was undoubtedly the occasion of saving his life. For as soon as the mob had got into the house, with a most irresistible fury they immediately looked about for him to murder him, and even made diligent inquiry whither he was gone. They went to work with a rage scarce to be exemplified by the most savage people. Everything movable was destroyed in the most minute manner except such things of value as were worth carrying off, among which was near £1,000 sterling in specie, besides a great quantity of family plate, etc.

But the loss to be most lamented is that there was in one room kept for that purpose a large and valuable collection of manuscripts and original papers which he had been gathering all his lifetime, and to which all persons who had been in possession of valuable papers of a public kind had been contributing as to a public museum. As these related to the history and policy of the country from the time of its settlement to the present and was the only collection of its kind, the loss to the public is great and irretrievable as it is to himself, the loss of the papers of a family which had made a figure in this province for 130 years.

As for the house, which from its structure and inside finishing seemed to be from a design of Inigo Jones or his successor, it appears that they were a long while resolved to level to the ground. They worked for three hours at the cupola before they could get it down, and they uncovered part of the roof; but I suppose that the thickness of the walls which were of very fine brickwork, adorned with Ionic pilasters worked into the wall, prevented their completing their purpose though they worked at it till daylight. The next day the streets were found scattered with money, plate, gold rings, etc., which had been dropped in carrying off. The whole loss in this house only is reckoned at £3,000 sterling.

As soon as I received advice of this at the Castle, I immediately sent an order to the secretary to summon a Council at Cambridge early in the afternoon, not thinking Boston a safe place to sit at. As I was going thither, on the road I received a letter from the secretary desiring that I would hold the Council in Boston; for that this affair had given such a turn to the town that all the gentlemen in the place were ready to support the government in detecting and punishing the actors in the last horrid scene, and there was a town meeting appointed to testify their abhorrence of it. I accordingly went to the Council and there issued orders to the colonel of the regiment of militia, the captain of the company of cadet guards, the captains of the batteries and of the companies of militia in Charles Town, Cambridge, and Roxbury to raise their several corps and make detachments therefrom to keep a constant guard. And I recommended to the gentlemen of the town who were excused from military duty to enroll themselves as volunteers in some of the corps, many of which did, especially in the cadets, which were doubled upon this occasion; to whom I assigned the guard of the Custom House where there were several thousand pounds of the King's money.

And these measures were but just taken in time for otherwise a much greater mischief would have happened the second night than the former. For, it seems, the mob had set down no less than fifteen houses in or near the town to be attacked the next night, among which was the Custom House and the houses of some of the most respectable persons in the government. It was now becoming a war of plunder, of general leveling and taking away the distinction of rich and poor so that those gentlemen who had promoted and approved the cruel treatment of Mr. Oliver became now as fearful for themselves as the most loyal person in the town could be. They found, as I told some of them, that they had raised the devil and could not lay him again. However, by means of the military guards the town was kept quiet that night without anything happening except that the cadets were obliged once to present their pieces, but did not fire.

After I had established these guards, which took up all that day, I considered whether it would not be proper to call in assistance from without. By an instruction I am directed to have the advice of Council whenever I call for military aid. I knew that the Council would never advise me to call in the King's troops in cases more desperate than this. Their own situation and dependence would make them afraid of being answerable to the people for so disagreeable a step. I therefore put the question whether it was expedient to advertise General Gage and Lord Colville of what had happened at Boston. But they advised in the negative, saying that such advertisement would amount to a tacit request for forces; and though they expected such forces would be ordered hither some time or other, they would not help to bring them here nor hasten them before their time.

I therefore transmitted to General Gage a copy of this resolution of Council, copies of my proclamations, with advice of the intention of lodging the stamps in the Castle, and augmenting the garrison for that purpose; from all which he will see the restraints I am under. I then acquainted the Council with the various reports I had heard of the Castle being threatened if the stamps were put in there, represented the present state of garrison, and proposed that an independent company should be raised for augmenting the garrison, which they readily came into, and I immediately dispatched orders for that purpose. I am also by all means in my power strengthening the Castle so that if I can get the reinforcement here in time, I shan't be afraid for the Castle against any number, though I cannot think that any people will be desperate enough to attack it, notwithstanding what has been given out.

When first the town took this new turn, I was in hopes that they would have disavowed all the riotous proceedings, that of the first night as well as the last. But it is no such thing: great pains are taken to separate the two riots; what was done against Mr. Oliver is still approved of as a necessary declaration of their resolution not to submit to the Stamp Act; and even the cruel treatment of him and his family is justified by its consequences — the frightening him into a resignation. And it has been publicly hinted that if a line is not drawn between the first riot and the last, the civil power will not be supported by the principal people of the town, as it is assured it shall be now. And indeed, if the last riot had been the only one, the civil government would appear to be in full power. Many people concerned in the last riot are daily taken up and committed to jail, where a constant guard is kept by the militia, and the town cries aloud for some of them to be made examples of. And yet if one was to offer to take one of the persons concerned in the first riot only, things would again be flung into confusion and the civil power would become as weak as ever. So that the present authority of the government is only exercised upon condition and with prescribed limitations.

It seems therefore that the horror of this last affair has not at all abated the spirit of the people against the Stamp Act. I am again and again assured that this town and country about it (how far deep I can't say) are as resolute as ever to oppose the execution of the Stamp Act and to suffer the utmost extremities rather than submit to it. There are but two things which are like to produce a change in these resolutions: the one is a nearer and fuller prospect of the anarchy and confusion which must take place when the courts of justice and public offices are shut up, as they must be on November 1 unless stamps are allowed to be used. These must necessarily alarm all serious people and especially those who have much property. The other is the meeting of the Assembly, which I believe I shall be obliged to call at the time it is prorogued to, September 25, though I could have wished that it might have been postponed till I could have received orders from England.

I should have much dependence upon the prudence of the Assembly in common cases, but I know not how to expect that they will act against the voice of the people, if it is such as I am told it is. On the other hand, they must be greatly staggered when they are called upon to assist the execution of an act of Parliament which is opposed by violence. Hitherto the opposition is chargeable upon private persons only; it will then be adopted by the legislature, and if that should fail in so important a duty, they must expect that a forfeiture of their rights will be the consequence. If these two causes — the apprehension of confusion when all business shall cease, and the prudence, or what is the same, the fear of the Assembly — should cooperate together, it is possible that the act may be yet carried into execution at its day. I shall watch every opportunity and improve every incident to produce so happy an event.

I labor under many difficulties, and none more than that the Council, which I have to advise with, is composed almost wholly of gentlemen whose connections and properties are in Boston. They that live out of

Boston will not come in; I have but two or three such since the last riot and I have known some that have been afraid to come to Boston. By these means nothing can pass the Council that is likely to be displeasing to Boston; expedients are thereby rendered very few and spirited measures are quite impracticable. I submitted to the Council whether it would not be best to call the Assembly at a distance from Boston, that it might sit free from intimidation or undue influence: it passed in the negative. I then asked if I should call a general council by summoning every member to meet at Cambridge, and I urged that several members, naming them, objected to coming to Boston: it passed in the negative. I then proposed calling such general council at Boston, which was approved of, and it is appointed for Thursday next, September 5. It is true that I can without advice of Council call the Assembly and the Council to what place I please, but it is the business of the Council, among other things, to guard the governor against popular odium from his taking unpopular measures necessary to government by concurring with him and advising such measures; and when they refuse so to do, it would be dangerous as well

as impolitic for the governor to expose himself solely to the resentment of the people by acting without or contrary to the advice of Council.

I must, however, add that it is become now much safer to meet at Boston than it was a week ago. The town is now become as quiet as ever it was, and the principal gentlemen have desired me, who have of late slept in the Castle, although I have been in town almost every day, and sometimes all day long, to live more at the Province House, assuring me that I shall have a guard of what number of gentlemen I please; and I shall go to the Province House on Monday and stay there some days, to show that I don't keep out of the town for fear of it. There will therefore remain only the objection to the Assembly's meeting at Boston upon account of undue influence, which I own has considerable weight with me; though perhaps it may not have so much weight with the Council, by whom I must be determined concerning the sitting of the Assembly.

P.S. — I have taken the liberty to use only initial letters in one name as the person is of no significance and has a brother who is a very faithful officer of the King.

This is the Place to affix the STAMP.

28.

JOHN ADAMS: A Burdensome and Unconstitutional Tax

The Stamp Act gave Adams his first opportunity to enter into Massachusetts politics and into the struggle between the mother country and the colonies. He drew up a set of resolutions of protest against the act for the town of Braintree, Massachusetts, on October 14, 1765. Similar resolutions were passed by other Massachusetts townships.

Source: C. F. Adams, III: "Instructions of the Town of Braintree to Their Representatives, 1765."

Sir,

In all the calamities which have ever befallen this country, we have never felt so great a concern, or such alarming apprehensions, as on this occasion. Such is our loyalty to the King, our veneration for both houses of Parliament, and our affection for all our fellow subjects in Britain that measures which discover any unkindness in that country toward us are the more sensibly and intimately felt. And we can no longer forbear complaining that many of the measures of the late Ministry, and some of the late acts of Parliament, have a tendency, in our apprehension, to divest us of our most essential rights and liberties. We shall confine ourselves, however, chiefly to the act of Parliament, commonly called the Stamp Act, by which a very burdensome and, in our opinion, unconstitutional tax is to be laid upon us all; and we [are to be] subjected to numerous and enormous penalties, to be prosecuted, sued for, and recovered at the option of an informer in a Court of Admiralty without a jury.

We have called this a burdensome tax, because the duties are so numerous and so high, and the embarrassments to business in this infant, sparsely settled country so great,

that it would be totally impossible for the people to subsist under it, if we had no controversy at all about the right and authority of imposing it. Considering the present scarcity of money, we have reason to think the execution of that act for a short space of time would drain the country of its cash, strip multitudes of all their property, and reduce them to absolute beggary. And what the consequence would be to the peace of the province, from so sudden a shock and such a convulsive change in the whole course of our business and subsistence, we tremble to consider.

We further apprehend this tax to be unconstitutional. We have always understood it to be a grand and fundamental principle of the constitution that no freeman should be subject to any tax to which he has not given his own consent, in person or by proxy. And the maxims of the law, as we have constantly received them, are to the same effect: that no freeman can be separated from his property but by his own act or fault. . . .

But the most grievous innovation of all is the alarming extension of the power of Courts of Admiralty. In these courts one judge presides alone! No juries have any concern there! The law and the fact are both to be decided by the same single judge, whose commission is only during pleasure, and with whom, as we are told, the most mischievous of all customs has become established, that of taking commissions on all condemnations; so that he is under a pecuniary temptation always against the subject. . . . We have all along thought the acts of trade in this respect a grievance; but the Stamp Act has opened a vast number of sources of new crimes, which may be committed by any man and cannot but be committed by multitudes, and prodigious penalties are annexed, and all these are to be tried by such a judge of such a court! . . .

We cannot help asserting, therefore, that this part of the act will make an essential change in the constitution of juries, and it is directly repugnant to the Great Charter itself; for, by that charter, "no amercement shall be assessed, but by the oath of honest and lawful men of the vicinage"; and, "no freeman shall be taken, or imprisoned, or disseized of his freehold, or liberties of free customs, nor passed upon, nor condemned, but by lawful judgment of his peers, or by the law of the land." So that this act will "make such a distinction, and create such a difference between" the subjects in Great Britain and those in America as we could not have expected from the guardians of liberty in "both."

As these, sir, are our sentiments of this act, we, the freeholders and other inhabitants, legally assembled for this purpose, must enjoin it upon you to comply with no measures or proposals for countenancing the same, or assisting in the execution of it but by all lawful means consistent with our allegiance to the King and relation to Great Britain to oppose the execution of it till we can hear the success of the cries and petitions of America for relief.

We further recommend the most clear and explicit assertion and vindication of our rights and liberties to be entered on the public records, that the world may know, in the present and all future generations, that we have a clear knowledge and a just sense of them, and, with submission to Divine Providence, that we never can be slaves.

Nor can we think it advisable to agree to any steps for the protection of stamped papers or stamp officers. Good and wholesome laws we have already for the preservation of the peace; and we apprehend there is no further danger of tumult and disorder, to which we have a well-grounded aversion; and that any extraordinary and expensive exertions would tend to exasperate the people and endanger the public tranquillity, rather than the contrary. Indeed, we cannot too often inculcate upon you our desires, that all extraordinary grants and expensive measures may, upon all occasions, as much as possible, be avoided. The public money of this country is the toil and labor of the people, who are under many uncommon difficulties and distresses at this time, so that all reasonable frugality ought to be observed. And we would recommend, particularly, the strictest care and the utmost firmness to prevent all unconstitutional drafts upon the public treasury.

The die was now cast; I had passed the Rubicon. Swim or sink, live or die, survive or perish with my country was my unalterable determination.

JOHN ADAMS. Daniel Webster, in his *Eulogy of Adams and Jefferson* (1826), paraphrased the words thus: "Sink or swim, live or die, survive or perish, I give my hand and my heart to this vote."

29.

Daniel Dulany: On the Propriety of Imposing Taxes in the British Colonies

In October, seven months after the passage of the Stamp Act, Daniel Dulany, a Maryland lawyer, produced a pamphlet entitled Considerations on the Propriety of Imposing Taxes in the British Colonies, for the Purpose of Raising a Revenue, by Act of Parliament. *Dulany opposed the Stamp Act, scoffing at the British idea that the colonists (like British industrial cities) were "virtually represented" in Parliament by strangers. Dulany's forceful arguments ranked foremost among political writings of the period. William Pitt supported Dulany's reasoning when he pleaded in England for the repeal of the Stamp Act.*

Source: *Considerations on the Propriety of Imposing Taxes in the British Colonies, for the Purpose of Raising a Revenue, by Act of Parliament,* London, 1766.

I shall undertake to disprove the supposed similarity of situation, whence the same kind of representation is deduced of the inhabitants of the colonies, and of the British nonelectors; and, if I succeed, the notion of a virtual representation of the colonies must fail, which, in truth, is a mere cobweb spread to catch the unwary and entangle the weak. I would be understood. I am upon a question of propriety, not of power; and though some may be inclined to think it is to little purpose to discuss the one when the other is irresistible, yet are they different considerations; and, at the same time that I invalidate the claim upon which it is founded, I may very consistently recommend a submission to the law, whilst it endures. . . .

Lessees for years, copyholders, proprietors of the public funds, inhabitants of Birmingham, Leeds, Halifax, and Manchester, merchants of the City of London, or members of the corporation of the East India Company, are, as such, under no personal incapacity to be electors; for they may acquire the right of election, and there are actually not only a considerable number of electors in each of the classes of lessees for years, etc., but in many of them, if not all, even members of Parliament. The interests, therefore, of the nonelectors, the electors, and the representatives are individually the same; to say nothing of the connection among neighbors, friends, and relations. The security of the nonelectors against oppression is that their oppression will fall also upon the electors and the representatives. The one cannot be injured and the other indemnified.

Further, if the nonelectors should not be taxed by the British Parliament, they would not be taxed at all; and it would be iniquitous, as well as a solecism in the political system, that they should partake of all the benefits resulting from the imposition and application of taxes, and derive an immunity from the circumstance of not being qualified to vote. Under this constitution, then, a double or virtual representation may be reasonably supposed.

The electors, who are inseparably connected in their interests with the nonelectors, may be justly deemed to be the representatives of the nonelectors, at the same time they exercise their personal privilege in their right of election, and the members chosen, therefore, the representatives of both. This is the only rational explanation of the expression "virtual representation." None has been advanced by the assertors of it, and their meaning can only be inferred from the instances by which they endeavor to elucidate it; and no other meaning can be stated to which the instances apply. . . .

The inhabitants of the colonies are, as such, incapable of being electors, the privilege of election being exercisable only in person, and, therefore, if every inhabitant of America had the requisite freehold, not one could vote but upon the supposition of his ceasing to be an inhabitant of America and becoming a resident in Great Britain, a supposition which would be impertinent because it shifts the question — Should the colonies not be taxed by parliamentary impositions; their respective legislatures have a regular, adequate, and constitutional authority to tax them; and therefore there would not necessarily be an iniquitous and absurd exemption from their not being represented by the House of Commons?

There is not that intimate and inseparable relation between the electors of Great Britain and the inhabitants of the colonies, which must inevitably involve both in the same taxation. On the contrary, not a single actual elector in England might be immediately affected by a taxation in America, imposed by a statute which would have a general operation and effect upon the properties of the inhabitants of the colonies.

But though it has been admitted that the Stamp Act is the first statute that has imposed an internal tax upon the colonies *for the single purpose of revenue,* yet the advocates for that law contend that there are many instances of the Parliament's exercising a supreme legislative authority over the colonies and actually imposing *internal taxes* upon their properties — that the duties upon any exports or imports are internal taxes; that an impost on a foreign commodity is as much an internal tax as a duty upon any production of the plantations; that no distinction can be supported between one kind of tax and another, an authority to impose the one extending to the other.

If these things are really as represented by the advocates for the Stamp Act, why did the chancellor of the Exchequer make it a question for the consideration of the House of Commons, whether the Parliament could impose an *internal tax* in the colonies or not for the *single purpose of revenue?*

It appears to me that there is a clear and necessary distinction between an act imposing a tax for the single purpose of revenue and those acts which have been made for the regulation of trade and have produced some revenue in consequence of their effect and operation as regulations of trade.

The colonies claim the privileges of British subjects. It has been proved to be inconsistent with those privileges to tax them without their own consent, and it has been demonstrated that a tax imposed by Parliament is a tax *without their consent.*

The subordination of the colonies and the authority of Parliament to preserve it have been fully acknowledged. Not only the welfare but perhaps the existence of the mother country, as an independent kingdom, may depend upon her trade and navigation, and these so far upon her intercourse with the colonies that if this should be neglected, there would soon be an end to that commerce, whence her greatest wealth is derived and upon which her maritime power is principally founded. From these considerations, the right of the British Parliament to regulate the trade of the colonies may be justly deduced; a denial of it would contradict the admission of the subordination and of the authority to preserve it, resulting from the nature of the relation between the mother country and her colonies. It is a common and frequently the most proper method to regulate trade by duties on imports and exports. The authority of the mother country to regulate the trade of the colonies being unquestionable, what regulations are the most proper are to be of course submitted to the determination of the Parliament; and if an incidental revenue should be produced by such regulations, these are not therefore unwarrantable.

A right to impose an internal tax on the colonies without their consent for the single purpose of revenue is denied; a right to regulate their trade without their consent is admitted. The imposition of a duty may, in some instances, be the proper regulation. If the claims of the mother country and the colonies should seem on such an occasion to interfere and the point of right to be doubtful (which I take to be otherwise), it is easy to guess that the determination will be on the side of power and that the inferior will be constrained to submit. . . .

Not only as a friend to the colonies but as an inhabitant having my all at stake upon their welfare, I desire an exemption from taxes imposed *without my consent,* and I have reflected longer than a moment upon the consequences. I value it as one of the dearest privileges I enjoy. I acknowledge dependence on Great Britain, but I can perceive a degree of it without slavery, and I disown all other. I do not expect that the interests of the colonies will be considered by some men but in subserviency to other regards. The effects of luxury, and venality, and oppression, posterity may perhaps experience, and *sufficient for the day will be the evil thereof.*

30.

No Taxation Without Representation

Formal opposition to the Stamp Act led to the Stamp Act Congress in New York, in October 1765. Delegates from nine colonies convened and wrote a moderate statement of colonial rights. In addition to the adoption of "The Declarations" on October 19, the delegates prepared petitions to the King, the House of Lords, and the House of Commons. Because the members of the congress were far more conservative in their sentiments than colonial legislatures had been, some of the delegates refused to sign even the moderate documents that were produced by the congress. Parliament rejected the petitions in spite of their mildness. The Stamp Act Congress was the first intercolonial congress to meet in America. It was a foundation from which the subsequent Continental Congresses arose.

Source: *Proceedings of the Congress at New-York,* Boston, 1765: "Saturday, October 19, 1765, A.M."

THE CONGRESS MET according to adjournment, and resumed, etc., as yesterday. And upon mature deliberation agreed to the following declarations of the rights and grievances of the colonists, in America, which were ordered to be inserted.

The members of this Congress, sincerely devoted with the warmest sentiments of affection and duty to His Majesty's person and government, inviolably attached to the present happy establishment of the Protestant succession, and with minds deeply impressed by a sense of the present and impending misfortunes of the British colonies on this continent, having considered as maturely as time will permit the circumstances of the said colonies, esteem it our indispensable duty to make the following declarations of our humble opinion, respecting the most essential rights and liberties of the colonists, and of the grievances under which they labor, by reason of several late acts of Parliament.

1. That His Majesty's subjects in these colonies owe the same allegiance to the Crown of Great Britain that is owing from his subjects born within the Realm, and all due subordination to that august body, the Parliament of Great Britain.

2. That His Majesty's liege subjects in these colonies are entitled to all the inherent rights and liberties of his natural-born subjects within the Kingdom of Great Britain.

3. That it is inseparably essential to the freedom of a people, and the undoubted right of Englishmen, that no taxes be imposed on them but with their own consent, given personally or by their representatives.

4. That the people of these colonies are not, and, from their local circumstances, cannot be represented in the House of Commons in Great Britain.

5. That the only representatives of the people of these colonies are persons chosen therein by themselves, and that no taxes ever have been or can be constitutionally imposed on them but by their respective legislature.

6. That all supplies to the Crown being free gifts of the people, it is unreasonable and inconsistent with the principles and spirit of the British constitution for the people of Great Britain to grant to His Majesty the property of the colonists.

7. That trial by jury is the inherent and invaluable right of every British subject in these colonies.

8. That the late act of Parliament entitled "An act for granting and applying certain stamp duties, and other duties, in the British colonies and plantations in America, etc.," by imposing taxes on the inhabitants of these colonies, and the said act and several other acts by extending the jurisdiction of the Courts of Admiralty beyond its ancient limits, have a manifest tendency to subvert the rights and liberties of the colonists.

9. That the duties imposed by several late acts of Parliament, from the peculiar circumstances of these colonies, will be extremely burdensome and grievous; and from the scarcity of specie, the payment of them absolutely impracticable.

10. That as the profits of the trade of these colonies ultimately center in Great Britain to pay for the manufactures which they are obliged to take from thence, they eventually contribute very largely to all supplies granted there to the Crown.

11. That the restrictions imposed by several late acts of Parliament on the trade of these colonies will render them unable to purchase the manufactures of Great Britain.

12. That the increase, prosperity, and happiness of these colonies depend on the full and free enjoyment of their rights and liberties, and an intercourse with Great Britain mutually affectionate and advantageous.

13. That it is the right of the British subjects in these colonies to petition the King or either house of Parliament.

Lastly. That it is the indispensable duty of these colonies, to the best of sovereigns, to the mother country, and to themselves, to endeavor by a loyal and dutiful address to His Majesty and humble applications to both houses of Parliament, to procure the repeal of the act for granting and applying certain stamp duties, of all clauses of any other acts of Parliament whereby the jurisdiction of the Admiralty is extended as aforesaid, and of the other late acts for the restriction of American commerce.

31.

SOAME JENYNS: The Objections to the Taxation of Our American Colonies Considered

Part of the American opposition to British taxation was based on the objection that, since the colonies were not represented in Parliament, that body has no right either to tax them or to legislate for them generally. One member of Parliament, Soame Jenyns, attempted to answer this argument with a theory of "virtual representation." His pamphlet on the objections to colonial taxation, excerpted here, was published in 1765.

Source: *The Objections to the Taxation of Our American Colonies, by the Legislature of Great Britain, Briefly Consider'd,* 2nd edition, London, 1765.

THE RIGHT OF THE LEGISLATURE of Great Britain to impose taxes on her American colonies, and the expediency of exerting that right in the present conjuncture, are propositions so indisputably clear that I should never have thought it necessary to have undertaken their defense had not many arguments been lately flung out, both in papers and conversation, which with insolence equal to their absurdity deny them both. As these are usually mixed up with several patriotic and favorite words, such as liberty, property, Englishmen, etc., which are apt to make strong impressions on that more numerous part of mankind who have ears but no understanding, it will not, I think, be improper to give them some answers. To this, therefore, I shall singly confine myself, and do it in as few words as possible. . . .

The great capital argument, which I find on this subject, and which, like an elephant at the head of a Nabob's army, being once overthrown must put the whole into confusion, is this: that no Englishman is or can be taxed but by his own consent, by which must be meant one of these three propositions — either that no Englishman can be taxed without his own consent as an individual; or that no Englishman can be taxed without the consent of the persons he chooses to represent him; or that no Englishman can be taxed without the consent of the majority of all those who are elected by himself and others of his fellow subjects to represent them. Now, let us impartially consider whether any of these propositions are in fact true. If not, then this wonderful structure which has been erected upon them falls at once to the ground, and like another Babel perishes by a confusion of words, which the builders themselves are unable to understand.

First, then, that no Englishman is or can be taxed but by his own consent as an individual: this is so far from being true, that it is the very reverse of truth, for no man that I know of is taxed by his own consent; and an Englishman, I believe, is as little likely to be so taxed as any man in the world.

Second, that no Englishman is or can be taxed but by the consent of those persons whom he has chosen to represent him: for the truth of this I shall appeal only to the candid representatives of those unfortunate counties which produce cider and shall willingly acquiesce under their determination.

Lastly, that no Englishman is or can be taxed without the consent of the majority of those who are elected by himself and others of his fellow subjects to represent them: this is certainly as false as the other two, for every Englishman is taxed, and not one in twenty represented: copyholders, leaseholders, and all men possessed of personal property only, choose no representatives. Manchester, Birmingham, and many more of our richest and most flourishing trading towns send no members to Parliament, consequently cannot consent by their representatives because they choose none to represent them. Yet are they not Englishmen? Or are they not taxed?

I am well aware that I shall hear Locke, Sidney, Selden, and many other great names quoted to prove that every Englishman, whether he has a right to vote for a representative or not, is still represented in the British Parliament; in which opinion they all agree. On what principle of common sense this opinion is founded I comprehend not, but on the authority of such respectable names I shall acknowledge its truth; but then I will ask one question, and on that I will rest the whole merits of the cause. Why does not this imaginary representation extend to America as well as over the whole island of Great Britain? If it can travel 300 miles, why not 3,000? If it can jump over rivers and mountains, why cannot it sail over the ocean? If the towns of Manchester and Birmingham, sending no representatives to Parliament, are notwithstanding there represented, why are not the cities of Albany and Boston equally represented in that assembly? Are they not alike British subjects? Are they not Englishmen? Or are they only Englishmen when they solicit for protection, but not Englishmen when taxes are required to enable this country to protect them?

But it is urged that the colonies are by their charters placed under distinct governments, each of which has a legislative power within itself, by which alone it ought to be taxed; that if this privilege is once given up, that liberty which every Englishman has a right to is torn from them, they are all slaves, and all is lost.

The liberty of an Englishman is a phrase of so various a signification, having within these few years been used as a synonymous term for blasphemy, bawdy, treason, libels, strong beer, and cider, that I shall not here presume to define its meaning; but I shall venture to assert what it cannot mean; that is, an exemption from taxes imposed by the authority of the Parliament of Great Britain. Nor is there any charter that ever pretended to grant such a privilege to any colony in America; and had they granted it, it could have had no force, their charters being derived from the Crown, and no charter from the Crown can possibly supersede the right of the whole legislature. Their charters are undoubtedly no more than those of all corporations, which empower them to make bylaws and raise duties for the purposes of their own police, forever subject to the superior authority of Parliament. And in some of their charters, the manner of exercising these powers is specified in these express words, "according to the course of other corporations in Great Britain"; and, therefore, they can have no more pretense to plead an exemption from this parliamentary authority than any other corporation in England.

It has been moreover alleged that, though Parliament may have power to impose taxes on the colonies, they have no right to use it because it would be an unjust tax; and no supreme or legislative power can have a right to enact any law in its nature unjust. To this I shall only make this short reply: that if Parliament can impose no taxes but what are equitable, and the persons taxed are to be the judges of that equity, they will in effect have no power to lay any tax at all. No tax can be imposed exactly equal on all, and if it is not equal, it cannot be just; and if it is not just, no power whatever can impose it; by which short syllogism, all taxation is at an end. But why it should not be used by Englishmen on this side the Atlantic as well as by those on the other I do not comprehend.

1766

32.

London Merchants Against the Stamp Act

As the colonies began to cooperate with one another in their opposition to the Crown and to the Stamp Act, resistance took many forms, the most effective being a well-enforced program on nonimportation. British merchants, who were suffering heavy losses through the American boycott of British goods, petitioned Parliament to repeal the Act on January 17, 1766.

Source: *The Parliamentary History of England, from the Earliest Period to the Year 1803*, Vol. XVI, London, 1813, pp. 133-136.

A PETITION OF THE MERCHANTS of London, trading to North America, was presented to the House, and read, setting forth:

That the petitioners have been long concerned in carrying on the trade between this country and the British colonies on the continent of North America; and that they have annually exported very large quantities of British manufactures, consisting of woolen goods of all kinds, cottons, linens, hardware, shoes, household furniture, and almost without exception of every other species of goods manufactured in these kingdoms, besides other articles imported from abroad, chiefly purchased with our manufactures and with the produce of our colonies. By all which, many thousand manufacturers, seamen, and laborers have been employed, to the very great and increasing benefit of this nation; and that, in return for these exports, the petitioners have received from the colonies rice, indigo, tobacco, na-

val stores, oil, whale fins, furs, and, lately, potash, with other commodities, besides remittances by bills of exchange and bullion obtained by the colonists in payment for articles of their produce not required for the British market and therefore exported to other places.

From the nature of this trade, consisting of British manufactures exported and of the import of raw materials from America, many of them used in our manufactures and all of them tending to lessen our dependence on neighboring states, it must be deemed of the highest importance in the commercial system of this nation; and that this commerce, so beneficial to the state and so necessary for the support of multitudes, now lies under such difficulties and discouragement that nothing less than its utter ruin is apprehended without the immediate interposition of Parliament. In consequence of the trade between the colonies and the mother country as established and as permitted for many years, and of the experience which the petitioners have had of the readiness of the Americans to make their just remittances to the utmost of their real ability, they have been induced to make and venture such large exportations of British manufactures as to leave the colonies indebted to the merchants of Great Britain in the sum of several millions sterling.

At this time the colonists, when pressed for payment, appeal to past experience in proof of their willingness; but declare it is not in their power, at present, to make good their engagements, alleging that the taxes and restrictions laid upon them, and the extension of the jurisdiction of Vice-Admiralty courts established by some late acts of Parliament, particularly by an act passed in the fourth year of His present Majesty for granting certain duties in the British colonies and plantations in America, and by an act passed in the fifth year of His present Majesty for granting and applying certain stamp duties and other duties in the British colonies and plantations in America, with several regulations and restraints, which, if founded in acts of Parliament for defined purposes, are represented to have

been extended in such a manner as to disturb legal commerce and harass the fair trader, have so far interrupted the usual and former most fruitful branches of their commerce, restrained the sale of their produce, thrown the state of the several provinces into confusion, and brought on so great a number of actual bankruptcies that the former opportunities and means of remittances and payments are utterly lost and taken from them.

The petitioners are, by these unhappy events, reduced to the necessity of applying to the House in order to secure themselves and their families from impending ruin; to prevent a multitude of manufacturers from becoming a burden to the community, or else seeking their bread in other countries, to the irretrievable loss of this kingdom; and to preserve the strength of this nation entire, its commerce flourishing, the revenues increasing, our navigation, the bulwark of the kingdom, in a state of growth and extension, and the colonies, from inclination, duty, and interest, firmly attached to the mother country; and therefore praying the consideration of the premises, and entreating such relief as to the House shall seem expedient.

33.

Northampton County Resolutions on the Stamp Act

Reaching into the business transactions of daily life, the Stamp Act was a continual assertion of Parliamentary authority that the colonists were unwilling to concede. Among various forms of local defiance was the following order by the court of Northampton County, Virginia, on February 11, 1766. In regarding the Act as "unconstitutional," the court expressed the widespread conviction of the colonies that England had no right to apply to them for revenue. It was one of the earliest declarations to the effect that an act considered unconstitutional is not binding.

Source: *Virginia Gazette,* March 21, 1766.

Williamsburg, March 21. The following is a copy of a late order of Northampton Court, on the eastern shore of this colony, which we are desired to insert. At a court held for Northampton County, Feb. 11, 1766:

On the motion of the clerk and other officers of this Court, praying their opinion whether the act entitled "An Act for granting and applying certain Stamp Duties, and other Duties, in America, etc.," was binding on the inhabitants of this colony, and whether they, the said officers, should incur any penalties by not using stamped paper agreeable to the directions of the said act, the Court unanimously declared it to be their opinion that the said act did not bind, affect, or concern the inhabitants of this colony, inasmuch as they conceive the same to be unconstitutional; and that the said several officers may proceed to the execution of their respective offices without incurring any penalties by means thereof; which opinion this court does order to be recorded.

34.

Francis Bernard: The Growing Opposition to England

Elaborate and accurate accounts of political events in the colonies during the 1760s were written by Governor Francis Bernard of Massachusetts to the British secretaries of state and the Board of Trade. He gave a detailed account of the actions of James Otis, blaming him for most of the opposition to the Stamp Act. Bernard's letters are a valuable source for the history of Massachusetts during the time he was governor. He directed the following one to the Earl of Shelburne on December 22, 1766.

Source: *British Public Record Office, C. O. 5/892.*

I am extremely sorry that I am obliged to enter minutely into the civil divisions of this province and the causes and effects of the same. I should have been glad to have saved Your Lordship the trouble of reading so unpleasing a report and myself the disagreeable task of making it. I should also have been glad to have concealed the present unhappy state of the province if there was any prospect of its amendment; although in truth the disgrace arising therefrom is chargeable but to few persons, for though the driven and the led are many, the drivers and the leaders are but few. But since the faction which has raised itself upon the public calamity knows no bounds and seems determined to persist in bringing all authority down to the level of the people (preserving nevertheless the form of the government which may be made consistent with such a scheme) and to make an example of a governor who has dared to stand in the gap, and to endeavor to support the royalty of the government, I cannot any longer excuse myself laying open this system to the bottom. Not only my own defense, for that I might have safely left to a review of my general conduct since I have been governor, but my duty in discovering designs and proceedings full of danger to the King's government require it of me.

I would avoid personalities, but in the present case it is impossible. The troubles of this country take their rise from and owe their continuance to one man, so much that his history alone would contain a full account of them. This man, James Otis, Esq., was a lawyer at Boston when I came to the government. He is by nature a passionate, violent, and desperate man, which qualities sometimes work him up to an absolute frenzy. I say nothing of him which is not known to be his certain character, confirmed by frequent experience. Soon after my entrance upon the government the place of chief justice of the province became vacant. The lieutenant governor was proposed for that office by the best men in the government. Mr. Otis (the father of *the* Otis) proposed himself for a seat on the bench in case one of the judges was made chief. Both these proposals could not be complied with and there was no balancing between the two candidates. But Mr. Otis, Senior, urged his pretensions by telling me and the lieutenant governor that if he (the lieutenant governor) was appointed, we should both of us repent it. Otis, Junior, did not confine himself to hints but declared publicly, with oaths, that "if his father was not appointed judge, he would set the whole province in a flame though he perished in the attempt." This was proved by the oaths of two gentlemen of credit, whose depositions are now in the public offices at home. However, I appointed the lieutenant governor with the general approbation of the whole province and Messrs. Otis immediately proceeded to make good their promises.

In less than half a year they stirred up a persecution against the Court of Admiralty and the Custom House, promising nothing less than the abolishment of the activity of both. In this it was unavoidable, as it was intended, that I should be involved as well as the chief justice. This persecution (it may be truly called so) lasted two years. In the course of it five actions were brought against different Custom House officers, one (made bailable) against the surveyor general (not the present) for £7,500 sterling, all by the advice and direction of Otis, Junior. In the course of these proceedings Otis everywhere appeared the principal. He was chief director, chamber council, counselor at the bar, popular haranguer, and Assembly orator; for the merit of this opposition to the King's officers procured him a seat in the House. However, after about two years' harassment this matter subsided with the maintenance of the King's rights, which were preserved, I may truly say, by my firmness and perseverance and by the steadiness of the chief justice and the other judges of the Superior Court. A full account of these proceedings, chiefly supported by oath, was returned to the Treasury and to the Board of Trade, and will appear further from my letters to the secretary of state and the Lords of trade, in 1761 and 1762.

When this was over he still continued in a constant opposition to government, except during an interval when his father was soliciting for two offices, which put him at the head of his county. These I gave to him, together with a good place to one of his sons, and was assured that this would wipe away all the ill humor which his former disappointment had occasioned. But no sooner were these patents sealed than Otis renewed his hostilities against government with fresh vigor; but to no purpose, as the Council and House were then filled with men of worth and ability, who greatly outweighed and outnumbered the opposers of government; and as I had at that time a credit with the province equal at least to any of my predecessors at any time. The business of the government was carried on with the utmost harmony and good humor, and I never met the Assembly without giving and receiving mutual testimonies of our satisfaction with one another. All this fair form of civil power, which had its chief foundation upon the prudence and good temper of the constituent members of the government and the confidence of the people, and had scarce any coercive power to resort to upon occasion, was at once overturned by the fatal and unfortunate Stamp Act. This let loose all the ill humors of the common people and put them into the hands of designing men to be employed not so much for the defense of their real and constitutional rights as to humble the government and bring it to the level of the very people.

I desire not to revive the disputes concerning the Stamp Act; I wish they were buried beyond the reach of memory, and they would have been buried before now if the opposition had not had further views than the defeat of the taxation. But, My Lord, the opposing [of] the Stamp Act has been made a mask for a battery, a stalking horse to take a better aim at the royalty of the government. This was apparent whilst the repeal was in suspense, but since it has passed, it is put out of all doubt. For this purpose, when the people's passions were thoroughly worked up, when their fears, jealousy, and credulity were got to such a pitch that it was dangerous as well as impracticable to reason with them, they were told that the scheme of the Stamp Act was formed in this province. The principal officers of the government and others of the first men of the province were pointed out as the contrivers of it. Otis himself said, in the House as well as out of it, that he knew the room (meaning in my house), the time, and the company when the plan was settled. All persons who had any weight or influence in the province, and had been used to exercise it in the support of the government, were branded by the name of friends to the Stamp Act; when the propagators of these calumnies knew in their conscience that there did not exist within the province a friend to the Stamp Act, not even in the stamp officer himself, who to my knowledge at no time wished for the continuance of the act.

These being the purposes of the faction, means were taken to distress the government quite foreign to the repeal of the Stamp Act, and such as if they had been known in Parliament, would have tended to prevent it. I shall mention a few particulars which will divide these matters into heads. Mr. Otis in a speech in the House directed against the government of Great Britain said that "he wished that the island was sunk in the sea so that the King and his family were saved." This proviso I suppose was to qualify the treasonableness of the wish. Of the King's governors he has said that "those who were appointed to the American governments were such as were obliged either by their crimes or their debts to fly their country." Of the Council (who had given no other offense than by assisting me to secure the stamp papers at the castle) he said in the House "it was an infernal

Courtesy, Christ Church, Oxford

Sir Francis Bernard (1712-1779); portrait by John Singleton Copley

divan and deserved to be sent to the place from whence they derived their councils." In the House it was common for him to tell a member who spoke on the side of government that he should not sit in that House the next year. And accordingly, as soon as the General Court was dissolved in order for a new election, there was published in a weekly paper conducted by Otis and his junto, a list of thirty-two members, the most respectable in the House and noted for their attachment to government, who were proscribed as enemies to their country because they had given their testimony against the violences lately committed. And of these thirty-two, nineteen lost their election.

Most of the foregoing passed whilst the event of the Stamp Act was in suspense and therefore might have well been forgotten if the party himself had desired that they should. But when the same violent measures are pursued after the repeal of the Stamp Act is made known, as before; when the King's government and all that bear office in it are persecuted with the same unrelenting acrimony as if nothing had been done for the people and they were under no obligations to the King and his Parliament; when the servant, to whom his King had forgiven 10,000 talents, takes his fellow servant by the throat for 100d., it is difficult not to connect the proceedings before and after the repeal. However, I shall draw a line between them in order to show that the repeal occasioned no relaxation in the disposition and designs of the faction which had raised itself by the Act.

It was the general opinion that Otis himself wished that the Act might not be repealed as that would answer his inflammatory purposes better. This was collected partly from a declaration he made about the time of the advice of the event being expected, that he hoped it would not be repealed; for, said he, "We will repeal it ourselves." As soon as the advice of the repeal came Otis published an advertisement which all the printers were obliged to insert under pain of mob execution. I enclose this advertisement which Otis owned to be his till he found it to be generally reprobated, after which he would neither own it nor deny it. By the terms of this, it is plain that the repeal was to produce no remission either of the pretensions against Parliament, or the persecution of the friends of the government. The week after this came out a republication of the list of the thirty-two members who had been proscribed as friends of the Stamp Act and therefore enemies to their country, accompanied with observations, among which it was said "that a general purgation in both houses was of absolute necessity." That is, that every member of either house who professed to have a regard for the support of the gov-

ernment and the royal rights thereof should lose his seat.

About this time Mr. Otis began to declare that they had fixed upon fifteen councilors who were to be turned out at the next election. This threat was continued almost to the day of election. I must add one transaction more which passed in this interval, which will properly conclude this paragraph. Mr. Otis at a meeting at the town hall (which I think was to fix a time for public rejoicings for the repeal) in a set speech told the people that "the distinction between inland taxes and port duties was without foundation, for whoever had a right to impose one had a right to impose the other. And therefore as the Parliament had given up the one (for he said the act for securing the dependency had no relation to taxes), they had given up the other; and the merchants were great fools if they submitted any longer to the laws restraining their trade, which ought to be free." This speech made a great deal of noise, and it was observed by serious men that Otis had thereby made himself answerable for all the disturbances which should thereafter happen in the execution of the laws of trade. But the natural consequence, and what immediately followed, was that a common talk prevailed among the people that there should be no more seizures in this town. There have been but two seizures made in the province since, and they have been both rescued with a high hand. In that at Boston it is remarkable that the man who opposed the officers sent for Otis and he went thither as his counselor. This is the manner in which this man and his faction, after they had heard of the repeal of the Stamp Act, prepared to make a return for it on the part of this province.

PAINTING

By the mid-18th century the demand for portraits in the colonies supported a small number of professionals of varying competence. In addition to the untrained native-born painters, several lesser English portraitists visited the colonies, bringing a semblance of the light, stylized techniques current in England, which the colonials had previously seen only in imported mezzotint engravings.

Lewis Morris by John Wollaston, who came from England about 1750 and was active in the middle and southern colonies for about 15 years

John Greenwood's portrait of Benjamin Pickman includes symbols of his subject's commercial interests

Charles Calvert, painted in 1761 by John Hesselius, who painted many of the wealthy families of Maryland and Pennsylvania

Brigadier General Joseph Dwight, by Joseph Blackburn, an Englishman painting in Boston in the 1750s and 1760s

"Isaac Winslow," by Robert Feke (1724-69) is derived from portraits by Hudson

"Mrs. David Chesebrough," by Blackburn, is also based on prevailing English styles

Miniature
self-portrait
by Copley

Copley

John Singleton Copley, the foremost colonial painter, was born in Boston in 1738 and grew up in the nearest thing to artistic surroundings that the colonies offered. His stepfather was Peter Pelham, whose engravings of his own and Smibert's portraits were the first American mezzotints.

"Mrs. Jerathmael Bowers," painted by Copley in 1765, is in the style of Joshua Reynolds

"Theodore Atkinson, Jr." by Copley, is derivative in its studied pose

Copley's portrait of James Otis, Sr. shows his developing skill at incisive and unadorned characterization

"Mrs. Seymour Fort," painted about 1776, is one of Copley's most compelling portraits

Like Feke and other colonials, Copley's early experiments with style were influenced by engravings of English portraits. Copley fused this strain with a straightforward, New England approach to create uncompromisingly realistic portraits of great strength. However, he grew restless in Boston, where painting, he felt, was valued only as a useful craft, and left for London in 1774.

"Mr. and Mrs. Isaac Winslow," by Copley

"The Copley Family," painted in London, combines full technical mastery with a new mannered self-consciousness in the pose and setting

West

Henry Laurens was painted by Copley in 1782 while he was in London as peace envoy and minister to Britain

Aside from a provincial's natural inclination to be at the center of his art world, an important influence in Copley's decision to leave Boston was the immense success of Benjamin West in London. West was born near Philadelphia in 1738. A rudimentary education in the classics and some instruction from local painters inspired him with the ambition to paint great historical pictures.

"The American School," depicting a session at West's studio in London, was painted by Matthew Pratt in 1765 and shows West standing on the left

Benjamin West, painted by Matthew Pratt, 1765

After traveling in Italy, West settled in London in 1763 and achieved instant fame with heroic canvases on classical and historical themes. The novelty of his work came in the application of neo-classical scale and grandeur to contemporary subjects. Additionally, West, who sympathized with the Revolution, greatly influenced the course of American painting by welcoming a succession of aspiring American painters to his studio.

"Sarah Ursula Rose" was painted by West on commission while he was still in his teens

"The Death of General Wolfe," painted by West in 1770

1766 - 1767

35.

The Artist in Colonial New England

During the colonial period, the portrait was virtually the only vehicle for the American painter's art. John Singleton Copley, a native-born colonial portraitist, was unhappy with the limits put upon him in the late 1760s by a public "entirely destitute of all just ideas of the arts." The reverence Copley had for "one of the most noble arts of the world" is expressed in an exchange of letters with Benjamin West, a Philadelphia artist, and Captain R. G. Bruce, who took Copley's paintings to London for an exhibition. The two paintings Copley sent were "The Boy With the Squirrel" and "Little Girl."

Source: *Letters and Papers of John Singleton Copley and Henry Pelham*,
      The Massachusetts Historical Society, 1914, pp. 41-45, 50-52, 65-66.

I.

R. G. BRUCE TO JOHN SINGLETON COPLEY

DON'T IMAGINE I have forgotten or neglected your interest by my long silence. I have delayed writing to you ever since the exhibition in order to forward the enclosed letter from Mr. West, which he has from time to time promised me, but which his extreme application to his art has hitherto prevented his finishing.

What he says will be much more conclusive to you than anything from me. I have only to add the general opinions which were pronounced on your picture when it was exhibited. It was universally allowed to be the best picture of its kind that appeared on that occasion, but the sentiments of Mr. Reynolds will, I suppose, weigh more with you than those of other critics. He says of it, "that in any collection of painting it will pass for an excellent picture, but considering the disadvantages" I told him "you had labored under, that it was a very wonderful performance"; "that it exceeded any portrait that Mr. West ever drew"; "that he did not know one painter at home who had all the advantages that Europe could give them that could equal it, and that if you are capable of producing such a piece by the mere efforts of your own genius, with the advantages of the example and instruction which you could have in Europe, you would be a valuable acquisition to the art, and one of the first painters in the world, provided you could receive these aids before it was too late in life, and before your manner and taste were corrupted or fixed by working in your little way at Boston."

He condemns your working either in crayons or water colors. Don't imagine I flatter you. I only repeat Mr. Reynolds' words, which are confirmed by the public voice. He, indeed, is a mere enthusiast when he speaks of you. At the same time he found faults. He observed a little hardness in the drawing, coldness in the shades, an overminuteness, all which example would correct. "But still," he added, "it is a wonderful picture to be sent by a young man who was never out of New England, and had only some bad copies to study."

I have begged of Mr. West to be copious in his criticisms and advices to you. Mr. Reynolds would have also written to you himself but his time is too valuable. The picture is at his house where I shall leave it till I have your directions how to dispose of it. I could sell it to advantage, but it is thought more for your interest to keep it as a specimen. You are greatly obliged to Lord Cardross, a friend of mine, to whom I first sent it. He showed it to the most eminent connoisseurs, then gave it to Mr. Reynolds, who sent it with his own pictures to the exhibition. You are best judge of your own affairs and whether you can with propriety accomplish a trip for a few years to Europe. Should you take that resolution, I believe I may venture to assure you that you will meet with much encouragement and patronage. Should it be in my little power to be of the least use to you, you may command me to the utmost. I am already very happy in having contributed to make your merit so far known to the world, and hope it has laid the foundation of your being the great man Mr. Reynolds prognosticates.

I am obliged to write this in a very great hurry as I set out tomorrow on a visit to Scotland. Pray remember me to my old ac-

quaintances at Boston. I have written to Mr. Scollay and Mrs. Melville. You have already my direction, and I shall expect to hear from you. Perhaps I may see you in Boston next year, but that at present is uncertain.

I had almost forgotten to tell you that, in case you don't appear yourself, the friends of your art wish that you will paint another picture to exhibit next year, and Mr. West has promised to point out a subject to you. Should you do so, send it to Mr. West, who seems sincerely disposed to be your friend. Mr. Reynolds is too busy and too great a man to be active for you, though he is also much disposed to serve you.

I have now a favor to beg of you in turn, which is that you will make me a copy of my picture I left with Mrs. Melville. I hope this will find you and your family well, and either in Europe or America assure yourself of my sincere friendship.

II.

BENJAMIN WEST TO COPLEY

ON SEEING a picture painted by you and meeting with Captain Bruce, I take the liberty of writing to you. The great honor the picture has gained you here in the art of painting I dare say must have been made known to you long before this time, and as you have made so great a progress in the art I am persuaded you are the more desirous of hearing the remarks that might have been made by those of the profession, and as I am here in the midst of the painting world have the greater opportunity of hearing them.

Your picture first fell into Mr. Reynolds' hands to have it put into the exhibition as the performance of a young American. He was great struck with the piece, and it was first concluded to have been painted by one Mr. Wright, a young man that has just made his appearance in the art in a surprising degree of merit. As your name was not given with the picture it was concluded a mistake, but before the exhibition opened the particulars were received from Captain Bruce.

While it was exhibited to view, the criticism was that at first sight the picture struck the eye as being too liny, which was judged to have arisen from there being so much neatness in the lines, which indeed as far as I was capable of judging was somewhat the case. For I very well know from endeavoring at great correctness in one's outline it is apt to produce a poverty in the look of one's work. Whenever great decision is attended to the lines are apt to be too fine and edgy. This is a thing in works of great painters I have remarked has been strictly avoided, and have given correctness in a breadth of outline, which is finishing out into the canvas by no determined line when closely examined; though when seen at a short distance, as when one looks at a picture, shall appear with the greatest beauty and freedom. For in nature everything is round, or at least partakes the most of that form which makes it impossible that nature, when seen in a light and shade, can ever appear liny.

As we have every April an exhibition where our works are exhibited to the public, I advise you to paint a picture of a half figure or two in one piece, of a boy and girl, or any other subject you may fancy. And be sure [to] take your subjects from nature as you did in your last piece, and don't trust any resemblance of anything to fancy, except the dispositions of the figures and the adjustments of draperies, so as to make an agreeable whole. For in this consists the work of fancy and taste.

If you should do anything of this kind, I beg you may send it to me, when you may be sure it shall have the greatest justice done it. Let it be painted in oil, and make it a rule to paint in that way as much as possible, for oil painting has the superiority over all other painting. As I am from America, and know the little opportunity to be had there in the way of painting, I make the inducement the more in writing to you in this manner. As you have got to that length in the art that nothing is wanting to perfect you now but a sight of what has been done by the great masters, if you could make a visit to Europe for this purpose for three or four years, you would find yourself then in possession of what will be highly valuable. If ever you should make a visit to Europe you may depend on my friendship in any way that's in my power to serve.

III.

COPLEY TO WEST

YOUR KIND FAVOR of Aug. 4, 1766, came to hand. It gave me great pleasure to receive without reserve your criticisms on the picture I sent to the exhibition. Mr. Powell informed me of your intention of writing, and the handsome things you were pleased to say in praise of that little performance, which has increased my estimation of it, and demands my thanks which previous to the receipt of your favor I acknowledged in a letter forwarded by Mr. Powell. It was remarked the picture was too lined. This I confess I was conscious of myself and think with you that it is the natural result of too great precision in the outline, which in my next picture I will endeavor to avoid, and perhaps should not have fallen into it in that had I not felt too great temerity at presenting a picture to the inspection of the first artists in the world, and where it was to come into competition with such masterly performances as generally appear in that collection.

In my last I promised to send another piece, the subject you have since pointed out, but I fear it will not be in my power to comply with your design, the time being too short for the execution of two figures, not having it in my power to spend all my time on it, and the days short and weather cold, and I must ship it by the middle of February at farthest, otherwise it will come too late for the exhibition. But I shall do something near what you propose. Your cautioning me against doing anything from fancy I take very kindly, being sensible of the necessity of attending to nature as the fountainhead of all perfection, and the works of the great masters as so many guides that lead to the more perfect imitation of her, pointing out to us in what she is to be copied, and where we should deviate from her. In this country, as you rightly observe, there are no examples of art, except what is to be met with in a few prints indifferently executed from which it is not possible to learn much, and must greatly enhance the value of free and unreserved criticism made with judgment and candor.

It would give me inexpressible pleasure to make a trip to Europe, where I should see those fair examples of art that have stood so long the admiration of all the world. The paintings, sculptures, and *basso relievos* that adorn Italy, and which you have had the pleasure of making your studies from, would, I am sure, animate my pencil and enable me to acquire that bold, free, and graceful style of painting that will, if ever, come much slower from the mere dictates of nature, which has hitherto been my only instructor. I was almost tempted the last year to take a tour to Philadelphia, and that chiefly to see some of your pictures, which I am informed are there. I think myself peculiarly unlucky in living in a place into which there has not been one portrait brought that is worthy to be called a picture within my memory, which leaves me at a great loss to guess the style that you, Mr. Reynolds, and the other artists practise. I shall be glad when you write next you will be more explicit on the article of cray-

ons, and why you disapprove the use of them, for I think my best portraits done in that way. And be kind enough to inform me what Count Algarotti means by the five points that he recommends for amusement and to assist the invention of postures, and whether any prints after Correggio or Titian are to be purchased. I fear I shall tire your patience and make you repent your writing to one who makes so many requests in one letter.

But I shall be exceedingly glad to know in general what the present state of painting in Italy is, whether the living masters are excellent as the dead have been. It is not possible my curiosity can be satisfied in this by anybody but yourself, not having any correspondence with any whose judgment is sufficient to satisfy me. I have been painting the head of a dissenting clergyman and his friends are desirous to subscribe for it to be scraped in mezzotint in the common size of fourteen inches by ten, but I cannot give them the terms till I know the price. I shall take it kindly if when you see any artist that you approve you mention it to him, and let me know. I have seen a well-executed print by Mr. Pether of a Jewish rabbi. If you think him a good hand, be kind enough to desire him to let me know by a few lines (as soon as convenient) his terms, as the portrait waits only for that in my hands, and I shall send it immediately with the money to defray the expense when I know what it is.

IV.

COPLEY TO BRUCE or WEST

I OBSERVE the criticisms made on my last picture were not the same as those made on the first. I hope I have not in this as in the last by striving to avoid one error fallen into another. I shall be sorry if I have. However, it must take its fate.

Perhaps you may blame me for not taking another subject that would have afforded me more time, but subjects are not so easily procured in this place. A taste of painting is too much wanting to afford any kind of helps; and was it not for preserving the resemblance of particular persons, painting would not be known in the place. The people generally regard it no more than any other useful trade, as they sometimes term it, like that of a carpenter, tailor, or shoemaker, not as one of the most noble arts in the world, which is not a little mortifying to me.

While the arts are so disregarded I can hope for nothing, either to encourage or assist me in my studies but what I receive from a thousand leagues distance, and be my improvements what they will, I shall not be benefited by them in this country, neither in point of fortune or fame. This is what I wrote at large in my last letter . . . as the only reason that discourages me from going to Europe, lest after going I shall not find myself so good an artist as to merit that encouragement that would make it worth my while.

It would by no means be [worthwhile] to go there to improve myself, and then return to America; but if I could make it worth my while to stay there, I would remove with mother and brother, who I am bound by all ties of duty and affection not to desert as long as I live. My income in this country is about 300 guineas a year, out of which I have been able to lay up as much as would carry me through and support me handsomely for a couple of years with a family.

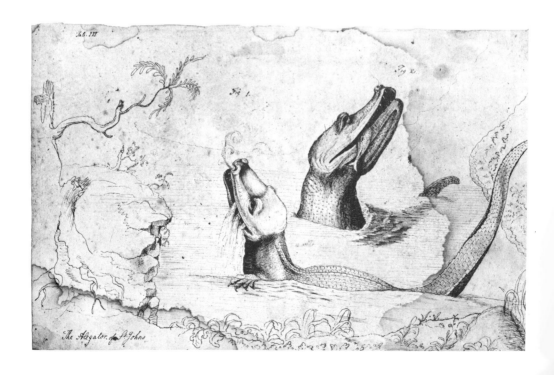

The Alegator of St Johns

1767

36.

Henry Moore: On the Progress of Manufacturing

The lack of capital was one of the main obstacles standing in the way of the development of large-scale manufacturing in the colonies. Furthermore, in situations where capital was not lacking, there was usually a more profitable employment for it in trade and land speculation. The governors of the colonies were ordered by the Board of Trade to report about the development of manufactures in their provinces since 1734 and about legislative encouragement of manufacturing. This letter of Governor Henry Moore of New York, dated January 12, 1767, is typical of the reports of the colonial governors.

Source: *Documents Relative to the Colonial History of the State of New-York,*
E. B. O'Callaghan, ed., Vol. VII, Albany, 1856, pp. 88-89.

Having received Your Lordships' command in a letter dated August 1 last, in which I was directed to prepare and transmit as soon as possible an account of the several manufactures set up and carried on within this colony since the year 1734, I took the liberty of giving Mr. Peter Hasenclaver a letter of introduction to Your Lordships, as he was then ready to sail for England, imagining that from his character and knowledge of the country, a more perfect account might be obtained from him of what was required in the before-mentioned letter than I could possibly give by that opportunity. I have since made all the inquiries I could, and the whole of the information given to me may be reduced to the following heads.

There is a small manufactory of linen in this city under the conduct of one Wells, and supported chiefly by the subscriptions of a set of men who call themselves the Society of Arts and Agriculture. No more than fourteen looms are employed in it, and it was established in order to give bread to several poor families which were a considerable charge to the city, and are now comfortably supported by their own daily labor in spinning of flax. It does not appear that there is any established fabric of broadcloth here, and some poor weavers from Yorkshire who came over lately in expectation of being engaged to make broadcloths could find no employment. But there is a general manufactory of woolen carried on here, and consists of two sorts, the first a coarse cloth entirely woolen, three-fourths of a yard wide, and the other a stuff which they call linsey-woolsey. The warp of this is linen, and the woof woolen; and a very small quantity of it is ever sent to market.

Last year when the riots and disorders here were at their height on the occasion of the Stamp Act, these manufactures were greatly boasted of, and the quantity then made greatly magnified by those who were desirous of distinguishing themselves as American patriots, and would wear nothing else. They were sometimes sold for three times their value; but the manufacturers themselves showed that they had more good sense than the persons who employed them, for they never clothed themselves with the work of their own hands but readily brought it to market, and selling it at an extravagant price there, bought English cloth for themselves and their families. The custom of making these coarse cloths in private families prevails throughout the whole province, and almost in every house a sufficient quantity is manufactured for the use of the family without the least design of sending any of it to market. This I had an opportunity of seeing during the late tour I made, and had the same accounts given me by all those persons of whom I made any inquiry, for every house swarms with children who are set to work as soon as they are able to spin and card; and as every family is furnished with a loom, the itinerant weavers who travel about the country put the finishing hand to the work.

There is a manufactory of hats in this city which is very considerable; for the hats are not so good as those made in England, and are infinitely dearer. Under such disadvantages as these it is easy to imagine with what difficulty it is supported, and how short the duration of it is like to be; the price of labor is so great in this part of the world that it will always prove the greatest obstacle to any manufactures attempted to be set up here, and the genius of the people in a country where everyone can have land to work upon leads them so naturally into agriculture that it prevails over every other occupation. There can be no stronger instances of this than in the servants imported from Europe of different trades; as soon as the time stipulated in their indentures is expired, they immediately quit their masters and get a small tract of land, in settling which for the first three or four years they lead miserable lives, and in the most abject poverty, but all this is patiently borne and submitted to with the greatest cheerfulness; the satisfaction of being landholders smooths every difficulty and makes them prefer this manner of living to that comfortable subsistence which they could procure for themselves and their families by working at the trades in which they were brought up.

The master of a glasshouse which was set up here a few years ago, now a bankrupt, assured me that his ruin was owing to no other cause than being deserted in this manner by his servants, which he had imported at a great expense; and that many others had suffered and been reduced as he was, by the same kind of misfortune.

The little foundry lately set up near this town for making small iron pots is under the direction of a few private persons, and as yet very inconsiderable.

As to the foundries which Mr. Hasenclaver has set up in the different parts of this country, I do not mention them as he will be able to give Your Lordships a full account of them and of the progress he has already made; I can only say that I think this province is under very great obligations to him for the large sums of money he has laid out here in promoting the cultivation of hemp and introducing the valuable manufactures of iron and potash.

37.

Act Suspending the New York Assembly

In 1765, Parliament passed a Quartering Act that required colonial legislatures to pay for specified articles used by British troops in the colonies. Among the legislatures refusing to obey the Quartering Act was that of New York. As New York was the headquarters of the British Army, Parliament decided to make an example of the colony, and on July 2, 1767, suspended the Colonial Assembly until it complied with the Act.

Source: Pickering, XXVII.

MAY IT PLEASE Your Majesty that it may be enacted . . . by and with the advice and consent of the Lords . . . and Commons, in this present Parliament assembled . . . that from and after Oct. 1, 1767, until provision shall have been made by the said assembly of New York for furnishing His Majesty's troops within the said province with all such necessaries as are required by the said acts of Parliament, or any of them, to be furnished for such troops, it shall not be lawful for the governor, lieutenant governor, or person presiding or acting as governor or commander in chief, or for the Council for the time being, within the colony, plantation, or province of New York in America, to pass, or give his or their assent to, or concurrence in, the making or passing of any act of Assembly; or his or their assent to any order, resolution, or vote, in concurrence with the House of Representatives for the time being within the said colony, plantation, or province; or for the said House of Representatives to pass or make

any bill, order, resolution, or vote (orders, resolutions, or votes for adjourning such house only excepted) of any kind, for any other purpose whatsoever; and that all acts of Assembly, orders, resolutions, and votes whatsoever, which shall or may be passed, assented to, or made, contrary to the tenor and meaning of this act, after the said Oct. 1, 1767, within the said colony, plantation, or province, before and until provision shall have been made for supplying His Majesty's troops with necessaries as aforesaid, shall be, and are hereby declared to be null and void, and of no force or effect whatsoever.

II. Provided nevertheless, and it is hereby declared to be the true intent and meaning of this act, that nothing herein before contained shall extend, or be construed to extend, to hinder, prevent, or invalidate, the choice, election, or approbation, of a speaker of the House of Representatives for the time being within the said colony, plantation, or province.

38.

JOHN DICKINSON: On the Suspension of the New York Assembly

Letters from a Farmer in Pennsylvania, *written by John Dickinson, though conciliatory in tone, did much to formulate the sense of wrong in British policies that led the colonies at last to strike for independence. Published first in newspapers during 1767 and 1768, the* Letters *were later brought out in a pamphlet that went rapidly through at least ten editions. In his letter of November 5, 1767, Dickinson discussed Parliament's suspension of the New York Assembly.*

Source: *Memoirs of the Historical Society of Pennsylvania,* Vol. XIV, Philadelphia, 1895, pp. 307-312.

My Dear Countrymen,

I am a farmer, settled after a variety of fortunes near the banks of the River Delaware in the province of Pennsylvania. I received a liberal education and have been engaged in the busy scenes of life; but am now convinced that a man may be as happy without bustle as with it. My farm is small; my servants are few and good; I have a little money at interest; I wish for no more; my employment in my own affairs is easy; and with a contented, grateful mind . . . I am completing the number of days allotted to me by divine goodness.

Being generally master of my time, I spend a good deal of it in a library, which I think the most valuable part of my small estate; and being acquainted with two or three gentlemen of abilities and learning who honor me with their friendship, I have acquired, I believe, a greater share of knowledge in history and the laws and constitution of my country than is generally attained by men of my class, many of them not being so fortunate as I have been in the opportunities of getting information.

From infancy I was taught to love humanity and liberty. Inquiry and experience have since confirmed my reverence for the lessons then given me by convincing me more fully of their truth and excellence. Benevolence toward mankind excites wishes for their welfare, and such wishes endear the means of fulfilling them. These can be found in liberty only, and therefore her sacred cause ought to be espoused by every man, on every occasion, to the utmost of his power. As a charitable but poor person does not withhold his mite because he cannot relieve *all* the distresses of the miserable, so should not any honest man suppress his sentiments concerning freedom, however small their influence is likely to be. Perhaps he may "touch some wheel" that will have an effect greater than he could reasonably expect.

These being my sentiments, I am encouraged to offer to you, my countrymen, my thoughts on some late transactions that appear to me to be of the utmost importance to you. Conscious of my defects, I have waited some time in expectation of seeing the subject treated by persons much better qualified for the task; but being therein disappointed, and apprehensive that longer delays will be injurious, I venture at length to request the attention of the public, praying that these lines may be read with the same zeal for the happiness of British America with which they were written.

With a good deal of surprise I have observed that little notice has been taken of an act of Parliament, as injurious in its principle to the liberties of these colonies as the Stamp Act was: I mean the act for suspending the legislation of New York.

The assembly of that government complied with a former act of Parliament, requiring certain provisions to be made for the troops in America, in every particular, I think, except the articles of salt, pepper, and vinegar. In my opinion they acted imprudently, considering all circumstances, in not complying so far as would have given satisfaction as several colonies did. But my dislike of their conduct in that instance has not blinded me so much that I cannot plainly perceive that they have been punished in a manner pernicious to American freedom and justly alarming to all the colonies.

If the British Parliament has a legal authority to issue an order that we shall furnish a single article for the troops here and to compel obedience to that order, they have the same right to issue an order for us to supply those troops with arms, clothes, and every necessary, and to compel obedience to that order also; in short, to lay any burdens they please upon us. What is this but taxing us at a certain sum and leaving to us only the manner of raising it? How is this mode more tolerable than the Stamp Act? Would that act have appeared more pleasing to Americans if, being ordered thereby to raise the sum total of the taxes, the mighty privilege had been left to them of saying how much should be paid for an instrument of writing on paper, and how much for another on parchment?

An act of Parliament commanding us to do a certain thing, if it has any validity, is a tax upon us for the expense that accrues in complying with it, and for this reason, I believe, every colony on the continent that chose to give a mark of their respect for Great Britain, in complying with the act relating to the troops, cautiously avoided the mention of that act, lest their conduct should be attributed to its supposed obligation.

The matter being thus stated, the assembly of New York either had or had not a right to refuse submission to that act. If they had, and I imagine no American will say they had not, then the Parliament had no right to compel them to execute it. If they had not that right, they had no right to punish them for not executing it; and therefore had no right to suspend their legislation, which is a punishment. In fact, if the people of New York cannot be legally taxed but by their own representatives, they cannot be legally deprived of the privilege of legislation, only for insisting on that exclusive privilege of taxation. If they may be legally deprived in such a case of the privilege of legislation, why may they not, with equal reason, be deprived of every other privilege? Or why may not every colony be treated in the same manner, when any of them shall dare to deny their assent to any impositions that shall be directed? Or what signifies the repeal of the Stamp Act, if these colonies are to lose their other privileges by not tamely surrendering that of taxation?

There is one consideration arising from the suspension which is not generally attended to but shows its importance very clearly. It was not necessary that this suspension should be caused by an act of Parliament. The Crown might have restrained the governor of New York even from calling the assembly together, by its prerogative in the royal governments. This step, I suppose, would have been taken if the conduct of the assembly of New York had been regarded as an act of disobedience to the Crown alone. But it is regarded as an act of "disobedience to the authority of the British legislature." This gives the suspension a consequence vastly more affecting. It is a parliamentary assertion of the supreme authority of the British legislature over these colonies in the point of taxation; and it is intended to compel New York into a submission to that authority. It seems therefore to me as much a violation of the liberty of the people of that province, and consequently of all these colonies, as if the Parliament had sent a number of regiments to be quartered upon them, till they should comply.

For it is evident that the suspension is meant as a compulsion; and the method of compelling is totally indifferent. It is indeed probable that the sight of red coats and the hearing of drums would have been most alarming, because people are generally more influenced by their eyes and ears than by their reason. But whoever seriously considers the matter must perceive that a dreadful stroke is aimed at the liberty of these colonies. I say of these colonies; for the cause of one is the cause of all. If the Parliament may lawfully deprive New York of any of her rights, it may deprive any or all the other colonies of their rights; and nothing can possibly so much encourage such attempts as a mutual inattention to the interest of each other. To divide and thus to destroy is the first political maxim in attacking those who are powerful by their union. He

certainly is not a wise man who folds his arms and reposes himself at home, seeing with unconcern the flames that have invaded his neighbor's house without using any endeavors to extinguish them. When Mr. Hampden's ship-money cause for 3s. 4d. was tried, all the people of England, with anxious expectations, interested themselves in the important decision; and when the slightest point touching the freedom of one colony is agitated, I earnestly wish that all the rest may with equal ardor support their sister. Very much may be said on this subject, but I hope more at present is unnecessary.

With concern I have observed that two assemblies of this province have sat and adjourned without taking any notice of this act. It may perhaps be asked: What would have been proper for them to do? I am by no means fond of inflammatory measures. I detest them. I should be sorry that anything should be done which might justly displease our sovereign or our mother country. But a firm, modest exertion of a free spirit should never be wanting on public occasions. It appears to me that it would have been sufficient for the assembly to have ordered our agents to represent to the King's ministers their sense of the suspending act and to pray for its repeal. Thus we should have borne our testimony against it; and might therefore reasonably expect that on a like occasion we might receive the same assistance from the other colonies.

Small things grow great by concord.

A FARMER

39.

Charles Woodmason: Lawlessness on the South Carolina Frontier

The back-country settlers of South Carolina in the 1760s complained frequently of the coastal aristocrats' indifference to establishing adequate local government. By 1764, the back-country men began to take matters into their own hands in order to enforce law and order by organizing "Regulator" associations. In the following petition, written by the Reverend Charles Woodmason, the Regulators asked the legislature for local governmental agencies. As a result, the government did establish a better court system, but the back-country men remained distrustful of the landowners and were reluctant to participate in the later revolutionary movement.

Source: *The Carolina Back country on the Eve of the Revolution: The Journal and Other Writings of Charles Woodmason, Anglican Itinerant,* Richard J. Hooker, ed., Chapel Hill, N.C., 1953, pp. 213-233.

THE REMONSTRANCE AND PETITION of the inhabitants of the upper and interior parts of this province on behalf of themselves, and all the other settlers of the back country, humbly shows:

That for many years past, the back parts of this province have been infested with an infernal gang of villains, who have committed such horrid depredations on our properties and estates, such insults on the persons of many settlers, and perpetrated such shocking outrages throughout the back settlements as is past description.

Our large stocks of cattle are either stolen and destroyed, our cow pens are broken up, and all our valuable horses are carried off. Houses have been burned by these rogues, and families stripped and turned naked into the woods. Stores have been broken open and rifled by them (wherefrom several traders are absolutely ruined). Private houses have been plundered; and the inhabitants wantonly tortured in the Indian manner to be made to confess where they secreted their effects from plunder. Married women have been ravished, virgins deflowered, and other unheard of cruelties committed by these barbarous ruffians, who, by being let loose among us (and connived at) by the acting magistrates, have hereby reduced numbers of individuals to poverty, and for these three years last past have laid (in a manner) this part of the province under contribution.

No trading persons (or others) with money or goods, no responsible persons and traders dare keep cash or any valuable articles by them. Nor can women stir abroad but with a guard, or in terror. The chastity of many beauteous maidens has been threatened by these rogues. Merchants' stores are obliged to be kept constantly guarded (which enhances the price of goods). And thus we live not as under a British government (every man sitting in peace and security under his own vine, his own fig tree), but as if we were in Hungary or Germany, and in a state of war, continually exposed to the incursions of Hussars and Pandours [Croatian soldiers]; obliged to be constantly on the watch and on our guard against these intruders and having it not in our power to call what we possess our own, not even for an hour; as being liable daily and hourly to be stripped of our property.

Representations of these grievances and vexations have often been made by us to those in power, but without redress. Our cries must have pierced their ears though not entered into their hearts. For, instead of public justice being executed on many of these notorious robbers (who have been taken by us at much labor and expense and committed) and on others (who with great difficulty and charge have been arraigned and convicted), we have to lament that such have, from time to time, been pardoned; and afresh set loose among us to repeat their villainies and strip us of the few remaining cattle, horses, and movables which, after their former visits, they had left us.

Thus distressed, thus situated and unrelieved by government, many among us have been obliged to punish some of these banditti and their accomplices in a proper manner; necessity (that first principle) compelling them to do what was expected that the executive branch of the legislature would long ago have done.

We are free men, British subjects, not born slaves. We contribute our proportion in all public taxations and discharge our duty to the public equally with our fellow provincials, yet we do not participate with them in the rights and benefits which they enjoy, though equally entitled to them.

Property is of no value, except it be secure. How ours is secured appears from the forementioned circumstances and from our now being obliged to defend our families by our own strength, as legal methods are beyond our reach, or not as yet extended to us.

We may be deemed too bold in saying, "That the present constitution of this province is very defective, and become a burden, rather than being beneficial to the back inhabitants." For instance: to have but one place of judicature in this large and growing colony, and that seated not central but in a nook by the seaside; the back inhabitants to travel 200-300 miles to carry down criminals, prosecute offenders, appear as witnesses (though secluded to serve as jurors), attend the courts and suits of law, the governor and Court of Ordinary, all land matters, and on every public occasion, are great grievances and call loudly for redress. For 'tis not only loss of time which the poor settlers sustain therefrom but the toil of traveling, and heavy expenses therefrom arising. Poor suitors are often driven to great distresses, even to the spending their last shilling, or to sell their only horse, to defray their traveling and town costs. After which, they are obliged to trudge home on foot and beg for subsistence by the way. And after being subpoenaed and then attending court as witnesses or as constables, they oft are never called for on trials but are put off to next court, and then the same services must be repeated. These are circumstances experienced by no individuals under British government save those in South Carolina.

It is partly owing to these burdens on our shoulders that the gangs of robbers who infest us have so long reigned without repression; for if a party has twenty cattle or the best of his stallions stolen from him, the time and charge consequent on a prosecution of the offenders is equal to or greater than his loss, as to prosecute would make him doubly a sufferer. And poor persons have not money to answer the cravings of rapacious lawyers. As proceedings at law are now managed, it may cost a private person £50 to bring a villain to justice; and in civil cases the recovery of £20 will frequently be attended with £70 costs, if not treble that sum.

When cattle and horses are stolen and the thief is publicly known (they will commit their robberies openly at noonday), persons who see and know of these evils are backward in making information as they thereby are certain to subject themselves to much trouble and expense, besides the risk they run of being plundered themselves by the rogues in revenge for informing against them. And in consequence of being subpoenaed to attend the courts of Charleston (under great disadvantages), they are often obliged to sell their substance at half-value to defray road charges, the public having made no provision on this head. These long journeys are often required, too, at some critical juncture, very detrimental to the poor planter, who, therefrom, will endeavor to avoid appearing against rogues when they are brought to trial. From which circumstances, many rogues have been acquitted at court for want of evidence, the trials of others delayed, the province (as well as individuals) put to grievous expense; and the gangs of robbers (herefrom recruited and spirited) have still reigned without control, ranging and plundering the country with impunity. We can truly say they reign, as by their menaces they intimidate many whom they have injured from laying hold on and bringing of them to justice.

If we are thus insecure; if our lives and properties are thus at stake; if we cannot be protected; if these villains are suffered to range the country uncontrolled and no redress to be obtained for our losses, all of us and our families must quit the province and retire where there are laws, religion, and government; for as the laws now stand, it is of no import to bind lawless, profligate persons to their good behavior. Recognizances are laughed at because never put in suit, nor can be but at the private expense of the suffering party. Wherefrom the clergy, magistracy, and all in public authority (who ought to be protected in execution of the laws and honored in their public stations) are insulted and abused by licentious and insolent persons without redress.

The trial of small and mean causes by a single magistrate (a wise institution in the infancy of the colony) is now become an intolerable grievance, partly through the ignorance of some justices and the bigotry and partiality of others. Individuals are rath-

er oppressed than relieved by their decisions, for persons are ofttimes saddled with £10 or £12 costs on a debt of as many shillings. Through the indolence, connivance, or corruption of several justices, it is owing that the thieves have gained such strength and risen to such a pitch of audacity. They well know that if warrants are issued out against them that they will be slowly pursued, or that they shall have timely notice given them for to avoid the officers. We could enumerate many flagrant instances of this sort, but as every complaint of this nature from the country have hitherto been disregarded, we can only close this article with saying that through the venality of mean persons now in the Commission, contempt instead of respect is thrown on this so honorable and necessary an office.

By poor persons being obliged to travel to Charleston to obtain patents for small tracts of land or to renew their warrants, His Majesty's kindness to his subjects is defeated as it causes land to come as dear, or prove as expensive in running out, as if for to be purchased, the same fees being paid on a grant of 10 as on one of 10,000 acres. The like grievance exists in respect to the proving of wills or taking out letters of administration, the fees on which are treble to what is charged at home, even though clogged with stamps. When effects of a deceased party do not exceed £40 or £50, half this sum must be expended in court fees, no distinction being made, it being alike the same if the effects are £50 or £50,000. These are great hardships on the poor, especially as the fees now claimed at the public offices are double to what were formerly demanded, which merits the serious attention of the legislature.

As the laws are now modeled, any malicious, malevolent party may arrest any stranger, any innocent person, for any sum whatever, without showing cause of action or making oath of his debt or giving security for joining issue, which often prevents persons from getting bail; for though the debt or balance may not be 6d., yet the sum alleged may be £6,000. This intimidates persons from becoming securities and subjects many to wrongful and injurious imprisonment, whereby their credit and families are entirely ruined, health impaired, lives sacrificed by lying in a close and stinking jail crowded with thieves and vagabonds! No separation, no distinction made of parties, not hardly even of the sexes. Who can boast of British liberty that is not safe one hour from so dreadful an oppression!

A stranger or vagrant in this province, who can pay a lawyer £10, may, at his pleasure or for his frolic, send to prison (at 200 miles distance) the best person here among us without his knowing on what account or for what reason, and this in as arbitrary a manner as in France, by a *lettre de cachet*, or in Spain, by warrant from the Inquisition. Most sore are these evils! Especially, too, when a poor wretch who has inadvertently broken the peace (for which in Britain he would be ordered a few lashes or a small fine and be dismissed) must lie five or six months in this loathsome jail amidst thieves and robbers, in the heat of summer, and then afterward be discharged by proclamation.

Punishments ought to bear some proportion to trespasses. Nor should small and great offenses be treated with equal severity. To be confined six months in Charleston jail at 200 or 300 miles distance from friends or family, and to live in this hot clime on bread and water, is a far heavier punishment than for to be in the French king's galleys, or a slave in Barbary. And for persons to lie there session after session for small sums or petty offenses is contrary to all humanity. And more so (as we observed) when persons of every class and each sex are promiscuously confined together in a space where they have not room to lie, and no distinction made between offenders; but thieves and murderers, debtors to the King, offenders in penal laws, va-

grants and idle persons are closely huddled in one mixed crowd.

When persons are unwarrantably arrested by vexatious pettifoggers or litigious miscreants (as such will infest every society) and bail is given, in this case, should the plaintiff discontinue and refuse joining issue and drop the suit, we apprehend (from the sufferings of many) that no remedy at present lies for relief of any innocent person who is so treated, consistent with the liberty of the subject. But the defendant must submit to £40 or £50 charge and loss. Or if he sue for damages or costs expended, or for false imprisonment after being ruined and undone, what satisfaction is to be obtained against insolvent prosecutors?

By our birthright as Britons we ought to be tried by a jury of our peers. This is the glorious liberty of freeborn subjects, the darling privilege that distinguishes Britain from all other nations. But we poor distressed settlers enjoy only the shadow, not the substance of this happiness. For can we truly be said to be tried by our peers when few or no persons on this north side of Santee River (containing half the province) are on the jury list? The juries of every court are generally composed of the inhabitants of Charleston or its environs — persons who never perhaps traveled beyond Charleston Neck, who know not even the geography much less the persons and concerns of the back country. These determine boundaries of our lands, without a view, and decide on matters of which they have no proper conception. We think these proceedings as absurd as if affairs of shipping and trade were to be settled by twelve residents in our woods who never saw a town, the sea, or a ship in their lives.

Herefrom, the lives and properties of us back settlers may accidentally be affected through the judge or jurors having no personal knowledge of parties who dispose in court, or of their quality, estate, or character they bear where they dwell. All persons, without exception, are now admitted to give evidence, according to the mode of their profession, and stand *recta in curia*. Now, as we are a mixed people, and many concealed Papists among us (especially in the disguise of Quakers), and as such are often admitted as witnesses and jurors, a wrong verdict may often pass through this general admission of persons of all countries' complexions and characters being suffered to be on juries, and so give evidence without distinction or restriction.

Nor can we be said to possess our legal rights as freeholders when we are so unequally represented in assembly. The south side of Santee River, electing forty-four members, and the north side, with these upper parts of the province (containing two-thirds of the white inhabitants), returning but six. It is to this great disproportion of representatives on our part that our interests have been so long neglected and the back country disregarded. But it is the number of free men, not black slaves, that constitute the strength and riches of a state.

The not laying out the back country into parishes is another most sensible grievance. This evil we apprehend to arise from the selfish views of those whose fortune and estates are in or near Charleston, which makes them endeavor that all matters and things shall center there, however detrimental to the body politic. Hence it arises that assemblies are kept sitting for six months when the business brought before them might be dispatched in six weeks, to oblige us (against inclination) to choose such persons for representatives who live in or contiguous to Charleston, and to render a seat in the assembly too heavy a burden for any country planter of a small estate to bear. From this, our nonrepresentation in the House, we conceive it is that £60,000 public money (of which we must pay the greater part, as being levied on the consumer) has lately been voted for to build an exchange for the merchants, and a ballroom for the ladies of Charleston; while near 60,000 of us back settlers have not a minis-

ter or a place of worship to repair to! As if we were not worth even the thought of, or deemed as savages and not Christians!

To leave our native countries, friends, and relations, the service of God, the enjoyment of our civil and religious rights to breathe here (as we hoped) a purer air of freedom, and possess the utmost enjoyment of liberty and independency; and instead hereof, to be set adrift in the wild woods among Indians and outcasts; to live in a state of heathenism, without law or government or even the appearance of religion; exposed to the insults of lawless and impudent persons, to the depredations of thieves and robbers, and to be treated by our fellow provincials who hold the reins of things as persons hardly worthy the public attention, not so much as their Negroes. These sufferings have broken the hearts of hundreds of our new settlers, made others quit the province; some return to Europe (and therefrom prevent others coming this way), and deterred numbers of persons of fortune and character (both at home and in America) from taking up of lands here and settling this, our back country, as otherwise they would have done.

But whatever regulations, whatever emoluments are offered for the embellishment or benefit of the metropolis, such are readily admitted while we are considered by its inhabitants (and if they could, they would make us) hewers of wood and drawers of water, for service of the town; who treat us not as brethren of the same kindred, united in the same interests, and subjects of the same prince, but as if we were of a different species from themselves; reproaching us for our ignorance and unpoliteness, while they themselves contribute to it, and would chain us to these oars, as unwilling that either us or our posterity should emerge from darkness to light, and from the power of Satan unto God. Their very follies and extravagances would afford us means of knowledge and refinement. What they waste and throw away would lay for us the foundations of good things. The sums trifled away in a playhouse there would have raised us fifty new churches. And the heavy annual charges which the public is saddled with, attending the conveying of prisoners to town, summoning juries, and other incident expenses, together with Mr. Provost Marshal's and Mr. Attorney General's bills, would, if thrown together for these last seven years, have defrayed the expense of building jails and courthouses in every parish of the province, and all other public edifices.

But this is not comparable to the damage done the mother country and the West India trade by the thieves stealing all of our best horses and then selling them to Dutch agents, to be transported to the French islands to work their sugar mills. Add to this the depression of our lands in value; prevention of their sale and culture of any improvements in planting or public works through the insecurity of all property by incursions of the thieves; the bad character which the back settlements have gained hereby (both in Britain and America); the rise of provisions through loss of our stocks of meat cattle; the length of time and great expense it will cost us to raise again a fine breed of horses; the dread which persons of condition and character entertain even of their persons should they travel among us (which deters them from sending of any slaves for to improve their lands in the back country through fear of their being stolen), prevents their paying us any attention or regard or attempting any new branches of commerce though excited thereto by the Society of Arts at home. In short, the dread impressed on all travelers, and which prevents itinerants from visiting us (and thereby making cash to circulate); the damp put on our spirits through the disregard shown us by the legislature which has prevented, as beforesaid, many thousands from settling among us and lessening thereby the weight of taxes, and adding to the increase of provisions and commodities for the market; the drawing of merchants and mechanics among us, thereby lowering the present exorbitant prices of goods and labor and opening new channels of trade; all these, and other striking circumstances, have been little thought of or considered in Charleston, midst scenes of luxury and dissipation.

Oppression will make wise men mad. And many sober persons among us are become almost desperate in seeing the nonattention given to these and other matters of serious concern, and which so nearly affects the foundation of things. They seem weary of living (as they have done for years past) without exercise of their civil and religious rights which they ought to share in common with the lower settlements, and being deemed and treated as if not members of the same body politic. For, can we vote for members of assembly, or choose vestrymen, or elect parish officers when we have no churches to repair to, or they are situated 100-200 miles from us? Can our poor be taken charge of when there has been neither minister, church wardens, or vestry in St. Marks or St. Matthews parish for these three years past; nor either a church built or parish laid out in any of the upper parts of the province? Does not hereby a great and heavy encumbrance fall on the generous and humane? On all who have feelings for the sufferings of others? For the poor, the sick, the aged and infirm must be relieved and supported in some manner and not left to perish. What care is or can be taken of poor orphans and their effects (no proper laws or provisions being yet made on this head)? Are they not liable to become the prey of every invader?

Nor is here any security to the merchant or trader who may credit out their goods, as knaves and villains may remove with their substance unmolested into the neighboring provinces and there bid defiance to their creditors. Herefrom, no credit can be given among us, for no writ can be obtained without going to Charleston. No attachment can be sued out but in Charleston, and while these are preparing, your debtor has taken flight and is quite out of reach. And no marriage license can be obtained but in Charleston, and there every person must repair to get married that would marry judicially and according to law, for we have not churches wherein to publish banns, or ministers to marry persons. Wherefrom, the generality marry each other, which causes the vilest abominations, and that whoredom and adultery overspreads our land.

Thus we live and have lived for years past as if without God in the world, destitute of the means of knowledge, without law or gospel, esteem or credit. For we know not even the laws of this country we inhabit, for where are they to be found but in the secretary's office in Charleston? The printing of a code of the laws has been long petitioned for, often recommended by the Crown, and delineated in the presentments of grand juries as a matter long wanting and of the utmost consequence. But like all their other presentments, it lies totally unregarded.

Of what service have been, of what use are the parish churches of Prince George, Prince Frederic, and St. Mark to the inhabitants of Williamsburgh, Great and Little Pedee, Lynch's Creek, Waccamaw, the Congarees, Waxhaws, Waterees, Saluday, Long Canes, Ninety-Six, or Broad River — places and settlements containing 50,000 souls? These fabrics were placed where they are to serve some local occasion or particular persons or purposes but are not (at least at present) of the least benefit to the back country. What church can we repair to for divine service nearer than Dorchester or Charleston, several parishes being now destitute of ministers and no effectual plan settled for their being properly supplied?

It is notorious that, through the want of churches and ministers, new sects have arisen and now greatly prevail, especially those called New Lights. Profaneness and infidelity abound; ignorance, vice, and idleness prevail; and to the great indifference shown by all ranks to promote the interests of religion and virtue, it is in great measure owing that such few checks have been given to the villains and outlaws who have devoured us. For the common people hardly know the first principles of religion; and so corrupt are their morals that a reformation of manners among them in our time is more to be wished for than expected.

Through want of churches and ministers many persons go into the north province, there to be married by magistrates; which has encouraged many of our magistrates (so venal are they) to take on them also to solemnize marriages, and this without any previous publication of banns or any set form, but each after his own fancy, which occasions much confusion as they ask no questions but couple persons of all ages and every complexion, to the ruin and grief of many families. Their examples have been followed by the low lay teachers of every petty sect and also copied by itinerant and straggling preachers of various denominations who traverse the back country (sent this way from Pennsylvania and New England to poison the minds of the people).

From these irregular practices the sacred bond of marriage is so greatly slighted as to be productive of many great and innumerable evils. For many loose wretches are fond of such marriages on supposition that they are only temporary, or *durante placito;* dissoluble whenever their interests or passions incite them to separate. Thus they live *ad libitum,* quitting each other at pleasure, intermarrying year after year with others; changing from hand to hand as they remove from place to place, and swapping away their wives and children as they would horses or cattle. Great scandal arises herefrom to the back country, and loss to the community; for the issue of such are too often exposed, deserted, and disowned; beggars are hereby multiplied, concubinage established (as it were) by law. The most sacred obligations are hereby trampled on, and bastardy, adultery, and other heinous vices become so common, so openly practised and avowed, as to lose the stigma annexed to their commission. These are some of the main roots from whence the reigning gangs of horse thieves have sprung up.

Through the nonestablishment of public schools, a great multitude of children are now grown up in the greatest ignorance of everything save vice, in which they are adepts. Consequently they lead idle and immoral lives, for they, having no sort of education, naturally follow hunting, shooting, racing, drinking, gaming, and every species of wickedness. Their lives are only one continual scene of depravity of manners and reproach to the country, being more abandoned to sensuality and more rude in manners than the poor savages around us. They will learn no trade or mechanic arts whereby to obtain an honest livelihood, or practise any means of industry; or if they know, they will not practise them, but range the country with their horse and gun, without home or habitation, all persons, all places, all women being alike to them.

These are other deep roots from which the hordes of mulattoes and villains we are pestered with have shot up, whereas, had we churches and ministers, schools and catechists, children would be early taught the principles of religion and goodness, and their heads and hands be employed in exercises of the manual and useful arts; tradesmen would increase; manufactures be followed up; agriculture be improved; the country wear a new face; and peace and plenty smile around us.

But in our present unsettled situation, when the bands of society and government hang loose and ungirt about us, when no regular police is established but everyone left to do as seems him meet, there is not the least encouragement for any individual to be industrious, emulous in well-doing, or enterprising in any attempt that is laudable or public-spirited. Cunning, rapine, fraud, and violence are now the studies and pursuits of the vulgar. If we save a little money

to bring down to town wherewith to purchase slaves, should it be known, our houses are beset and robbers plunder us even of our clothes. If we buy liquor to retail, or for hospitality, they will break into our dwellings and consume it. If we purchase bedding, linen, or decent furniture, they have early notice, and we are certain to be stripped of it. Should we raise fat cattle or prime horses for the market, they are constantly carried off, though well-guarded (as a small force is insufficient for their security). Or if we collect gangs of hogs to kill and to barrel up for sale, or plant orchards or gardens, the rogues, and other idle, worthless, vagrant people with whom we are overrun, are continually destroying them, and subsisting on the stocks and labors of the industrious planter.

If we are in any wise injured in our persons, fame, or fortune, what remedy have we? What redress can be obtained without traveling 200 miles to Charleston? Where (through the chicanery of lawyers, slowness of law proceedings, and expenses thence arising) we are greater sufferers than before, and only thereby add evil to evil. Nay, we have had, and daily do see those very horses and creatures which have been stolen from us (and for which we have endeavored to bring villains to justice); we have seen these our creatures sold before our faces to raise money to fee lawyers to plead against us and to save rogues from the halter. And what defense are the laws (as they are now dispensed) to us against such as are below the law? For, in many cases (as in branding and killing of cattle), fines only being imposed and no provision made for the sufferer, should the injurer be a vagrant, or insolvent, incapable of paying the fine, what redress lies in this case? The confining of the transgressor for six months (at the private expense of the sufferer, besides his charges of prosecution) in the common jail of Charleston, where it is as agreeable to him to live an idle life in as out of it, work being the article he would avoid at any rate, and we have not a bridewell, whipping post, or pair of stocks in the province, and the workhouse of Charleston is only so in name.

As the back country is now daily increasing by imports of people from Ireland and elsewhere (most of whom are very poor), the number of the idle and worthless must also increase if our settlements long remain in their present neglected state. Many of these new settlers greatly repent their coming out here, to languish away life in a country that falls so very short of their expectations; and the sober part of them would more willingly return than remain here. They have, indeed, land given them, and may with industry raise a bare subsistence; but they are discouraged from any bold pursuits or exerting their laudable endeavors to make improvements through the uncertainty that attends us all, *i.e.,* whether in the end they may reap the fruits of their labor; for such number of idle and vagrant persons from the northern colonies traverse and infest this province that if a spot of ground be planted (especially with fruit trees for cider, etc.), the proprietor cannot be certain of gathering the produce but may see it carried off before his face without control. So great is the weakness of government in these parts that our magistrates are weary of committing persons to Charleston for petty offenses, and they have no authority to inflict punishments. It is therefore in vain for us to attempt the laying out of vineyards, sheepwalks, or bleaching grounds, as it would only be working for these indolent, unsettled, roving wretches.

Property being thus insecure, no improvements are attempted, no new plans can take place, nothing out of the common road can be executed till legislation is extended to us. A damp is now put on all spirited endeavors to make matters run in their proper channel. And (shameful to say) our lands (some of the finest in America) lie useless and uncleared, being rendered of small value from the many licentious persons intermixed among us whom we cannot drive off without force or violence.

But these our lands would be of infinite value, and in time, the most desirable in the province, were proper regulations to take place and good manners and order be introduced among us. Our soil is not only fruitful but capable of producing any grain whatever. Our vales and woods are delightful, our hills healthful and pleasant. This single consideration merits the public attention. For, was the country to be once cleared of lawless and idle people (or were they only to be put under proper restraint), were courts of justice once established, the roads repaired and improved, bridges built in proper places, and traveling rendered safe and commodious, we should no longer be pestered with insolvent and licentious persons from the neighboring governments. Nor would this province be the sink (as now it is) of the refuse of other colonies. Such abandoned wretches would no longer seek shelter or find protection here, nor set bad examples to our rising progeny. We should chase them away as beasts of prey. And was the country once cleared of such vermin, it would induce genteel persons to make the tour of their native country and not embark annually for Rhode Island or New York for the benefit of cool air. They may breathe equal as salubrious on our hills. And the specie which is now carried out of the province by our traveling gentry (never to return!) would circulate among the poor back inhabitants and quickly find its way down to Charleston.

We may be despised or slighted for our poverty but poor the country ever will be if it long remains in its present disordered state, as the few persons of property among us must be obliged to quit their farms instead of their engaging new adventurers to sit down among us. Were our interest (which is the interest of the community) but properly attended to and the laws duly administered among us, our industry and application to raise staple articles for the foreign market would render this province in few years a most valuable country and one of the brightest jewels in the crown of Great Britain.

By our urging of these particulars and thus bringing them home to the attention of the legislature, we do not presume to reflect on or to censure the conduct, much less to prescribe or dictate to those in authority; but we humbly submit ourselves and our cause to the wisdom of our superiors, professing ourselves dutiful and loyal subjects to His Majesty, King George, true lovers of our country, zealous for its true interests, the rights and liberties of the subject, and the stability of our present happy constitution in church and state. We only enumerate plain and glaring facts, and all we crave is the enjoyment of those native rights which as freeborn subjects we are entitled unto but at present are debarred of; and also the proper establishment of religion and dispensation of the laws in the upper part of the country. All which our petitions we humbly beg leave (with the greatest deference and submission) to sum up in the following articles, humbly praying that the legislature would be pleased to grant us such relief as may be conducive to the public welfare, the honor of the Crown, the good of the church, and the peace and prosperity of all His Majesty's liege people in this his province.

With all due respect, we humbly request:

1. That circuit or county courts for the due and speedy administration of justice be established in this, as is in the neighboring provinces.

2. That some subordinate courts, to consist of justices and freeholders, be erected in each parish for the trial of slaves, small and mean causes, and other local matters; and that (under the governor) they may grant probate of wills and letters of administration for all effects under £100; also to pass small grants of lands, renew warrants, etc., paying the common fees, to prevent poor

persons from traveling down to Charleston on account of these and other such petty matters.

3. That these circuit or county courts may decide all suits not exceeding £100 currency without appeal, and that no *nolle prosequis* or *traverses* be filed against informations made against transgressors of the local or penal laws.

4. That the clerk of the circuit or county court may issue writs or attachments for any sum, all above £100 currency to be made returnable to the Supreme Court in Charleston, and all under that sum returnable by the sheriff of each county to his particular court, and that justices of the peace or clerk of the court may issue attachments (as now they do executions) for sums under £20 currency.

5. That the poor laws be amended and some better provision made for the care of poor orphans and their estates; also of the effects of strangers, travelers, and transient persons dying within the province.

6. That courthouses, jails, and bridewells be built in proper places and coercive laws framed for the punishment of idleness and vice and for lessening the number of vagrant and indolent persons who now prey on the industrious. And that none such be allowed to traverse the province without proper licenses or passes.

7. That the laws respecting public houses and taverns be amended, and the prices of articles vended by them to be ascertained as to quality and quantity. And that none be permitted to retail liquors on the public roads but such as can lodge travelers and provide entertainment for man and horse.

8. That the laws concerning the stealing and branding of cattle, tolling of horses, taking up of strays, etc., be amended; that hunters be put under some restrictions and obliged not to leave carcasses unburied in the woods; and that some few regulations be made in respect to swine.

9. That the provincial laws be digested into a regular code and be printed as soon as possible.

10. That gentlemen who may be elected as members of assembly, commissioners of the roads, and into other public offices be obliged to serve or be fined.

11. That the interior and upper parts of the province, and all beyond Black River, be laid out into parishes, or chapels, churches, and parsonages be founded among them.

12. That ministers be provided for these new as well as vacant old parishes, and that some method be devised for an immediate supply of parishes with ministers, on the death or cession of incumbents; also for the better care (than at present) of vacant churches and parsonages.

13. That the salaries of the country clergy be augmented and some provision made for their widows, thereby that learned and goodly men may be excited to come over to us, and not profligates.

14. That all magistrates, lay persons, and itinerant preachers and teachers be inhibited from marrying, and the mode and authenticity of marriages be settled; and that dissenting teachers be obliged to register their meeting houses and to take the state oaths agreeable to the statute (1 William and Mary); and that none but such settled pastors be allowed to teach or preach among the people.

15. That some expedient be devised for His Majesty's attorney general to put recognizances in suit; and that he may be empowered to prosecute on all recognizances given for the observance of the provincial laws.

16. That a proper table of fees be framed for all ministers, ecclesiastical and civil, to govern themselves by; and that the length and enormous expense of lawsuits be moderated, this province being harder ridden at present by lawyers than Spain or Italy by priests.

17. That juries be impaneled from, and all offenses tried in, that county wherein crimes, trespasses, and damages have been committed or sustained — agreeable to Magna Charta.

18. That no attorney be put into commission of the peace, and that their number be limited in the Commons House of Assembly.

19. That some public schools be founded in the back settlements for training up of the rising generation in the true principles of things, that so they may become useful and not pernicious members of society.

20. That proper premiums be annually distributed for promoting agriculture, the raising of articles for exportation, and establishing useful arts on the plan of the Dublin Society and that of Arts and Commerce in London.

21. That the statute for limitation of actions and that for preventing frivolous and vexatious suits be enforced and elucidated; and that the liberty of the subject as to arrests and wrongful imprisonments be better secured.

22. That the lines of the several counties be run out from the sea to the Cherokee boundary; also that the lines of each old and new parish be ascertained and known, that we may no longer wander in the mazes of supposition.

23. Lastly, we earnestly pray that the legislature would import a quantity of Bibles, Common Prayers, and devotional tracts, to be distributed by the ministers among the poor, which will be of far greater utility to the province than erecting the statue of Mr. Pitt.

The above particulars are with the greatest deference and respect submitted to the wisdom of the legislature.

In the name, by desire, and on behalf of the back inhabitants, and signed in their presence, by us, their deputies.

1768

40.

Benjamin Rush: On Medical Education in the Colonies

In 1775, the American colonies had about 3,500 physicians. Of these, less than 400 held medical degrees, most of them earned in London and Edinburgh. Medical schools in the colonies initially grew out of apprenticeship training and lecture courses. Dr. Benjamin Rush had a major interest in medical education in the colonies. While studying medicine at Edinburgh he wrote the following letter on January 20, 1768, to John Morgan, who established America's first medical school in 1765.

Source: Butterfield, I.

Your most agreeable favor came safe to hand by Captain Faulkner. I wish I had time to dwell upon each of the particulars in it. At present I can only assure you how much I esteem and how desirous I am of cultivating your friendship.

I exult in the happy prospects which now open upon you of the success of the medical schools you have established in Philadelphia. The scheme you have published for conferring degrees in physic has met with the approbation of Dr. Cullen himself, who interests himself warmly in everything that relates to your reputation or success in life. He thinks himself very happy, he says, in educating those young men to whom so important a medical college as that in Philadelphia will give its foundation and future credit.

I thank you for the pains you have taken to secure me the professorship of chemistry. I think I am now master of the science and could teach it with confidence and ease. I am not surprised at Dr. Redman's behavior. It corresponds with the rest of his conduct to me, both before I left him and since I came to Edinburgh. I have written to him seven or eight times and have received but one letter from him, which was last summer. What can this mean? I fear each of us will have reason to say with the poet:

> O! had we served our God
> With but half that earnestness
> we served our master,
> He would not thus have left us.

I wrote to him about the professorship at the same time I wrote to you, and desired him to use his interest to secure it for me. It was the first favor I ever implored from him, and I am resolved it shall be the last. I would not, however, urge your interest too warmly in this affair. Perhaps I may disappoint the expectations of the trustees and prevent a person better qualified from filling the chair. I should like to teach chemistry as a professor because I think I could show its application to medicine and philosophy in a stronger light than ever has yet been done. I should likewise be able more fully (from having a seat in the college) to cooperate with you in advancing the medical sciences in general. But I would not condescend to implore that as a favor which I am sure will contribute much more to the emolument of the college than my own.

I can with pleasure inform you that your schools begin to attract the notice of the professors here not a little. Boarding is now become so excessive high in Edinburgh that few students will be able to come here hereafter from America. This will evidently throw an advantage in favor of the College of Philadelphia of which the professors here are very sensible.

You have little to fear from the coalition in New York. Dr. Clossy is full of the old mechanical doctrines, and Dr. Bard had not entirely rejected them when he went from Edinburgh. The rest of the professors don't deserve a stricture.

I am now busily employed in translating my thesis. The subject of it is digestion, in which I hope to publish a discovery that will admit of some useful inductions in pathology and the practice of physic. I shall beg leave to prefix your name to it together with Dr. Franklin's, Dr. Black's, Dr. Shippen's, and Redman's. The thesis will contain little more than a few experiments on which the whole of my doctrine is founded. I expect to stand forth in a few nights to defend my papers in the Medical Society.

One of them is on the bilious fever, the other on venereal disease, in each of which I have ventured upon *loca nullo antea trita solo* [areas never before explored by anyone]. But of this you shall hear more hereafter.

You cannot conceive, my dear sir, with what pleasure I look forward into life when I think I shall pass through it hand in hand with you. I have a thousand things to communicate to you in physic. I am attending Dr. Cullen's lectures a second time and am daily surprised with some new discovery from him. His lectures upon the nervous system and upon pathology are worth their weight in gold. I am in hopes I shall be able to transplant most of his doctrines to Philadelphia. Dr. Gregory's lectures abound with excellent practical observations, but are by no means equal to the unrivaled Dr. Cullen's, whose merit is beyond all praise. I am likewise attending Dr. Black a second course. This very amiable and learned gentleman has honored me with his particular friendship. Modesty forbids me to tell you of the many distinguishing marks of favor I have received from him.

I have thought much of the advantages that would arise from establishing a literary and physical society in Philadelphia, in imitation of the Edinburgh society of the same name. Nothing but publications in medicine will ever attract the notice of the literati to the college. I could mention many other advantages that would accrue from such an institution, but want of room forbids.

Dr. Cullen desires to be remembered to you in the most affectionate manner, as do also Mr. Hogg and Mr. Scott with their respective families.

41.

THOMAS GAGE: On the Growing Economic Competition with England

Many of the colonies resisted the Stamp Act by signing nonimportation agreements and relying for their needs on domestic manufactures. The fear of economic competition alarmed Great Britain. Colonial governors therefore were ordered to report on the progress of American manufacturing. In the following letter to the Earl of Shelburne, dated January 23, 1768, General Thomas Gage confirmed British fears of the potential rivalry and made suggestions about how to stem the tide.

Source: Carter, I.

DURING MY STAY AT PHILADELPHIA, I could not help being surprised at the great increase of that city in buildings, mechanics, and manufacturers. The emigrations from Great Britain and Ireland and the importation of Germans every year from Holland contribute to the constant increase of mechanics and manufacturers in this province beyond any of the rest. The discharged soldiers too have contributed not a little to this increase in Philadelphia, as well as in other cities of the continent. Instead of clearing uncultivated lands, which it was expected they would do, they have for the most part crowded into the towns to work at trades, and help to supply the inhabitants with necessaries, which should be imported from the mother country. I would take the liberty to propose to Your Lordship, that no soldier who has any trade should receive his discharge in America, and that the men of war and packets should have orders to receive such discharged soldiers on the return to England and transport them thither. The Pennsylvanians complain that the Dutch have laid a duty upon all emigrants who embark in their ports, but they import them notwithstanding.

They talk and threaten much in other provinces of their resolution to lessen the importation of British manufactures, and to manufacture for themselves; but they are by no means able to do it. The people of Pennsylvania lay their plans with more temper and judgment, and pursue with patience and steadiness. They don't attempt impossibilities, or talk of what they will do, but are silently stealing in mechanics and manufacturers; and if they go on as they have hitherto done, they will probably in a few years supply themselves with many necessary articles which they now import from Great Britain.

42.

A Circular Letter Against Taxation

In 1767, the British government passed what were known as the Townshend Acts, named for Charles Townshend, Chancellor of the Exchequer. These acts added new taxes to those that had already been levied on the colonies, but their chief affront was in creating a Board of Customs Commissioners in Boston to enforce the British trade laws with heavy penalties. As the burden of this provision fell hardest upon the merchants of Boston, they decided, with the agreement of other merchants, that no further imports from abroad would be accepted in America. At the same time the Massachusetts General Court adopted a circular letter, drafted by Samuel Adams, protesting the idea of taxation without representation. For circulating this letter among the colonies, the Massachusetts General Court was dissolved by the royal governor, Francis Bernard, in 1768. The Assembly of Virginia met the same fate for receiving the letter with approval.

Source: *The Writings of Samuel Adams*, Harry A. Cushing, ed., Vol. I, New York, 1904, pp. 184-188.

THE HOUSE OF REPRESENTATIVES of this province have taken into their serious consideration the great difficulties that must accrue to themselves and their constituents by the operation of several acts of Parliament imposing duties and taxes on the American colonies. As it is a subject in which every colony is deeply interested, they have no reason to doubt but your Assembly is deeply impressed with its importance, and that such constitutional measures will be come into as are proper. It seems to be necessary that all possible care should be taken that the representations of the several assembl[ies] upon so delicate a point should harmonize with each other. The House, therefore, hope that this letter will be candidly considered in no other light than as expressing a disposition freely to communicate their mind to a sister colony, upon a common concern in the same manner as they would be glad to receive the sentiments of your or any other house of assembly on the continent.

The House have humbly represented to the Ministry their own sentiments that His Majesty's High Court of Parliament is the supreme legislative power over the whole Empire; that in all free states the constitution is fixed; and as the supreme legislative derives its power and authority from the constitution, it cannot overleap the bounds of it without destroying its own foundation; that the constitution ascertains and limits both sovereignty and allegiance, and, therefore, His Majesty's American subjects, who acknowledge themselves bound by the ties of allegiance, have an equitable claim to the full enjoyment of the fundamental rules of the British constitution; that it is an essential, unalterable right in nature, engrafted into the British constitution as a fundamental law, and ever held sacred and irrevocable by the subjects within the Realm, that what a man has honestly acquired is absolutely his own, which he may freely give, but cannot be taken from him without his consent; that the American subjects may, therefore, exclusive of any consideration of charter rights, with a decent firmness adapted to the character of free men and subjects, assert this natural and constitutional right.

It is, moreover, their humble opinion, which they express with the greatest deference to the wisdom of the Parliament, that the acts made there imposing duties on the people of this province, with the sole and express purpose of raising a revenue, are infringements of their natural and constitutional rights; because, as they are not represented in the British Parliament, His Majesty's Commons in Britain, by those acts, grant their property without their consent.

This House further are of opinion that their constituents, considering their local circumstances, cannot by any possibility be represented in the Parliament, and that it will forever be impracticable that they should be equally represented there, and consequently not at all, being separated by an ocean of a thousand leagues; and that His Majesty's royal predecessors, for this reason, were graciously pleased to form a subordinate legislature here, that their subjects might enjoy the unalienable right of a representation. Also that considering the utter impracticability of their ever being fully and equally represented in Parliament, and the great expense that must unavoidably attend even a partial representation there, this House think that a taxation of their constituents, even without their consent, grievous as it is, would be preferable to any representation that could be admitted for them there.

Upon these principles, and also considering that were the right in Parliament ever so clear, yet, for obvious reasons, it would be beyond the rules of equity that their constituents should be taxed on the manufactures of Great Britain here, in addition

to the duties they pay for them in England, and other advantages arising to Great Britain from the acts of trade, this House have preferred a humble, dutiful, and loyal petition to our most gracious Sovereign, and made such representations to His Majesty's ministers as they apprehended would tend to obtain redress.

They have also submitted to consideration whether any people can be said to enjoy any degree of freedom if the Crown, in addition to its undoubted authority of constituting a governor, should appoint him such a stipend as it may judge proper without the consent of the people and at their expense; and whether, while the judges of the land and other civil officers hold not their commissions during good behavior, their having salaries appointed for them by the Crown independent of the people, has not a tendency to subvert the principles of equity and endanger the happiness and security of the subject.

In addition . . . the House have written a letter to their agent . . . the sentiments of which he is directed to lay before the Ministry; wherein they take notice of the hardships of the act for preventing mutiny and desertion, which requires the governor and Council to provide enumerated articles for the King's marching troops and the people to pay the expenses; and also of the commission of the gentlemen appointed [as] commissioners of the customs to reside in America, which authorizes them to make as many appointments as they think fit and to pay the appointees what sum they please . . . from whence it may happen that officers of the Crown may be multiplied to such a degree as to become dangerous to the liberty of the people. . . .

These are the sentiments and proceedings of this House; and as they have too much reason to believe that the enemies of the colonies have represented them to His Majesty's ministers and the Parliament as factious, disloyal, and having a disposition to make themselves independent of the mother country, they have taken occasion, in the most humble terms, to assure His Majesty and his ministers that with regard to the people of this province and as they doubt not, of all the colonies, the charge is unjust.

The House is fully satisfied that your Assembly is too generous and enlarged in sentiment to believe that this letter proceeds from an ambition of taking the lead, or dictating to the other assemblies. They freely submit their opinions to the judgment of others, and shall take it kind in your House to point out to them anything further which may be thought necessary.

This House cannot conclude without expressing their firm confidence in the King, our common head and father, that the united and dutiful supplications of his distressed American subjects will meet with his royal and favorable acceptance.

43.

Boston Boycott Agreement

The nonimportation agreements were the colonies' main weapon against Great Britain in the struggle for American liberty. The renewal of these agreements, which had been employed at the time of the Stamp Act, was a result of the enactment of the Townshend measures. In March of 1768, merchants of Boston agreed not to import from England if similar promises were made by New York and Philadelphia merchants. By August 1, the Boston merchants were acting independently and had ceased trade with England; similar action was later taken by merchants of other New England towns. The nonimportation agreements reduced imports from England by about one-half during 1768 and 1769.

Source: *The Annual Register . . . for the Year 1768*, London, 1768, pp. 235-236.

THE MERCHANTS AND TRADERS in the town of Boston having taken into consideration the deplorable situation of the trade, and the many difficulties it at present labors under on account of the scarcity of money, which is daily increasing for want of the other remittances to discharge our debts in Great Britain, and the large sums collected by the officers of the customs for duties on goods imported; the heavy taxes levied to discharge the debts contracted by the government in the late war; the embarrassments and restrictions laid on the trade by several late acts of Parliament; together with the bad success of our cod fishery this season, and the discouraging prospect of the whale fishery, by which our principal sources of remittance are like to be greatly diminished, and we thereby rendered unable to pay the debts we owe the merchants in Great Britain, and to continue the importation of goods from thence:

We, the subscribers, in order to relieve the trade under those discouragements, to promote industry, frugality, and economy, and to discourage luxury and every kind of extravagance, do promise and engage to and with each other as follows:

First, that we will not send for or import from Great Britain, either upon our own account or upon commission this fall, any other goods than what are already ordered for the fall supply.

Second, that we will not send for or import any kind of goods or merchandise from Great Britain, either on our own account or on commissions or any other wise, from the 1st of January, 1769, to the 1st of January, 1770, except salt, coals, fishhooks and lines, hemp, and duck-bar lead and shot, wool cards and card wire.

Third, that we will not purchase of any factor, or others, any kind of goods imported from Great Britain from January 1769 to January 1770.

Fourth, that we will not import, on our own account or on commissions, or purchase of any who shall import from any other colony in America, from January 1769 to January 1770, any tea, glass, paper, or other goods commonly imported from Great Britain.

Fifth, that we will not, from and after the 1st of January, 1769, import into this province any tea, paper, glass, or painter's colors until the act imposing duties on those articles shall be repealed.

In witness whereof, we have hereunto set our hands, this 1st day of August, 1768.

44.

Resolutions of a Boston Town Meeting Against the King

Because Boston had become the focal point of colonial opposition to British tax policies, General Gage ordered British troops to be stationed there in the spring of 1768. This news caused an immediate reaction in Massachusetts. When the Boston town meeting requested Governor Bernard to call a special session of the legislature, he refused on the grounds that he had to have permission from Britain. On September 13, the town meeting adopted resolutions stating the rights of the colonists, and proceeded to call a provincial convention to meet in Boston on September 22. These revolutionary proceedings were printed in town newspapers, and copies were circulated throughout the colony.

Source: *The Annual Register . . . for the Year 1768*, London, 1768, pp. 238-241.

THE COMMITTEE appointed to take the state of our public affairs into consideration reported the following declaration and resolves:

Whereas it is the first principle in civil society, founded in nature and reason, that no law of the society can be binding on any individual without his consent, given by himself in person or by his representative of his own free election; *and whereas* in and by an act of the British Parliament passed in the first year of the reign of King William and Queen Mary, of glorious and blessed memory, entitled "An Act declaring the Rights and Liberties of the Subject, and Settling the Succession of the Crown," the preamble of which act is in these words, viz.: "*Whereas* the late King James II, by the assistance of diverse evil councilors, judges, and ministers employed by him did endeavor to subvert and extirpate the Protestant religion, and the laws and liberties of this kingdom," it is expressly among other things declared that the levying money for the use of the Crown by pretense of prerogative, without grant of Parliament for a longer time or in other manner than the same is granted, is illegal.

And whereas in the third year of the reign of the same King William and Queen Mary, Their Majesties were graciously pleased by their royal charter to give and grant to the inhabitants of His Majesty's province all the territory therein described to be held in free and common socage; and also to ordain and grant to the said inhabitants certain rights, liberties, and privileges therein expressly mentioned, among which it is granted, established, and ordained that all and every the subjects of Them, Their Heirs, and Successors, which shall go to inhabit within said province and territory, and every of their children which shall happen to be born there, or on the seas in going thither or returning from thence, shall have and enjoy all liberties and immunities of free and natural subjects, within any of the dominions of Them, Their Heirs, and Successors, to all intents, purposes, and constructions whatever, as if they and every of them were born within the Realm of England.

And whereas by the aforesaid act of Parliament made in the first year of the said King William and Queen Mary, all and singular the premises contained therein are claimed, demanded, and insisted on as the undoubted rights and liberties of the subjects born within the Realm.

And whereas the freeholders and other inhabitants of this town, the metropolis of the province in said charter mentioned, do hold all the rights and liberties therein contained to be sacred and inviolable; at the same time publicly and solemnly acknowledging their firm and unshaken allegiance to their alone and rightful sovereign King George III, the lawful successor of the said King William and Queen Mary to the British throne: Therefore,

Resolved, that the said freeholders and other inhabitants of the town of Boston will at the utmost peril of their lives and fortunes take all legal and constitutional measures to defend and maintain the person, family, crown, and dignity of our said sovereign Lord George III; and all and singular the rights, liberties, privileges, and immunities granted in the said royal charter, as well as those which are declared to be belonging to us as British subjects by birthright, as all others therein specially mentioned.

And whereas by the said royal charter it is specially granted to the Great and General Court or assembly therein constituted to impose and levy proportionable and reasonable assessments, rates, and taxes upon the estates and persons of all and every the proprietors and inhabitants of said province or territory for the service of the King in the necessary defense and support of his government of this province and the protection and preservation of his subjects therein: Therefore:

Voted, as the opinion of this town, that the levying money within this province for the use and service of the Crown in other manner than the same is granted by the Great and General Court or assembly of this province is in violation of the said royal charter; and the same is also in violation of the undoubted natural rights of subjects, declared in the aforesaid act of Parliament, freely to give and grant their own money for the service of the Crown, with their own consent, in person or by representatives of their own free election.

And whereas in the aforesaid act of Parliament it is declared that the raising or keeping a standing army within the Kingdom in time of peace, unless it be with the consent of Parliament, is against law, it is the opinion of this town that the said declarations are founded in the indefeasible right of the subjects to be *consulted*, and to give their *free consent in person* or by representatives of their own free election to the raising and keeping a standing army among them; and the inhabitants of this town being free subjects have the same right derived from nature and confirmed by the British constitution, as well as the said royal charter; and, therefore, the raising or keeping a standing army without their consent in person or by representatives of their own free election would be an infringement of their natural, constitutional, and charter rights; and the employing such army for the enforcing of laws made without the consent of the people, in person or by their representatives, would be a grievance.

The foregoing report being diverse times distinctly read and considered by the town, the question was put whether the same shall be accepted and recorded, and passed unanimously in the affirmative.

Upon a motion made and seconded, the following vote was unanimously passed, viz.:

Whereas by an act of Parliament of the first of King William and Queen Mary, it is declared that for the redress of all grievances, and for amending, strengthening, and preserving the laws, parliaments ought to be held frequently; and inasmuch as it is the opinion of this town that the people labor under many intolerable grievances which unless speedily redressed threaten the total destruction of our invaluable natural, constitutional, and charter rights:

And furthermore as His Excellency the Governor has declared himself unable, at the request of this town, to call a General Court, which is the assembly of the states of this province for the redress of such grievances:

Voted, that this town will now make choice of a suitable number of persons to act for them as a committee in convention, with such as may be sent to join them from the several towns in this province, in order that such measures may be consulted and advised as His Majesty's service, and the peace and safety of his subjects in this province may require; whereupon the Hon. James Otis, Esq., the Hon. Thomas Cushing, Esq., Mr. Samuel Adams, and John Hancock, Esq., were appointed a committee for the said purpose, the town hereafter to take into consideration what recompense shall be made them for the service they may perform.

Voted, that the selectmen be directed to write to the selectmen of the several towns within this province informing them of the foregoing vote, and to propose that a convention be held, if they shall think proper, at Faneuil Hall, in this town, on . . . the 22nd day of September, instant, at 10 o'clock before noon.

1770

45.

Thomas Gage: Rioting in Boston

Thomas Gage, commander in chief of the British Army in America, had been sent to Boston in 1768 to quell any disturbances that might arise from the presence of British troops. Antagonism between the populace and the troops came to a head in the spring of 1770. On March 5, a mob attacked a group of soldiers. In the ensuing confusion the soldiers opened fire, leaving several Bostonians dead. The event, termed the Boston Massacre, was quickly seized upon as a source of anti-British propaganda and came to symbolize, in the years that followed, the clash between Britain and America over colonial rights. In a letter of April 10, 1770, to the Earl of Hillsborough, one of the King's principal secretaries of state, General Gage described the riots in Boston.

Source: Carter, I.

YOUR LORDSHIP will have received by the way of Boston much earlier intelligence than it has been in my power to transmit, of an unhappy quarrel between the people of that town and the soldiers, in which several of the former were killed and wounded. But I take the first opportunity to send Your Lordship the best account I have been able to procure of this unfortunate accident, as well as to represent the critical situation of the troops, and the hatred of the people towards them.

The occasion which brought the regiments to Boston rendered them obnoxious to the people, and they may have increased the odium themselves, as the disorders of that place have mostly sprung from disputes with Great Britain. The officers and soldiers are Britons, and the people found no advocates amongst them. It was natural for them, without examining into the merits of a political dispute, to take the part of their country; which probably they have often done with more zeal than discretion, considering the circumstances of the place they were in; for in matters of dispute with the mother country, or relative thereto, government is at end in Boston, and in the hands of the people, who have only to assemble to execute any designs. No person dares to oppose them, or call them to account; the whole authority of government, the governor excepted, and magistracy supporting them. The people, prejudiced against the troops, laid every snare to entrap and distress them, and frequent complaints have been made that the soldiers were daily insulted, and the people encouraged to insult them even by magistrates; that no satisfaction could be obtained, but the soldier, if found in fault, punished with the rigor of the law. Such proceedings could not fail to irritate, but the troops were restrained by their discipline; and though accidental quarrels happened, matters were prevented going to extremities.

In my letter to Your Lordship . . . I mentioned a misunderstanding between the inhabitants and soldiers in this town, soon after which advice was transmitted from Boston that the people there had quarreled with the troops, and lay in wait for them in the streets to knock them down; insomuch that it was unsafe for officers or soldiers to appear in the streets after dark. A particular quarrel happened at a rope walk with a few soldiers of the 29th Regiment; the provocation was given by the ropemakers, though it may be imagined in the course of it that there were faults on both sides. This quarrel, it is supposed, excited the people to concert a general rising on the night of March 5. They began by falling upon a few soldiers in a lane, contiguous to a barrack of the 29th Regiment, which brought some officers of the said regiment out of their quarters; who found some of their men greatly hurt, but carried all the soldiers to their barrack. The mob followed, menacing and brandishing their clubs over the officers' heads, to the barrack door, the officers endeavoring to pacify them, and desiring them to retire. Part of the mob broke into a meetinghouse and rang the fire bell, which appears to have been the alarm concerted; for numerous bodies immediately assembled in the streets, armed, some with muskets, but most with clubs, bludgeons, and suchlike weapons.

Many people came out of their houses supposing a fire in the town, and several officers on the same supposition were re-

pairing to their posts; but meeting with mobs were reviled, attacked, and those who could not escape, knocked down, and treated with great inhumanity. Different mobs paraded through the streets, passing the several barracks, and provoking the soldiers to come out. One body went to the main guard, where every provocation was given, without effect, for the guard remained quiet. From thence the mob proceeded to a sentinel posted upon the customhouse, at a small distance from the guard, and attacked him. He defended himself as well as he could, calling out for help; and people ran to the guard to give information of his danger. Captain Preston of the 29th Regiment, being Captain of the Day, his duty upon the alarm carried him to the main guard, and hearing the sentinel was in danger of being murdered, he detached a sergeant and twelve men to relieve him, and soon after followed himself, to prevent any rash act on the part of the troops. This party as well as the sentinel was immediately attacked, some throwing bricks, stones, pieces of ice and snowballs at them, whilst others advanced up to their bayonets, and endeavored to close with them, to use their bludgeons and clubs; calling out to them to fire if they dared, and provoking them to it by the most opprobrious language.

Captain Preston stood between the soldiers and the mob, parleying with the latter, and using every conciliating method to persuade them to retire peaceably. Some amongst them asked him if he intended to order the men to fire, he replied by no means, and observed he stood between the troops and them. All he could say ·had no effect, and one of the soldiers, receiving a violent blow, instantly fired. Captain Preston turned round to see who fired, and received a blow upon his arm, which was aimed at his head; and the mob, at first seeing no execution done, and imagining the soldiers had only fired powder to frighten, grew more bold and attacked with greater violence, continually striking at the soldiers and pelting them, and calling out to them to fire. The soldiers at length perceiving their lives in danger, and hearing the word fire all round them, three or four of them fired one after another, and again three more in the same hurry and confusion. Four or five persons were unfortunately killed, and more wounded. Captain Preston and the party were soon afterward delivered into the hands of the magistrates, who committed them to prison.

The misunderstanding between the people and the troops in this place was contrived by one party, not only to wound their adversaries who had voted to supply the troops according to act of Parliament through the sides of the soldiers, by making them and their measures odious to the people, but also to have a pretence to desire the removal of the troops; which I am assured was mentioned, if not moved at the time, in the Council. This plan of getting the troops removed by quarreling with them was soon transmitted to Boston; where they immediately put it in execution, by endeavors to bring on a general quarrel between them and the townspeople. We fortunately found not only magistrates but many people of consequence in this place, who discovered the designs of the adverse party, and exerted themselves in keeping the people quiet and, preventing mischief; without whose assistance I am confident something very disagreeable must have happened here, notwithstanding the uncommon pains taken with the soldiers. And had the magistrates and those who have influence over the populace in Boston taken as much trouble to appease and restrain as they have on too many occasions to inflame and excite the people to tumults and mischief, I am as confident that no blood would have been shed in that place. But it appears, unfortunately, that their schemes were not to be brought about through peace and tranquility, but by promoting disorders.

Some have sworn that Captain Preston gave orders to fire; others who were near, that the soldiers fired without orders from the provocation they received. None can deny the attack made upon the troops, but differ in the degree of violence in the attack.

I hope and believe that I have given Your Lordship in general a true relation of this unhappy affair; and sorry I am to say, there is too much reason to apprehend neither Captain Preston nor the soldiers, can have a fair and impartial trial for their lives. The utmost malice and malevolence has been shown already, in endeavors to bring on the trials whilst the people are heated by resentment, and the thirst of revenge. And attempts have been made to overawe the judges. The inveteracy of the people against the commissioners has also appeared in this affair, for there is information that the Grand Jury took pains to bring them in as conspiring with the army to massacre, as they term it, the inhabitants. And an officer of the Customs belonging to Gaspée with a gentleman of his acquaintance, and two servants of the Board have been committed to prison; where they have lain some days as accessories for firing out of the customhouses; upon the evidence of a French serving boy of fourteen years of age, notwithstanding the officer, by name Manwaring, was apprehended by a warrant from a popular justice, and dismissed upon the detection of the villainy of the boy.

Lieutenant Governor Hutchinson, and Lieutenant Colonel Dalrymple, having acquainted His Majesty's ministers with the reasons for removing the troops from Boston to the island of Castle-Williams, it is needless for me to trouble Your Lordship with a repetition of them. His Majesty alone can judge whether the lieutenant colonel, who acted contrary to his own opinion, should have refused to comply with the desires of every part of the civil government in that respect, as well as of most of the officers of the Crown, in order to avoid greater evils than they should suffer from the absence of the troops.

Conceiving the troops to be of no use at the island, I proposed to the lieutenant governor to remove them out of the province, and one of them immediately. The last measure I shall be obliged to take shortly, or run the risk of some contagious disorders getting amongst the men from their being so much crowded in small rooms. Not finding the proposal agreeable, I have consented to let both regiments remain till the arrival of the February mail from England; though I can't perceive any service is hoped for from them, unless it is to serve in the last extremity as an asylum, to which the officers of the Crown might fly for the security of their persons. But if there are any reasons to apprehend dangers of the kind, I am ignorant of them. It has indeed been proved that they were of no other use in the town of Boston, for the people were as lawless and licentious after the troops arrived as they were before. The troops could not act by military authority, and no person in civil authority would ask their aid. They were there contrary to the wishes of the Council, Assembly, magistrates and people, and seemed only offered to abuse and ruin, and the soldiers were either to suffer ill usage, and even assaults upon their persons till their lives were in danger, or by resisting and defending themselves, to run almost a certainty of suffering by the law.

46.

Thomas Gage: On the Desirability of Closing the Frontier

Thomas Gage held the post of commander in chief of the British Army in North America from 1763 to 1775. In a letter of November 10, 1770, to his superior, the Earl of Hillsborough, he expressed fears over the likelihood of colonial expansion to the west. Should the frontier territories be increasingly explored and settled, he pointed out to His Lordship, allegiance to the mother country would weaken as the colonies became economically independent.

Source: Carter, I.

As to increasing the settlements to respectable provinces, and colonization in general terms in the remote countries, I conceive it altogether inconsistent with sound policy; for there is little appearance that the advantages will arise from it, which nations expect when they send out colonies into foreign countries. They can give no encouragement to the fishery; though the country might afford some kind of naval stores, the distance would be too far to transport them; and for the same reason, they could not supply the Sugar Islands with lumber and provision. As for the raising of wine, silk or other commodities, the same may be said of the present colonies, without planting others for the purpose, at so vast a distance; but on the supposition that they would be raised, their very long transportation must probably make them too dear for any market. I do not apprehend the inhabitants could have any commodities to barter for manufactures, except skins and furs, which will naturally decrease in proportion as the country increases in people, and the deserts are cultivated so that in the course of a few years, necessity would force them to provide manufactures of some kind for themselves; and when all connection, upheld by commerce, with the mother country shall cease, it may be suspected that an independency on her government will soon follow. The pretense of forming barriers will have no end; wherever we settle, however remote, there must be a frontier, and there is room enough for the colonists to spread within our present limits, for a century to come.

If we reflect how the people of themselves have gradually retired from the coast, we shall be convinced they want no encouragement to desert the seacoasts, and go into the back countries, where the lands are better, and got upon easier terms. They are already almost out of reach of law and government; neither the endeavors of government, or fear of Indians has kept them properly within bounds; and it is apparently most for the interest of Great Britain to confine the colonists on the side of the back country, and to direct their settlements along the seacoast, where millions of acres are yet uncultivated. The lower provinces are still thinly inhabited, and not brought to the point of perfection that has been aimed at for the mutual benefit of Great Britain and themselves. Although America may supply the mother country with many articles, few of them are yet supplied in quantities equal to her consumption. The quantity of iron transported is not great, of hemp very small, and there are many other commodities not necessary to enumerate, which America has not yet been able to raise, notwithstanding the encouragement given her by bounties and premiums. The laying open new tracts of fertile territory in moderate climates might lessen her present produce, for it is the passion of every man to be a landholder, and the people have a natural disposition to rove in search of good lands, however distant.

It may be a question likewise whether colonizations of the kind could be effected without an Indian war, and fighting for every inch of ground. The Indians have long been jealous of our power, and have no patience in seeing us approach their towns and settle upon their hunting grounds. Atonements may be made for a fraud discovered in a trader, and even the murder of some of their tribes, but encroachments upon their lands have often produced serious consequences; the springs of the last general war are to be discovered, near the Allegheny Mountains and upon the banks of the Ohio.

It is so obvious that settlers might raise provision to feed the troops cheaper than it can be transported from the country below it is not necessary to explain it. But I must own, I know no other use in settlements; or can give any other reason for supporting forts than to protect the settlements and keep the settlers in subjection to government.

I conceive that to procure all the commerce it will afford, and at as little expense to ourselves as we can, is the only object we should have in view in the interior country for a century to come. And I imagine it might be effected by proper management, without either forts or settlements. Our manufactures are as much desired by the Indians as their peltry is sought for by us; what was originally deemed a superfluity or a luxury to the natives is now become a necessary; they are disused to the bow, and can neither hunt nor make war, without firearms, powder, and lead. The British provinces only can supply them with their necessaries, which they know, and for their own sakes they would protect the trade, which they actually do at present. It would remain with us to prevent the traders being guilty of frauds and impositions, and to pursue the same methods to that end, as are taken in the southern district. And I must confess, though the plan pursued in that district might be improved by proper laws to support it, that I don't know a better or more economical plan for the management of the trade. There are neither forts nor settlements in the southern department, and there are both in the northern department, and Your Lordship will be the best judge which of them has given you the least trouble; in which we have had the fewest quarrels with, or complaints from, the Indians.

I know of nothing so liable to bring in a serious quarrel with Indians as an invasion of their property. Let the savages enjoy their deserts in quiet; little bickerings that will unavoidably sometimes happen may soon be accommodated. And I am of opinion, independent of the motives of common justice and humanity, that the principles of interest and policy should induce us rather to protect than molest them. Were they driven from their forests, the peltry trade would decrease, and not impossible that worse savages would take refuge in them; for they might then become the asylum of fugitive Negroes, and idle vagabonds escaped from justice, who in time might become formidable, and subsist by rapine, and plundering the lower countries. . . .

The method Your Lordship has pointed out, to lead the trade going down the Mississippi into a British fort by the aid of a canal to join that river with the Ibbeville, I believe to be the most effectual that can be devised; and that it would answer many desirable ends, if the canal would have the effect pretended by those who argue in favor of it. They say, by cutting a channel from a point upon which the Mississippi strikes with violence to the Ibbeville, that the

former would in a short time make itself a new bed, and possibly change course.

It is said, on the other side, that the practicability of the scheme is very doubtful, and in all events could not succeed without a vast expense. If the cut is made only deep enough to introduce the waters when the freshets come down, it would be of no more use than the present overflowings into the Ibbeville. And also, that there is a height of land, nine miles in length, between the upper part of the Ibbeville and the River Amite; and unless the canal is continued to the junction of the Amite, and cut as deep as the bed of the Mississippi at low water, the waters will naturally flow back into the Mississippi, in the manner they do now, when the freshets subside. It is to be considered likewise that the Ibbeville with the lakes forms one side of the island of New Orleans. The Spaniards will naturally object to our carrying on any works on their side, especially as they are works which may be prejudicial to them. And if the channel, though cut, should be narrow, they might throw more obstructions into it in a few days, than could be removed in months.

I have taken pains to be informed of the possibility of making a canal that would be of real use, but I have not procured anything satisfactory concerning it. Lieutenant Pitman's report ought to obtain as much credit as that of any other person, but I believe the levels have never been taken, nor the soils examined, nor the project in general considered upon the spot with that accuracy and intelligence that it deserves. And I am of opinion that an intelligent person skilled in works of the kind, and whose report can be depended on, should examine the country and make an estimate of the expense, before anything is undertaken. If any such person can be found in West Florida, I have desired Brigadier Haldimand to send him to inspect the country, and to examine into the project.

1772

47.

JOSEPH WARREN: Against a British Army in the Colonies

Until some time after the Revolution, the anniversary of the Boston Massacre was the occasion for a commemorative oration. On March 5, 1772, Joseph Warren, a Revolutionary patriot, delivered an eloquent speech designed to arouse bitter feelings against the British troops and against Britain.

Source: Niles: "Oration Delivered at Boston, March 5, 1772."

WHEN WE TURN OVER the historic page and trace the rise and fall of states and empires, the mighty revolutions which have so often varied the face of the world strike our minds with solemn surprise, and we are naturally led to endeavor to search out the causes of such astonishing changes.

That man is formed for social life is an observation which, upon our first inquiry, presents itself immediately to our view, and our reason approves that wise and generous principle which actuated the first founders of civil government; an institution which has its origin in the weakness of individuals, and has for its end the strength and security of all; and so long as the means of effecting this important end are thoroughly known, and religiously attended to, government is one of the richest blessings to mankind, and ought to be held in the highest veneration.

In young and new-formed communities, the grand design of this institution is most generally understood and the most strictly regarded; the motives which urged to the social compact cannot be at once forgotten, and that equality which is remembered to have subsisted so lately among them prevents those who are clothed with authority from attempting to invade the freedom of their brethren; or if such an attempt is made, it prevents the community from suffering the offender to go unpunished. Every member feels it to be his interest and knows it to be his duty to preserve inviolate the constitution on which the public safety depends, and he is equally ready to assist the magistrate in the execution of the laws, and the subject in defense of his right; and so long as this noble attachment to a constitution, founded on free and benevolent principles, exists in full vigor in any state, that state must be flourishing and happy. . . .

It was this attachment to a constitution founded on free and benevolent principles which inspired the first settlers of this country. They saw with grief the daring outrages committed on the free constitution of their native land; they knew nothing but a civil war could at that time restore its pristine purity. So hard was it to resolve to embrue their hands in the blood of their brethren that they chose rather to quit their fair possessions and seek another habitation in a distant clime. When they came to this New World, which they fairly purchased of the Indian natives, the only rightful proprietors, they cultivated the then barren soil by their incessant labor, and defended their dear-bought possessions with the fortitude of the Christian and the bravery of the hero.

After various struggles which, during the tyrannic reigns of the House of Stuart, were constantly kept up between right and wrong, between liberty and slavery, the connection between Great Britain and this colony was settled in the reign of King William and Queen Mary by a compact, the conditions of which were expressed in a charter by which all the liberties and immunities of British subjects were confided to this province as fully and as absolutely as they possibly could be by any human instrument which can be devised. And it is undeniably true that the greatest and most important right of a British subject is that he shall be governed by no laws but those to which he, either in person or by his representatives, has given his consent. And this, I will venture to assert, is the great basis of British freedom; it is interwoven with the constitution, and whenever this is lost, the constitution must be destroyed.

The British constitution (of which ours is a copy) is a happy compound of the three forms (under some of which all governments may be ranged), viz., monarchy, aris-

tocracy, and democracy; of these three the British legislature is composed, and without the consent of each branch, nothing can carry with it the force of a law; but when a law is to be passed for raising a tax, that law can originate only in the democratic branch, which is the House of Commons in Britain, and the House of Representatives here. The reason is obvious: they and their constituents are to pay much the largest part of it; but as the aristocratic branch, which in Britain is the House of Lords, and in this province, the Council, are also to pay some part, their consent is necessary; and as the monarchic branch, which in Britain is the king, and with us, either the king in person or the governor whom he shall be pleased to appoint to act in his stead, is supposed to have a just sense of his own interest, which is that of all the subjects in general, his consent is also necessary, and when the consent of these three branches is obtained, the taxation is most certainly legal.

Let us now allow ourselves a few moments to examine the late acts of the British Parliament for taxing America. Let us with candor judge whether they are constitutionally binding upon us; if they are, in the name of justice let us submit to them, without one murmuring word.

First, I would ask whether the members of the British House of Commons are the democracy of this province. If they are, they are either the people of this province, or are elected by the people of this province to represent them, and have therefore a constitutional right to originate a bill for taxing them; it is most certain they are neither; and therefore nothing done by them can be said to be done by the democratic branch of our constitution. I would next ask whether the lords, who compose the aristocratic branch of the legislature, are peers of America. I never heard it was (even in those extraordinary times) so much as pretended, and if they are not, certainly no act of theirs can be said to be the act of the aristocratic branch of our constitution. The power of the monarchic branch, we with pleasure acknowledge, resides in the king, who may act either in person or by his representative; and I freely confess that I can see no reason why a proclamation for raising in America issued by the king's sole authority would not be equally consistent with our own constitution, and therefore equally binding upon us with the late acts of the British Parliament for taxing us; for it is plain that if there is any validity in those acts, it must arise altogether from the monarchical branch of the legislature. . . .

I further think that it would be at least as equitable; for I do not conceive it to be of the least importance to us by whom our property is taken away, so long as it is taken without our consent; and I am very much at a loss to know by what figure of rhetoric the inhabitants of this province can be called free subjects when they are obliged to obey implicitly such laws as are made for them by men 3,000 miles off, whom they know not, and whom they never empowered to act for them, or how they can be said to have property, when a body of men over whom they have not the least control, and who are not in any way accountable to them, shall oblige them to deliver up any part or the whole of their substance without even asking their consent. . . .

Yet whoever pretends that the late acts of the British Parliament for taxing America ought to be deemed binding upon us must admit at once that we are absolute slaves, and have no property of our own; or else that we may be freemen, and at the same time under a necessity of obeying the arbitrary commands of those over whom we have no control or influence, and that we may have property of our own which is entirely at the disposal of another. Such gross absurdities, I believe, will not be relished in this enlightened age; and it can be no matter of wonder that the people quickly perceived and seriously complained of the inroads which these acts must unavoidably make upon their liberty, and of the hazard to which their whole property is by them exposed; for, if they may be taxed without their consent, even in the smallest trifle, they may also, without their consent, be deprived of everything they possess, although never so valuable, never so dear.

Certainly it never entered the hearts of our ancestors that after so many dangers in this then desolate wilderness, their hard-earned property should be at the disposal of the British Parliament; and as it was soon found that this taxation could not be supported by reason and argument, it seemed necessary that one act of oppression should be enforced by another, and therefore, contrary to our just rights as possessing, or at least having a just title to possess, all the liberties and immunities of British subjects, a standing army was established among us in time of peace; and evidently for the purpose of effecting that which it was one principal design of the founders of the constitution to prevent (when they declared a standing army in a time of peace to be against law), namely, for the enforcement of obedience to acts which, upon fair examination, appeared to be unjust and unconstitutional.

The ruinous consequences of standing armies to free communities may be seen in the histories of Syracuse, Rome, and many other once flourishing states, some of which have now scarce a name! Their baneful influence is most suddenly felt when they are placed in populous cities; for, by a corruption of morals, the public happiness is immediately affected! And that this is one of the effects of quartering troops in a populous city is a truth to which many a mourning parent, many a lost despairing child in this metropolis must bear a very melancholy testimony.

Soldiers are also taught to consider arms

as the only arbiters by which every dispute is to be decided between contending states; they are instructed implicitly to obey their commanders without inquiring into the justice of the cause they are engaged to support; hence it is that they are ever to be dreaded as the ready engines of tyranny and oppression. And it is too observable that they are prone to introduce the same mode of decision in the disputes of individuals, and from thence have often arisen great animosities between them and the inhabitants, who, whilst in a naked, defenseless state, are frequently insulted and abused by an armed soldiery. And this will be more especially the case when the troops are informed that the intention of their being stationed in any city is to overawe the inhabitants. That this was the avowed design of stationing an armed force in this town is sufficiently known; and we, my fellow citizens, have seen, we have felt the tragical effects!

The fatal 5th of March, 1770, can never be forgotten. The horrors of that dreadful night are but too deeply impressed on our hearts. Language is too feeble to paint the emotion of our souls when our streets were stained with the blood of our brethren, when our ears were wounded by the groans of the dying, and our eyes were tormented with the sight of mangled bodies of the dead.

When our alarmed imagination presented to our view our houses wrapped in flames, our children subjected to the barbarous caprice of the raging soldiery, our beauteous virgins exposed to all the insolence of unbridled passion, our virtuous wives, endeared to us by every tender tie, falling a sacrifice to worse than brutal violence, and perhaps like the famed Lucretia, distracted with anguish and despair, ending their wretched lives by their own fair hands. When we beheld the authors of our distress parading in our streets, or drawn up in a regular battalia, as though in a hostile city, our hearts beat to arms; we snatched our weapons, al-

most resolved by one decisive stroke to avenge the death of our slaughtered brethren, and to secure from future danger all that we held most dear. But propitious heaven forbade the bloody carnage and saved the threatened victims of our too keen resentment, not by their discipline, not by their regular array. No, it was royal George's livery that proved their shield — it was that which turned the pointed engines of destruction from their breasts. The thoughts of vengeance were soon buried in our inbred affection to Great Britain, and calm reason dictated a method of removing the troops more mild than an immediate resource to the sword. With united efforts you urged the immediate departure of the troops from the town — you urged it, with a resolution which ensured success — you obtained your wishes, and the removal of the troops was effected without one drop of their blood being shed by the inhabitants.

The immediate actors in the tragedy of that night were surrendered to justice. It is not mine to say how far they were guilty. They have been tried by the country and *acquitted* of murder! And they are not to be again arraigned at an earthly bar; but, surely the men who have promiscuously scattered death amidst the innocent inhabitants of a populous city ought to see well to it that they be prepared to stand at the bar of an omniscient judge! And all who contrived or encouraged the stationing troops in this place have reasons of eternal importance to reflect with deep contrition on their base designs, and humbly to repent of their impious machinations.

The infatuation which has seemed for a number of years to prevail in the British councils with regard to us is truly astonishing! What can be proposed by the repeated attacks made upon our freedom, I really cannot surmise, even leaving justice and humanity out of question. I do not know one single advantage which can arise to the British nation from our being enslaved. I

Courtesy, Museum of Fine Arts, Boston

Joseph Warren, portrait by John Singleton Copley

the British nation will not suffer the reputation of their justice and their honor to be thus sported away by a capricious ministry; no, they will in a short time open their eyes to their true interest. They nourish in their own breasts a noble love of liberty; they hold her dear, and they know that all who have once possessed her charms had rather die than suffer her to be torn from their embraces. They are also sensible that Britain is so deeply interested in the prosperity of the colonies that she must eventually feel every wound given to their freedom; they cannot be ignorant that more dependence may be placed on the affections of a brother than on the forced service of a slave; they must approve your efforts for the preservation of your rights; from a sympathy of soul they must pray for your success. And I doubt not but they will, ere long, exert themselves effectually to redress your grievances. Even in the dissolute reign of King Charles II, when the House of Commons impeached the earl of Clarendon of high treason, the first article on which they founded their accusation was that "he had designed a standing army to be raised, and to govern the kingdom thereby." And the eighth article was that "he had introduced an arbitrary government into His Majesty's plantation." A terrifying example to those who are now forging chains for this country.

You have, my friends and countrymen, frustrated the designs of your enemies by your unanimity and fortitude. It was your union and determined spirit which expelled those troops who polluted your streets with innocent blood. You have appointed this anniversary as a standard memorial of the bloody consequences of placing an armed force in a populous city, and of your deliverance from the dangers which then seemed to hang over your heads; and I am confident that you never will betray the least want of spirit when called upon to guard your freedom. None but they who set a just

know not of any gains which can be wrung from us by oppression which they may not obtain from us by our own consent in the smooth channel of commerce. We wish the wealth and prosperity of Britain; we contribute largely to both. Does what we contribute lose all its value because it is done voluntarily? The amazing increase of riches to Britain, the great rise of the value of her lands, the flourishing state of her Navy, are striking proofs of the advantages derived to her from her commerce with the colonies; and it is our earnest desire that she may still continue to enjoy the same emoluments, until her streets are paved with American gold; only let us have the pleasure of calling it our own whilst it is in our own hands; but this it seems is too great a favor. We are to be governed by the absolute command of others; our property is to be taken away without our consent. If we complain, our complaints are treated with contempt; if we assert our rights, that assertion is deemed insolence; if we humbly offer to submit the matter to the impartial decision of reason, the sword is judged the most proper argument to silence our murmurs!

But this cannot long be the case. Surely

value upon the blessings of liberty are worthy to enjoy her. Your illustrious fathers were her zealous votaries. When the blasting frowns of tyranny drove her from public view they clasped her in their arms, they cherished her in their generous bosoms, they brought her safe over the rough ocean and fixed her seat in this then dreary wilderness; they nursed her infant age with the most tender care; for her sake they patiently bore the severest hardships; for her support they underwent the most rugged toils; in her defense they boldly encountered the most alarming dangers; neither the ravenous beasts that ranged the woods for prey, nor the more furious savages of the wilderness could damp ardor!

Whilst with one hand they broke the stubborn glebe [land], with the other they grasped their weapons, ever ready to protect her from danger. No sacrifice, not even their own blood, was esteemed too rich a libation for her altar! God prospered their valor, they preserved her brilliancy unsullied; they enjoyed her whilst they lived, and dying, bequeathed the dear inheritance to your care. And as they left you this glorious legacy, they have undoubtedly transmitted to you some portion of their noble spirit to inspire you with virtue to merit her and courage to preserve her. You surely cannot, with such examples before your eyes as every page of the history of this country affords, suffer your liberties to be ravished from you by lawless force, or cajoled away by flattery and fraud.

The voice of your fathers' blood cries to you from the ground: my sons, scorn to be slaves! In vain we met the frowns of tyrants. In vain we crossed the boisterous ocean, found a new world, and prepared it for the happy residence of liberty. In vain

we toiled. In vain we fought. We bled in vain, if you, our offspring, want valor to repel the assaults of her invaders! Stain not the glory of your worthy ancestors, but like them resolve never to part with your birthright; be wise in your deliberations, and determined in your exertions for the preservation of your liberties. Follow not the dictates of passion, but enlist yourselves under the sacred banner of reason; use every method in your power to secure your rights; at least prevent the curses of posterity from being heaped upon your memories.

If you, with united zeal and fortitude, oppose the torrent of oppression; if you feel the true fire of patriotism burning in your breasts; if you, from your souls, despise the most gaudy dress that slavery can wear; if you really prefer the lonely cottage (whilst blessed with liberty) to gilded palaces surrounded with the ensigns of slavery, you may have the fullest assurance that tyranny, with her whole accursed train, will hide their hideous heads in confusion, shame, and despair. If you perform your part, you must have the strongest confidence that the same Almighty Being who protected your pious and venerable forefathers, who enabled them to turn a barren wilderness into a fruitful field, who so often made bare his arm for their salvation, will still be mindful of you, their offspring.

May this Almighty Being graciously preside in all our councils. May He direct us to such measures as He Himself shall approve, and be pleased to bless. May we ever be a people favored of God. May our land be a land of liberty, the seat of virtue, the asylum of the oppressed, a name and a praise in the whole earth, until the last shock of time shall bury the empires of the world in one common undistinguished ruin!

48.

SAMUEL ADAMS: The Rights of the Colonists

On November 2, 1772, the Boston town meeting, upon Samuel Adams' motion, appointed "a committee of correspondence . . . . to state the rights of the Colonists and of this Province in particular, as men, as Christians, and as subjects; and to communicate the same to the several towns and to the world." On November 20, Adams presented the declaration of rights which he, as a member of the committee, had drafted. In Adams' paper, observed William V. Wells, is "embodied the whole philosophy of human rights, condensed from the doctrines of all times, and applied to the immediate circumstances of America. Upon this paper was based all that was written or spoken on human liberty in the Congress which declared independence" (Life of Samuel Adams).

Source: OSL 173.

NATURAL RIGHTS OF THE COLONISTS AS MEN

AMONG THE NATURAL RIGHTS of the colonists are these: first, a right to life; second, to liberty; third, to property; together with the right to support and defend them in the best manner they can. These are evident branches of, rather than deductions from, the duty of self-preservation, commonly called the first law of nature.

All men have a right to remain in a state of nature as long as they please; and in case of intolerable oppression, civil or religious, to leave the society they belong to, and enter into another.

When men enter into society, it is by voluntary consent; and they have a right to demand and insist upon the performance of such conditions and previous limitations as form an equitable original compact.

Every natural right not expressly given up, or, from the nature of a social compact, necessarily ceded, remains.

All positive and civil laws should conform, as far as possible, to the law of natural reason and equity.

As neither reason requires nor religion permits the contrary, every man living in or out of a state of civil society has a right peaceably and quietly to worship God according to the dictates of his conscience.

"Just and true liberty, equal and impartial liberty," in matters spiritual and temporal, is a thing that all men are clearly entitled to by the eternal and immutable laws of God and nature, as well as by the law of nations and all well-grounded municipal laws, which must have their foundation in the former.

In regard to religion, mutual toleration in the different professions thereof is what all good and candid minds in all ages have ever practised, and, both by precept and example, inculcated on mankind. And it is now generally agreed among Christians that this spirit of toleration, in the fullest extent consistent with the being of civil society, is the chief characteristical mark of the church. Insomuch that Mr. Locke has asserted and proved, beyond the possibility of contradiction on any solid ground, that such toleration ought to be extended to all whose doctrines are not subversive of society. The only sects which he thinks ought to be, and which by all wise laws are excluded from such toleration, are those who teach doctrines subversive of the civil government under which they live. The Roman Catholics or Papists are excluded by reason of such doctrines as these: that princes excommunicated may be deposed, and those that they call heretics may be destroyed without mercy; besides their recognizing the pope in so absolute a manner, in subversion of government, by introducing, as far as possible into the states under whose protection they enjoy life, liberty, and property, that solecism in politics, *imperium in imperio*, leading directly to the worst anarchy and confusion, civil discord, war, and bloodshed.

The natural liberty of man, by entering into society, is abridged or restrained so far only as is necessary for the great end of society, the best good of the whole.

In the state of nature every man is, under God, judge and sole judge of his own rights and of the injuries done him. By entering into society he agrees to an arbiter or indifferent judge between him and his neighbors; but he no more renounces his original right than by taking a cause out of the ordinary course of law, and leaving the decision to referees or indifferent arbitrators. In the last case, he must pay the referees for time and trouble. He should also be willing to pay his just quota for the support of government, the law, and the constitution; the end of which is to furnish indifferent and impartial judges in all cases that may happen, whether civil, ecclesiastical, marine, or military.

The *natural* liberty of man is to be free from any superior power on earth, and not to be under the will or legislative authority of man, but only to have the law of nature for his rule.

In the state of nature men may, as the patriarchs did, employ hired servants for the defense of their lives, liberties, and property; and they should pay them reasonable wages. Government was instituted for the purposes of common defense, and those who hold the reins of government have an equitable, natural right to an honorable support from the same principle that "the laborer is worthy of his hire." But then the same community which they serve ought to be the assessors of their pay. Governors have no right to seek and take what they please; by this, instead of being content with the station assigned them, that of honorable servants of the society, they would soon become absolute masters, despots, and tyrants. Hence, as a private man has a right to say what wages he will give in his private affairs, so has a community to determine what *they* will give and grant of their substance for the administration of public affairs. And, in both cases, more are ready to offer their service at the proposed and stipulated price than are able and willing to perform their duty.

In short, it is the greatest absurdity to suppose it in the power of one or any number of men, at the entering into society, to renounce their essential natural rights, or the means of preserving those rights, when the grand end of civil government, from the very nature of its institution, is for the support, protection, and defense of those very rights; the principal of which, as is before observed, are life, liberty, and property. If men, through fear, fraud, or mistake, should in terms renounce or give up any essential natural right, the eternal law of reason and the grand end of society would absolutely vacate such renunciation. The right to freedom being the gift of God Almighty, it is not in the power of man to alienate this gift and voluntarily become a slave.

THE RIGHTS OF THE COLONISTS AS CHRISTIANS

THESE MAY BE BEST understood by reading and carefully studying the institutes of the great Lawgiver and Head of the Christian Church, which are to be found clearly written and promulgated in the New Testament.

By the act of the British Parliament, commonly called the Toleration Act, every subject in England, except Papists, etc., was restored to, and reestablished in, his natural right to worship God according to the dictates of his own conscience. And, by the charter of this province, it is granted, ordained, and established (that is, declared as an original right) that there shall be liberty of conscience allowed in the worship of God to all Christians, except Papists, inhabiting, or which shall inhabit or be resident within, such province or territory. Magna Charta itself is in substance but a constrained declaration or proclamation and promulgation in the name of the King, Lords, and Commons, of the sense the latter had of their original, inherent, indefeasible natural rights as also those of free citizens equally perdurable with the other. That great author, that great jurist, and even that court writer, Mr. Justice Blackstone, holds that this recognition was justly obtained of King John, sword in hand. And peradventure it must be one day, sword in hand, again rescued and preserved from total destruction and oblivion.

THE RIGHTS OF THE COLONISTS AS SUBJECTS

A COMMONWEALTH or state is a body politic, or civil society of men, united together to promote their mutual safety and prosperity by means of their union.

The absolute rights of Englishmen and all freemen, in or out of civil society, are principally personal security, personal liberty, and private property.

All persons born in the British American colonies are, by the laws of God and nature and by the common law of England, exclusive of all charters from the Crown, well entitled, and by acts of the British Parliament are declared to be entitled, to all the natural, essential, inherent, and inseparable rights, liberties, and privileges of subjects born in Great Britain or within the Realm. Among those rights are the following, which no man, or body of men, consistently with their own rights as men and citizens, or members of society, can for themselves give up or take away from others.

First, "the first fundamental positive law of all commonwealths or states is the establishing the legislative power. As the first fundamental *natural* law, also, which is to govern even the legislative power itself, is the preservation of the society."

Second, the legislative has no right to absolute, arbitrary power over the lives and fortunes of the people; nor can mortals assume a prerogative not only too high for men, but for angels, and therefore reserved for the exercise of the Deity alone.

"The legislative cannot justly assume to itself a power to rule by extempore arbitrary decrees; but it is bound to see that justice is dispensed, and that the rights of the subjects be decided by promulgated, standing, and known laws, and authorized *independent judges*"; that is, independent, as far as possible, of prince and people. "There should be one rule of justice for rich and poor, for the favorite at court, and the countryman at the plough."

Third, the supreme power cannot justly take from any man any part of his property, without his consent in person or by his representative.

These are some of the first principles of natural law and justice, and the great barriers of all free states and of the British constitution in particular. It is utterly irreconcilable to these principles and to many other fundamental maxims of the common law, common sense, and reason that a British House of Commons should have a right at pleasure to give and grant the property of the colonists. (That the colonists are well entitled to all the essential rights, liberties, and privileges of men and freemen born in Britain is manifest not only from the colony charters in general, but acts of the British Parliament.) The statute of the 13th year of George II, chap. 7, naturalizes even foreigners after seven years' residence. The words of the Massachusetts charter are these:

And further, our will and pleasure is, and we do hereby for Us, Our Heirs, and Successors, grant, establish, and ordain that all and every of the subjects of Us, Our Heirs, and Successors, which shall go to, and inhabit within our said province or territory, and every of their children, which shall happen to be born there or on the seas in going thither or returning from thence, shall have and enjoy all liberties and immunities of free and natural subjects within any of the dominions of Us, Our Heirs, and Successors, to all intents, constructions, and purposes whatsoever, as if they and every one of them were born within this Our Realm of England.

Now what liberty can there be where property is taken away without consent? Can it be said with any color of truth and justice that this continent of 3,000 miles in length, and of a breadth as yet unexplored, in which, however, it is supposed there are 5,000,000 people, has the least voice, vote, or influence in the British Parliament? Have they all together any more weight or power to return a single member to that House of Commons who have not inadvertently, but deliberately, assumed a power to dispose of their lives, liberties, and properties, than to choose an emperor of China? Had the colonists a right to return members to the British Parliament, it would only be hurtful; as, from their local situation and circumstances, it is impossible they should ever be truly and properly represented there.

The inhabitants of this country, in all probability, in a few years will be more numerous than those of Great Britain and Ireland together; yet it is absurdly expected by the promoters of the present measures that these, with their posterity to all generations, should be easy, while their property shall be disposed of by a House of Commons at 3,000 miles' distance from them, and who cannot be supposed to have the least care or concern for their real interest; who have not only no natural care for their interest, but must be in effect bribed against it, as every burden they lay on the colonists is so much saved or gained to themselves. Hitherto, many of the colonists have been free from quitrents; but if the breath of a British House of Commons can originate an act for taking away all our money, our lands will go next, or be subject to rack rents from haughty and relentless landlords, who will ride at ease, while we are trodden in the dirt. The colonists have been branded with the odious names of traitors and rebels only for complaining of their grievances. How long such treatment will or ought to be borne is submitted.

1773

49.

BENJAMIN FRANKLIN: Rules by Which a Great Empire May Be Reduced to a Small One

Franklin spent the better part of the years between 1757 and 1775 in London as a sort of ambassador extraordinary from various colonial assemblies to Great Britain, attempting to bring about some alteration in its colonial policy. During these years he gradually lost faith in the wisdom of the British government, reluctantly coming to feel that America could no longer profit by its rule. Rebuffed at nearly every turn by ministers whose incivility betrayed their ignorance of American affairs, he lost heart for his mission, though he did not actually return home until he had decided that all hope for conciliation was gone. It was at the height of his difficulties that he turned to political satire as a weapon in his negotiations. An Edict by the King of Prussia, *parodying the English King's arbitrary acts with respect to America, and* Rules by Which a Great Empire May Be Reduced to a Small One, *which is reprinted here, appeared originally in the* London Public Advertiser *in 1773. While tactically a mistake, since their immediate effect was only to antagonize the pro-American party in London, these pieces have long survived their occasion by virtue of their brilliant and incisive irony.*

Source: Sparks, IV, pp. 387-398.

AN ANCIENT SAGE valued himself upon this, that though he could not fiddle, he knew how to make a great city of a little one. The science that I, a modern simpleton, am about to communicate, is the very reverse.

I address myself to all ministers who have the management of extensive dominions, which from their very greatness are become troublesome to govern, because the multi-plicity of their affairs leaves no time for fiddling.

1. In the first place, gentlemen, you are to consider that a great empire, like a great cake, is most easily diminished at the edges. Turn your attention, therefore, first to your remotest provinces; that as you get rid of them, the next may follow in order.

2. That the possibility of this separation

may always exist, take special care the provinces are never incorporated with the mother country; that they do not enjoy the same common rights, the same privileges in commerce; and that they are governed by severer laws, all of your enacting, without allowing them any share in the choice of the legislators. By carefully making and preserving such distinctions, you will (to keep to my simile of the cake) act like a wise gingerbread baker, who, to facilitate a division, cuts his dough half through in those places where, when baked, he would have it broken to pieces.

3. Those remote provinces have perhaps been acquired, purchased, or conquered at the sole expense of the settlers, or their ancestors, without the aid of the mother country. If this should happen to increase her strength, by their growing numbers, ready to join in her wars; her commerce, by their growing demand for her manufactures; or her naval power, by greater employment for her ships and seamen, they may probably suppose some merit in this, and that it entitles them to some favor; you are therefore to forget it all, or resent it, as if they had done you injury. If they happen to be zealous Whigs, friends of liberty, nurtured in revolution principles, remember all that to their prejudice, and resolve to punish it; for such principles, after a revolution is thoroughly established, are of no more use; they are even odious and abominable.

4. However peaceably your colonies have submitted to your government, shown their affection to your interests, and patiently borne their grievances, you are to suppose them always inclined to revolt, and treat them accordingly. Quarter troops among them who by their insolence may provoke the rising of mobs, and by their bullets and bayonets suppress them. By this means, like the husband who uses his wife ill from suspicion, you may in time convert your suspicions into realities.

5. Remote provinces must have governors and judges to represent the royal person, and execute everywhere the delegated parts of his office and authority. You ministers know that much of the strength of government depends on the opinion of the people; and much of that opinion on the choice of rulers placed immediately over them. If you send them wise and good men for governors, who study the interest of the colonists, and advance their prosperity, they will think their king wise and good, and that he wishes the welfare of his subjects. If you send them learned and upright men for judges, they will think him a lover of justice. This may attach your provinces more to his government. You are therefore to be careful whom you recommend for those offices. If you can find prodigals who have ruined their fortunes, broken gamesters, or stockjobbers, these may do well as governors, for they will probably be rapacious, and provoke the people by their extortions. Wrangling proctors and pettifogging lawyers, too, are not amiss, for they will be for ever disputing and quarreling with their little parliaments. If withal they should be ignorant, wrongheaded, and insolent, so much the better. Attorneys' clerks and Newgate solicitors will do for chief justices, especially if they hold their places during your pleasure; and all will contribute to impress those ideas of your government that are proper for a people you would wish to renounce it.

6. To confirm these impressions and strike them deeper, whenever the injured come to the capital with complaints of maladministration, oppression, or injustice, punish such suitors with long delay, enormous expense, and a final judgment in favor of the oppressor. This will have an admirable effect every way. The trouble of future complaints will be prevented, and governors and judges will be encouraged to further acts of oppression and injustice; and thence the people may become more disaffected, and at length desperate.

7. When such governors have crammed their coffers and made themselves so odious to the people that they can no longer remain among them with safety to their person, recall and reward them with pensions. You may make them baronets, too, if that respectable order should not think fit to resent it. All will contribute to encourage new governors in the same practice, and make the supreme government detestable.

8. If, when you are engaged in war, your colonies should vie in liberal aids of men and money against the common enemy upon your simple requisition, and give far beyond their abilities, reflect that a penny taken from them by your power is more honorable to you than a pound presented by their benevolence; despise therefore their voluntary grants, and resolve to harass them with novel taxes. They will probably complain to your Parliament, that they are taxed by a body in which they have no representative, and that this is contrary to common right. They will petition for redress. Let the parliaments flout their claims, reject their petitions, refuse even to suffer the reading of them, and treat the petitioners with the utmost contempt. Nothing can have a better effect in producing the alienation proposed; for though many can forgive injuries, none ever forgave contempt.

9. In laying these taxes, never regard the heavy burdens those remote people already undergo in defending their own frontiers, supporting their own provincial governments, making new roads, building bridges, churches, and other public edifices, which in old countries have been done to your hands by your ancestors, but which occasion constant calls and demands on the purses of a new people. Forget the restraints you lay on their trade for your own benefit, and the advantage a monopoly of this trade gives your exacting merchants. Think nothing of the wealth those merchants and your manufacturers acquire by the colony commerce; their increased ability

thereby to pay taxes at home; their accumulating, in the price of their commodities, most of those taxes, and so levying them from their consuming customers; all this, and the employment and support of thousands of your poor by the colonists, you are entirely to forget. But remember to make your arbitrary tax more grievous to your provinces by public declarations importing that your power of taxing them has no limits; so that when you take from them without their consent one shilling in the pound, you have a clear right to the other nineteen. This will probably weaken every ideal of security in their property, and convince them that under such a government they have nothing they can call their own — which can scarce fail of producing the happiest consequences!

10. Possibly, indeed, some of them might still comfort themselves and say, "Though we have no property, we have yet something left that is valuable; we have constitutional liberty, both of person and of conscience. This King, these Lords, and these Commons, who it seems are too remote from us to know us and feel for us, cannot take from us our habeas corpus right, or our right of trial by a jury of our neighbors; they cannot deprive us of the exercise of our religion, alter our ecclesiastical constitution, and compel us to be Papists, if they please, or Mahometans." To annihilate this comfort, begin by laws to perplex their commerce with infinite regulations, impossible to be remembered and observed; ordain seizures of their property for every failure; take away the trial of such property by jury, and give it to arbitrary judges of your own appointing, and of the lowest characters in the country, whose salaries and emoluments are to arise out of the duties or condemnations, and whose appointments are during pleasure. Then let there be a formal declaration of both houses that opposition to your edicts is treason, and that any person suspected of treason in the provinces may, ac-

cording to some obsolete law, be seized and sent to the metropolis of the empire for trial; and pass an act that those there charged with certain other offenses, shall be sent away in chains from their friends and country to be tried in the same manner for felony. Then erect a new court of inquisition among them, accompanied by an armed force, with instructions to transport all such suspected persons, to be ruined by the expense if they bring over evidences to prove their innocence, or be found guilty and hanged, if they cannot afford it.

And, lest the people should think you cannot possibly go any farther, pass another solemn declaratory act, "that King, Lords, Commons had, have, and of right ought to have, full power and authority to make statutes of sufficient force and validity to bind the unrepresented provinces in all cases whatsoever." This will include spiritual with temporal, and, taken together, must operate wonderfully to your purpose by convincing them that they are at present under a power something like that spoken of in the Scriptures, which can not only kill their bodies, but damn their souls to all eternity, by compelling them, if it pleases, to worship the devil.

11. To make your taxes more odious and more likely to procure resistance, send from the capital a board of officers to superintend the collection, composed of the most indiscreet, ill-bred, and insolent you can find. Let these have large salaries out of the extorted revenue, and live in open, grating luxury upon the sweat and blood of the industrious, whom they are to worry continually with groundless and expensive prosecutions before the above-mentioned arbitrary revenue judges — all at the cost of the party prosecuted, though acquitted, because the King is to pay no costs. Let these men, by your order, be exempted from all the common taxes and burdens of the province, though they and their property are protected by its laws. If any revenue officers

are suspected of the least tenderness for the people, discard them. If others are justly complained of, protect and reward them. If any of the under officers behave so as to provoke the people to drub them, promote those to better offices. This will encourage others to procure for themselves such profitable drubbings, by multiplying and enlarging such provocations, and all will work toward the end you aim at.

12. Another way to make your tax odious is to misapply the produce of it. If it was originally appropriated for the defense of the provinces, the better support of government, and the administration of justice, where it may be necessary, then apply none of it to that defense, but bestow it where it is not necessary, in augmented salaries or pensions to every governor who had distinguished himself by his enmity to the people, and by calumniating them to their sovereign. This will make them pay it more unwillingly, and be more apt to quarrel with those that collect it and those that imposed it, who will quarrel again with them, and all shall contribute to your main purpose, of making them weary of your government.

13. If the people of any province have been accustomed to support their own governors and judges to satisfaction, you are to apprehend that such governors and judges may be thereby influenced to treat the people kindly, and to do them justice. This is another reason for applying part of that revenue in larger salaries to such governors and judges, given, as their commissions are, during your pleasure only; forbidding them to take any salaries from their provinces; that thus the people may no longer hope any kindness from their governors, or (in Crown cases) any justice from their judges. And, as the money thus misapplied in one province is extorted from all, probably all will resent the misapplication.

14. If the parliaments of your provinces should dare to claim rights, or complain of

New York Historical Society

Sons of Liberty organized resistance to the Tea Act, which would have given the East India Co. a monopoly of tea trade

your administration, order them to be harassed with repeated dissolutions. If the same men are continually returned by new elections, adjourn their meetings to some country village, where they cannot be accommodated, and there keep them during pleasure; for this, you know, is your prerogative, and an excellent one it is, as you may manage it to promote discontents among the people, diminish their respect, and increase their disaffection.

15. Convert the brave, honest officers of your Navy into pimping tide-waiters and colony officers of the customs. Let those who in time of war fought gallantly in defense of the commerce of their countrymen, in peace be taught to prey upon it. Let them learn to be corrupted by great and real smugglers; but (to show their diligence) scour with armed boats every bay, harbor, river, creek, cove, or nook throughout the coast of your colonies; stop and detain every coaster, every wood boat, every fisherman, tumble their cargoes and even their ballast inside out and upside down; and, if a pennyworth of pins is found unentered, let the whole be seized and confiscated.

Thus shall the trade of your colonists suffer more from their friends in time of peace than it did from their enemies in war. Then let these boats' crews land upon every farm in their way, rob the orchards, steal the pigs and the poultry, and insult the inhabitants.

If the injured and exasperated farmers, unable to procure other justice, should attack the aggressors, drub them, and burn their boats; you are to call this high treason and rebellion, order fleets and armies into their country, and threaten to carry all the offenders 3,000 miles to be hanged, drawn, and quartered. O! this will work admirably!

16. If you are told of discontents in your colonies, never believe that they are general, or that you have given occasion for them; therefore, do not think of applying any remedy, or of changing any offensive measure. Redress no grievance, lest they should be encouraged to demand the redress of some other grievance. Grant no request that is just and reasonable, lest they should make another that is unreasonable. Take all your informations of the state of the colonies from your governors and officers in enmity with them. Encourage and reward these leasing makers; secrete their lying accusations, lest they should be confuted; but act upon them as the clearest evidence; and believe nothing you hear from the friends of the people. Suppose all *their* complaints to be invented and promoted by a few factious demagogues, whom if you could catch and hang, all would be quiet. Catch and hang a few of them accordingly; and the blood of the martyrs shall work miracles in favor of your purpose.

17. If you see rival nations rejoicing at

the prospect of your disunion with your provinces, and endeavoring to promote it; if they translate, publish, and applaud all the complaints of your discontented colonists, at the same time privately stimulating you to severer measures, let not that alarm or offend you. Why should it, since you all mean the same thing?

18. If any colony should at their own charge erect a fortress to secure their port against the fleets of a foreign enemy, get your governor to betray that fortress into your hands. Never think of paying what it cost the country, for that would look at least like some regard for justice; but turn it into a citadel to awe the inhabitants and curb their commerce.

If they should have lodged in such fortress the very arms they bought and used to aid you in your conquests, seize them all; it will provoke like ingratitude added to robbery. One admirable effect of these operations will be to discourage every other colony from erecting such defenses, and so your enemies may more easily invade them, to the great disgrace of your government, and of course the furtherance of your project.

19. Send armies into their country under pretence of protecting the inhabitants; but, instead of garrisoning the forts on their frontiers with those troops, to prevent incursions, demolish those forts, and order the troops into the heart of the country, that the savages may be encouraged to attack the frontiers, and that the troops may be protected by the inhabitants. This will seem to proceed from your ill will or your ignorance, and contribute farther to produce and strengthen an opinion among them that you are no longer fit to govern them.

20. Lastly, invest the general of your army in the provinces with great and unconstitutional powers, and free him from the control of even your own civil governors. Let him have troops enough under his command, with all the fortresses in his possession; and who knows but (like some provincial generals in the Roman Empire, and encouraged by the universal discontent you have produced) he may take it into his head to set up for himself? If he should, and you have carefully practised these few excellent rules of mine, take my word for it, all the provinces will immediately join him; and you will that day (if you have not done it sooner) get rid of the trouble of governing them, and all the plagues attending their commerce and connection from henceforth and forever.

Q.E.D.

You are a member of Parliament, and one of that majority which has doomed my country to destruction. You have begun to burn our towns, and murder our people, — Look upon your hands! — They are stained with the blood of your relations! — You and I were long friends: — you are now my enemy, — and I am, Yours, B. Franklin.

BENJAMIN FRANKLIN, letter to William Strahan, July 5, 1775. This letter, to an old friend, was never sent.

The Colonies Reduced
Design'd & Engrav'd for the Political Register.

RULE AND REBELLION

The successful conclusion of the French and Indian War left England with considerable debts and increased responsibilities in America. The loose control that had distinguished British colonial rule from that of the French and Spanish was tightened in an effort to ease the burden of defense and administration. Settlement west of the Alleghenies was forbidden by the Proclamation of 1763, and new taxes were established to increase revenue from the colonies.

However reasonable these measures were to Parliament, many colonists thought them a burdensome violation of their rights. Conflict between the mother country and the colonies was based on differences of principle and self-interest, but was increased by the presence in the colonies of skilled propagandists, and in England by a proud and corrupt Parliament. When the first disputes arose, few men on either side believed, or hoped, that in only a decade the united colonies would declare themselves free and independent.

The British Museum

Royal Academy of Arts, London

The British Museum

(Both) Library of Congress

(Top left) **Cartoon: Americans being robbed by the King's agents;** (top right) **King George III;** (above) **George Grenville, promoter of the Stamp Act; a tax stamp and an American parody**

The Stamp Act

The Stamp Act of 1765, like the Sugar Act of the previous year, brought to a head the dispute over whether Parliament, in addition to regulating and governing the American colonies, could tax them for revenue as well. Unfortunately for Parliament, the stamp tax had its most serious effects on the most articulate and influential Americans: the lawyers, publishers, and tavern keepers.

v. United Provinces

[No *Stamped Paper* to be had.]

From the PUBLIC LEDGER, August 16.

A Dialogue between a North-American *and a* Courtier.

North-American.

YOU remember that at our laſt meeting, we agreed upon this day candidly to enquire into the juſtice as well as policy of Great-Britain, in taxing the North-Americans; and as this is a matter of the greateſt importance to both countries, I ſhall with pleaſure hear you endeavour to defend the meaſures that have been taken to the utmoſt of my power, I mean as far as is conſiſtent with truth or right reaſon; but if I ſhould differ with you in opinion, I hope you will hear me with the ſame candor that I ſhall you.

Courtier.

Upon theſe principles, Sir, I join iſſue; and firſt, as to

LONDON, August 29.

His Excellency the Earl of Hertford, Lord Lieutenant of Ireland, has appointed the Hon. Col. Cunningham, and Capt. Fleming, to be his Aids de Camp.

Very large Orders from Spain are come over for the purchaſe of corn, ſo great a ſcarcity of which has not been known there for many years.

A Letter from on board the Hardwicke Indiaman, in St. Jago road, capital of the Cape de Verd Iſlands, dated May 16, mentions, that ſhe touched there the 8th of that Month for Water, (having had a very good paſſage) where ſhe found the Hector and True Briton. The Royal Charlotte came in there for water a few days after.

and not chiming in with the *oppreſſive* Meaſures of thoſe in Power, having had many broad Hints and Overtures, to bring them over for that Purpoſe. Which they rejected with Diſdain. I ſhou'd be very ſorry to find your Paper under ſo much *undue* Influence, as to omit inferring Things of ſo great Conſequence to the Peace, Happineſs, and Tranquility of the Public in general. I cannot in Juſtice to theſe Gentlemen's Characters, read your Papers, without making ſome Reply to ſo great a Falaſy.

I am, Sir, Your obedient Servant,

A Citizen of Montreal.

N. B. For Conveniency, we have new Commiſſion of the Peace every Quarter Seſſions; ſuppoſe it is ſo in the other Colonies.

St. Jago, (Jamaica) Auguſt 24.

Extract from the Proceedings of the Aſſembly of the 16th Auguſt.

And Colonial Resistance

Daniel Dulany

Resistance to the Stamp Act was both practical and philosophical. Men designated as stamp agents found their property and health endangered by mobs, which also burned stamped paper whenever possible. And the British argument that the colonists were "virtually represented" in Parliament was countered by the constitutional reasoning of Daniel Dulany, James Otis, and other colonial thinkers.

(Top) Cartoon: Boston and the colonies attack the Stamp Act monster, which holds English freedom in its claws; (bottom left) engraving showing rioters burning stamped paper; (center) newspaper notice following such a riot

Courtesy, the British Museum

Etching in celebration of the repeal of the Stamp Act which appeared at the head of a song entitled "The World Turned Upside Down, or, the Old Woman Taught Wisdom"

Stamp Act Repeal

While Parliament would not officially heed colonial protests against the Stamp Act, they did listen to English merchants who suffered from colonial boycotts. Important also were Parliamentary politics: a change of ministries brought in compromis-ers who soon repealed the Stamp Act. The repeal was celebrated throughout the colonies. In their triumph, the colonists failed to take note of the Declaratory Act, passed at the same time, which reaffirmed the absolute rule of Parliament over the colonies.

Lord Rockingham, rival and successor of George Grenville, who repealed the Stamp Act

Public Records Office, London

National Portrait Gallery, London

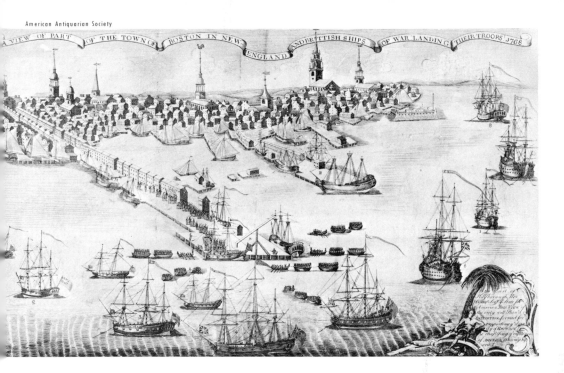

The Townshend Duties

The notion that Americans objected only to "internal" taxes, such as on newspaper printing, but not to "external" taxes on foreign trade, was dispelled by the reaction to the "Townshend Duties" on imported goods.

Named after Charles Townshend, unpredictable Chancellor of the Exchequer, the duties were unpopular even in England, and after another period of boycotts, were repealed in 1770, except for the one on tea.

(Top) 1768 engraving by Paul Revere shows British troops landing in Boston to enforce law and order; (bottom left) John Hancock, wealthy Boston merchant and backer of the Sons of Liberty, whose income was derived in part by smuggling goods in violation of British trade regulations; portrait by John Singleton Copley

To the PUBLIC.

AS I am convinced that my refusing to store my Goods, was wrong; I do promise and consent, That they shall be deposited in the public Store with other Goods which were imported contrary to the *Non-importation Agreement*;---which I hope will appease the Minds of my injured Fellow Citizens, and convince them that I do not regard sacrificing my private Interest for the *Good of the Public.*

Simeon Coley.

New-York, 21st July, 1769.
Afternoon, 2 o'Clock.

(Top left) Efforts to install a bishop in America were resisted even by Anglicans here as an unnecessary extension of British rule; (top right) Samuel Adams, the colonial agitator, shown here in 1770 demanding that Gov. Hutchinson remove British troops from Boston, in a portrait by J. S. Copley; (center right) Thomas Hutchinson, governor of Massachusetts during this troubled period; (bottom left) Green Dragon Inn in Boston, meeting place for the Sons of Liberty

The BLOODY MASSACRE perpetrated in King — Street BOSTON on March 5th 1770 by a party of the 29th REG.

Engrav'd Printed & Sold by PAUL REVERE BOSTON

Unhappy Boston! see thy Sons deplore,
Thy hallow'd Walks besmear'd with guiltless Gore.
While faithless P——n and his savage Bands,
With murd'rous Rancour stretch their bloody Hands,
Like fierce Barbarians grinning o'er their Prey,
Approve the Carnage and enjoy the Day.

If scalding drops from Rage from Anguish Wrung
If speechless Sorrows lab'ring for a Tongue
Or if a weeping World can ought appease
The plaintive Ghosts of Victims such as these;
The Patriot's copious Tears for each are shed,
A glorious Tribute which embalms the Dead.

But know Fate summons to that awful Goal.
Where Justice strips the Murd'rer of his Soul
Should venal C——ts the scandal of the Land,
Snatch the relentless Villain from her Hand,
Keen Execrations on this Plate inscrib'd,
Shall reach a JUDGE who never can be brib'd.

The unhappy Sufferers were Mess.rs SAM.L GRAY SAM.L MAVERICK, JAM.S CALDWELL, CRISPUS ATTUCKS & PAT.K CARR
Killed Six wounded, two of them (CHRIST.R MONK & JOHN CLARK) Mortally

Boston "Massacre"

The British soldiers stationed in Boston to preserve order found little to do: the Bostonians practised a form of passive resistance, often taunting the Redcoats, but rarely caused violence. An exception was the "Boston Massacre," in which beleaguered soldiers fired into a threatening mob. The incident was publicly attacked by Paul Revere and Samuel Adams as wanton British brutality, but the soldiers were defended by John Adams and Robert Auchmuty and acquitted.

(Top left) Robert Auchmuty, portrait attributed to Robert Feke; (center left) youthful portrait of John Adams by Joseph Badger; (top right) Paul Revere's interpretation of the incident he calls a "Bloody Massacre," in one of the most widely circulated pieces of propaganda before the Revolution; (bottom left) Paul Revere, by John Singleton Copley

A NEW METHOD OF MACARONY MAKING AS PRACTISED AT BOSTON

*See the Custom House officers landing the Tea
They Tar'd him and feather'd him just as you see
And they Drench'd him so well both behind and before
That he begg'd for God's sake they would drench him no more*

A Party in Protest

Colonials torture a customs house agent for accepting a tea shipment

The famous Tea Party was well planned, probably by Samuel Adams, the colonial master of propaganda and agitation. Dumping the tea was an illegal extension of the boycott on tea occasioned, not by a tax, but by the granting of a tea monopoly to the East India Company. This hurt colonial merchants, and seemed an ominous precedent to sellers of other goods; therefore, protest did not stop with the Tea Party.

Monday Morning, December 27, 1773.

THE Tea-Ship being arrived, every Inhabitant who wishes to preserve the Liberty of America, is desired to meet at the STATE-HOUSE, This Morning, precisely at TEN o'Clock, to advise what is best to be done on this alarming Crisis.

General Gage, made governor of Massachusetts to enforce the Coercive Acts

The Coercive Acts Backfire

British cartoon lampoons the "Bostonians in distress"

Parliament was not amused by the Tea Party, and in retaliation passed the Coercive Acts (1774), closing Boston harbor and placing Massachusetts under close British rule. With bad timing, Parliament also passed the Quebec Act, extending the boundaries of that centrally ruled Catholic province down to the Ohio River. This made Boston a cause instead of an example, and united the Protestant colonies in her aid.

THE Massachusetts Spy

Or, Thomas's Boston Journal.

Do thou Great LIBERTY inspire our Souls—And make our Lives in THY Possession happy—Or, our Deaths glorious in THY just Defence.

VOL. IV.)　　THURSDAY, July 7, 1774.　　(NUMB. 179.

JOIN OR DIE

The First Continental Congress

The Coercive Acts were thought to endanger all the colonies, so a congress was convened in Philadelphia in September 1774 to decide a course of action. For many delegates the question was no longer whether Parliament could tax the colonies, but whether it could legislate for them at all. Enough radicals, such as Patrick Henry of Virginia, were present to ensure the defeat of a proposal for conciliation by Joseph Galloway of Pennsylvania. After adopting a declaration of rights, an address to the people of Great Britain, and an agreement not to buy or use English goods, the Congress resolved to meet again if their grievances were not redressed.

(Above left) Joseph Galloway; (left) Patrick Henry; (below) a portion of the "Address to the People of Great Britain," from the "Extracts," (bottom) Carpenters' Hall in Philadelphia, meeting place of the first Congress

To the People of GREAT-BRITAIN,

From the DELEGATES appointed by the several English Colonies of New-Hampshire, Massachusetts-Bay, Rhode-Island and Providence Plantations, Connecticut, New-York, New-Jersey, Pennsylvania, the Lower Counties on Delaware, Maryland, Virginia, North-Carolina, and South-Carolina, to consider of their Grievances in GENERAL CONGRESS, at Philadelphia, September 5th, 1774.

FRIENDS and FELLOW SUBJECTS,

WHEN a Nation, led to greatness by the hand of Liberty, and possessed of all the glory that heroism, munificence, and humanity can bestow, descends to the ungrateful task of forging chains for her Friends and Children, and instead of giving support to Freedom, turns advocate for Slavery and Oppression, there is reason to suspect she has either ceased to be virtuous, or been extremely negligent in the appointment of her rulers.
In

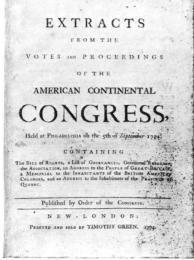

EXTRACTS

FROM THE

VOTES AND PROCEEDINGS

OF THE

AMERICAN CONTINENTAL

CONGRESS,

Held at PHILADELPHIA on the 5th of September 1774.

CONTAINING

The BILL of RIGHTS, a List of GRIEVANCES, Occasional ADDRESSES, the ASSOCIATION, an ADDRESS to the PEOPLE of GREAT-BRITAIN, a MEMORIAL to the Inhabitants of the BRITISH AMERICAN COLONIES, and an ADDRESS to the Inhabitants of the Province of QUEBEC.

Published by Order of the CONGRESS.

NEW-LONDON:

PRINTED AND SOLD BY TIMOTHY GREEN. 1774.

"A view of the south part of Lexington," engraved by Amos Dolittle from sketches by Ralph Earl

The First Shots

The first shots between provincials and British regulars were exchanged in confusion at Lexington, as soldiers marched past on their way to seize colonial military stores in Concord. On their retreat to Boston, the regulars were trailed by sharpshooting colonists firing from cover. The emboldened colonists then determined to drive the small British garrison from Boston, but failed at Bunker Hill, for lack of ammunition.

America burns while Parliament fiddles and argues; "Bunker's Hill, or America's Head-Dress"

Conciliation Fails

The second meeting of the Continental Congress began in May 1775, after the battles of Lexington and Concord. At this late date the delegates attempted conciliation — not with Parliament, but with the King as loyal subjects entitled to their own legislature — and sent the "Olive Branch Petition" to George III. But the King would not read it.

In January of 1776, an uncompromising pamphlet by Thomas Paine became a best seller and helped convince thousands of Americans that their continent should be independent of the little British island.

Stokes Collection, New York Public Library

(Left) Signature page of the "Olive Branch Petition"; **(below)** Edmund Burke, supporter of the colonies in Parliament; **(bottom)** Thomas Paine and title page from his influential pamphlet, "Common Sense"

National Portrait Gallery, London

National Portrait Gallery, London

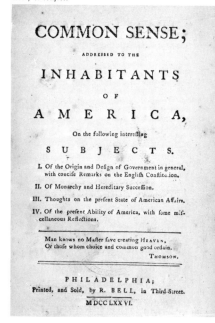

Library of Congress

COMMON SENSE;

ADDRESSED TO THE

INHABITANTS

OF

AMERICA,

On the following interesting

SUBJECTS.

I. Of the Origin and Design of Government in general,
with concise Remarks on the English Constitution.

II. Of Monarchy and Hereditary Succession.

III. Thoughts on the present State of American Affairs.

IV. Of the present Ability of America, with some miscellaneous Reflections.

Man knows no Master save creating HEAVEN,
Or those whom choice and common good ordain.
THOMSON.

PHILADELPHIA;
Printed, and Sold, by R. BELL, in Third-Street.
MDCCLXXVI.

Declaration of Independence

Independence Hall, Philadelphia, meeting place of 2nd Continental Congress

A draft of the Declaration including a portion, later omitted, condemning the slave trade

On July 2, 1776, the Congress formally resolved for independence, and on July 4 adopted a declaration supporting that resolution. A committee had been appointed to draw up the declaration, but it was primarily the work of Thomas Jefferson. Intended to justify independence, the document blamed the colonies' troubles on the King, though all of their disputes had been with Parliament.

"Congress Voting Independence" by Robert Edge Pine and Edward Savage; (below) a sketch of Thomas Jefferson by Benjamin Latrobe and a draft of the Lee resolution for independence, June 7, 1776

1773 - 1774

50.

Resistance to the Tax on Tea

The Tea Act of 1773 was passed by Parliament to save the British East India Company from bankruptcy. The effect of the act would have been to undersell any competition in America and thus benefit both the consumer and the company. American colonials who were in favor of a revolution decided to use this act to maneuver Britain into a difficult position. Rumors were planted to the effect that the Tea Act created an illegal monopoly. Resistance to the importation of tea was encouraged throughout the colonies, and resolutions against tea imports were drawn up in several ports. It was in Boston that, under the leadership of Sam Adams, the most drastic action occurred. On December 16, 1773, American patriots, masquerading as African Americans and Native Americans, raided the ships of the East India Company that were docked in the harbor and dumped the tea into the ocean. Two sets of resolutions against importing tea are reprinted below. The resolutions of the New York Sons of Liberty were the result of a meeting held in late November; those of the citizens of Philadelphia are dated January 3, 1774, and reinforce a position taken the previous October.

Source: Niles: "Association of the Sons of Liberty to the Public."
　　　　Niles: "Action of the Citizens of Philadelphia, in Opposition to the Importation of Tea."

I.

Resolutions of the New York Sons of Liberty

THE FOLLOWING ASSOCIATION is signed by a great number of the principal gentlemen of the city, merchants, lawyers, and other inhabitants of all ranks, and it is still carried about the city, to give an opportunity to those who have not yet signed to unite with their fellow citizens, to testify their abhorrence to the diabolical project of enslaving America.

The Association of the Sons of Liberty of New York

It is essential to the freedom and security of a free people that no taxes be imposed upon them but by their own consent, or [that of] their representatives. For "what property have they in that which another may, by right, take when he pleases to himself?" The former is the undoubted right of Englishmen, to secure which they expended millions and sacrificed the lives of thousands. And yet, to the astonishment of all the world and the grief of America, the

Commons of Great Britain, after the repeal of the memorable and detestable Stamp Act, reassumed the power of imposing taxes on the American colonies; and, insisting on it as a necessary badge of parliamentary supremacy, passed a bill in the seventh year of His present Majesty's reign, imposing duties on all glass, painters' colors, paper, and teas that should, after November 20, 1767, be "imported from Great Britain into any colony or plantation in America."

This bill, after the concurrence of the Lords, obtained the royal assent. And thus they who, from time immemorial, have exercised the right of giving to or withholding from the Crown their aids and subsidies, according to their own free will and pleasure, signified by their representatives in Parliament, do, by the act in question, deny us, their brethren in America, the enjoyment of the same right. As this denial, and the execution of that act, involves our slavery, and would sap the foundation of our freedom whereby we should become slaves to our brethren and fellow subjects born to no greater stock of freedom than the Americans, the merchants and inhabitants of this city, in conjunction with the merchants and inhabitants of the ancient American colonies, entered into an agreement to decline a part of their commerce with Great Britain until the above mentioned act should be totally repealed. This agreement operated so powerfully to the disadvantage of the manufacturers of England that many of them were unemployed.

To appease their clamors, and to provide the subsistence for them, which the nonimportation had deprived them of, the Parliament, in 1770, repealed so much of the revenue act as imposed a duty on glass, painters' colors, and paper, and left the duty on tea, as a test of the parliamentary right to tax us. The merchants of the cities of New York and Philadelphia, having strictly adhered to the agreement, so far as it is related to the importation of articles subject to an American duty, have convinced the Ministry that some other measures must be adopted to execute parliamentary supremacy over this country, and to remove the distress brought on the East India Company by the ill policy of that act.

Accordingly, to increase the temptation to the shippers of tea from England, an act of Parliament passed the last session which gives the whole duty on tea the company were subject to pay, upon the importation of it into England, to the purchasers and exporters; and when the company have 10 million pounds of tea in their warehouses exclusive of the quantity they may want to ship, they are allowed to export tea, discharged from the payment of that duty with which they were before chargeable. In hopes of aid in the execution of this project by the influence of the owners of the American ships, application was made by the company to the captains of those ships to take the tea on freight; but they virtuously rejected it. Still determined on the scheme, they have chartered ships to bring the tea to this country, which may be hourly expected, to make an important trial of our virtue. If they succeed in the sale of that tea, we shall have no property that we can call our own, and then we may bid adieu to American liberty.

Therefore, to prevent a calamity which, of all others, is the most to be dreaded — slavery, and its terrible concomitants — we, the subscribers, being influenced from a regard to liberty, and disposed to use all lawful endeavors in our power to defeat the pernicious project; and to transmit to our posterity those blessings of freedom which our ancestors have handed down to us; and to contribute to the support of the common liberties of America which are in danger to be subverted, do, for those important purposes, agree to associate together, under the name and style of the Sons of New York, and engage our honor to and with each other faithfully to observe and perform the following resolutions, viz.:

1. *Resolved,* that whoever shall aid, or

abet, or in any manner assist in the introduction of tea from any place whatsoever into this colony, while it is subject by a British act of Parliament to the payment of a duty for the purpose of raising a revenue in America, he shall be deemed an enemy to the liberties of America.

2. *Resolved,* that whoever shall be aiding or assisting in the landing or carting of such tea from any ship or vessel, or shall hire any house, storehouse, or cellar or any place whatsoever to deposit the tea, subject to a duty as aforesaid, he shall be deemed an enemy to the liberties of America.

3. *Resolved,* that whoever shall sell, or buy, or [in] any manner contribute to the sale or purchase of tea subject to a duty as aforesaid, or shall aid or abet in transporting such tea by land or water from this city until the statute of the seventh year of George III, chap. 46, commonly called the Revenue Act, shall be totally and clearly repealed, he shall be deemed an enemy to the liberties of America.

4. *Resolved,* that whether the duties on tea imposed by this act be paid in Great Britain or in America our liberties are equally affected.

5. *Resolved,* that whoever shall transgress any of these resolutions, we will not deal with, or employ, or have any connection with him.

II.

Resolutions of the Citizens of Philadelphia

THE UNANIMITY, spirit, and zeal which have heretofore animated all the colonies from Boston to South Carolina have been so eminently displayed in the opposition to the pernicious project of the East India Company in sending tea to America, while it remains subject to a duty, and the Americans at the same time confined by the strongest prohibitory laws to import it only from Great Britain, that a particular account of

the transactions of this city cannot but be acceptable to all our readers, and every other friend of American liberty.

Upon the first advice of this measure, a general dissatisfaction was expressed that, at a time when we were struggling with this oppressive act and an agreement not to import tea while subject to the duty, our fellow subjects in England should form a measure so directly tending to enforce that act, and again embroil us with our parent state. When it was also considered that the proposed mode of disposing of the tea tended to a monopoly, ever odious in a free country, a universal disapprobation showed itself throughout the city. A public meeting of the inhabitants was held at the State House on October 18 [1773], at which great numbers attended, and the sense of the city was expressed in the following resolves:

1. That the disposal of their own property is the inherent right of freemen; that there can be no property in that which another can, of right, take from us without our consent; that the claim of Parliament to tax America is, in other words, a claim of right to levy contributions on us at pleasure.

2. That the duty imposed by Parliament upon tea landed in America is a tax on the Americans, or levying contributions on them without their consent.

3. That the express purpose for which the tax is levied on the Americans, namely, for the support of government, administration of justice, and defense of His Majesty's dominions in America, has a direct tendency to render assemblies useless, and to introduce arbitrary government and slavery.

4. That a virtuous and steady opposition to this ministerial plan of governing America is absolutely necessary to preserve even the shadow of liberty, and is a duty which every freeman in America owes to his country, to himself, and to his posterity.

5. That the resolution lately entered into by the East India Company to send out their tea to America, subject to the payment of duties on its being landed here, is an

open attempt to enforce this ministerial plan, and a violent attack upon the liberties of America.

6. That it is the duty of every American to oppose this attempt.

7. That whoever shall directly or indirectly countenance this attempt, or in any wise aid or abet in unloading, receiving, or vending the tea sent, or to be sent out by the East India Company, while it remains subject to the payment of duty here, is an enemy to his country.

8. That a committee be immediately chosen to wait on those gentlemen who, it is reported, are appointed by the East India Company to receive and sell the said tea, and request them from a regard to their own character, and the peace and good order of the city and province, immediately to resign their appointment.

In consequence of this appointment, the committee waited upon the gentlemen in this city, who had been appointed consignees of the expected cargo. They represented to them the detestation and abhorrence in which this measure was held by their fellow citizens, the danger and difficulties which must attend the execution of so odious a trust, and expressed the united desires of the city that they would renounce the commission and engage not to intermeddle with the ship or cargo in any shape whatever. Some of the commissioners resigned, in a manner that gave general satisfaction, others in such equivocal terms as required further explanation. However, in a few days the resignation was complete. In this situation things remained for a few days.

In the meantime, the general spirit and indignation rose to such a height that it was thought proper to call another general meeting of the principal citizens to consider and resolve upon such farther steps as might give weight and insure success to the unanimous opposition now formed. Accordingly a meeting was held for the above purpose at which a great number of respectable inhabitants attended, and it appeared to be

the unanimous opinion that the entry of the ship at the customhouse, or the landing any part of her cargo, would be attended with great danger and difficulty, and would directly tend to destroy that peace and good order which ought to be preserved. An addition of twelve other gentlemen was then made to the former committee, and the general meeting adjourned till the arrival of the tea ship. Information being given of that, the price of tea was suddenly advanced, though it was owing to a general scarcity of that article; yet all the possessors of tea, in order to give strength to the opposition, readily agreed to reduce the price, and sell what remained in their hands at a reasonable rate. Nothing now remained but to keep up a proper correspondence and connection with the other colonies, and to take all prudent and proper precautions on the arrival of the tea ship.

It is not easy to describe the anxiety and suspense of the city in this interval. Sundry reports of her arrival were received which proved premature. But on Saturday evening, the 25th ult, an express came up from Chester to inform the town that the tea ship, commanded by Captain Ayres, with her detested cargo, was arrived there, having followed another ship up the river so far.

The committee met early the next morning, and being apprized of the arrival of Mr. Gilbert Barclay, the other consignee, who came passenger in the ship, they immediately went in a body to request his renunciation of the commission. Mr. Barclay politely attended the committee at the first request; and being made acquainted with the sentiments of the city, and the danger to which the public liberties of America were exposed by this measure, he, after expressing the particular hardship of his situation, also resigned the commission, in a manner which affected everyone present.

The committee then appointed three of their members to go to Chester, and two others to Gloucester Point, in order to have the earliest opportunity of meeting Captain Ayres, and representing to him the sense of the public respecting his voyage and cargo. The gentlemen who had set out for Chester, receiving intelligence that the vessel had weighed anchor about 12 o'clock, and proceeded to town, returned. About 2 o'clock she appeared in sight of Gloucester Point, where a number of inhabitants from the town had assembled with the gentlemen from the committee. As she passed along, she was hailed, and the captain requested not to proceed further, but to come on shore. This the captain complied with, and was handed through a lane made by the people to the gentlemen appointed to confer with him. They represented to him the general sentiments, together with the danger and difficulties that would attend his refusal to comply with the wishes of the inhabitants, and finally desired him to proceed with them to town, where he would be more fully informed of the temper and resolution of the people.

He was accordingly accompanied to town by a number of persons, where he was soon convinced of the truth and propriety of the representations which had been made to him, and agreed that, upon the desire of the inhabitants being publicly expressed, he would conduct himself accordingly. Some small rudeness being offered to the captain afterwards in the street by some boys, several gentlemen interposed and suppressed it before he received the least injury. Upon an hour's notice on Monday morning, a public meeting was called, and the State House not being sufficient to hold the numbers assembled, they adjourned into the square. This meeting is allowed by all to be the most respectable, both in the numbers and rank of those who attended it, that has been known in this city. After a short introduction, the following resolutions were not only agreed to, but the public approbation testified in the warmest manner:

1. *Resolved*, that the tea on board the ship *Polly*, Captain Ayres, shall not be landed.

2. That Captain Ayres shall neither enter nor report his vessel at the customhouse.

3. That Captain Ayres shall carry back the tea immediately.

4. That Captain Ayres shall immediately send a pilot on board his vessel with orders to take charge of her, and proceed to Reedy Island next high water.

5. That the captain shall be allowed to stay in town till tomorrow to provide necessaries for his voyage.

6. That he shall then be obliged to leave the town and proceed to his vessel, and make the best of his way out of our river and bay.

7. That a committee of four gentlemen be appointed to see these resolves carried into execution.

The Assembly were then informed of the spirit and resolution of New York, Charleston, South Carolina, and the conduct of the people of Boston, whereupon it was unanimously *resolved*:

That this assembly highly approve of the conduct and spirit of the people of New York, Charleston, and Boston, and return their hearty thanks to the people of Boston for their resolution in destroying the tea rather than suffering it to be landed.

The whole business was conducted with a decorum and order worthy the importance of the cause. Captain Ayres being present at this meeting, solemnly and publicly engaged that he would literally comply with the sense of the city, as expressed in the above resolutions.

A proper supply of necessaries and fresh provisions being then procured, in about two hours the tea ship weighed anchor from Gloucester Point, where she lay within sight of the town, and has proceeded, with her whole cargo, on her return to the East India Company.

The public think the conduct of those gentlemen whose goods are returned on board the tea ship ought not to pass unnoticed, as they have, upon this occasion, generously sacrificed their private interest to the public good.

Thus this important affair, in which there has been so glorious an exertion of public virtue and spirit, has been brought to a happy issue, by which the force of a law so obstinately persisted in to the prejudice of the national commerce, for the sake of the principle on which it is founded (a right of taxing the Americans without their consent), has been effectually broken, and the foundations of American liberty more deeply laid than ever.

51.

"Revolutionary Tea"

Boston's violent resistance against the Tea Act met with varied reactions among the colonists. The destruction of private property was condemned by many Americans, but most of them supported the principle, if not the practice, of Boston's position. "Revolutionary Tea" is a song that expressed the feelings of many of the patriots.

Source: *Father Kemp's Old Folks Concert Music*, Boston, n.d.

✿ REVOLUTIONARY TEA

There was an old lady lived over the sea,
And she was an Island Queen;
Her daughter lived off in a new country,
With an ocean of water between.
The old lady's pockets were full of gold,
But never contented was she,
So she called on her daughter to pay her
    a tax
Of three pence a pound on her tea,
Of three pence a pound on her tea.

"Now mother, dear mother," the
    daughter replied,
"I shan't do the thing that you ax;
I'm willing to pay a fair price for the tea,
But never the three penny tax."
"You shall," quoth the mother, and
    reddened with rage,
"For you're my own daughter, you see,
And sure 'tis quite proper the daughter
    should pay
Her mother a tax on her tea,
Her mother a tax on her tea."

And so the old lady her servant called up,
And packed off a budget of tea;
And eager for three pence a pound, she
    put in
Enough for a large family.
She ordered her servants to bring home
    the tax,
Declaring her child should obey,
Or old as she was, and almost woman
    grown,
She'd half whip her life away,
She'd half whip her life away.

The tea was conveyed to the daughter's
    door,
All down by the ocean's side;
And the bouncing girl poured out every
    pound
In the dark and boiling tide.
And then she called out to the Island
    Queen,
"Oh, mother, dear mother," quoth she,
"Your tea you may have when 'tis
    steeped enough,
But never a tax from me,
But never a tax from me."

1774

52.

The Independence of the Massachusetts Legislature

The Bay Colony was a leader in the growing resistance to royal authority. The legislature of Massachusetts attempted during 1773 to stimulate intercolonial cooperation through committees of correspondence. Governor Hutchinson contested the determination of the legislature to exercise its prerogative in appointing such committees. In reply to the governor's criticism of the Massachusetts House of Representatives, a committee consisting of Sam Adams, John Hancock, and others submitted the following report on February 5, 1774.

Source: Niles: "Extract from the Answer of the House of Representatives to the Governor, February 5, 1774."

IT AFFORDS GREAT SATISFACTION to this house to find that His Majesty has been pleased to put an end to an undue claim, heretofore made by the governors of this province, grounded upon a supposition that the consent of the chair was necessary to the validity of the judicial acts of the Governor and Council. Whereby their proceedings, when sitting as the Supreme Court of Probate, and as the court for determining in cases of marriage and divorce, have been so often impeded. The royal order, that the governor shall acquiesce in the determination of the majority of the Council, respects not the Council only but the body of the people of this province. And His Majesty has herein showed his regard to justice, as well as the interest and convenience of his subjects, in rescuing a clause in the charter from a construction which, in the opinion of this house, was repugnant to the express meaning and intent of the charter, inconsistent with the idea of a court of justice, and dangerous to the rights and property of the subject.

Your Excellency is pleased to inform the two houses that you are required to signify to them His Majesty's disapprobation of the appointment of committees of correspondence, in various instances, which sit and act during the recess of the General Court by prorogation. You are not pleased to explain to us the grounds and reasons of His Majesty's disapprobation; until we shall have such explanation laid before us, a full answer to this part of your speech will not be expected from us. We cannot, however, omit saying upon this occasion that while the common rights of the American subjects continue to be attacked in various instances, and at times when the several assemblies are not sitting, it is highly necessary that they should correspond with each other in order to unite in the most effectual means for the obtaining a redress of their grievances. And as the sitting of the general assemblies in this and most of the colonies depends upon the pleasure of the governors, who hold themselves under the direction of administration, it is to be expected that the meeting of the assemblies will be so ordered, as that the intention proposed by a correspondence between them will be impracticable but by committees to sit and act in the recess.

We would, moreover, observe that, as it has been the practice for years past for the governor and lieutenant governor of this province, and other officers of the Crown, at all times, to correspond with ministers of state and persons of influence and distinction in the nation in order to concert and carry on such measures of the British administration as have been deemed by the colonists to be grievous to them, it cannot be thought unreasonable or improper for the colonists to correspond with their agents, as well as with each other, to the end that their grievances may be so explained to His Majesty, as that, in his justice, he may afford them necessary relief. As this province has heretofore felt the great misfortune of the displeasure of our sovereign by means of misrepresentations, permit us further to say there is room to apprehend that His Majesty has, in this instance, been misinformed and that there are good grounds to suspect that those who may have misinformed him have had in meditation further measures destructive to the colonies, which they were apprehensive would be defeated by means of committees of correspondence sitting and acting in the recess of the respective assemblies.

It must be pleasing to the good people of this province to find that the heavy debt which had been incurred by their liberal aids, through the course of the late war for the subduing His Majesty's inveterate enemies and extending his territory and dominion in America, is so nearly discharged. Whenever the house of representatives shall deem it incumbent upon them to provide for any future charges, it will be done, as it ought, by such ways and means as, after due deliberation, to them shall seem meet.

In the meantime, this House will employ the powers with which they are entrusted in supporting His Majesty's just authority in the province, according to the royal charter, and in dispatching such public business as now properly lies before us. And, while we pursue such measures as tend, by God's blessing, to the redress of grievances and to the restoration and establishment of the public liberty, we persuade ourselves that we shall, at the same time, as far as in us lies, most effectually secure the tranquility and good order of the government, and the great end for which it was instituted, the safety and welfare of the people.

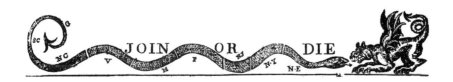

53.

Lord Dartmouth: On Securing the Submission of Massachusetts

The cumulative effect of the reports of colonial resistance to British rule during the winter of 1773-1774 was to make Parliament more determined than ever to assert its authority in America. The main force of their actions fell on Boston which seemed to be the center of colonial hostility. General Thomas Gage, commander in chief of the British Army in America, was appointed governor of Massachusetts. In the following letter to Gage of April 9, 1774, Lord Dartmouth, the secretary of state for the colonies, spoke of the ministry's determination to make Massachusetts submit.

Source: Carter, II.

The King, having thought fit that you should return immediately to your command in North America and that you should proceed directly to Boston on board His Majesty's ship *Lively* (now lying at Plymouth ready to sail with the first fair wind), I send you herewith by His Majesty's command a commission under the great seal appointing you captain-general and governor-in-chief of His Majesty's province of Massachusetts Bay, together with such instructions as have been usually given to governors of that province for their guidance in the exercise of the ordinary and more permanent powers and authorities incident to that command.

What is further necessary for your direction in the present state of disorder and commotion within that province, and for enabling you to carry into execution the measures that have been and probably will be adopted for reducing it to a state of obedience to lawful authority, is of a more delicate and important nature, and requires more precise and particular instructions. With this letter you will receive an act of Parliament passed in the present session for

discontinuing the loading and unloading of goods and merchandise at the town and within the harbor of Boston; and also a minute of the Treasury Board, containing the substance of such instructions as their lordships have thought fit to give their officers in consequence thereof; and it is the King's command that you do give them all proper and necessary assistance and support in the execution thereof.

To this end it will be expedient that you do, immediately upon your arrival and so soon as your commission has been read and published in the usual form, appoint a meeting either at the town or within the castle (as circumstances shall point out) with the commander in chief of His Majesty's ships, the lieutenant governor, the commissioners of the customs, the chief justice, and the secretary of the province in order to consider what steps it may be proper to take for carrying the act into execution, and for enforcing, if necessary, a due obedience thereto. And if Mr. Hutchinson should not be come away in consequence of the leave he has obtained for that purpose, his advice and assistance in this case, as well as in the execution of every other part of your instructions, will be of very great use and advantage to you.

His Majesty trusts that no opposition will, or can, with any effect, be made to the carrying the law into execution, nor any violence or insult offered to those to whom the execution of it is entrusted. Should it happen otherwise, your authority as the first magistrate, combined with your command over the King's troops, will, it is hoped, enable you to meet every opposition and fully to preserve the public peace by employing those troops with effect, should the madness of the people on the one hand, or the timidity or want of strength of the peace officers on the other hand, make it necessary to have recourse to their assistance. The King trusts, however, that such necessity will not occur and commands me to say that it will be your duty to use every endeavor to avoid it; to quiet the minds of the people; to remove their prejudices; and, by mild and gentle persuasion, to induce such a submission on their part to this law and such a proper compliance with the just requisitions it contains as may give full scope to His Majesty's clemency, and enable His Majesty to exercise the discretionary power given him by the act of again restoring to the town of Boston those commercial privileges and advantages which it has so long enjoyed and which have raised it to its present state of opulence and importance.

At the same time, the sovereignty of the King, in his Parliament, over the colonies requires a full and absolute submission; and His Majesty's dignity demands that, until that submission be made, the town of Boston, where so much anarchy and confusion have prevailed, should cease to be the place of the residence of his governor or of any other officer of government who is not obliged by law to perform his functions there. It is therefore His Majesty's further pleasure that so soon as the law for discon-

Courtesy, Lord Dartmouth

The 2nd Earl of Dartmouth, portrait by Thomas Gainsborough

tinuing the port shall have taken place, and every step has been pursued that is necessary to insure the execution of it, you do make the town of Salem the place of your residence; that you do require all officers (not included in the above exception) to attend you there; and that the General Court and all other courts and offices which are not by law fixed at Boston be appointed and held at Salem until His Majesty, satisfied upon your representation that the laws of this Kingdom will be duly observed and government be again administered at the town of Boston without opposition, shall have signified his royal will and pleasure for the return of his governor to, and for holding of the General Court at that town.

The proceedings of the body of the people at the town of Boston in the months of November and December last were of such a nature and criminality as to have fixed a deep degree of guilt upon those who were the principal ringleaders and abettors of those proceedings, and the measures proper to be taken for inducing the punishment of such guilt become a very necessary part of the present consideration relative to the state of the province of Massachusetts Bay.

The enclosed copy of a report made to me by His Majesty's attorney and solicitor general will point out to you their opinion of the extent of the criminality attending those transactions; and the copy of the narrative on which that opinion was given, accompanied with copies of certain depositions taken before the lords of the Council (all of which are herewith enclosed), will fully inform you as well of the facts as of the persons to which the opinion applies.

The object of the inquiry made here was to have established such a charge against the ringleaders in those violences as might have enabled His Majesty to have proceeded against them in this Kingdom. It was found, however, upon the result that it would be difficult (clear and positive as the evidence was with respect to some parts of the proceedings) to establish such a connection between the acts of the body of the people and the destruction of the tea as to have no doubt of the propriety and effect of bringing over the persons charged to be tried here.

In this dilemma there seemed to be no other method of proceeding against them but in the ordinary courts of justice within the colony. It will therefore be your duty, with the advice and assistance of such of His Majesty's law servants as it may be proper for you to consult upon such occasion, to make all possible inquiry into every particular of the transactions pointed out in the attorney and solicitor generals' report, and to employ your utmost endeavors to obtain sufficient evidence against the principal actors therein; and in case the acts, stated in the report of the attorney and solicitor general to have been acts of treason, can by full and clear evidence be brought home to any individuals, or that such transactions have been attended with any other degree of guilt that is an object of criminal prosecution against any persons, and you shall be of opinion that upon indictment of them there is a probability of their being brought

to punishment, it is His Majesty's pleasure that you do, in such case, direct the proper steps to be taken for their prosecution.

The King considers the punishment of these offenders as a very necessary and essential example to others of the ill consequences that must follow from such open and arbitrary usurpations as tend to the subversion of all government and the rendering civil liberty unsafe and precarious. And His Majesty's subjects in the province of Massachusetts Bay in general cannot give a better test of their love of justice and respect for the constitution than in their zealous endeavors to render effectual a due prosecution of such offenders.

If, however, the prejudices of the people should appear to you to be such as would, in all probability, prevent a conviction, however clear and full the evidence might be, in that case it would be better to desist from prosecution, seeing that an ineffectual attempt would only be triumph to the faction and disgraceful to government.

You will observe, sir, that I have throughout the whole of this letter avoided making any mention of the Council for the province of Massachusetts Bay, and I have been thus silent with regard to them from an apprehension that, from what has already appeared respecting their conduct, any hope of proper advice or assistance from them would be vain. At the same time, I do not mean that any constitutional power or authority, vested in them, should be set aside by any part of these instructions, or that you should not be at liberty to give them full confidence and communication in case you shall perceive such an alteration in their conduct as will justify such a behavior toward them.

There are, however, some amongst those who constitute the present Council there upon whose attachment to the constitution no reliance can be had in any case where the sovereignty of the King in his Parliament is in question; and His Majesty thinks it essential to the due support of that sovereignty that the principal of those who insisted upon the report of the committee of the Council on the 27th day of September last, in which report that sovereignty is questioned, at a time when the execution of the laws was openly opposed by force and violence, should not have seats at the Council Board. It is therefore His Majesty's pleasure that if those persons, or any of them, shall be chosen at the next general election, you do put your negative upon such election.

The foregoing is all that I have at present in command from the King to say to you. I need not suggest to you the very great advantage that will result from your obtaining a just and perfect knowledge of the characters, inclinations and tempers of the principal people in the colony; such information must, of necessity, be of great benefit, and your own discretion will point out to you the use that is to be made of it.

The last advices from Boston are of a nature to leave but little room to hope that order and obedience are soon likely to take the place of anarchy and usurpation. His Majesty, however, confides in your fortitude and discretion, and doubts not that all other officers, civil and military, animated by your example, will exert themselves in such manner, in support of the constitution, and for enforcing obedience to the laws, as will recommend them to His Majesty's royal grace and favor.

54.

GOUVERNEUR MORRIS: Against Revolutionary Enthusiasm

Gouverneur Morris of New York feared the social upheaval that he thought likely to occur in the event of a "democratic" revolution. Morris was a member of the colonial aristocracy and believed "that if the disputes with Britain continue, we shall be under the worst of all possible dominions . . . . the domination of a riotous mob." But when the break with England came, Morris supported the American cause. The occasion of the following letter of May 20, 1774, to [John] Penn was a meeting in New York called to consider Boston's proposals to stop all trade with Britain.

Source: *Archives*, I, pp. 342-343.

YOU HAVE HEARD, and you will hear, a great deal about politics, and in the heap of chaff you may find some grains of good sense. Believe me, sir, freedom and religion are only watchwords. We have appointed a committee, or rather we have nominated one. Let me give you the history of it. It is needless to premise that the lower orders of mankind are more easily led by specious appearances than those of a more exalted station. This, and many similar propositions, you know better than your humble servant.

The troubles in America, during Grenville's administration, put our gentry upon this finesse. They stimulated some daring coxcombs to rouse the mob into an attack upon the bounds of order and decency. These fellows became the Jack Cades of the day, the leaders in all the riots, the bellwethers of the flock. The reason of the maneuver in those who wished to keep fair with the government, and at the same time to receive the incense of popular applause, you will readily perceive. On the whole, the shepherds were not much to blame in a politic point of view. The bellwethers jingled merrily and roared out liberty, and property, and religion, and a multitude of cant terms, which everyone thought he understood and was egregiously mistaken. For you must know the shepherds kept the dictionary of the day, and, like the mysteries of the ancient mythology, it was not for profane eyes or ears. This answered many purposes; the simple flock put themselves entirely under the protection of these most excellent shepherds.

By and by, behold a great metamorphosis, without the help of Ovid or his divinities, but entirely effectuated by two modern genii — the God of Ambition and the Goddess of Faction. The first of these prompted the shepherds to shear some of their flock, and then, in conjunction with the other, converted the bellwethers into shepherds. That we have been in hot water with the British Parliament ever since everybody knows. Consequently, these new shepherds had their hands full of employment. The old ones kept themselves least in sight, and a want of confidence in each other was not the least evil which followed. The port of Boston has been shut up. These sheep, simple as they are, cannot be gulled as heretofore. In short, there is no ruling them; and now, to leave the metaphor, the heads of the mobility [the mob] grow dangerous to the gentry, and how to keep them down is the question. While

Courtesy, New York Historical Society

Gouverneur Morris, portrait by Ezra Ames

they correspond with the other colonies, call and dismiss popular assemblies, make resolves to bind the consciences of the rest of mankind, bully poor printers, and exert with full force all their other tribunitial powers, it is impossible to curb them.

But art sometimes goes farther than force, and, therefore, to trick them handsomely, a committee of patricians was to be nominated, and into their hands was to be committed the majesty of the people, and the highest trust was to be reposed in them by a mandate that they should take care *quod respublica non capiat injuriam* [that the republic should not suffer injury]. The tribunes, through the want of good legerdemain in the senatorial order, perceived the finesse; and, yesterday, I was present at a grand division of the city, and there I beheld my fellow citizens very accurately counting all their chickens, not only before any of them were hatched but before above one-half of the eggs were laid. In short, they fairly contended about the future forms of our government, whether it should be founded upon aristocratic or democratic principles.

I stood in the balcony, and on my right hand were ranged all the people of property, with some few poor dependents, and on the other all the tradesmen, etc., who thought it worth their while to leave daily labor for the good of the country. The spirit of the English constitution has yet a little influence left, and but a little. The remains of it, however, will give the wealthy people a superiority this time, but would they secure it they must banish all schoolmasters and confine all knowledge to themselves. This cannot be. The mob begin to think and to reason. Poor reptiles! it is with them a vernal morning; they are struggling to cast off their winter's slough, they bask in the sunshine, and ere noon they will bite, depend upon it.

The gentry begin to fear this. Their committee will be appointed; they will deceive the people and again forfeit a share of their confidence. And if these instances of what with one side is policy, with the other perfidy, shall continue to increase and become more frequent, farewell aristocracy. I see, and I see it with fear and trembling, that if the disputes with Great Britain continue, we shall be under the worst of all possible dominions; we shall be under the domination of a riotous mob.

It is the interest of all men, therefore, to seek for reunion with the parent state. A safe compact seems, in my poor opinion, to be now tendered. Internal taxation is to be left with ourselves; the right of regulating trade to be vested in Great Britain, where alone is found the power of protecting it. I trust you will agree with me, that this is the only possible mode of union. Men by nature are free as air. When they enter into society, there is, there must be, an implied compact, for there never yet was an express one, that a part of this freedom shall be given up for the security of the remainder. But what part? The answer is plain. The least possible, considering the circumstances of the society, which constitute what may be called its political necessity.

And what does this political necessity require in the present instance? Not that Britain should lay imposts upon us for the support of government, nor for its defense; not that she should regulate our internal police. These things affect us only. She can have no right to interfere. To these things we ourselves are competent. But can it be said that we are competent to the regulating of trade? The position is absurd, for this affects every part of the British Empire, every part of the habitable earth. If Great Britain, if Ireland, if America, if all of them are to make laws of trade, there must be a collision of these different authorities, and then who is to decide the *vis major?* To recur to this, if possible to be avoided, is the greatest of all great absurdities.

Political necessity, therefore, requires that this power should be placed in the hands of one part of the Empire. Is it a question which part? Let me answer by taking another. Pray, which part of the Empire protects trade? Which part of the Empire receives almost immense sums to guard the rest? And what danger is in the trust? Some men object that England will draw all the profits of our trade into her coffers. All that she can, undoubtedly. But unless a reasonable compensation for his trouble be left to the merchant here, she destroys the trade, and then she will receive no profit from it.

If I remember, in one of those kind letters with which you have honored me, you desire my thoughts on matters as they rise. How much pleasure I take in complying with your requests let my present letter convince you. If I am faulty in telling things which you know better than I do, you must excuse this fault, and a thousand others, for which I can make no apology.

55.

A Proposal for a Continental Congress

Early in May of 1774 the Boston Committee of Correspondence sent a circular letter throughout the colonies urging a stoppage of trade with Britain. This appeal was met with a mixed response. In New York, a committee of fifty-one, dominated by merchants, drafted a reply on May 23. While this committee had no desire to halt trade, it was determined to maintain control of the anti-British sentiments of the populace. The reply, therefore, sympathized with Boston's situation, but implied that only a continental congress could suitably handle the matter.

Source: *Archives,* I, pp. 297-298.

THE ALARMING MEASURES of the British Parliament relative to your ancient and respectable town, which has so long been the seat of freedom, fill the inhabitants of this city with inexpressible concern. As a sister colony, suffering in defense of the rights of America, we consider your injuries as a common cause, to the redress of which it is equally our duty and our interest to contribute. But what ought to be done in a situation so truly critical, while it employs the anxious thoughts of every generous mind, is very hard to be determined.

Our citizens have thought it necessary to appoint a large committee, consisting of fifty-one persons, to correspond with our sister colonies on this and every other matter of public moment, and at ten o'clock this forenoon we were first assembled. Your letter, enclosing the vote of the town of Boston, and the letter of your Committee of Correspondence were immediately taken into consideration.

While we think you justly entitled to the thanks of your sister colonies for asking their advice on a case of such extensive con-

sequences, we lament our inability to relieve your anxiety by a decisive opinion. The cause is general, and concerns a whole continent, who are equally interested with you and us; and we foresee that no remedy can be of avail unless it proceeds from the joint act and approbation of all; from a virtuous and spirited union which may be expected while the feeble efforts of a few will only be attended with mischief and disappointment to themselves and triumph to the adversaries of our liberty.

Upon these reasons we conclude that a congress of deputies from the colonies in general is of the utmost moment; that it ought to be assembled without delay, and some unanimous resolution formed in this fatal emergency, not only respecting your deplorable circumstances, but for the security of our common rights. Such being our sentiments, it must be premature to pronounce any judgment on the expedient which you have suggested. We beg, however, that you will do us the justice to believe that we shall continue to act with a firm and becoming regard to American freedom, and to cooperate with our sister colonies in every measure which shall be thought salutary and conducive to the public good.

We have nothing to add, but that we sincerely condole with you in your unexampled distress, and to request your speedy opinion of the proposed congress, that if it should meet with your approbation, we may exert our utmost endeavors to carry it into execution.

56.

The Quartering Act

When news of colonial opposition in 1773 and 1774 reached England, Parliament rapidly passed four acts, labeled by the colonists as the "Intolerable Acts." One of these was the Quartering Act of June 2, 1774, which applied to all British America and gave colonial governors the right to requisition unoccupied buildings to house British troops. However, in Massachusetts the British troops were forced to remain camped on the Boston Common until the following November because the Boston patriots refused to allow workmen to repair the vacant buildings General Gage had obtained for quarters.

Source: Pickering, XXX.

Whereas doubts have been entertained whether troops can be quartered otherwise than in barracks, in case barracks have been provided sufficient for the quartering of all the officers and soldiers within any town, township, city, district, or place within His Majesty's dominions in North America; and *whereas* it may frequently happen from the situation of such barracks that, if troops should be quartered therein they would not be stationed where their presence may be necessary and required: *be it therefore enacted* by the King's Most Excellent Majesty, by and with the advice and consent of the Lords . . . and Commons, in this present Parliament assembled . . . that, in such cases, it shall and may be lawful for the persons who now are, or may be hereafter, authorized by law, in any of the provinces within His Majesty's dominions in North America, and they are hereby respectively authorized, empowered, and directed, on the requisition of the officer who, for the time being, has the command of His Majesty's forces in North America, to cause any officers or soldiers in His Majesty's service to be quartered and billeted in such manner as is now directed by law where no barracks are provided by the colonies.

2. *And be it further enacted* by the authority aforesaid that, if it shall happen at any time that any officers or soldiers in His Majesty's service shall remain within any of the said colonies without quarters for the space of twenty-four hours after such quarters shall have been demanded, it shall and may be lawful for the governor of the province to order and direct such and so many uninhabited houses, outhouses, barns, or other buildings as he shall think necessary

to be taken (making a reasonable allowance for the same) and make fit for the reception of such officers and soldiers, and to put and quarter such officers and soldiers therein for such time as he shall think proper.

3. *And be it further enacted* by the authority aforesaid that this act, and everything herein contained, shall continue and be in force in all His Majesty's dominions in North America, until March 24, 1776.

57.

Resolutions Against Trade with England

The Virginia House of Burgesses at its meeting of May 27, 1774, had proposed a gathering of delegates in a continental congress to discuss British-colonial relations. Members of the House were asked to determine the opinion of their constituents on such a congress. One favorable response came in the form of the resolutions from Albemarle County on July 26. This document, which was drafted by Thomas Jefferson, summed up colonial grievances against Britain and urged a stoppage in trade.

Source: Ford, I, pp. 318-320: "Resolution of Albemarle County."

AT A MEETING OF THE FREEHOLDERS of the County of Albemarle, assembled in their collective body, at the court house of the said county, on the 26th of July, 1774:

Resolved, that the inhabitants of the several states of British America are subject to the laws which they adopted at their first settlement, and to such others as have been since made by their respective legislatures, duly constituted and appointed with their own consent. That no other legislature whatever can rightly exercise authority over them; and that these privileges they hold as the common rights of mankind, confirmed by the political constitutions they have respectively assumed, and also by several charters of compact from the Crown.

Resolved, that these their natural and legal rights have in frequent instances been invaded by the Parliament of Great Britain and particularly that they were so by an act lately passed to take away the trade of the inhabitants of the town of Boston, in the province of Massachusetts Bay; that all such assumptions of unlawful power are dangerous to the right of the British Empire in general, and should be considered as its common cause, and that we will ever be ready to join with our fellow subjects in every part of the same, in executing all those rightful powers which God has given us, for the reestablishment and guaranteeing such their constitutional rights, when, where, and by whomsoever invaded.

It is the opinion of this meeting that the most eligible means of effecting these purposes will be to put an immediate stop to all imports from Great Britain (cotton, osnaburgs [a coarse cloth], striped duffel, medicines, gunpowder, lead, books and printed papers, the necessary tools and implements for the handicraft arts and manufactures excepted, for a limited term), and to all exports thereto, after the 1st day of

October, which shall be in the year of our Lord, 1775; and immediately to discontinue all commercial intercourse with every part of the British Empire which shall not in like manner break off their commerce with Great Britain.

It is the opinion of this meeting, that we immediately cease to import all commodities from every part of the world, which are subjected by the British Parliament to the payment of duties in America.

It is the opinion of this meeting, that these measures should be pursued until a repeal be obtained of the act for blocking up the harbor of Boston; of the acts prohibiting or restraining internal manufactures in America; of the acts imposing on any commodities duties to be paid in America; and of the act laying restrictions on the American trade; and that on such repeal it will be

reasonable to grant to our brethren of Great Britain such privileges in commerce as may amply compensate their fraternal assistance, past and future.

Resolved, however, that this meeting do submit these their opinions to the Convention of Deputies from the several counties of this colony, and appointed to be held at Williamsburg on the 1st day of August next, and also to the General Congress of Deputies from the several American states, when and wheresoever held; and that they will concur in these or any other measures which such convention or such congress shall adopt as most expedient for the American good; and we do appoint Thomas Jefferson and John Walker our deputies to act for this county at the said convention, and instruct them to conform themselves to these our resolutions and opinions.

THE ALTERNATIVE OF WILLIAMS-BURG.

Plate IV.

(Left) "The Alternative of Williams Burg," 1775 mezzotint by Phillip Dawe

Courtesy, Library of Congress

(Below) Blacklist of merchants published in "North American Almanack," 1770

Courtesy, New York Public Library

A LIST of the Names of *those* who AUDACIOUSLY continue to counteract the UNITED SENTIMENTS of the BODY of Merchants thro'out NORTH-AMERICA; by importing British Goods contrary to the Agreement.

John Bernard,
(In King-Street, almost opposite Vernon's Head.
James McMasters,
(On Treat's Wharf.
Patrick McMasters,
(Opposite the Sign of the Lamb.
John Mein,
(Opposite the White-Horse, and in King-Street.
Nathaniel Rogers,
(Opposite Mr. Henderson Inches Store lower End King-Street.
William Jackson,
At the Brazen Head, Cornhill, near the Town-House.
Theophilus Lillie,
(Near Mr. Pemberton's Meeting-House, North-End.
John Taylor,
(Nearly opposite the Heart and Crown in Cornhill.
Ame & Elizabeth Cummings,
(Opposite the Old Brick Meeting House, all of Buston.
Israel Williams, Esq; & Son,
(Traders in the Town of Hatfield.
And, Henry Barnes,
(Trader in the Town of Marlboro'.

The following Names should have been inserted in the List of Justices.

County of Middlesex.	County of Lincoln.
Samuel Hendley	
John Borland	John Kingsbury
Henry Barnes	
Richard Cary	County of Berkshire.
County of Bristol.	Mark Hopkins
George Brightman	Elijah Dwight
County of Worcester.	Israel Stoddard
Daniel Bliss	

58.

THOMAS JEFFERSON: A Summary View of the Rights of British America

News of the Boston Port Bill, closing and otherwise punishing Boston until it apologized for the Tea Party of the previous December, reached Williamsburg, Virginia, in May 1774. In response, certain younger members of the Virginia House of Burgesses, among them Thomas Jefferson, submitted a resolution calling for June 1 to be set aside as a day of fasting and humiliation for this and "every injury to American rights." Lord Dunmore, the royal governor of the province, promptly dissolved the House. Under the leadership of Patrick Henry, the members adjourned to the Raleigh Tavern, where they resolved to call for a general congress of the colonies to consider "those measures which the united interests of America may from time to time require." They also summoned a special Virginia revolutionary convention for August 1, to decide what might be done to help the people of Boston and to elect delegates to the general or Continental Congress when it met in Philadelphia in September. Jefferson's constituents of Albemarle County elected him to represent them at the Virginia convention. He drew up a "draft of instructions" in July which he planned to lay before the members, hoping it might serve to guide the delegates at Philadelphia. The result was the Summary View of the Rights *of British America. While the Virginia convention eventually rejected the* View *as too radical, the effort established Jefferson's reputation as a revolutionary pamphleteer.*

Source: Ford, I, pp. 429-447.

Resolved that it be an instruction to the said deputies when assembled in General Congress with the deputies from the other states of British America to propose to the said Congress that a humble and dutiful address be presented to His Majesty begging leave to lay before him as chief magistrate of the British empire the united complaints of His Majesty's subjects in America; complaints which are excited by many unwarrantable encroachments and usurpations, attempted to be made by the legislature of one part of the empire, upon those rights which God and the laws have given equally and independently to all. To represent to His Majesty that these his states have often individually made humble application to his imperial throne, to obtain through its intervention some redress of their injured rights; to none of which was ever even an answer condescended. Humbly to hope that this their joint address, penned in the language of truth, and divested of those expressions of servility which would persuade His Majesty that we are asking favors and not rights, shall obtain from His Majesty a more respectful acceptance. And this His Majesty will think we have reason to expect when he reflects that he is no more than the chief officer of the people, appointed by the laws, and circumscribed with definite powers, to assist in working the great machine of government erected for their use, and consequently subject to their superintendence. And in order that these our rights, as well as the invasions of them, may be laid more fully before His Majesty, to take a view of them from the origin and first settlement of these countries.

To remind him that our ancestors, before their emigration to America, were the free inhabitants of the British dominions in Europe, and possessed a right, which nature has given to all men, of departing from the country in which chance, not choice has placed them; of going in quest of new habitations, and of there establishing new societies, under such laws and regulations as to them shall seem most likely to promote public happiness. That their Saxon ancestors had under this universal law, in like manner, left their native wilds and woods in the north of Europe, had possessed themselves of the island of Britain then less charged with inhabitants, and had established there that system of laws which has so long been the glory and protection of that country. Nor was ever any claim of superiority or dependence asserted over them by that mother country from which they had migrated: and were such a claim made it is believed that His Majesty's subjects in Great Britain have too firm a feeling of the rights derived to them from their ancestors to bow down the sovereignty of their state before such visionary pretensions. And it is thought that no circumstance has occurred to distinguish materially the British from the Saxon emigration.

America was conquered, and her settlements made and firmly established, at the expense of individuals, and not of the British public. Their own blood was spilled in acquiring lands for their settlements, their own fortunes expended in making that settlement effectual. For themselves they fought, for themselves they conquered, and for themselves alone they have right to hold. No shilling was ever issued from the public treasures of His Majesty or his ancestors for their assistance, till of very late times, after the colonies had become established on a firm and permanent footing. That then indeed, having become valuable to Great Britain for her commercial purposes, his Parliament was pleased to lend them assistance against an enemy who would fain have drawn to herself the benefits of their commerce to the great aggrandisement of herself and danger of Great Britain. . . . We do not however mean to underrate those aids which to us were doubtless valuable, on whatever principles granted: but we would show that they cannot give a title to that authority which the British Parliament would arrogate over us; and that they may amply be repaid, by our giving to the inhabitants of Great Britain such exclusive privileges in trade as may be advantageous to them, and at the same time not too restrictive to ourselves. That settlements having been thus effected in the wilds of America, the emigrants thought proper to adopt that system of laws under which they had hitherto lived in the mother country, and to continue their union with her by submitting themselves to the same common sovereign, who was thereby made the central link connecting the several parts of the empire thus newly multiplied.

But that not long were they permitted, however far they thought themselves removed from the hand of oppression, to hold undisturbed the rights thus acquired at the hazard of their lives and loss of their fortunes. . . . That country which had been acquired by the lives, the labors, and the fortunes of individual adventurers was by these princes at several times parted out and distributed among favorites and followers of their fortunes; and by an assumed right to the Crown alone were erected into distinct and independent governments; a measure which it is believed His Majesty's prudence and understanding would prevent him from imitating at this day. . . .

That the exercise of a free trade with all parts of the world possessed by the American colonists as of natural right, and which no law of their own had taken away or abridged, was next the object of unjust encroachment. . . . This arbitrary act, however, they soon recalled, and by solemn treaty entered into on March 12, 1651, between the said Commonwealth by their commissioners and the colony of Virginia by their House of Burgesses, it was expressly stipulated by the 8th Article of the said treaty that they should have "free trade as the people of England do enjoy to all places and with all nations according to the laws of that Commonwealth." But that, upon the restoration of His Majesty King Charles II, their rights of free commerce fell once more a victim to arbitrary power: and by several acts of his reign as well as of some of his successors the trade of the colonies was laid under such restrictions as show what hopes they might form from the justice of a British Parliament were its uncontrolled power admitted over these states.

History has informed us that bodies of men as well as individuals are susceptible of the spirit of tyranny. A view of these acts of Parliament for regulation, as it has been affectedly called, of the American trade, if all other evidence were removed out of the case, would undeniably evince the truth of this observation. Besides the duties they impose on our markets of export and import, they prohibit our going to any markets northward of Cape Finesterre in the kingdom of Spain for the sale of commodities which Great Britain will not take from us, and for the purchase of others with which she cannot supply us. . . . That these acts prohibit us from carrying in quest of other purchasers the surplus of our tobaccos remaining after the consumption of Great Britain is supplied: so that we must leave them with the British merchant for whatever he will please to allow us, to be by him reshipped to foreign markets, where he will reap the benefits of making sale of them for full value.

That to heighten still the idea of parliamentary justice, and to show with what moderation they are like to exercise power, where themselves are to feel no part of its weight, we take leave to mention to His Majesty certain other acts of British Parliament, by which they would prohibit us from manufacturing for our own use the articles we raise on our own lands with our own labor. . . . We do not point out to His Majesty the injustice of these acts with intent to rest on that principle the cause of their nullity, but to show that experience confirms the propriety of those political principles which exempt us from the jurisdiction of the British Parliament. The true ground on which we declare these acts void is that the British Parliament has no right to exercise its authority over us.

That these exercises of usurped power have not been confined to instances alone in which themselves were interested; but they have also intermeddled with the regulation of the internal affairs of the colonies. The act of the ninth year of Anne for establishing a post office in America seems to have had little connection with British convenience, except that of accommodating His Majesty's ministers and favorites with the sale of a lucrative and easy office.

That thus have we hastened through the reigns which preceded His Majesty's, during which the violations of our rights were less alarming, because repeated at more distant intervals, than that rapid and bold succession of injuries which is likely to distinguish the present from all other periods of American story. Scarcely have our minds been able to emerge from the astonishment into which one stroke of parliamentary thunder has involved us, before another more heavy and more alarming is fallen on us. Single acts of tyranny may be ascribed to the accidental opinion of a day; but a series of oppressions, begun at a distinguished period, and pursued unalterably through every change of ministers, too plainly prove a deliberate, systematical plan of reducing us to slavery. . . .

But that one other act passed in the seventh year of his reign, having been a peculiar attempt, must ever require peculiar mention. It is entitled "An Act for Suspending the Legislature of New York." One free and independent legislature hereby takes upon itself to suspend the powers of another, free and independent as itself, thus exhibiting a phenomenon unknown in nature, the creator and creature of his own power. Not only the principles of common sense, but the common feelings of human nature must be surrendered up, before His Majesty's subjects here can be persuaded to believe that they hold their political existence at the will of a British Parliament.

Shall these governments be dissolved, their property annihilated, and their people reduced to a state of nature, at the imperious breath of a body of men whom they never saw, in whom they never confided, and over whom they have no powers of punishment or removal, let their crimes against the American public be ever so great? Can any one reason be assigned why 160,000 electors in the island of Great Britain should give law to 4,000,000 in the states of America, every individual of whom is equal to every individual of them in virtue, in understanding, and in bodily strength? . . .

An act of Parliament had been passed imposing duties on teas to be paid in America, against which act the Americans had protested as inauthoritative. The East India Company, who till that time had never sent a pound of tea to America on their own account, stepped forth on that occasion as the asserters of parliamentary right, and sent hither many ship loads of that obnoxious commodity. The masters of their several vessels, however, on their arrival in America, wisely attended to admonition, and returned with their cargoes.

In the province of New England alone the remonstrances of the people were disregarded, and a compliance, after being many days waited for, was flatly refused. Whether in this the master of the vessel was governed by his obstinacy or his instructions, let those who know, say. There are extraordinary situations which require extraordinary interposition. An exasperated people, who feel that they possess power, are not easily restrained within limits strictly regular. A number of them assembled in the town of Boston, threw the tea into the ocean, and dispersed without doing any other act of violence.

If in this they did wrong, they were known, and were amenable to the laws of the land, against which it could not be objected that they had ever in any instance been obstructed or diverted from their regular course in favor of popular offenders. They should therefore not have been distrusted on this occasion. But that ill-fated colony had formerly been bold in their enmities against the House of Stuart, and were now devoted to ruin by that unseen hand which governs the momentous affairs of this great Empire.

On the partial representations of a few worthless ministerial dependents, whose constant office it has been to keep that government embroiled, and who by their treacheries hope to obtain the dignity of the British knighthood, without calling for the party accused, without asking a proof, without attempting a distinction between the guilty and the innocent, the whole of that ancient and wealthy town is in a moment reduced from opulence to beggary. Men who had spent their lives in extending the British commerce, who had invested in that place the wealth their honest endeavors had merited, found themselves and their families thrown at once on the world for subsistence by its charities. Not the hundredth part of the inhabitants of that town had been concerned in the act complained of; many of them were in Great Britain and in other parts beyond sea; yet all were involved in one indiscriminate ruin, by a new executive power unheard of till then, that of a British Parliament. A property of the value of many millions of money was sacrificed to revenge, not repay, the loss of a few thousands. . . .

By the act for the suppression of riots and tumults in the town of Boston, passed also in the last session of Parliament, a murder committed there is, if the governor pleases, to be tried in a Court of King's Bench in the island of Great Britain, by a jury of Middlesex. The witnesses too, on receipt of such a sum as the governor shall think it reasonable for them to expend, are to enter into recognizance to appear at the trial. This is, in other words, taxing them to the amount of their recognizance; and that amount may be whatever a governor pleases. For who does His Majesty think can be prevailed on to cross the Atlantic for the sole purpose of bearing evidence to a fact? His expenses are to be borne indeed as they shall be estimated by a governor; but who are to feed the wife and children whom he leaves behind, and who have had no other subsistence but his daily labor? . . .

And the wretched criminal, if he happen to have offended on the American side, stripped of his privilege of trial by peers, of his vicinage, removed from the place where alone full evidence could be obtained, without money, without counsel, without friends, without exculpatory proof, is tried before judges predetermined to condemn. The cowards who would suffer a countryman to be torn from the bowels of their society in order to be thus offered a sacrifice to parliamentary tyranny, would merit that everlasting infamy now fixed on the authors of the act! . . .

That these are the acts of power assumed by a body of men foreign to our constitutions, and unacknowledged by our laws; against which we do, on behalf of the inhabitants of British America, enter this our solemn and determined protest. And we do earnestly entreat His Majesty, as yet the only mediatory power between the several states of the British empire, to recommend to his Parliament of Great Britain the total revocation of these acts, which however nugatory they be, may yet prove the cause of further discontents and jealousies among us.

That we next proceed to consider the conduct of His Majesty, as holding the executive powers of the laws of these states, and mark out his deviations from the line of duty. By the constitution of Great Britain as well as of the several American states, His Majesty possesses the power of refusing to pass into a law any bill which has already passed the other two branches of legislature. . . . The addition of new states to the British empire has produced an addition of new, and sometimes opposite interests. It is now therefore the great office of His Majesty to resume the exercise of his negative power, and to prevent the passage of laws by any one legislature of the empire which might bear injuriously on the rights and interests of another.

Yet this will not excuse the wanton exercise of this power which we have seen His Majesty practise on the laws of the American legislatures. For the most trifling reasons, and sometimes for no conceivable reason at all, His Majesty has rejected laws of the most salutary tendency. The abolition of domestic slavery is the great object of desire in those colonies where it was unhappily introduced in their infant state. But previous to the enfranchisement of the slaves we have, it is necessary to exclude all further importations from Africa. Yet our repeated attempts to effect this by prohibitions, and by imposing duties which might amount to a prohibition, have been hitherto defeated by His Majesty's negative, thus preferring the immediate advantages of a few British corsairs to the lasting interests of the American states, and to the rights of human nature deeply wounded by this infamous practice. . . .

With equal inattention to the necessities of his people here has His Majesty permitted our laws to lie neglected in England for years, neither confirming them by his assent, nor annulling them by his negative. . . .

And to render this grievance still more oppressive, His Majesty by his instructions has laid his governors under such restrictions that they can pass no law of any moment unless it has such suspending clause; so that, however immediate may be the call for legislative interposition, the law cannot be executed till it has twice crossed the Atlantic, by which time the evil may have spent its whole force.

But in what terms reconcilable to majesty, and at the same time to truth, shall we speak of a late instruction to His Majesty's governor of the colony of Virginia, by which he is forbidden to assent to any law for the division of a county, unless the new county will consent to have no representative in assembly? That colony has as yet affixed no boundary to the westward. Their western counties therefore are of indefinite extent. Some of them are actually seated many hundred miles from their eastward limits. Is it possible then that His Majesty can have bestowed a single thought on the situation of those people who, in order to obtain justice for injuries however great or small, must, by the laws of that colony, attend their county court at such a distance, with all their witnesses, monthly, till their litigation be determined? Or does His Majesty seriously wish, and publish it to the world, that his subjects should give up the glorious right of representation, with all the benefits derived from that, and submit themselves the absolute slaves of his sovereign will? Or is it rather meant to confine the legislative body to their present numbers, that they may be the cheaper bargain

whenever they shall become worth a purchase? . . .

To declare as their duty required, the known rights of their country, to oppose the usurpations of every foreign judicature, to disregard the imperious mandates of a minister or governor, have been the avowed causes of dissolving houses of representatives in America. But if such powers be really vested in His Majesty, can he suppose they are there placed to awe the members from such purposes as these? When the representative body have lost the confidence of their constituents, when they have notoriously made sale of their most valuable rights, when they have assumed to themselves powers which the people never put into their hands, then indeed their continuing in office becomes dangerous to the state, and calls for an exercise of the power of dissolution. Such being the causes for which the representative body should and should not be dissolved, will it not appear strange to an unbiased observer that that of Great Britain was not dissolved, while those of the colonies have repeatedly incurred that sentence?

But Your Majesty or your governors have carried this power beyond every limit known or provided for by the laws. After dissolving one house of representatives, they have refused to call another, so that for a great length of time the legislature provided by the laws has been out of existence. From the nature of things, every society must at all times possess within itself the sovereign powers of legislation. The feelings of human nature revolt against the supposition of a state so situated as that it may not in any emergency provide against dangers which perhaps threaten immediate ruin. While those bodies are in existence to whom the people have delegated the powers of legislation, they alone possess and may exercise those powers. But when they are dissolved by the lopping off one or more of their branches, the power reverts to the people, who may exercise it to unlimited extent, either assembling together in person, sending deputies, or in any other way they may think proper. We forbear to trace consequences further; the dangers are conspicuous with which this practice is replete.

That we shall at this time also take notice of an error in the nature of our landholdings, which crept in at a very early period of our settlement. . . . Our ancestors who emigrated hither were farmers, not lawyers. The fictitious principle that all lands belong originally to the king, they were early persuaded to believe real, and accordingly took grants of their own lands from the Crown. And while the Crown continued to grant for small sums and on reasonable rents, there was no inducement to arrest the error and lay it open to the public view. But His Majesty has lately taken on him to advance the terms of purchase and of holding to the double of what they were, by which means the acquisition of lands being rendered difficult, the population of our country is likely to be checked. It is time therefore for us to lay this matter before His Majesty, and to declare that he has no right to grant lands of himself. From the nature and purpose of civil institutions, all the lands within the limits which any particular society has circumscribed around itself are assumed by that society, and subject to their allotment only. This may be done by themselves assembled collectively, or by their legislature to whom they may have delegated sovereign authority: and, if they are allotted in neither of these ways, each individual of the society may appropriate to himself such lands as he finds vacant, and occupancy will give him title.

That in order to enforce the arbitrary measures before complained of, His Majesty has from time to time sent among us large bodies of armed forces, not made up of the people here, nor raised by the authority of our laws. Did His Majesty possess such a right as this, it might swallow up all our

other rights whenever he should think proper. But His Majesty has no right to land a single armed man on our shores; and those whom he sends here are liable to our laws for the suppression and punishment of riots, and unlawful assemblies, or are hostile bodies invading us in defiance of the law. When in the course of the late war it became expedient that a body of Hanoverian troops should be brought over for the defense of Great Britain, His Majesty's grandfather, our late sovereign, did not pretend to introduce them under any authority he possessed. Such a measure would have given just alarm to his subjects in Great Britain, whose liberties would not be safe if armed men of another country, and of another spirit, might be brought into the Realm at any time without the consent of their legislature.

He therefore applied to Parliament who passed an act for that purpose, limiting the number to be brought in and the time they were to continue. In like manner is His Majesty restrained in every part of the empire. He possesses indeed the executive power of the laws in every state; but they are the laws of the particular state which he is to administer within that state, and not those of any one within the limits of another. Every state must judge for itself the number of armed men which they may safely trust among them, of whom they are to consist, and under what restrictions they shall be laid.

To render these proceedings still more criminal against our laws, instead of subjecting the military to the civil powers, His Majesty has expressly made the civil subordinate to the military. But can His Majesty thus put down all law under his feet? Can he erect a power superior to that which erected himself? He has done it indeed by force; but let him remember that force cannot give right.

That these are our grievances which we have thus laid before His Majesty with that freedom of language and sentiment which becomes a free people, claiming their rights as derived from the laws of nature, and not as the gift of their chief magistrate. Let those flatter, who fear: it is not an American art. . .

You are surrounded by British counselors, but remember that they are parties. You have no minister for American affairs, because you have none taken from among us, nor amenable to the laws on which they are to give you advice. It behooves you therefore to think and to act for yourself and your people. The great principles of right and wrong are legible to every reader: to pursue them requires not the aid of many counselors. The whole art of government consists in the art of being honest. . . .

Let no act be passed by any one legislature which may infringe on the rights and liberties of another. This is the important post in which fortune has placed you, holding the balance of a great, if a well-poised empire. This, sire, is the advice of your great American council, on the observance of which may perhaps depend your felicity and future fame, and the preservation of that harmony which alone can continue both in Great Britain and America and reciprocal advantages of their connection. It is neither our wish nor our interest to separate from her. We are willing on our part to sacrifice everything which reason can ask to the restoration of that tranquillity for which all must wish. . . . . The God who gave us life, gave us liberty at the same time: the hand of force may destroy, but cannot disjoin them.

This, sire, is our last, our determined resolution: and that you will be pleased to interpose with that efficacy which your earnest endeavors may insure to procure redress of these our great grievances, to quiet the minds of your subjects in British America against any apprehensions of future encroachment to establish fraternal love and harmony through the whole empire, and that these may continue to the latest ages of time, is the fervent prayer of all British America.

. . . its soul, its climate, its equality, liberty, laws, people, and manners. My God! how little do my countrymen know what precious blessings they are in possession of, and which no other people on earth enjoy!

THOMAS JEFFERSON, letter to Monroe, June 17, 1785

59.

Resistance and Reprisal

A special convention of delegates from the counties of Virginia met at Williamsburg on August 1, 1774. The convention agreed to an association for the cessation of trade with Great Britain similar to the agreement adopted two months later by the Continental Congress. In addition, delegates for this first congress were elected and given the instructions printed below.

Source: Niles: "Instructions to the Delegates to Congress, Williamsburg, 1774."

THE UNHAPPY DISPUTES between Great Britain and her American colonies, which began about the third year of the reign of His present Majesty, and since continually increasing, have proceeded to lengths so dangerous and alarming as to excite just apprehensions in the minds of His Majesty's faithful subjects of this colony, that they are in danger of being deprived of their natural, ancient, constitutional, and chartered rights, have compelled them to take the same into their most serious consideration; and being deprived of their usual and accustomed mode of making known their grievances [the Virginians] have appointed us their representatives to consider what is proper to be done in this dangerous crisis of American affairs. It being our opinion that the united wisdom of North America should be collected in a general congress of all the colonies, we have appointed the Honorable Peyton Randolph, Esquire, Richard Henry Lee, George Washington, Patrick Henry, Richard Bland, Benjamin Harrison, and Edmund Pendleton, Esquires, deputies to represent this colony in the said congress, to be held at Philadelphia on the first Monday in September next.

And that they be the better informed of our sentiments, touching the conduct we wish them to observe on this important occasion, we desire they will express, in the first place, our faith and true allegiance to His Majesty King George the Third, our lawful and rightful sovereign; and that we are determined, with our lives and fortunes, to support him in the *legal* exercise of all his just rights and prerogatives; and however misrepresented, we sincerly approve of a constitutional connection with Great Britain, and wish most ardently a return of that intercourse of affection and commercial connection that formerly united both countries, which can only be affected by a removal of those causes of discontent which have of late unhappily divided us.

It cannot admit of a doubt but that British subjects in America are entitled to the same rights and privileges as their fellow subjects possess in Britain; and, therefore, that the power assumed by the British Parliament to bind America by their statutes in all cases whatsoever is unconstitutional, and the source of these unhappy differences.

The end of government would be defeated by the British Parliament exercising a power over the lives, the property, and the liberty of the American subjects who are not, and from their local circumstances cannot be, there represented. Of this nature we consider the several acts of Parliament for raising a revenue in America, for extending the jurisdiction of the Courts of Admiralty, for seizing American subjects and transporting them to Britain to be tried for crimes committed in America, and the several late oppressive acts respecting the town of Boston and province of the Massachusetts Bay.

The original constitution of the American colonies possessing their assemblies with the sole right of directing their internal polity, it is absolutely destructive of the end of their institution that their legislatures should be suspended or prevented, by hasty dissolutions, from exercising their legislative power.

Wanting the protection of Britain, we have long acquiesced in their acts of navigation restrictive of our commerce, which we consider as an ample recompense for such protection; but as those acts derive their efficacy from that foundation alone, we have reason to expect they will be restrained so as to produce the reasonable purposes of Britain without being injurious to us.

To obtain a redress of those grievances, without which the people of America can neither be safe, free, nor happy, they are willing to undergo the great inconvenience that will be derived to them from stopping all imports whatsoever from Great Britain after the 1st day of November next, and also to cease exporting any commodity whatsoever to the same place after August 10, 1775. The earnest desire we have, to make as quick and full payment as possible of our debts to Great Britain, and to avoid

the heavy injury that would arise to this country from an earlier adoption of the nonexportation plan, after the people have already applied so much of their labor to the perfecting of the present crop, by which means they have been prevented from pursuing other methods of clothing and supporting their families, have rendered it necessary to restrain you in this article of nonexportation; but it is our desire that you cordially cooperate with our sister colonies, in General Congress, in such other just and proper methods as they, or the majority, shall deem necessary for the accomplishment of these valuable ends.

The proclamation issued by General Gage, in the government of the province of the Massachusetts Bay, declaring it treason for the inhabitants of that province to assemble themselves to consider of their grievances, and form associations for their common conduct on the occasion, and requiring the civil magistrates and officers to apprehend all such persons to be tried for their supposed offenses, is the most alarming process that ever appeared in a British government. . . .

That, if the said General Gage conceives he is empowered to act in this manner, as the commander in chief of His Majesty's forces in America, this odious and illegal proclamation must be considered as a plain and full declaration that this despotic viceroy will be bound by no law nor regard the constitutional rights of His Majesty's subjects whenever they interfere with the plan he had formed for oppressing the good people of the Massachusetts Bay; and, therefore, that the executing, or attempting to execute such proclamation, will justify resistance and reprisal.

There is a time to pray and a time to fight. This is the time to fight.
JOHN PETER GABRIEL MUHLENBERG, sermon, 1775

60.

JOSEPH GALLOWAY: A Plan for the Union of Great Britain and the Colonies

To solve the difficulties with Great Britain, Joseph Galloway of Pennsylvania proposed a Plan of Union in the Continental Congress that had convened in Philadelphia in September 1774. Though favorably received by many delegates, the plan was defeated by a six to five vote of colonies. It was the sudden arrival of news concerning the resolutions passed in Suffolk County (Boston), Massachusetts, that turned sentiment away from this effort at compromise. Six years later Galloway reminisced on the fate of this plan, which is reprinted here. "While the two parties in Congress [Loyalist and Republican] remained thus during three weeks on an equal balance," he wrote in 1780, "the republicans were calling to their assistance the aid of their factions without. Continual expresses were employed between Philadelphia and Boston. These were under the management of Samuel Adams — a man, who though by no means remarkable for brilliant abilities, yet is equal to most men in popular intrigue and the management of a faction. . . . It was this man, who by his superior application managed at once the faction in Congress at Philadelphia and the factions in New England. Whatever these patriots in Congress wished to have done by their colleagues without, to induce General Gage, then at the head of his Majesty's army at Boston, to give them a pretext for violent opposition or to promote their measures in Congress, Mr. Adams advised and directed to be done; and when done, it was dispatched by express to Congress. By one of these expresses came the inflammatory resolves of the county of Suffolk, which contained a complete declaration of war against Great Britain."

Source: *Archives*, I, pp. 905-906.

Resolved, that this Congress will apply to His Majesty for a redress of grievances under which his faithful subjects in America labor; and assure him that the colonies hold in abhorrence the idea of being considered independent communities on the British government, and most ardently desire the establishment of a political union, not only among themselves but with the mother state, upon those principles of safety and freedom which are essential in the constitution of all free governments, and particular-

ly that of the British legislature. And as the colonies from their local circumstances cannot be represented in the Parliament of Great Britain, they will humbly propose to His Majesty and his two houses of Parliament the following plan, under which the strength of the whole empire may be drawn together on any emergency, the interest of both countries advanced, and the rights and liberties of America secured: *A Plan for a Proposed Union between Great Britain and the Colonies of New Hampshire, the Massa-*

chusetts Bay, Rhode Island, Connecticut, New York, New Jersey, Pennsylvania, Maryland, the Three Lower Counties on the Delaware, Virginia, North Carolina, South Carolina, and Georgia.

That a British and American legislature, for regulating the administration of the general affairs of America, be proposed and established in America, including all the said colonies; within and under which government each colony shall retain its present constitution and powers of regulating and governing its own internal police, in all cases whatever.

That the said government be administered by a president general, to be appointed by the King, and a Grand Council, to be chosen by the representatives of the people of the several colonies, in their respective assemblies, once in every three years.

That the several assemblies shall choose members for the Grand Council in the following proportions, viz.:

New Hampshire ——, Massachusetts Bay ——, Rhode Island ——, Connecticut ——, New York ——, New Jersey   , Pennsylvania ——, Delaware Counties ——, Maryland ——, Virginia ——, North Carolina ——, South Carolina ——, Georgia ——, who shall meet at the city of ——— for the first time, being called by the president general as soon as conveniently may be after his appointment.

That there shall be a new election of members for the Grand Council every three years; and on the death, removal, or resignation of any member, his place shall be supplied by a new choice at the next sitting of assembly of the colony he represented.

That the Grand Council shall meet once in every year if they shall think it necessary, and oftener if occasions shall require, at such time and place as they shall adjourn to at the last preceding meeting, or as they shall be called to meet at by the president general on any emergency.

That the Grand Council shall have power to choose their speaker, and shall hold and exercise all the like rights, liberties, and privileges as are held and exercised by and in the House of Commons of Great Britain.

That the president general shall hold his office during the pleasure of the King and his assent shall be requisite to all acts of the Grand Council, and it shall be his office and duty to cause them to be carried into execution.

That the president general, by and with the advice and consent of the Grand Council, hold and exercise all the legislative rights, powers, and authorities necessary for regulating and administering all the general police and affairs of the colonies in which Great Britain and the colonies, or any of them, the colonies in general, or more than one colony, are in any manner concerned, as well civil and criminal as commercial.

That the said president general and the Grand Council be an inferior and distinct branch of the British legislature, united and incorporated with it for the aforesaid general purposes; and that any of the said general regulations may originate and be formed and digested, either in the Parliament of Great Britain or in the said Grand Council, and being prepared, transmitted to the other for their approbation or dissent; and that the assent of both shall be requisite to the validity of all such general acts and statutes.

That in time of war, all bills for granting aid to the Crown, prepared by the Grand Council and approved by the president general, shall be valid and passed into a law, without the assent of the British Parliament.

61.

Declaration and Resolves of the Continental Congress

After the rejection of the Galloway Plan of Union the Continental Congress, on October 14, 1774, adopted the following declaration of colonial rights. Major John Sullivan, delegate from New Hampshire, drafted the resolutions. The Congress voted to reconvene the following year unless the grievances set forth in the declaration were settled.

Source: *Journals,* I: "Friday, October 14, 1774."

Whereas, since the close of the last war, the British Parliament, claiming a power of right to bind the people of America by statutes in all cases whatsoever, has in some acts expressly imposed taxes on them, and in others, under various pretenses but in fact for the purpose of raising a revenue, has imposed rates and duties payable in these colonies; established a Board of Commissioners with unconstitutional powers; and extended the jurisdiction of Courts of Admiralty, not only for collecting the said duties but for the trial of causes merely arising within the body of a county.

And whereas, in consequence of other statutes, judges, who before held only estates at will in their offices, have been made dependent on the Crown alone for their salaries, and standing armies kept in times of peace. *And whereas* it has lately been resolved in Parliament that, by force of a statute made in the thirty-fifth year of the reign of King Henry the Eighth, colonists may be transported to England and tried there upon accusations for treasons, and misprisions, or concealments of treasons committed in the colonies; and by a late statute, such trials have been directed in cases therein mentioned.

And whereas, in the last session of Parliament, three statutes were made; one, entitled "An act to discontinue, in such manner and for such time as are therein mentioned, the landing and discharging, lading, or shipping of goods, wares, and merchandise at the town, and within the harbor of Boston, in the province of Massachusetts Bay, in North America"; another, entitled "An act for the better regulating the government of the province of Massachusetts Bay in New England"; and another, entitled "An act for the impartial administration of justice in the cases of persons questioned for any act done by them in the execution of the law, or for the suppression of riots and tumults in the province of the Massachusetts Bay in New England"; and another statute was then made, "for making more effectual provision for the government of the province of Quebec, etc."; all which statutes are impolitic, unjust, and cruel, as well as unconstitutional, and most dangerous and destructive of American rights.

And whereas, assemblies have been frequently dissolved, contrary to the rights of the people, when they attempted to deliberate on grievances; and their dutiful, humble, loyal, and reasonable petitions to the

Crown for redress have been repeatedly treated with contempt by His Majesty's ministers of state:

The good people of the several colonies of New Hampshire; Massachusetts Bay; Rhode Island and Providence Plantations; Connecticut; New York; New Jersey; Pennsylvania; Newcastle, Kent, and Sussex on Delaware; Maryland; Virginia; North Carolina; and South Carolina, justly alarmed at these arbitrary proceedings of Parliament and administration, have severally elected, constituted, and appointed deputies to meet and sit in General Congress in the city of Philadelphia in order to obtain such establishment as that their religion, laws, and liberties may not be subverted:

Whereupon the deputies so appointed being now assembled, in a full and free representation of these colonies, taking into their most serious consideration the best means of attaining the ends aforesaid, do, in the first place, as Englishmen, their ancestors in like cases have usually done, for affecting and vindicating their rights and liberties, declare,

That the inhabitants of the English colonies in North America, by the immutable laws of nature, the principles of the English constitution, and the several charters or compacts, have the following rights:

Resolved:

1. That they are entitled to life, liberty, and property, and they have never ceded to any sovereign power whatever a right to dispose of either without their consent.

2. That our ancestors, who first settled these colonies, were at the time of their emigration from the mother country entitled to all the rights, liberties, and immunities of free and natural-born subjects, within the Realm of England.

3. That by such emigration they by no means forfeited, surrendered, or lost any of those rights, but that they were, and their descendants now are, entitled to the exercise and enjoyment of all such of them as their local and other circumstances enable them to exercise and enjoy.

4. That the foundation of English liberty, and of all free government, is a right in the people to participate in their legislative council; and as the English colonists are not represented, and from their local and other circumstances cannot properly be represented in the British Parliament, they are entitled to a free and exclusive power of legislation in their several provincial legislatures, where their right of representation can alone be preserved, in all cases of taxation and internal polity, subject only to the negative of their sovereign, in such manner as has been heretofore used and accustomed. But, from the necessity of the case and a regard to the mutual interest of both countries, we cheerfully consent to the operation of such acts of the British Parliament as are bona fide, restrained to the regulation of our external commerce, for the purpose of securing the commercial advantages of the whole empire to the mother country, and the commercial benefits of its respective members, excluding every idea of taxation, internal or external, for raising a revenue on the subjects in America without their consent.

5. That the respective colonies are entitled to the common law of England, and more especially to the great and inestimable privilege of being tried by their peers of the vicinage according to the course of that law.

6. That they are entitled to the benefit of such of the English statutes as existed at the time of their colonization; and which they have, by experience, respectively found to be applicable to their several local and other circumstances.

7. That these, His Majesty's colonies, are likewise entitled to all the immunities and privileges granted and confirmed to them by royal charters, or secured by their several codes of provincial laws.

8. That they have a right peaceably to assemble, consider of their grievances, and

Peyton Randolph (1721-1775), president of the 1st
Continental Congress; portrait by Wollaston

petition the King; and that all prosecutions,
prohibitory proclamations, and commitments for the same are illegal.

9. That the keeping of a standing army
in these colonies, in times of peace, without
the consent of the legislature of that colony
in which such army is kept is against law.

10. It is indispensably necessary to good
government, and rendered essential by the
English constitution, that the constituent
branches of the legislature be independent
of each other; that, therefore, the exercise of
legislative power in several colonies, by a
council appointed during pleasure by the
Crown, is unconstitutional, dangerous, and
destructive to the freedom of American legislation.

All and each of which the aforesaid deputies, in behalf of themselves and their constituents, do claim, demand, and insist on as
their indubitable rights and liberties; which
cannot be legally taken from them, altered
or abridged by any power whatever, without their own consent, by their representatives in their several provincial legislatures.

In the course of our inquiry, we find
many infringements and violations of the
foregoing rights, which, from an ardent desire that harmony and mutual intercourse of
affection and interest may be restored, we
pass over for the present, and proceed to
state such acts and measures as have been
adopted since the last war, which demonstrate a system formed to enslave America.

Resolved, that the following acts of Parliament are infringements and violations of the
rights of the colonists; and that the repeal
of them is essentially necessary in order to
restore harmony between Great Britain and
the American colonies, viz.:

The several acts . . . which impose duties
for the purpose of raising a revenue in
America, extend the powers of the Admiralty Courts beyond their ancient limits, deprive the American subject of trial by jury,
authorize the judge's certificate to indemnify
the prosecutor from damages that he might
otherwise be liable to, requiring oppressive
security from a claimant of ships and goods
seized, before he shall be allowed to defend
his property, and are subversive of American rights.

Also [the act] entitled "An act for the
better securing His Majesty's dockyards,
magazines, ships, ammunition, and stores,"
which declares a new offense in America,
and deprives the American subject of a constitutional trial by jury of the vicinage, by
authorizing the trial of any person, charged
with the committing any offense described
in the said act, out of the Realm, to be indicted and tried for the same in any shire or
county within the Realm.

Also the three acts passed in the last session of Parliament for stopping the port
and blocking up the harbor of Boston, for
altering the charter and government of
Massachusetts Bay, and that which is entitled "An act for the better administration of
justice, etc."

Also the act passed the same session for establishing the Roman Catholic religion in the province of Quebec, abolishing the equitable system of English laws, and erecting a tyranny there to the great danger, from so total a dissimilarity of religion, law, and government of the neighboring British colonies, by the assistance of whose blood and treasure the said country was conquered from France.

Also the act passed the same session for the better providing suitable quarters for officers and soldiers in His Majesty's service in North America.

Also, that the keeping a standing army in several of these colonies, in time of peace, without the consent of the legislature of that colony in which the army is kept, is against law.

To these grievous acts and measures Americans cannot submit, but in hopes that their fellow subjects in Great Britain will, on a revision of them, restore us to that state in which both countries found happiness and prosperity, we have for the present only resolved to pursue the following peaceable measures:

1. To enter into a nonimportation, nonconsumption, and nonexportation agreement or association.

2. To prepare an address to the people of Great Britain and a memorial to the inhabitants of British America.

3. To prepare a loyal address to His Majesty, agreeable to resolutions already entered into.

62.

The Association of the Continental Congress

Most members of the First Continental Congress hoped that a commercial boycott would induce the British government to accede to their demands. On October 20, 1774, the Congress voted for nonimportation, nonconsumption, and nonexportation, virtually cutting off trade with Britain. It was hoped that this economic maneuver would bring about repeal of the Intolerable Acts. The nonintercourse agreement differed from previous colonial boycotts inasmuch as it derived from the people, working through committees, rather than from the merchants. The Continental Association was perhaps more successful politically than economically, since it helped to weld the colonies together into an American union.

Source: *Journals*, I: "Thursday, October 20, 1774."

WE, HIS MAJESTY'S MOST LOYAL SUBJECTS, the delegates of the several colonies of New Hampshire, Massachusetts Bay, Rhode Island, Connecticut, New York, New Jersey, Pennsylvania, the three lower counties of Newcastle, Kent, and Sussex on Delaware, Maryland, Virginia, North Carolina, and South Carolina, deputed to represent them in a Continental Congress, held in the city of Philadelphia, on the 5th day of September, 1774, avowing our allegiance to His Majesty, our affection and regard for our fellow subjects in Great Britain and elsewhere, affected with the deepest anxiety and most alarming apprehensions at those grievances and distresses, with which His Majesty's American subjects are oppressed; and having taken under our most serious deliberation the state of the whole continent, find that the present unhappy situation of our affairs is occasioned by a ruinous system of colony administration, adopted by the British Ministry about the year 1763, evidently calculated for enslaving these colonies and with them, the British empire.

In prosecution of which system, various acts of Parliament have been passed for raising a revenue in America; for depriving the American subjects, in many instances, of the constitutional trial by jury; exposing their lives to danger by directing a new and illegal trial beyond the seas for crimes alleged to have been committed in America. And in prosecution of the same system, several late, cruel, and oppressive acts have been passed respecting the town of Boston and the Massachusetts Bay, and also an act for extending the province of Quebec, so as to border on the western frontiers of these colonies, establishing an arbitrary government therein, and discouraging the settlement of British subjects in that wide-extended country; thus, by the influence of civil principles and ancient prejudices to dispose the inhabitants to act with hostility against the free Protestant colonies, whenever a wicked Ministry shall choose to direct them.

To obtain redress of these grievances which threaten destruction to the lives, liberty, and property of His Majesty's subjects in North America, we are of opinion that a nonimportation, nonconsumption, and nonexportation agreement, faithfully adhered to, will prove the most speedy, effectual, and peaceable measure. And, therefore, we do, for ourselves and the inhabitants of the several colonies whom we represent, firmly agree and associate, under the sacred ties of virtue, honor, and love of our country, as follows:

1. That from and after the 1st day of December next, we will not import into British America from Great Britain or Ireland any goods, wares, or merchandise whatsoever, or from any other place, any such goods, wares, or merchandise, as shall have been exported from Great Britain or Ireland. Nor will we, after that day, import any East India tea from any part of the world; nor any molasses, syrups, paneles, coffee, or pimento from the British plantations or from Dominica; nor wines from Madeira or the Western Islands; nor foreign indigo.

2. We will neither import nor purchase any slave imported after the 1st day of December next; after which time, we will wholly discontinue the slave trade and will neither be concerned in it ourselves, nor will we hire our vessels, nor sell our commodities or manufactures to those who are concerned in it.

3. As a nonconsumption agreement, strictly adhered to, will be an effectual security for the observation of the nonimportation, we, as above, solemnly agree and associate that from this day we will not purchase or use any tea imported on account of the East India Company, or any on which a duty has been or shall be paid. And from and after the 1st day of March next, we will not purchase or use any East India tea whatever; nor will we, nor shall any person for or under us, purchase or use any of those goods, wares, or merchandise we have agreed not to import, which we shall know or have cause to suspect, were imported after the 1st day of December, except such as come under the rules and directions of the 10th Article hereafter mentioned.

4. The earnest desire we have not to injure our fellow subjects in Great Britain, Ireland, or the West Indies induces us to suspend a nonexportation [agreement] until the 10th day of September, 1775; at which time, if the said acts and parts of acts of the British Parliament hereinafter mentioned

are not repealed, we will not directly or indirectly export any merchandise or commodity whatsoever to Great Britain, Ireland, or the West Indies, except rice to Europe.

5. Such as are merchants and use the British and Irish trade will give orders, as soon as possible, to their factors, agents, and correspondents in Great Britain and Ireland not to ship any goods to them, on any pretense whatsoever, as they cannot be received in America; and if any merchant residing in Great Britain or Ireland shall directly or indirectly ship any goods, wares, or merchandise for America in order to break the said nonimportation agreement or in any manner contravene the same, on such unworthy conduct being well attested, it ought to be made public; and, on the same being so done, we will not, from thenceforth, have any commercial connection with such merchant.

6. That such as are owners of vessels will give positive orders to their captains or masters not to receive on board their vessels any goods prohibited by the said nonimportation agreement, on pain of immediate dismission from their service.

7. We will use our utmost endeavors to improve the breed of sheep and increase their number to the greatest extent; and to that end, we will kill them as seldom as may be, especially those of the most profitable kind; nor will we export any to the West Indies or elsewhere; and those of us who are or may become overstocked with, or can conveniently spare any, sheep will dispose of them to our neighbors, especially to the poorer sort, on moderate terms.

8. We will, in our several stations, encourage frugality, economy, and industry, and promote agriculture, arts, and the manufactures of this country, especially that of wool; and will discountenance and discourage every species of extravagance and dissipation, especially all horse racing, and all kinds of gaming, cockfighting, exhibitions of shows, plays, and other expensive diversions and entertainments. And on the death of any relation or friend, none of us, or any of our families, will go into any further mourning dress than a black crape or ribbon on the arm or hat for gentlemen, and a black ribbon and necklace for ladies, and we will discontinue the giving of gloves and scarves at funerals.

9. Such as are vendors of goods or merchandise will not take advantage of the scarcity of goods that may be occasioned by this association, but will sell the same at the rates we have been respectively accustomed to do for twelve months last past. And if any vendor of goods or merchandise shall sell such goods on higher terms, or shall, in any manner or by any device whatsoever, violate or depart from this agreement, no person ought nor will any of us deal with any such person, or his or her factor or agent, at any time thereafter, for any commodity whatever.

10. In case any merchant, trader, or other person shall import any goods or merchandise after the 1st day of December and before the 1st day of February next, the same ought forthwith, at the election of the owner, to be either reshipped or delivered up to the committee of the country or town wherein they shall be imported, to be stored at the risk of the importer until the nonimportation agreement shall cease or be sold under the direction of the committee aforesaid. And in the last-mentioned case, the owner or owners of such goods shall be reimbursed out of the sales the first cost and charges, the profit, if any, to be applied toward relieving and employing such poor inhabitants of the town of Boston as are immediate sufferers by the Boston port bill; and a particular account of all goods so returned, stored, or sold to be inserted in the public papers. And if any goods or merchandises shall be imported after the said 1st day of February, the same ought forthwith to be sent back again, without break-

ing any of the packages thereof.

11. That a committee be chosen in every county, city, and town by those who are qualified to vote for representatives in the legislature, whose business it shall be attentively to observe the conduct of all persons touching this association. And when it shall be made to appear, to the satisfaction of a majority of any such committee, that any person within the limits of their appointment has violated this association, that such majority do forthwith cause the truth of the case to be published in the gazette; to the end that all such foes to the rights of British America may be publicly known and universally contemned as the enemies of American liberty; and thenceforth we respectively will break off all dealings with him or her.

12. That the Committee of Correspondence, in the respective colonies, do frequently inspect the entries of their customhouses, and inform each other, from time to time, of the true state thereof, and of every other material circumstance that may occur relative to this association.

13. That all manufactures of this country be sold at reasonable prices, so that no undue advantage be taken of a future scarcity of goods.

14. And we do further agree and resolve that we will have no trade, commerce, dealings, or intercourse whatsoever with any colony or province in North America which shall not accede to, or which shall hereafter violate, this association, but will hold them as unworthy of the rights of freemen and as inimical to the liberties of their country.

And we do solemnly bind ourselves and our constituents, under the ties aforesaid, to adhere to this association until such parts of the several acts of Parliament passed since the close of the last war, as impose or continue duties on tea, wine, molasses, syrups, paneles, coffee, sugar, pimento, indigo, foreign paper, glass, and painters' colors imported into America, and extend the powers of the Admiralty Courts beyond their ancient limits, deprive the American subject of trial by jury, authorize the judge's certificate to indemnify the prosecutor from damages, that he might otherwise be liable to from a trial by his peers, require oppressive security from a claimant of ships or goods seized, before he shall be allowed to defend his property, are repealed.

And until that part of the act . . . entitled "An act for the better securing His Majesty's dockyards, magazines, ships, ammunition, and stores," by which any persons charged with committing any of the offenses therein described, in America, may be tried in any shire or county within the Realm, is repealed; and until the four acts, passed the last session of Parliament, viz.: that for stopping the port and blocking up the harbor of Boston; that for altering the charter and government of the Massachusetts Bay; that which is entitled "An act for the better administration of justice, etc."; and that "for extending the limits of Quebec, etc.," are repealed. And we recommend it to the provincial conventions, and to the committees in the respective colonies, to establish such further regulations as they may think proper, for carrying into execution this association.

The foregoing association being determined upon by the Congress, was ordered to be subscribed by the several members thereof; and thereupon, we have hereunto set our respective names accordingly.

We must indeed all hang together, or most assuredly we will all hang separately.

BENJAMIN FRANKLIN, at signing of Declaration of Independence

63.

JOHN JAY: Address to the People of Great Britain

John Jay, of New York, favored effective central government in the interests of the merchants and property owners. He supported the colonial cause, although he deplored violence in the quarrel between Great Britain and America, hoping, until the eve of independence, for a reconciliation with the mother country. As a member of the First Continental Congress, Jay was appointed in October 1774 to draft the following address, stating the rights of the colonists in a spirit of moderation and conciliation.

Source: Johnston, I, pp. 17-31.

WHEN A NATION, led to greatness by the hand of liberty, and possessed of all the glory that heroism, munificence, and humanity can bestow, descends to the ungrateful task of forging chains for her friends and children, and instead of giving support to freedom, turns advocate for slavery and oppression, there is reason to suspect she has either ceased to be virtuous, or been extremely negligent in the appointment of her rulers.

In almost every age, in repeated conflicts, in long and bloody wars, as well civil as foreign, against many and powerful nations, against the open assaults of enemies and the more dangerous treachery of friends, have the inhabitants of your island, your great and glorious ancestors, maintained their independence, and transmitted the rights of men and the blessings of liberty to you, their posterity.

Be not surprised, therefore, that we, who are descended from the same common ancestors, that we, whose forefathers participated in all the rights, the liberties, and the constitution you so justly boast of, and who have carefully conveyed the same fair inheritance to us, guaranteed by the plighted faith of government and the most solemn compacts with British sovereigns, should refuse to surrender them to men who found their claims on no principles of reason, and who prosecute them with a design that, by having *our* lives and property in their power, they may with the greater facility enslave *you.*

The cause of America is now the object of universal attention; it has at length become very serious. This unhappy country has not only been oppressed but abused and misrepresented; and the duty we owe to ourselves and posterity, to your interest, and the general welfare of the British empire, leads us to address you on this very important subject.

Know then, that we consider ourselves, and do insist that we are and ought to be, as free as our fellow subjects in Britain, and that no power on earth has a right to take our property from us without our consent.

That we claim all the benefits secured to the subject by the English constitution, and particularly that inestimable one of trial by jury.

That we hold it essential to English liberty that no man be condemned unheard, or punished for supposed offenses without having an opportunity of making his defense.

That we think the legislature of Great Britain is not authorized by the constitution to establish a religion fraught with sanguinary and impious tenets, or to erect an arbitrary form of government in any quarter of the globe. These rights we, as well as you, deem sacred. And yet, sacred as they are, they have, with many others, been repeatedly and flagrantly violated.

Are not the proprietors of the soil of Great Britain lords of their own property? Can it be taken from them without their consent? Will they yield it to the arbitrary disposal of any man or number of men whatever? You know they will not.

Why then are the proprietors of the soil of America less lords of their property than you are of yours? Or why should they submit it to the disposal of your Parliament, or any other parliament or council in the world not of their election? Can the intervention of the sea that divides us cause disparity in rights? Or can any reason be given why English subjects who live 3,000 miles from the royal palace should enjoy less liberty than those who are 300 miles distant from it?

Reason looks with indignation on such distinctions, and freemen can never perceive their propriety. And yet, however chimerical and unjust such discriminations are, the Parliament assert that they have a right to bind us in all cases without exception, whether we consent or not; that they may take and use our property when and in what manner they please; that we are pensioners on their bounty for all that we possess, and can hold it no longer than they vouchsafe to permit. Such declarations we consider as heresies in English politics, and which can no more operate to deprive us of our property, than the interdicts of the pope can divest kings of scepters which the laws of the land and the voice of the people have placed in their hands.

At the conclusion of the late war — a war rendered glorious by the abilities and integrity of a minister to whose efforts the British empire owes its safety and its fame — at the conclusion of this war, which was succeeded by an inglorious peace, formed under the auspices of a minister of principles and of a family unfriendly to the Protestant cause and inimical to liberty; we say, at this period, and under the influence of that man, a plan for enslaving your fellow subjects in America was concerted, and has ever since been pertinaciously carrying into execution.

Prior to this era, you were content with drawing from us the wealth produced by our commerce. You restrained our trade in every way that could conduce to your emolument. You exercised unbounded sovereignty over the sea. You named the ports and nations to which alone our merchandise should be carried, and with whom alone we should trade; and though some of these restrictions were grievous, we nevertheless did not complain. We looked up to you as to our parent state, to which we were bound by the strongest ties; and were happy in being instrumental to your prosperity and grandeur.

We call upon you yourselves to witness our loyalty and attachment to the common interest of the whole empire. Did we not, in the last war, add all the strength of this vast continent to the force which repelled our common enemy? Did we not leave our native shores, and meet disease and death, to promote the success of British arms in foreign climates? Did you not thank us for our zeal, and even reimburse us large sums of money which, you confessed, we had advanced beyond our proportion; and far beyond our abilities? You did.

To what causes, then, are we to attribute

the sudden changes of treatment, and that system of slavery which was prepared for us at the restoration of peace?

Before we had recovered from the distresses which ever attend war, an attempt was made to drain this country of all its money by the oppressive Stamp Act. Paint, glass, and other commodities which you would not permit us to purchase of other nations were taxed; nay, although no wine is made in any country subject to the British state, you prohibited our procuring it of foreigners without paying a tax imposed by your Parliament on all we imported. These and many other impositions were laid upon us most unjustly and unconstitutionally for the express purpose of raising a revenue. In order to silence complaint, it was indeed provided that this revenue should be expended in America for its protection and defense. These exactions, however, can receive no justification from a pretended necessity of protecting and defending us. They are lavishly squandered on court favorites and ministerial dependents, generally avowed enemies to America, and employing themselves by partial representations to traduce and embroil the colonies.

For the necessary support of government here, we ever were and ever shall be ready to provide. And whenever the exigencies of the state may require it, we shall, as we have heretofore done, cheerfully contribute our full proportion of men and money. To enforce this unconstitutional and unjust scheme of taxation, every fence that the wisdom of our British ancestors had carefully erected against arbitrary power has been violently thrown down in America, and the inestimable right of trial by jury taken away in cases that touch life and property. It was ordained that whenever offenses should be committed in the colonies against particular acts imposing various duties and restrictions upon trade, the prosecutor might bring his action for the penalties in the Courts of Ad-

miralty; by which means the subject lost the advantage of being tried by an honest, uninfluenced jury of the vicinage, and was subjected to the sad necessity of being judged by a single man, a creature of the Crown, and according to the course of a law which exempts the prosecutor from the trouble of proving his accusation, and obliges the defendant either to evince his innocence or to suffer. To give this new judicatory the greater importance, and as if with design to protect false accusers, it is further provided that the judge's certificate of there having been probable causes of seizure and prosecution shall protect the prosecutor from actions at common law for recovery of damages.

By the course of our law, offenses committed in such of the British dominions in which courts are established and justice duly and regularly administered shall be there tried by a jury of the vicinage. There the offenders and witnesses are known, and the degree of credibility to be given to their testimony can be ascertained.

In all these colonies, justice is regularly and impartially administered; and yet, by the construction of some, and the direction of other acts of Parliament, offenders are to be taken by force, together with all such persons as may be pointed out as witnesses, and carried to England, there to be tried in a distant land, by a jury of strangers, and subject to all the disadvantages that result from want of friends, want of witnesses, and want of money.

When the design of raising a revenue from the duties imposed on the importation of tea into America had in a great measure been rendered abortive by our ceasing to import that commodity, a scheme was concerted by the Ministry with the East India Company, and an act passed enabling and encouraging them to transport and vend it in the colonies. Aware of the danger of giving success to this insidious maneuver, and of permitting a precedent of taxation thus to be established among us, various methods were adopted to elude the stroke. The people of Boston, then ruled by a governor whom, as well as his predecessor Sir Francis Bernard, all America considers as her enemy, were exceedingly embarrassed. The ships which had arrived with the tea were by his management prevented from returning. The duties would have been paid, the cargoes landed and exposed to sale; a governor's influence would have procured and protected many purchasers.

While the town was suspended by deliberations on this important subject, the tea was destroyed. Even supposing a trespass was thereby committed, and the proprietors of the tea entitled to damages, the courts of law were open, and judges appointed by the Crown presided in them. The East India Company, however, did not think proper to commence any suits, nor did they even demand satisfaction either from individuals or from the community in general. The Ministry, it seems, officiously made the case their own, and the great council of the nation descended to intermeddle with a dispute about private property.

Diverse papers, letters, and other unauthenticated *ex parte* evidence were laid before them; neither the persons who destroyed the tea nor the people of Boston were called upon to answer the complaint. The Ministry, incensed by being disappointed in a favorite scheme, were determined to recur from the little arts of finesse to open force and unmanly violence. The port of Boston was blocked up by a fleet, and an army placed in the town. Their trade was to be suspended, and thousands reduced to the necessity of gaining subsistence from charity till they should submit to pass under the yoke, and consent to become slaves by confessing the omnipotence of Parliament and acquiescing in whatever disposition they might think proper to make of their lives and property.

Let justice and humanity cease to be the boast of your nation! Consult your history, examine your records of former transactions, nay, turn to the annals of the many arbitrary states and kingdoms that surround you, and show us a single instance of men being condemned to suffer for imputed crimes, unheard, unquestioned, and without even the specious formality of a trial; and that, too, by laws made expressly for the purpose, and which had no existence at the time of the fact committed. If it be difficult to reconcile these proceedings to the genius and temper of your laws and constitution, the task will become more arduous when we call upon our ministerial enemies to justify not only condemning men untried and by hearsay but involving the innocent in one common punishment with the guilty, and for the act of 30 or 40, to bring poverty, distress, and calamity on 30,000 souls, and those not your enemies but your friends, brethren, and fellow subjects.

It would be some consolation to us if the catalogue of American oppressions ended here. It gives us pain to be reduced to the necessity of reminding you that under the confidence reposed in the faith of government, pledged in a royal charter from a British sovereign, the forefathers of the present inhabitants of the Massachusetts Bay left their former habitations and established that great, flourishing, and loyal colony. Without incurring or being charged with a forfeiture of their rights, without being heard, without being tried, without law, and without justice, by an act of Parliament their charter is destroyed, their liberties violated, their constitution and form of government changed. And all this upon no better pretense than because in one of their towns a trespass was committed on some merchandise said to belong to one of the companies, and because the Ministry were of opinion that such high political regulations were necessary to compel due subordination and obedience to their mandates.

Nor are these the only capital grievances under which we labor. We might tell of dissolute, weak, and wicked governors having been set over us; of legislatures being suspended for asserting the rights of British subjects; of needy and ignorant dependents on great men advanced to the seats of justice and to other places of trust and importance; of hard restrictions on commerce, and a great variety of lesser evils, the recollection of which is almost lost under the weight and pressure of greater and more poignant calamities.

Now mark the progression of the ministerial plan for enslaving us. Well aware that such hardy attempts to take our property from us, to deprive us of the valuable right of trial by jury, to seize our persons and carry us for trial to Great Britain, to blockade our ports, to destroy our charters, and change our forms of government would occasion, and had already occasioned, great discontent in the colonies, which might produce opposition to these measures; an act was passed to protect, indemnify, and screen from punishment such as might be guilty even of murder, in endeavoring to carry their oppressive edicts into execution; and by another act the Dominion of Canada is to be so extended, modeled, and governed, as that by being disunited from us, detached from our interests by civil as well as religious prejudices, that by their numbers daily swelling with Catholic emigrants from Europe, and by their devotion to an administration so friendly to their religion, they might become formidable to us, and, on occasion, be fit instruments in the hands of power to reduce the ancient, free, Protestant colonies to the same state of slavery with themselves.

This was evidently the object of the act; and in this view, being extremely dangerous to our liberty and quiet, we cannot forbear complaining of it as hostile to British America. Superadded to these considerations, we cannot help deploring the unhappy condition to which it has reduced the many English settlers who, encouraged by the royal proclamation promising the enjoyment of all their rights, have purchased estates in that country. They are now the subjects of an arbitrary government, deprived of trial by jury, and when imprisoned, cannot claim the benefit of the Habeas Corpus Act, that great bulwark and palladium of English liberty. Nor can we suppress our astonishment that a British Parliament should ever consent to establish in that country a religion that has deluged your island in blood, and dispersed impiety, bigotry, persecution, murder, and rebellion through every part of the world.

This being a state of facts, let us beseech you to consider to what end they lead. Admit that the Ministry, by the powers of Britain and the aid of our Roman Catholic neighbors, should be able to carry the point of taxation, and reduce us to a state of perfect humiliation and slavery. Such an enterprise would doubtless make some addition to your national debt which already presses down your liberties and fills you with pensioners and placemen. We presume, also, that your commerce will somewhat be diminished. However, suppose you should prove victorious, in what condition will you then be? What advantages or what laurels will you reap from such a conquest? May not a Ministry with the same armies enslave you? It may be said you will cease to pay them; but remember, the taxes from America, the wealth, and we may add the men, and particularly the Roman Catholics of this vast continent, will then be in the power of your enemies; nor will you have any reason to expect that after making slaves of us, many among us should refuse to assist in reducing you to the same abject state.

Do not treat this as chimerical. Know that in less than half a century the quitrents reserved to the Crown from the numberless grants of this vast continent will pour large streams of wealth into the royal coffers.

And if to this be added the power of taxing America at pleasure, the Crown will be rendered independent of you for supplies, and will possess more treasure than may be necessary to purchase the remains of liberty in your island. In a word, take care that you do not fall into the pit that is preparing for us.

We believe there is yet much virtue, much justice, and much public spirit in the English nation. To that justice we now appeal. You have been told that we are seditious, impatient of government, and desirous of independence. Be assured that these are not facts, but calumnies. Permit us to be as free as yourselves, and we shall ever esteem a union with you to be our greatest glory, and our greatest happiness; we shall ever be ready to contribute all in our power to the welfare of the empire; we shall consider your enemies as our enemies, and your interest as our own.

But if you are determined that your ministers shall wantonly sport with the rights of mankind; if neither the voice of justice, the dictates of the law, the principles of the constitution, or the suggestions of humanity can restrain your hands from shedding human blood in such an impious cause, we must then tell you that we will never submit to be hewers of wood or drawers of water for any ministry or nation in the world.

Place us in the same situation that we were at the close of the last war, and our former harmony will be restored.

But lest the same supineness and the same inattention to our common interest which you have for several years shown should continue, we think it prudent to anticipate the consequences.

By the destruction of the trade of Boston the Ministry have endeavored to induce submission to their measures. The like fate may befall us all. We will endeavor, therefore, to live without trade, and recur for subsistence to the fertility and bounty of our native soil, which affords us all the necessaries and some of the conveniences of life. We have suspended our importation from Great Britain and Ireland; and in less than a year's time, unless our grievances should be redressed, shall discontinue our exports to those kingdoms and the West Indies.

It is with the utmost regret, however, that we find ourselves compelled by the overruling principles of self-preservation to adopt measures detrimental in their consequences to numbers of our fellow subjects in Great Britain and Ireland. But we hope that the magnanimity and justice of the British nation will furnish a Parliament of such wisdom, independence, and public spirit as may save the violated rights of the whole empire from the devices of wicked ministers and evil counselors, whether in or out of office, and thereby restore that harmony, friendship, and fraternal affection between all the inhabitants of His Majesty's kingdoms and territories so ardently wished for by every true and honest American.

By the waters of Babylon we sit down and weep, when we think of thee, O America!

HORACE WALPOLE, letter to Mason, 1775

64.

On the Depravity of Kings and the Sovereignty of the People

Fearing the loss of popular support and the collapse of organized opposition to Britain, the delegates to the Continental Congress of 1774 could not openly express their desire for independence. Newspaper writers, however, who could remain anonymous, did not hesitate to affirm their goal of independence. The following newspaper article, of November 14, would seem to indicate that popular opinion was moving far in advance of the conciliatory documents produced by the Congress.

Source: *Archives*, I, pp. 976-977: "Political Observations Without Order."

1. All power of government is derived from God through the instrumentality of kings or the people. Has the impartial Governor of the universe communicated His attributes of power, wisdom, justice, and mercy to kings only, and denied the least portion of them to every other class of mankind? Let history decide this question. The history of kings is nothing but the history of the folly and depravity of human nature.

2. To live (says Bishop Hoadly) by one man's will became the cause of all men's misery. If the Bible was silent, analogy would teach us that the depravity and misery of one man could contaminate and render miserable a whole race of men. Look up then, mortals, to kings with humility. They are living histories of your first calamity. One man still continues to be the source of misery and depravity in all the kingdoms of the world. God deals with all mankind as He did with the Jews. He gives them kings only in His anger. We read now and then, it is true, of a good king; so we read likewise of a prophet escaping unhurt from a lion's den, and of three men

walking in a fiery furnace without having even their garments singed. The order of nature is as much inverted in the first as it was in the last two cases. A good king is a miracle.

3. The American Congress derives all its power, wisdom, and justice, not from scrolls of parchment signed by kings but from the people. A more august and a more equitable legislative body never existed in any quarter of the globe. It is founded upon the principles of the most perfect liberty. A freeman, in honoring and obeying the Congress, honors and obeys himself. The man who refuses to do both is a slave. He knows nothing of the dignity of his nature. He cannot govern himself. Expose him for sale at a public vendue. Send him to plant sugar with his fellow slaves in Jamaica. Let not the air of America be contaminated with his breath.

4. The Congress, like other legislative bodies, have annexed penalties to their laws. They do not consist of the gallows, the rack, and the stake. These punishments belong to vindictive states, and are proper

only for a corrupted people. They have held out no punishments but infamy, a species of infamy which sounds more dreadful to a freeman than the gallows, the rack, or the stake. It is this; he shall be declared in the public papers to be an enemy to his country.

5. The wisdom and revenge of man have been exhausted to find out a suitable punishment for treason, or for those crimes which affect the liberty and happiness of a people. The least deviation from the resolves of the Congress will be treason — such treason as few villains have ever had an opportunity of committing. It will be treason against the present inhabitants of the colonies — against the millions of unborn generations who are to exist hereafter in America; against the only liberty and happiness which remain to mankind; against the last hopes of the wretched in every corner of the world. In a word, it will be treason against God. It will be to take from Him (with reverence be it spoken) the power of making His creatures happy. I do not attempt to hint a punishment for such extensive and complicated guilt. Infamy is a punishment of the soul. It can only affect a free man. The body of the wretch who is capable of violating the resolves of the Congress is the only part of him which can be punished. But here all ingenuity fails us. The tortures of Damien and Ravaillac would be rendered abortive for this purpose by the longest possible duration of human life.

6. There is a strange veneration for antiquity and disinclination for innovations in all civil as well as religious bodies. We are now laying the foundation of an American constitution. Let us therefore hold up everything we do to the eye of posterity. They will probably measure their liberties and happiness by the most careless of our footsteps. Let no unhallowed hand touch the precious seed of liberty. Let us form the glorious tree in such a manner, and impreg-

nate it with such principles of life that it shall last forever. Greece, Rome, and Britain would still have been free had not the principles of corruption been concealed in the elements of their constitutions. Let us not avail ourselves of the just spirit of the times, but bind up posterity to be freemen. Our Congress were actuated with this prophetic benevolence when they dissolved themselves and recommended a new choice of delegates in the spring.

7. There is some reason to fear that the steps we are obliged to take to defend our liberties will render us careless in establishing them. Wise and good men in Britain have lifted up the curtain of futurity in America. Let us not be afraid to look through it. Ye intuitive spirits who see through the connection of cause and effect; ye holy spirits who have been accustomed to trace the operations of Divine Providence; ye decisive spirits who resolve and execute at once — ye know what I mean. . . . Let us neither think, write, speak, nor act without keeping our eyes fixed upon the period which shall dissolve our connection with Great Britain. The delirium of the present Ministry may precipitate it, but the ordinary course of human things must accomplish it. Britain may relax from her present arbitrary measures, but political necessity, not justice, must hereafter be the measure of her actions. Freemen cannot bear a middle state between liberty and slavery. It is essential to the happiness of liberty that it should be secure and perpetual.

8. A rotation of offices is one of the lifeguards of liberty. The right as well as the obligations to legislation are alike binding upon all men. To prevent pride and excessive popularity, and to diffuse knowledge and virtue are the surest methods of securing and perpetuating public liberty. These are to be obtained only by a constant rotation of offices.

9. I almost wish to live to hear the tri-

umphs of the jubilee in the year 1874; to see the medals, pictures, fragments of writings, etc., that shall be displayed to revive the memory of the proceedings of the Congress in the year 1774. If any adventitious circumstance shall give precedency on that day, it shall be to inherit the blood or even to possess the name of a member of that glorious assembly. I cannot after this be understood to mean the least reflection upon any one of that body when I urge that only one-half, or at most two-thirds of the old members should be returned from each colony to attend the next Congress. The good dispositions in human nature sometimes lead us astray in public affairs. Do not, illustrious senators, avail yourselves of the gratitude and veneration of your countrymen. You have, we trust, made them free. But a nobler task awaits you. Instruct them, instruct posterity in the great science of securing and perpetuating freedom.

65.

Proposals for Manufacturing

Despite the attempts at reconciliation with Britain, the outbreak of hostilities seemed inevitable by the end of 1774. The various colonies were preparing for war by collecting arms and ammunition and encouraging local manufactures. In October the Assembly of Massachusetts, dissolved by Governor Gage, met at Concord as a provincial congress and took over the government of the colony. It appointed a committee of safety to collect guns and ammunition and organize select militia (minutemen) for immediate action. The following resolutions were adopted by that congress on December 8. By the end of 1775 almost every colony had adopted similar resolutions.

Source: *Archives,* I, pp. 1001-1002.

AS THE HAPPINESS of particular families arises in a great degree from their being more or less dependent upon others; and as the less occasion they have for any article belonging to others, the more independent; and consequently the happier they are; so the happiness of every political body of men upon earth is to be estimated in a great measure upon their greater or less dependence upon any other political bodies; and from hence arises a forcible argument, why every state ought to regulate their internal policy in such a manner as to furnish themselves, within their own body, with every necessary article for subsistence and defense. Otherwise, their political existence will depend upon others who may take advantage of such weakness and reduce them to the lowest state of vassalage and slavery. For preventing so great an evil, more to be dreaded than death itself, it must be the wisdom of this colony at all times, more especially at this time, when the hand of power is lashing us with the scorpions of despotism, to encourage agriculture, manufactures, and economy, so as to render this state as independent of every other state as the nature of our country will admit. From the consideration thereof, and trusting that the virtue of the people of this colony is such that the following resolutions of this congress, which must be productive of the greatest good, will by them be effectually carried into execution. And it is therefore resolved:

1. That we do recommend to the people the improvement of their breed of sheep, and the greatest possible increase of the same; and also the preferable use of our own woolen manufactures; and to manufacturers, that the manufacturers ask only reasonable prices for their goods; and especially a very careful sorting of the wool, so that it may be manufactured to the greatest advantage, and as much as may be, into the best goods.

2. We do also recommend to the people the raising of hemp and flax; and as large quantities of flaxseed, more than may be wanted for sowing, may be produced, we would also further recommend the manufacturing the same into oil.

3. We do likewise recommend the making of nails; which we do apprehend must meet with the strongest encouragement from the public, and be of lasting benefit both to the manufacturer and the public.

4. The making of steel, and the preferable use of the same, we do also recommend to the inhabitants of this colony.

5. We do in like manner recommend the making tinplate, as an article well worth the attention of this people.

6. As firearms have been manufactured in several parts of this colony, we do recommend the use of such, in preference to any imported. And we do recommend the making gunlocks, and furniture and other locks, with other articles in the iron way.

7. We do also earnestly recommend the making of saltpeter, as an article of vast importance to be encouraged, as may be directed hereafter.

8. That gunpowder is also an article of such importance that every man among us who loves his country must wish the establishment of manufactories for that purpose, and, as there are the ruins of several powder mills, and sundry persons among us who are acquainted with that business, we do heartily recommend its encouragement by repairing one or more of said mills, or erecting others, and renewing said business as soon as possible.

9. That as several paper mills are now usefully employed, we do likewise recommend a preferable use of our own manufactures in this way; and a careful saving and collecting of rags, etc., and also that the manufacturers give a generous price for such rags, etc.

10. That it will be the interest, as well as the duty of this body, or of such as may succeed us, to make such effectual provision for the further manufacturing of the several sorts of glass, as that the same may be carried on to the mutual benefit of the undertaker and the public, and firmly established in this colony.

11. Whereas buttons of excellent qualities and of various sorts are manufactured among us, we do earnestly recommend the general use of the same; so that the manufactories may be extended to the advantage of the people and the manufacturers.

12. And whereas salt is an article of vast consumption within this colony, and in its fisheries, we do heartily recommend the making the same, in the several ways wherein it is made in several parts of Europe; especially in the method used in that part of France where they make bay-salt.

13. We do likewise recommend an encouragement of hornsmiths in all their various branches, as what will be of public utility.

14. We do also recommend the establishment of one or more manufactories for making wool-comber's combs, as an article necessary in our woolen manufactures.

15. We do in like manner heartily recommend the preferable use of the stockings

and other hosiery woven among ourselves, so as to enlarge the manufactories thereof, in such a manner as to encourage the manufacturers and serve the country.

16. As madder is an article of great importance in the dyer's business, and which may be easily raised and cured among ourselves, we do therefore earnestly recommend the raising and curing the same.

17. In order the more effectually to carry these resolutions into effect, we do earnestly recommend that a society or societies be established for the purposes of introducing and establishing such arts and manufactures as may be useful to this people and are not yet introduced, and the more effectually establishing such as we already have among us.

18. We do recommend to the inhabitants of this province to make use of our own manufactures, and those of our sister colonies, in preference to all other manufactures.

66.

Maryland Endorses Resistance

On December 12, 1774, the deputies of the province of Maryland met at Annapolis. The following report of their meeting constitutes an endorsement of the Association of the Continental Congress. In resolving to form a provincial militia, the Maryland delegates went beyond the express recommendations of Congress.

Source: Niles: "Patriotic Recommendation, Full Meeting of Deputies Respecting Manufactures, and Home Industry."

AT A MEETING OF THE DEPUTIES appointed by the several counties of the province of Maryland, at the city of Annapolis, by adjournment, on the 8th day of December, 1774, and continued till the 12th day of the same month, were present, eighty-five members: Mr. John Hall in the chair, and Mr. John Duckett, clerk.

The proceedings of the Continental Congress were read, considered, and unanimously approved. *Resolved*, that every member of this convention will, and every person in the province ought strictly and inviolably to observe and carry into execution the association agreed on by the said Continental Congress.

On motion, unanimously *resolved*, that the thanks of this convention be given, by the chairman, to the gentlemen who represented this province as deputies in the late Continental Congress for their faithful discharge of that important trust; and the same was done accordingly.

To increase our flocks of sheep, and thereby promote the woolen manufacture in this province, *resolved*, that no person ought to kill any lamb dropped before the 1st day of May yearly, or other sheep, after the 1st day of January next, under four years of age.

To increase the manufacture of linen and cotton, *resolved*, that every planter and farmer ought to raise as much flax, hemp, and cotton as he conveniently can; and the cultivation thereof is particularly recommended to such inhabitants of this province, whose lands are best adapted to that purpose. And *resolved*, that no flaxseed of the growth of the present year ought to be purchased for exportation, after the 12th day of this month.

It being represented to this convention that many merchants and traders of this province, from a scarcity of cash to make their remittances and other causes, had sold their goods within twelve months next before the 20th day of October last, at, and sometimes even below, the prime cost; and that, in many different parts of this province, merchants had vended their goods at a very different advance on the prime cost; and it appearing to this convention to be unjust to compel such merchants to sell their goods at prime cost, and that one general rule, allowing a reasonable profit to the trader, and preventing him from taking advantage of the scarcity of goods which may be occasioned by the nonimportation, would give great satisfaction to the merchants and people of this province, *resolved* unanimously; that no merchant ought to sell his goods, at wholesale, for more than 112½ percent — at retail, for cash, for more than 13 percent — on credit, for more than 150 percent, advance on the prime cost; and that no merchant, or other person, ought to engross any goods, wares, or merchandise whatsoever. And in case any question should arise respecting the prime cost of goods, every merchant or factor possessing or owning such goods ought to ascertain the same on oath, if requested to do it by the committee.

As a further regulation to enforce an observance of the late Continental association *resolved* unanimously, that in all cases where breaches of the Continental association or the resolves of this convention shall happen and be declared such by any committee of a county, no gentleman of the law ought to bring or prosecute any suit whatever for such offender. And if any factor shall commit any breach of the said association or resolves, that no gentleman of the law ought to bring or prosecute any suit for any debt due to the store of which the said factor has the management, after notice as aforesaid.

Resolved, that it is earnestly recommended by this convention to the people of this province, that the determinations of the several county committees be observed and acquiesced in. That no persons, except members of the committees, undertake to meddle with or determine any question respecting the construction of the association entered into by the Continental Congress. And that peace and good order be inviolably maintained throughout this congress.

Resolved unanimously, that if the late acts of Parliament, relative to the Massachusetts Bay, shall be attempted to be carried into execution by force in that colony, or if the assumed power of Parliament to tax the colonies shall be attempted to be carried into execution by force, in that colony or any other colony, that in such case, this province will support such colony to the utmost of their power.

Resolved unanimously, that a well-regulated militia, composed of the gentlemen, freeholders, and other freemen, is the natural strength and only stable security of a free government, and that such militia will relieve our mother country from any expense in our protection and defense; will obviate the pretense of a necessity for taxing us on that account, and render it unnecessary to keep any standing army (ever dangerous to liberty) in this province. And therefore, it is recommended to such of the said inhabitants of this province as are from sixteen to fifty years of age, to form themselves into companies of sixty-eight men; to choose a captain, two lieutenants, an ensign, four sergeants, four corporals, and one drummer for each company; and use their utmost endeavors to make themselves masters of the military exercise. That each man be provided with a good firelock and bayonet fitted thereon, half a pound of powder, two pounds of lead, and a cartouch box, or powder horn and bag for ball, and be in readiness to act on any emergency.

Resolved unanimously, that it is recommended to the committees of each county to raise by subscription, or in such other voluntary manner as they think proper, and will be most agreeable to their respective counties. . . .

Resolved unanimously, that it is recommended to the several colonies and provinces to enter into such or the like resolutions, for mutual defense and protection, as are entered into by this province. As our opposition to the settled plan of the British administration to enslave America will be strengthened by a union of all ranks of men in this province, we do most earnestly recommend that all former differences about religion or politics, and all private animosities and quarrels of every kind, from henceforth cease and be forever buried in oblivion; and we entreat, we conjure every man by his duty to God, his country, and his posterity, cordially to unite in defense of our common rights and liberties.

67.

SAMUEL SEABURY: The Controversy Between Great Britain and Her Colonies

In spite of the Intolerable Acts, Samuel Seabury and other Tories devoted their literary efforts to keeping the colonies loyal to the Crown. Seabury, who signed his pamphlets "A Westchester Farmer," tried to convince the colonists that their greatest freedom and good lay in their submission to British rule. He believed the Americans could secure the changes they wanted through peaceful and orderly petitions to Parliament. The following selection, dated December 24, 1774, is a letter in reply to the anonymous author of a pamphlet that had taken the other side.

Source: *A View of the Controversy Between Great-Britain and Her Colonies, etc., etc.,* London, 1775.

I WISH YOU HAD explicitly declared to the public your ideas of the natural rights of mankind. Man in a state of nature may be considered as perfectly free from all restraints of law and government; and then the weak must submit to the strong. From such a state, I confess, I have a violent aversion. I think the form of government we lately enjoyed a much more eligible state to live in, and cannot help regretting our having lost it by the equity, wisdom, and authority of the Congress, who have introduced in the room of it confusion and violence, where all must submit to the power of a mob.

You have taken some pains to prove what would readily have been granted you — that liberty is a very good thing, and slavery a very bad thing. But then I must think that liberty under a king, Lords, and Commons is as good as liberty under a republican Congress; and that slavery under a republican Congress is as bad, at least, as slavery under a king, Lords, and Commons; and, upon the whole, that liberty under the supreme authority and protection of Great Britain is infinitely preferable to slavery under an American Congress. I will also agree with you "that Americans are entitled to freedom." I will go further: I will own and acknowledge that not only Americans but Africans, Europeans, Asiatics, all men of all countries and degrees, of all sizes and complexions, have a right to as much freedom as is consistent with the security of civil society. And I hope you will not think me an "enemy" to the natural "rights of mankind" because I cannot wish them more. We must, however, remember that more liberty may, without inconvenience, be allowed to individuals in a small government than can be admitted of in a large empire.

But when you assert that "since Americans have not by any act of theirs empowered the British Parliament to make laws for them, it follows they can have no just authority to do it," you advance a position subversive of that dependence which all colonies must, from their very nature, have on the mother country. By the British Parliament, I suppose you mean the supreme legislative authority, the King, Lords, and Commons, because no other authority in England has a right to make laws to bind the kingdom, and consequently no authority to make laws to bind the colonies. In this sense I shall understand and use the phrase "British Parliament."

Now the dependence of the colonies on the mother country has ever been acknowledged. It is an impropriety of speech to talk of an independent colony. The words "independency" and "colony" convey contradictory ideas: much like killing and sparing. As soon as a colony becomes independent on its parent state, it ceases to be any longer a colony; just as when you kill a sheep, you cease to spare him. The British colonies make a part of the British Empire. As parts of the body they must be subject to the general laws of the body. To talk of a colony independent of the mother country is no better sense than to talk of a limb independent of the body to which it belongs.

In every government there must be a supreme, absolute authority lodged somewhere. In arbitrary governments this power is in the monarch; in aristocratical governments, in the nobles; in democratical, in the people or the deputies of their electing. Our own government being a mixture of all these kinds, the supreme authority is vested in the King, nobles, and people; i.e., the King, House of Lords, and House of Commons elected by the people. This supreme authority extends as far as the British dominions extend. To suppose a part of the British dominions which is not subject to the power of the British legislature is no better sense than to suppose a country, at one and the same time, to be and not to be a part of the British dominions. If, therefore, the colony of New York be a part of the British dominions, the colony of New York is subject and dependent on the supreme legislative authority of Great Britain.

Legislation is not an inherent right in the colonies. Many colonies have been established, and subsisted long without it. . . .

The position that we are bound by no laws to which we have not consented, either by ourselves or our representatives, is a novel position, unsupported by any authoritative record of the British constitution, ancient or modern. It is republican in its very nature, and tends to the utter subversion of the English monarchy.

This position has arisen from an artful change of terms. To say that an Englishman is not bound by any laws but those to which the representatives of the nation have given their consent is to say what is true. But to say that an Englishman is bound by no laws but those to which *he* has consented in person, or by *his* representative, is saying what never was true, and never can be true. A great part of the people in England have no vote in the choice of representatives and therefore are governed by laws to which they never consented either by *themselves* or by *their* representatives.

The right of colonists to exercise a legislative power is no natural right. They derive it not from nature but from the indulgence or grant of the parent state, whose subjects they were when the colony was settled, and by whose permission and assistance they made the settlement.

Upon supposition that every English colony enjoyed a legislative power independent of the Parliament; and that the Parliament has no just authority to make laws to bind them, this absurdity will follow: that there is no power in the British Empire which has authority to make laws for the whole Empire, *i.e.*, we have an Empire without government; or, which amounts to the same thing, we have a government which has no supreme power. All our colonies are independent of each other. Suppose them independent of the British Parliament — what power do you leave to govern the whole? None at all. You split and divide the Empire into a number of petty, insignificant states. This is the direct, the necessary tendency of refusing submission to acts of Parliament. Every man who can see one inch beyond his nose must see this consequence. And every man who endeavors to accelerate the independency of the colonies on the British Parliament endeavors to accelerate the ruin of the British Empire.

To talk of being liege subjects to King George while we disavow the authority of Parliament is another piece of Whiggish nonsense. I love my King as well as any Whig in America or England either, and am as ready to yield him all lawful submission. But, while I submit to the King, I submit to the authority of the laws of the state, whose guardian the King is. The difference between a good and a bad subject is only this, that the one obeys, the other transgresses the law. The difference between a loyal subject and a rebel is that the one yields obedience to and faithfully supports the supreme authority of the state, and the other endeavors to overthrow it. If we obey the laws of the King, we obey the laws of the Parliament. If we disown the authority of the Parliament, we disown the authority of the King. There is no medium without ascribing powers to the King which the constitution knows nothing of, without

making him superior to the laws and setting him above all restraint. These are some of the ridiculous absurdities of American Whiggism.

I am utterly at a loss what ideas to annex to the phrases "dependence on Great Britain"; "subordination to the Parliament"; "submission to the supreme legislative power" — unless they mean some degree of subjection to the British Parliament, some acknowledgment of its right to make laws to bind the colonies.

Give me leave, sir, to transcribe for your perusal an extract from a petition to the House of Commons, sent by the General Congress, who met at New York the 19th of October, 1765. Whether this Congress was equal in wisdom, dignity, and authority to that lately assembled at Philadelphia, you can determine for yourself. However that be, they express themselves thus:

> It is from and under the English constitution we derive all our civil and religious rights and liberties; we glory in being subjects of the best of kings and having been born under the most perfect form of government. We esteem our connections with, and dependence on, Great Britain as one of our greatest blessings; and apprehend the latter will appear to be sufficiently secure when it is considered that the inhabitants in the colonies have the most unbounded affection for His Majesty's person, family, and government; and that their subordination to the Parliament is universally acknowledged.

A still more respectable body, viz., the General Assembly of New York, in the preamble to their resolutions of the 18th of December 1765, declare:

> That they think it their indispensable duty to make a declaration of their faith and allegiance to His Majesty, King George III, and their submission to the supreme legislative power; and at the same time to show that the rights claimed by them are in no manner inconsistent with either.

Trinity College Press

Bishop Samuel Seabury, portrait by an unknown artist

You have utterly failed in proving that "the clear voice of natural justice" and "the fundamental principles of the English constitution" set us free from the subordination here acknowledged. Let us see the success of your next attempt.

You appeal to "our charters, the express conditions on which our progenitors relinquished their native countries and came to settle in this," and our charters, you say, "preclude every claim of ruling and taxing us without our assent." Did you examine all the charters of the different colonies before you made this bold assertion? I fear you did not read one of them.

I presume the province of New York has no charter; at least I never heard of any. The claim, then, of the Parliament "of ruling and taxing us without our assent," is not precluded by charter. . . .

A person diseased with the jaundice sees no color but yellow. Party heat, the fever of liberty, may, for anything I know, vitiate the mind as much as the jaundice does the eyes. I flatter myself, however, that all reasonable Americans will . . . not be led by positive assertions without proof, nor declamatory harangues without argument, into rebellion against the supreme authority of the nation; nor be beguiled of their present free and happy government by the loud clamors of unrestrained licentiousness under the specious name of liberty. Tyranny and

slavery must be the consequence of the present system of conduct. If we wantonly throw off that subordination to the British Parliament which our present state requires, we shall inevitably fall under the dominion of some foreign tyrant, or the more intolerable despotism of a few American demagogues. . . .

Let it be considered that, in every government, legislation and taxation, or the right of raising a revenue, must be conjoined. If you divide them, you weaken and finally destroy the government; for no government can long subsist without power to raise the supplies necessary for its defense and administration.

It has been proved that the supreme authority of the British Empire extends over all the dominions that compose the Empire. The power, or right, of the British Parliament to raise such a revenue as is necessary for the defense and support of the British government in all parts of the British dominions is therefore incontestable. For, if no government can subsist without a power to raise the revenues necessary for its support, then, in fact, no government can extend any further than its power of raising such a revenue extends. If, therefore, the British Parliament has no power to raise a revenue in the colonies, it has no government over the colonies; i.e., no government that can support itself. The burden of supporting its government over the colonies must lie upon the other parts of the Empire.

But this is unreasonable. Government implies not only a power of making and enforcing laws but defense and protection. Now protection implies tribute. Those that share in the protection of any government are in reason and duty bound to maintain and support the government that protects them; otherwise they destroy their own protection; or else they throw an unjust burden on their fellow subjects, which they ought to bear in common with them. While, therefore, the colonies are under the British government and share in its protection, the British government has a right to raise, and they are in reason and duty bound to pay, a reasonable and proportionable part of the expense of its administration.

The authority of the British Parliament, that is, of the supreme sovereign authority of the British Empire, over the colonies, and its right to raise a proportional part of its revenue for the support of its government in the colonies being established, it is to be considered what is the most reasonable and equitable method of doing it. . . .

Good policy will require that the heavier duties be laid upon articles of luxury, especially foreign ones; and that as little as possible be laid upon the raw materials for manufactures and upon our own exports. . . .

When it is considered that Great Britain is a maritime power; that the present flourishing state of her trade and of the trade of her colonies depends in a great measure upon the protection which they receive from her Navy; that her own security depends upon her Navy; and that it is principally a naval protection that we receive from her, there will appear a peculiar propriety in laying the chief burden of supporting her Navy upon her commerce, and in requesting us to bear a part of the expense, proportional to our ability, and to that protection and security which we receive from it.

There are but two objections that can reasonably be made to what has been said upon this subject. The first is that, if the British Parliament has a right to make laws to bind the whole Empire, our assemblies become useless. But a little consideration will remove this difficulty.

Our assemblies, from the very nature of things, can have but a legated, subordinate, and local authority of legislation. Their power of making laws in conjunction with the other branches of the legislature cannot extend beyond the limits of the province to which they belong. Their authority must be subordinate to the supreme sovereign authority of the nation, or there is *imperium in imperio* — two sovereign authorities in the same state — which is a contradiction. Everything that relates to the internal policy and government of the province which they represent comes properly before them, whether they be matters of law or revenue. But all laws relative to the Empire in general, or to all the colonies conjunctively, or which regulate the trade of any particular colony, in order to make it compatible with the general good of the whole Empire, must be left to the Parliament. There is no other authority which has a right to make such regulations or weight sufficient to carry them into execution.

Our assemblies are also the true, proper, legal guardians of our rights, privileges, and liberties. . . . They are the real, not the pretended, representatives of the people. They are bodies known and acknowledged by the public laws of the Empire. Their representations will be attended to and their remonstrances heard.

To the honor of the assemblies of this province, as far back as I am able to judge . . . they have always discharged this duty with fidelity, prudence, and firmness; and with such success as ought to encourage us to rely upon their wisdom and good conduct, to deliver us from our present embarrassed state with our mother country; and from that abject slavery and cruel oppression which the tyranny of the late Congress has brought upon us.

Considered in this light, they are a body of real dignity, and of the utmost importance; and whoever attempts to lessen their influence or disparage their authority ought to be considered as an enemy to the liberties of his country. Had our present contests with Great Britain been left to their management, I would not have said a word. But their authority is contravened and superseded by a power from without the province.

Virginia and Massachusetts madmen met

at Philadelphia, have made laws for the province of New York, and have rendered our assembly useless and, unless they exert their proper authority with a spirit becoming their own dignity, insignificant. . . .

You, sir, affect to consider the gentlemen that went from this province to the Congress as the representatives of the province. You know in your conscience that they were not chosen by a hundredth part of the people. You know also that their appointment was in a way unsupported by any law, usage, or custom of the province. You know also that the people of this province had already delegated their power to the members of their Assembly, and therefore had no right to choose delegates, to contravene the authority of the Assembly by introducing a foreign power of legislation. Yet you consider those delegates in a point of light equal to our legal representatives; for you say that "our representatives in General Assembly cannot take any wiser or better course to settle our differences than our representatives in the Continental Congress have taken." Then I affirm that our representatives ought to go to school for seven years before they are returned to serve again. No wiser or better course? Then they must take just the course that the Congress have taken; for a worse, or more foolish, they cannot take should they try; if they act any way different from the Congress, they must act better and wiser. . . .

The other objection to what has been said upon the legislative authority of the British Parliament is this: that if the Parliament have authority to make laws to bind the whole Empire; to regulate the trade of the whole Empire; and to raise a revenue upon the whole Empire, then we have nothing that we can call our own. By the same authority that they can take a penny, they can take a pound, or all we have got.

Let it be considered that no scheme of human policy can be so contrived and guarded but that something must be left to the integrity, prudence, and wisdom of those who govern. We are apt to think, and I believe justly, that the British constitution is the best scheme of government now subsisting. The rights and liberties of the people are better secured by it than by any other system now subsisting. . . .

The colonies have become so considerable by the increase of their inhabitants and commerce, and by the improvement of their lands, that they seem incapable of being governed in the same lax and precarious manner as formerly. They are arrived to that mature state of manhood which requires a different and more exact policy of ruling than was necessary in their infancy and childhood. They want, and are entitled to, a fixed, determinate constitution of their own — a constitution which shall unite them firmly with Great Britain and with one another, which shall mark out the line of British supremacy and colonial dependence, giving, on the one hand, full force to the supreme authority of the nation over all its dominions, and, on the other, securing effectually the rights, liberty, and property of colonists. This is an event devoutly to be wished by all good men, and which all ought to labor to obtain by all prudent and probable means. Without obtaining this, it is idle talk of obtaining a redress of the grievances complained of. They naturally, they necessarily result from the relation which at present stand in to Great Britain.

You, sir, argue through your whole pamphlet upon an assumed point: viz., that the British government — the King, Lords, and Commons — have laid a regular plan to enslave America; and that they are now deliberately putting it in execution. This point has never been proved, though it has been asserted over and over and over again. If you say that they have declared their right of making laws to bind us in all cases whatsoever, I answer that the declarative act here referred to means no more than to assert the supreme authority of Great Britain over all her dominions. If you say that they have exercised this power in a wanton, oppressive manner, it is a point that I am not enough acquainted with the minutiae of government to determine.

It may be true. The colonies are undoubtedly alarmed on account of their liberties. Artful men have availed themselves of the opportunity and have excited such scenes of contention between the parent state and the colonies as afford none but dreadful prospects. Republicans smile at the confusion that they themselves have in a great measure made and are exerting all their influence, by sedition and rebellion, to shake the British Empire to its very basis, that they may have an opportunity of erecting their beloved commonwealth on its ruins. If greater security to our rights and liberties be necessary than the present form and administration of the government can give us, let us endeavor to obtain it; but let our endeavors be regulated by prudence and probability of success. In this attempt all good men will join, both in England and America. All who love their country and wish the prosperity of the British Empire will be glad to see it accomplished.

Before we set out to obtain this security we should have had prudence enough to settle one point among ourselves. We should have considered what security it was we wanted, what concessions on the part of Great Britain would have been sufficient to have fixed our rights and liberties on a firm and permanent foundation. This was the proper business of our assemblies, and to them we ought to have applied. And why we did not apply to them, no one tolerable reason can be assigned — a business which our Assembly, at least, is equal to, whether we consider their abilities as men or their authority as representatives of the province; and a business which, I doubt not, they would have executed with prudence, firmness, and success. I say nothing of the other assemblies on the continent, for I know little of them; only that they were the proper persons to have managed this affair. . . .

I will here, sir, venture to deliver my sentiments upon the line that ought to be drawn between the supremacy of Great Britain and the dependency of the colonies. And I shall do it with the more boldness because I know it to be agreeable to the opinions of many of the warmest advocates for America, both in England and in the colonies, in the time of the Stamp Act. I imagine that if all internal taxation be vested in our own legislatures, and the right of regulating trade by duties, bounties, etc., be left in the power of the Parliament, and also the right of enacting all general laws for the good of all the colonies, that we shall have all the security for our rights, liberties, and property which human policy can give us. The dependence of the colonies on the mother country will be fixed on a firm foundation; the sovereign authority of Parliament over all the dominions of the Empire will be established; and the mother country and all her colonies will be knit together, in *one grand, firm, and compact body.* . . .

If we should succeed in depriving Great Britain of the power of regulating our trade, the colonies will probably be soon at variance with each other. Their commercial interests will interfere; there will be no supreme power to interpose, and discord and animosity must ensue.

And upon the whole, if the Parliament can regulate our trade so as to make it conduce to the general good of the whole Empire as well as to our particular profit; if they can protect us in the secure enjoyment of an extensive and lucrative commerce, and at the same time can raise a part of the revenue necessary to support their naval power, without which our commerce cannot be safe, every reasonable man, I should imagine, would think it best to let them enjoy it in peace without descending to the mean, paltry, narrow, stupid design of the Congress.

68.

John Trumbull: "An Elegy on the Times"

John Trumbull's first poem about national affairs, An Elegy on the Times, *written in 1774, was a "glittering, bombastic piece" that bore a patriotic message. In the role of a liberal, Trumbull attacked British economic policies but was still, at this time, hopeful of avoiding open conflict.*

Source: *Poetical Works,* Hartford, Conn., 1820, Vol. II, p. 205-217.

AN ELEGY ON THE TIMES

Oh Boston! late with every beauty crowned,
   Where Commerce triumphed on the favoring gales;
And each pleased eye, that roved in prospect round,
   Hailed thy bright spires and blessed thy opening sails!

Thy splendid mart with rich profusion smiled,
   The gay throng crowded in thy spacious streets,
From either Ind, thy cheerful stores were filled,
   Thy haven joyous with unnumbered fleets.

For here, more fair than in their native vales,
   Tall groves of masts arose in beauteous pride;
Glad ocean shone beneath the swelling sails,
   And wafted plenty on the bordering tide.

Alas how changed! the swelling sails no more
   Catch the soft airs and wanton in the sky:
But hostile beaks affright the guarded shore,
   And pointed thunders all access deny.

Where the bold cape its warning forehead rears,
   Where tyrant vengeance waved her fatal wand,
Far from the sight each friendly vessel veers,
   And flies averse the interdicted strand.

Along thy fields, which late in beauty shone,
  With lowing herds and grassy vesture fair,
The insulting tents of barbarous troops are strown,
  And bloody standards stain the peaceful air.

Are these thy deeds, oh Britain? this the praise,
  That gilds the fading luster of thy name,
These the bold trophies of thy later days,
  That close the period of thine early fame?

Shall thy strong fleets, with awful sails unfurled,
  On freedom's shrine the unhallowed vengeance bend,
And leave forlorn the desolated world,
  Crushed every foe and ruined every friend?

And quenched, alas, the soul-inspiring ray,
  Where virtue kindled and where genius soared;
Or damped by darkness and the dismal sway
  Of senates venal and liveried lord?

There pride sits blazoned on the unmeaning brow,
  And over the scene thy factious nobles wait,
Prompt the mixed tumult of the noisy show,
  Guide the blind vote and rule the mock debate.

To these how vain, in weary woes forlorn,
  With abject fear the fond complaint to raise,
Lift fruitless offerings to the ear of scorn
  Of servile vows and well-dissembled praise!

Will the grim savage of the nightly fold
  Learn from their cries the blameless flock to spare?
Will the deaf gods, that frown in molten gold,
  Heed the duped votary and the prostrate prayer?

With what pleased hope before the throne of pride,
  We reared our suppliant hands with filial awe,
While loud Disdain with ruffian voice replied,
  And falsehood triumphed in the garb of law?

While Peers enraptured hail the unmanly wrong,
  See Ribaldry, vile prostitute of shame,
Stretch the bribed hand and dart the envenomed tongue,
  To blast the laurels of a Franklin's fame!

But will the Sage, whose philosophic soul
   Controlled the lightning in its fierce career,
Over heaven's dread vault bade harmless thunders roll,
   And taught the bolts ethereal where to steer;

Will he, while echoing to his just renown,
   The voice of kingdoms swells the loud applause,
Heed the weak malice of a courtier's frown,
   Or dread the insolence of wrested laws?

Yet nought avail the virtues of the heart,
   The vengeful bolt no muse's laurels ward;
From Britain's rage, like death's relentless dart,
   No worth can save us and no fame can guard.

Over hallowed bounds see dire oppression roll,
   Fair Freedom buried in the whelming flood;
Nor chartered rights her tyrant course control,
   Tho' sealed by kings and witnessed in our blood.

In vain we hope from ministerial pride
   A hand to save us or a heart to bless:
'Tis strength, our own, must stem the rushing tide,
   'Tis our own virtue must command success.

But oh my friends, the arm of blood restrain,
   (No rage intemperate aids the public weal;)
Nor basely blend, too daring but in vain,
   The assassin's madness with the patriot's zeal.

Ours be the manly firmness of the sage,
   From shameless foes ungrateful wrongs to bear;
Alike removed from baseness and from rage,
   The flames of faction and the chills of fear.

Repel the torrent of commercial gain,
   That buys our ruin at a price so rare,
And while we scorn Britannia's servile chain,
   Disdain the livery of her marts to wear.

For shall the lust of fashion and of show,
   The curst idolatry of silks and lace,
Bid our gay robes insult our country's woe,
   And welcome slavery in the glare of dress?

No — the rich produce of our fertile soil
   Shall clothe in neat array the cheerful train,
While heaven-born virtues bless the sacred toil,
   And gild the humble vestures of the plain.

No foreign labor in the Asian field
   Shall weave her silks to deck the wanton age:
But as in Rome, the furrowed vale shall yield
   The conquering hero and paternal sage.

And ye, whose heaven in golden pomp to shine,
   And warmly press the dissipated round,
Grace the ripe banquet with the charms of wine,
   And roll the thundering chariot over the ground;

For this, while guised in sycophantic smile,
   With heart regardless of your country's pain,
Your flattering falsehoods feed the ears of guile,
   And barter freedom for the dreams of gain!

Are these the joys on vassal-realms that wait;
   In downs of ease and dalliance to repose,
Quaff streams nectareous in the domes of state,
   And blaze in grandeur of imperial shows?

No — the hard hand, the tortured brow of care,
   The thatch-roofed hamlet and defenseless shed,
The tattered garb, that meets the inclement air,
   The famished table and the matted bed —

These are their fate. In vain the arm of toil
   With gifts autumnal crowns the bearded plain,
In vain glad summer warms the genial soil,
   And spring dissolves in softening showers in vain;

There savage power extends a dreary shade,
   And chill oppression, with her frost severe,
Sheds a dire blast, that nips the rising blade,
   And robs the expecting labors of the year.

So must we sink? and at the stern command,
   That bears the terror of a tyrant's word,
Bend the weak knee and raise the suppliant hand;
   The scorned, dependent vassals of a lord?

The wintry ravage of the storm to mee
   Brave the scorched vapor of the autı
Then pour the hard-earned harvest at
   And beg some pittance from our p

But not for this, by heaven and virtue led,
   From the mad rule of hierarchal pride,
Over pathless seas our injured fathers fled,
   And followed freedom on the adventurous tide;

Dared the wild horrors of the clime unknown,
   The insidious savage, and the crimson plain,
To us bequeathed the prize their woes had won,
   Nor deemed they suffered, or they bled in vain.

And thinks't thou, *North*,[1] the sons of such a race,
   Whose beams of glory blessed their purpled morn,
Will shrink unnerved before a despot's face,
   Nor meet thy louring insolence with scorn?

Look through the circuit of the extended shore,
   That checks the surges of the Atlantic deep;
What weak eye trembles at the frown of power,
   What torpid soul invites the bands of sleep?

What kindness warms each heaven-illumined heart!
   What generous gifts the woes of want assuage,
And sympathetic tears of pity start,
   To aid the destined victims of thy rage!

No faction, clamorous with unhallowed zeal,
   To wayward madness wakes the impassioned throng;
No thoughtless furies sheath our breasts in steel,
   Or call the sword to avenge the oppressive wrong.

Fraternal bands with vows accordant join,
   One guardian genius, one pervading soul
Nerves the bold arm, inspires the just design,
   Combines, enlivens, and illumes the whole.

Now meet the Fathers of the western clime,
   Nor names more noble graced the rolls of fame,
When Spartan firmness braved the wrecks of time,
   Or Latian virtue fanned the heroic flame.

1. Lord North, prime minister of Great Britain.

Not deeper thought the immortal sage inspired,
  On Solon's lips when Grecian senates hung;
Nor manlier eloquence the bosom fired,
  When genius thundered from the Athenian tongue.

And hopes thy pride to match the patriot strain,
  By the bribed slave in pensioned lists enrolled;
Or awe their councils by the voice profane,
  That wakes to utterance at the call of gold?

Can frowns of terror daunt the warrior's deeds,
  Where guilt is stranger to the ingenuous heart,
Or craft illude, where godlike science sheds
  The beams of knowledge and the gifts of art?

Go, raise thy hand, and with its magic power
  Pencil with night the sun's ascending ray,
Bid the broad veil eclipse the noon-tide hour,
  And damps of Stygian darkness shroud the day;

Bid heaven's dread thunder at thy voice expire,
  Or chain the angry vengeance of the waves;
Then hope thy breath can quench the immortal fire,
  And free souls pinion with the bonds of slaves.

Thou canst not hope! Attend the flight of days,
  View the bold deeds, that wait the dawning age,
Where Time's strong arm, that rules the mighty maze,
  Shifts the proud actors on this earthly stage.

Then tell us, *North:* for thou art sure to know,
  For have not kings and fortune made thee great;
Or lurks not wisdom in the ennobled brow,
  And dwells no prescience in the robes of state?

Tell how the powers of luxury and pride
  Taint thy pure zephyrs with their baleful breath,
How deep corruption spreads the envenomed tide,
  And whelms thy land in darkness and in death.

And tell how rapt by freedom's sacred flame,
  And fostering influence of propitious skies,
This western world, the last recess of fame,
  Sees in her wilds a newborn empire rise —

A newborn empire, whose ascendant hour
   Defies its foes, assembled to destroy,
And like Alcides, with its infant power
   Shall crush those serpents, who its rest annoy.

Then look through time, and with extended eye,
   Pierce the dim veil of fate's obscure domain:
The morning dawns, the effulgent star is nigh,
   And crimson glories deck our rising reign.

Behold, emerging from the cloud of days,
   Where rest the wonders of ascending fame,
What heroes rise, immortal heirs of praise!
   What fields of death with conquering standards flame!

See our thronged cities' warlike gates unfold;
   What towering armies stretch their banners wide,
Where cold Ontario's icy waves are rolled,
   Or far Altama's silver waters glide!

Lo, from the groves, the aspiring cliffs that shade,
   Descending pines the surging ocean brave,
Rise in tall masts, the floating canvas spread,
   And rule the dread dominions of the wave!

Where the clear rivers pour their mazy tide,
   The smiling lawns in full luxuriance bloom;
The harvest wantons in its golden pride,
   The flowery garden breathes a glad perfume.

Behold that coast, which seats of wealth surround,
   That haven, rich with many a flowing sail,
Where friendly ships, from earth's remotest bound,
   Float on the cheerly pinions of the gale;

There Boston smiles, no more the sport of scorn,
   And meanly prisoned by thy fleets no more,
And far as ocean's billowy tides are borne,
   Lifts her dread ensigns of imperial power.

So smile the shores, where lordly Hudson strays,
   Whose floods fair York and deep Albania lave,
Or Philadelphia's happier clime surveys
   Her splendid seats in Delaware's lucid wave:

Or southward far extend thy wondering eyes,
   Where fertile streams the gardened vales divide,
And mid the peopled fields, distinguished rise
   Virginian towers and Charleston's spiry pride.

Genius of arts, of manners and of arms,
   See dressed in glory and the bloom of grace,
This virgin clime unfolds her brightest charms,
   And gives her beauties to thy fond embrace.

Hark, from the glades and every listening spray,
   What heaven-born muses wake the raptured song.
The vocal groves attune the warbling lay,
   And echoing vales the rising strains prolong.

Through the vast series of descending years,
   That lose their currents in the eternal wave,
Till heaven's last trump shall rend the affrighted spheres,
   And ope each empire's everlasting grave;

Propitious skies the joyous field shall crown,
   And robe our valleys in perpetual prime,
And ages blest of undisturbed renown
   Arise in radiance over the imperial clime.

And where is Britain? In the skirt of day,
   Where stormy Neptune rolls his utmost tide,
Where suns oblique diffuse a feeble ray,
   And lonely streams the fated coasts divide,

Seest thou yon Isle, whose desert landscape yields
   The mournful traces of the fame she bore,
Where matted thorns oppress the uncultured fields,
   And piles of ruin load the dreary shore?

From those loved seats, the Virtues sad withdrew
   From fell Corruption's bold and venal hand;
Reluctant Freedom waved her last adieu,
   And devastation swept the vassalled land.

On her white cliffs, the pillars once of fame,
   Her melancholy Genius sits to wail,
Drops the fond tear, and over her latest shame,
   Bids dark Oblivion draw the eternal veil.

1775

69.

DANIEL LEONARD: The Dangers of Rebellion

The case for submission to the British Crown was argued in Massachusetts by Daniel Leonard, a wealthy and aristocratic lawyer, in a series of weekly "Letters Addressed to the Inhabitants of Massachusetts Bay" which were published in the Massachusetts Gazette *under the pen name of "Massachusettensis" between December 1774 and April 1775. Leonard's real sympathies were probably always with the Tories. But in 1769, upon his election to the general court, with an apparent ear for popular opinion he had spoken strongly in opposition to the King At the urging of Governor Thomas Hutchinson, he definitely sided with the Tories in 1774 and thereby secured for himself an appointment in the provincial government. The "Letter" that follows is Number V and appeared on January 9, 1775.*

Source: [Daniel Leonard] *Massachusettensis: or A Series of Letters, etc., etc..* 3rd edition, Boston, 1776.

PERHAPS THE WHOLE STORY of empire does not furnish another instance of a forcible opposition to government with so much specious and so little real cause, with such apparent probability without any possibility of success. The Stamp Act gave the alarm. The instability of the public counsels, from the Grenvillian administration to the appointment of the Earl of Hillsborough to the American department, afforded as great a prospect of success as the heavy duties imposed by the Stamp Act did a color for the opposition. It was necessary to give the history of this matter in its course, offend who it would, because those acts of government that are called the greatest grievances became proper and necessary through the misconduct of our politicians; and the justice of Great Britain toward us could not be made apparent without first pointing out that. I intend to consider the acts of the British government, which are held up as the principal grievances, and inquire whether Great Britain is chargeable with injustice in any one of them; but must first ask your attention to the authority of Parliament. I suspect many of our politicians are wrong in their first principle, in denying that the constitutional authority of Parliament extends to the colonies; if so, it must not be wondered at, that their whole fabric is so ruinous. I shall not travel through all the arguments that have been adduced for and against this question, but attempt to reduce the substance of them to a narrow compass, after having taken a cursory view of the British constitution.

The security of the people from internal rapacity and violence, and from foreign invasion, is the end and design of government. The simple forms of government are monarchy, aristocracy, and democracy; that is, where the authority of the state is vested in one, a few, or the many. Each of these species of government has advantages peculiar to itself, and would answer the ends of government were the persons entrusted with the authority of the state always guided themselves by unerring wisdom and public virtue; but rulers are not always exempt from the weakness and depravity which made government necessary to society. Thus monarchy is apt to rush headlong into tyranny; aristocracy to beget faction and multiplied usurpations; and democracy to degenerate into tumult, violence, and anarchy. A government formed upon these three principles, in due proportion, is the best calculated to answer the ends of government and to endure.

Such a government is the British constitution, consisting of King, Lords, and Commons, which at once includes the principal excellencies and excludes the principal defects of the other kinds of government. It is allowed, both by Englishmen and foreigners, to be the most perfect system that the wisdom of ages has produced. The distributions of power are so just, and the proportions so exact, as at once to support and control each other. An Englishman glories in being subject to, and protected by, such a government. The colonies are a part of the British Empire. The best writers upon the law of nations tell us that when a nation takes possession of a distant country and settles there, that country, though separated from the principal establishment or mother country, naturally becomes a part of the state, equal with its ancient possessions.

Two supreme or independent authorities cannot exist in the same state. It would be what is called *imperium in imperio* [government within a government], and the height of political absurdity. The analogy between the political and human bodies is great. Two independent authorities in a state would be like two distinct principles of volition and action in the human body dissenting, opposing, and destroying each other. If, then, we are a part of the British Empire, we must be subject to the supreme power of the state which is vested in the estates of Parliament, notwithstanding each of the colonies have legislative and executive powers of their own, delegated or granted to them for the purposes of regulating their own internal police, which are subordinate to, and must necessarily be subject to, the checks, control, and regulation of the supreme authority.

This doctrine is not new, but the denial of it is. It is beyond a doubt that it was the sense both of the parent country and our ancestors that they were to remain subject to Parliament. It is evident from the charter itself, and this authority has been exercised by Parliament, from time to time, almost ever since the first settlement of the country, and has been expressly acknowledged by our provincial legislatures. It is not less our interest than our duty to continue subject to the authority of Parliament which will be more fully considered hereafter. The principal argument against the authority of Parliament is this: The Americans are entitled to all the privileges of an Englishman; it is the privilege of an Englishman to be exempt from all laws that he does not consent to in person, or by representative; the Americans are not represented in Parliament, and therefore are exempt from acts of Parliament, or in other words, not subject to its authority. This appears specious; but [it] leads to such absurdities as demonstrate its fallacy.

If the colonies are not subject to the authority of Parliament, Great Britain and the colonies must be distinct states, as completely so as England and Scotland were before the union, or as Great Britain and Hanover are now. The colonies in that case will owe no allegiance to the imperial Crown, and perhaps not to the person of the King, as the title of the Crown is derived from an act of Parliament, made since the settlement of this province, which act respects the imperial Crown only. Let us waive this difficulty, and suppose allegiance due from the colonies to the person of the King of Great Britain, he then appears in a new capacity, as King of America, or rather in several new capacities, as King of Massachusetts, King of Rhode Island, King of Connecticut, etc. For if our connection with Great Britain by the Parliament be dissolved, we shall have none among ourselves but each colony will become as distinct from the others as England was from Scotland before the union.

Some have supposed that each state having one and the same person for its king, it is a sufficient connection. Were he an absolute monarch, it might be; but, in a mixed government, it is no union at all. For, as the king must govern each state by its parliament, those several parliaments would pursue the particular interest of its own state; and however well-disposed the king might be to pursue a line of interest that was common to all, the checks and control that he would meet with would render it impossible. If the King of Great Britain has really these new capacities, they ought to be added to his titles; and then another difficulty will arise: the prerogatives of these new crowns have never been defined or limited. Is the monarchical part of the several provincial constitutions to be nearer or more remote from absolute monarchy, in an inverted ratio to each one's approaching to, or receding from, a republic?

But let us suppose the same prerogatives inherent in the several American crowns as are in the imperial Crown of Great Britain, where shall we find the British constitution that we all agree we are entitled to? We shall seek for it in vain in our provincial assemblies. They are but faint sketches of the estates of Parliament. The houses of representatives or burgesses have not all the powers of the House of Commons; in the charter governments they have no more than what is expressly granted by their several charters. The first charters granted to this province did not empower the assembly to tax the people at all. Our council boards are as destitute of the constitutional authority of the House of Lords as their several members are of the noble independence and splendid appendages of peerage. The House of Peers is the bulwark of the British constitution, and through successive ages has withstood the shocks of monarchy and the sappings of democracy, and the constitution gained strength by the conflict.

Thus the supposition of our being independent states, or exempt from the authority of Parliament, destroys the very idea of our having a British constitution. The provincial constitutions, considered as subordinate, are generally well adapted to those purposes of government for which they were intended, that is, to regulate the internal police of the several colonies; but having no principle of stability within themselves, though they may support themselves in moderate times, would be merged by the violence of turbulent ones, and the several colonies become wholly monarchial, or wholly republican, were it not for the checks, controls, regulations, and support of the supreme authority of the Empire. Thus the argument that is drawn from their first principle of our being entitled to English liberties destroys the principle itself; it deprives us of the Bill of Rights and all the benefits resulting from the revolution of English laws and of the British constitution.

Our patriots have been so intent upon

building up American rights that they have overlooked the rights of Great Britain and our own interest. Instead of proving that we are entitled to privileges that our fathers knew our situation would not admit us to enjoy, they have been arguing away our most essential rights. If there be any grievance, it does not consist in our being subject to the authority of Parliament but in our not having an actual representation in it. Were it possible for the colonies to have an equal representation in Parliament, and were [they] refused it upon proper application, I confess I should think it a grievance; but at present it seems to be allowed by all parties to be impracticable, considering the colonies are distant from Great Britain a thousand transmarine leagues. If that be the case, the right or privilege that we complain of being deprived of is not withheld by Britain, but the first principles of government and the immutable laws of nature render it impossible for us to enjoy it.

This is apparently the meaning of that celebrated passage in Governor Hutchinson's letter, that rang through the continent; viz., there must be an abridgment of what is called English liberties. He subjoins that he had never yet seen the projection whereby a colony, 3,000 miles from the parent state, might enjoy all the privileges of *that* parent state and be subject to it, or

in words to that effect. The obnoxious sentence, taken detached from the letter, appears very unfriendly to the colonies; but, considered in connection with the other parts of the letter, is but a necessary result from our situation.

Allegiance and protection are reciprocal. It is our highest interest to continue a part of the British Empire, and equally our duty to remain subject to the authority of Parliament. Our own internal police may generally be regulated by our provincial legislatures, but in national concerns, or where our own assemblies do not answer the ends of government with respect to ourselves, the ordinance or interposition of the great council of the nation is necessary. In this case, the major must rule the minor. After many more centuries shall have rolled away, long after we, who are now bustling upon the stage of life, shall have been received to the bosom of mother earth and our names are forgotten, the colonies may be so far increased as to have the balance of wealth, numbers, and power in their favor, the good of the Empire make it necessary to fix the seat of government here; and some future George, equally the friend of mankind with him that now sways the British scepter, may cross the Atlantic and rule Great Britain by an American Parliament.

70.

JOHN ADAMS: The Rule of Law and the Rule of Men

As a result of the resolutions of protest against the Stamp Act that he had written for the town of Braintree, Massachusetts, Adams was already identified by 1774 with the patriotic cause. He was therefore selected as a delegate to the First Continental Congress at Philadelphia in that year. Upon his return, he read the "Letters" by "Massachusettensis" [Daniel Leonard] in the Massachusetts Gazette, *arguing the Loyalist point of view. Though he did not then know who the author of the "Letters" was, Adams prepared letters of his own in reply, of which the following appeared in the same paper on February 6, 1775, under the pen name of "Novanglus." He had not yet come to believe in complete independence, as the letter shows. The remarks that he quotes in order to refute them are all those of "Massachusettensis."*

Source: C. F. Adams, IV: "Novanglus, No. VII."

AMERICA HAS ALL ALONG CONSENTED, still consents, and ever will consent that Parliament, being the most powerful legislature in the dominions, should regulate the trade of the dominions. This is founding the authority of Parliament to regulate our trade upon *compact* and *consent* of the colonies, not upon any principle of common or statute law; not upon any original principle of the English constitution; not upon the principle that Parliament is the supreme and sovereign legislature over them in all cases whatsoever. The question is not, therefore, whether the authority of Parliament extends to the colonies in any case, for it is admitted by the Whigs that it does in that of commerce, but whether it extends in all cases. . . .

If the English Parliament were to govern us, where did they get the right, without our consent, to take the Scottish Parliament into a participation of the government over us? When this was done, was the American share of the democracy of the constitution consulted? If not, were not the Americans deprived of the benefit of the democratical part of the constitution? And is not the de-

mocracy as essential to the English constitution as the monarchy or aristocracy? Should we have been more effectually deprived of the benefit of the British or English constitution if one or both houses of Parliament, or if our House and Council, had made this union with the two houses of Parliament in Scotland, without the King?

If a new constitution was to be formed for the whole British dominions, and a supreme legislature coextensive with it, upon the general principles of the English constitution, an equal mixture of monarchy, aristocracy, and democracy, let us see what would be necessary. England has 6,000,000 people, we will say; America had 3,000,000. England has 500 members in the House of Commons, we will say; America must have 250. Is it possible she should maintain them there, or could they at such a distance know the state, the sense, or exigencies of their constituents? Ireland, too, must be incorporated and send another hundred or two of members. . . .

Yet, without such a union, a legislature which shall be sovereign and supreme in all cases whatsoever and coextensive with the empire can never be established upon the general principles of the English constitution which Massachusettensis lays down, namely, an equal mixture of monarchy, aristocracy, and democracy. Nay, further, in order to comply with this principle, this new government, this mighty colossus, which is to bestride the narrow world, must have a House of Lords, consisting of Irish, East and West Indian, African, American, as well as English and Scottish noblemen; for the nobility ought to be scattered about all the dominions, as well as the representatives of the Commons.

If, in twenty years more, America should have 6,000,000 inhabitants, as there is a boundless territory to fill up, she must have 500 representatives. Upon these principles, if in forty years she should have 12,000,000 — 1,000; and if the inhabitants of the three kingdoms remain as they are, being already full of inhabitants, what will become of your supreme legislative? It will be translated, Crown and all, to America. This is a sublime system for America. It will flatter those ideas of independency which the Tories impute to them, if they have any such, more than any other plan of independency that I have ever heard projected. . . .

I agree that "two supreme and independent authorities cannot exist in the same state," any more than two supreme beings in one universe; and, therefore, I contend that our provincial legislatures are the only supreme authorities in our colonies. Parliament, notwithstanding this, may be allowed an authority supreme and sovereign over the ocean, which may be limited by the banks of the ocean or the bounds of our charters; our charters give us no authority over the high seas. Parliament has our consent to assume a jurisdiction over them. And here is a line fairly drawn between the rights of Britain and the rights of the colonies, namely, the banks of the ocean, or low watermark; the line of division between common law and civil or maritime law. If this is not sufficient — if Parliament are at

a loss for any principle of natural, civil, maritime, moral, or common law on which to ground any authority over the high seas, the Atlantic especially, let the colonies be treated like reasonable creatures, and they will discover great ingenuity and modesty. The acts of trade and navigation might be confirmed by provincial laws and carried into execution by our own courts and juries, and, in this case, illicit trade would be cut up by the roots forever.

I knew the smuggling Tories in New York and Boston would cry out against this, because it would not only destroy their profitable game of smuggling but their whole place and pension system. But the Whigs, that is, a vast majority of the whole continent, would not regard the smuggling Tories. In one word, if public principles and motives and arguments were alone to determine this dispute between the two countries, it might be settled forever in a few hours; but the everlasting clamors of prejudice, passion, and private interest drown every consideration of that sort and are precipitating us into a civil war.

"If, then, we are a part of the British empire, we must be subject to the supreme power of the state, which is vested in the estates in Parliament."

Here, again, we are to be conjured out of our senses by the magic in the words "British empire," and "supreme power of the state." But, however it may sound, I say we are not a part of the British empire; because the British government is not an empire. The governments of France, Spain, etc., are not empires but monarchies, supposed to be governed by fixed fundamental laws, though not really. The British government is still less entitled to the style of *an empire*. It is a limited monarchy.

If Aristotle, Livy, and Harrington knew what a republic was, the British constitution is much more like a republic than an empire. They define a republic to be a *government of laws*, and *not of men*. If this definition be just, the British constitution is nothing more nor less than a republic, in which the king is first magistrate. This office being hereditary, and being possessed of such ample and splendid prerogatives, is no objection to the government's being a republic, as long as it is bound by fixed laws, which the people have a voice in making, and a right to defend. An empire is a despotism, and an emperor a despot, bound by no law or limitation but his own will; it is a stretch of tyranny beyond absolute monarchy. For, although the will of an absolute monarch is law, yet his edicts must be registered by parliaments. Even this formality is not necessary in an empire. . . .

To say that we "must be" subject seems to betray a consciousness that we are not by any law or upon any principles but those of mere power; and an opinion that we ought to be, or that it is necessary that we should be. But if this should be admitted for argument's sake only, what is the consequence? The consequences that may fairly be drawn are these: that Britain has been imprudent enough to let colonies be planted until they are become numerous and important without ever having wisdom enough to concert a plan for their government consistent with her own welfare; that now it is necessary to make them submit to the authority of Parliament; and, because there is no principle of law or justice or reason by which she can effect it, therefore, she will resort to war and conquest — to the maxim, *delenda est Carthago.*

These are the consequences, according to this writer's idea. We think the consequences are, that she has, after 150 years, discovered a defect in her government, which ought to be supplied by some just and reasonable means, that is, by the consent of the colonies; for metaphysicians and politicians may dispute forever, but they will never find any other moral principle or foundation of rule or obedience than the consent of governors and governed. She has found out that the great machine will not

go any longer without a new wheel. She will make this herself. We think she is making it of such materials and workmanship as will tear the whole machine to pieces. We are willing, if she can convince us of the necessity of such a wheel, to assist with artists and materials in making it, so that it may answer the end. But she says we shall have no share in it; and, if we will not let her patch it up as she pleases, her Massachusettensis, and other advocates tell us, she will tear it to pieces herself by cutting our throats. To this kind of reasoning, we can only answer that we will not stand still to be butchered. We will defend our lives as long as Providence shall enable us. . . .

That the authority of Parliament "has been exercised almost ever since the first settlement of the country" is a mistake; for there is no instance, until the first Navigation Act, which was in 1660, more than forty years after the first settlement. This act was never executed nor regarded until seventeen years afterwards, and then it was not executed as an act of Parliament but as a law of the colony, to which the King agreed.

This "has been expressly acknowledged by our provincial legislatures." There is too much truth in this. It has been twice acknowledged by our House of Representatives, that Parliament was the supreme legislative; but this was directly repugnant to a multitude of other votes, by which it was denied. This was in conformity to the distinction between taxation and legislation, which has since been found to be a distinction without a difference.

When a great question is first started, there are very few, even of the greatest minds, which suddenly and intuitively comprehend it, in all its consequences.

It is both "our interest and our duty to continue subject to the authority of Parliament," as far as the regulation of our trade, if it will be content with that, but no longer.

"If the colonies are not subject to the authority of Parliament, Great Britain and the colonies must be distinct states, as completely so as England and Scotland were before the union, or as Great Britain and Hanover are now." There is no need of being startled at this consequence. It is very harmless. There is no absurdity at all in it. Distinct states may be united under one king. And those states may be further cemented and united together by a treaty of commerce. This is the case. We have, by our own express consent, contracted to observe the Navigation Act and, by our implied consent, by long usage and uninterrupted acquiescence, have submitted to the other acts of trade however grievous some of them may be. This may be compared to a treaty of commerce, by which those distinct states are cemented together, in perpetual league and amity. And if any further ratifications of this pact or treaty are necessary, the colonies would readily enter into them, provided their other liberties were inviolate. . . .

The only proposition in all this writer's long string of pretended absurdities, which he says follows from the position that we are distinct states, is this: That "as the king must govern each state by its parliament, those several parliaments would pursue the particular interest of its own state; and however well-disposed the king might be to pursue a line of interest that was common to all, the checks and control that he would meet with would render it impossible." Every argument ought to be allowed its full weight; and therefore candor obliges me to acknowledge that here lies all the difficulty that there is in this whole controversy. There has been, from first to last, on both sides of the Atlantic, an idea, an apprehension that it was necessary there should be some superintending power to draw together all the wills and unite all the strength of the subjects in all the dominions, in case of war and in the case of trade.

The necessity of this, in case of trade, has been so apparent that, as has often been said, we have consented that Parliament should exercise such a power. In case of war, it has by some been thought necessary. But, in fact and experience, it has not been found so. What though the proprietary colonies, on account of disputes with the proprietors, did not come in so early to the assistance of the general cause in the last war as they ought, and perhaps one of them not at all? The inconveniences of this were small in comparison of the absolute ruin to the liberties of all which must follow the submission to Parliament, in all cases, which would be giving up all the popular limitations upon the government.

These inconveniences fell chiefly upon New England. She was necessitated to greater exertions; but she had rather suffer these again and again than others infinitely greater. However, this subject has been so long in contemplation that it is fully understood now in all the colonies; so that there is no danger, in case of another war, of any colony's failing of its duty.

But, admitting the proposition in its full force, that it is absolutely necessary there should be a supreme power, coextensive with all the dominions, will it follow that Parliament, as now constituted, has a right to assume this supreme jurisdiction? By no means.

A union of the colonies might be projected, and an American legislature; for, if America has 3,000,000 people, and the whole dominions, 12,000,000, she ought to send a quarter part of all the members to the House of Commons; and, instead of holding parliaments always at Westminster, the haughty members for Great Britain must humble themselves, one session in four, to cross the Atlantic, and hold the Parliament in America.

There is no avoiding all inconveniences in human affairs. The greatest possible, or conceivable, would arise from ceding to Parliament power over us without a representation in it. The next greatest would accrue from any plan that can be devised for a representation there. The least of all would arise from going on as we began and fared well for 150 years, by letting Parliament regulate trade, and our own assemblies all other matters. . . .

That a representation in Parliament is impracticable, we all agree; but the consequence is that we must have a representation in our supreme legislatures here. This was the consequence that was drawn by kings, ministers, our ancestors, and the whole nation more than a century ago, when the colonies were first settled, and continued to be the general sense until the last peace; and it must be the general sense again soon, or Great Britain will lose her colonies.

71.

EDMUND BURKE: On Conciliation with America

"To reconcile British superiority with American liberty will be my great object,"
Edmund Burke told his constituents of Bristol in 1774, and this may be regarded as the
purpose of his famous Speech on Conciliation with America, *reprinted here in part, which*
was delivered to the House of Commons on March 22, 1775. The occasion was the
belated proposal by Lord North's ministry to exempt from taxation any colony that would
voluntarily undertake some of the expenses of civil and military rule. Because the
amounts of such expenditures were not specified and because at the moment the colonies
were under subjection by force, Burke thought this proposal ignominious — "a method of
ransom by auction." He believed that Parliament had the right to tax the colonies, but
that the right was not worth insisting upon at the cost of military suppression.

Source: Niles: "Edmund Burke, His Celebrated Speech Delivered in the
       House of Commons, on Moving his Resolution for Conciliation
       with the American Colonies."

TO RESTORE ORDER and repose to an empire so great and so distracted as ours, is, merely in the attempt, an undertaking that would ennoble the flights of the highest genius, and obtain pardon for the efforts of the meanest understanding. Struggling a good while with these thoughts, by degrees I felt myself more firm. I derived, at length, some confidence from what in other circumstances usually produces timidity. I grew less anxious, even from the idea of my own insignificance. For, judging of what you are by what you ought to be, I persuaded myself that you would not reject a reasonable proposition because it had nothing but its reason to recommend it. . . .

The proposition is peace. Not peace through the medium of war; not peace to be hunted through the labyrinth of intricate and endless negotiations; not peace to arise out of universal discord fomented from principle in all parts of the empire; not peace to depend on the juridical determination of perplexing questions, or the precise marking the shadowy boundaries of a complex government. It is simple peace, sought in its natural course, and in its ordinary haunts. It is peace sought in the spirit of peace, and laid in principles purely pacific. I propose, by removing the ground of the [difference] and by restoring the former unsuspecting [confidence] of the colonies in the mother country, to give permanent satisfaction to your people; and (far from a scheme of ruling by discord) to reconcile them to each other in the same act and by the bond of the very same interest which reconciles them to British government. . . .

The first thing we have to consider with regard to the nature of the object is the number of people in the colonies. I have taken for some years a good deal of pains on that point. I can by no calculation justify myself in placing the number below 2,000,000 inhabitants of our own European blood and color, besides at least 500,000 others, who form no inconsiderable part of the strength and opulence of the whole. . . . Whilst we spend our time in deliberating on the mode of governing 2,000,000, we shall find we have millions more to manage. Your children do not grow faster from infancy to manhood than they spread from families to communities, and from villages to nations. . . .

But the population of this country, the great and growing population, though a very important consideration, will lose much of its weight if not combined with other circumstances. The commerce of your colonies is out of all proportion beyond the numbers of the people. . . .

The export trade to the colonies consists of three great branches: the African, which, terminating almost wholly in the colonies, must be put to the account of their commerce; the West Indian; and the North American. All these are so interwoven that the attempt to separate them would tear to pieces the contexture of the whole; and, if not entirely destroy, would very much depreciate the value of all the parts. . . .

I pass . . . to the colonies in another point of view, their agriculture. This they have prosecuted with such a spirit that, besides feeding plentifully their own growing multitude, their annual export of grain, comprehending rice, has some years ago exceeded £1,000,000 in value. Of their last harvest I am persuaded they will export much more. At the beginning of the century some of these colonies imported corn from the mother country. For some time past the Old World has been fed from the New. . . .

As to the wealth which the colonies have drawn from the sea by their fisheries, you had all that matter fully opened at your bar. You surely thought those acquisitions of value, for they seemed even to excite your envy; and yet the spirit by which that enterprising employment has been exercised ought rather, in my opinion, to have raised your esteem and admiration. . . .

I am sensible, sir, that all which I have asserted in my detail is admitted in the gross, but that quite a different conclusion is drawn from it. America, gentlemen say, is a noble object. It is an object well worth fighting for. Certainly it is, if fighting a people be the best way of gaining them. Gentlemen in this respect will be led to their choice of means by their complexions and their habits. Those who understand the military art will of course have some predilection for it. Those who wield the thunder of the state may have more confidence in the efficacy of arms. But I confess, possibly for want of this knowledge, my opinion is much more in favor of prudent management than of force; considering force not as an odious but a feeble instrument for preserving a people so numerous, so active, so growing, so spirited as this in a profitable and subordinate connection with us.

First, sir, permit me to observe that the use of force alone is but temporary. It may subdue for a moment, but it does not remove the necessity of subduing again; and a nation is not governed which is perpetually to be conquered.

My next objection is its uncertainty. Terror is not always the effect of force, and an armament is not a victory. If you do not succeed, you are without resource; for, conciliation failing, force remains; but, force failing, no further hope of reconciliation is left. Power and authority are sometimes bought by kindness; but they can never be begged as alms by an impoverished and defeated violence.

A further objection to force is that you impair the object by your very endeavors to preserve it. The thing you fought for is not the thing which you recover; but depreciated, sunk, wasted, and consumed in the contest. Nothing less will content me than whole America. . . .

Lastly, we have no sort of experience in favor of force as an instrument in the rule of our colonies. Their growth and their utility has been owing to methods altogether different. Our ancient indulgence has been said to be pursued to a fault. It may be so. But we know, if feeling is evidence, that our fault was more tolerable than our attempt to mend it; and our sin far more salutary than our penitence.

These, sir, are my reasons for not entertaining that high opinion of untried force by which many gentlemen, for whose sentiments in other particulars I have great respect, seem to be so greatly captivated. But there is still behind a third consideration concerning this object which serves to determine my opinion on the sort of policy which ought to be pursued in the management of America, even more than its population and its commerce — I mean its temper and character.

In this character of the Americans, a love of freedom is the predominating feature which marks and distinguishes the whole; and as an ardent is always a jealous affection, your colonies become suspicious, restive, and untractable whenever they see the least attempt to wrest from them by force, or shuffle from them by chicane, what they

think the only advantage worth living for. This fierce spirit of liberty is stronger in the English colonies probably than in any other people of the earth, and this from a great variety of powerful causes; which, to understand the true temper of their minds and the directions which this spirit takes, it will not be amiss to lay open somewhat more largely.

First, the people of the colonies are descendants of Englishmen. England, sir, is a nation which still, I hope, respects, and formerly adored, her freedom. The colonists emigrated from you when this part of your character was most predominant; and they took this bias and direction the moment they parted from your hands. They are therefore not only devoted to liberty, but to liberty according to English ideas, and on English principles. Abstract liberty, like other mere abstractions, is not to be found. Liberty inheres in some sensible object; and every nation has formed to itself some favorite point which by way of eminence becomes the criterion of their happiness. It happened, you know, sir, that the great contests for freedom in this country were from the earliest times chiefly upon the question of taxing. Most of the contests in the ancient commonwealths turned primarily on the right of election of magistrates, or on the balance among the several orders of the state. The question of money was not with them so immediate.

But in England it was otherwise. On this point of taxes the ablest pens and most eloquent tongues have been exercised; the greatest spirits have acted and suffered. In order to give the fullest satisfaction concerning the importance of this point, it was not only necessary for those who in argument defended the excellence of the English constitution to insist on this privilege of granting money as a dry point of fact, and to prove that the right had been acknowledged in ancient parchments and blind usages to reside in a certain body called a House of

Commons. They went much further; they attempted to prove, and they succeeded, that in theory it ought to be so, from the particular nature of a House of Commons as an immediate representative of the people, whether the old records had delivered this oracle or not. They took infinite pains to calculate, as a fundamental principle, that in all monarchies the people must in effect themselves, mediately or immediately, possess the power of granting their own money, or no shadow of liberty could subsist.

The colonies draw from you, as with their lifeblood, these ideas and principles. Their love of liberty, as with you, fixed and attached on this specific point of taxing. Liberty might be safe or might be endangered in twenty other particulars without their being much pleased or alarmed. Here they felt its pulse; and as they found that beat, they thought themselves sick or sound. I do not say whether they were right or wrong in applying your general arguments to their own case. It is not easy, indeed, to make a monopoly of theorems and corollaries. The fact is that they did thus apply those general arguments; and your mode of governing them, whether through lenity or indolence, through wisdom or mistake, confirmed them in the imagination that they, as well as you, had an interest in these common principles.

They were further confirmed in this pleasing error by the form of their provincial legislative assemblies. Their governments are popular in a high degree; some are merely popular; in all, the popular representative is the most weighty; and this share of the people in their ordinary government never fails to inspire them with lofty sentiments, and with a strong aversion from whatever tends to deprive them of their chief importance.

If anything were wanting to this necessary operation of the form of government, religion would have given it a complete effect. Religion, always a principle of energy, in this new people is no way worn out or impaired; and their mode of professing it is also one main cause of this free spirit. The people are Protestants; and of that kind which is the most adverse to all implicit submission of mind and opinion. This is a persuasion not only favorable to liberty, but built upon it. I do not think, sir, that the reason of this averseness in the dissenting churches from all that looks like absolute government is so much to be sought in their religious tenets as in their history. . . .

All Protestantism, even the most cold and passive, is a sort of dissent. But the religion most prevalent in our northern colonies is a refinement on the principle of resistance; it is the dissidence of dissent, and the protestantism of the Protestant religion. This religion, under a variety of denominations agreeing in nothing but in the communion of the spirit of liberty, is predominant in most of the northern provinces, where the Church of England, notwithstanding its legal rights, is in reality no more than a sort of private sect, not composing most probably the tenth of the people. . . .

Sir, I can perceive by their manner that some gentlemen object to the latitude of this description, because in the southern colonies the Church of England forms a large body, and has a regular establishment. It is certainly true. There is, however, a circumstance attending these colonies which, in my opinion, fully counterbalances this difference, and makes the spirit of liberty still more high and haughty than in those to the northward. It is that in Virginia and the Carolinas they have a vast multitude of slaves. Where this is the case in any part of the world, those who are free are by far the most proud and jealous of their freedom. Freedom is to them not only an enjoyment but a kind of rank and privilege. Not seeing there that freedom, as in countries where it is a common blessing and as broad and general as the air, may be united with much abject toil, with great misery, with all the exterior of servitude; liberty looks, amongst them, like something that is more noble and liberal. I do not mean, sir, to commend the superior morality of this sentiment, which has at least as much pride as virtue in it; but I cannot alter the nature of man. The fact is so; and these people of the southern colonies are much more strongly, and with a higher and more stubborn spirit, attached to liberty than those of the northward. . . .

Permit me, sir, to add another circumstance in our colonies which contributes no mean part toward the growth and effect of this untractable spirit. I mean their education. In no country perhaps in the world is the law so general a study. The profession itself is numerous and powerful; and in most provinces it takes the lead. The greater number of the deputies sent to the Congress were lawyers. But all who read, and most do read, endeavor to obtain some smattering in that science. I have been told by an eminent bookseller that in no branch of his business, after tracts of popular devotion, were so many books as those on the law exported to the plantations. The colonists have now fallen into the way of printing them for their own use. I hear that they have sold nearly as many of Blackstone's *Commentaries* in America as in England. General Gage marks out this disposition very particularly in a letter on your table. He states that all the people in his government are lawyers, or smatterers in law; and that in Boston they have been enabled, by successful chicane, wholly to evade many parts of one of your capital penal constitutions. The smartness of debate will say that this knowledge ought to teach them more clearly the rights of legislature, their obligations to obedience, and the penalties of rebellion. . . . This study renders men acute, inquisitive, dexterous, prompt in attack, ready in defense, full of resources. In other countries, the people, more simple and of a less mercurial cast, judge of an ill principle in government only by an actual grievance; here they anticipate the evil, and judge of the pressure of the grievance by the badness of the principle. They augur misgovernment at a distance, and snuff the approach of tyranny in every tainted breeze.

The last cause of this disobedient spirit in the colonies is hardly less powerful than the rest, as it is not merely moral but laid deep in the natural constitution of things. Three thousand miles of ocean lie between you and them. No contrivance can prevent the effect of this distance in weakening government. . . .

Then, sir, from these six capital sources — of descent, of form of government, of religion in the northern provinces, of manners in the southern, of education, of the remoteness of situation from the first mover of government — from all these causes a fierce spirit of liberty has grown up. It has grown with the growth of the people in your colonies, and increased with the increase of their wealth; a spirit that unhappily meeting with an exercise of power in England which, however lawful, is not reconcilable to any ideas of liberty, much less with theirs, has kindled this flame that is ready to consume us. . . .

Until very lately all authority in America seemed to be nothing but an emanation from yours. Even the popular part of the colony constitution derived all its activity and its first vital movement from the pleasure of the Crown. We thought, sir, that the utmost which the discontented colonists could do was to disturb authority; we never dreamed they could of themselves supply it — knowing in general what an operose business it is to establish a government absolutely new. But having for our purposes in this contention resolved that none but an obedient assembly should sit, the humors of the people there, finding all passage through the legal channel stopped, with great violence broke out another way. Some provinces have tried their experiment, as we have tried ours; and theirs has succeeded. They have formed a government sufficient for its purposes without the bustle of a revolution or the troublesome formality of an election. Evident necessity and tacit consent have done the business in an instant.

So well they have done it that Lord Dunmore — the account is among the fragments on your table — tells you that the new institution is infinitely better obeyed than the ancient government ever was in its most fortunate periods. Obedience is what makes government, and not the names by which it is called; not the name of governor, as formerly, or committee, as at present. This new government has originated directly from the people, and was not transmitted through any of the ordinary artificial media of a positive constitution. It was not a manufacture ready formed and transmitted to them in that condition from England. The evil arising from hence is this: that the colonists having once found the possibility of enjoying the advantages of order in the midst of a struggle for liberty, such struggles will not henceforward seem so terrible to the settled and sober part of mankind as they had appeared before the trial. . . .

As the growing population in the colonies is evidently one cause of their resistance, it was last session mentioned in both houses by men of weight, and received not without applause, that in order to check this evil it would be proper for the Crown to make no further grants of land. But to this scheme there are two objections. The first, that there is already so much unsettled land in private hands as to afford room for an immense future population, although the Crown not only withheld its grants, but annihilated its soil. If this be the case, then the only effect of this avarice of desolation, this hoarding of a royal wilderness, would be to raise the value of the possessions in the hands of the great private monopolists,

without any adequate check to the growing and alarming mischief of population.

But if you stopped your grants, what would be the consequence? The people would occupy without grants. They have already so occupied in many places. You cannot station garrisons in every part of these deserts. If you drive the people from one place, they will carry on their annual tillage, and remove with their flocks and herds to another. Many of the people in the back settlements are already little attached to particular situations. Already they have topped the Appalachian Mountains. From thence they behold before them an immense plain, one vast, rich, level meadow; a square of 500 miles. Over this they would wander without a possibility of restraint; they would change their manners with the habits of their life; they would soon forget a government by which they were disowned; would become hordes of English Tartars and, pouring down upon your unfortified frontiers a fierce and irresistible cavalry, become masters of your governors and your counselors, your collectors and comptrollers, and of all the slaves that adhered to them. . . . .

Adhering, sir, as I do, to this policy, as well as for the reasons I have just given, I think this new project of hedging in population to be neither prudent nor practicable.

To impoverish the colonies in general, and in particular to arrest the noble course of their marine enterprises, would be a more easy task. I freely confess it. We have shown a disposition to a system of this kind, a disposition even to continue the restraint after the offense, looking on ourselves as rivals to our colonies, and persuaded that of course we must gain all that they shall lose. Much mischief we may certainly do. The power inadequate to all other things is often more than sufficient for this. I do not look on the direct and immediate power of the colonies to resist our violence as very formidable. In this, however, I may be mistaken. But when I consider that we have colonies for no purpose but to be serviceable to us, it seems to my poor understanding a little preposterous to make them unserviceable in order to keep them obedient. . . .

I think it is nearly as little in our power to change their republican religion as their free descent; or to substitute the Roman Catholic as a penalty, or the Church of England as an improvement. . . .

If, then, the removal of the causes of this spirit of American liberty be for the greater part, or rather entirely, impracticable; if the ideas of criminal process be inapplicable — or, if applicable, are in the highest degree inexpedient — what way yet remains? No way is open but the third and last — to comply with the American spirit as necessary; or, if you please, to submit to it as a necessary evil.

If we adopt this mode — if we mean to conciliate and concede — let us see of what nature the concession ought to be. To ascertain the nature of our concession, we must look at their complaint. The colonies complain that they have not the characteristic mark and seal of British freedom. They complain that they are taxed in a Parliament in which they are not represented. If you mean to satisfy them at all, you must satisfy them with regard to this complaint. If you mean to please any people, you must give them the boon which they ask; not what you may think better for them, but of a kind totally different. Such an act may be a wise regulation, but it is no concession; whereas our present theme is the mode of giving satisfaction. . . .

My idea, therefore, without considering whether we yield it as a matter of right or grant as matter of favor, is to admit the people of our colonies into an interest in the constitution; and, by recording that admission in the journals of Parliament, to give them as strong an assurance as the nature of the thing will admit that we mean

forever to adhere to that solemn declaration of systematic indulgence. . . .

One fact is clear and indisputable. The public and avowed origin of this quarrel was on taxation. This quarrel has indeed brought on new disputes on new questions; but certainly the least bitter, and the fewest of all, on the trade laws. To judge which of the two be the real radical cause of quarrel, we have to see whether the commercial dispute did, in order of time, precede the dispute on taxation. There is not a shadow of evidence for it. Next, to enable us to judge whether at this moment a dislike to the trade laws be the real cause of quarrel, it is absolutely necessary to put the taxes out of the question by a repeal. See how the Americans act in this position, and then you will be able to discern correctly what is the true object of the controversy, or whether any controversy at all will remain. Unless you consent to remove this cause of difference, it is impossible, with decency, to assert that the dispute is not upon what it is avowed to be. And I would, sir, recommend to your serious consideration whether it be prudent to form a rule for punishing people, not on their own acts, but on your conjectures. Surely it is preposterous at the very best. It is not justifying your anger by their misconduct, but it is converting your ill will into their delinquency.

But the colonies will go further. Alas! Alas! when will this speculation against fact and reason end? What will quiet these panic fears which we entertain of the hostile effect of a conciliatory conduct? Is it true that no case can exist in which it is proper for a sovereign to accede to the desires of his discontented subjects? Is there anything peculiar in this case to make a rule for itself? Is all authority of course lost when it is not pushed to the extreme? Is it a certain maxim that the fewer causes of dissatisfaction are left by government, the more the subject will be inclined to resist and rebel? . . .

You will now, sir, perhaps imagine that I am on the point of proposing to you a scheme for a representation of the colonies in Parliament. Perhaps I might be inclined to entertain some such thought; but a great flood stops me in my course. *Opposuit natura* [Nature opposed], I cannot remove the eternal barriers of the creation. The thing, in that mode, I do not know to be possible. As I meddle with no theory, I do not absolutely assert the impracticability of such a representation; but I do not see my way to it, and those who have been more confident have not been more successful. However, the arm of public benevolence is not shortened, and there are often several means to the same end. What nature has disjoined in one way, wisdom may unite in another. When we cannot give the benefit as we would wish, let us not refuse it altogether. If we cannot give the principal, let us find a substitute. But how? Where? What substitute? . . .

My resolutions, therefore, mean to establish the equity and justice of a taxation of America by grant, and not by imposition; to mark the legal competency of the colony assemblies for the support of their government in peace, and for public aids in time of war; to acknowledge that this legal competency has had a dutiful and beneficial exercise; and that experience has shown the benefit of their grants, and the futility of parliamentary taxation as a method of supply. . . .

The first is a resolution:

That the colonies and plantations of Great Britain in North America, consisting of fourteen separate governments, and containing 2,000,000 and upward of free inhabitants, have not had the liberty and privilege of electing and sending any knights and burgesses, or others, to represent them in the high court of Parliament. . . .

The second is like unto the first:

That the said colonies and plantations have been liable to, and bounden by, several subsidies, payments, rates, and taxes given and granted by Parliament, though the said colonies and plantations have not their knights and burgesses in the said high court of Parliament, of their own election, to represent the condition of their country; by lack whereof they have been oftentimes touched and grieved by subsidies given, granted, and assented to in the said court, in a manner prejudicial to the Commonwealth, quietness, rest, and peace of the subjects inhabiting within the same. . . .

The next proposition is:

That, from the distance of the said colonies, and from other circumstances, no method has hitherto been devised for procuring a representation in Parliament for the said colonies. . . .

The fourth resolution is:

That each of the said colonies has within itself a body chosen in part or in the whole by the freemen, freeholders, or other free inhabitants thereof, commonly called the General Assembly or General Court, with powers legally to raise, levy, and assess, according to the several usage of such colonies, duties and taxes toward defraying all sorts of public services. . . .

The fifth resolution is also a resolution of fact:

That the said general assemblies, general courts, or other bodies legally qualified as aforesaid, have at sundry times freely granted several large subsidies and public aids for His Majesty's service, according to their abilities, when required thereto by letter from one of His Majesty's principal secretaries of state; and that their right to grant the same, and their cheerfulness and sufficiency in the said grants, have been at sundry times acknowledged by Parliament. . . .

That it has been found by experience that the manner of granting the said supplies and aids, by the said general assemblies, has been more agreeable to the said colonies, and more beneficial and conducive to the public service, than the mode of giving and granting aids in Parliament, to be raised and paid in the said colonies.

This makes the whole of the fundamental part of the plan. The conclusion is irresistible. You cannot say that you were driven by any necessity to an exercise of the utmost rights of legislature. You cannot assert that you took on yourselves the task of imposing colony taxes from the want of another legal body that is competent to the purpose of supplying the exigencies of the state without wounding the prejudices of the people. Neither is it true that the body so qualified, and having that competence, had neglected the duty. . . .

The Americans will have no interest contrary to the grandeur and glory of England, when they are not oppressed by the weight of it; and they will rather be inclined to respect the acts of a superintending legislature when they see them the acts of that power which is itself the security, not the rival, of their secondary importance. In this assurance my mind most perfectly acquiesces, and I confess I feel not the least alarm from the discontents which are to arise from putting people at their ease, nor do I apprehend the destruction of this empire from giving, by an act of free grace and indulgence, to 2,000,000 of my fellow citizens some share of those rights upon which I have always been taught to value myself. . . .

All this, I know well enough, will sound wild and chimerical to the profane herd of those vulgar and mechanical politicians who have no place among us; a sort of people who think that nothing exists but what is gross and material, and who, therefore, far from being qualified to be directors of the great movement of empire, are not fit to turn a wheel in the machine. But to men truly initiated and rightly taught, these ruling and master principles which, in the opinion of such men as I have mentioned, have no substantial existence, are in truth everything, and all in all. Magnanimity in politics is not seldom the truest wisdom; and a great empire and little minds go ill together. If we are conscious of our situation, and glow with zeal to fill our places as becomes our station and ourselves, we ought to auspicate all our public proceedings on America with the old warning of the church, *Sursum corda* [Lift up your hearts!]. We ought to elevate our minds to the greatness of that trust to which the order of Providence has called us. By adverting to the dignity of this high calling our ancestors have turned a savage wilderness into a glorious empire, and have made the most extensive and the only honorable conquests — not by destroying but by promoting the wealth, the number, the happiness of the human race. Let us get an American revenue as we have got an American empire. English privileges have made it all that it is; English privileges alone will make it all it can be.

When we assumed the soldier, we did not lay aside the citizen.
    GEORGE WASHINGTON, address to the provincial Congress of New York, June 26, 1775; inscribed in the Memorial Amphitheater, Arlington Cemetery

72.

Patrick Henry: Give Me Liberty or Give Me Death

Like Samuel Adams, his counterpart in Massachusetts, Patrick Henry dominated the assembly of his province for ten years before independence was declared. Repeatedly, he overcame the doubts of more cautious leaders — the Randolphs, Pendletons, Harrisons, Carys, and Braxtons — with an eloquence that made him a legend. Unhappily, some of his best speeches were never taken down but survive only as they were remembered. This is the case with what was perhaps the greatest of them, his address on March 23, 1775, to the convention that gathered at Richmond after Lord Dunmore suspended the Virginia Assembly. The speech is best known in the reconstruction, reprinted here, by Henry's early biographer, William Wirt, originally published in 1817. Its last paragraph is among the two or three most famous perorations in American history.

Source: William Wirt, *The Life and Character of Patrick Henry*, Philadelphia, n.d., pp. 137-142.

Mr. Henry was fitted to raise the whirlwind, as well as to ride in and direct it. His was that comprehensive view, that unerring prescience, that perfect command over the actions of men, which qualified him not merely to guide but almost to create the destinies of nations.

He rose at this time with a majesty unusual to him in an exordium, and with all that self-possession by which he was so invariably distinguished. No man, he said, thought more highly than he did of the patriotism, as well as abilities, of the very worthy gentlemen who had just addressed the House. But different men often saw the same subject in different lights; and, therefore, he hoped it would not be thought disrespectful to those gentlemen if, entertaining as he did opinions of a character very opposite to theirs, he should speak forth *his* sentiments freely and without reserve. This, he said, was no time for ceremony. The question before this House was one of awful moment to the country. For his own part, he considered it as nothing less than a question of freedom or slavery. And, in proportion to the magnitude of the subject, ought to be the freedom of the debate. It was only in this way that they could hope to arrive at truth, and fulfill the great responsibility which they held to God and their country. Should he keep back his opinions at such a time through fear of giving offense, he should consider himself as guilty of treason toward his country and of an act of disloyalty toward the Majesty of Heaven, which he revered above all earthly kings.

"Mr. President," said he, "it is natural to man to indulge in the illusions of hope. We are apt to shut our eyes against a painful truth and listen to the song of that siren, till she transforms us into beasts. Is this," he asked, "the part of wise men, engaged in a great and arduous struggle for liberty?" Were we disposed to be of the number of those, who having eyes, see not, and having ears, hear not, the things which so nearly concern their temporal salvation? For his part, whatever anguish of spirit it might cost, *he* was willing to know the whole truth; to know the worst, and to provide for it.

He had, he said, but one lamp by which his feet were guided; and that was the lamp of experience. He knew of no way of judging of the future but by the past. And judging by the past, he wished to know what there had been in the conduct of the British Ministry for the last ten years to justify those hopes with which gentlemen had been pleased to solace themselves and the House?

Is it that insidious smile with which our petition has been lately received? Trust it not, sir; it will prove a snare to your feet. Suffer not yourselves to be betrayed with a kiss. Ask yourselves how this gracious reception of our petition comports with those warlike preparations which cover our waters and darken our land. Are fleets and armies necessary to a work of love and reconciliation? Have we shown ourselves so unwilling to be reconciled that force must be called in to win back our love? Let us not deceive ourselves, sir. These are the implements of war and subjugation — the last arguments to which kings resort. I ask gentlemen, sir, what means this martial array, if its purpose be not to force us to submission? Can gentlemen assign any other possible motive for it? Has Great Britain any enemy in this quarter of the world to call for all this accumulation of navies and armies? No, sir, she has none. They are meant for us; they can be meant for no other. They are sent over to bind and rivet upon us those chains which the British Ministry have been so long forging.

And what have we oppose to them? Shall we try argument? Sir, we have been trying that for the last ten years. Have we anything new to offer upon the subject? Nothing. We have held the subject up in every light of which it is capable; but it has been all in vain. Shall we resort to entreaty and humble supplication? What terms shall we find which have not been already exhausted? Let us not, I beseech you, sir, deceive ourselves longer. Sir, we have done everything that could be done to avert the storm which is now coming on. We have petitioned; we have remonstrated; we have supplicated; we have prostrated ourselves before the throne and have implored its interposition to arrest the tyrannical hands of the Ministry and Parliament. Our petitions have been slighted; our remonstrances have produced additional violence and insult; our supplications have been disregarded; and we have been spurned, with contempt, from the foot of the throne. In vain, after these things, may we indulge the fond hope of peace and reconciliation.

There is no longer any room for hope. If we wish to be free; if we mean to preserve inviolate those inestimable privileges for which we have been so long contending; if we mean not basely to abandon the noble struggle in which we have been so long engaged, and which we have pledged ourselves never to abandon, until the glorious object of our contest shall be obtained; we must fight! I repeat it, sir, we must fight!! An appeal to arms and to the God of hosts is all that is left us!

They tell us, sir . . . that we are weak, unable to cope with so formidable an adversary. But when shall we be stronger. Will it be the next week or the next year? Will it be when we are totally disarmed, and when a British guard shall be stationed in every house? Shall we gather strength by irresolution and inaction? Shall we acquire the means of effectual resistance by lying supinely on our backs and hugging the delusive phantom of hope, until our enemies shall have bound us hand and foot? Sir, we are not weak if we make a proper use of those means which the God of nature has placed in our power. Three millions of people armed in the holy cause of liberty and in such a country as that which we possess are invincible by any force which our enemy can send against us.

Besides, sir, we shall not fight our battles alone. There is a just God who presides over the destinies of nations, and who will raise up friends to fight our battles for us. The battle, sir, is not to the strong alone; it is to the vigilant, the active, the brave. Besides, sir, we have no election. If we were base enough to desire it, it is now too late to retire from the contest. There is no retreat but in submission and slavery! Our chains are forged. Their clanking may be heard on the plains of Boston! The war is inevitable — and let it come!! I repeat it, sir, let it come!!!

It is vain, sir, to extenuate the matter. Gentlemen may cry, peace, peace; but there is no peace. The war is actually begun! The next gale that sweeps from the north will bring to our ears the clash of resounding arms! Our brethren are already in the field! Why stand we here idle? What is it that gentlemen wish?

What would they have? Is life so dear or peace so sweet as to be purchased at the price of chains and slavery?

"Forbid it, Almighty God — I know not what course others may take; but as for me," cried he, with both his arms extended aloft, his brows knit, every feature marked with the resolute purpose of his soul, and his voice swelled to its boldest note of exclamation — "give me liberty, or give me death!"

He took his seat. No murmur of applause was heard. The effect was too deep. After the trance of a moment, several members started from their seats. The cry, "To arms!" seemed to quiver on every lip and gleam from every eye.

73.

Preamble to the Massachusetts Articles of War

In February of 1775, a second Massachusetts provincial congress met to prepare for war. It directed the appointed generals to oppose the British by force, if necessary. Directions were also given to gather such military stores as could be procured. On April 5, the congress adopted fifty-three articles of war, to which the following preamble was affixed.

Source: *The Journals of Each Provincial Congress of Massachusetts in 1774 and 1775, etc., etc.,* Boston, 1838, pp. 120-121.

Whereas the lust of power, which of old oppressed, persecuted, and exiled our pious and virtuous ancestors from their fair possessions in Britain, now pursues with tenfold severity us, their guiltless children, who are unjustly and wickedly charged with licentiousness, sedition, treason, and rebellion, and being deeply impressed with a sense of the almost incredible fatigues and hardships our venerable progenitors encountered, who fled from oppression for the sake of civil and religious liberty for themselves and their offspring, and began a settlement here on bare creation, at their own expense; and having seriously considered the duty we owe to God, to the memory of such invincible worthies, to the King, to Great Britain, our country, ourselves, and posterity, do think it our indispensable duty, by all lawful ways and means in our power, to recover, maintain, defend, and preserve the free exercise of all those civil and religious rights and liberties for which many of our forefathers fought, bled, and died, and to hand them down entire for the free enjoyment of the latest posterity;

And whereas the keeping a standing army in any of these colonies in times of peace, without the consent of the legislature of that colony in which such army is kept is against law; *and whereas* such an army with a large naval force is now placed in the town and harbor of Boston for the purpose of subjecting us to the power of the British Parliament; *and whereas* we are frequently told by the tools of administration, dupes to ministerial usurpation, that Great Britain will not, in any degree, relax in her measures until we acknowledge her "right of making laws binding upon us in all cases whatever"; and that if we refuse by our denial of her claim, the dispute must be decided by arms, in which, it is said by our enemies, "we shall have no chance, being undisciplined, cowards, disobedient, impatient of command, and possessed of that spirit of leveling which admits of no order, subordination, rule, or government"; *and whereas,* from the ministerial army and fleet now at Boston, the large reenforcement of troops expected, the late circular letters to the governors upon the continent, the general tenor of intelligence from Great Britain, and the hostile preparations making here, as also from the threats and repeated insults of our

enemies in the capital town, we have reason to apprehend that the sudden destruction of this province is in contemplation, if not determined upon;

And whereas the great law of self-preservation may suddenly require our raising and keeping an army of observation and defense in order to prevent or repel any further attempts to enforce the late cruel and oppressive acts of the British Parliament, which are evidently designed to subject us and the whole continent to the most ignominious slavery; *and whereas* in case of raising and keeping such an army it will be necessary that the officers and soldiers in the same be fully acquainted with their duty, and that the articles, rules, and regulations thereof be made as plain as possible; and having great confidence in the honor and public virtue of the inhabitants of this colony that they will readily obey the officers chosen by themselves, and will cheerfully do their duty when known, without any such severe articles and rules (except in capital cases), and cruel punishments as are usually practised in standing armies; and will submit to all such rules and regulations as are founded in reason, honor, and virtue — :

It is therefore resolved, that the following articles, rules, and regulations for the army that may be raised for the defense and security of our lives, liberties, and estates be, and hereby are, earnestly recommended to be strictly adhered to by all officers, soldiers, and others concerned, as they regard their own honor and the public good.

———◆———

Stand your ground. Don't fire unless fired upon, but if they mean to have a war let it begin here.

CAPTAIN JOHN PARKER, to his Minute Men on Lexington Green, April 19, 1775

74.

Joseph Warren: The Battles of Lexington and Concord

At the battles of Lexington and Concord, "the shot heard 'round the world" began the bloody clash that would bring on independence. Certainly the political effect of these battles was more significant than the military outcome. American public opinion everywhere was aroused in support of the revolutionary cause. British and American accounts varied greatly in their descriptions of what happened. This account, written on April 26, 1775, by Joseph Warren, president of the Massachusetts Provincial Congress, presents the American version of the event.

Source: Niles: "Address of Provincial Congress of Massachusetts, to the Inhabitants of Great Britain."

Friends and Fellow Subjects:

Hostilities are at length commenced in this colony by the troops under the command of General Gage, and it being of the greatest importance, that an early, true, and authentic account of this inhuman proceeding should be known to you, the Congress of this colony have transmitted the same, and from want of a session of the honorable Continental Congress, think it proper to address you on the alarming occasion.

By the clearest depositions relative to this transaction, it will appear that on the night preceding the 19th of April instant, a body of the King's troops, under the command of Colonel Smith, were secretly landed at Cambridge, with an apparent design to take or destroy the military and other stores provided for the defense of this colony, and deposited at Concord; that some inhabitants of the colony, on the night aforesaid, whilst traveling peaceably on the road between Boston and Concord were seized and greatly abused by armed men, who appeared to be officers of General Gage's army; that the town of Lexington, by these means, was alarmed, and a company of the inhabitants mustered on the occasion; that the regular troops on their way to Concord marched into the said town of Lexington, and the said company, on their approach, began to disperse; that, notwithstanding this, the regulars rushed on with great violence and first began hostilities by firing on said Lexington company, whereby they killed eight, and wounded several others; that the regulars continued their fire, until those of said company, who were neither killed nor wounded, had made their escape; and that Colonel Smith, with the detachment, then marched to Concord, where a number of provincials were again fired on by the troops, two of them killed and several wounded before the provincials fired on them, and that these hostile measures of the troops, produced an engagement that lasted through the day, in which many of the provincials and more of the regular troops were killed and wounded.

To give a particular account of the ravages of the troops as they retreated from Concord to Charlestown would be very difficult, if not impracticable. Let it suffice to say that a great number of the houses on the road were plundered and rendered unfit for use, several were burned, women in childbed were driven by the soldiery naked into the streets, old men peaceably in their houses were shot dead, and such scenes exhibited as would disgrace the annals of the most uncivilized nation.

These, brethren, are marks of ministerial vengeance against this colony for refusing, with her sister colonies, a submission to slavery; but they have not yet detached us from our royal sovereign. We profess to be his loyal and dutiful subjects, and, so hardly dealt with as we have been, are still ready, without lives and fortunes, to defend his person, family, Crown, and dignity. Nevertheless, to the persecution and tyranny of his cruel Ministry we will not tamely submit — appealing to Heaven for the justice of our cause, we determine to die or be free.

We cannot think that the honor, wisdom, and valor of Britons will suffer them to be longer inactive spectators of measures in which they themselves are so deeply interested — measures pursued in opposition to the solemn protests of many noble lords and expressed sense of conspicuous commoners whose knowledge and virtue have long characterized them as some of the greatest men in the nation; measures executed contrary to the interest, petitions, and resolves of many large, respectable, and opulent counties, cities, and boroughs in Great Britain; measures highly incompatible with justice, but still pursued with a specious pretense of easing the nation of its burdens; measures which, if successful, must end in the ruin and slavery of Britain, as well as the persecuted American colonies.

We sincerely hope that the Great Sovereign of the universe, who has so often appeared for the English nation, will support you in every rational and manly exertion with these colonies for saving it from ruin, and that, in a constitutional connection with the mother country, we shall soon be altogether a free and happy people.

Two views of the battles of Lexington and Concord: (left) the first encounter between rebels and British regulars on the Lexington Green; (below) the battle at Concord Bridge. Engravings by Amos Doolittle from sketches by Ralph Earl

75.

An Appeal to Canada

During the early years of the war, Americans had the impression that the Canadians wished to join the American Union. On May 29, 1775, the Second Continental Congress sent an appeal for cooperation, drafted by John Jay, to the inhabitants of Canada. With Canada in the Union, Britain would have been deprived of a northern base of attack. However, military expeditions in 1775, culminating in Benedict Arnold's unsuccessful assault on Quebec, failed to win Canada for the colonies.

Source: *Journals*, I: "Monday, May 29, 1775."

Friends and Countrymen,

Alarmed by the designs of an arbitrary Ministry to extirpate the rights and liberties of all America, a sense of common danger conspired with the dictates of humanity in urging us to call your attention, by our late address, to this very important object.

Since the conclusion of the late war, we have been happy in considering you as fellow subjects, and from the commencement of the present plan for subjugating the continent, we have viewed you as fellow sufferers with us. As we were both entitled by the bounty of an indulgent Creator to freedom, and being both devoted by the cruel edicts of a despotic administration, to common ruin, we perceived the fate of the Protestant and Catholic colonies to be strongly linked together; and therefore invited you to join with us in resolving to be free, and in rejecting, with disdain, the fetters of slavery, however artfully polished.

We most sincerely condole with you on the arrival of that day, in the course of which the sun could not shine on a single freeman in all your extensive dominion. Be assured that your unmerited degradation has engaged the most unfeigned pity of your sister colonies; and we flatter ourselves you will not, by tamely bearing the yoke, suffer that pity to be supplanted by contempt.

When hardy attempts are made to deprive men of rights bestowed by the Almighty, when avenues are cut through the most solemn compacts for the admission of despotism, when the plighted faith of government ceases to give security to dutiful subjects, and when the insidious stratagems and maneuvers of peace become more terrible than the sanguinary operations of war, it is high time for them to assert those rights, and, with honest indignation, oppose the torrent of oppression rushing in upon them.

By the introduction of your present form of government, or rather present form of tyranny, you and your wives and your children are made slaves. You have nothing that you can call your own, and all the fruits of your labor and industry may be taken from you whenever an avaricious governor and a rapacious council may incline to demand them. You are liable by their edicts to be transported into foreign countries to fight battles in which you have no interest, and to spill your blood in conflicts from which neither honor nor emolument can be derived.

Nay, the enjoyment of your very religion, in the present system, depends on a legislature in which you have no share and over which you have no control; and your priests are exposed to expulsion, banishment, and ruin whenever their wealth and possessions furnish sufficient temptation. They cannot be sure that a virtuous prince will always fill the throne; and should a wicked or a careless king concur with a wicked Ministry in extracting the treasure and strength of your country, it is impossible to conceive to what variety and to what extremes of wretchedness you may, under the present establishment, be reduced.

We are informed you have already been called upon to waste your lives in a contest with us. Should you, by complying in this instance, assent to your new establishment, and a war break out with France, your wealth and your sons may be sent to perish in expeditions against their islands in the West Indies.

It cannot be presumed that these considerations will have no weight with you, or that you are so lost to all sense of honor. We can never believe that the present race of Canadians are so degenerated as to possess neither the spirit, the gallantry, nor the courage of their ancestors. You certainly will not permit the infamy and disgrace of such pusillanimity to rest on your own heads and the consequences of it on your children, forever.

We, for our parts, are determined to live free, or not at all; and are resolved that posterity shall never reproach us with having brought slaves into the world.

Permit us again to repeat that we are your friends, not your enemies, and be not imposed upon by those who may endeavor to create animosities. The taking of the fort and military stores at Ticonderoga and Crown Point and the armed vessels on the lake was dictated by the great law of self-preservation. They are intended to annoy us and to cut off that friendly intercourse and communication which has hitherto subsisted between you and us. We hope it has given you no uneasiness, and you may rely on our assurances that these colonies will pursue no measures whatever but such as friendship and a regard for our mutual safety and interest may suggest.

As our concern for your welfare entitles us to your friendship, we presume you will not, by doing us injury, reduce us to the disagreeable necessity of treating you as enemies.

We yet entertain hopes of your uniting with us in the defense of our common liberty, and there is yet reason to believe that, should we join in imploring the attention of our sovereign to the unmerited and unparalleled oppressions of his American subjects, he will at length be undeceived, and forbid a licentious Ministry any longer to riot in the ruins of the rights of mankind.

76.

John Adams: The Formation of New State Governments

Most of the colonies in 1775 were still operating under their original charters. As relations with Britain deteriorated, several colonies appealed to the Continental Congress for aid in forming new state governments. John Adams, in the Autobiography *he wrote many years after these events, recalled that Congress neither claimed nor offered any leadership in this matter but referred each state back to its own constituents. The new state constitutions that were devised during the Revolution were not the result of popular democratic movements but were produced by those who already held positions of authority to provide the political unity necessary to fight the war with England.*

Source: C. F. Adams, III, pp. 13-23.

Friday, June 2, 1775. Journals of Congress, page 112. The president laid before Congress a letter from the provincial convention of Massachusetts Bay dated May 16, which was read, setting forth the difficulties they labor under for want of a regular form of government; and as they and the other colonies are now compelled to raise an army to defend themselves from the butcheries and devastations of their implacable enemies, which renders it still more necessary to have a regular established government, requesting the Congress to favor them with explicit advice respecting the taking up and exercising the powers of civil government, and declaring their readiness to submit to such a general plan as the Congress may direct for the colonies, or make it their great study to establish such a form of government there as shall not only promote their advantage but the union and interest of all America.

This subject had engaged much of my attention before I left Massachusetts, and had been frequently the subject of conversation between me and many of my friends: Dr. Winthrop, Dr. Cooper, Colonel Otis, the two Warrens, Major Hawley, and others, besides my colleagues in Congress, and lay with great weight upon my mind as the most difficult and dangerous business that we had to do (for from the beginning I always expected we should have more difficulty and danger in our attempts to govern ourselves and in our negotiations and connections with foreign powers than from all the fleets and armies of Great Britain). It lay, therefore, with great weight upon my mind; and when this letter was read, I embraced the opportunity to open myself in Congress, and most earnestly to entreat the serious attention of all the members and of all the continent to the measures which the times demanded. For my part I thought there was great wisdom in the adage: When the sword is drawn throw away the scabbard. Whether we threw it away voluntarily or not, it was useless now and would be useless forever. The pride of Britain, flushed with late triumphs and conquests, their infinite contempt of all the power of America, with an insolent, arbitrary Scotch faction with a Bute and Mansfield at their head for a Ministry, we might depend upon it, would force us to call forth every energy and resource of the country, to seek the friendship of England's enemies, and we had no rational hope but from the *ratio ultima regum et rerum publicarum* [the last consideration of kings and governments].

These efforts could not be made without government, and as I supposed no man would think of consolidating this vast continent under one national government, we should probably, after the example of the Greeks, the Dutch, and the Swiss, form a confederacy of states, each of which must have a separate government. That the case of Massachusetts was the most urgent, but that it could not be long before every other colony must follow her example. That with a view to this subject I had looked into the ancient and modern confederacies for examples; but they all appeared to me to have been huddled up in a hurry by a few chiefs. But we had a people of more intelligence, curiosity, and enterprise, who must be all consulted, and we must realize the theories of the wisest writers and invite the people to erect the whole building with their own hands upon the broadest foundation. That this could be done only by conventions of representatives chosen by the people in the several colonies, in the most exact proportions. That it was my opinion that Congress ought now to recommend to the people of every colony to call such conventions immediately and set up governments of their own, under their own authority, for the people were the source of all authority and original of all power. These were new, strange, and terrible doctrines to the greatest part of the members, but not a very small number heard them with apparent pleasure, and none more than Mr. John Rutledge of South Carolina and Mr. John Sullivan of New Hampshire.

Congress however ordered the letter to lie on the table for further consideration.

Saturday, June 3, 1775; the letter from the convention of the Massachusetts Bay, dated the 16th of May, being again read, the subject was again discussed, and then resolved that a committee of five persons be chosen to consider the same and report what in their opinion is the proper advice to be given to that convention. The following persons were chosen by ballot to compose that committee, viz.: Mr. J. Rutledge, Mr. Johnson, Mr. Jay, Mr. Wilson, and Mr. Lee. These gentlemen had several conferences with the delegates from our state, in the course of which I suppose the hint was suggested that they adopted in their report.

Wednesday, June 7, 1775; on motion resolved that Thursday, the 20th of July next, be observed throughout the twelve united colonies as a day of humiliation, fasting, and prayer; and that Mr. Hooper, Mr. J. Adams, and Mr. Paine be a committee to bring in a resolve for that purpose.

The committee appointed to prepare advice in answer to the letter from the convention of Massachusetts Bay brought in their report, which was read and ordered to lie on the table for consideration.

Friday, June 9, 1775; the report of the committee on the letter from the convention of Massachusetts Bay being again read, the Congress came into the following resolution:

Resolved, that no obedience being due to the act of Parliament for altering the charter of the colony of Massachusetts Bay, nor to a governor or lieutenant governor who will not observe the directions of but endeavor to subvert that charter, the governor and lieutenant governor of that colony are to be considered as absent and their offices vacant. And as there is no council there and the inconveniences arising from the suspension of the powers of government are intolerable, especially at a time when General Gage has actually levied war and is carrying on hostilities against His Majesty's peaceable and loyal subjects of that colony, that in order to conform as near as may be to the spirit and substance of the charter, it be recommended to the provincial convention to write letters to the inhabitants of the several places, which are entitled to representation in assembly, requesting them to choose such representatives; and that the assembly, when chosen, do elect councilors; and that such assembly or council exercise the powers of government until a governor of His Majesty's appointment will consent to govern the colony according to its charter.

Ordered that the president transmit a copy of the above to the convention of Massachusetts Bay.

Although this advice was in a great degree conformable to the New York and Pennsylvania system, or in other words to the system of Mr. Dickinson and Mr. Duane, I thought it an acquisition, for it was a precedent of advice to the separate states to institute governments, and I doubted not we should soon have more occasions to follow this example. Mr. John Rutledge and Mr. Sullivan had frequent conversations with me upon this subject. Mr. Rutledge asked me my opinion of a proper form of government for a state. I answered him that any form that our people would consent to institute would be better than none, even if they placed all power in a house of representatives and they should appoint governors and judges; but I hoped they would be wiser and preserve the English constitution in its spirit and substance, as far as the circumstances of this country required or would admit. That no hereditary powers ever had existed in America, nor would they or ought they to be introduced or proposed. But that I hoped the three branches of a legislature would be preserved, an executive, independent of the senate or council and the house and, above all things, the independence of the judges. Mr. Sullivan was fully agreed

with me in the necessity of instituting governments and he seconded me very handsomely in supporting the argument in Congress.

Mr. Samuel Adams was with us in the opinion of the necessity and was industrious in conversation with the members out of doors; but he very rarely spoke much in Congress, and he was perfectly unsettled in any plan to be recommended to a state, always inclining to the most democratical forms, and even to a single sovereign assembly, until his constituents, afterward in Boston, compelled him to vote for three branches. Mr. Cushing was also for one sovereign assembly, and Mr. Paine was silent and reserved upon the subject, at least to me.

Not long after this Mr. John Rutledge returned to South Carolina, and Mr. Sullivan went with General Washington to Cambridge; so that I lost two of my able coadjutors. But we soon found the benefit of their cooperation at a distance.

Wednesday, October 18, 1775, the delegates from New Hampshire laid before the Congress a part of the instructions delivered to them by their colony, in these words:

> We would have you immediately use your utmost endeavors to obtain the advice and direction of the Congress with respect to a method for our administering justice and regulating our civil police. We press you not to delay this matter, as its being done speedily will probably prevent the greatest confusion among us.

This instruction might have been obtained by Mr. Langdon or Mr. Whipple, but I always supposed it was General Sullivan who suggested the measure, because he left Congress with a stronger impression upon his mind of the importance of it than I ever observed in either of the others. Be this, however, as it may have been, I embraced with joy the opportunity of haranguing on the subject at large, and of urging

Congress to resolve on a general recommendation to all the states to call conventions and institute regular governments.

I reasoned from various topics, many of which perhaps I could not now recollect. Some I remember as: (1) The danger to the morals of the people, from the present loose state of things and general relaxation of laws and government through the union. (2) The danger of insurrections in some of the most disaffected parts of the colonies in favor of the enemy or, as they called them, the mother country, an expression that I thought it high time to erase out of our language. (3) Communications and intercourse with the enemy from various parts of the continent could not be wholly prevented, while any of the powers of government remained in the hands of the King's servants. (4) It could not well be considered as a crime to communicate intelligence, or to act as spies or guides to the enemy, without assuming all the powers of government. (5) The people of America would never consider our union as complete, but our friends would always suspect divisions among us, and our enemies, who were scattered in larger or smaller numbers not only in every state and city but in every village through the whole union, would forever represent Congress as divided and ready to break to pieces, and in this way would intimidate and discourage multitudes of our people who wished us well. (6) The absurdity of carrying on war against a king, when so many persons were daily taking oaths and affirmations of allegiance to him. (7) We could not expect that our friends in Great Britain would believe us united and in earnest, or exert themselves very strenuously in our favor, while we acted such a wavering, hesitating part. (8) Foreign nations, particularly France and Spain, would not think us worthy of their attention while we appeared to be deceived by such fallacious hopes of redress of grievances, of pardon for our offenses, and of reconciliation with our enemies. (9) We could not command the natural resources of our own country; we could not establish manufactories of arms, cannon, saltpeter, powder, ships, etc., without the powers of government, and all these and many other preparations ought to be going on in every state or colony, if you will, in the country.

Although the opposition was still inveterate, many members of Congress began to hear me with more patience, and some began to ask me civil questions: How can the people institute governments?

My answer was: By conventions of representatives, freely, fairly, and proportionally chosen.

When the convention has fabricated a government, or a constitution rather, how do we know the people will submit to it?

If there is any doubt of that, the convention may send out their project of a constitution to the people in their several towns, counties, or districts, and the people may make the acceptance of it their own act.

But the people know nothing about constitutions. I believe you are much mistaken in that supposition; if you are not, they will not oppose a plan prepared by their own chosen friends; but I believe that in every considerable portion of the people, there will be found some men who will understand the subject as well as their representatives, and these will assist in enlightening the rest. . . .

But what plan of a government would you advise?

A plan as nearly resembling the governments under which we were born and have lived as the circumstances of the country will admit. Kings we never had among us; nobles we never had. Nothing hereditary ever existed in the country, nor will the country require or admit of any such thing; but governors and councils we have always had, as well as representatives. A legislature in three branches ought to be preserved, and independent judges.

Where and how will you get your governors and councils?

By elections.

How, who shall elect?

The representatives of the people in a convention will be the best qualified to contrive a mode.

After all these discussions and interrogations, Congress was not prepared nor disposed to do anything as yet. They must consider farther.

Resolved, that the consideration of this matter be referred to Monday next. Monday arrived and Tuesday and Wednesday passed over, and Congress not yet willing to do anything.

Thursday, October 26, 1775; the subject again brought on the carpet, and the same discussions repeated, for very little new was produced. After a long discussion in which Mr. John Rutledge, Mr. Ward, Mr. Lee, Mr. Sherman, Mr. Gadsden, Mr. Dyer, and some others had spoken on the same side with me, Congress resolved that a committee of five members be appointed to take into consideration the instructions given to the delegates of New Hampshire, and report their opinion thereon. The members chosen: Mr. John Rutledge, Mr. J. Adams, Mr. Ward, Mr. Lee, and Mr. Sherman.

Although this committee was entirely composed of members as well-disposed to encourage the enterprise as could have been found in Congress, yet they could not be brought to agree upon a report and to bring it forward in Congress till Friday, November 3, 1775, when Congress, taking into consideration the report of the committee on the New Hampshire instructions, after another long deliberation and debate, resolved that it be recommended to the provincial convention of New Hampshire to call a full and free representation of the people, and that the representatives, if they think it necessary, establish such a form of government as in their judgment will best produce the happiness of the people and

Massachusetts Historical Society

John Adams, pastel portrait by Benjamin Blyth

most effectually secure peace and good order in the province during the continuance of the present dispute between Great Britain and the colonies.

By this time, I mortally hated the words "province," "colonies," and "mother country," and strove to get them out of the report. The last was indeed left out, but the other two were retained even by this committee, who were all as high Americans as any in the House, unless Mr. Gadsden should be excepted. Nevertheless, I thought this resolution a triumph and a most important point gained.

Mr. John Rutledge was now completely with us in our desire of revolutionizing all the governments, and he brought forward immediately some representations from his own state, when Congress, then taking into consideration the state of South Carolina, and sundry papers relative thereto being read and considered:

Resolved that a committee of five be appointed to take the same into consideration and report what in their opinion is necessary to be done. The members chosen: Mr.

Harrison, Mr. Bullock, Mr. Hooper, Mr. Chase, and Mr. S. Adams.

November 4, 1775; the committee appointed to take into consideration the state of South Carolina brought in their report, which being read a number of resolves were passed. . . .

Resolved that if the convention of South Carolina shall find it necessary to establish a form of government in that colony, it be recommended to that convention to call a full and free representation of the people, and that the said representatives, if they think it necessary, shall establish such a form of government as in their judgment will produce the happiness of the people and most effectually secure peace and good order in the colony, during the continuance of the present dispute between Great Britain and the colonies.

Although Mr. John Rutledge united with me and others in persuading the committee to report this resolution, and the distance of Carolina made it convenient to furnish them with this discretionary recommendation, I doubt whether Mr. Harrison or Mr. Hooper were as yet sufficiently advanced to agree to it. Mr. Bullock, Mr. Chase, and Mr. Samuel Adams were very ready for it. When it was under consideration, I labored afresh to expunge the words "colony" and "colonies," and insert the words "states" and "state," and the word "dispute" to make way for that of "war," and the word "colonies" for the word "America" or "states." But the child was not yet weaned.

I labored also to get the resolution enlarged and extended into a recommendation to the people of all the states to institute governments, and this occasioned more interrogations from one part and another of the House.

What plan of government would you recommend? Here it would have been the most natural to have made a motion that Congress should appoint a committee to prepare a plan of government to be reported to Congress and there discussed paragraph by paragraph, and that which should be adopted should be recommended to all the states. But I dared not make such a motion, because I knew that if such a plan was adopted it would be if not permanent yet of long duration; and it would be extremely difficult to get rid of it. And I knew that every one of my friends, and all those who were the most zealous for assuming government, had at that time no idea of any other government but a contemptible legislature in one assembly, with committees for executive, magistrates, and judges. These questions, therefore, I answered by sporting offhand a variety of short sketches of plans which might be adopted by the conventions; and as this subject was brought into view in some way or other, almost every day, and these interrogations were frequently repeated, I had in my head and at my tongue's end many projects of government. . . . I took care, however, always to bear my testimony against every plan of an unbalanced government.

Men, you are all marksmen — don't one of you fire until you see the whites of their eyes.

Israel Putnam, Battle of Bunker Hill, June 17, 1775

77.

NATHANIEL NILES: "The American Hero"

The Battle of Bunker Hill was the first stand-up battle between the untrained New England troops and the British regulars. The battle was a tactical victory for the British, but, because of the manner in which the militia resisted the regulars, it came to be regarded as an important moral victory for the Americans. Nathaniel Niles, a New England theologian, politician, and businessman, wrote an ode in celebration of Bunker Hill entitled "The American Hero." Set to music by Andrew Law and under the title "Bunker Hill," the song gained wide popularity during the Revolutionary War. Niles composed his ode in a verse form, English Sapphics, not commonly found in military songs; however, the measure would have been familiar because of Isaac Watts's use of it in several hymns, and perhaps it was Niles's intention to make his readers think of a hymn.

Source: *Songs, Odes, and Other Poems, on National Subjects,* compiled by Wm. McCarty, Philadelphia, 1842, pp. 457-459.

THE AMERICAN HERO

Why should vain mortals tremble at the sight of
Death and destruction in the field of battle,
Where blood and carnage clothe the ground in crimson,
    Sounding with death groans?

Death will invade us by the means appointed,
And we must all bow to the king of terrors;
Nor am I anxious, if I am preparèd,
    What shape he comes in.

Infinite Goodness teaches us submission,
Bids us be quiet under all His dealings;
Never repining, but forever praising
    God, our Creator.

Well may we praise Him; all His ways are perfect;
Though a resplendence, infinitely glowing,
Dazzles in glory on the sight of mortals,
    Struck blind by luster.

Good is Jehovah in bestowing sunshine,
Nor less His goodness in the storm and thunder.
Mercies and judgment both proceed from kindness,
    Infinite kindness.

O, then, exult that God forever reigneth;
Clouds which, around Him, hinder our perception,
Bind us the stronger to exalt His name, and
    Shout louder praises.

Then to the wisdom of my Lord and Master
I will commit all that I have or wish for,
Sweetly as babes' sleep will I give my life up,
    When called to yield it.

Now, Mars, I dare thee, clad in smoky pillars,
Bursting from bombshells, roaring from the cannon,
Rattling in grapeshot like a storm of hailstones,
    Torturing ether.

Up the bleak heavens let the spreading flames rise,
Breaking, like Aetna, through the smoky columns,
Lowering, like Egypt, o'er the falling city,
    Wantonly burned down.

Let oceans waft on all your fleeting castles,
Fraught with destruction, horrible to nature;
Then, with your sails filled by a storm of vengeance,
    Bear down to battle.

From the dire caverns made by ghostly miners,
Let the explosion, dreadful as volcanoes,
Heave the broad town, with all its wealth and people,
    Quick to destruction.

Still shall the banner of the King of Heaven
Never advance where I am afraid to follow;
While that precedes me, with an open bosom,
    War, I defy thee.

Fame and dear freedom lure me on to battle,
While a fell despot, grimmer than a death's-head,
Stings me with serpents, fiercer than Medusa's,
    To the encounter.

Life, for my country and the cause of freedom,
Is but a trifle for a worm to part with;
And, if preservèd in so great a contest,
    Life is redoubled.

78.

The Necessity for Taking Up Arms

*A Declaration . . . Setting Forth the Causes and Necessity of Their Taking Up Arms
held out a hope of reconciliation with Britain, but at the same time approved the use
of armed resistance to obtain recognition of the rights of the colonists. The final
draft of the* Declaration *was the work of Thomas Jefferson and John Dickinson.
Approved by the Second Continental Congress on July 6, 1775, the* Declaration
*disavowed all thoughts of independence. The colonists claimed to be fighting a
"ministerial army" and not the King, who they felt had been misled by evil counselors.
The Americans promised to lay down their arms when the liberties they claimed as
a birthright had been secured.*

Source: *Journals,* I: "Thursday, July 6, 1775."

IF IT WAS POSSIBLE for men who exercise their reason to believe that the Divine Author of our existence intended a part of the human race to hold an absolute property in and an unbounded power over others, marked out by His infinite goodness and wisdom, as the objects of a legal domination never rightfully resistible, however severe and oppressive, the inhabitants of these colonies might at least require from the Parliament of Great Britain some evidence that this dreadful authority over them has been granted to that body. But a reverence for our great Creator, principles of humanity, and the dictates of common sense must convince all those who reflect upon the subject that government was instituted to promote the welfare of mankind and ought to be administered for the attainment of that end.

The legislature of Great Britain, however, stimulated by an inordinate passion for a power not only unjustifiable but which they know to be peculiarly reprobated by the very constitution of that kingdom, and desperate of success in any mode of contest where regard should be had to truth, law, or right, have at length, deserting those, attempted to effect their cruel and impolitic purpose of enslaving these colonies by violence, and have thereby rendered it necessary for us to close with their last appeal from reason to arms. Yet, however blinded that assembly may be by their intemperate rage for unlimited domination so to slight justice and the opinion of mankind, we esteem ourselves bound, by obligations of respect to the rest of the world, to make known the justice of our cause.

Our forefathers, inhabitants of the island of Great Britain, left their native land to seek on these shores a residence for civil and religious freedom. At the expense of their blood, at the hazard of their fortunes, without the least charge to the country from which they removed, by unceasing labor and an unconquerable spirit, they effected settlements in the distant and inhospitable wilds of America, then filled with numerous and warlike nations of barbarians. Societies or governments, vested with perfect legislatures, were formed under charters from the Crown, and a harmonious intercourse was established between the colonies and the kingdom from which they derived their origin. The mutual benefits of this union became in a short time so extraordinary as to excite astonishment. It is universally confessed that the amazing increase of the wealth, strength, and navigation of the Realm arose from this source; and the minister, who so wisely and successfully directed the measures of Great Britain in the late war, publicly declared that these colonies enabled her to triumph over her enemies.

Toward the conclusion of that war, it pleased our sovereign to make a change in his counsels. From that fatal moment, the affairs of the British empire began to fall into confusion, and gradually sliding from the summit of glorious prosperity to which they had been advanced by the virtues and abilities of one man, are at length distracted by the convulsions that now shake it to its deepest foundations. The new Ministry finding the brave foes of Britain though frequently defeated yet still contending, took up the unfortunate idea of granting them a hasty peace, and of then subduing her faithful friends.

These devoted colonies were judged to be in such a state as to present victories without bloodshed and all the easy emoluments of statuteable plunder. The uninterrupted tenor of their peaceable and respectful behavior from the beginning of colonization; their dutiful, zealous, and useful services during the war, though so recently and amply acknowledged in the most honorable manner by His Majesty, by the late King, and by Parliament, could not save them from the meditated innovations. Parliament was influenced to adopt the pernicious project, and, assuming a new power over them, have, in the course of eleven years, given

such decisive specimens of the spirit and consequences attending this power as to leave no doubt concerning the effects of acquiescence under it. They have undertaken to give and grant our money without our consent, though we have ever exercised an exclusive right to dispose of our own property; statutes have been passed for extending the jurisdiction of Courts of Admiralty and Vice-Admiralty beyond their ancient limits; for depriving us of the accustomed and inestimable privilege of trial by jury, in cases affecting both life and property; for suspending the legislature of one of the colonies; for interdicting all commerce to the capital of another; and for altering fundamentally the form of government established by charter, and secured by acts of its own legislature solemnly confirmed by the Crown; for exempting the "murderers" of colonists from legal trial and, in effect, from punishment; for erecting in a neighboring province, acquired by the joint arms of Great Britain and America, a despotism dangerous to our very existence; and for quartering soldiers upon the colonists in time of profound peace. It has also been resolved in Parliament that colonists charged with committing certain offenses shall be transported to England to be tried.

But why should we enumerate our injuries in detail? By one statute it is declared that Parliament can "of right make laws to bind us in all cases whatsoever." What is to defend us against so enormous, so unlimited a power? Not a single man of those who assume it is chosen by us, or is subject to our control or influence; but, on the contrary, they are all of them exempt from the operation of such laws; and an American revenue, if not diverted from the ostensible purposes for which it is raised, would actually lighten their own burdens in proportion as they increase ours. We saw the misery to which such despotism would reduce us. We for ten years incessantly and ineffectually besieged the throne as suppliants; we reasoned, we remonstrated with Parliament, in the most mild and decent language.

Administration, sensible that we should regard these oppressive measures as freemen ought to do, sent over fleets and armies to enforce them. The indignation of the Americans was roused, it is true; but it was the indignation of a virtuous, loyal, and affectionate people. A congress of delegates from the United Colonies was assembled at Philadelphia, on the 5th day of last September. We resolved again to offer a humble and dutiful petition to the King, and also addressed our fellow subjects of Great Britain. We have pursued every temperate, every respectful measure; we have even proceeded to break off our commercial intercourse with our fellow subjects, as the last peaceable admonition, that our attachment to no nation upon earth should supplant our attachment to liberty. This, we flattered ourselves, was the ultimate step of the controversy; but subsequent events have shown how vain was this hope of finding moderation in our enemies.

Several threatening expressions against the colonies were inserted in His Majesty's speech; our petition, though we were told it was a decent one, and that His Majesty had been pleased to receive it graciously, and to promise laying it before his Parliament, was huddled into both houses among a bundle of American papers and there neglected. The Lords and Commons in their address, in the month of February, said, that "a rebellion at that time actually existed within the province of Massachusetts Bay; and that those concerned in it had been countenanced and encouraged by unlawful combinations and engagements, entered into by His Majesty's subjects in several of the other colonies; and therefore they besought His Majesty that he would take the most effectual measures to enforce due obedience to the laws and authority of the supreme legislature." Soon after, the commercial intercourse of whole colonies with foreign countries, and with each other, was cut off by an act of Parliament; by another, several of them were entirely prohibited from the fisheries in the seas near their coasts, on which they always depended for their sustenance; and large reinforcements of ships and troops were immediately sent over to General Gage.

Fruitless were all the entreaties, arguments, and eloquence of an illustrious band of the most distinguished peers and commoners, who nobly and strenuously asserted the justice of our cause to stay, or even to mitigate, the heedless fury with which these accumulated and unexampled outrages were hurried on. Equally fruitless was the interference of the City of London, of Bristol, and many other respectable towns in our favor. Parliament adopted an insidious maneuver calculated to divide us, to establish a perpetual auction of taxations where colony should bid against colony, all of them uninformed what ransom would redeem their lives; and thus to extort from us, at the point of the bayonet, the unknown sums that should be sufficient to gratify, if possible to gratify, ministerial rapacity, with the miserable indulgence left to us of raising, in our own mode, the prescribed tribute. What terms more rigid and humiliating could have been dictated by remorseless victors to conquered enemies? In our circumstances to accept them would be to deserve them.

Soon after intelligence of these proceedings arrived on this continent, General Gage, who in the course of the last year had taken possession of the town of Boston in the province of Massachusetts Bay, and still occupied it as a garrison, on the 19th day of April, sent out from that place a large detachment of his army, who made an unprovoked assault on the inhabitants of the said province, at the town of Lexington, as appears by the affidavits of a great number of persons, some of whom were officers and soldiers of that detachment, murdered eight of the inhabitants, and wounded many others. From thence the troops proceeded in warlike array to the town of Concord, where they set upon another party of the inhabitants of the same province, killing several and wounding more, until compelled to retreat by the country people suddenly assembled to repel this cruel aggression. Hostilities, thus commenced by the British troops, have been since prosecuted by them without regard to faith or reputation.

The inhabitants of Boston being confined within that town by the general their governor, and having, in order to procure their dismission, entered into a treaty with him, it was stipulated that the said inhabitants having deposited their arms with their own magistrates, should have liberty to depart, taking with them their other effects. They accordingly delivered up their arms; but in open violation of honor, in defiance of the obligation of treaties, which even savage nations esteemed sacred, the governor ordered the arms deposited as aforesaid, that they might be preserved for their owners, to be seized by a body of soldiers; detained the greatest part of the inhabitants in the town, and compelled the few who were permitted to retire to leave their most valuable effects behind. By this perfidy, wives are separated from their husbands, children from their parents, the aged and the sick from their relations and friends who wish to attend and comfort them; and those who have been used to live in plenty and even elegance are reduced to deplorable distress.

The general, further emulating his ministerial masters by a proclamation bearing date on the 12th day of June, after venting the grossest falsehoods and calumnies against the good people of these colonies, proceeds to "declare them all, either by name or description, to be rebels and traitors, to supersede the course of the common law, and instead thereof to publish and order the use and exercise of the law martial." His troops have butchered our countrymen, have wantonly burned Charlestown, besides a considerable number of houses in other places; our ships and vessels are seized; the necessary supplies of provisions are intercepted; and he is exerting his utmost power to spread destruction and devastation around him.

We have received certain intelligence that General Carleton, the governor of Canada, is instigating the people of that province and the Indians to fall upon us; and we have but too much reason to apprehend that schemes have been formed to excite domestic enemies against us. In brief, a part of these colonies now feel, and all of them are sure of feeling, as far as the vengeance of administration can inflict them, the complicated calamities of fire, sword, and famine. We are reduced to the alternative of choosing an unconditional submission to the tyranny of irritated ministers, or resistance by force.

The latter is our choice. We have counted the cost of this contest and find nothing so dreadful as voluntary slavery. Honor, justice, and humanity forbid us tamely to surrender that freedom which we received from our gallant ancestors, and which our innocent posterity have a right to receive from us. We cannot endure the infamy and guilt of resigning succeeding generations to that wretchedness which inevitably awaits them, if we basely entail hereditary bondage upon them.

Our cause is just. Our union is perfect. Our internal resources are great; and, if necessary, foreign assistance is undoubtedly attainable. We gratefully acknowledge, as signal instances of the divine favor toward us, that His providence would not permit us to be called into this severe controversy until we were grown up to our present strength, had been previously exercised in warlike operation, and possessed of the means of defending ourselves. With hearts fortified with these animating reflections, we most solemnly, before God and the world, *declare* that, exerting the utmost energy of those powers which our beneficent Creator has graciously bestowed upon us, the arms we have been compelled by our enemies to assume, we will, in defiance of every hazard, with unabating firmness and perseverance, employ for the preservation of our liberties; being with one mind resolved to die free men rather than live slaves.

Lest this declaration should disquiet the minds of our friends and fellow subjects in any part of the empire, we assure them that we mean not to dissolve that union which has so long and so happily subsisted between us and which we sincerely wish to see restored. Necessity has not yet driven us into that desperate measure, or induced us to excite any other nation to war against them. We have not raised armies with ambitious designs of separating from Great Britain and establishing independent states. We fight not for glory or for conquest. We exhibit to mankind the remarkable spectacle of a people attacked by unprovoked enemies, without any imputation or even suspicion of offense. They boast of their privileges and civilization, and yet proffer no milder conditions than servitude or death.

In our own native land, in defense of the freedom that is our birthright and which we ever enjoyed till the late violation of it, for the protection of our property acquired solely by the honest industry of our forefathers and ourselves, against violence actually offered, we have taken up arms. We shall lay them down when hostilities shall cease on the part of the aggressors and all danger of their being renewed shall be removed, and not before.

With a humble confidence in the mercies of the supreme and impartial Judge and Ruler of the universe, we most devoutly implore His divine goodness to protect us happily through this great conflict, to dispose our adversaries to reconciliation on reasonable terms, and thereby to relieve the empire from the calamities of civil war.

On a motion made, *Resolved*, that a letter be prepared to the lord mayor, aldermen, and livery of the City of London expressing the thanks of this Congress for their virtuous and spirited opposition to the oppressive and ruinous system of colony administration adopted by the British Ministry.

Ordered, that the committee appointed to draft an address to the people of Great Britain do prepare this.

As to pay, sir, I beg to assure the Congress, that, as no pecuniary consideration could have tempted me to accept this arduous employment, at the expense of my domestic ease and happiness, I do not wish to make any profit from it. I will keep an exact account of my expenses. Those, I doubt not, they will discharge; and that is all I desire.

GEORGE WASHINGTON, answer to Congress on his appointment as commander in chief, June 16, 1775

79.

Horatio Gates: On Recruiting an American Army

As the theater of war expanded in America, the need became evident for an intercolonial military establishment. The Second Continental Congress established the Continental Army in 1775, composing it of the scattered colonial forces outside Boston and appointing George Washington commander in chief. As military organization was developed and funds were raised, fresh units were authorized to supplement the forces already in the field. Horatio Gates, adjutant general of the army, issued instructions to the recruiters on July 10, 1775.

Source: Niles: "Instruction of Adjutant General Horatio Gates for Recruiting Troops, Massachusetts Bay, July 10, 1775."

You ARE NOT TO ENLIST any deserter from the ministerial army, nor any stroller, Negro, or vagabond, or person suspected of being an enemy to the liberty of America, nor any under eighteen years of age.

As the cause is the best that can engage men of courage and principle to take up arms, so it is expected that none but such will be accepted by the recruiting officer; the pay, provision, etc., being so ample, it is not doubted but the officers set upon this service will without delay complete their respective corps, and march the men forthwith to the camp.

You are not to enlist any person who is not an American born, unless such person has a wife and family, and is a settled resident in this country.

The person you enlist must be provided with good and complete arms.

Given at the headquarters at Cambridge, this 10th day of July, 1775.

XXII. *Charge your Bayonet.*

80.

Jonathan Boucher: Civil Liberty and Nonresistance

By temper a snob and in practice a social opportunist, Jonathan Boucher (who had come to Virginia from England in 1759) nevertheless brought considerable courage and eloquence to bear against the revolutionary spirit that gathered in his adopted country after 1765. He himself was always a supporter of authority, declaring that "to suffer grievances nobly is proper, to disobey the established government is simply to resist the ordinances of God." Such doctrine offended his congregation, and Boucher preached his last sermons in America with loaded pistols on his pulpit. In 1797, he published thirteen of those sermons under the title, A View of the Causes and Consequences of the American Revolution. *The following extract is taken from the twelfth sermon, delivered shortly before his return to England in September 1775.*

Source: *A View of the Causes and Consequences of the American Revolution, etc., etc.,* London, 1797: "On Civil Liberty; Passive Obedience, and Non-Resistance."

Stand fast, therefore, in the liberty wherewith Christ hath made us free.

Gal. 5:1

To HAVE BECOME NOTED either as a political writer or preacher, as some (who at least are unacquainted with my preaching) are pleased to tell you I now am, is a circumstance that gives me no pleasure. I was sorry to hear the observation, not (I thank God!) from any consciousness of my having ever written or preached anything of which (at least in point of principle) I have reason to be ashamed but because it is painful to reflect that it should have fallen to my lot to live in times, and in a country, in which such subjects demand the attention of every man. Convinced in my judgment that it is my duty to take the part which I have taken, though I cannot but lament its not having produced all the beneficial consequences which I fondly flattered myself it might, I dare not allow myself to discontinue it. The time, I know, has been when addresses of this sort from English pulpits were much more frequent than they now are. Even now, however, they are not wholly discontinued. Sermons on political topics, on certain stated days, are still preached, and with the authority of government. This is mentioned to obviate a charge that I am singular in continuing this practice as it proves that such preaching is not yet proscribed from our pulpits. . . .

As the liberty here spoken of [in the passage] respected the Jews, it denoted an exemption from the burdensome services of the ceremonial law; as it respected the gentiles, it meant a manumission from bondage under the weak and beggarly elements of the world and an admission into the covenant of grace. And as it respected both in common, it meant a freedom from the servitude of sin. Every sinner is, literally, a slave; for, *His servants ye are to whom ye obey* — and the only true liberty is the liberty of being the servants of God, for, *His service is perfect freedom.* The passage cannot, without infinite perversion and torture, be made to refer to any other kind of liberty, much less to that liberty of which every man now talks, though few understand it. . . .

The word "liberty," as meaning civil liberty, does not, I believe, occur in all the Scriptures. With the aid of a Concordance, I find only two or three passages, in two apocryphal writers, that look at all like it. . . .

I entreat your indulgence, whilst, without too nicely scrutinizing the propriety of deducing from a text a doctrine which it clearly does not suggest, I once more adopt a plan already chalked out for me, and deliver to you what occurs to me as proper for a Christian audience to attend to on the subject of liberty.

It has just been observed that the liberty inculcated in the Scriptures (and which alone the Apostle had in view in this text) is wholly of the spiritual or religious kind. This liberty was the natural result of the new religion in which mankind were then instructed, which certainly gave them no new civil privileges. They remained subject to the governments under which they lived, just as they had been before they became Christians, and just as others were who never became Christians, with this difference only — that the duty of submission and obedience to government was enjoined on the converts to Christianity with new and stronger sanctions. The doctrines of the Gospel make no manner of alteration in the nature or form of civil government, but enforce afresh, upon all Christians, that obedience which is due to the respective constitutions of every nation in which they may happen to live. . . .

Obedience to government is every man's duty, because it is every man's interest; but it is particularly incumbent on Christians, because (in addition to its moral fitness) it is enjoined by the positive commands of God; and, therefore, when Christians are disobedient to human ordinances, they are also disobedient to God. If the form of government under which the good providence of God has been pleased to place us be mild and free, it is our duty to enjoy it with gratitude and with thankfulness and, in particular, to be careful not to abuse it by licentiousness. If it be less indulgent and less liberal than in reason it ought to be, still it is our duty not to disturb and destroy the peace of the community by becoming refractory and rebellious subjects and resisting the ordinances of God. However humiliating such acquiescence may seem to men of warm and eager minds, the wisdom of God in having made it our duty is manifest. For, as it is the natural temper and bias of the human mind to be impatient under restraint, it was wise and merciful in the Blessed Author of our religion not to add any new impulse to the natural force of this prevailing propensity, but, with the whole weight of His authority, altogether to discountenance every tendency to disobedience.

If it were necessary to vindicate the Scriptures for this their total unconcern about a principle which so many other writings seem to regard as the first of all human considerations, it might be observed that, avoiding the vague and declamatory manner of such writings, and avoiding also the useless and impracticable subtleties of metaphysical definitions, these Scriptures have better consulted the great general interests of mankind by summarily recommending and enjoining a conscientious reverence for law whether human or divine. To respect the laws is to respect liberty in the only rational sense in which the term can be used, for liberty consists in a subserviency to law. "Where there is no law," says Mr. Locke, "there is no freedom." The mere man of nature (if such a one there ever was) has no freedom: all his lifetime he is subject to bondage. It is by being included within the pale of civil polity and government that he takes his rank in society as a free man.

Hence it follows that we are free, or otherwise, as we are governed by law, or by the mere arbitrary will or wills of any individual or any number of individuals. And liberty is not the setting at nought and despising established laws — much less the making our own wills the rule of our own actions, or the actions of others — and not bearing (whilst yet we dictate to others) the being dictated to, even by the laws of the land; but it is the being governed by law and by law only. . . . The more carefully well-devised restraints of law are enacted, and the more rigorously they are executed in any country, the greater degree of civil liberty does that country enjoy. To pursue liberty, then, in a manner not warranted by law, whatever the pretense may be, is clearly to be hostile to liberty; and those persons who thus promise you liberty are themselves the servants of corruption.

Says an excellent writer:

Civil liberty is a severe and a restrained thing; implies, in the notion of it, authority, settled subordinations, subjection, and obedience; and is altogether as much hurt by too little of this kind as by too much of it. And the love of liberty, when it is indeed the love of liberty, which carries us to withstand tyranny, will as much carry us to reverence authority and to support it, for this most obvious reason, that one is as necessary to the being of liberty as the other is destructive of it.

And, therefore, the love of liberty which does not produce this effect, the love of liberty which is not a real principle of dutiful behavior toward authority, is as hypocritical as the religion which is not productive of a good life. Licentiousness is, in truth, such an excess of liberty as is of the same nature with tyranny.

For what is the difference betwixt them but that one is lawless power exercised under pretense of authority, or by persons vested with it; the other, lawless power exercised under pretense of liberty, or without any pretense at all? A people, then, must always be less free in proportion as they are more licentious, licentiousness being not only different from liberty but directly contrary to it — a direct breach upon it.

True liberty, then, is a liberty to do everything that is right, and the being restrained from doing anything that is wrong. So far from our having a right to do everything that we please, under a notion of liberty, liberty itself is limited and confined; but limited and confined only by laws which are at the same time both its foundation and its support. It can, however, hardly be necessary to inform you that ideas and notions respecting liberty very different from these are daily suggested in the speeches and the writings of the times; and also that some opinions on the subject of government at large, which appear to me to be particularly loose and dangerous, are advanced in the sermon now under consideration; and that, therefore, you will acknowledge the propriety of my bestowing some further notice on them both.

It is laid down in this sermon as a settled maxim that the end of government is "the common good of mankind." I am not sure that the position itself is indisputable; but, if it were, it would by no means follow that "this common good being matter of common feeling, government must therefore have been instituted by common consent." There is an appearance of logical accuracy and precision in this statement; but it is only an appearance. The position is vague and loose; and the assertion is made without an attempt to prove it. If by men's "common feelings" we are to understand that principle in the human mind called common sense, the assertion is either unmeaning and insignificant, or it is false. In no instance have mankind ever yet agreed as to what is or is not "the common good."

A form or mode of government cannot be named which these "common feelings" and "common consent," the sole arbiters, as it seems, of "common good," have not, at one time or another, set up and established, and again pulled down and reprobated. What one people in one age have concurred in establishing as the "common good," another in another age have voted to be mischievous and big with ruin. The premises, therefore, that "the common good is matter of common feeling," being false, the consequence drawn from it, viz., that government was instituted by "common consent," is of course equally false.

This popular notion that government was originally formed by the consent or by a compact of the people rests on, and is supported by, another similar notion, not less popular nor better founded. This other notion is that the whole human race is born equal; and that no man is naturally inferior or, in any respect, subjected to another; and that he can be made subject to another only by his own consent. The position is equally ill-founded and false both in its premises and conclusions. In hardly any sense that can be imagined is the position strictly true; but, as applied to the case under consideration, it is demonstrably not true.

Man differs from man in everything that can be supposed to lead to supremacy and subjection, as one star differs from another star in glory. It was the purpose of the Creator that man should be social; but, without government, there can be no society; nor, without some relative inferiority and superiority, can there be any government. A musical instrument composed of chords, keys, or pipes, all perfectly equal in size and power, might as well be expected to produce harmony as a society composed of members all perfectly equal to be productive of order and peace.

If (according to the idea of the advocates'

of this chimerical scheme of equality) no man could rightfully be compelled to come in and be a member even of a government to be formed by a regular compact, but by his own individual consent, it clearly follows from the same principles that neither could he rightfully be made or compelled to submit to the ordinances of any government already formed to which he has not individually or actually consented. On the principle of equality, neither his parents, nor even the vote of a majority of the society (however virtuously and honorably that vote might be obtained), can have any such authority over any man. Neither can it be maintained that acquiescence implies consent; because acquiescence may have been extorted from impotence or incapacity. Even an explicit consent can bind a man no longer than he chooses to be bound. The same principle of equality that exempts him from being governed without his own consent clearly entitles him to recall and resume that consent whenever he sees fit; and he alone has a right to judge when and for what reasons it may be resumed.

Any attempt, therefore, to introduce this fantastic system into practice would reduce the whole business of social life to the wearisome, confused, and useless task of mankind's first expressing and then withdrawing their consent to an endless succession of schemes of government. Governments, though always forming, would never be completely formed; for the majority today might be the minority tomorrow, and, of course, that which is now fixed might and would be soon unfixed.

Mr. Locke indeed says that, "by consenting with others to make one body-politic under government, a man puts himself under an obligation to every one of that society to submit to the determination of the majority, and to be concluded by it." For the sake of the peace of society, it is undoubtedly reasonable and necessary that this should be the case; but, on the principles of the system now under consideration, before Mr. Locke or any of his followers can have authority to say that it actually is the case, it must be stated and proved that every individual man, on entering into the social compact, did first consent and declare his consent to be concluded and bound in all cases by the vote of the majority. In making such a declaration, he would certainly consult both his interest and his duty; but at the same time he would also completely relinquish the principle of equality, and eventually subject himself to the possibility of being governed by ignorant and corrupt tyrants.

Mr. Locke himself afterward disproves his own position respecting this supposed obligation to submit to the "determination of the majority" when he argues that a right of resistance still exists in the governed; for what is resistance but a recalling and resuming the consent heretofore supposed to have been given, and in fact refusing to submit to the "determination of the majority"? It does not clearly appear what Mr. Locke exactly meant by what he calls "the determination of the majority"; but the only rational and practical public manner of declaring "the determination of the majority" is by law. The laws, therefore, in all countries, even in those that are despotically governed, are to be regarded as the declared "determination of a majority" of the members of that community; because, in such cases, even acquiescence only must be looked upon as equivalent to a declaration. A right of resistance, therefore, for which Mr. Locke contends, is incompatible with the duty of submitting to the determination of "the majority," for which he also contends.

It is indeed impossible to carry into effect any government which, even by compact, might be framed with this reserved right of resistance. Accordingly, there is no record that any such government ever was so formed. If there had, it must have carried the seeds of its decay in its very constitu-

tion. For, as those men who make a government (certain that they have the power) can have no hesitation to vote that they also have the right to unmake it, and as the people, in all circumstances, but more especially when trained to make and unmake governments, are at least as well-disposed to do the latter as the former, it is morally impossible that there should be anything like permanency or stability in a government so formed. Such a system, therefore, can produce only perpetual dissensions and contests and bring back mankind to a supposed state of nature, arming every man's hand, like Ishmael's, against every man, and rendering the world an *aceldama*, or field of blood.

Such theories of government seem to give something like plausibility to the notions of those other modern theorists who regard all governments as invasions of the natural rights of men, usurpations, and tyranny. On this principle it would follow, and could not be denied, that government was indeed fundamentally, as our people are sedulously taught it still is, an evil. Yet it is to government that mankind owe their having, after their fall and corruption, been again reclaimed from a state of barbarity and war to the conveniency and the safety of the social state; and it is by means of government that society is still preserved, the weak protected from the strong, and the artless and innocent from the wrongs of proud oppressors. It was not without reason, then, that Mr. Locke asserted that a greater wrong cannot be done to prince and people than is done by "propagating wrong notions concerning government."

Ashamed of this shallow device, that government originated in superior strength and violence, another party, hardly less numerous, and certainly not less confident than the former, fondly deduce it from some imaginary compact. They suppose that, in the decline perhaps of some fabulous age of gold, a multitude of human beings, who, like their brother beasts, had hitherto

Jonathan Boucher (1738-1804), portrait by Daniel Gardner

ranged the forests, without guide, overseer, or ruler, at length convinced by experience of the impossibility of living either alone with any degree of comfort or security, or together in society with peace, without government, had (in some lucid interval of reason and reflection) met together in a spacious plain for the express purpose of framing a government. Their first step must have been the transferring to some individual or individuals some of those rights which are supposed to have been inherent in each of them. Of these it is essential to government that they should be divested. Yet can they not, rightfully, be deprived of them, otherwise than by their own consent.

Now, admitting this whole supposed assembly to be perfectly equal as to rights, yet all agreed as to the propriety of ceding some of them, on what principles of equality is it possible to determine either who shall relinquish such a portion of his rights, or who shall be invested with such new accessory rights? By asking another to exercise jurisdiction over me, I clearly confess that I do not think myself his equal; and, by his consenting to exercise such authority, he also virtually declares that he thinks himself superior. And, to establish this hypothesis of a compact, it is further necessary that the whole assembly should concur in this opinion — a concurrence so extremely improbable that it seems to be barely possible. The supposition that a large concourse of people, in a rude and imperfect state of society, or even a majority of them, should thus rationally and unanimously concur to subject themselves to various restrictions, many of them irksome and unpleasant, and all of them contrary to all their former habits, is to suppose them possessed of more wisdom and virtue than multitudes in any instance in real life have ever shown.

Another difficulty respecting this notion may yet be mentioned. Without a power of life and death, it will, I presume, be readily admitted that there could be no government. Now, admitting it to be possible that men, from motives of public and private utility, may be induced to submit to many heavy penalties, and even to corporal punishment, inflicted by the sentence of the law, there is an insuperable objection to any man's giving to another a power over his life. This objection is that no man has such a power over his own life and cannot therefore transfer to another, or to others, be they few or many, on any conditions, a right which he does not himself possess. He only who gave life can give the authority to take it [a]way; and as such authority is essential to government, this argument seems very decidedly to prove, not only that government did not originate in any compact but also that it was originally from God. . . .

Kings and princes (which are only other words for supreme magistrates) were doubtless created and appointed not so much for their own sakes as for the sake of the people committed to their charge; yet are they not, therefore, the creatures of the people? So far from deriving their authority from any supposed consent or suffrage of men, they receive their commission from Heaven; they receive it from God, the source and origin of all power. However obsolete, therefore, either the sentiment or the language may now be deemed, it is with the most perfect propriety that the supreme magistrate, whether consisting of one or of many, and whether denominated an emperor, a king, an archon, a dictator, a consul, or a senate, is to be regarded and venerated as the vicegerent of God. . . .

When it is asserted that Christianity made no alteration in the civil affairs of the world, the assertion should neither be made nor understood without some qualification. The injunction to "render unto Caesar the things that are Caesar's" is no doubt very comprehensive, implying that unless we are good subjects we cannot be good Christians. But then we are to render unto Caesar, or the supreme magistrate, that obedience only to which God has given him a just claim. Our paramount duty is to God, to whom we are to render the things that are God's. If, therefore, in the course of human affairs, a case should occur (and no doubt such cases do often occur) in which the performance of both these obligations becomes incompatible, we cannot long be at a loss in determining that it is our duty to obey God rather than men. . . .

As Christians, solicitous to tread in the steps in which our Savior trod, the tribute of civil obedience is as much due to our civil rulers, even though they should happen to be invaders . . . and though . . . the ministers of government should chance to be oppressors, as the duty of religious obedience is a debt which we owe to the King of kings, and Lord of lords.

Nor let this be deemed a degrading and servile principle. It is the very reverse; and it is this its superior dignity which proves its celestial origin. For whilst other doctrines and other systems distract the world with disputes and debates which admit of no decision, and of wars and fightings which are almost as endless as they are useless, it is the glory of Christianity to teach her votaries patiently to bear imperfections, inconveniences, and evils in government, as in everything else that is human. This patient acquiescence under some remediless evils is not more our duty than it is our interest. For the only very intolerable grievance in government is when men allow themselves to disturb and destroy the peace of the world by vain attempts to render that perfect which the laws of our nature have ordained to be imperfect.

And there is more magnanimity, as well as more wisdom, in enduring some present and certain evils than can be manifested by any projects of redress that are uncertain; but which, if they fail, may bring down irretrievable ruin on thousands of others, as well as on ourselves, since to suffer nobly indicates more greatness of mind than can be shown even by acting valiantly. Wise men, therefore, in the words of a noted philosopher, will "rather choose to brook with patience some inconveniences under government" (because human affairs cannot possibly be without some) than self-opinionatedly disturb the quiet of the public. And, weighing the justice of those things you are about, not by the persuasion and advice of private men but by the laws of the realm, you will no longer suffer ambitious men, through the streams of your blood, to wade to their own power but esteem it better to enjoy yourselves in the present state, though perhaps not the best, than, by waging war, endeavor to procure a reformation in another age, yourselves "in the meanwhile either killed, or consumed with age."

This long inquiry concerning the divine origin and authority of government might perhaps have been deemed rather curious than useful were it not of acknowledged moment that some dangerous inferences which are usually drawn from the contrary opinion should be obviated. One of these dangerous inferences it seems to have been the aim of the sermon now before me to inculcate. Government being assumed to be a mere human ordinance, it is thence inferred that "rulers are the servants of the public." And, if they be, no doubt it necessarily follows that they may (in the coarse phrase of the times) be cashiered or continued in pay, be reverenced or resisted, according to the mere whim or caprice of those over whom they are appointed to rule. Hence the author of this sermon also takes occasion to enter his protest against "passive obedience and nonresistance."

It really is a striking feature in our national history that, ever since the Revolution, hardly any person of any note has preached or published a sermon into which it was possible to drag this topic without declaring against this doctrine. It seems to have been made a kind of criterion or test of principle, and the watchword of a party. For, it cannot well be said that the circumstances of the times, or the temper of men's minds, either lately have been, or now are, such as particularly to call for these studied and repeated protestations. What is not less remarkable is that, while the right of resistance has thus incessantly been delivered from the pulpit, insisted on by orators and inculcated by statesmen, the contrary position is still (I believe) the dictate of religion, and certainly the doctrine of the Established Church, and still also the law of the land. . . .

All government, whether lodged in one or in many, is in its nature absolute and irresistible. It is not within the competency even of the supreme power to limit itself, because such limitation can emanate only from a superior. For any government to make itself irresistible and to cease to be absolute it must cease to be supreme, which is but saying in other words that it must

dissolve itself or be destroyed. If, then, to resist government be to destroy it, every man who is a subject must necessarily owe to the government under which he lives an obedience either active or passive: active, where the duty enjoined may be performed without offending God; and passive (that is to say, patiently to submit to the penalties annexed to disobedience), where that which is commanded by man is forbidden by God.

No government upon earth can rightfully compel any one of its subjects to an active compliance with anything that is, or that appears to his conscience to be, inconsistent with or contradictory to the known laws of God, because every man is under a prior and superior obligation to obey God in all things. When such cases of incompatible demands of duty occur, every well-informed person knows what he is to do; and every well-principled person will do what he ought; viz., he will submit to the ordinances of God rather than comply with the commandments of men In thus acting, he cannot err, and this alone is "passive obedience," which I entreat you to observe is so far from being "unlimited obedience" (as its enemies willfully persist to miscall it) that it is the direct contrary. Resolute not to disobey God, a man of good principles determines, in case of competition, as the lesser evil, to disobey man; but he knows that he should also disobey God, were he not, at the same time, patiently to submit to any penalties incurred by his disobedience to man.

With the fancies or the follies of the injudicious defenders of this doctrine who, in the heat of controversy, have argued for the exclusive irresistibility of kings, merely in their personal capacity, I have no concern. Such arguments are now to be met with only in the answers of those equally injudicious, but less candid, opposers of the doctrine, who (as though there were any gallantry in taking a fortress that is no longer defended) persist to combat a phantom which, now at least, may be said to be of their own creating. In the present state of things, when a resistance is recommended, it must be, not against the king alone, but against the laws of the land. To encourage undistinguishing multitudes by the vague term of resistance, to oppose all such laws as happen not to be agreeable to certain individuals, is neither more nor less than, by a regular plan, to attempt the subversion of the government. And I am not sure but that such attacks are more dangerous to free than to absolute governments. . . .

What dreadful confusions and calamities must have been occasioned in the world had such strong and dangerous natural propensities been directly encouraged by any positive law! It was surely, then, merciful and wise in the Almighty Ruler of the world to impose on His creatures the general law of obedience without any exceptions.

A nonresisting spirit never yet made any man a bad subject. And if men of such mild and yielding tempers have shown less ardor than many others do in the pursuit of that liberty which makes so conspicuous a figure in the effusions of orators and poets, it can be only for this reason: that they think it is precisely that kind of liberty which has so often set the world in an uproar, and that therefore it would be better for the world if it were never more heard of. . . .

Be it (for the sake of argument) admitted that the government under which till now you have lived happily is, most unaccountably, all at once become oppressive and severe; did you, of yourselves, make the discovery? No. I affirm, without any apprehension of being contradicted, that you are acquainted with these oppressions only from the report of others. For what, then (admitting you have a right to resist in any case), are you now urged to resist and rise against those whom you have hitherto always regarded (and certainly not without reason) as your nursing fathers and nursing mothers? Often as you have already heard it repeated without expressing any disapprobation, I assure myself it will afford you no pleasure to be reminded that it is on account of an insignificant duty on tea, imposed by the British Parliament, and which, for aught we know, may or may not be constitutionally imposed, but which, we well know, two-thirds of the people of America can never be called on to pay. Is it the part of an understanding people, of loyal subjects, or of good Christians instantly to resist and rebel for a cause so trivial?

O my brethren, consult your own hearts and follow your own judgments! And learn not your "measures of obedience" from men who weakly or wickedly imagine there can be liberty unconnected with law — and whose aim it is to drive you on, step by step, to a resistance which will terminate, if it does not begin, in rebellion! On all such trying occasions, learn the line of conduct which it is your duty and interest to observe, from our constitution itself, which, in this particular, is a fair transcript or exemplification of the ordinance of God. Both the one and the other warn you against resistance; but you are not forbidden either to remonstrate or to petition. And can it be humiliating to any man, or any number of men, to ask when we have but to *ask and it shall be given?*

Is prayer an abject duty, or do men ever appear either so great, or so amiable, as when they are modest and humble? However meanly this privilege of petitioning may be regarded by those who claim everything as a right, they are challenged to show an instance in which it has failed when it ought to have succeeded. If, however, our grievances, in any point of view, be of such moment as that other means of obtaining redress should be judged expedient, happily we enjoy those means. In a certain sense, some considerable portion of legislation is still in our own hands. We are supposed to have chosen "fit and able" persons to represent us in the Great Council of our country; and they only can constitutionally interfere either to obtain the enacting of what is right or the repeal of what is wrong.

If we and our fellow subjects have been conscientiously faithful in the discharge of our duty, we can have no reason to doubt that our delegates will be equally faithful in the discharge of theirs. Our provincial assemblies, it is true, are but one part of our colonial legislature; they form, however, that part which is the most efficient. If the present general topic of complaint be, in their estimation, well-founded, and a real and great grievance, what reason have you to imagine that all the assemblies on the continent will not concur and be unanimous in so representing it? And if they should all concur so to represent it, it is hardly within the reach of supposition that all due attention will not be paid to their united remonstrances. So many and such large concessions have often been made, at the instance only of individual assemblies, that we are warranted in relying that nothing which is reasonable and proper will ever be withheld from us, provided only it be asked for with decency; and that we do not previously forfeit our title to attention by becoming refractory and rebellious.

Let it be supposed, however, that even the worst may happen which can happen: that our remonstrances are disregarded, our petitions rejected, and our grievances unredressed. What, you will naturally ask — what, in such a case, would I advise you to do? — Advice, alas, is all I have to give; which, however, though you may condescend to ask and to regard it, will neither be asked nor accepted by those who alone can give it great effect. Yet, circumscribed as our sphere of influence is, we are not wholly without influence; and, therefore, even in our humble department, we have some duties to perform.

To your question, therefore, I hesitate not to answer that I wish and advise you to act the part of reasonable men and of Christians. You will be pleased to observe, however, that I am far from thinking that your virtue will ever be brought to so severe a test and trial. The question, I am aware, was an ensnaring one, suggested to you by those who are as little solicitous about your peace as they are for my safety; the answer which, in condescension to your wishes, I have given to it is direct and plain and not more applicable to you than it is to all the people of America.

If you think the duty of 3d. a pound upon tea laid on by the British Parliament a grievance, it is your duty to instruct your members to take all the constitutional means in their power to obtain redress; if those means fail of success, you cannot but be sorry and grieved, but you will better bear your disappointment by being able to reflect that it was not owing to any misconduct of your own. . . .

I affirm with great authority that "there can be no better way of asserting the people's lawful rights than the disowning unlawful commands, by thus patiently suffering." When this doctrine was more generally embraced, our holy religion gained as much by submission as it is now in a fair way of losing for want of it.

Having, then, my brethren, thus long been tossed to and fro in a wearisome circle of uncertain traditions or in speculations and projects still more uncertain concerning government, what better can you do than, following the Apostle's advice, to submit yourselves to every ordinance of man, for the Lord's sake; whether it be to the King as supreme, or unto *governors,* as unto them that are *sent* by Him for the punishment of evildoers and for the praise of them that do well? For, so is the will of God, that with well-doing you may put to silence the ignorance of foolish men; as free and not using your liberty for a cloak of maliciousness but as the servants of God.

Honor all men — love the brotherhood — fear God — honor the King.

81.

Reconciliation Rejected

Lord North, the prime minister of Great Britain during the Revolutionary War, made an offer for reconciliation to the colonies in May of 1775. Evidence indicates that the purpose of this gesture was to divide parliamentary opposition to ministerial policy and to win support in England for further coercive measures. The Continental Congress was divided between those who favored compromise and those who favored war. On July 31, Congress finally rejected Lord North's motion upon the advice of a committee consisting of Benjamin Franklin, Thomas Jefferson, Richard Henry Lee, and John Adams. In the following document, Congress repeated the colonial claim to the right of self-government and denounced the hypocrisy involved in offering reconciliation while at the same time passing the Restraining Acts.

Source: *Journals*, I: "Monday, July 31, 1775."

THE SEVERAL ASSEMBLIES of New Jersey, Pennsylvania, and Virginia, having referred to the Congress a resolution of the House of Commons of Great Britain, which resolution is in these words:

The House in a committee on the American papers. Motion made, and question proposed:

That it is the opinion of this committee that when the General Council and Assembly, or General Court of any of His Majesty's provinces or colonies in America shall propose to make provision, according to the condition, circumstance, or situation of such province or colony, for contributing their proportion to the common defense (such proportion to be raised under the authority of the General Court or General Assembly of such province or colony and disposable by Parliament) and shall engage to make provision also for the support of the civil government, and the administration of justice in such province or colony, it will be proper, if such proposal shall be approved by His Majesty, and the two houses of Parliament, and for so long as such provision shall be made accordingly, to forbear in respect to such province or colony to lay any duty, tax, or assessment, or to impose any further duty, tax, or assessment, except only such duties as it may be expedient to continue to levy or impose for the regulation of commerce; the net produce or the duties last mentioned to be carried to the account of such province or colony respectively.

The Congress took the said resolution into consideration, and are thereupon of opinion:

That the colonies of America are entitled to the sole and exclusive privilege of giving and granting their own money; that this involves a right of deliberating whether they will make any gift, for what purposes it shall be made, and what shall be its amount; and that it is a high breach of this privilege for any body of men, extraneous to their constitutions, to prescribe the purposes for which money shall be levied on them, to take to themselves the authority of judging of their conditions, circumstances, and situations, and of determining the amount of the contribution to be levied.

That as the colonies possess a right of appropriating their gifts, so are they entitled at all times to inquire into their application, to see that they be not wasted among the venal and corrupt for the purpose of undermining the civil rights of the givers, nor yet be diverted to the support of standing armies, inconsistent with their freedom and subversive of their quiet. To propose, therefore, as this resolution does, that the monies given by the colonies shall be subject to the disposal of Parliament alone, is to propose that they shall relinquish this right of inquiry and put it in the power of others to render their gifts ruinous, in proportion as they are liberal.

That this privilege of giving or of withholding our monies is an important barrier against the undue exertion of prerogative, which, if left altogether without control, may be exercised to our great oppression; and all history shows how efficacious is its intercession for redress of grievances and reestablishment of rights, and how improvident it would be to part with so powerful a mediator.

We are of opinion that the proposition contained in this resolution is unreasonable and insidious: unreasonable, because if we declare we accede to it, we declare without reservation we will purchase the favor of Parliament, not knowing at the same time at what price they will please to estimate their favor. It is insidious because individual colonies, having bid and bidden again till they find the avidity of the seller too great for all their powers to satisfy, are then to return into opposition, divided from their sister colonies whom the minister will have previously detached by a grant of easier terms, or by an artful procrastination of a definitive answer.

That the suspension of the exercise of their pretended power of taxation being ex-

pressly made commensurate with the continuance of our gifts, these must be perpetual to make that so. Whereas no experience has shown that a gift of perpetual revenue secures a perpetual return of duty or of kind disposition. On the contrary, the Parliament itself, wisely attentive to this observation, are in the established practice of granting their supplies from year to year only.

Desirous and determined as we are to consider, in the most dispassionate view, every seeming advance toward a reconciliation made by the British Parliament, let our brethren of Britain reflect what would have been the sacrifice to men of free spirits had even fair terms been proffered, as these insidious proposals were, with circumstances of insult and defiance. A proposition to give our money, accompanied with large fleets and armies, seems addressed to our fears rather than to our freedom. With what patience would Britons have received articles of treaty from any power on earth when borne on the point of the bayonet by military plenipotentiaries?

We think the attempt unnecessary to raise upon us, by force or by threats, our proportional contributions to the common defense, when all know, and themselves acknowledge, we have fully contributed whenever called upon to do so in the character of freemen.

We are of opinion it is not just that the colonies should be required to oblige themselves to other contributions while Great Britain possesses a monopoly of their trade. This of itself lays them under heavy contribution. To demand, therefore, additional aids in the form of a tax is to demand the double of their equal proportion. If we are to contribute equally with the other parts of the empire, let us equally with them enjoy free commerce with the whole world. But while the restrictions on our trade shut to us the resources of wealth, is it just we should bear all other burdens equally with those to whom every resource is open?

We conceive that the British Parliament has no right to intermeddle with our provisions for the support of civil government or administration of justice. The provisions we have made are such as please ourselves, and are agreeable to our own circumstances. They answer the substantial purposes of government and of justice, and other purposes than these should not be answered. We do not mean that our people shall be burdened with oppressive taxes to provide sinecures for the idle or the wicked, under color of providing for a civil list. While Parliament pursue their plan of civil government within their own jurisdiction, we also hope to pursue ours without molestation.

We are of opinion the proposition is altogether unsatisfactory because it imports only a suspension of the mode, not a renunciation of the pretended right to tax us: because, too, it does not propose to repeal the several acts of Parliament passed for the purposes of restraining the trade and altering the form of government of one of our colonies; extending the boundaries and changing the government of Quebec; enlarging the jurisdiction of the Courts of Admiralty and Vice-Admiralty; taking from us the rights of trial by a jury of the vicinage in cases affecting both life and property; transporting us into other countries to be tried for criminal offenses; exempting by mock trial the murderers of colonists from punishment; and quartering soldiers on us in times of profound peace. Nor do they renounce the power of suspending our own legislatures, and for legislating for us themselves in all cases whatsoever. On the contrary, to show they mean no discontinuance of injury, they pass acts, at the very time of holding out this proposition, for restraining the commerce and fisheries of the provinces of New England, and for interdicting the trade of other colonies with all foreign nations, and with each other. This proves unequivocally they mean not to relinquish the exercise of indiscriminate legislation over us.

Upon the whole, this proposition seems to have been held up to the world to deceive it into a belief that there was nothing in dispute between us but the *mode* of levying taxes, and that the Parliament having now been so good as to give up this, the colonies are unreasonable if not perfectly satisfied. Whereas, in truth our adversaries still claim a right of demanding *ad libitum,* and of taxing us themselves to the full amount of their demand if we do not comply with it. This leaves us without anything we can call property. But what is of more importance, and what in this proposal they keep out of sight, as if no such point was now in contest between us, they claim a right to alter our charters and established laws and leave us without any security for our lives or liberties.

The proposition seems also to have been calculated more particularly to lull into fatal security our well-affected fellow subjects on the other side the water till time should be given for the operation of those arms which a British minister pronounced would instantaneously reduce the "cowardly" sons of America to unreserved submission. But when the world reflects how inadequate to justice are these vaunted terms; when it attends to the rapid and bold succession of injuries which during the course of eleven years have been aimed at these colonies; when it reviews the pacific and respectful expostulations which during that whole time were the sole arms we opposed to them; when it observes that our complaints were either not heard at all or were answered with new and accumulated injuries; when it recollects that the minister himself on an early occasion declared "that he would never treat with America, till he had brought her to his feet," and that an avowed partisan of ministry has more lately denounced against us the dreadful sentence, *Delenda est Carthago"* [Let Carthage be destroyed]; that was done in the presence of a British senate, and being unreproved by them must be taken to be their own sentiment (especially as the purpose has already in part been carried into execution by their treatment of Boston and burning of Charlestown); when it considers the great armaments with which they have invaded us and the circumstances of cruelty with which these have commenced and prosecuted hostilities; when these things, we say, are laid together and attentively considered, can the world be deceived into an opinion that we are unreasonable, or can it hesitate to believe with us that nothing but our own exertions may defeat the ministerial sentence of death or abject submission?

82.

The Authority of the People

The Revolution was the occasion for attempts in many of the colonies to make their governments more democratic. That they were insufficiently so was felt with particular passion in North Carolina, where a group of seaboard gentry, allied with the royal governor and his handpicked council, had for all practical purposes ruled the colony. This small minority controlled four-fifths of the representation in the provincial government, since the coastal counties had five members for every two that the inland counties could send to the legislature. The same group taxed the inland region unfairly, was corrupt in its administration of the laws (in 1770 there was at least one defaulting sheriff in every county in the province), and held hard by the established religion. Although the bulk of the population consisted of dissenters, as late as 1769 no marriage was legal unless celebrated by an Anglican clergyman, of whom there were but six to serve a colony of 230,000 persons. The royal governor and the gentry managed to put down the Regulator revolt, but with the coming of the war, the back country was no longer to be denied. On May 31, 1775, only seven weeks after the battles of Lexington and Concord, the Scots-Irish of Mecklenburg County drafted militant resolves declaring that British government was suspended in America. Three months later, on September 1, the same county prepared the following instructions for its delegates to the provincial congress that would consider, among other things, a new constitution for the province. When such a constitution was adopted on December 18, 1776, the province had become a state, and the Mecklenburg demands, at least in principle, were law.

Source: *The Colonial Records of North Carolina, etc., etc.,* William L. Saunders, ed., Vol. X, Raleigh, 1890: "Instructions for the Delegates of Mecklenburg County Proposed to the Consideration of the County."

1. You are instructed to vote that the late province of North Carolina is, and of right ought to be, a free and independent state invested with all the power of legislation capable of making laws to regulate all its internal policy, subject only in its external connections and foreign commerce to a negative of a continental senate.

2. You are instructed to vote for the execution of a civil government under the authority of the people for the future security of all the rights, privileges, and prerogatives

of the state and the private, natural, and un-alienable rights of the constituting members thereof, either as men or Christians. If this should not be confirmed in Congress or Convention, protest.

3. You are instructed to vote that an equal representation be established, and that the qualifications required to enable any person or persons to have a voice in legislation may not be secured too high but that every freeman who shall be called upon to support government, either in person or property, may be admitted thereto. If this should not be confirmed, protest and remonstrate.

4. You are instructed to vote that legislation be not a divided right, and that no man or body of men be invested with a negative on the voice of the people duly collected, and that no honors or dignities be conferred for life or made hereditary on any person or persons either legislative or executive. If this should not be confirmed, protest and remonstrate.

5. You are instructed to vote that all and every person or persons seized or possessed of any estate, real or personal, agreeable to the last establishment, be confirmed in their seizures and possession to all intents and purposes in law who have not forfeited their right to the protection of the state by their criminal practice toward the same. If this should not be confirmed, protest.

6. You are instructed to vote that deputies to represent this state in a Continental Congress be appointed in and by the supreme legislative body of the state; the form of nomination to be submitted to if free and also that all officers the influence of whose office is equally to extend to every part of the state be appointed in the same manner and form; likewise give your consent to the establishing the old political divisions if it should be voted in Convention or to new ones if similar. On such establishments taking place, you are instructed to vote in the general that all officers who are

to exercise their authority in any of the said districts be recommended to the trust only by the freemen of the said division — to be subject, however, to the general laws and regulations of the state. If this should not be substantially confirmed, protest.

7. You are instructed to move and insist that the people you immediately represent be acknowledged to be a distinct county of this state, as formerly of the late province, with the additional privilege of annually electing their own officers, both civil and military, together with the elections of clerks and sheriffs by the freemen of the same. The choice to be confirmed by the sovereign authority of the state, and the officers so invested to be under the jurisdiction of the state and liable to its cognizance and inflictions in case of malpractice. If this should not be confirmed, protest and remonstrate.

8. You are instructed to vote that no chief justice, no secretary of state, no auditor general, no surveyor general, no practicing lawyer, no clerk of any court of record, no sheriff, and no person holding a military office in this state shall be a representative of the people in Congress or Convention. If this should not be confirmed, contend for it.

9. You are instructed to vote that all claims against the public, except such as accrue upon attendance upon Congress or Convention, be first submitted to the inspection of a committee of nine or more men, inhabitants of the county where said claimant is a resident, and without the approbation of said committee, it shall not be accepted by the public; for which purpose you are to move and insist that a law be enacted to empower the freemen of each county to choose a committee of not less than nine men, of whom none are to be military officers. If this should not be confirmed, protest and remonstrate.

10. You are instructed to refuse to enter into any combinations of secrecy as members of Congress or Convention and also to

refuse to subscribe any ensnaring tests binding you to an unlimited subjection to the determination of Congress or Convention.

11. You are instructed to move and insist that the public accounts fairly stated shall be regularly kept in proper books open to the inspection of all persons whom it may concern. If this should not be confirmed, contend for it.

12. You are instructed to move and insist that the power of county courts be much more extensive than under the former constitution, both with respect to matters of property and breaches of the peace. If not confirmed, contend for it.

13. You are instructed to assert and consent to the establishment of the Christian religion as contained in the Scriptures of the Old and New Testaments and more briefly comprised in the Thirty-Nine Articles of the Church of England, excluding the 37th Article, together with all the articles excepted, and not to be imposed on dissenters, by the Act of Toleration and clearly held forth in the confession of faith compiled by the Assembly of Divines at Westminster, to be the religion of the state, to the utter exclusion forever of all and every other (falsely so-called) religion, whether pagan or papal; and that the full, free, and peaceable enjoyment thereof be secured to all and every constituent member of the state as their unalienable right as freemen without the imposition of rites and ceremonies, whether claiming civil or ecclesiastic power for their source; and that a confession and profession of the religion so established shall be necessary in qualifying any person for public trust in the state. If this should not be confirmed, protest and remonstrate.

14. You are instructed to oppose to the utmost any particular church or set of clergymen being invested with power to decree rites and ceremonies and to decide in controversies of faith to be submitted to under the influence of penal laws. You are also to oppose the establishment of any mode of worship to be supported to the opposition of the rights of conscience together with the destruction of private property. You are to understand that under modes of worship are comprehended the different forms of swearing by law required. You are, moreover, to oppose the establishing an ecclesiastic supremacy in the sovereign authority of the state. You are to oppose the toleration of the popish idolatrous worship. If this should not be confirmed, protest and remonstrate.

15. You are instructed to move and insist that not less than four-fifths of the body of which you are members shall in voting be deemed a majority. If this should not be confirmed, contend for it.

16. You are instructed to give your voices to and for every motion and bill made or brought into the Congress or Convention where they appear to be for public utility and in no ways repugnant to the above instruction.

17. Gentlemen, the foregoing instructions you are not only to look on as instructions but as charges to which you are desired to take special heed as the general rule of your conduct as our representatives, and we expect you will exert yourselves to the utmost of your ability to obtain the purposes given you in charge. And wherein you fail either in obtaining or opposing, you are hereby ordered to enter your protest against the vote of the Congress or Convention as is pointed out to you in the above instructions.

83.

Thomas Gage: The Rebellion in America

Thomas Gage was relieved of his post as commander in chief of the British forces in America in 1775. On board ship, returning to England, he addressed the following letter of October 15 to Lord Dartmouth, describing the rebellion in America. Gage wanted to convince his superiors that the colonial rebellion could not be disposed of quickly and that a general war would be necessary to insure British domination in North America.

Source: *Archives,* III, pp. 1069-1070.

IT WILL GIVE ME PLEASURE, as I think it my duty, to send Your Lordship every hint or intelligence that can be of use at this important crisis. Nor am I disposed to do it in a secret manner, as it behooves every man in such times as these to declare his sentiments openly.

People agree now that there has been a scheme for a revolt from the mother country long conceived between those who have most influence in the American councils, which has been preparing the people's minds by degrees, for events that at first view they regarded with horror and detestation. If the Boston Port Bill had not furnished a pretext for rebellion, something else would have brought it forward. Unfortunately, few could believe it possible for them to prevail with the people to rise, and to the last the friends of government assured them it was only threats and menaces meant to intimidate.

Misfortune has arisen from this incredulity, for the rebels have been prepared to exercise their plan, while the government, not apprehensive of so general a revolt, has been unprepared to oppose it. The conduct of the leaders on the 19th of April evinced

their intention to begin hostilities, and had they not commenced then, they would only have been deferred. Your Lordship has a perfect idea of the transactions of that day, which were so far unlucky as it put an immediate stop to supplies of every kind; otherwise, our magazines would have been better filled.

I am convinced that the promoters of the rebellion have no real desire of peace, unless they have a *carte blanche.* Their whole conduct has been one scene of fallacy, duplicity, and dissimulation, by which they have duped many well-inclined people. Your Lordship will judge if the last petition of the Congress to the King is to be relied upon. And yet we are told that this petition was obtained by the most moderate of the members with great difficulty, and after very long debate.

There has been much heat and division in the Congress and a jealousy of the New England members, and I am told it was owing to jealousy that Washington was appointed to the command of the rebel army, in which there is much discontent. Lee is neither respected nor esteemed among them, though it is said that he is supported by the Boston rulers in opposition to Washington, and that he is for making an attack without delay upon the troops, but that the rest think it too desperate an undertaking. The rebel forces are well fed, but in general ill clothed and badly paid, though paper money has been issued to them lately. The credit of the paper is now kept up by force, and I have not heard that any plan has been fixed upon to redeem it.

They give out that they expect peace on their own terms through the inability of Britain to contend with them; and it is no wonder that such reports gain credit with the people, when letters from England and English newspapers give so much encouragement to rebellion.

Many people are of the opinion that the rebels will not hold together another year; but though the country will be very greatly distressed, and the people tired of the work, I will take the liberty to say, that from their presumption, arrogance, and encouragement from England, we can rely on nothing but our own force to procure even decent terms of peace; and that if it was ever necessary to obtain peace through the means of war, it is highly so in the present juncture.

I transmit to Your Lordship a packet of letters that were picked out from a number of papers scattered about Cushing's house. They contain no intelligence of present transactions but show the nature of the correspondence that the two Lees, Dr. Franklin, and others kept up with the leaders of this rebellion.

84.

LORD DUNMORE: Martial Law in Virginia

Lord Dunmore, Loyalist governor of Virginia, by mid-1775 had succeeded in alienating the whole colony. In June, he and his family had to flee to safety aboard a British ship which thereafter became the seat of government. On November 7, Dunmore issued the following proclamation. He hoped to intimidate the rebels by declaring martial law and by offering freedom to any slave who would desert his master and bear arms in the British cause.

Source: Niles: "Proclamation of Lord Dunmore Offering Freedom to the Slaves Belonging to the Rebels in Virginia, November 7, 1775."

As I HAVE EVER ENTERTAINED HOPES that an accommodation might have taken place between Great Britain and this colony, without being compelled by my duty to do this most disagreeable, but now absolutely necessary, duty, rendered so by a body of men, unlawfully assembled, firing on His Majesty's tenders, and the formation of an army, and an army now on its march to attack His Majesty's troops and destroy the well-disposed subjects of this colony. To defeat such treasonable purposes, and that all such traitors and their abettors may be brought to justice, and that the peace and good order of this colony may be again restored, which the ordinary course of the civil law is unable to effect, I have thought fit to issue this my proclamation, hereby declaring that, until the aforesaid good purposes can be obtained, I do, in virtue of the power and authority to me given by His Majesty, determine to execute martial law, and cause the same to be executed throughout this colony.

And to the end that peace and good order may the sooner be restored, I do require every person capable of bearing arms to resort to His Majesty's standard, or be looked upon as traitors to His Majesty's crown and government, and thereby become liable to the penalty the law inflicts upon such offenses; such as forfeiture of life, confiscation of lands, etc.

And I do hereby further declare all inden-tured servants, Negroes, or others (appertaining to rebels) free, that are able and willing to bear arms, they joining His Majesty's troops as soon as may be, for the more speedily reducing his colony to a proper sense of their duty to His Majesty's crown and dignity. I do further order and require all His Majesty's liege subjects to retain their quitrents or other taxes due, or that may become due in their own custody, till such a time may again be restored to this at present most unhappy country, or demanded of them for their former salutary purposes, by officers properly authorized to receive the same.

Given under my hand, on board the ship *William,* off Norfolk, the 7th day of November, in the 16th year of His Majesty's reign.

85.

Instructions to Vote Against Independence

Well into 1776, there was still some reluctance to declare openly for independence. Apart from their determined opposition to British policy, other factors were operative in the thinking of the colonial leadership. First was an anti-democratic bias: the fear of a popular upheaval in the transition to new forms of government. Second was a fear that strife between the colonies would lead to civil war at a time when Britain was the common enemy. Among the moves which delayed a declaration of independence for some months were the instructions issued November 9, 1775, to the Pennsylvania delegates to the Second Continental Congress.

Source: *Archives,* III, p. 1408.

THE TRUST REPOSED IN YOU is of such a nature and the modes of executing it may be so diversified in the course of your deliberations, that it is scarcely possible to give you particular instructions respecting it.

We, therefore, in general, direct that you, or any four of you, meet in Congress the delegates of the several colonies now assembled in this city and any such delegates as may meet in Congress next year; that you consult together on the present critical and alarming state of public affairs; that you exert your utmost endeavors to agree upon and recommend such measures as you shall judge to afford the best prospect of obtaining redress of American grievances, and restoring that union and harmony between Great Britain and the colonies so essential to the welfare and happiness of both countries.

Though the oppressive measures of the British Parliament and administration have compelled us to resist their violence by force of arms, yet we strictly enjoin you that you, in behalf of this colony, dissent from and utterly reject any propositions, should such be made, that may cause or lead to a separation from our mother country or a change of the form of this government.

You are directed to make report of your proceedings to this House.

86.

ABIGAIL ADAMS: Doubts About Independence

Although Abigail Adams had little formal education, she was intelligent and broadminded and became a terse and vigorous letter writer. That she was concerned with the growth of the new nation can be seen in her numerous letters to her husband John Adams. In the following letter, written November 27, 1775, Mrs. Adams expresses her doubts about the ability of the Americans to form a viable government.

Source: *Letters of Mrs. Adams, the Wife of John Adams,* Charles Francis Adams, ed., 4th edition, Boston, 1848.

COLONEL WARREN RETURNED last week to Plymouth, so that I shall not hear anything from you until he goes back again, which will not be till the last of this month. He damped my spirits greatly by telling me that the court had prolonged your stay another month. I was pleasing myself with the thought that you would soon be upon your return. It is in vain to repine. I hope the public will reap what I sacrifice.

I wish I knew what mighty things were fabricating. If a form of government is to be established here, what one will be assumed? Will it be left to our assemblies to choose one? And will not many men have many minds? And shall we not run into dissensions among ourselves?

I am more and more convinced that man is a dangerous creature; and that power, whether vested in many or a few, is ever grasping, and, like the grave, cries "Give, give." The great fish swallow up the small; and he who is most strenuous for the rights of the people when vested with power, is as eager after the prerogatives of government. You tell me of degrees of perfection to which human nature is capable of arriving, and I believe it, but, at the same time, lament that our admiration should arise from the scarcity of the instances.

The building up a great empire, which was only hinted at by my correspondent, may now, I suppose, be realized even by the unbelievers. Yet, will not ten thousand difficulties arise in the formation of it? The reins of government have been so long slackened that I fear the people will not quietly submit to those restraints which are necessary for the peace and security of the community. If we separate from Britain, what code of laws will be established? How shall we be governed so as to retain our liberties? Can any government be free which is not administered by general stated laws? Who shall frame these laws? Who will give them force and energy? It is true your resolutions, as a body, have hitherto had the force of laws; but will they continue to have?

When I consider these things, and the prejudices of people in favor of ancient customs and regulations, I feel anxious for the fate of our monarchy or democracy, or whatever is to take place. I soon get lost in a labyrinth of perplexities; but, whatever occurs, may justice and righteousness be the stability of our times, and order arise out of confusion. Great difficulties may be surmounted by patience and perseverance.

I believe I have tired you with politics. As to news, we have not any at all. I shudder at the approach of winter, when I think I am to remain desolate.

I must bid you good night; 'tis late for me, who am much of an invalid. I was disappointed last week in receiving a packet by the post, and, upon unsealing it, finding only four newspapers. I think you are more cautious than you need be. All letters, I believe, have come safe to hand. I have sixteen from you, and wish I had as many more.

87.

Funds for Scientific Research

The American Philosophical Society was founded in 1743 by Benjamin Franklin "for the promotion of useful knowledge among the British plantations in America." On March 6, 1775, the Society petitioned the Pennsylvania General Assembly for financial support to erect an observatory. David Rittenhouse, an astronomer and member of the Society, was to be the "Public Astronomical Observer" and receive an annual salary. The plans received encouragement from Lord North and from Nevil Maskelyne, the royal astronomer, but war intervened before they could be adopted.

Source: *Memoirs of the Life of David Rittenhouse, etc., etc.,* William Barton, ed., Philadelphia, 1813, pp. 248-254.

Gentlemen,

It must yield a sensible satisfaction to the good people of this province, whom you represent, to find that although it be among the youngest of our American settlements, its reputation has risen high among the sister colonies, and has extended even to the remotest part of Europe, on account of our many public-spirited institutions and our rapid improvements in all useful arts. This satisfaction is also greatly increased when we consider that notwithstanding these institutions, through the necessity of the case, were generally obliged to derive much of their first support from the benevolence of individuals; yet a liberal spirit for their encouragement and final establishment has gone forth among our representatives, in proportion to the increase of our provincial funds. And indeed the savings of public money, after supplying the exigencies of the state, are never more laudably directed than toward the promoting whatever is useful and ornamental in society.

It is with unfeigned gratitude that your petitioners recollect the repeated occasions you have given them, of acknowledging your bounty and protection, in carrying on their designs "for the advancement of useful knowledge"; and it is their firm resolution never to abuse your former indulgence, by any future unnecessary or unimportant applications. By the means now in their own power, they hope, in general, to be able to prosecute their plan; except so far as they may sometimes find it incumbent on them humbly to suggest to you the encouragement of useful inventions, and the patronizing [of] undertakings beneficial to the whole community: And it is in this last view that they presume to address you at this time.

Amidst the variety of fields which, in this new world, lie open to the investigation of your petitioners, they have for several years turned their views toward one, wherein they hope to gather some of their chief laurels and to make discoveries alike honorable to their country and themselves. Our distance from the chief observatories in the world, the purity and serenity of our atmosphere, invite us, nay loudly call upon us, to institute a series of regular astronomical observations; the comparison of which with those made in Europe and elsewhere might settle some very important points and contribute greatly to give a last perfection to geography and navigation. The advantages derived to those noble and useful sciences from such observations are so obvious that there is scarce a civilized nation in the world that has not made some provision for prosecuting them; and your petitioners have been honored with repeated solicitations from some of the greatest men in Europe to join with them in this great work, and in a mutual communication of our labors.

It would be inexcusable, therefore, in your petitioners to neglect the present opportunity of endeavoring to set such a design on foot, when we have a gentleman among us, whose abilities, speculative as well as practical, would do honor to any country, and who is, nevertheless, indebted for bread to his daily toil in an occupation the most unfriendly both to health and study. Under his auspices, the work may now be undertaken with the greatest advantages; and others may be bred up by him to prosecute it in future times: but if the present opportunity is neglected, perhaps whole centuries may not afford such another. To rescue such a man from the drudgery of manual labor, and give him an occasion of indulging his bent of genius with advantage to his country is an honor which crowned heads might glory in — but it is an honor also which it is hoped, in the case of a native, Pennsylvania would not yield to the greatest prince or people on earth!

The design which your petitioners have projected and now humbly beg leave to lay before your honorable house is as follows, viz.:

First, that the honorable proprietaries be petitioned to grant a lot of ground, for erecting a public observatory, and to give such other encouragement to the design as they may think proper. And from their known attachment to the interest of this country, as well as their professed readiness to serve the gentleman who is proposed to conduct the design, your petitioners cannot have any doubt of their kind compliance with this humble request.

Second, that the assistance of your honorable house be requested, agreeably to the concluding prayer of this petition.

Third, that a subscription be promoted for erecting a public observatory, and furnishing it with such instruments as may be wanted, in addition to those valuable ones now in the province. Of the success of this subscription among our benevolent fellow citizens, there can be no doubt; and the expense of the additional instruments will not be great, as the gentleman proposed to conduct the design is capable of constructing them all with his own hand, in the most masterly manner.

Fourth, that the observatory shall be at all times open to the curious; and, particularly, that captains and mates of vessels, and young gentlemen desirous of obtaining a practical knowledge in astronomy, shall have admittance, and (under proper rules, to be framed for that purpose) be taught the use of instruments, and the method of making observations, especially the *new method* of ascertaining the longitude at sea; for the perfecting of which the Parliament of Great Britain has of late given such ample rewards, to the singular advantage of trade and navigation.

Fifth, that the observations to be made by the public observer shall be annually published, under the inspection of the American Philosophical Society, and communicated to the learned societies in Europe, with such remarks as may render them generally useful and entertaining.

Sixth, that the same person might also be appointed surveyor of the high roads and waters, in order that when any public proposals are to be made for improving navigation and shortening the communications between capital trading places, there be always a person who has leisure and is skilled in measuring and reducing distances, taking heights and levels, and who may be employed in conjunction with others, when necessary, to make report on all such matters, either at the expense of those who request such service, or at the public expense, as the case may require.

Your petitioners therefore humbly pray, that your honorable house would take the premises into your consideration, and allow a yearly salary for such person, at least as a public astronomer, if you should not view the additional office of surveyor of the high roads and waters in the same important light as it is viewed by your petitioners; and they further pray that you would give them leave to bring in a bill for the legislative appointment of such public observer, and for regulating his duty in the execution of his trust.

He snatched the lightning from heaven and the sceptre from tyrants. (Eripuit coelo fulmen sceptrumque tyrannis.)

ANNE MARIE JACQUES TURGOT, inscription on Houdon's bust of Franklin

88.

Isaac Backus: Civil Government and Religious Taxes

The liberating tendencies of the revolutionary crisis provided an opportunity for arguments promoting the separation of church and state and total religious freedom for Protestants. The Reverend Isaac Backus, a Massachusetts Baptist, insisted that freedom from tyranny meant freedom from religious taxation for dissenters. Following is his memorial in behalf of the Warren Association to the Massachusetts Assembly in September 1775.

Source: *A Church History of New-England*, Providence, 1784, Vol. II, pp. 304-305.

OUR REAL GRIEVANCES are that we, as well as our fathers, have from time to time been taxed on religious accounts where we were not represented; and when we have sued for our rights, our causes have been tried by interested judges. That the representatives in former assemblies, as well as the present, were elected by virtue only of civil and worldly qualifications is a truth so evident that we presume it need not be proved to this Assembly; and for a civil legislature to impose religious taxes, is, we conceive, a power which their constituents never had to give; and is therefore going entirely out of their jurisdiction. Under the legal dispensation, where God himself prescribed the exact proportion of what the people were to give, yet none but persons of the worst characters ever attempted to take it by force (I Sam. 2:12, 16; Mic. 3:5-9). How daring then must it be for any to do it for Christ's ministers, who says, my kingdom is not of this world! We beseech this honorable Assembly to take these matters into their wise and serious consideration, before Him who has said, With what measure ye mete it shall be measured to you again.

Is not all America now appealing to Heaven against the injustice of being taxed where we are not represented, and against being judged by men who are interested in getting away our money? And will heaven approve of your doing the same thing to your fellow servants? No, surely. We have no desire of representing this government as the worst of any who have imposed religious taxes; we fully believe the contrary. Yet, as we are persuaded that an entire freedom from being taxed by civil rulers to religious worship is not a mere favor from any man or men in the world but a right and property granted us by God, who commands us to *stand fast in it,* we have not only the same reason to refuse an acknowledgment of such a taxing power here, as America has the abovesaid power, but also, according to our present light, we should wrong our consciences in allowing that power to men, which we believe belongs only to God.

89.

John Adams: The Virtues of New England

John Adams revealed a lifelong fascination with the political and social institutions of New England and their influence on the character of the people. His partiality for his birthplace was a constant theme in his private and public writings, for example, in a letter to his wife Abigail, written on October 29, 1775.

Source: *The Adams Papers*, L. H. Butterfield, ed., Cambridge, 1963, Vol. V.

THERE IS, IN THE HUMAN BREAST, a social affection which extends to our whole species. Faintly indeed; but in some degree. The nation, kingdom, or community to which we belong is embraced by it more vigorously. It is stronger still toward the province to which we belong and in which we had our birth. It is stronger and stronger as we descend to the county, town, parish, neighborhood, and family which we call our own. And here we find it often so powerful as to become partial, to blind our eyes, to darken our understanding and pervert our wills.

It is to this infirmity in my own heart that I must perhaps attribute that local attachment, that partial fondness, that overweening prejudice in favor of New England, which I feel very often and which I fear sometimes leads me to expose myself to just ridicule.

New England has in many respects the advantage of every other colony in America, and indeed of every other part of the world, that I know anything of.

1. The people are of purer English blood, less mixed with Scotch, Irish, Dutch, French, Danish, Swedish, etc., than any other; and descended from Englishmen too who left Europe in purer times than the present and less tainted with corruption than those they left behind them.

2. The institutions in New England for the support of religion, morals, and decency exceed any other, obliging every parish to have a minister, and every person to go to meeting, etc.

3. The public institutions in New England for the education of youth, supporting colleges at the public expense and obliging towns to maintain grammar schools, are not equaled and never were, in any part of the world.

4. The division of our territory, that is, our counties into townships, empowering towns to assemble, choose officers, make laws, mend roads, and twenty other things, gives every man an opportunity of showing and improving that education which he received at college or at school, and makes knowledge and dexterity at public business common.

5. Our laws for the distribution of intestate estates occasion a frequent division of landed property and prevent monopolies of land.

But in opposition to these, we have labored under many disadvantages — the exorbitant prerogatives of our governors, etc., which would have overborne our liberties if they had not been opposed by the five preceding particulars.

90.

BENJAMIN FRANKLIN: Autobiography

Franklin wrote his Autobiography, *which was never completed, at four different periods of his life. The first half, more or less, was written in two weeks during an interval spent with friends at Twyford, England, in 1771. It is in the form, later abandoned, of a letter to his son. At the same time or a little later, Franklin also composed an outline of the rest, or most of the rest, of the work. Subsequent portions were written at Passy, France, in 1784 and at Philadelphia in 1786 and 1788. All but the last were published without authorization in a French edition the year after Franklin died. The first edition of these three parts in English was brought out by William Temple Franklin in 1818. The fourth part was not printed until 1868, when it was recovered by John Bigelow, then American minister to France. The* Autobiography *has long been a part of American literary history and one of the best-known works of its kind in the world. Five relatively short passages from the* Autobiography *are reprinted here, dealing with well-known occurrences in Franklin's life. The first two passages were written in 1771 and were brought by Franklin to Philadelphia in 1775; hence the placement of the selection at this point in the volume. The last three selections had been outlined in 1775 but were not actually written out until the 1780s.*

Source: *Memoirs of Benjamin Franklin*, New York, 1839, Vol. I, pp. 32-43, 89-90, 118-120, 125-127. Sparks,. I, pp. 151-156.

MY BROTHER HAD, in 1720 or 1721, begun to print a newspaper. It was the second that appeared in America, and was called the *New-England Courant.* The only one before it was the *Boston News-Letter.* I remember his being dissuaded by some of his friends from the undertaking as not likely to succeed, one newspaper being, in their judgment, enough for America. At this time (1771) there are not less than five-and-twenty. He went on, however, with the undertaking. I was employed to carry the papers to the customers, after having worked in composing the types and printing off the sheets.

He had some ingenious men among his friends, who amused themselves by writing little pieces for his paper, which gained it credit and made it more in demand; and these gentlemen often visited us. Hearing their conversations and their accounts of the approbation their papers were received with, I was excited to try my hand among them; but, being still a boy, and suspecting that my brother would object to printing anything of mine in his paper if he knew it to be mine, I contrived to disguise my hand, and, writing an anonymous paper, I put it in at night under the door of the printing house. It was found in the morning and committed to his writing friends when they called in as usual. They read it, commented on it in my hearing, and I had the exquisite pleasure of finding it had met with their approbation, and that, in their different guesses at the author, none were named but men of some character among us for learning and ingenuity. I suppose that I was rather lucky in my judges, and they were not really so very good as I then believed them to be.

Encouraged, however, by this attempt, I wrote and sent in the same way to the press several other pieces that were equally approved; and I kept my secret till all my fund of sense for such performances was exhausted, and then discovered it, when I began to be considered with a little more attention by my brother's acquaintance. However, that did not quite please him as he thought it tended to make me too vain. This might be one occasion of the differences we began to have about this time. Though a brother, he considered himself as my master, and me as his apprentice, and, accordingly, expected the same services from me as he would from another, while I thought he degraded me too much in some he required of me, who from a brother required more indulgence. Our disputes were often brought before our father, and I fancy I was either generally in the right, or else a better pleader, because the judgment was generally in my favor. But my brother was passionate and had often beaten me, which I took extremely amiss; and, thinking my apprenticeship very tedious, I was continually wishing for some opportunity of shortening it, which at length offered in a manner unexpected.

Perhaps the harsh and tyrannical treatment of me might be a means of impressing me with the aversion to arbitrary power that has stuck to me through my whole life.

One of the pieces in our newspaper on some political point, which I have now forgotten, gave offense to the Assembly. He was taken up, censured, and imprisoned for a month, by the speaker's warrant, I suppose, because he would not discover the author. I too was taken up and examined before the Council; but, though I did not give them any satisfaction, they contented themselves with admonishing me, and dismissed me, considering me, perhaps, as an apprentice who was bound to keep his master's secrets.

During my brother's confinement, which I resented a good deal notwithstanding our differences, I had the management of the paper; and I made bold to give our rulers some rubs in it, which my brother took very kindly, while others began to consider me in an unfavorable light, as a youth that had a turn for libeling and satire. My brother's discharge was accompanied with an order (a very odd one) that "James Franklin should no longer print the paper called the *New-England Courant.*"

On a consultation held in our printing office among his friends, what he should do in this conjuncture, it was proposed to elude the order by changing the name of the paper; but my brother, seeing inconveniences in this, came to a conclusion, as a better way, to let the paper in future be printed in the name of Benjamin Franklin. And, in order to avoid the censure of the Assembly that might fall on him as still printing it by his apprentice, he contrived and consented that my old indenture should be returned to me, with a full discharge on the back of it, to show in case of necessity. And, in order to secure to him the benefit of my service, I should sign new indentures for the remainder of my time, which was to be kept private. A very flimsy scheme it was; however, it was immediately executed, and the paper was printed, accordingly, under my name for several months.

At length, a fresh difference arising between my brother and me, I took upon me to assert my freedom, presuming that he would not venture to produce the new indentures. It was not fair in me to take this advantage, and this I therefore reckon as one of the first errata of my life; but the unfairness of it weighed little with me, when under the impression of resentment for the blows his passion too often urged him to bestow upon me, though he was otherwise not an ill-natured man — perhaps I was too saucy and provoking.

When he found I would leave him, he took care to prevent my getting employment in any other printing house in town by going round and speaking to every master, who accordingly refused to give me work. I then thought of going to New York, as the nearest place where there was a printer; and I was rather inclined to leave Boston when I reflected that I had already made myself a little obnoxious to the governing party, and, from the arbitrary proceedings of the Assembly in my brother's case, it was likely I might, if I stayed, soon bring myself into scrapes; and, further, that my indiscreet disputations about religion began to make me pointed at with horror by good people as an infidel or atheist.

I concluded, therefore, to remove to New York; but my father now siding with my brother, I was sensible that, if I attempted to go openly, means would be used to prevent me. My friend Collins, therefore, undertook to manage my flight. He agreed with the captain of a New York sloop to take me. I sold my books to raise a little money, was taken on board the sloop privately, had a fair wind, and in three days found myself at New York, near 300 miles from my home, at the age of seventeen, without the least recommendation or knowledge of any person in the place, and very little money in my pocket.

The inclination I had felt for the sea was by this time done away, or I might now have gratified it. But, having another profession, and conceiving myself a pretty good workman, I offered my services to a printer of the place, old Mr. W. Bradford, who had been the first printer in Pennsylvania, but had removed thence in consequence of a quarrel with the governor, General Keith. He could give me no employment, having little to do and hands enough already; but, he said, "My son at Philadelphia has lately lost his principal hand, Aquilla Rose, by death; if you go thither, I believe he may employ you." Philadelphia was 100 miles farther. I set out, however, in a boat for Amboy, leaving my chest and things to follow me round by sea.

In crossing the bay, we met with a squall that tore our rotten sails to pieces, prevented our getting into the Kill, and drove us upon Long Island. In our way, a drunken Dutchman, who was a passenger too, fell overboard; when he was sinking, I reached through the water to his shock pate [thick hair], and drew him up, so that we got him in again. His ducking sobered him a little, and he went to sleep, taking first out of his pocket a book, which he desired I would dry for him. It proved to be my old favorite author, Bunyan's *Pilgrim's Progress,* in Dutch, finely printed on good paper, copper cuts, a dress better than I had ever seen it wear in its own language. I have since found that it has been translated into most of the languages of Europe, and suppose it has been more generally read than any other book, except perhaps the Bible. Honest John was the first that I know of who mixed narration and dialogue; a method of writing very engaging to the reader, who, in the most interesting parts, finds himself, as it were, admitted into the company and present at the conversation. Defoe has imitated him successfully in his *Robinson Crusoe,* in his *Moll Flanders,* and other pieces; and Richardson has done the same in his *Pamela,* etc.

On approaching the island, we found it was in a place where there could be no landing, there being a great surf on the stony beach. So we dropped anchor and swung out our cable toward the shore. Some people came down to the shore and halloed to us, as we did to them; but the wind was so high and the surf so loud that we could not understand each other. There were some small boats near the shore, and we made signs and called to them to fetch us; but they either did not comprehend us, or it was impracticable, so they went off. Night approaching, we had no remedy but to have patience till the wind abated; and, in the meantime, the boatmen and myself concluded to sleep, if we could; and so we crowded into the hatches, where we joined the Dutchman, who was still wet, and the spray breaking over the head of our boat leaked through to us, so that we were soon almost as wet as he. In this manner we lay all night with very little rest; but, the wind abating the next day, we made a shift to reach Amboy before night, having been thirty hours on the water without victuals or any drink but a bottle of filthy rum, the water we sailed on being salt.

In the evening I found myself very feverish and went to bed; but, having read somewhere that cold water drunk plentifully was good for a fever, I followed the prescription and sweat plentifully most of the night. My fever left me, and, in the morning, crossing the ferry, I proceeded on my journey on foot, having fifty miles to Burlington, where I was told I should find boats that would carry me the rest of the way to Philadelphia.

It rained very hard all the day. I was thoroughly soaked, and by noon a good deal tired, so I stopped at a poor inn where I stayed all night, beginning now to wish I had never left home. I made so miserable a figure, too, that I found, by the questions asked me, I was suspected to be some runaway indentured servant and in danger of being taken up on that suspicion. However, I proceeded next day, and got in the evening to an inn within eight or ten miles of Burlington, kept by one Dr. Brown. He entered into conversation with me while I took some refreshment, and, finding I had read a little, became very obliging and friendly. Our acquaintance continued all the rest of his life. He had been, I imagine, an

ambulatory quack doctor, for there was no town in England or any country in Europe of which he could not give a very particular account. He had some letters, and was ingenious, but he was an infidel, and wickedly undertook, some years after, to turn the Bible in doggerel verse, as Cotton had done formerly with Virgil. By this means he set many facts in a ridiculous light, and might have done mischief with weak minds if his work had been published; but it never was.

At his house I lay that night, and arrived the next morning at Burlington, but had the mortification to find that the regular boats had gone a little before, and no other expected to go before Tuesday, this being Saturday. Wherefore, I returned to an old woman in the town, of whom I had bought some gingerbread to eat on the water, and asked her advice. She proposed to lodge me till a passage by some other boat occurred. I accepted her offer, being much fatigued by traveling on foot. Understanding I was a printer, she would have had me remain in that town and follow my business, being ignorant what stock was necessary to begin with. She was very hospitable, gave me a dinner of ox-cheek with great goodwill, accepting only of a pot of ale in return; and I thought myself fixed till Tuesday should come.

However, walking in the evening by the side of the river, a boat came by, which I found was going toward Philadelphia, with several people in her. They took me in, and, as there was no wind, we rowed all the way; and, about midnight, not having yet seen the city, some of the company were confident we must have passed it, and would row no farther. The others knew not where we were; so we put toward the shore, got into a creek, landed near an old fence, with the rails of which we made a fire, the night being cold in October, and there we remained till daylight. Then one of the company knew the place to be

Cooper's Creek, a little above Philadelphia, which we saw as soon as we got out of the creek, and arrived there about 8 or 9 o'clock on the Sunday morning, and landed at Market Street wharf.

I have been the more particular in this description of my journey, and shall be so of my first entry into that city, that you may in your mind compare such unlikely beginnings with the figure I have since made there. I was in my working dress, my best clothes coming round by sea. I was dirty from my being so long in the boat; my pockets were stuffed out with shirts and stockings; and I knew no one, nor where to look for lodging. Fatigued with walking, rowing, and want of sleep, I was very hungry; and my whole stock of cash consisted in a single dollar and about a shilling in copper coin, which I gave to the boatmen for my passage. At first they refused it on account of my having rowed; but I insisted on their taking it. Man is sometimes more generous when he has little money than when he has plenty, perhaps to prevent his being thought to have but little.

I walked toward the top of the street, gazing about, still in Market Street, where I met a boy with bread, I had often made a meal of dry bread, and, inquiring where he had bought it, I went immediately to the baker's he directed me to. I asked for biscuits, meaning such as we had at Boston; that sort, it seems, was not made in Philadelphia. I then asked for a threepenny loaf, and was told they had none. Not knowing the different prices nor the names of the different sorts of bread, I told him give me threepenny worth of any sort. He gave me, accordingly, three great puffy rolls. I was surprised at the quantity, but took it, and, having no room in my pockets, walked off with a roll under each arm and eating the other. Thus I went up Market Street as far as Fourth Street, passing by the door of Mr. Read, my future wife's father; when she, standing at the door, saw me, and

thought I made, as I certainly did, a most awkward, ridiculous appearance. Then I turned and went down Chestnut Street and part of Walnut Street, eating my roll all the way, and coming round, found myself again at Market Street wharf, near the boat I came in, to which I went for a draft of the river water; and, being filled with one of my rolls, gave the other two to a woman and her child that came down the river in the boat with us and were waiting to go farther.

Thus refreshed, I walked again up the street, which by this time had many clean-dressed people in it, who were all walking the same way. I joined them, and thereby was led into the great meetinghouse of the Quakers near the market. I sat down among them, and, after looking round awhile and hearing nothing said, being very drowsy through labor and want of rest the preceding night, I fell fast asleep, and continued so till the meeting broke up, when someone was kind enough to rouse me. This, therefore, was the first house I was in, or slept in, in Philadelphia.

I then walked down toward the river, and, looking in the faces of everyone, I met a young Quaker man, whose countenance pleased me, and, accosting him, requested he would tell me where a stranger could get a lodging. We were then near the sign of the Three Mariners. "Here," said he, "is a house where they receive strangers, but it is not a reputable one; if thou wilt walk with me, I'll show thee a better one." And he conducted me to the Crooked Billet in Water Street. There I got a dinner; and, while I was eating, several questions were asked me, as from my youth and appearance I was suspected of being a runaway.

After dinner, my host having shown to a bed, I lay myself on it without undressing, and slept till six in the evening, was called to supper. I went to bed again very early, and slept very soundly till next morning. Then I dressed myself as neat as I could, and went to Andrew Bradford, the printer's. I found in the shop the old man, his father, whom I had seen at New York and who, traveling on horseback, had got to Philadelphia before me. He introduced me to his son, who received me civilly, gave me a breakfast, but told me he did not at present want a hand, being lately supplied with one; but there was another printer in town lately set up, one Keimer, who perhaps might employ me. If not, I should be welcome to lodge at his house, and he would give me a little work to do now and then till fuller business should offer.

The old gentleman said he would go with me to the new printer; and when we found him, "Neighbor," said Bradford, "I have brought to see you a young man of your business; perhaps you may want such a one." He asked me a few questions, put a composing stick in my hand to see how I worked, and then said he would employ me soon, though he had just then nothing for me to do; and taking old Bradford, whom he had never seen before, to be one of the townspeople that had a goodwill for him, entered into conversation on his present undertaking and prospects; while Bradford (not discovering that he was the other printer's father), on Keimer's saying he expected soon to get the greatest part of the business into his own hands, drew him on by artful questions, and starting little doubts, to explain all his views, what influence he relied on, and in what manner he intended to proceed. I, who stood by and heard all, saw immediately that one was a crafty old sophister and the other a true novice. Bradford left me with Keimer, who was greatly surprised when I told him who the old man was.

Keimer's printing house, I found, consisted of an old damaged press, and a small, worn-out font of English types which he was using himself, composing an elegy on Aquilla Rose, before mentioned, an ingenious young man of excellent character, much respected in the town, secretary to the Assembly, and a pretty poet. Keimer made verses, too, but very indifferently. He could not be said to *write* them, for his method was to *compose* them in the types directly out of his head; there being no copy but one pair of cases, and the elegy probably requiring all the letter, no one could help him. I endeavored to put his press (which he had not yet used and of which he understood nothing) into order to be worked with; and promising to come and print off his elegy as soon as he should have got it ready, I returned to Bradford's, who gave me a little job to do for the present, and there I lodged and dieted. A few days after, Keimer sent for me to print off the elegy. And now he had got another pair of cases, and a pamphlet to reprint, on which he set me to work.

These two printers I found poorly qualified for their business. Bradford had been bred to it and was very illiterate; and Keimer, though something of a scholar, was a mere compositor, knowing nothing of presswork. He had been one of the French prophets and could act their enthusiastic agitations. At this time he did not profess any particular religion, but something of all on occasion; was very ignorant of the world, and had, as I afterward found, a good deal of the knave in his composition. He did not like my lodging at Bradford's while I worked with him. He had a house, indeed, but without furniture, so he could not lodge me; but he got me a lodging at Mr. Read's, before mentioned, who was the owner of his house; and my chest and clothes being come by this time, I made rather a more respectable appearance in the eyes of Miss Read than I had done when she first happened to see me eating my roll in the street.

I began now to have some acquaintance among the young people of the town that were lovers of reading, with whom I spent my evenings very pleasantly; and gained money by my industry and frugality. I lived very contented and forgot Boston as much as I could, and did not wish it should be known where I resided, except to my friend Collins, who was in the secret and kept it faithfully.

At length, however, an incident happened that occasioned my return home much sooner than I had intended. I had a brother-in-law, Robert Holmes, master of a sloop that traded between Boston and Delaware. He being at Newcastle, forty miles below Philadelphia, and hearing of me, wrote me a letter mentioning the grief of my relations and friends in Boston at my abrupt departure, assuring me of their goodwill toward me and that everything would be accommodated to my mind if I would return, to which he entreated me earnestly. I wrote an answer to his letter, thanking him for his advice, but stated my reasons for quitting Boston so fully and in such a light as to convince him that I was not so wrong as he had apprehended. . . .

About this time [1730], our club, meeting not at a tavern but in a little room of Mr. Grace's set apart for that purpose, a proposition was made by me that, since our books were often referred to in our disquisitions upon the queries, it might be convenient to us to have them all together when we met, that, upon occasion, they might be consulted. And, by thus clubbing our books to a common library, we should, while we liked to keep them together, have each of us the advantage of using the books of all the other members, which would be nearly as beneficial as if each owned the whole. It was liked and agreed to, and we filled one end of the room with such books as we could best spare. The number was not so great as we expected; and, though they had been of great use, yet some inconveniences occuring for want of due care of them, the collection, after about a year, was separated and each took his books home again.

And now I set on foot my first project of a public nature — that for a subscription library. I drew up the proposals, got them put into form by our great scrivener Brockden, and, by the help of my friends in the Junto, procured fifty subscribers of 40s. each to begin with and 10s. a year for fifty years, the term our company was to continue. We afterward obtained a charter, the company being increased to one hundred. This was the mother of all the North American subscription libraries, now so numerous. It is become a great thing itself and continually goes on increasing. These libraries have improved the general conversation of the Americans, made the common tradesmen and farmers as intelligent as most gentlemen from other countries, and perhaps have contributed in some degree to the stand so generally made throughout the colonies in defense of their privileges. . . .

In 1732 I first published my *Almanac*, under the name of Richard Saunders; it was continued by me about twenty-five years and commonly called *Poor Richard's Almanac*. I endeavored to make it both entertaining and useful, and it accordingly came to be in such demand that I reaped considerable profit from it, vending annually near 10,000. And observing that it was generally read (scarce any neighborhood in the province being without it), I considered it as a proper vehicle for conveying instruction among the common people, who bought scarcely any other books. I therefore filled all the little spaces that occurred between the remarkable days in the calendar with proverbial sentences, chiefly such as inculcated industry and frugality as the means of procuring wealth, and thereby securing virtue, it being more difficult for a man in want to act always honestly, as (to use here one of those proverbs) "it is hard for an empty sack to stand upright."

These proverbs, which contained the wisdom of many ages and nations, I assembled and formed into a connected discourse pre-fixed to the *Almanac* of 1757, as the harangue of a wise old man to the people attending an auction. The bringing all these scattered counsels thus into a focus enabled them to make greater impression. The piece, being universally approved, was copied in all the newspapers of the American continent; reprinted in Britain on a large sheet of paper to be stuck up in houses; two translations were made of it in French; and great numbers bought by the clergy and gentry to distribute gratis among their poor parishioners and tenants. In Pennsylvania, as it discouraged useless expense in foreign superfluities, some thought it had its share of influence in producing that growing plenty of money which was observable for several years after its publication.

I considered my newspaper, also, another means of communicating instruction, and, in that view, frequently reprinted in it extracts from the *Spectator* and other moral writers; and sometimes published little pieces of mine own, which had been first composed for reading in our Junto. Of these are a Socratic dialogue, tending to prove that, whatever might be his parts and abilities, a vicious man could not properly be called a man of sense; and a discourse on self-denial, showing that virtue was not secure till its practice became a habitude and was free from the opposition of contrary inclinations. These may be found in the papers about the beginning of 1735.

In the conduct of my newspaper, I carefully excluded all libeling and personal abuse, which is of late years become so disgraceful to our country. Whenever I was solicited to insert anything of that kind, and the writers pleaded (as they generally did) the liberty of the press, and that a newspaper was like a stagecoach in which anyone who would pay had a right to a place, my answer was that I would print the piece separately if desired, and the author might have as many copies as he pleased to dis-

Benjamin Franklin's birthplace depicted in a 19th-century lithograph

tribute himself, but that I would not take upon me to spread his detraction; and that, having contracted with my subscribers to furnish them with what might be either useful or entertaining, I could not fill their papers with private altercation, in which they had no concern, without doing them manifest injustice.

Now, many of our printers make no scruple of gratifying the malice of individuals by false accusations of the fairest characters among ourselves, augmenting animosity even to the producing of duels; and are, moreover, so indiscreet as to print scurrilous reflections on the government of neighboring states, and even on the conduct of our best national allies, which may be attended with the most pernicious consequences. These things I mention as a caution to young printers, and that they may be encouraged not to pollute the presses and disgrace their profession by such infamous practices, but refuse steadily, as they may see by my example that such a course of conduct will not, on the whole, be injurious to their interests. . . .

In 1737, Colonel Spotswood, late governor of Virginia, and then postmaster general, being dissatisfied with his deputy at Philadelphia, respecting some negligence in rendering and want of exactness in framing his accounts, took from him his commission and offered it to me. I accepted it readily, and found it of great advantage; for, though the salary was small, it facilitated the correspondence that improved my newspaper, [and] increased the number demanded, as well as the advertisements to be inserted, so that it came to afford me a considerable income. My old competitor's newspaper declined proportionally, and I was satisfied without retaliating his refusal, while postmaster, to permit my papers being carried by the riders. Thus he suffered greatly from his neglect in due accounting; and I mention it as a lesson to those young men who may be employed in managing affairs for others, that they should always render accounts and make remittances with great clearness and punctuality. The character of observing such a conduct is the most powerful of all recommendations to new employments and increase of business.

I began now to turn my thoughts to public affairs, beginning, however, with small matters. The city watch was one of the first things that I conceived to want regulation. It was managed by the constables of the respective wards in turn; the constable summoned a number of housekeepers to attend him for the night. Those who chose never to attend, paid him 6s. a year to be excused, which was supposed to go for hiring substitutes, but was, in reality, much more than was necessary for that purpose, and made the constableship a place of profit; and the constable, for a little drink, often got such ragamuffins about him as a watch that respectable housekeepers did not choose to

mix with. Walking the rounds, too, was often neglected, and most of the nights spent in tippling. I thereupon wrote a paper, to be read in Junto, representing these irregularities, but insisting more particularly on the inequality of this 6s. tax of the constables, respecting the circumstances of those who paid it, since a poor widow housekeeper, all whose property to be guarded by the watch did not perhaps exceed the value of £50, paid as much as the wealthiest merchant, who had thousands of pounds' worth of goods in his stores.

On the whole, I proposed as a more effectual watch, the hiring of proper men to serve constantly in that business; and, as a more equitable way of supporting the charge, the levying of a tax that should be proportioned to the property. This idea, being approved by the Junto, was communicated to the other clubs, but as originating in each of them; and though the plan was not immediately carried into execution, yet, by preparing the minds of people for the change, it paved the way for the law obtained a few years after, when the members of our clubs were grown into more influence.

About this time I wrote a paper (first to be read in Junto, but it was afterward published) on the different accidents and carelessnesses by which houses were set on fire, with cautions against them, and means proposed of avoiding them. This was spoken of as a useful piece, and gave rise to a project, which soon followed it, of forming a company for the more ready extinguishing of fires and mutual assistance in removing and securing of goods when in danger. Associates in this scheme were presently found, amounting to thirty. Our articles of agreement obliged every member to keep always in good order and fit for use a certain number of leather buckets, with strong bags and baskets (for packing and transporting goods), which were to be brought to every fire; and we agreed about once a month to spend a social evening together in discoursing and communicating such ideas as occurred to us upon the subject of fires as might be useful in our conduct on such occasions.

The utility of this institution soon appeared, and many more desiring to be admitted than we thought convenient for one company, they were advised to form another, which was accordingly done; and thus went on one new company after another, till they became so numerous as to include most of the inhabitants who were men of property. And now, at the time of my writing this (though upward of fifty years since its establishment), that which I first formed, called the Union Fire Company, still subsists, though the first members are all deceased but one, who is older by a year than I am. The fines that have been paid by members for absence at the monthly meetings have been applied to the purchase of fire engines, ladders, fire hooks, and other useful implements for each company, so that I question whether there is a city in the world better provided with the means of putting a stop to beginning conflagrations; and, in fact, since these institutions, the city has never lost by fire more than one or two houses at a time, and the flames have often been extinguished before the house in which they began has been half consumed. . . .

It had been proposed that we should encourage the scheme for building a battery [cannon] by laying out the present stock, then about £60, in tickets of the lottery. By our rules, no money could be disposed of till the next meeting after the proposal. The company consisted of thirty members, of whom twenty-two were Quakers and eight only of other persuasions. We eight punctually attended the meeting; but, though we thought that some of the Quakers would join us, we were by no means sure of a majority. Only one Quaker, Mr.

James Morris, appeared to oppose the measure. He expressed much sorrow that it had ever been proposed, as he said Friends were all against it, and it would create such discord as might break up the company. We told him that we saw no reason for that; we were the minority, and if Friends were against the measure and outvoted us, we must and should, agreeably to the usage of all societies, submit. When the hour for business arrived, it was moved to put this to the vote; he allowed we might do it by the rules, but, as he could assure us that a number of members intended to be present for the purpose of opposing it, it would be but candid to allow a little time for their appearing.

While we were disputing this, a waiter came to tell me that two gentlemen below desired to speak with me. I went down and found there two of our Quaker members. They told me there were eight of them assembled at a tavern just by; that they were determined to come and vote with us if there should be occasion, which they hoped would not be the case; and desired we would not call for their assistance if we could do without it, as their voting for such a measure might embroil them with their elders and friends. Being thus secure of a majority, I went up, and, after a little seeming hesitation, agreed to a delay of another hour. This Mr. Morris allowed to be extremely fair. Not one of his opposing friends appeared, at which he expressed great surprise; and, at the expiration of the hour, we carried the resolution eight to one; and as, of the twenty-two Quakers, eight were ready to vote with us and thirteen, by their absence, manifested that they were not inclined to oppose the measure, I afterward estimated the proportion of Quakers sincerely against defense as one to twenty-one only; for these were all regular members of that society, and in good reputation among them, and who had notice of what was proposed at that meeting.

The honorable and learned Mr. Logan, who had always been of that sect, wrote an address to them, declaring his approbation of *defensive* war and supporting his opinion by many strong arguments. He put into my hands £60 to be laid out in lottery tickets for the battery, with directions to apply what prizes might be drawn wholly to that service. He told me the following anecdote of his old master, William Penn, respecting defense. He came over from England when a young man, with that proprietary, and as his secretary. It was wartime, and their ship was chased by an armed vessel, supposed to be an enemy. Their captain prepared for defense; but told William Penn and his company of Quakers that he did not expect their assistance and they might retire into the cabin, which they did, except James Logan, who chose to stay upon deck, and was quartered to a gun. The supposed enemy proved a friend, so there was no fighting; but, when the secretary went down to communicate the intelligence, William Penn rebuked him severely for staying upon deck and undertaking to assist in defending the vessel, contrary to the principles of Friends, especially as it had not been required by the captain. This reprimand, being before all the company, piqued the secretary, who answered, "I, being thy servant, why did thee not order me to come down? But thee was willing enough that I should stay and help to fight the ship when thee thought there was danger."

My being many years in the Assembly, the majority of which were constantly Quakers, gave me frequent opportunities of seeing the embarrassment given them by their principle against war, whenever application was made to them, by order of the Crown, to grant aids for military purposes. They were unwilling to offend government, on the one hand, by a direct refusal; and their friends, the body of the Quakers, on the other, by a compliance contrary to their principles, using a variety of evasions to avoid complying, and modes of disguising the compliance when it became unavoidable. The common mode at last was to grant money under the phrase of its being "for the King's use," and never to inquire how it was applied.

But, if the demand was not directly from the Crown, that phrase was found not so proper, and some other was to be invented. Thus, when powder was wanting (I think it was for the garrison at Louisburg), and the government of New England solicited a grant of some from Pennsylvania, which was much urged on the House by Governor Thomas, they could not grant money to buy *powder* because that was an ingredient of war; but they voted an aid to New England of £3,000 to be put into the hands of the governor, and appropriated it for the purchasing of bread, flour, wheat, or *other grain.* Some of the Council, desirous of giving the House still further embarrassment, advised the governor not to accept provision as not being the thing he had demanded; but he replied, "I shall take the money, for I understand very well their meaning; *other grain* is gunpowder," which he accordingly bought, and they never objected to it.

It was in allusion to this fact that, when in our fire company we feared the success of our proposal in favor of the lottery, and I had said to a friend of mine, one of our members, "If we fail, let us move the purchase of a fire engine with the money; the Quakers can have no objection to that; and then, if you nominate me and I you as a committee for that purpose, we will buy a great gun, which is certainly a *fire engine.*"

"I see," said he, "you have improved by being so long in the Assembly; your equivocal project would be just a match for their wheat or *other grain.*"

Those embarrassments that the Quakers suffered from having established and published it as one of their principles, that no kind of war was lawful, being once published, they could not afterward, however they might change their minds, easily get rid of, reminds me what I think a more prudent conduct in another sect among us, that of the Dunkers. I was acquainted with one of its founders, Michael Weffare, soon after it appeared. He complained to me that they were grievously calumniated by the zealots of other persuasions, and charged with abominable principles and practices, to which they were utter strangers. I told him this had always been the case with new sects, and that, to put a stop to such abuse, I imagined it might be well to publish the articles of their belief and the rules of their discipline. He said that it had been proposed among them but not agreed to for this reason:

> When we were first drawn together as a society [said he], it had pleased God to enlighten our minds so far as to see that some doctrines, which were esteemed truths, were errors; and that others, which we had esteemed errors, were real truths. From time to time He has been pleased to afford us further light, and our principles have been improving and our errors diminishing. Now we are not sure that we are arrived at the end of this progression and at the perfection of spiritual or theological knowledge; and we fear that, if we should once print our confession of faith, we should feel ourselves as if bound and confined by it, and perhaps be unwilling to receive further improvement, and our successors still more so, as conceiving what their elders and founders had done to be something sacred, never to be departed from.

This modesty in a sect is perhaps a singular instance in the history of mankind, every other sect supposing itself in possession of all truth, and that those who differ are so far in the wrong; like a man traveling in foggy weather, those at some distance before him on the road he sees wrapped up in the fog, as well as those behind him, and also the people in the fields on each side, but near him all appear clear, though in truth he is as much in the fog as any of them. To avoid this kind of embarrassment, the Quakers have of late years been gradually declining the public service in the Assembly and in the magistracy, choosing rather to quit their power than their principle.

George Washington — the Joshua, who commanded the sun and the moon to stand still, and they obeyed him.

> BENJAMIN FRANKLIN, at an official dinner. The British Ambassador proposed as a toast: "England — the sun — whose bright beams enlighten and fructify the remotest corners of the earth." The French Ambassador proposed: "France — the moon — whose mild, steady, and cheering rays are the delight of all nations, consoling them in darkness." Franklin then proposed the above toast.

Oh, very well, Doctor, I had rather relate your stories than other men's truths.

> ABBÉ RAYNAL, when told by Benjamin Franklin that Polly Baker was a fabrication

I succeed Dr. Franklin. No man can replace him.

> THOMAS JEFFERSON, at the Court of France when asked if he replaced Franklin as American ambassador, 1785

1776

91.

"Yankee Doodle"

France, Spain, the Netherlands, Germany, and Hungary have all claimed "Yankee Doodle," but the melody seems to have come first from England, where it was a children's game song called "Lucy Locket." Brought to America by the English soldiers who fought in the French and Indian War, the song became popular among the colonists, each settlement having its own set of lyrics. During the Revolutionary War, the British soldiers used a derisive set of lyrics to mock the shabby colonial soldiers, and the colonists in turn had another set of words that eventually became their battle cry. "Yankee" was a contemptuous nickname the British used for the New Englanders, and "doodle" meant "dope, half-wit, fool."

YANKEE DOODLE

Father and I went down to camp
Along with Captain Gooding,
And there we saw the men and boys
As thick as hasty pudding.

    Yankee Doodle keep it up,
    Yankee Doodle Dandy,
    Mind the music and the step,
    And with the girls be handy.

There was Captain Washington
Upon a slapping stallion
A-giving orders to his men —
There must have been a million.

Then I saw a swamping gun
As large as logs of maple
Upon a very little cart,
A load for Father's cattle.

Every time they shot it off
It took a horn of powder
And made a noise like father's gun
Only a nation louder.

There I saw a wooden keg
With heads made out of leather;
They knocked upon it with some sticks
To call the folks together.

Then they'd fife away like fun
And play on cornstalk fiddles,
And some had ribbons red as blood
All bound around their middles.

I can't tell you all I saw —
They kept up such a smother.
I took my hat off, made a bow,
And scampered home to mother.

92.

Massachusetts Suspends the Royal Authority

Early in 1776, most features of royal authority had vanished in the colonies, although reconciliation with Britain still seemed possible. On January 23, the General Court of Massachusetts, at the urging of the Continental Congress, issued a proclamation ousting the royal governor. The management of the colony's affairs reverted to the assembly until such time as the King would appoint a new governor compatible with the spirit of the old charter.

Source: Niles: "Proclamation by the Great and General Court of the Colony of Massachusetts Bay, January 23, 1776."

As THE HAPPINESS of the people is the sole end of government, so the consent of the people is the only foundation of it, in reason, morality, and the natural fitness of things. And, therefore, every act of government, every exercise of sovereignty against or without the consent of the people is injustice, usurpation, and tyranny.

It is a maxim that in every government there must exist, somewhere, a supreme, sovereign, absolute, and uncontrollable power; but this power resides always in the body of the people; and it never was, or can be delegated to one man, or a few; the great Creator has never given to men a right to vest others with authority over them, unlimited either in duration or degree.

When kings, ministers, governors, or legislators, therefore, instead of exercising the powers entrusted with them, according to the principles, forms and proportions stated by the constitution, and established by the original compact, prostitute those powers to the purposes of oppression — to subvert, instead of supporting a free constitution; to destroy, instead of preserving the lives, liberties and properties of the people — they are no longer to be deemed magistrates vested with a sacred character, but become public enemies, and ought to be resisted.

The administration of Great Britain, despising equally the justice, humanity, and magnanimity of their ancestors, and the rights, liberties, and courage of *Americans,* have, for a course of years, labored to establish a sovereignty in America, not founded in the consent of the people but in the mere will of persons, a thousand leagues from us, whom we know not, and have endeavored to establish this sovereignty over us, against our consent, in all cases whatsoever.

The colonies, during this period, have recurred to every peaceable resource in a free constitution, by petitions and remonstrances, to obtain justice; which has been not only denied to them but they have been treated with unexampled indignity and contempt; and, at length, open war of the most atrocious, cruel, and sanguinary kind has been commenced against them. To this an open, manly, and successful resistance has hitherto been made; thirteen colonies are now firmly united in the conduct of this most just and necessary war, under the wise councils of their Congress.

It is the will of Providence for wise, righteous, and gracious ends that this colony should have been singled out, by the enemies of America, as the first object, both of their envy and their revenge; and, after having been made the subject of several merciless and vindictive statutes, one of which was intended to subvert our constitution by charter, is made the seat of war.

No effectual resistance to the system of tyranny prepared for us could be made without either instant recourse to arms or a temporary suspension of the ordinary powers of government and tribunals of justice. To the last of which evils, in hope of a speedy reconciliation with Great Britain, upon equitable terms, the Congress advised us to submit: — And mankind has seen a phenomenon, without example in the political world, a large and populous colony, subsisting in great decency and order, for more than a year, under such a suspension of government.

But as our enemies have proceeded to such barbarous extremities, commencing hostilities upon the good people of this colony, and with unprecedented malice exerting their power to spread the calamities of fire, sword, and famine through the land, and no reasonable prospect remains of a speedy reconciliation with Great Britain, the Congress have resolved:

That no obedience being due to the act of Parliament for altering the charter of the colony of Massachusetts Bay, nor to a governor or lieutenant governor, who will not observe the directions of, but endeavor to subvert that charter, the governor and lieutenant governor of that colony are to be considered as absent, and their offices vacant. And as there is no council there, and inconveniences arising from the suspension of the powers of government are intolerable, especially at a time when General Gage has actually levied war, and is carrying on hostilities against His Majesty's peaceable and loyal subjects of that colony: that, in order to conform as near as may be to the spirit and substance of the charter, it be recommended to the provincial convention to write letters to the inhabitants of the several places which are entitled to representation in assembly, requesting them to choose such representatives; and that the assembly, when chosen, elect counselors; and that such assembly and council exercise the powers of government, until a governor of His Majesty's appointment will consent to govern the colony according to its charter.

In pursuance of which advice, the good people of this colony have chosen a full and free representation of themselves, who, being convened in assembly, have elected a Council; who, as the executive branch of government, have constituted necessary officers through the colony. The present generation, therefore, may be congratulated on the acquisition of a form of government more immediately, in all its branches, under the influence and control of the people; and therefore more free and happy than was enjoyed by their ancestors. But as a government so popular can be supported only by universal knowledge and virtue in the body of the people, it is the duty of all ranks to promote the means of education, for the rising generation, as well as true religion, purity of manners, and integrity of life among all orders and degrees.

As an army has become necessary for our defense, and in all free states the civil must provide for and control the military power, the major part of the Council have appointed magistrates and courts of justice in every county whose happiness is so connected with that of the people that it is difficult to suppose they can abuse their trust. The business of it is to see those laws enforced which are necessary for the preservation of peace, virtue, and good order. And the

Great and General Court expects and requires that all necessary support and assistance be given, and all proper obedience yielded to them; and will deem every person who shall fail of his duty in this respect toward them a disturber of the peace of this colony, and deserving of exemplary punishment.

That piety and virtue, which alone can secure the freedom of any people, may be encouraged, and vice and immorality suppressed, the Great and General Court have thought fit to issue this proclamation, commanding and enjoining it upon the good people of this colony, that they lead sober, religious, and peaceable lives, avoiding all blasphemies, contempt of the Holy Scriptures, and of the Lord's Day, and all other crimes and misdemeanors, all debauchery, profaneness, corruption, venality, all riotous and tumultuous proceedings, and all immoralities whatsoever; and that they decently and reverently attend the public worship of God, at all times acknowledging with gratitude His merciful interposition in their behalf, devoutly confiding in Him, as the God of armies, by whose favor and protection alone they may hope for success in their present conflict.

93.

Virginia Opposes the Arming of Slaves

Virginia's Governor Dunmore had declared martial law in November 1775 and had offered freedom to any slave who would desert his master. These actions infuriated the colonists, and in December, troops met and defeated the governor's forces in a battle at Great Bridge. In retaliation the governor bombarded and fired Norfolk. The heightening colonial animosity toward royal authority is reflected in the resolution of the Virginia Convention at Williamsburg, January 25, 1776.

Source: Niles: "Proceedings in the Convention of Virginia Relating to the Proclamation of Lord Dunmore."

Resolved unanimously, that this Convention do highly approve of Colonel Woodford's conduct manifested as well in the success of the troops under his command as in the humane treatment of, and kind attention to, the unfortunate though brave officers and soldiers who were made prisoners in the late action near the Great Bridge, and that the president communicate to Colonel Woodford the sense of his country on this occasion.

Whereas Lord Dunmore, by his proclamation, dated on board the ship *William*, the 7th day of November, 1775, has presumed, in direct violation of the constitution and the laws of this country, to declare martial law in force, and to be executed throughout this colony, whereby our lives, our liberty, and our property are arbitrarily subjected to his power and direction; *and whereas* the said Lord Dunmore, assuming powers which the King himself cannot exercise, to intimidate the good people of this colony into a compliance with his arbitrary will, has declared those who do not immediately repair to his standard, and submit in all things to a government not warranted by the constitution, to be in actual rebellion, and thereby to have incurred the penalties inflicted by the laws for such offenses; and has offered freedom to the servants and slaves of those he is pleased to term rebels, arming them against their masters, and destroying the peace and happiness of His Majesty's good and faithful subjects whose property is rendered insecure and whose lives are exposed to the dangers of a general insurrection. We, as guardians of the lives and liberty of the people, our constituents, conceived it to be indispensably our duty to protect them against every species of despotism, and to endeavor to remove those fears with which they are so justly alarmed. . . .

Impressed with a just and ardent zeal for the welfare and happiness of our countrymen, we trust they will, on their part, exert themselves in defense of our common cause, and that we shall all acquit ourselves like freemen, being compelled by a disagreeable but absolute necessity of repelling force by force, to maintain our just rights and privileges; and we appeal to God, who is the Sovereign Disposer of all events, for the justice of our cause, trusting to His unerring wisdom to direct our councils and give success to our arms.

Whereas Lord Dunmore, by his proclamation, dated on board the ship *William* off Norfolk, the 7th day of November, 1775, has offered freedom to such ablebodied slaves as are willing to join him and take up arms against the good people of this colony, giving thereby encouragement to a general insurrection which may induce a necessity of inflicting the severest punishments upon those unhappy people already deluded by his base and insidious arts, *and whereas*, by an act of the General Assembly now in force in this colony, it is enacted that all Negro or other slaves conspiring to rebel or make insurrection shall suffer death and be excluded all benefit of clergy — we think it proper to declare that all slaves who have been, or shall be, seduced by His Lordship's proclamation, or other arts, to desert their master's service, and take up arms against the inhabitants of this colony, shall be liable to such punishment as shall hereafter be directed by the Convention. And to the end that all such who have taken this unlawful and wicked step may return in safety to their duty, and escape the punishment due to their crimes, we hereby promise pardon to them, they surrendering themselves to Col. William Woodford or any other commander of our troops, and not appearing in arms after the publication hereof. And we do further earnestly recommend it to all humane and benevolent persons in this colony to explain and make known this our offer of mercy to those unfortunate people.

And whereas, notwithstanding the favorable and kind dispositions shown by the convention and the natives of this colony, and the extraordinary and unexampled indulgence by them held out to the natives of Great Britain residing in this colony (the Scotch who gave themselves this title in their petition), many of these have lately become strict adherents to the Lord Dunmore and the most active promoters of all his cruel and arbitrary persecutions of the good people of this colony, not only by violating the Continental association, to which they had solemnly subscribed, in many the most flagrant instances; not merely by giving intelligence to our enemies and furnishing them with provisions, but by propagating, as well in Great Britain as in this colony, many of the most mischievous falsehoods, to the great prejudice and dishonor of this country. And moreover, many of these natives of Great Britain, instead of giving their assistance in suppressing insurrections, have contrary to all faith solemnly plighted in their petition excited our slaves to rebellion, and some of them have daringly led those slaves in arms against our inhabitants; the committee having these things in full proof, and considering their alarming and dangerous tendency, do give it as their opinion, and *it is accordingly resolved,* that the former resolution in their favor ought from henceforth to be totally abrogated and rescinded; that none of the freemen, inhabitants of this country, wherever born, ought to be exempted from any of the burdens or dangers to which the colony is exposed: but that as good citizens, it is incumbent on them to use every exertion of their power and abilities in the common defense; and should any persons of ability decline or shrink from so necessary a duty to the community, that all such, except those who have taken up arms against our inhabitants, or shown themselves to us, may be permitted, under a license of the committee of safety, to leave the country.

94.

Tom Paine: Epistle to the Quakers

A January 1776 meeting of Quakers in New Jersey issued a statement ". . . touching the commotions now prevailing in these and other parts of America." This tract urged Americans to nonviolence in their dealings with Britain. Tom Paine, himself of Quaker descent, took the Quakers to task for their position and asked them to reexamine their own principles for a lack of consistent thinking. His Epistle to Quakers was published later in the same year.

Source: *The Political Writings of Thomas Paine,* New York, 1830, Vol. I.

THE WRITER of this is one of those few who never dishonors religion either by ridiculing or caviling at any denomination whatsoever. To God, and not to man, are all men accountable on the score of religion. Wherefore, this epistle is not so properly addressed to you as a religious but as a political body, dabbling in matters which the professed quietude of your principles instruct you not to meddle with.

As you have, without a proper authority for so doing, put yourselves in the place of the whole body of the Quakers, so the writer of this, in order to be in an equal rank with yourselves, is under the necessity of putting himself in the place of all those who approve the very writings and principles against which your testimony is directed. And he has chosen their singular situation in order that you might discover in him that presumption of character which you cannot see in yourselves. For neither he nor you have any claim or title to political representation.

When men have departed from the right way, it is no wonder that they stumble and fall. And it is evident from the manner in which ye have managed your testimony that politics (as a religious body of men) is not your proper walk; for however well adapted it might appear to you, it is, nevertheless, a jumble of good and bad unwisely put together, and the conclusion drawn therefrom both unnatural and unjust.

The first two pages (and the whole does make but four) we give you credit for, and expect the same civility from you, because the love and desire of peace is not confined to Quakerism; it is the natural as well as the religious wish of all denominations of men. And on this ground, as men laboring to establish an independent constitution of our own, do we exceed all others in our hope, end, and aim. *Our plan is peace forever.* We are tired of contention with Britain, and can see no real end to it but in a final separation. We act consistently, because for the sake of introducing an endless and uninterrupted peace, do we bear the evils and the burdens of the present day. We are endeavoring, and will steadily continue to endeavor, to separate and dissolve a connection which has already filled our land with blood; and which, while the name of it remains, will be the fatal cause of future mischiefs to both countries.

We fight neither for revenge nor conquest; neither from pride nor passion; we are not insulting the world with our fleets and armies, nor ravaging the globe for plunder. Beneath the shade of our own vines are we attacked; in our own houses and on our own lands is the violence committed against us. We view our enemies in the characters of highwaymen and housebreakers, and having no defense for ourselves in the civil law, are obliged to punish them by the military one, and apply the sword, in the very case where you have before now applied the halter. Perhaps we feel for the ruined and insulted sufferers in all and every part of the continent with a degree of tenderness which has not yet made its way into some of your bosoms. But be ye sure that ye mistake not the cause and ground of your testimony. Call not coldness of soul religion; nor put the bigot in the place of the Christian.

O ye partial ministers of your own acknowledged principles! If the bearing arms be sinful, the first going to war must be more so, by all the difference between willful attack and unavoidable defense. Wherefore, if ye really preach from conscience, and mean not to make a political hobbyhorse of your religion, convince the world thereof by proclaiming your doctrine to our enemies, *for they likewise bear arms.* Give us proof of your sincerity by publishing it at St. James's, to the commanders in chief at Boston, to the admirals and captains who are piratically ravaging our coasts, and to all the murdering miscreants who are acting in authority under Him whom ye profess to serve. Had ye the honest soul of Barclay ye would preach repentance to your king: ye would tell the Royal Tyrant his sins, and warn him of eternal ruin. Ye would not spend your partial invectives against the injured and insulted only, but, like faithful ministers, would cry aloud and spare none. Say not that ye are persecuted, neither endeavor to make us the authors of that reproach which ye are bringing upon yourselves; for we testify unto all men that we do not complain against you because ye are Quakers but because ye pretend to be and are not Quakers.

Alas! it seems by the particular tendency of some part of your testimony, and other parts of your conduct, as if all sin was reduced to, and comprehended in, the act of bearing arms, and that by the people only. Ye appear to us to have mistaken party for conscience; because the general tenor of your actions wants uniformity: and it is exceedingly difficult for us to give credit to many of your pretended scruples; because we see them made by the same men who, in the very instant that they are exclaiming against the mammon of this world, are nevertheless hunting after it with a step as steady as time, and an appetite as keen as death.

The quotation which ye have made from Proverbs, in the third page of your testimony, that "when a man's ways please the Lord, he maketh even his enemies to be at peace with him," is very unwisely chosen on your part; because it amounts to a proof that the King's ways (whom ye are so desirous of supporting) do *not* please the Lord, otherwise his reign would be in peace.

I now proceed to the latter part of your testimony, and that for which all the foregoing seems only an introduction, viz.:

> It hath ever been our judgment and principle, since we were called to profess the light of Christ Jesus, manifested in our consciences unto this day, that the setting up and putting down kings and governments is God's peculiar prerogative, for causes best known to himself. And that it is not our business to have any hand or contrivance therein; nor to be busybodies above our station, much less to plot and contrive the ruin, or overturn of any of them, but to pray for the king, and safety of our nation, and good of all men that we may live a quiet and peaceable life, in all godliness and honesty, *under the government which God is pleased to set over us.*

If these are really your principles why do ye not abide by them? Why do ye not leave that which ye call God's work, to be managed by himself? These very principles instruct you to wait with patience and humility for the event of all public measures, and to receive that event as the divine will toward you. Wherefore, what occasion is there for your political testimony, if you fully believe what it contains? And the very publishing it proves that either ye do not believe what ye profess, or have not virtue enough to practise what ye believe.

The principles of Quakerism have a direct tendency to make a man the quiet and inoffensive subject of any and every government which is set over him. And if the setting up and putting down of kings and governments is God's peculiar prerogative, he most certainly will not be robbed thereof by us; wherefore, the principle itself leads you to approve of everything which ever happened, or may happen to kings, as being His work.

Oliver Cromwell thanks you. Charles, then, died not by the hands of man; and should the present proud imitator of him come to the same untimely end, the writers and publishers of the testimony are bound, by the doctrine it contains, to applaud the fact. Kings are not taken away by miracles, neither are changes in governments brought about by any other means than such as are common and human; and such as we now are using. Even the dispersing of the Jews, though foretold by our Savior, was effected by arms.

Wherefore, as ye refuse to be the means on one side, ye ought not to be meddlers on the other; but to wait the issue in silence; and, unless you can produce divine authority to prove that the Almighty, who has created and placed this New World at the greatest distance it could possibly stand, east and west, from every part of the Old, does nevertheless, disapprove of its being independent of the corrupt and abandoned court of Britain; unless, I say, ye can show this, how can ye, on the ground of your principles, justify the exciting and stirring up the people

> firmly to unite in the *abhorrence* of all such *writings* and *measures* as evince a desire and design to break off the *happy* connection we have hitherto enjoyed with the Kingdom of Great Britain, and our just and necessary subordination to the King, and those who are lawfully placed in authority under him.

What a slap in the face is here! The men who, in the very paragraph before have quietly and passively resigned up the ordering, altering, and disposal of kings and governments into the hands of God, are now recalling their principles, and putting in for a share of the business. Is it possible that the conclusion which is here justly quoted can any ways follow from the doctrine laid down! The inconsistency is too glaring not to be seen; the absurdity too great not to be laughed at; and such as could only have been made by those whose understandings were darkened by the narrow and crabbed spirit of a despairing political party; for ye are not to be considered as the whole body of the Quakers, but only as a factional and fractional part thereof.

Here ends the examination of your testimony (which I call upon no man to abhor, as ye have done, but only to read and judge of fairly), to which I subjoin the following remark "that the setting up and putting down of kings" must certainly mean the making him a king who is yet not so, and the making him no king who is already one. And pray what has this to do in the present case? We neither mean to *set up* nor to *put down*, neither to *make* nor to *unmake*, but to have nothing to do with them. Wherefore, your testimony, in whatever light it is viewed, serves only to dishonor your judgment, and for many other reasons had better have been let alone than published.

First, because it tends to decrease and reproach of all religion whatever, and is of the utmost danger to society, to make it a party in political disputes.

Second, because it exhibits a body of men, numbers of whom disavow the publishing of political testimonies, as being concerned therein and approvers thereof.

Third, because it has a tendency to undo that continental harmony and friendship which yourselves, by your late liberal and charitable donations, have lent a hand to establish, and the preservation of which is of the utmost consequence to us all.

And here, without anger or resentment, I bid you farewell, sincerely wishing, that as men and Christians ye may always fully and uninterruptedly enjoy every civil and religious right, and be, in your turn, the means of securing it to others; but that the example which ye have unwisely set of mingling religion with politics may be disavowed and reprobated by every inhabitant of America.

95.

Tom Paine: Plain Arguments for Independence

As the Revolutionary War progressed, the attitude of the British authorities made it apparent that no concessions could be expected. The idea of complete independence, which was beginning to win more and more support, was the subject of discussion in a pamphlet written by a newly arrived English immigrant Tom Paine. Published in January 1776, Common Sense *pressed the argument for independence in logically compelling terms. Paine's reasoning convinced George Washington who wrote to Joseph Reed of Pennsylvania on January 31, 1776: "A few more of such flaming arguments, as were exhibited at Falmouth and Norfolk, added to the sound doctrine and unanswerable reasoning contained in the pamphlet* Common Sense, *will not leave numbers at a loss to decide upon the propriety of a separation."*

Source: *Common Sense,* Boston, 1856, pp. 33-47.

IN THE FOLLOWING PAGES I offer nothing more than simple facts, plain arguments, and common sense; and have no other preliminaries to settle with the reader than that he will divest himself of prejudice and prepossession, and suffer his reason and his feelings to determine for themselves; that he will put *on*, or rather that he will not put *off*, the true character of a man, and generously enlarge his views beyond the present day.

Volumes have been written on the subject of the struggle between England and America. Men of all ranks have embarked in the controversy, from different motives and with various designs; but all have been ineffectual, and the period of debate is closed. Arms, as the last resource, must decide the contest; the appeal was the choice of the king, and the continent has accepted the challenge.

It has been reported of the late Mr. Pelham (who, though an able minister, was not without his faults) that on his being attacked in the House of Commons, on the score that his measures were only of a temporary kind, replied, "They will last my time." Should a thought so fatal and unmanly possess the colonies in the present contest, the name of ancestors will be remembered by future generations with detestation.

The sun never shone on a cause of greater worth. 'Tis not the affair of a city, a county, a province, or a kingdom but of a continent — of at least one-eighth part of the habitable globe. 'Tis not the concern of a day, a year, or an age; posterity are virtually involved in the contest and will be more or less affected even to the end of time by the proceedings now. Now is the seedtime of continental union, faith, and honor. The least fracture now will be like a name engraved with the point of a pin on the tender rind of a young oak; the wound will enlarge with the tree, and posterity read it in full-grown characters.

By referring the matter from argument to

arms, a new area for politics is struck; a new method of thinking has arisen. All plans, proposals, etc., prior to the 19th of April, *i.e.*, to the commencement of hostilities, are like the almanacs of last year; which, though proper then, are superseded and useless now. Whatever was advanced by the advocates on either side of the question then terminated in one and the same point, viz., a union with Great Britain. The only difference between the parties was the method of effecting it, the one proposing force, the other friendship; but it has so far happened that the first has failed, and the second has withdrawn her influence.

As much has been said of the advantages of reconciliation, which, like an agreeable dream, have passed away and left us as we were, it is but right that we should examine the contrary side of the argument, and inquire into some of the many material injuries which these colonies sustain, and always will sustain, by being connected with and dependent on Great Britain. To examine that connection and dependence, on the principles of nature and common sense, to see what we have to trust to if separated, and what we are to expect if dependent.

I have heard it asserted by some that as America has flourished under her former connection with Great Britain, the same connection is necessary toward her future happiness, and will always have the same effect. Nothing can be more fallacious than this kind of argument. We may as well assert that because a child has thrived upon milk . . . it is never to have meat, or that the first twenty years of our lives is to become a precedent for the next twenty. But even this is admitting more than is true, for I answer roundly that America would have flourished as much, and probably much more, had no European power had anything to do with her. The articles of commerce, by which she has enriched herself, are the necessaries of life, and will always have a market while eating is the custom of Europe.

But she has protected us, say some. That she has engrossed us is true, and defended the continent at our expense as well as her own is admitted, and she would have defended Turkey from the same motives, viz., for the sake of trade and dominion.

Alas! we have been long led away by ancient prejudices, and made large sacrifices to superstition. We have boasted the protection of Great Britain without considering that her motive was *interest* not *attachment;* and that she did not protect us from *our enemies* on *our account* but from *her enemies* on *her own account,* from those who had no quarrel with us on any *other account,* and who will always be our enemies on the *same account.* Let Britain waive her pretensions to the continent, or the continent throw off the dependence, and we should be at peace with France and Spain, were they at war with Britain. The miseries of Hanover last war ought to warn us against connections.

It has lately been asserted in Parliament that the colonies have no relation to each other but through the parent country, *i.e.,* that Pennsylvania and the Jerseys, and so on for the rest, are sister colonies by the way of England. This is certainly a very roundabout way of proving relationship, but it is the nearest and only true way of proving enemyship, if I may so call it. France and Spain never were, nor perhaps ever will be, our enemies as *Americans* but as our being the *subjects of Great Britain.*

But Britain is the parent country, say some. Then the more shame upon her conduct. Even brutes do not devour their young, nor savages make war upon their families; wherefore, the assertion, if true, turns to her reproach. But it happens not to be true, or only partly so, and the phrase "parent" or "mother country" has been jesuitically adopted by the king and his parasites, with a low papistical design of gaining an unfair bias on the credulous weakness of our minds. Europe, and not England, is the parent country of America. This New

World has been the asylum for the persecuted lovers of civil and religious liberty from *every part* of Europe. Hither have they fled, not from the tender embraces of the mother but from the cruelty of the monster; and it is so far true of England that the same tyranny which drove the first emigrants from home pursues their descendants still.

In this extensive quarter of the globe, we forget the narrow limits of 360 miles (the extent of England) and carry our friendship on a larger scale; we claim brotherhood with every European Christian, and triumph in the generosity of the sentiment.

It is pleasant to observe by what regular gradations we surmount local prejudices as we enlarge our acquaintance with the world. A man born in any town in England divided into parishes will naturally associate most with his fellow parishioners (because their interests in many cases will be common) and distinguish him by the name of "neighbor"; if he meet him but a few miles from home, he drops the narrow idea of a street and salutes him by the name of "townsman"; if he travel out of the county and meet him in any other, he forgets the minor divisions of street and town and calls him "countryman," *i.e.*, "countyman." But if in their foreign excursions they should associate in France or any other part of Europe, their local remembrance would be enlarged into that of "Englishmen." And by a just parity of reasoning, all Europeans meeting in America, or any other quarter of the globe, are "countrymen"; for England, Holland, Germany, or Sweden, when compared with the whole, stand in the same places on the larger scale, which the divisions of street, town, and county do on the smaller one — distinctions too limited for continental minds. Not one-third of the inhabitants, even of this province, are of English descent. Wherefore, I reprobate the phrase of "parent" or "mother country" applied to England only as being false, selfish, narrow, and ungenerous.

But, admitting that we were all of English descent, what does it amount to? Nothing. Britain, being now an open enemy, extinguishes every other name and title; and to say that reconciliation is our duty is truly farcical. The first king of England, of the present line (William the Conqueror), was a Frenchman, and half the peers of England are descendants from the same country; wherefore, by the same method of reasoning, England ought to be governed by France.

Much has been said of the united strength of Britain and the colonies — that in conjunction they might bid defiance to the world. But this is mere presumption. The fate of war is uncertain, neither do the expressions mean anything; for this continent would never suffer itself to be drained of inhabitants to support the British arms in either Asia, Africa, or Europe.

Besides, what have we to do with setting the world at defiance? Our plan is commerce, and that, well attended to, will secure us the peace and friendship of all Europe; because it is the interest of all Europe to have America a *free port.* Her trade will always be a protection, and her barrenness of gold and silver secure her from invaders.

I challenge the warmest advocate for reconciliation to show a single advantage that this continent can reap by being connected with Great Britain. I repeat the challenge; not a single advantage is derived. Our corn will fetch its price in any market in Europe, and our imported goods must be paid for, buy them where we will.

But the injuries and disadvantages which we sustain by that connection are without number; and our duty to mankind at large, as well as to ourselves, instructs us to renounce the alliance, because any submission to or dependence on Great Britain tends directly to involve this continent in European wars and quarrels, and sets us at variance with nations who would otherwise seek our friendship, and against whom we have neither anger nor complaint. As Europe is our market for trade, we ought to form no partial connection with any part of it. It is the true interest of America to steer clear of European contentions which she never can do, while, by her dependence on Britain, she is made the makeweight in the scale of British politics.

Europe is too thickly planted with kingdoms to be long at peace; and whenever a war breaks out between England and any foreign power, the trade of America goes to ruin *because of her connection with Britain.* The next war may not turn out like the last, and should it not, the advocates for reconciliation now will be wishing for separation then, because neutrality in that case would be a safer convoy than a man-of-war. Everything that is right or natural pleads for separation. The blood of the slain, the weeping voice of nature cries, "tis time to part." Even the distance at which the Almighty has placed England and America is a strong and natural proof that the authority of the one over the other was never the design of Heaven. The time, likewise, at which the continent was discovered adds weight to the argument, and the manner in which it was peopled increases the force of it. The Reformation was preceded by the discovery of America, as if the Almighty graciously meant to open a sanctuary to the persecuted in future years, when home should afford neither friendship nor safety.

The authority of Great Britain over this continent is a form of government which sooner or later must have an end; and a serious mind can draw no true pleasure by looking forward, under the painful and positive conviction that what he calls "the present constitution" is merely temporary. As parents, we can have no joy knowing that *this government* is not sufficiently lasting to ensure anything which we may bequeath to posterity; and by a plain method of argument, as we are running the next generation into debt, we ought to do the work of it, otherwise we use them meanly and pitifully.

In order to discover the line of our duty rightly, we should take our children in our hand and fix our station a few years further into life; that eminence will present a prospect which a few present fears and prejudices conceal from our sight.

Though I would carefully avoid giving unnecessary offense, yet I am inclined to believe that all those who espouse the doctrine of reconciliation may be included within the following descriptions: Interested men who are not to be trusted; weak men who *cannot* see; prejudiced men who *will not* see; and a certain set of moderate men who think better of the European world than it deserves; and this last class, by an ill-judged deliberation, will be the cause of more calamities to this continent than all the other three.

It is the good fortune of many to live distant from the scene of sorrow; the evil is not sufficiently brought to *their* doors to make *them* feel the precariousness with which all American property is possessed. But let our imaginations transport us a few moments to Boston; that seat of wretchedness will teach us wisdom and instruct us forever to renounce a power in whom we can have no trust. The inhabitants of that unfortunate city, who but a few months ago were in ease and affluence, have now no other alternative than to stay and starve, or turn out to beg. Endangered by the fire of their friends if they continue within the city, and plundered by the soldiery if they leave it, in their present situation they are prisoners without the hope of redemption, and in a general attack for their relief, they would be exposed to the fury of both armies.

Men of passive tempers look somewhat lightly over the offenses of Britain, and, still hoping for the best, are apt to call out, "Come, come, we shall be friends again for all this." But examine the passions and feelings of mankind, bring the doctrine of reconciliation to the touchstone of nature, and then tell me whether you can hereafter love, honor, and faithfully serve the power that has carried fire and sword into your land. If you cannot do all these then are you only deceiving yourselves, and by your delay bringing ruin upon your posterity. Your future connection with Britain, whom you can neither love nor honor, will be forced and unnatural, and being formed only on the plan of present convenience, will in a little time fall into a relapse more wretched than the first. But if you say you can still pass the violations over, then I ask, has your house been burned? Has your property been destroyed before your face? Are your wife and children destitute of a bed to lie on or bread to live on? Have you lost a parent or child by their hands, and yourself the ruined and wretched survivor? If you have not, then are you not a judge of those who have? But if you have, and can still shake hands with the murderers, then are you unworthy the name of husband, father, friend, or lover, and whatever may be your rank or title in life, you have the heart of a coward and the spirit of a sycophant.

This is not inflaming or exaggerating matters but trying them by those feelings and affections which nature justifies, and without which we should be incapable of discharging the social duties of life or enjoying the felicities of it. I mean not to exhibit horror for the purpose of provoking revenge but to awaken us from fatal and unmanly slumbers, that we may pursue determinately some fixed object. It is not in the power of Britain or of Europe to conquer America, if she does not conquer herself by *delay* and *timidity*. The present winter is worth an age if rightly employed, but if lost or neglected, the whole continent will partake of the misfortune; and there is no punishment which that man will not deserve, be he who or what or where he will, that may be the means of sacrificing a season so precious and useful.

It is repugnant to reason and the univer-sal order of things [and] to all examples from former ages to suppose that this continent can longer remain subject to any external power. The most sanguine in Britain do not think so. The utmost stretch of human wisdom cannot, at this time, compass a plan short of separation which can promise the continent even a year's security. Reconciliation is *now* a fallacious dream. Nature has deserted the connection, and art cannot supply her place. For, as Milton wisely express-es, "never can true reconcilement grow, where wounds of deadly hate have pierced so deep."

Every quiet method for peace has been ineffectual. Our prayers have been rejected with disdain, and only tended to convince us that nothing flatters vanity or confirms obstinacy in kings more than repeated petitioning; nothing has contributed more than this very measure to make the kings of Europe absolute — witness Denmark and Sweden. Wherefore, since nothing but blows will do, for God's sake let us come to a final separation and not leave the next generation to be cutting throats under the violated unmeaning names of parent and child.

To say they will never attempt it again is idle and visionary. We thought so at the repeal of the Stamp Act, yet a year or two undeceived us, as well may we suppose that nations which have been once defeated will never renew the quarrel.

As to government matters, it is not in the power of Britain to do this continent justice. The business of it will soon be too weighty and intricate to be managed with any tolerable degree of convenience by a power so distant from us, and so very ignorant of us; for if they cannot conquer us, they cannot govern us. To be always running 3,000 or 4,000 miles with a tale or a petition, waiting four or five months for an answer, which, when obtained, requires five or six more to explain it in, will in a few years be looked upon as folly and childishness — there was a time when it was proper, and there is a proper time for it to cease.

Small islands not capable of protecting themselves are the proper objects for kingdoms to take under their care; but there is something absurd in supposing a continent to be perpetually governed by an island. In no instance has nature made the satellite larger than its primary planet; and as England and America, with respect to each other, reverses the common order of nature, it is evident that they belong to different systems: England to Europe, America to itself.

I am not induced by motives of pride, party, or resentment to espouse the doctrine of separation and independence; I am clearly, positively, and conscientiously persuaded that it is the true interest of this continent to be so; that everything short of *that* is mere patchwork; that it can afford no lasting felicity; that it is leaving the sword to our children and shrinking back at a time when going a little further would have rendered this continent the glory of the earth.

As Britain has not manifested the least inclination toward a compromise, we may be assured that no terms can be obtained worthy the acceptance of the continent, or anyway equal to the expense of blood and treasure we have been already put to.

The object contended for ought always to bear some just proportion to the expense. The removal of North, or the whole detestable junto, is a matter unworthy the millions we have expended. A temporary stoppage of trade was an inconvenience which would have sufficiently balanced the repeal of all the acts complained of had such repeals been obtained; but if the whole continent must take up arms, if every man must be a soldier, it is scarcely worth our while to fight against a contemptible Ministry only. Dearly, dearly do we pay for the repeal of the acts, if that is all we fight for; for, in a just estimation, it is as great a folly to pay a Bunker-Hill price for law as for

land. I have always considered the independency of this continent as an event which sooner or later must take place, and, from the late rapid progress of the continent to maturity, the event cannot be far off. Wherefore, on the breaking out of hostilities, it was not worth the while to have disputed a matter which time would have finally redressed, unless we meant to be in earnest; otherwise, it is like wasting an estate on a suit at law to regulate the trespasses of a tenant whose lease is just expiring. No man was a warmer wisher for a reconciliation than myself before the fatal 19th of April, 1775; but the moment the event of that day was made known, I rejected the hardened, sullen-tempered Pharaoh of England forever; and disdain the wretch, that with the pretended title of "Father of his people" can unfeelingly hear of their slaughter, and composedly sleep with their blood upon his soul.

But admitting that matters were now made up, what would be the event? I answer, the ruin of the continent. And that for several reasons.

First, the powers of governing still remaining in the hands of the king, he will have a negative over the whole legislation of this continent. And as he has shown himself such an inveterate enemy to liberty, and discovered such a thirst for arbitrary power, is he, or is he not, a proper person to say to these colonies, "You shall make no laws but what I please!" And is there any inhabitant of America so ignorant as not to know that according to what is called the *present constitution*, this continent can make no laws but what the king gives leave to? And is there any man so unwise as not to see that (considering what has happened) he will suffer no law to be made here but such as suits *his* purpose? We may be as effectually enslaved by the want of laws in America as by submitting to laws made for us in England. After matters are made up (as it is called), can there be any doubt but the whole power of the Crown will be exerted to keep this continent as low and humble as possible? Instead of going forward we shall go backward, or be perpetually quarreling, or ridiculously petitioning. We are already greater than the king wishes us to be, and will he not hereafter endeavor to make us less? To bring the matter to one point: Is the power who is jealous of our prosperity a proper power to govern us? Whoever says "No" to this question is an *independent*, for independency means no more than this — whether we shall make our own laws, or, whether the king, the greatest enemy which this continent has or can have, shall tell us "There shall be no laws but such as I like."

But the king, you will say, has a negative in England; the people there can make no laws without his consent. In point of right and good order, it is something very ridiculous that a youth of twenty-one (which has often happened) shall say to several millions of people, older and wiser than himself, I forbid this or that act of yours to be law. But in this place I decline this sort of reply, though I will never cease to expose the absurdity of it; and only answer that England being the king's residence, and America not, makes quite another case. The king's negative *here* is ten times more dangerous and fatal than it can be in England; for *there* he will scarcely refuse his consent to a bill for putting England into as strong a state of defense as possible, and in America he would never suffer such a bill to be passed.

America is only a secondary object in the system of British politics; England consults the good of *this* country no further than it answers her *own* purpose. Wherefore, her own interest leads her to suppress the growth of *ours* in every case which does not promote her advantage, or in the least interferes with it. A pretty state we should soon be in under such a secondhand government, considering what has happened! Men do not change from enemies to friends by the

alteration of a name; and in order to show that reconciliation *now* is a dangerous doctrine, I affirm *that it would be policy in the king at this time to repeal the acts, for the sake of reinstating himself in the government of the provinces, in order that he may accomplish by craft and subtlety, in the long run, what he cannot do by force in the short one.* Reconciliation and ruin are nearly related.

Second, that as even the best terms which we can expect to obtain can amount to no more than a temporary expedient, or a kind of government by guardianship which can last no longer than till the colonies come of age, so the general face and state of things, in the interim, will be unsettled and unpromising. Emigrants of property will not choose to come to a country whose form of government hangs but by a thread, and which is every day tottering on the brink of commotion and disturbance; and numbers of the present inhabitants would lay hold of the interval to dispose of their effects and quit the continent.

But the most powerful of all arguments is that nothing but independence, *i.e.*, a continental form of government, can keep the peace of the continent and preserve it inviolate from civil wars. I dread the event of a reconciliation with Britain now, as it is more than probable that it will be followed by a revolt somewhere or other, the consequences of which may be far more fatal than all the malice of Britain.

Thousands are already ruined by British barbarity. (Thousands more will probably suffer the same fate.) Those men have other feelings than us who have nothing suffered. All they *now* possess is liberty; what they before enjoyed is sacrificed to its service; and having nothing more to lose, they disdain submission. Besides, the general temper of the colonies toward a British government will be like that of a youth who is nearly out of his time; they will care very little about her. And a government which cannot preserve the peace is no government at all, and in that case we pay our money for nothing. And pray what is it that Britain can do, whose power will be wholly on paper, should a civil tumult break out the very day after reconciliation?

I have heard some men say, many of whom I believe spoke without thinking, that they dreaded an independence, fearing that it would produce civil wars. It is but seldom that our first thoughts are truly correct, and that is the case here; for there is ten times more to dread from a patched up connection than from independence. I make the sufferer's case my own, and I protest that were I driven from house and home, my property destroyed, and my circumstances ruined, that as a man sensible of injuries, I could never relish the doctrine of reconciliation, or consider myself bound thereby.

The colonies have manifested such a spirit of good order and obedience to continental government as is sufficient to make every reasonable person easy and happy on that head. No man can assign the least pretense for his fears on any other grounds than such as are truly childish and ridiculous, viz., that one colony will be striving for superiority over another.

Where there are no distinctions there can be no superiority; perfect equality affords no temptation. The republics of Europe are all (and we may say always) in peace. Holland and Switzerland are without wars, foreign or domestic; monarchical governments, it is true, are never long at rest; the crown itself is a temptation to enterprising ruffians at home; and that degree of pride and insolence ever attendant on regal authority swells into a rupture with foreign powers in instances where a republican government, by being formed on more natural principles, would negotiate the mistake.

If there is any true cause of fear respecting independence, it is because no plan is yet laid down. Men do not see their way out; wherefore, as an opening into that business, I offer the following hints, at the same time modestly affirming that I have no other opinion of them myself than that they may be the means of giving rise to something better. Could the straggling thoughts of individuals be collected, they would frequently form materials for wise and able men to improve into useful matter.

Let the assemblies be annual, with a president only; the representation more equal; their business wholly domestic and subject to the authority of a continental congress.

Let each colony be divided into six, eight, or ten convenient districts, each district to send a proper number of delegates to Congress, so that each colony send at least 30. The whole number in Congress will be at least 390. Each Congress to sit ――― and to choose a president by the following method. When the delegates are met, let a colony be taken from the whole thirteen colonies by lot, after which, let the Congress choose (by ballot) a president from out of the delegates of that province. In the next Congress, let a colony be taken by lot from twelve only, omitting that colony from which the president was taken in the former Congress, and so proceeding on till the whole thirteen shall have had their proper rotation. And in order that nothing may pass into a law but what is satisfactorily just, not less than three-fifths of the Congress to be called a majority. He that will promote discord, under a government so equally formed as this, would have joined Lucifer in his revolt.

But as there is a peculiar delicacy from whom, or in what manner, this business must first arise, and as it seems most agreeable and consistent that it should come from some intermediate body between the governed and the governors, that is, between the Congress and the people, let a continental conference be held, in the following manner, and for the following purpose:

A committee of twenty-six members of Congress, viz., two for each colony; two members from each house of assembly, or provincial convention; and five representatives of the people at large, to be chosen in the capital city or town of each province, for and in behalf of the whole province, by as many qualified voters as shall think proper to attend from all parts of the province for that purpose; or, if more convenient, the representatives may be chosen in two or three of the most populous parts thereof. In this conference, thus assembled, will be united the two grand principles of business, *knowledge* and *power*. The members of Congress, assemblies, or conventions, by having had experience in national concerns, will be able and useful counselors; and the whole, being empowered by the people, will have a truly legal authority.

The conferring members being met, let their business be to frame a continental charter, or charter of the united colonies (answering to what is called the Magna Charta of England), fixing the number and manner of choosing members of congress and members of assembly, with their date of sitting, and drawing the line of business and jurisdiction between them (always remembering that our strength is continental, not provincial), securing freedom and property to all men, and, above all things, the free exercise of religion, according to the dictates of conscience, with such other matter as it is necessary for a charter to contain. Immediately after which, the said conference to dissolve, and the bodies which shall be chosen conformable to the said charter to be the legislators and governors of this continent for the time being, whose peace and happiness may God preserve. Amen.

Should any body of men be hereafter delegated for this or some similar purpose, I offer them the following extracts from that wise observer on governments, Dragonetti.

The science of the politician consists in fixing the true point of happiness and freedom. Those men would deserve the gratitude of ages who should discover a mode of government that contained the greatest sum of individual happiness, with the least national expense.

But where, say some, is the king of America? I'll tell you, friend, He reigns above, and does not make havoc of mankind like the royal brute of Britain. Yet, that we may not appear to be defective even in earthly honors, let a day be solemnly set apart for proclaiming the charter; let it be brought forth placed on the divine law, the word of God; let a crown be placed thereon, by which the world may know that so far as we approve of monarchy, that in America *the law is king*. For as in absolute governments the king is law, so in free countries the law ought to be king; and there ought to be no other. But lest any ill use should afterward arise, let the crown at the conclusion of the ceremony be demolished and scattered among the people whose right it is.

A government of our own is our natural right; and when a man seriously reflects on the precariousness of human affairs, he will become convinced that it is infinitely wiser and safer, to form a constitution of our own in a cool deliberate manner, while we have it in our power, than to trust such an interesting event to time and chance. If we omit it now, some Massanello [Thomas Anello] may hereafter arise, who, laying hold of popular disquietudes, may collect together the desperate and the discontented, and by assuming to themselves the powers of government, finally sweep away the liberties of the continent like a deluge. Should the government of America return again into the hands of Britain, the tottering situation of things will be a temptation for some desperate adventurer to try his fortune; and in such a case, what relief can Britain give? 'Ere she could hear the news, the fatal business might be done; and ourselves suffering like the wretched Britons under the oppression of the Conqueror. Ye that oppose independence now, ye know not what ye do; ye are opening a door to eternal tyranny by keeping vacant the seat of government. There are thousands and tens of thousands who would think it glorious to expel from the continent that barbarous and hellish power which has stirred up the Indians and Negroes to destroy us; the cruelty has a double guilt — it is dealing brutally by us and treacherously by them.

To talk of friendship with those in whom our reason forbids us to have faith, and our affections, wounded through a thousand pores, instruct us to detest, is madness and folly. Every day wears out the little remains of kindred between us and them; and can there be any reason to hope that as the relationship expires, the affection will increase, or that we shall agree better when we have ten times more and greater concerns to quarrel over than ever?

Ye that tell us of harmony and reconciliation, can ye restore to us the time that is past? Can ye give to prostitution its former innocence? Neither can ye reconcile Britain and America. The last cord now is broken; the people of England are presenting addresses against us. There are injuries which nature cannot forgive; she would cease to be nature if she did. As well can the lover forgive the ravisher of his mistress as the continent forgive the murders of Britain. The Almighty has implanted in us these unextinguishable feelings, for good and wise purposes. They are the guardians of His image in our hearts, and distinguish us from the herd of common animals. The social compact would dissolve and justice be extirpated from the earth, or have only a casual existence, were we callous to the touches of affection. The robber and the murderer would often escape unpunished did not the injuries which our tempers sustain provoke us into justice.

O! ye that love mankind! Ye that dare oppose, not only the tyranny but the tyrant, stand forth! Every spot of the Old World is overrun with oppression. Freedom has been haunted round the globe. Asia and Africa have long expelled her. Europe regards her like a stranger, and England has given her warning to depart. O! receive the fugitive, and prepare in time an asylum for mankind

---

E Pluribus Unum.

ANON., used on title page of *Gentleman's Journal*, January 1692. Motto for seal of U.S. proposed originally on Aug. 10, 1776, by a committee composed of Franklin, Adams and Jefferson; adopted June 20, 1782; the motto added to certain coins, 1796. The actual selection of the motto for the seal is sometimes credited to Pierre Eugène du Simitière, who submitted a design for the seal that was not accepted, but that is said to have contained the words.

96.

Replies to Tom Paine

Loyalist pamphleteers in the colonies were not afraid to argue their point of view, as is evidenced by the following two documents. The Reverend William Smith, signing himself "Cato," wrote a series of articles in reply to Tom Paine's Common Sense. *The articles appeared in the form of letters to the people of Pennsylvania. He dealt not only with Paine but also with "Cassandra," the pseudonym adopted by James Cannon, a tutor at Smith's own College of Philadelphia. The selection below is taken from Letters II, III, and IV, written in March 1776. The second selection is by Charles Inglis who published his pamphlet anonymously in 1776. He was a prolific writer of essays designed to convince the patriots of the error of their ways. His argument, calmly set forth, was doubtless more impressive before events went beyond it, but his pamphlet remains one of the most cogent statements of the loyalist position.*

Source: *Archives*, V, pp. 514-517.
    The True Interest of America Impartially Stated, in Certain Strictures on a Pamphlet Intitled Common Sense, 2nd edition, Philadelphia, 1776.

I.

WILLIAM SMITH: The Advantages of Union with England

THE AUTHORS or, if I must say, author of what is called *Common Sense* has certainly had fair play. Full time has been allowed him by the sale of his pamphlet to reap the fruits of his labors and gratify that avidity with which many are apt to devour doctrines that are out of the common way — bold, marvelous, and flattering. What was intended as a compliment to the public — to give them time to gaze with their own eyes and reason with their own faculties upon this extraordinary appearance — the author's vanity has construed wholly in his own favor. He has called repeatedly for answers and announced his second edition to the world in the following strain of self-adulation: "That, as no answer hath yet appeared, it is now presumed that none will";

and, therefore, as may be fairly implied, that he is unanswerable.

Why, then, when his challenge is accepted, will not he and his seconds fight upon fair terms? Why will they seek to draw the attention of the public from things to men, refusing that quarter to others which the author of *Common Sense* craves for himself? "Who the author of this publication is (says he) is wholly unnecessary to the public, as the object of attention is the doctrine itself, and not the man!" Can this sentence be reconciled to all the pother made about *Cato* — who and what he is? Or does it not rather betray some symptoms of fear and cowardice, to beset him at the threshold and seek to stop him in his march to the field? What, although he attempts to walk forth humbly with his staff in his hand and has been somewhat late in filling his scrip with stones to meet this Goliath, should he therefore be tauntingly defied? If what is called *Common Sense* be really *com-*

mon sense, it is invulnerable, and every attack upon it will but add to the author's triumph. If it should be proved, in any instances, to be *nonsense*, millions will be interested in the discovery; and to them I appeal.

Once more I repeat the design of these letters, in which I conceive a question to be involved of the greatest importance that ever came before us — a question not yet decided and which ought, therefore, to be fully discussed. Opprobrious names can prove nothing here, except that they who use them have nothing better to say and are afraid of their cause. It is probable that some may see their interest upon one side of the question and some upon the other; but that the great body of the people can have any interest separate from their country, or (when fairly understood) pursue any other, is not to be imagined. If *Cato* may be believed, he can conscientiously class himself with this great body and can assure his readers that the guesses hitherto made concerning him are rather unlucky.

Great pains have been taken to engage him in a contest with our Committee; but, as nothing has been quoted from him which concerns that body in general, he leaves his letters to answer for themselves; and, if his comments on the circular letter to the County Committees should appear to the public not to be well warranted, he will submit to their judgment. But he finds it would be endless to answer all the silly queries and daily scribble of his opponents, and has learned better than to be drawn from his main object by indulging them in this way. It would be too great a trespass upon the reader's patience. He has viewed the ground on which he stands and is not afraid to tread it in the sight of the most vigilant son of liberty, making that free use of the press which is promised to him, without the least violation of any resolve of this continent hitherto made.

One side of a great question has been held up to us. We are told that it can never be our interest to have any future connection with Great Britain and are pressed immediately to declare our total separation; for now is the time, and the time has found us. Could it be expected that all America would instantly take a leap in the dark, or that any who had not a predilection for the doctrine, or were capable of reasoning upon it, would swallow it in the gross, without wishing to hear the arguments on the other side? I am sure this is the wish of multitudes of good men — particularly of those who may be principally concerned in deciding the question, and whose earnest desire it is not only to know the sense of individuals but the clear sense of their country upon it; without which, they could not think themselves at liberty to give their decision.

Upon this ground, then, I proceed and shall rest the cause with my adversaries on the present general defense, which (although I am sorry it was necessary) I have reason to think will be more acceptable to the public than the misspending time in private altercation. Those who oppose me may enjoy, for a while (perhaps unnoticed), all the triumph of the answers they may give; and, if it is found at last, as has been already hinted, that I have said nothing to the purpose, their side of the question will only be strengthened.

In my remarks upon the pamphlet before me, I shall first consider those arguments on which the author appears to lay his chief stress; and these are collected under four heads, in his conclusion:

> It is the custom of nations, when any two are at war, for some other powers, not engaged in the quarrel, to step in as mediators and bring about the preliminaries of peace. But while America calls herself a subject of Great Britain, no power, however well-disposed she may be, can offer her mediation.

Is this *common sense* or common nonsense? Surely peace with Great Britain cannot be the object of this writer, after the horrible character he has given us of the people of that country and telling us that reconciliation with them would be ruin. The latter part of the paragraph seems to cast some light upon the former, although it contradicts it; for these mediators are not to interfere for making up the quarrel but to widen it by supporting us in a declaration that we are not subjects of Great Britain. A new sort of business, truly, for mediators!

But this leads us directly to the inquiry — What foreign powers are able to give us this support? Whether they can be persuaded to engage with us? What will be their terms? Is an alliance with them safe; or is it to be preferred to an honorable and firm renewal of that ancient connection under which we have so long flourished?

These questions cannot but employ the most serious thoughts of men whose all is at stake in the resolution of them; and they ought to be answered to the general satisfaction before we are launched out into a tempestuous ocean, of which we know not the other shore. That a continuance of mutual violence and hate may at last force us upon such an ocean is not altogether improbable; and it is possible we may gain some port of safety, although in a shattered condition. Not a word shall be drawn from me to discredit our own strength or resources. Although the accounts given of them by the author of *Common Sense* appear incredible to some, I will even go beyond him in expressing my good opinion of our situation. He thinks foreign assistance necessary to us. I think we should but be injured by it. We are able to defend our own rights and to frustrate the attempt of any nation upon earth to govern us by force. For my part, I would risk my all in resisting every attempt of this kind at every hazard.

But let us see what assistance he offers us, and we find France and Spain held out for that purpose, although not as mediators to "strengthen the connection between Great Britain and America," but wholly to dissolve it.

As to Spain, it is well known that the government of her own unwieldy colonies is already a weight which she can hardly bear; and some profound politicians have thought that, from the first, she has rather been weakened than strengthened by them; and that all her returns of gold and silver from America are but a poor compensation for the lives and cost with which they are purchased. It may well be questioned, then (supposing Spain were able to assist us in erecting an independent empire in America), whether her jealousy would permit her to risk the possibility of our seducing her own American subjects into an alliance with us for the purpose of a future revolt from herself. But our author mentions France, as well as Spain, and thus proposes that both branches of the Bourbon family, so long the terror of Protestants and freemen, should now join as their protectors. By what means, or at what price, is this marvelous revolution in the system of politics, religion, and liberty to be accomplished? How are these two powers to divide these colonies between them? Is their guardianship to be joint or separate? Under whose wing is Pennsylvania to fall — that of the most Catholic or most Christian King?

I confess that those questions stagger me; and, till answered to satisfaction, cannot but give every good man the most painful apprehensions concerning the future fate of his country. To be told by the author of *Common Sense* that all this is mere prejudice; that we must divest ourselves of every opinion in which we have been educated in order to digest his pure doctrine, and throw down what our fathers and we have been building up for ages to make room for his visionary fabric; I say, to be told this is only insult instead of argument and can be tolerated by none but those who are so far inflamed or interested that separation from Great Britain, at any risk, is their choice rather than reconciliation, upon whatever terms.

This, I much fear, is the temper of those

who are constantly dinning in our ears the necessity of an immediate Declaration of Independence for the sake of procuring foreign assistance, especially that of France. Their real desire is to shut the door against all further reconciliation, by this precipitate step. The matter of foreign assistance is a mere decoy. Can we imagine that, if France thought it her interest to quarrel with Great Britain for any benefits to be derived from us, her delicacy would stand in her way? Was she ever restricted by such delicacy in any of the former civil wars of her neighbors, especially those of Great Britain? But the truth is that, in the present ruinous state of her finances and feeble condition of her fleets, she will scarce think it prudent (for any prospects we can yield her) to rush into a new and expensive war, when so ill recruited, after the blood and treasure which she lavished so ineffectually in the last.

Would it be wise, then, to risk a refusal from her, or to mix our affairs with those of any foreign power whatever in this contest with Great Britain? No. I conceive this would only protract our wars, increase our dangers, weaken our force, and probably end in our ruin. And, of all nations in the world, France is the last from which we should seek assistance, even if it were necessary. What kind of assistance do we expect from her? Gold and silver she can but ill afford to give us; her men we have no occasion for; and, in a word, until she has a fleet able to contend with that of England, she can do us no essential service. The want of such a fleet has been the great bar to her numerous projects for universal empire. Can any Protestant — can you, my countrymen — ever wish to see her possessed of such a fleet, assist her in attaining it, or willingly give her footing in America? Would she then be contented to be the humble ally of these colonies; or would she not, in her own right, resume Canada, which, according to the limits she formerly claimed, is larger than all our provinces together? Could we hinder her from introducing what multitudes of her people she might think proper into that country, where they have already a great body of their friends to receive them? In that case, we should soon be left without room for the increasing number of our posterity; hemmed in upon the seashore; and, with armies behind us and fleets before us, be either crushed to pieces, obliged to submit to the absolute dominion of France, or to throw ourselves back upon the protection of Great Britain.

This consideration is truly alarming, and France has never shown herself so worthy of confidence among the nations of Europe as to induce us to run such risks by throwing ourselves precipitately into her arms. She is so notorious to the whole world for her disregard of the most sacred treaties that *Gallica fides,* or French faith, is become as proverbial now as *Punica fides,* or Carthagenian faith, of old. It could scarce have been imagined that the author of *Common Sense,* after telling us that "the blood of the slain, the weeping voice of nature, cries, 'tis time to part" — eternally to part — from the limited monarchy of Great Britain (whatever future terms might be offered us) would so soon have recommended to us a new alliance with the arbitrary monarchs of France and Spain. Bloody massacres, the revocation of sacred edicts, and the most unrelenting persecutions have certainly taught American Protestants (and especially our German brethren) what sort of faith we are to expect from popish princes, and from nations who are strangers to liberty themselves and envy the enjoyment of it to others.

In short, I am not able, with all the pains I have taken, to understand what is meant by a Declaration of Independence; unless it is to be drawn up in the form of a solemn abjuration of Great Britain as a nation with which we can never more be connected. And this seems the doctrine of the author of *Common Sense.* But I believe he has made but a few converts to this part of his scheme; for who knows to what vicissitudes of fortune we may yet be subjected?

We have already declared ourselves independent, as to all useful purposes, by resisting our oppressors upon our own foundation. And while we keep upon this ground, without connecting ourselves with any foreign nations, to involve us in fresh difficulties and endanger our liberties still further, we are able, in our own element (upon the shore), to continue this resistance; and it is our duty to continue it till Great Britain is convinced (as she must soon be) of her fatal policy, and open her arms to reconciliation, upon the permanent and sure footing of mutual interest and safety.

Upon such a footing, we may again be happy. Our trade will be revived. Our husbandmen, our mechanics, our artificers will flourish. Our language, our laws, and manners being the same with those of the nation with which we are again to be connected, that connection will be natural; and we shall the more easily guard against future innovations. Pennsylvania has much to lose in this contest and much to hope from a proper settlement of it. We have long flourished under our charter government. What may be the consequences of another form we cannot pronounce with certainty; but this we know, that it is a road we have not traveled and may be worse than it is described.

CATO

II.

CHARLES INGLIS: The True Interest of America

I THINK IT NO DIFFICULT MATTER to point out many advantages which will certainly attend our reconciliation and connection with Great Britain on a firm, constitutional plan. I shall select a few of these; and, that their importance may be more clearly discerned, I shall afterward point out some of the evils which inevitably must attend our separating from Britain and declaring for independency. On each article I shall study brevity.

1. By a reconciliation with Britain, a period would be put to the present calamitous war, by which so many lives have been lost, and so many more must be lost if it continues. This alone is an advantage devoutly to be wished for. This author [Paine] says: "The blood of the slain, the weeping voice of nature cries, 'Tis time to part." I think they cry just the reverse. The blood of the slain, the weeping voice of nature cries: It is time to be reconciled; it is time to lay aside those animosities which have pushed on Britons to shed the blood of Britons; it is high time that those who are connected by the endearing ties of religion, kindred, and country should resume their former friendship and be united in the bond of mutual affection, as their interests are inseparably united.

2. By a reconciliation with Great Britain, peace — that fairest offspring and gift of heaven — will be restored. In one respect peace is like health — we do not sufficiently know its value but by its absence. What uneasiness and anxiety, what evils has this short interruption of peace with the parent state brought on the whole British Empire! Let every man only consult his feelings — I except my antagonist — and it will require no great force of rhetoric to convince him that a removal of those evils and a restoration of peace would be a singular advantage and blessing.

3. Agriculture, commerce, and industry would resume their wonted vigor. At present, they languish and droop, both here and in Britain; and must continue to do so while this unhappy contest remains unsettled.

4. By a connection with Great Britain, our trade would still have the protection of the greatest naval power in the world. England has the advantage, in this respect, of every other state, whether of ancient or modern times. Her insular situation, her nurseries for seamen, the superiority of

those seamen above others — these circumstances, to mention no other, combine to make her the first maritime power in the universe — such exactly is the power whose protection we want for our commerce. To suppose, with our author, that we should have no war were we to revolt from England is too absurd to deserve a confutation. I could just as soon set about refuting the reveries of some brainsick enthusiast. Past experience shows that Britain is able to defend our commerce and our coasts; and we have no reason to doubt of her being able to do so for the future.

5. The protection of our trade, while connected with Britain, will not cost us a *fiftieth* part of what it must cost were we ourselves to raise a naval force sufficient for the purpose.

6. While connected with Great Britain, we have a bounty on almost every article of exportation; and we may be better supplied with goods by her than we could elsewhere. What our author says is true, "that our imported goods must be paid for, buy them where we will"; but we may buy them dearer, and of worse quality, in one place than another. The manufactures of Great Britain confessedly surpass any in the world, particularly those in every kind of metal, which we want most; and no country can afford linens and woolens of equal quality cheaper.

7. When a reconciliation is effected, and things return into the old channel, a few years of peace will restore everything to its pristine state. Emigrants will flow in as usual from the different parts of Europe. Population will advance with the same rapid progress as formerly, and our lands will rise in value.

These advantages are not imaginary but real. They are such as we have already experienced; and such as we may derive from a connection with Great Britain for ages to come. Each of these might easily be enlarged on, and others added to them; but I only mean to suggest a few hints. . . .

Let us now, if you please, take a view of the other side of the question. Suppose we were to revolt from Great Britain, declare ourselves independent, and set up a republic of our own — what would be the consequence? I stand aghast at the prospect; my blood runs chill when I think of the calamities, the complicated evils that must ensue, and may be clearly foreseen — it is impossible for any man to foresee them all.

Our author cautiously avoids saying anything of the inconveniences that would attend a separation. He does not even suppose that any inconvenience would attend it. Let us only declare ourselves independent, break loose from Great Britain, and, according to him, a paradisiacal state will follow! But a prudent man will consider and weigh matters well before he consents to such a measure — when on the brink of such a dreadful precipice, he must necessarily recoil and think of the consequences before he advances a step forward. Supposing then we declared for independency, what would follow? I answer:

1. All our property throughout the continent would be unhinged; the greatest confusion and most violent convulsions would take place. It would not be here as it was in England at the Revolution in 1688. That Revolution was not brought about by a defeasance or disannulling the right of succession. James II, by abdicating the throne, left it vacant for the next in succession; accordingly, his eldest daughter and her husband stepped in. Every other matter went on in the usual, regular way; and the constitution, instead of being dissolved, was strengthened. But in case of our revolt, the old constitution would be totally subverted. The common bond that tied us together, and by which our property was secured, would be snapped asunder. It is not to be doubted but our Congress would endeavor to apply some remedy for those evils; but, with all deference to that respectable body, I do not apprehend that any remedy in their power would be adequate, at least for some time. I

do not choose to be more explicit; but I am able to support my opinion.

2. What a horrid situation would thousands be reduced to who have taken the oath of allegiance to the King; yet, contrary to their oath as well as inclination, must be compelled to renounce that allegiance or abandon all their property in America! How many thousands more would be reduced to a similar situation, who, although they took not that oath, yet would think it inconsistent with their duty and a good conscience to renounce their sovereign. I dare say these will appear trifling difficulties to our author; but, whatever he may think, there are thousands and thousands who would sooner lose all they had in the world, nay, life itself, than thus wound their conscience. A declaration of independency would infallibly disunite and divide the colonists.

3. By a declaration for independency, every avenue to an accommodation with Great Britain would be closed; the sword only could then decide the quarrel; and the sword would not be sheathed till one had conquered the other.

The importance of these colonies to Britain need not be enlarged on — it is a thing so universally known. The greater their importance is to her, so much the more obstinate will her struggle be not to lose them. The independency of America would, in the end, deprive her of the West Indies, shake her empire to the foundation, and reduce her to a state of the most mortifying insignificance. Great Britain, therefore, must, for her own preservation, risk everything, and exert her whole strength to prevent such an event from taking place. This being the case,

4. Devastation and ruin must mark the progress of this war along the seacoast of America. Hitherto, Britain has not exerted her power. Her number of troops and ships of war here at present is very little more than she judged expedient in time of peace — the former does not amount to 12,000

Courtesy, Trinity Church, New York

Rev. Charles Inglis

men — nor the latter to 40 ships, including frigates. Both she and the colonies hoped for and expected an accommodation; neither of them has lost sight of that desirable object. The seas have been open to our ships; and, although some skirmishes have unfortunately happened, yet a ray of hope still cheered both sides that peace was not distant. But, as soon as we declare for independency, every prospect of this kind must vanish. Ruthless war, with all its aggravated horrors, will ravage our once happy land; our seacoasts and ports will be ruined, and our ships taken. Torrents of blood will be spilled, and thousands reduced to beggary and wretchedness.

This melancholy contest would last till one side conquered. Supposing Britain to be victorious; however high my opinion is of British generosity, I should be exceedingly sorry to receive terms from her in the haughty tone of a conqueror. Or supposing such a failure of her manufactures, commerce, and strength, that victory should incline to the side of America; yet, who can say, in that case, what extremities her sense of resentment and self-preservation will drive Great Britain to? For my part, I should not in the least be surprised if, on such a prospect as the independency of America, she would parcel out this continent to the different European powers. Canada might be restored to France, Florida to Spain, with additions to each; other states also might come in for a portion. Let no man think this chimerical or improbable. The independency of America would be so fatal to Britain that she would leave nothing in her power undone to prevent it. I believe as firmly as I do my own existence that, if every other method failed, she would try some such expedient as this to disconcert our scheme of independency; and let any man figure to himself the situation of these British colonies, if only Canada were restored to France!

5. But supposing once more that we were able to cut off every regiment that Britain can spare or hire, and to destroy every ship she can send, that we could beat off any other European power that would presume to intrude upon this continent; yet, a republican form of government would neither suit the genius of the people nor the extent of America.

In nothing is the wisdom of a legislator more conspicuous than in adapting his government to the genius, manners, disposition, and other circumstances of the people with whom he is concerned. If this important point is overlooked, confusion will ensue; his system will sink into neglect and ruin. Whatever check or barriers may be interposed, nature will always surmount them and finally prevail. . . .

The Americans are properly Britons. They have the manners, habits, and ideas of Britons; and have been accustomed to a similar form of government. But Britons never could bear the extremes, either of monarchy or republicanism. Some of their kings have aimed at despotism, but always failed. Repeated efforts have been made . toward democracy, and they equally failed. Once, indeed, republicanism triumphed over the constitution; the despotism of one per-

son ensued; both were finally expelled. The inhabitants of Great Britain were quite anxious for the restoration of royalty in 1660, as they were for its expulsion in 1642, and for some succeeding years. If we may judge of future events by past transactions, in similar circumstances, this would most probably be the case of America were a republican form of government adopted in our present ferment. After much blood was shed, those confusions would terminate in the despotism of some one successful adventurer; and should the Americans be so fortunate as to emancipate themselves from that thralldom, perhaps the whole would end in a limited monarchy, after shedding as much more blood. Limited monarchy is the form of government which is most favorable to liberty, which is best adapted to the genius and temper of Britons; although here and there among us a crackbrained zealot for democracy or absolute monarchy may be sometimes found.

Besides the unsuitableness of the republican form to the genius of the people, America is too extensive for it. That form may do well enough for a single city or small territory, but would be utterly improper for such a continent as this. America is too unwieldy for the feeble, dilatory administration of democracy. . . . .

It is well known that wages and the price of labor, in general, are much higher in America than in England. Labor must necessarily be dear in every country where land is cheap and large tracts of it unsettled, as is the case here. Hence an American regiment costs us *double* what a British regiment, of equal number, costs Britain. Were it proper to be explicit and descend to particulars, I could evince this past all possibility of doubt; and I appeal for the truth of it to those gentlemen among us who are acquainted with these matters.

Where the money is to come from which will defray this enormous annual expense of *three millions* sterling, and all those other debts, I know not; unless the author of

Common Sense, or some other ingenious projector, can discover the Philosopher's Stone, by which iron and other base metals may be transmuted into gold. Certain I am that our commerce and agriculture, the two principal sources of our wealth, will not support such an expense. The whole of our exports from the Thirteen United Colonies, in the year 1769, amounted only to £ 2,887,898 sterling; which is not so much, by near half a million, as our annual expense would be were we independent of Great Britain. Those exports, with no inconsiderable part of the profits arising from them, it is well known, centered finally in Britain to pay the merchants and manufacturers there for goods we had imported thence — and yet left us still in debt! What then must our situation be, or what the state of our trade, when oppressed with such a burden of annual expense! When every article of commerce, every necessary of life, together with our lands, must be heavily taxed to defray that expense!

Such is the load of debt and expense we should incur by this writer's hopeful exchange of our connection with Great Britain for independency and republicanism! And all this, after being exhausted by a tedious war, and perhaps our shipping and seaports destroyed! This is a very serious matter, which is obvious to every understanding, and which no sophistry can evade. All who have any prudence or common sense left, or any property to lose, will pause and consider well before they plunge themselves into such a dreadful situation. How little do those who desire this situation know what they are about or what they desire.

Our author frequently refers us to Holland, as if that were the only land of liberty — crowned with every blessing and exempt from every evil. But hear a little plain truth. The national debt of Holland is much greater, in proportion, than that of England. The taxes in Holland far exceed not only those in England but even those in France,

insomuch that a certain writer declares he scarcely knows anything they have which has escaped taxation, "except the air they breathe." Nay, more — the people at large have no voice in choosing the members of their several senates, as we have in choosing representatives. The members of each senate, upon any vacancy, elect new members; and the deputies from those senates constitute the States General. So that, in fact, the people have no share in the government, as with us, "they have nothing to do but pay and grumble," as Lord Chesterfield observes. Yet this is the country our author holds up for imitation; and, if we were to follow his advice, I have not the least doubt but we should soon resemble them in paying heavy taxes, as well as in every other matter.

But here it may be said *that all the evils above specified are more tolerable than slavery.* With this sentiment I sincerely agree — any hardships, however great, are preferable to slavery. But then I ask — Is there no other alternative in the present case? Is there no choice left us but slavery, or those evils? I am confident there is; and that both may be equally avoided. Let us only show a disposition to treat or negotiate in earnest — let us fall upon some method to set a treaty or negotiation with Great Britain on foot; and, if once properly begun, there is moral certainty that this unhappy dispute will be settled to the mutual satisfaction and interest of both countries. For my part, I have not the least doubt about it.

It would be improper and needless for me to enlarge on the particulars that should be adjusted at such a treaty. The maturest deliberation will be necessary on the occasion, as well as a generous regard to every part of the Empire. I shall just beg leave to suggest my opinion on a few points — I think America should insist that the claim of parliamentary taxation be either explicitly relinquished, or else such security given as the case will admit, and may be equivalent to a formal relinquishment, that this claim shall not be exerted. When this most important point is gained, America should consider that there is a great difference between having her money wrested from her by others and not giving any of it herself when it is proper to give. While she is protected and shares in the advantages resulting from being a part of the British Empire, she should contribute something for that protection and those advantages; and I never heard a sensible American deny this. Moreover, she should stipulate for such a freedom of trade as is consistent with the general welfare of the State; and that this interesting object be settled in such a manner as to preclude, as much as possible, any impolitic or injurious infringements hereafter. All this may be easily done if both sides are only disposed for peace; and there are many other particulars which would be exceedingly beneficial to America, and might be obtained, as they could not interfere with the interest of Great Britain or any other part of the Empire. We have abundant proof of this, as well as several good hints to proceed on, in the late concessions to Nova Scotia from government.

But it may be asked — What probability is there that Britain will enter on such a treaty or listen to proposals of this kind? Is she not preparing for war and fitting out a formidable armament against the colonies? I answer — There is every reason to believe that she will enter on such a treaty, if it is desired; and that she will listen to reasonable proposals. It is her interest to do so. To hold these colonies by the sword only, were she ever so powerful, would be holding them by a very precarious, expensive tenure. Such a union with the colonies as will promote their interest equally with hers is the only effectual way of attaching them to her. Is it reasonable to suppose that Great Britain does not see this? Or that she is not sensible of it? Besides, it has been openly and expressly declared in Parliament that *taxation is given up* by the Ministry; we

are also assured that some very respectable names have been lately added to the advocates of America, and commissioners have been appointed to treat with us. All these things are in our favor and promise a prosperous issue to a negotiation, if once begun.

The British armament will not in the least impede a treaty. Belligerent powers, when on the eve of peace, always make as vigorous preparations for war as if there were no thoughts of peace. America also is preparing for war, which is no more than a prudent step. It need not prevent her from treating; and she may thereby obtain better terms.

But a declaration for independency on the part of America would preclude treaty entirely and could answer no good purpose. We actually have already every advantage of independency, without its inconveniences. By a declaration of independency, we should instantly lose all assistance from our friends in England. It would stop their mouths; for, were they to say anything in our favor, they would be deemed rebels and treated accordingly.

Our author is much elated with the prospect of foreign succor, if we once declare ourselves independent, and from thence promises us mighty matters. This, no doubt, is intended to spirit up the desponding — all who might shrink at the thought of America encountering, singly and unsupported, the whole strength of Great Britain. I believe, in my conscience, that he is as much mistaken in this as in anything else; and that this expectation is delusive, vain, and fallacious. My reasons are these, and I submit them to the reader's judgment:

The only European power from which we can possibly receive assistance is France. But France is now at peace with Great Britain; and is it probable that France would interrupt that peace and hazard a war with the power which lately reduced her so low, from a disinterested motive of aiding and protecting these colonies? . . .

It is well known that some of the French and Spanish colonists, not long since, offered to put themselves under the protection of England and declare themselves independent of France and Spain; but England rejected both offers. The example would be rather dangerous to states that have colonies — to none could it be more so than to France and Spain, who have so many and such extensive colonies. "The practice of courts are as much against us" in this as in the instance our author mentions. Can anyone imagine that, because we declared ourselves independent of England, France would *therefore* consider us as really independent! And before England had acquiesced, or made any effort worth mentioning to reduce us? Or can anyone be so weak as to think that France would run the risk of a war with England, unless she (France) were sure of some extraordinary advantage by it, in having the colonies under her *immediate jurisdiction?* If England will not protect us for our trade, surely France will not. . . .

The several European states who have colonies on this continent, or the adjacent islands, are exceedingly jealous of those colonies, lest they should aspire to independency. He must be totally ignorant of the state of things in Europe who is not sensible of this. The great distance of America from Europe contributes to raise that jealousy; and it is heightened by our growing strength and importance, and our enterprising spirit. Hence it was that France lately sent such a number of regular troops to Martinico [Martinique] and disarmed all the inhabitants, to whom the defense of that island was chiefly committed formerly. The professed reason for disarming the inhabitants was to prevent their joining the North Americans in their contest with Great Britain. . . . The inhabitants of the French West Indies, it is probable, would willingly join us and shake off the despotic yoke under which they groan; but this disposition in them will only serve to alarm France the more, and induce the latter to oppose rather than assist us. . . .

America is far from being yet in a desperate situation. I am confident she may obtain honorable and advantageous terms from Great Britain. A few years of peace will soon retrieve all her losses. She will rapidly advance to a state of maturity whereby she may not only repay the parent state amply for all past benefits but also lay under the greatest obligations.

America, till very lately, has been the happiest country in the universe. Blessed with all that nature could bestow with the profusest bounty, she enjoyed, besides, more liberty, greater privileges than any other land. How painful is it to reflect on these things, and to look forward to the gloomy prospects now before us! But it is not too late to hope that matters may mend. By prudent management her former happiness may again return; and continue to increase for ages to come, in a union with the parent state.

However distant humanity may wish the period, yet, in the rotation of human affairs, a period may arrive when (both countries being prepared for it) some terrible disaster, some dreadful convulsion in Great Britain may transfer the seat of empire to this Western Hemisphere — where the British constitution, like the Phoenix from its parent's ashes, shall rise with youthful vigor and shine with redoubled splendor.

But if America should now mistake her real interest — if her sons, infatuated with romantic notions of conquest and empire, ere things are ripe, should adopt this republican's scheme — they will infallibly destroy this smiling prospect. They will dismember this happy country, make it a scene of blood and slaughter, and entail wretchedness and misery on millions yet unborn.

97.

JOHN ADAMS: The Foundation of Government

The prospect of independence meant more than fighting a war with Britain. It also entailed the formation of new governments in America. In January of 1776, George Wythe, of Virginia, asked John Adams to draw up a plan that would enable the colonies to make this transition. Adams responded with the following letter.

Source: C. F. Adams, IV, pp. 193-200.

IF I WAS EQUAL TO THE TASK of forming a plan for the government of a colony, I should be flattered with your request, and very happy to comply with it; because, as the divine science of politics is the science of social happiness, and the blessings of society depend entirely on the constitutions of government, which are generally institutions that last for many generations, there can be no employment more agreeable to a benevolent mind than a research after the best. . . .

We ought to consider what is the end of government before we determine which is the best form. Upon this point all speculative politicians will agree, that the happiness of society is the end of government, as all divines and moral philosophers will agree that the happiness of the individual is the end of man. From this principle it will follow that the form of government which communicates ease, comfort, security, or, in one word, happiness to the greatest number of persons, and in the greatest degree, is the best.

All sober inquirers after truth, ancient and modern, pagan and Christian, have declared that the happiness of man, as well as his dignity, consists in virtue. . . . If there is a form of government, then, whose principle and foundation is virtue, will not every sober man acknowledge it better calculated to promote the general happiness than any other form?

Fear is the foundation of most governments; but it is so sordid and brutal a passion, and renders men in whose breasts it predominates so stupid and miserable, that Americans will not be likely to approve of any political institution which is founded on it.

Honor is truly sacred, but holds a lower rank in the scale of moral excellence than virtue. Indeed, the former is but a part of the latter and, consequently, has not equal pretensions to support a frame of government productive of human happiness.

The foundation of every government is some principle or passion in the minds of the people. The noblest principles and most generous affections in our nature, then, have the fairest chance to support the noblest and most generous models of government. . . . That, as a republic is the best of governments, so that particular arrangement of the powers of society, or, in other words, that form of government which is best contrived to secure an impartial and exact execution of the laws, is the best of republics.

Of republics there is an inexhaustible variety, because the possible combinations of the powers of society are capable of innumerable variations.

As good government is an empire of laws, how shall your laws be made? In a large society inhabiting an extensive country, it is impossible that the whole should assemble to make laws. The first necessary step, then, is to depute power from the many to a few of the most wise and good. But by what rules shall you choose your representatives? Agree upon the number and qualifications of persons who shall have the benefit of choosing, or annex this privilege to the inhabitants of a certain extent of ground.

The principal difficulty lies, and the greatest care should be employed, in constituting this representative assembly. It should be in miniature an exact portrait of the people at large. It should think, feel, reason, and act like them. That it may be the interest of this assembly to do strict justice at all times, it should be an equal representation, or, in other words, equal interests among the people should have equal interests in it. Great care should be taken to effect this, and to prevent unfair, partial, and corrupt elections. Such regulations, however, may be better made in times of greater tranquillity than the present; and they will spring up themselves naturally when all the powers of government come to be in the hands of the people's friends. At present, it will be safest to proceed in all established modes to which the people have been familiarized by habit.

A representation of the people in one assembly being obtained, a question arises, whether all the powers of government, legislative, executive, and judicial, shall be left in this body? I think a people cannot be long free, nor ever happy, whose government is in one assembly. My reasons for this opinion are as follow:

1. A single assembly is liable to all the vices, follies, and frailties of an individual; subject to fits of humor, starts of passion, flights of enthusiasm, partialities, or prejudice, and consequently productive of hasty results and absurd judgments. And all these errors ought to be corrected and defects supplied by some controlling power.

2. A single assembly is apt to be avaricious, and in time will not scruple to exempt itself from burdens which it will lay, without compunction, on its constituents.

3. A single assembly is apt to grow ambitious, and after a time will not hesitate to vote itself perpetual. . . .

To avoid these dangers, let a distinct assembly be constituted as a mediator between the two extreme branches of the legislature, that which represents the people, and that which is vested with the executive power. . . .

The dignity and stability of government in all its branches, the morals of the people, and every blessing of society depend so much upon an upright and skilful administration of justice that the judicial power ought to be distinct from both the legislative and executive, and independent upon both, that so it may be a check upon both, as both should be checks upon that. . . .

A militia law requiring all men, or with very few exceptions besides cases of conscience, to be provided with arms and ammunition, to be trained at certain seasons; and requiring counties, towns, or other small districts to be provided with public stocks of ammunition and entrenching utensils, and with some settled plans for transporting provisions after the militia, when marched to defend their country against sudden invasions; and requiring certain districts to be provided with fieldpieces, companies of matrosses [gunner's mates], and perhaps some regiments of light-horse [men], is always a wise institution, and, in the present circumstances of our country, indispensable.

Laws for the liberal education of youth, especially of the lower class of people, are so extremely wise and useful that, to a humane and generous mind, no expense for this purpose would be thought extravagant. . . .

A constitution founded on these principles introduces knowledge among the people and inspires them with a conscious dignity becoming freemen; a general emulation takes place which causes good humor, sociability, good manners, and good morals to be general. That elevation of sentiment inspired by such a government makes the common people brave and enterprising. That ambition which is inspired by it makes them sober, industrious, and frugal. You will find among them some elegance, perhaps, but more solidity; a little pleasure, but a great deal of business; some politeness, but more civility. If you compare such a country with the regions of domination, whether monarchical or aristocratical, you will fancy yourself in Arcadia or Elysium.

If the colonies should assume governments separately, they should be left entirely to their own choice of the forms; and if a continental constitution should be formed, it should be a congress containing a fair and adequate representation of the colonies, and its authority should sacredly be confined to these cases; namely, war, trade, disputes between colony and colony, the post office, and the unappropriated lands of the Crown, as they used to be called.

These colonies under such forms of government, and in such a union, would be unconquerable by all the monarchies of Europe.

You and I, my dear friend, have been sent into life at a time when the greatest lawgivers of antiquity would have wished to live. How few of the human race have ever enjoyed an opportunity of making an election of government, more than of air, soil, or climate, for themselves or their children! When, before the present epoch, had 3,000,000 people full power and a fair opportunity to form and establish the wisest and happiest government that human wisdom can contrive? I hope you will avail yourself and your country of that extensive learning and indefatigable industry which you possess to assist her in the formation of the happiest governments and the best character of a great people.

In the new code of laws which I suppose it will be necessary for you to make I desire you would remember the ladies and be more generous and favorable to them than your ancestors.

ABIGAIL ADAMS, letter to John Adams, March 31, 1776

98.

James Wilson: The Legal Right to Form a Government

James Wilson was a delegate from Pennsylvania to the Second Continental Congress. On February 13, 1776, he prepared an address to the inhabitants of all the colonies that was meant to prepare public opinion for eventual independence. However, as public sentiment had already anticipated his position, the address was not published at the time.

Source: *Selected Political Essays of James Wilson,* Randolph G. Adams, ed., New York, 1930: "An Address to the Inhabitants of the Colonies of New Hampshire, etc., etc."

Friends and Countrymen:

History, we believe, cannot furnish an example of a trust higher and more important than that which we have received from your hands. It comprehends in it everything that can rouse the attention and interest the passions of a people, who will not reflect disgrace upon their ancestors, nor degrade themselves, nor transmit infamy to their descendants. It is committed to us at a time when everything dear and valuable to such a people is in imminent danger. This danger arises from those whom we have been accustomed to consider as our friends; who really were so while they continued friendly to themselves; and who will again be so when they shall return to a just sense of their own interests. The calamities which threaten us would be attended with a total loss of those constitutions, formed upon the venerable model of British liberty, which have been long our pride and felicity. To avert those calamities we are under the disagreeable necessity of making temporary deviations from those constitutions.

Such is the trust reposed in us. Much does it import you and us that it be executed with skill and with fidelity. That we have discharged it with fidelity, we enjoy the testimony of a good conscience. How far we have discharged it with skill must be determined by you, who are our principals and judges, to whom we esteem it our duty to render an account of our conduct. To enable you to judge of it, as we would wish you to do, it is necessary that you should be made acquainted with the situation in which your affairs have been placed; the principles on which we have acted; and the ends, which we have kept and still keep in view.

That all power was originally in the people — that all the powers of government are derived from them — that all power, which they have not disposed of, still continues theirs — are maxims of the English constitution, which, we presume, will not be disputed. The share of power which the king derives from the people, or, in other words, the prerogative of the Crown, is well known and precisely ascertained. It is the same in Great Britain and in the colonies. The share of power which the House of Commons derives from the people is likewise well known — the manner in which it is conveyed is by election.

But the House of Commons is not elected by the colonists; and, therefore, from them that body can derive no authority.

Besides, the powers which the House of Commons receives from its constituents are entrusted by the colonies to their assemblies in the several provinces. Those assemblies have authority to propose and assent to laws for the government of their electors, in the same manner as the House of Commons has authority to propose and assent to laws for the government of the inhabitants of Great Britain. Now the same collective body cannot delegate the same powers to distinct representative bodies. The undeniable result is that the House of Commons neither has nor can have any power derived from the inhabitants of these colonies.

In the instance of imposing taxes, this doctrine is clear and familiar; it is true and just in every other instance. If it would be incongruous and absurd that the same property should be liable to be taxed by two bodies independent of each other, would less incongruity and absurdity ensue if the same offense were to be subjected to different and perhaps inconsistent punishments? Suppose the punishment directed by the laws of one body to be death, and that directed by those of the other body be banishment for life; how could both punishments be inflicted?

Though the Crown possesses the same prerogative over the colonies which it possesses over the inhabitants of Great Britain; though the colonists delegate to their assemblies the same powers which our fellow subjects in Britain delegate to the House of Commons; yet by some inexplicable mystery in politics, which is the foundation of the odious system that we have so much reason to deplore, additional powers over you are ascribed to the Crown, as a branch of the British legislature. And the House of Commons — a body which acts solely by derivative authority — is supposed entitled to exert over you an authority which you

cannot give and which it cannot receive.

The sentence of universal slavery gone forth against you is: *that the British Parliament have power to make laws, without your consent, building you in all cases whatever.* Your fortunes, your liberties, your reputations, your lives, everything that can render you and your posterity happy, all are the objects of the laws; all must be enjoyed, impaired, or destroyed as the laws direct. And are you the wretches who have nothing that you can or ought to call your own? Were all the rich blessings of nature, all the bounties of indulgent Providence poured upon you, not for your own use but for the use of those upon whom neither nature nor Providence has bestowed qualities or advantages superior to yours?

From this root of bitterness numerous are the branches of oppression that have sprung. Your most undoubted and highest-prized rights have been invaded; heavy and unnecessary burdens have been imposed on you; your interests have been neglected and sometimes wantonly sacrificed to the interests and even to the caprice of others. When you felt, for your enemies have not yet made any laws to divest you of feeling, uneasiness under your grievances, and expressed it in the natural tone of complaint, your murmurs were considered and treated as the language of faction, and your uneasiness was ascribed to a restive disposition, impatient of control.

In proportion, however, as your oppressions were multiplied and increased, your opposition to them became firm and vigorous. Remonstrances succeeded petitions; a resolution carried into effect not to import goods from Great Britain succeeded both. The acts of Parliament then complained of were in part repealed. Your good humor and unsuspicious fondness returned. Short — alas! too short — was the season allowed for indulging them. The former system of rigor was renewed.

The colonies, wearied with presenting

fruitless supplications and petitions separately; or prevented by arbitrary and abrupt dissolutions of their assemblies from using even those fruitless expedients for redress, determined to join their counsels and their efforts. Many of the injuries flowing from the unconstitutional and ill-advised acts of the British legislature affected all the provinces equally; and even in those cases in which the injuries were confined, by the acts to one or to a few, the principles on which they were made extended to all. If common rights, common interests, common dangers and common sufferings are principles of union, what could be more natural than the union of the colonies?

Delegates authorized by the several provinces from Nova Scotia to Georgia to represent them and act in their behalf met in General Congress.

It has been objected that this measure was unknown to the constitution; that the Congress was, of consequence, an illegal body; and that its proceedings could not, in any manner, be recognized by the government of Britain. To those who offer this objection and have attempted to vindicate, by its supposed validity, the neglect and contempt with which the petition of that Congress to His Majesty was treated by the Ministry, we beg leave, in our turn, to propose that they would explain the principles of the constitution, which warranted the Assembly of the Barons at Runnymede, when Magna Charta was signed, the Convention-Parliament that recalled Charles II, and the Convention of Lords and Commons that placed King William on the throne. When they shall have done this, we shall perhaps be able to apply their principles to prove the necessity and propriety of a congress.

But the objections of those who have done so much and aimed so much against the liberties of America are not confined to the meeting and the authority of the Congress; they are urged with equal warmth against the views and inclinations of those who composed it. We are told, in the name of majesty itself, "that the authors and promoters of this desperate conspiracy," as those who have framed His Majesty's speech are pleased to term our laudable resistance, "have, in the conduct of it, derived great advantage from the difference of His Majesty's intentions and theirs. That they meant only to amuse by vague expressions of attachment to the parent state, and the strongest protestations of loyalty to the King, whilst they were preparing for a general revolt. That on the part of His Majesty and the Parliament, the wish was rather to reclaim than to subdue." It affords us some pleasure to find that the protestations of loyalty to His Majesty which have been made are allowed to be strong; and that attachment to the parent state is owned to be expressed. Those protestations of loyalty and expressions of attachment ought, by every rule of candor, to be presumed to be sincere, unless proofs evincing their insincerity can be drawn from the conduct of those who used them.

In examining the conduct of those who directed the affairs of the colonies at the time when, it is said, they were preparing for a general revolt, we find it an easy undertaking to show that they merited no reproach from the British Ministry by making any preparations for that purpose. We wish it were as easy to show that they merited no reproach from their constituents by neglecting the necessary provisions for their security. Has a single preparation been made which has not been found requisite for our defense? Have we not been attacked in places where fatal experience taught us we were not sufficiently prepared for a successful opposition? On which side of this unnatural controversy was the ominous intimation first given that it must be decided by force? Were arms and ammunition imported into America, before the importation of them was prohibited? What reason can

Miniature portrait of James Wilson by an unidentified artist

be assigned for this prohibition, unless it be this, that those who made it had determined upon such a system of oppression as they knew would force the colonies into resistance? And yet, they "wished only to reclaim!"

The sentiments of the colonies, expressed in the proceedings of their delegates assembled in 1774, were far from being disloyal or disrespectful. Was it disloyal to offer a petition to your sovereign? Did your still-anxious impatience for an answer, which your hopes, founded only on your wishes, as you too soon experienced, flattered you would be a gracious one — did this impatience indicate a disposition only to amuse? Did the keen anguish with which the fate of the petition filled your breasts betray an inclination to avail yourselves of the indignity with which you were treated for forwarding favorite designs of revolt?

Was the agreement not to import merchandise from Great Britain or Ireland, nor after the 10th day of September last to ex-

port our produce to those kingdoms and the West Indies — was this a disrespectful or a hostile measure? Surely we have a right to withdraw or to continue our own commerce. Though the British Parliament have exercised a power of directing and restraining our trade; yet, among all their extraordinary pretensions, we recollect no instance of their attempting to force it contrary to our inclinations. It was well known, before this measure was adopted, that it would be detrimental to our own interest, as well as to that of our fellow subjects. We deplored it on both accounts. We deplored the necessity that produced it. But we were willing to sacrifice our interest to any probable method of regaining the enjoyment of those rights which, by violence and injustice, had been infringed.

Yet even this peaceful expedient, which faction surely never suggested, has been represented, and by high authority too, as a seditious and unwarrantable combination. We are, we presume, the first rebels and conspirators who commenced their conspiracy and rebellion with a system of conduct immediately and directly frustrating every aim which ambition or rapaciousness could propose. Those whose fortunes are desperate may upon slight evidence be charged with desperate designs; but how improbable is it that the colonists, who have been happy, and have known their happiness in the quiet possession of their liberties; who see no situation more to be desired than that in which, till lately, they have been placed; and whose warmest wish is to be reinstalled in the enjoyment of that freedom which they claim and are entitled to as men and as British subjects — how improbable is it that such would, without any motives that could tempt even the most profligate minds to crimes, plunge themselves headlong into all the guilt and danger and distress with which those that endeavor to overturn the constitution of their country are always surrounded and frequently overwhelmed?

The humble, unaspiring colonists asked only for "peace, liberty and safety." This, we think, was a reasonable request. Reasonable as it was, it has been refused. Our ministerial foes, dreading the effects which our commercial opposition might have upon their favorite plan of reducing the colonies to slavery, were determined not to hazard it upon that issue. They employed military force to carry it into execution. Opposition of force by force or unlimited subjection was now our only alternative. Which of them did it become freemen, determined never to surrender that character, to choose? The choice was worthily made. We wish for peace — we wish for safety; but we will not, to obtain either or both of them, part with our liberty. The sacred gift descended to us from our ancestors; we cannot dispose of it; we are bound by the strongest ties to transmit it, as we have received it, pure and inviolate to our posterity.

We have taken up arms in the best of causes. We have adhered to the virtuous principles of our ancestors, who expressly stipulated in their favor, and in ours, a right to resist every attempt upon their liberties. We have complied with our engagements to our sovereign. He should be the ruler of a free people; we will not, as far as his character depends upon us, permit him to be degraded into a tyrant over slaves.

Our troops are animated with the love of freedom. They have fought and bled and conquered in the discharge of their duty as good citizens as well as brave soldiers. Regardless of the inclemency of the seasons, and of the length and fatigue of the march, they go with cheerfulness wherever the cause of liberty and their country requires their service. We confess that they have not the advantages arising from experience and discipline. But facts have shown that native courage warmed with patriotism is sufficient to counterbalance these advantages. The experience and discipline of our troops will daily increase; their patriotism will receive no diminution; the longer those who have forced us into this war oblige us to continue it, the more formidable we shall become.

The strength and resources of America are not confined to operations by land. She can exert herself likewise by sea. Her sailors are hardy and brave; she has all the materials for shipbuilding; her artificers can work them into form. We pretend not to vie with the Royal Navy of England though that navy had its beginnings; but still we may be able in a great measure to defend our own coasts, and may intercept, as we have been hitherto successful in doing, transports and vessels laden with stores and provisions.

Possessed of so many advantages; favored with the prospect of so many more; threatened with the destruction of our constitutional rights; cruelly and illiberally attacked because we will not subscribe to our own slavery — ought we to be animated with vigor or to sink into despondency? When the forms of our governments are, by those entrusted with the direction of them, perverted from their original design, ought we to submit to this perversion? Ought we to sacrifice the forms when the sacrifice becomes necessary for preserving the spirit of our constitution? Or ought we to neglect and, neglecting, to lose the spirit by a superstitious veneration for the forms? We regard those forms and wish to preserve them as long as we can consistently with higher objects. But much more do we regard essential liberty, which, at all events, we are determined not to lose but with our lives. In contending for this liberty, we are willing to go through good report and through evil report.

In our present situation, in which we are called to oppose an attack upon your liberties, made under bold pretensions of authority from that power, to which the executive part of government is, in the ordinary course of affairs, committed — in the situation, every mode of resistance, though directed by necessity and by prudence, and authorized by the spirit of the constitution, will be exposed to plausible objections drawn from its forms. Concerning such objections, and the weight that may be allowed to them, we are little solicitous. It will not discourage us to find ourselves represented as "laboring to inflame the minds of the people of America, and openly avowing revolt, hostility, and rebellion." We deem it an honor to "have raised troops, and collected a naval force"; and, clothed with the sacred authority of the people, from whom all legitimate authority proceeds, "to have exercised legislative, executive and judicial powers." For what purposes were those powers instituted? For your safety and happiness. You and the world will judge whether those purposes have been best promoted by us; or by those who claim the powers which they charge us with assuming.

But while we feel no mortification at being misrepresented with regard to the measures employed by us for accomplishing the great ends which you have appointed us to pursue, we cannot sit easy under an accusation which charges us with laying aside those ends and endeavoring to accomplish such as are very different. We are accused of carrying on the war "for the purpose of establishing an independent empire."

We disavow the intention. We declare that what we aim at, and what we are entrusted by you to pursue, is the defense and the reestablishment of the constitutional rights of the colonies. Whoever gives impartial attention to the facts we have already stated, and to the observations we have already made, must be fully convinced that all the steps which have been taken by us in this unfortunate struggle can be accounted for as rationally and as satisfactorily by supposing that the defense and reestablishment of their rights were the objects which the colonists and their representatives had in view, as by supposing that an independent

empire was their aim. Nay, we may safely go farther and affirm, without the most distant apprehension of being refuted, that many of those steps can be accounted for rationally and satisfactorily only upon the former supposition, and cannot be accounted for in that manner upon the latter. The numerous expedients that were tried, though fruitlessly, for avoiding hostilities; the visible and unfeigned reluctance and horror with which we entered into them; the caution and reserve with which we have carried them on; the attempts we have made by petitioning the Throne and by every other method which might probably, or could possibly, be of any avail for procuring an accommodation — these are not surely the usual characteristics of ambition.

In what instance have we been the aggressors? Did our troops take the field before the ministerial forces began their hostile march to Lexington and Concord? Did we take possession or did we form any plan for taking possession of Canada before we knew that it was a part of the ministerial system to pour the Canadians upon our frontiers? Did we approach the Canadians, or have we treated them as enemies? Did we take the management of the Indian tribes into our hands before we were well assured that the emissaries of administration were busy in persuading them to strike us? When we treated with them, did we imitate the barbarous example? Were not our views and persuasions confined to keeping them in a state of neutrality? Did we seize any vessel of our enemies before our enemies had seized some of ours? Had we yet seized any, except such as were employed in the service of administration, and in supplying those that were in actual hostilities against us? Cannot our whole conduct be reconciled to principles and views of self-defense? Whence then the uncandid imputation of aiming at an independent empire?

Is no regard to be had to the professions and protestations made by us, on so many different occasions, of attachment to Great

Britain, of allegiance to His Majesty; and of submission to his government upon the terms on which the constitution points it out as a duty, and on which alone a British sovereign has the right to demand it?

When the hostilities commenced by the ministerial forces in Massachusetts Bay and the imminent dangers threatening the other colonies rendered it absolutely necessary that they should be put into a state of defense — even on that occasion, we did not forget our duty to His Majesty and our regard for our fellow subjects in Britain. Our words are these:

But as we most ardently wish for a restoration of the harmony formerly subsisting between our mother country and these colonies, the interruption of which must at all events be exceedingly injurious to both countries: resolved, that with a sincere design of contributing, by all means in our power not incompatible with a just regard for the undoubted rights and true interests of these colonies, to the promotion of this most desirable reconciliation, a humble and dutiful address be presented to His Majesty

If the purposes of establishing an independent empire had lurked in our breasts, no fitter occasion could have been found for giving intimations of them than in our declaration setting forth the causes and necessity of our taking up arms. Yet even there no pretense can be found for fixing such an imputation on us.

Lest this declaration should disquiet the minds of our friends and fellow subjects in any part of the empire, we assure them that we mean not to dissolve that union which has so long and so happily subsisted between us, and which we sincerely wish to see restored. Necessity has not yet driven us into that desperate measure, or induced us to excite any other nation to war against them. We have not raised armies with the ambitious designs of separating from Great Britain and establishing independent states.

Our petition to the King has the following asseveration:

By such arrangements as Your Majesty's wisdom can form for collecting the united sense of your American people, we are convinced Your Majesty would receive such satisfactory proofs of the disposition of the colonists toward their Sovereign and the parent state, that the wished for opportunity would be soon restored to them, of evincing the sincerity of their professions by every testimony of devotion becoming the most dutiful subjects and the most affectionate colonists.

In our address to the inhabitants of Great Britain, we say:

We are accused of aiming at independence. But how is this accusation supported? By the allegations of your ministers, not by our actions. Give us leave most solemnly to assure you that we have not yet lost sight of the object we have ever had in view, a reconciliation with you on constitutional principles, and a restoration of that friendly intercourse which to the advantage of both we till lately maintained.

If we wished to detach you from your allegiance to His Majesty and to wean your affections from a connection with your fellow subjects in Great Britain, is it likely that we would have taken so much pains, upon every proper occasion, to place those objects before you in the most agreeable points of view?

If any equitable terms of accommodation had been offered us, and we had rejected them, there would have been some foundation for the charge that we endeavored to establish an independent empire. But no means have been used either by Parliament or by administration for the purpose of bringing this contest to a conclusion besides penalties directed by statutes or devastations occasioned by war. Alas! how long will Britons forget that kindred blood flows in your veins? How long will they strive with hostile fury to sluice it out from bosoms that have already bled in their cause; and, in their cause, would still be willing to pour out what remains, to the last precious drop?

We are far from being insensible of the advantages which have resulted to the colonies as well as to Britain from the connection which has hitherto subsisted between them; we are far from denying them, or wishing to lessen the ideas of their importance. But the nature of this connection, and the principles on which it was originally formed and on which alone it can be maintained, seem unhappily to have been misunderstood or disregarded by those who laid or conducted the late destructive plan of colony administration. It is a connection founded upon mutual benefits; upon religion, laws, manners, customs and habits common to both countries. Arbitrary exertions of power on the part of Britain, and servile submission on the part of the colonies, if the colonies should ever become degenerate enough to accept it, would immediately rend every generous bond asunder. An intimate connection between freemen and slaves cannot be continued without danger and, at last, destruction to the former. Should your enemies be able to reduce you to slavery, the baneful contagion would spread over the whole empire. We verily believe that the freedom, happiness, and glory of Great Britain, and the prosperity of His Majesty and his family, depend upon the success of your resistance. You are now expending your blood and your treasure in promoting the welfare and the true interests of your sovereign and your fellow subjects in Britain in opposition to the most dangerous attacks that have been ever made against them.

The ideas of deriving emolument to the mother country by taxing you and depriving you of your constitutions and liberties were not introduced till lately. The experiments to which those ideas have given birth have proved disastrous; the voice of wisdom calls loudly that they should be laid aside. Let them not, however, be removed from view. They may serve as beacons to prevent future shipwrecks.

Britain and these colonies have been blessings to each other. Sure we are that they might continue to be so. Some salutary system might certainly be devised which would remove from both sides jealousies that are ill-founded and causes of jealousies that are well-founded; which would restore to both countries those important benefits that nature seems to have intended them reciprocally to confer and to receive; and which would secure the continuance and the increase of those benefits to numerous succeeding generations. That such a system may be formed is our ardent wish.

But as such a system must affect the interest of the colonies as much as that of the mother country, why should the colonies be excluded from a voice in it? Should not, to say the least upon this subject, their consent be asked and obtained as to the general ends which it ought to be calculated to answer? Why should not its validity depend upon us as well as upon the inhabitants of Great Britain? No disadvantage will result to them; an important advantage will result to us. We shall be affected by no laws, the authority of which, as far as they regard us, is not founded on our own consent. This consent may be expressed as well by a solemn compact, as if the colonists, by their representatives, had an immediate voice in passing the laws. In a compact we would concede liberally to Parliament, for the bounds of our concessions would be known.

We are too much attached to the English laws and constitution, and know too well their happy tendency to diffuse freedom, prosperity, and peace wherever they prevail, to desire an independent empire. If one part of the constitution be pulled down, it is impossible to foretell whether the other parts of it may not be shaken, and, perhaps, overthrown. It is a part of our constitution to be under allegiance to the Crown, limited and ascertained as the prerogative is, the position — that a king can do no wrong — may be founded in fact as well as in law, if you are not wanting to yourselves.

We trace your calamities to the House of Commons. They have undertaken to give and grant your money. From a supposed virtual representation in their House it is argued that you ought to be bound by the acts of the British Parliament in all cases whatever. This is no part of the constitution. This is the doctrine to which we will never subscribe our assent; this is the claim to which we adjure you, as you tender your own freedom and happiness and the freedom and happiness of your posterity, never to submit. The same principles which directed your ancestors to oppose the exorbitant and dangerous pretensions of the Crown should direct you to oppose the no less exorbitant and dangerous claims of the House of Commons. Let all communication of despotic power through that channel be cut off, and your liberties will be safe.

Let neither our enemies nor our friends make improper inferences from the solicitude which we have discovered to remove the imputation of aiming to establish an independent empire. Though an independent empire is not our wish, it may — let your oppressors attend — it may be the fate of our countrymen and ourselves. It is in the power of your enemies to render independency or slavery your and our alternative. Should we — will you, in such an event — hesitate a moment about the choice? Let those who drive us to it answer to their King and to their country for the consequences. We are desirous to continue subjects; but we are determined to continue freemen. We shall deem ourselves bound to renounce, and we hope you will follow our example in renouncing, the former character whenever it shall become incompatible with the latter.

While we shall be continued by you in the very important trust which you have committed to us, we shall keep our eyes constantly and steadily fixed upon the grand object of the union of the colonies — the reestablishment and security of their constitutional rights. Every measure that we employ shall be directed to the attainment of this great end; no measure necessary, in our opinion, for attaining it shall be declined. If any such measure should, against our principal intention, draw the colonies into engagements that may suspend or dissolve their union with their fellow subjects in Great Britain, we shall lament the effect, but shall hold ourselves justified in adopting the measure. That the colonies may continue connected, as they have been, with Britain is our second wish. Our first is — *That America may be free.*

99.

John Adams: On the Importance of Property for the Suffrage

James Sullivan, a member of the provincial congress of Massachusetts, corresponded with John Adams in May 1776 when the latter was a member of the Second Continental Congress. On May 6, Sullivan wrote a letter to Adams in which he discussed the principles of representation and legislation and called for some alterations in the qualifications for voters. Adams replied in the following letter of May 26, 1776.

Source: C. F. Adams, IX, pp. 375-378.

IT IS CERTAIN, in theory, that the only moral foundation of government is the consent of the people. But to what an extent shall we carry this principle? Shall we say that every individual of the community, old and young, male and female, as well as rich and poor, must consent, expressly, to every act of legislation? No, you will say, this is impossible. How, then, does the right arise in the majority to govern the minority against their will? Whence arises the right of the men to govern the women without their consent? Whence the right of the old to bind the young without theirs?

But let us first suppose that the whole community, of every age, rank, sex, and condition, has a right to vote. This community is assembled. A motion is made, and carried by a majority of one voice. The minority will not agree to this. Whence arises the right of the majority to govern, and the obligation of the minority to obey?

From necessity, you will say, because there can be no other rule.

But why exclude women?

You will say, because their delicacy renders them unfit for practice and experience in the great businesses of life, and the hardy enterprises of war, as well as the arduous cares of state. Besides, their attention is so much engaged with the necessary nurture of their children that nature has made them fittest for domestic cares. And children have not judgment or will of their own. True. But will not these reasons apply to others? Is it not equally true that men in general, in every society, who are wholly destitute of property are also too little acquainted with public affairs to form a right judgment, and too dependent upon other men to have a will of their own? If this is a fact, if you give to every man who has no property a vote, will you not make a fine encouraging provision for corruption by your fundamental law? Such is the frailty of the human heart that very few men who have no property have any judgment of their own. They talk and vote as they are directed by some man of property who has attached their minds to his interest.

Upon my word, sir, I have long thought an army a piece of clockwork, and to be governed only by principles and maxims, as fixed as any in mechanics; and, by all that I have read in the history of mankind, and in authors who have speculated upon society and government, I am much inclined to think a government must manage a society in the same manner; and that this is machinery too.

Harrington has shown that power always follows property. This I believe to be as infallible a maxim in politics, as that action and reaction are equal is in mechanics. Nay, I believe we may advance one step farther, and affirm that the balance of power in a society accompanies the balance of property in land. The only possible way, then, of preserving the balance of power on the side of equal liberty and public virtue is to make the acquisition of land easy to every member of society; to make a division of the land into small quantities, so that the multitude may be possessed of landed estates. If the multitude is possessed of the balance of real estate, the multitude will have the balance of power, and in that case the multitude will take care of the liberty, virtue, and interest of the multitude in all acts of government. I believe these principles have been felt, if not understood, in the Massachusetts Bay from the beginning; and therefore I should think that wisdom and policy would dictate in these times to be very cautious of making alterations. Our people have never been very rigid in scrutinizing into the qualifications of voters, and I presume they will not now begin to be so. But I would not advise them to make any alteration in the laws, at present, respecting the qualifications of voters.

Your idea that those laws which affect the lives and personal liberty of all, or which inflict corporal punishment, affect those who are not qualified to vote, as well as those who are, is just. But so they do women as well as men; children as well as adults. What reason should there be for excluding a man of twenty years eleven months and twenty-seven days old from a vote, when you admit one who is twenty-one? The reason is you must fix upon some period in life when the understanding and will of men in general is fit to be trusted by the public. Will not the same reason justify the state in fixing upon some certain quantity of property as a qualification?

The same reasoning which will induce you to admit all men who have no property to vote with those who have, for those laws which affect the person, will prove that you ought to admit women and children; for, generally speaking, women and children have as good judgments, and as independent minds, as those men who are wholly destitute of property; these last being to all intents and purposes as much dependent upon others who will please to feed, clothe, and employ them, as women are upon their husbands, or children on their parents.

As to your idea of proportioning the votes of men, in money matters, to the property they hold, it is utterly impracticable. There is no possible way of ascertaining, at any one time, how much every man in a community is worth; and if there was, so fluctuating is trade and property that this state of it would change in half an hour. The property of the whole community is shifting every hour, and no record can be kept of the changes.

Society can be governed only by general rules. Government cannot accommodate itself to every particular case as it happens, nor to the circumstances of particular persons. It must establish general comprehensive regulations for cases and persons. The only question is, which general rule will accommodate most cases and most persons.

Depend upon it, sir, it is dangerous to open so fruitful a source of controversy and altercation as would be opened by attempting to alter the qualifications of voters; there will be no end of it. New claims will arise; women will demand a vote; lads from twelve to twenty-one will think their rights not enough attended to; and every man who has not a farthing will demand an equal voice with any other, in all acts of state. It tends to confound and destroy all distinctions and prostrate all ranks to one common level.

100.

The People as Constitution Makers

In New York, the provincial congress met in May 1776 and called for the formation of a new state government. The following address was made public on June 14 by a gathering of the mechanics' union in New York City. They were much concerned about the right of all the people to devise and ratify their own constitution. American patriots were fearful lest a loyalist oligarchy create a constitution that excluded the masses of people from government.

Source: Niles: "Address of the Mechanics of New York City, June 14, 1776."

To the honorable the delegates elected by the several counties and districts within the government of New York, in Colonial Congress convened. The respectful address of the mechanics in union, for the city and county of New York, represented by their general committee.

Elected Delegates:

With due confidence in the declaration which you lately made to the chairman of our general committee, that you are at all times ready and willing to attend to every request of your constituents, or any part of them; we, the mechanics in union, though a very inconsiderable part of your constituents, beg leave to represent that one of the clauses in your resolve, respecting the establishment of a new form of government, is erroneously construed, and for that reason may serve the most dangerous purposes; for it is well known how indefatigable the emissaries of the British Parliament are in the pursuit of every scheme which is likely to bring disgrace upon our rulers and ruin upon us all. At the same time, we cheerfully acknowledge that the genuine spirit of liberty which animates the other part of that resolve did not permit us to interpret it in any other sense than that which is the most

obvious, and likewise the most favorable to the natural rights of man.

We could not, we never can believe you intended that the future delegates, or yourselves, should be vested with the power of framing a new constitution for this colony; and that its inhabitants at large should not exercise the right which God has given them, in common with all men, to judge whether it be consistent with their interest to accept or reject a constitution framed for that state of which they are members. This is the birthright of every man to whatever state he may belong. There, he is, or ought to be, by inadmissible right, a colegislator with all the other members of that community.

Conscious of our own want of abilities, we are, alas! but too sensible that every individual is not qualified for assisting in the framing of a constitution; but that share of common sense which the Almighty has bountifully distributed among mankind in general is sufficient to quicken everyone's feeling and enable him to judge rightly what degree of safety and what advantages he is likely to enjoy, or be deprived of, under any constitution proposed to him. For this reason, should a preposterous confidence in the abilities and integrity of our future delegates delude us into measures which might imply a renunciation of our inalienable right to ratify our laws, we believe that your wisdom, your patriotism, your own interest, nay, your ambition itself, would urge you to exert all the powers of persuasion you possess, and try every method which, in your opinion, could deter us from perpetrating that impious and frantic act of self-destruction; for, as it would precipitate us into a state of absolute slavery, the lawful power which, till now, you have received from your constituents, to be exercised over a free people, would be annihilated by that unnatural act. It might probably accelerate our political death; but it must immediately cause your own.

The continued silence of the bodies which are, by election, vested with an authority subordinate to that of your House would strike us with amazement should we suppose that, in their presence, your resolve ever was interpreted by a sense that was not favorable to the free exercise of our inalienable rights. But we, who daily converse with numbers who have been deceived by such misconstruction, conceive that we ought to inform you in due time that it has alarmed many zealous friends to the general cause which the United Colonies are defending with their lives and fortunes.

As the general opinion of your uprightness depends, in a great measure, on your explanation of that matter; and it being self-evident that the political happiness or misery of the people under your government must be deeply affected by the measures which they may adopt in consequence of such explanation, we trust that you will receive this respectful address with indulgence, and that all our brethren in this and the other colonies in the union will do us the justice to believe that it was dictated by the purest sentiments of unconfined patriotism.

The resolve which contains the obnoxious clause already mentioned is, together with the introduction to it, in the following words, to wit:

> *And whereas* doubts have arisen whether this Congress are invested with sufficient power and authority to deliberate and determine on so important a subject as the necessity of erecting and constituting a new form of government and internal police, to the exclusion of all foreign jurisdiction, dominion, and control whatever; *and whereas* it appertains of right, solely to the people of this colony to determine the said doubts; therefore,
>
> *Resolved,* that it be recommended to the electors in the several counties in this colony, by election in the manner and form prescribed for the election of the present Congress, either to authorize (in addition to the powers vested in this Congress) their present deputies, or others in the stead of their present deputies, or either of them, to take into consideration the necessity and propriety of instituting such new government as in and by the said resolution of the Continental Congress is described and recommended: And if the majority of the counties, by their deputies in provincial congress, shall be of the opinion that such new government ought to be instituted and established, then to institute and establish such a government as they shall deem best calculated to secure the rights, liberties, and happiness of the good people of this colony, and to continue in force until a future peace with Great Britain shall render the same unnecessary.

We cannot forbear expressing our astonishment at the existence of the doubts alluded to in the introduction just quoted. But, when in comparison to those weak minds which gave them birth, you condescended to declare that "It appertains solely to the people of this colony to determine the said doubts," you have, in the spirit of the recommendations of the General Congress, demonstrated to your constituents that you will on all occasions warn them to destroy in its embryo every scheme that you may discover to have the least tendency toward promoting the selfish views of any foreign or domestic oligarchy. Your enemies never can persuade people of reflection that you fully instructed the most ignorant among us by such a positive declaration of our rights for the purpose of surreptitiously obtaining our renunciation of them. Human nature, depraved as it is, has not yet, and we hope never will be, guilty of so much hypocrisy and treachery.

We observe on the contrary, that your resolve is perfectly consistent with the liberal principle on which it is introduced; for, after having set forth what relates to the election of deputies, you recommend to the electors: If the majority of the counties shall be of opinion that such new government ought to be instituted, then to institute and establish such a government.

Posterity will behold that resolve as the test of their rectitude. It will prove that you have fully restored to us the exercise of our right, finally to determine on the laws by which this colony is to be governed; a right of which, by the injustice of the British government, we have till now been deprived. But a forced and most unnatural misconstruction, which is artfully put upon your resolve, has deceived many, who really believe that we will not be allowed to approve or reject the new constitution; they are terrified at the consequences, although a sincere zeal for the general cause inspire them to suppress their remonstrances, lest the common enemy should avail himself of that circumstance to undermine your authority.

Impressed with a just fear of the consequences which result from that error, we conceive it would be criminal in us to continue silent any longer; and, therefore, we beseech you to remove by a full and timely explanation the groundless jealousies which arise from a misconception of your patriotic resolve.

As to us, who do not entertain the least doubt of the purity of your intentions, who well know that your wisdom could not suffer you to aim at obtaining powers of which we cannot lawfully divest ourselves; which, if repeatedly declared by us to have been freely granted, would only proclaim our insanity and, for that reason, be void of themselves; we beg leave, as a part of your constituents, to tender you that tribute of esteem and respect to which you are justly entitled, for your zeal in so nobly asserting the rights which the people at large have to legislation, and in promoting their free exercise of those rights.

You have most religiously followed the lines drawn by the General Congress of the United Colonies. Their laws, issued in the style of recommendations, leave inviolate, in the conventions, the committees, and finally the people at large the right of rejection or ratification. But though it be decreed by that august body that the punishments of death shall, in some cases be inflicted, the people have not rejected any of their laws, nor even remonstrated against them. The reason of such general submission is that the whole of their proceedings is calculated to promote the greatest good to be expected from the circumstances which occasion their resolves, and scarcely admit the delays attending more solemn forms. The conduct of their constituents in this instance clearly shows what an unbounded confidence virtuous rules may place in the sound judgment, integrity, and moderation of a free people.

Whatever the interested supporters of oligarchy may assert to the contrary, there is not, perhaps, one man, nor any set of men, upon earth who, without the special inspiration of the Almighty, could frame a constitution which in all its parts would be truly unexceptionable by the majority of the people for whom it might be intended. And should God bless any man, or any set men, with such eminent gifts, that man, or those men, having no separate interest to support in opposition to the general good, would fairly submit the work to the collective judgment of all the individuals who might be interested in its operation. These, it is probable, would, after due examination, unanimously concur in establishing that constitution. It would become their own joint work, as soon as the majority of them should have freely accepted it; and, by its having received their free assent, the only characteristic of the true lawfulness and legality that can be given to human institutions, it would be truly binding on the people.

Any other concurrence in the acts of legislation is illusory and tyrannical; it proceeds from the selfish principles of corrupt oligarchy; and should a system of laws appear, or even be good in every other respect, which is scarcely admissible, yet it would be imperfect. It could be lawfully binding on none but the legislators themselves and must continue in that state of imperfection which disgraces the best laws, now and then made in governments established on oligarchic principles, and deprives them of true legality. As such is the case with Great Britain herself, it is evident that her Parliament are so far from having a lawful claim to our obedience that they have it not to that of their own constituents; that all our former laws have but a relative legality; and that not one of them is lawfully binding upon us, though even now for the sake of common conveniency the operation of most of them be and ought to be tolerated, until a new system of government shall have been freely ratified by the colegislative power of the people, the sole lawful legislature of this colony. It would be an act of despotism to put it in force by any other means, which God avert! The people, it is true, might be awed, or openly forced to obey, but they would abhor the tyranny and execrate its authors. They would justly think that they were no longer bound to submit than despotism could be maintained by the same violent or artful means which would have produced its existence.

But the free ratification of the people will not be sufficient to render the establishment lawful, unless they exercise in its fullness an uncontrolled power to alter the constitution in the same manner that it shall have been received. This power necessarily involves that of every district occasionally to renew their deputies to committees and congresses when the majority of such district shall think fit; and, therefore, without the intervention of the executive, or any other power, foreign to the body of the respective electors, that right is so essential to our safety that we firmly believe you will recommend to all your constituents immediately to exercise it and never suffer its being wrested from them; otherwise the sensibility of our delegates could not allow them to say that they hold their offices from the voluntary choice of a free people.

We likewise conceive that this measure will, more effectually and more speedily than any other, remove disaffected persons from all our councils and give our public proceedings a much greater weight than they have hitherto obtained among our neighbors.

We never did as a body, nor never will, assume any authority whatsoever in the public transactions of the present times. Common sense teaches us that the absurdity of the claim would not only destroy our usefulness as a body of voluntary associators, who are warmly attached to the cause of liberty, but that it would likewise expose every one of us to deserved derision. At the same time, we assure your honorable House that on all occasions we will continue to testify our zeal in supporting the measures adopted by congresses and committees in the prosecution of their grand object, the restoration of human rights in the United Colonies. And if, at any future time, the silence of the bodies in power give us reason to conceive that our representations may be useful, we then will endeavor to discharge our duty with propriety and rely on public indulgence for any imperfection which cannot affect our uprightness.

101.

Instructions for a Declaration of Independence

Pressure for a complete break with Britain gained momentum in the early months of 1776. Rhode Island took matters into its own hands by declaring its independence early in May. Several of the other colonies sent instructions to their delegates in the Continental Congress to call for a declaration of independence. On May 9, the Massachusetts House of Representatives, in an effort to ascertain the sentiments of the colony with respect to independence, requested each town to instruct its representatives. The instructions from the town of Malden, on May 27, were typical of many voted in Massachusetts.

Source: Niles: "Instructions of the Inhabitants of Malden, Mass. to Their Representative in Congress, May 27, 1776."

Sir:

A resolution of the honorable House of Representatives, calling upon the several towns in this colony to express their minds with respect to the important question of American independence, is the occasion of our now instructing you. The time was, sir, when we loved the King and the people of Great Britain with an affection truly filial; we felt ourselves interested in their glory; we shared in their joys and sorrows; we cheerfully poured the fruit of all our labors into the lap of our mother country, and without reluctance expended our blood and our treasure in their cause.

These were our sentiments toward Great Britain while she continued to act the part of a parent state; we felt ourselves happy in our connection with her, nor wished it to be dissolved; but our sentiments are altered. It is now the ardent wish of our souls that America may become a free and independent state.

A sense of unprovoked injuries will arouse the resentment of the most peaceful.

Such injuries these colonies have received from Britain. Unjustifiable claims have been made by the King and his minions to tax us without our consent; these claims have been prosecuted in a manner cruel and unjust to the highest degree. The frantic policy of administration has induced them to send fleets and armies to America; that, by depriving us of our trade, and cutting the throats of our brethren, they might awe us into submission and erect a system of despotism in America which should so far enlarge the influence of the Crown as to enable it to rivet their shackles upon the people of Great Britain.

This plan was brought to a crisis upon the ever memorable 19th of April. We remember the fatal day! The expiring groans of our countrymen yet vibrate on our ears! And we now behold the flames of their peaceful dwellings ascending to Heaven! We hear their blood crying to us from the ground for vengeance! And charging us, as we value the peace of their [names], to have no further connection with [him], who can unfeelingly hear of the slaughter of [them], and composedly sleep with their blood upon his soul. The manner in which the war has been prosecuted has confirmed us in these sentiments; piracy and murder, robbery and breach of faith, have been conspicuous in the conduct of the King's troops. Defenseless towns have been attacked and destroyed, the ruins of Charlestown, which are daily in our view, daily remind of this. The cries of the widow and the orphan demand our attention; they demand that the hand of pity should wipe the tear from their eye, and that the sword of their country should avenge their wrongs. We long entertained hopes that the spirit of the British nation would once more induce them to assert their own and our rights, and bring to condign punishment the elevated villains who have trampled upon the sacred rights of men and affronted the majesty of the people. We hoped in vain; they have lost their love to freedom, they have lost their spirit of just resentment; we therefore renounce with disdain our connection with a kingdom of slaves; we bid a final adieu to Britain.

Could an accommodation now be effected, we have reason to think that it would be fatal to the liberties of America; we should soon catch the contagion of venality and dissipation, which has subjected Britons to lawless domination. Were we placed in the situation we were in 1763, were the powers of appointing to offices and commanding the militia in the hands of governors, our arts, trade and manufactures would be cramped; nay, more than this, the life of every man who has been active in the cause of his country would be endangered.

For these reasons, as well as many others which might be produced, we are confirmed in the opinion that the present age would be deficient in their duty to God, their posterity, and themselves if they do not establish an American republic. This is the only form of government which we wish to see established; for we can never be willingly subject to any other king than He who, being possessed of infinite wisdom, goodness and rectitude, is alone fit to possess unlimited power.

We have freely spoken our sentiments upon this important subject, but we mean not to dictate; we have unbounded confidence in the wisdom and uprightness of the Continental Congress: with pleasure we recollect that this affair is under their direction; and we now instruct you, sir, to give them the strongest assurance that, if they should declare America to be a free and independent republic, your constituents will support and defend the measure to the last drop of their blood and the last farthing of their treasure.

Don't give up the ship! You will beat them off!
JAMES MUGFORD, last words, as he lay dying in his schooner, the *Franklin,* during a British attack in Boston Harbor, May 19, 1776

102.

Boston's Instructions to Its Delegates to the Continental Congress

Along with the debate over independence that concerned the Continental Congress was the equally weighty problem of providing for the civil government of the colonies. Early in June 1776, a committee composed of members from each colony was appointed to draft articles of confederation. The instructions from Boston, of May 23, to its delegates in the provincial General Assembly are indicative of the thinking of the colonists concerning representative government.

Source: *Archives*, V, pp. 556-558.

Gentlemen:

At a time when, in all probability, the whole United Colonies of America are upon the verge of a glorious revolution, and when, consequently, the most important questions that were ever agitated before the representative body of this colony, touching its internal police, will demand your attention, your constituents think it necessary to instruct you in several matters what part to act, that the path of your duty may be plain before you. . . .

We therefore think it absolutely impracticable for these colonies to be ever again subject to or dependent upon Great Britain without endangering the very existence of the state. Placing, however, unbounded confidence in the supreme councils of the Congress, we are determined to wait, most patiently to wait, till their wisdom shall dictate the necessity of making a Declaration of Independence. Nor should we have ventured to express our sentiments upon this subject but from the presumption that the Congress would choose to feel themselves supported by the people of each colony be-fore they adopt a resolution so interesting to the whole. The inhabitants of this town, therefore, unanimously instruct and direct you that, at the approaching session of the General Assembly, you use your endeavors that the delegates of this colony at the Congress be advised that, in case the Congress should think it necessary for the safety of the United Colonies to declare them independent of Great Britain, the inhabitants of this colony, with their lives and the remnant of their fortunes, will cheerfully support them in the measure.

Touching the internal police of this colony, it is essentially necessary, in order to preserve harmony among ourselves, that the constituent body be satisfied that they are fairly and fully represented.

The right to legislate is originally in every member of the community, which right is always exercised in the infancy of a state. But, when the inhabitants are become numerous, it is not only inconvenient but impracticable for all to meet in one assembly; and hence arose the necessity and practice of legislating by a few, freely chosen by the many. When this choice is free and the representation equal, it is the people's fault if they are not happy. We therefore instruct you to devise some means to obtain an equal representation of the people of this colony in the legislature. But care should be taken that the Assembly be not unwieldy, for this would be an approach to the evil meant to be cured by representation. The largest bodies of men do not always dispatch business with the greatest expedition, nor conduct it in the wisest manner.

It is essential to liberty that the legislative, judicial, and executive powers of government be, as nearly as possible, independent of and separate from each other; for, where they are united in the same person or number of persons, there would be wanting that mutual check which is the principal security against the making of arbitrary laws, and a wanton exercise of power in the execution of them. It is also of the highest importance that every person in a judiciary department employ the greatest part of his time and attention in the duties of his office.

We therefore further instruct you to procure the enacting such law or laws as shall make it incompatible for the same persons to hold a seat in the Legislative and Executive departments of government at one and the same time; that shall render the judges, in every judicatory through the colony, dependent, not on the uncertain tenure of caprice or pleasure but on an unimpeachable deportment in the important duties of their station, for their continuance in office; and to prevent the multiplicity of offices in the same person; that such salaries be settled upon them as will place them above the necessity of stooping to any indirect or collateral means for subsistence. We wish to avoid a profusion of the public moneys on the one hand, and the danger of sacrificing our liberties to a spirit of parsimony, on the other.

Not doubting of your zeal and abilities in the common cause of our country, we leave your discretion to promote such exertions in promoting any military operations as the exigencies of our public affairs may require. And, in the same confidence of your fervor and attachment to the public weal, we readily submit all other matters of public moment that may require your consideration to your own wisdom and discretion.

You will think me transported with enthusiasm, but I am not. I am well aware of the toil, and blood, and treasure, that it will cost us to maintain this declaration, and support and defend these States. Yet, through all the gloom, I can see the rays of ravishing light and glory. I can see that the end is more than worth all the means, and that posterity will triumph in that day's transaction, even although we should rue it, which I trust in God we shall not. . . . The second day of July 1776, will be the most memorable epoch in the history of America. I am apt to believe that it will be celebrated by succeeding generations as the great anniversary festival. It ought to be commemorated as the day of deliverance, by solemn acts of devotion to God Almighty. It ought to be solemnized with pomp and parade, with shows, games, sports, guns, bells, bonfires, and illuminations, from one end of this continent to the other, from this time forward forevermore.
JOHN ADAMS, letter to Mrs. Adams, July 3, 1776

103.

Virginia Declaration of Rights

Virginia's Declaration of Rights was in many ways a central document of its era. Drawn upon by Jefferson for the opening paragraphs of the Declaration of Independence, it was widely copied by the other colonies, became the basis of the Bill of Rights in the Constitution, and had considerable influence in France at the time of the French Revolution. It was written by George Mason and adopted by the Virginia Constitutional Convention on June 12, 1776, as the theoretical foundation of all government.

Source: Thorpe, VII, pp. 3812-3814.

A DECLARATION OF RIGHTS made by the representatives of the good people of Virginia, assembled in full and free convention: which rights do pertain to them and their posterity, as the basis and foundation of government.

Section 1. That all men are by nature equally free and independent and have certain inherent rights, of which, when they enter into a state of society, they cannot, by any compact, deprive or divest their posterity; namely, the enjoyment of life and liberty, with the means of acquiring and possessing property, and pursuing and obtaining happiness and safety.

Section 2. That all power is vested in, and consequently derived from, the people; that magistrates are their trustees and servants and at all times amenable to them.

Section 3. That government is, or ought to be, instituted for the common benefit, protection, and security of the people, nation, or community; of all the various modes and forms of government, that is best which is capable of producing the greatest degree of happiness and safety and is most effectually secured against the danger of maladministration. And that, when any government shall be found inadequate or contrary to these purposes, a majority of the community has an indubitable, inalienable, and indefeasible right to reform, alter, or abolish it, in such manner as shall be judged most conducive to the public weal.

Section 4. That no man, or set of men, is entitled to exclusive or separate emoluments or privileges from the community, but in consideration of public services; which, not being descendible, neither ought the offices of magistrate, legislator, or judge to be hereditary.

Section 5. That the legislative and executive powers of the state should be separate and distinct from the judiciary; and that the members of the two first may be restrained from oppression, by feeling and participating the burdens of the people, they should, at fixed periods, be reduced to a private station, return into that body from which they were originally taken, and the vacancies be supplied by frequent, certain, and regular elections, in which all, or any part, of the former members, to be again eligible, or ineligible, as the laws shall direct.

Section 6. That elections of members to serve as representatives of the people, in assembly, ought to be free; and that all men, having sufficient evidence of permanent common interest with, and attachment to, the community, have the right of suffrage and cannot be taxed or deprived of their property for public uses without their own consent, or that of their representatives so elected, nor bound by any law to which they have not, in like manner, assembled for the public good.

Section 7. That all power of suspending laws, or the execution of laws, by any authority, without consent of the representatives of the people, is injurious to their rights and ought not to be exercised.

Section 8. That in all capital or criminal prosecutions a man has a right to demand the cause and nature of his accusation, to be confronted with the accusers and witnesses, to call for evidence in his favor, and to a speedy trial by an impartial jury of twelve men of his vicinage, without whose unanimous consent he cannot be found guilty; nor can he be compelled to give evidence against himself; that no man be deprived of his liberty except by the law of the land or the judgment of his peers.

Section 9. That excessive bail ought not to be required, nor excessive fines imposed, nor cruel and unusual punishments inflicted.

Section 10. That general warrants, whereby an officer or messenger may be commanded to search suspected places without evidence of a fact committed, or to seize any person or persons not named, or whose offense is not particularly described and supported by evidence, are grievous and oppressive and ought not to be granted.

Section 11. That in controversies respecting property, and in suits between man and man, the ancient trial by jury is preferable to any other and ought to be held sacred.

Section 12. That the freedom of the press is one of the great bulwarks of liberty and can never be restrained but by despotic governments.

Section 13. That a well-regulated militia, composed of the body of the people, trained to arms, is the proper, natural, and safe defense of a free state; that standing armies, in time of peace, should be avoided as dangerous to liberty; and that in all cases the military should be under strict subordination to, and governed by, the civil power.

Section 14. That the people have a right to uniform government; and, therefore, that no government separate from or independent of the government of Virginia ought to be erected or established within the limits thereof.

Section 15. That no free government, or the blessings of liberty, can be preserved to any people but by a firm adherence to justice, moderation, temperance, frugality, and virtue, and by frequent recurrence to fundamental principles.

Section 16. That religion, or the duty which we owe to our Creator, and the manner of discharging it, can be directed only by reason and conviction, not by force or violence; and therefore all men are equally entitled to the free exercise of religion, according to the dictates of conscience; and that it is the mutual duty of all to practise Christian forbearance, love, and charity toward each other.

This day the Continental Congress declared the United Colonies free and independent states.

Anon., notice, quoted in its entirety, on the last page of the Pennsylvania *Evening Post*, July 2, 1776

104.

The First Virginia Constitution

Virginia's was probably the most famous of early constitutions, and it served as a model for other states. As a reaction to the tyranny of the royal governors, the legislature was given virtually all the governing power. Members of the executive and judicial branches were chosen by the House of Burgesses. A provincial convention drafted this constitution in May and adopted it on June 29, 1776, without submitting it to a referendum.

Source: Thorpe, VII, pp. 3814-3819.

Whereas, George III, King of Great Britain and Ireland, and elector of Hanover, heretofore entrusted with the exercise of the kingly office in this government, has endeavored to prevent the same into a detestable and insupportable tyranny by putting his negative on laws the most wholesome and necessary for the public good:

By denying his governors permission to pass laws of immediate and pressing importance, unless suspended in their operation for his assent, and, when so suspended neglecting to attend to them for many years;

By refusing to pass certain other laws, unless the persons to be benefited by them would relinquish the inestimable right of representation in the legislature;

By dissolving legislative assemblies repeatedly and continually, for opposing with manly firmness his invasions of the rights of the people;

When dissolved, by refusing to call others for a long space of time, thereby leaving the political system without any legislative head;

By endeavoring to prevent the population of our country, and, for that purpose, obstructing the laws for the naturalization of foreigners;

By keeping among us, in times of peace, standing armies and ships of war;

By effecting to render the military independent of, and superior to, the civil power;

By combining with others to subject us to a foreign jurisdiction, giving his assent to their pretended acts of legislation;

For quartering large bodies of armed troops among us;

For cutting off our trade with all parts of the world;

For imposing taxes on us without our consent;

For depriving us of the benefits of trial by jury;

For transporting us beyond seas to be tried for pretended offenses;

For suspending our own legislatures, and declaring themselves invested with power to legislate for us in all cases whatsoever;

By plundering our seas, ravaging our coasts, burning our towns, and destroying the lives of our people;

By inciting insurrections of our fellow subjects, with the allurements of forfeiture and confiscation;

By prompting our Negroes to rise in arms against us, those very Negroes whom, by an inhuman use of his negative, he has refused us permission to exclude by law;

By endeavoring to bring on the inhabitants of our frontiers the merciless Indian savages, whose known rule of warfare is an undistinguished destruction of all ages, sexes, and conditions of existence;

By transporting, at this time, a large army of foreign mercenaries to complete the works of death, desolation, and tyranny already begun with circumstances of cruelty and perfidy unworthy the head of a civilized nation;

By answering our repeated petitions for redress with a repetition of injuries;

And finally, by abandoning the helm of government and declaring us out of his allegiance and protection;

By which several acts of misrule, the government of this country, as formerly exercised under the Crown of Great Britain, is *totally dissolved.*

We, therefore, the delegates and representatives of the good people of Virginia, having maturely considered the premises, and viewing with great concern the deplorable conditions to which this once happy country must be reduced, unless some regular, adequate mode of civil polity is speedily adopted, and in compliance with a recommendation of the General Congress, do ordain and declare the future form of government of Virginia to be as follows:

The legislative, executive, and judiciary department shall be separate and distinct, so that neither exercise the powers properly belonging to the other; nor shall any person exercise the powers of more than one of them, at the same time, except that the justices of the county courts shall be eligible to either house of assembly.

The legislative shall be formed of two distinct branches, who, together, shall be a complete legislature. They shall meet once, or oftener, every year, and shall be called the General Assembly of Virginia. One of these shall be called the House of Delegates, and consist of two representatives to be chosen for each county, and for the district of West-Augusta, annually, of such men as actually reside in and are freeholders of the same, or duly qualified according to law; and also of one delegate or representative to be chosen annually for the city of Williamsburgh, and one for the borough of Norfolk, and a representative for each of such other cities and boroughs as may hereafter be allowed particular representation by the legislature. But when any city or borough shall so decrease, as that the number of persons having right of suffrage therein shall have been, for the space of seven years successively, less than half the number of voters in some one county in Virginia, such city or borough thenceforward shall cease to send a delegate or representative to the Assembly.

The other shall be called the Senate, and consist of twenty-four members, of whom thirteen shall constitute a House to proceed on business; for whose election the different counties shall be divided into twenty-four districts. And each county of the respective district, at the time of the election of its delegates, shall vote for one senator, who is actually a resident and freeholder within the district, or duly qualified according to law, and is upward of twenty-five years of age. And the sheriffs of each county, within five days at furthest, after the last county election in the district, shall meet at some convenient place, and from the poll so taken in their respective counties return, as a senator, the man who shall have the greatest number of votes in the whole district. To keep up this Assembly by rotation, the districts shall be equally divided into four classes and numbered by lot. At the end of one year after the general election, the six members, elected by the first division, shall be displaced, and the vacancies thereby occasioned supplied from such class or division, by new election, in the manner aforesaid. This rotation shall be applied to each division according to its number, and continued in due order annually.

The right of suffrage in the election of

members for both houses shall remain as exercised at present; and each house shall choose its own speaker, appoint its own officers, settle its own rules of proceeding, and direct writs of election for the supplying intermediate vacancies.

All laws shall originate in the House of Delegates, to be approved of or rejected by the Senate, or to be amended, with consent of the House of Delegates; except money bills, which in no instance shall be altered by the Senate, but wholly approved or rejected.

A governor, or chief magistrate shall be chosen annually by joint ballot of both houses (to be taken in each house respectively) deposited in the conference room; the boxes examined jointly by a committee of each house; and the numbers severally reported to them, that the appointments may be entered (which shall be the mode of taking the joint ballot of both houses, in all cases) who shall not continue in that office longer than three years successively, nor be eligible until the expiration of four years after he shall have been out of that office. An adequate but moderate salary shall be settled on him during his continuance in office; and he shall, with the advice of a council of state, exercise the executive powers of government, according to the laws of this Commonwealth; and shall not, under any pretense, exercise any power or prerogative, by virtue of any law, statute, or custom of England. But he shall, with the advice of the Council of State, have the power of granting reprieves or pardons, except where the prosecution shall have been carried on by the House of Delegates, or the law shall otherwise particularly direct; in which cases, no reprieve or pardon shall be granted but by resolve of the House of Delegates.

Either house of the General Assembly may adjourn themselves respectively. The governor shall not prorogue or adjourn the Assembly during their sitting, nor dissolve them at any time; but he shall, if necessary, either by advice of the Council of State, or on application of a majority of the House of Delegates, call them before the time to which they shall stand prorogued or adjourned.

A Privy Council, or Council of State, consisting of eight members, shall be chosen, by joint ballot of both houses of assembly, either from their own members or the people at large, to assist in the administration of government. They shall annually choose, out of their own members, a president, who, in case of death, inability, or absence of the governor from the government, shall act as lieutenant governor. Four members shall be sufficient to act, and their advice and proceedings shall be entered on record and signed by the members present (to any part whereof any member may enter his dissent) to be laid before the General Assembly, when called for by them. This Council may appoint their own clerk, who shall have a salary settled by law, and take an oath of secrecy in such matters as he shall be directed by the board to conceal. A sum of money, appropriated to that purpose, shall be divided annually among the members, in proportion to their attendance; and they shall be incapable, during their continuance in office, of sitting in either house of assembly. Two members shall be removed, by joint ballot of both houses of assembly, at the end of every three years, and be ineligible for the three next years. These vacancies, as well as those occasioned by death or incapacity, shall be supplied by new elections in the same manner.

The delegates for Virginia to the Continental Congress shall be chosen annually, or superseded in the meantime, by joint ballot of both houses of assembly.

The present militia officers shall be continued, and vacancies supplied by appointment of the governor, with the advice of the Privy Council, on recommendations from the respective county courts; but the governor and Council shall have a power of suspending any officer and ordering a court-martial on complaint of misbehavior or inability, or to supply vacancies of officers happening when in actual service.

The governor may embody the militia, with the advice of the Privy Council; and when embodied, shall alone have the direction of the militia, under the laws of the country.

The two houses of assembly shall, by joint ballot, appoint judges of the Supreme Court of Appeals and General Court, judges in chancery, judges of admiralty, secretary, and the attorney general, to be commissioned by the governor, and continue in office during good behavior. In case of death, incapacity, or resignation, the governor, with the advice of the Privy Council, shall appoint persons to succeed in office, to be approved or displaced by both houses. These officers shall have fixed and adequate salaries, and, together with all others holding lucrative offices, and all ministers of the gospel of every denomination, be incapable of being elected members of either house of assembly or the Privy Council.

The governor, with the advice of the Privy Council, shall appoint justices of the peace for the counties; and in case of vacancies, or a necessity of increasing the number hereafter, such appointments to be made upon the recommendation of the respective county courts. The present acting secretary in Virginia and clerks of all the county courts shall continue in office. In case of vacancies, either by death, incapacity, or resignation, a secretary shall be appointed, as before directed, and the clerks, by the respective courts. The present and future clerks shall hold their offices during good behavior, to be judged of and determined in the General Court. The sheriffs and coroners shall be nominated by the respective courts, approved by the governor, with the advice of the Privy Council, and commissioned by the governor. The justices shall appoint constables, and all fees of the aforesaid officers be regulated by law.

The governor, when he is out of office, and others offending against the state, either by maladministration, corruption, or other means, by which the safety of the state may be endangered, shall be impeachable by the House of Delegates. Such impeachment to be prosecuted by the attorney general, or such other person or persons as the House may appoint in the General Court, according to the laws of the land. If found guilty, he or they shall be either forever disabled to hold any office under government, or be removed from such office *pro tempore,* or subjected to such pains or penalties as the laws shall direct.

If all or any of the judges of the General Court should on good grounds (to be judged of by the House of Delegates) be accused of any of the crimes or offenses above mentioned, such House of Delegates may, in like manner, impeach the judge or judges so accused, to be prosecuted in the Court of Appeals; and he or they, if found guilty, shall be punished in the same manner as is prescribed in the preceding clause.

Commissions and grants shall run, "In the name of the Commonwealth of Virginia," and bear test by the governor, with the seal of the Commonwealth annexed. Writs shall run in the same manner, and bear test by the clerks of the several courts. Indictments shall conclude, "Against the peace and dignity of the Commonwealth."

A treasurer shall be appointed annually by joint ballot of both houses.

All escheats, penalties, and forfeitures heretofore going to the King shall go to the Commonwealth, save only such as the legislature may abolish or otherwise provide for.

The territories contained within the charters erecting the colonies of Maryland, Pennsylvania, North and South Carolina are hereby ceded, released, and forever confirmed to the people of these colonies respectively, with all the rights of property, jurisdiction, and government, and all other rights whatsoever which might, at any time heretofore, have been claimed by Virginia, except the free navigation and use of the rivers Patomaque and Pokomoke, with the property of the Virginia shores and strands, bordering on either of the said rivers, and all improvements, which have been or shall be made thereon. The western and northern extent of Virginia shall, in all other respects, stand as fixed by the Charter of King James I, in the year 1609, and by the public treaty of peace between the courts of Britain and France, in the year 1763; unless by act of this legislature, one or more governments be established westward of the Allegheny Mountains. And no purchases of lands shall be made of the Indian natives, but on behalf of the public, by authority of the General Assembly.

In order to introduce this government, the representatives of the people met in the Convention shall choose a governor and Privy Council, also such other officers directed to be chosen by both houses as may be judged necessary to be immediately appointed. The Senate to be first chosen by the people to continue until the last day of March next, and the other officers until the end of the succeeding session of Assembly. In case of vacancies, the speaker of either house shall issue writs for new elections.

105.

JOHN DICKINSON: Specch Against Independence

On June 7, 1776, following the instructions of the Virginia Convention, Richard Henry Lee submitted to the Second Continental Congress three resolutions calling for American independence. There was an initial two-day debate, but a vote on the issue was successfully delayed for three weeks by a few delegations that still opposed independence. When debate resumed on July 1, John Dickinson of Pennsylvania made his last protest against a declaration. The speech was probably not published at the time it was given. The text that follows is a reconstruction, printed — with his comments — by Hezekiah Niles in his Principles and Acts of the Revolution in America.

Source: Niles: "Speech of John Dickinson of Pennsylvania, Favoring a Condition of Union with England, Delivered July 1, 1776."

JOHN DICKINSON, one of the deputies of the province to the General Congress, a man of prompt genius, of extensive influence, and one of the most zealous partisans of American liberty, restricted, however, to the condition of union with England, harangued, it is said, in the following manner against independence:

It too often happens, fellow citizens, that men, heated by the spirit of party, give more importance in their discourses, to the surface and appearance of objects, than either to reason or justice; thus evincing that their aim is not to appease tumults but to excite them; not to repress the passions but to inflame them; not to compose ferocious discords but to exasperate and embitter them more and more. They aspire but to please the powerful, to gratify their own ambition, to flatter the caprices of the multitude in order to captivate their favor. Accordingly, in popular commotions, the party of wisdom and of equity is commonly found in the minority; and, perhaps, it would be safer, in difficult circumstances, to consult the smaller instead of the greater number. Upon this principle I invite the attention of those who hear me, since my opinion may differ from that of the majority; but I dare believe it will be shared by all impartial and moderate citizens who condemn this tumultuous proceeding, this attempt to coerce our opinions, and to drag us, with so much precipitation, to the most serious and important of decisions.

But, coming to the subject in controversy, I affirm that prudent men do not abandon objects which are certain to go in pursuit of those which offer only uncertainty. Now, it is an established fact that America can be well and happily governed by the English laws, under the same king and the same Parliament. Two hundred years of happiness furnish the proof of it; and we find it also in the present prosperity, which is the result of these venerable laws and of this ancient union. It is not as independent, but as subjects; not as republic, but as monarchy, that we have arrived at this degree of power and of greatness. What then is the object of these chimeras, hatched in the days of discord and war? Shall the transports of fury have more power over us than the experience of ages? Shall we destroy, in a moment of anger, the work cemented and tested by time?

I know the name of liberty is dear to each one of us; but have we not enjoyed liberty even under the English monarchy? Shall we this day renounce that to go and seek it in I know not what form of republic, which will soon change into a licentious anarchy and popular tyranny? In the human body the head only sustains and governs all the members, directing them, with admirable harmony, to the same object, which is self-preservation and happiness; so the head of the body politic, that is the king, in concert with the Parliament, can alone maintain the union of the members of this Empire, lately so flourishing, and prevent civil war by obviating all the evils produced by variety of opinions and diversity of interests. And so firm is my persuasion of this that I fully believe the most cruel war which Great Britain could make upon us would be that of not making any; and that the surest means of bringing us back to her obedience would be that of employing none. For the dread of the English arms, once removed, provinces would rise up against provinces and cities against cities; and we shall be seen to turn against ourselves the arms we have taken up to combat the common enemy.

Insurmountable necessity would then compel us to resort to the tutelary authority which we should have rashly abjured, and, if it consented to receive us again under its aegis, it would be no longer as free citizens but as slaves. Still inexperienced and in our infancy, what proof have we given of our ability to walk without a guide? None, and, if we judge the future by the past, we must conclude that our concord will continue as long as the danger, and no longer.

Even when the powerful hand of England supported us, for the paltry motives of territorial limits and distant jurisdictions, have we not abandoned ourselves to discords, and sometimes even to violence? And what must we not expect, now that minds are heated, ambitions roused, and arms in the hands of all?

If, therefore, our union with England offers us so many advantages for the maintenance of internal peace, it is no less necessary to procure us, with foreign powers, that condescension and respect which is so essential to the prosperity of our commerce,

John Dickinson, portrait by Charles Willson Peale

to the enjoyment of any consideration, and to the accomplishment of any enterprise. Hitherto in our intercourse with the different nations of the world, England has lent us the support of her name and of her arms. We have presented ourselves in all the ports and in all the cities of the globe, not as Americans, a people scarcely heard of, but as English. Under shadow of this respected name, every port was open to us, every way was smooth, every demand was heard with favor. From the moment when our separation shall take place, everything will assume a contrary direction. The nations will accustom themselves to look upon us with disdain; even the pirates of Africa and Europe will fall upon our vessels, will massacre our seamen, or lead them into a cruel and perpetual slavery.

There is in the human species, often so inexplicable in their affections, a manifest propensity to oppress the feeble as well as to flatter the powerful. Fear always carries it against reason, pride against moderation, and cruelty against clemency.

Independence, I am aware, has attractions for all mankind; but I maintain that, in the present quarrel, the friends of independence are the promoters of slavery, and that those who desire to separate us would but render us more dependent, if independence means the right of commanding and not the necessity of obeying, and if being dependent is to obey and not command. If, in rendering ourselves independent of England, supposing, however, that we should be able to effect it, we might be so, at the same time, of all other nations, I should applaud the project; but to change the condition of English subjects for that of slaves to the whole world is a step that could only be counseled by insanity. If you would reduce yourselves to the necessity of obeying, in all things, the mandates of supercilious France, who is now kindling fire under our feet, declare yourselves independent. If, to British liberty, you prefer the liberty of Holland, of Venice, of Genoa, or of Ragusa, declare yourselves independent. But, if we would not change the signification of words, let us preserve and carefully maintain this dependence which has been, down to this very hour, the principle and source of our prosperity, of our liberty, of our real independence.

But here I am interrupted and told that no one questions the advantages which America derived at first from her conjunction with England; but that the new pretensions of the ministers have changed all, have subverted all. If I should deny that, for the last twelve years, the English government has given the most fatal direction to the affairs of the colonies, and that its measures toward us savor of tyranny, I should deny not only what is the manifest truth but even what I have so often advanced and supported. But is there any doubt that it already feels a secret repentance? These arms, these soldiers it prepares against us are not designed to establish tyranny upon our shores but to vanquish our obstinacy, and to compel us to subscribe to conditions of accommodation.

In vain is it asserted that the Ministry will employ all means to make themselves quite sure of us in order to exercise upon us, with impunity, all the rigor of their power; for to pretend to reduce us to an absolute impossibility of resistance, in cases of oppression, would be, on their part, a chimerical project. The distance of the seat of government, the vast extent of intervening seas, the continual increase of our population, our warlike spirit, our experience in arms, the lakes, the rivers, the forests, the defiles which abound in our territory, are our pledges that England will always prefer to found her power upon moderation and liberty rather than upon rigor and oppression. An uninterrupted succession of victories and of triumphs could alone constrain England to acknowledge American independence; which, whether we can expect, whoever knows the instability of fortune can easily judge.

If we have combated successfully at Lexington and at Boston, Quebec and all Canada have witnessed our reverses. Everyone sees the necessity of opposing the extraordinary pretensions of the ministers; but does everybody see also that of fighting for independence?

It is to be feared that, by changing the object of the war, the present harmony will be interrupted, that the ardor of the people will be chilled by apprehensions for their new situation. By substituting a total dismemberment to the revocation of the laws we complain of, we should fully justify the ministers; we should merit the infamous name of rebels, and all the British nation would arm, with an unanimous impulse, against those who, from oppressed and complaining subjects, should have become all at once irreconcilable enemies. The English cherish the liberty we defend; they respect the dignity of our cause; but they will blame, they will detest our recourse to in-

dependence, and will unite with one consent to combat us.

The propagators of the new doctrine are pleased to assure us that, out of jealousy toward England, foreign sovereigns will lavish their succors upon us, as if these sovereigns could sincerely applaud rebellion; as if they had not colonies, even here in America, in which it is important for them to maintain obedience and tranquility. Let us suppose, however, that jealousy, ambition, or vengeance should triumph over the fear of insurrection; do you think these princes will not make you pay dear for the assistance with which they flatter you? Who has not learned, to his cost, the perfidy and the cupidity of Europeans? They will disguise their avarice under pompous words; under the most benevolent pretexts they will despoil us of our territories, they will invade our fisheries and obstruct our navigation, they will attempt our liberty and our privileges. We shall learn too late what it costs to trust to those European flatteries, and to place that confidence in inveterate enemies which has been withdrawn from long tried friends.

There are many persons who, to gain their ends, extol the advantages of a republic over monarchy. I will not here undertake to examine which of these two forms of government merits the preference. I know, however, that the English nation, after having tried them both, has never found repose except in monarchy. I know, also, that in popular republics themselves, so necessary is monarchy to cement human society, it has been requisite to institute monarchical powers, more or less extensive, under the names of *archons*, of *consuls*, of *doges*, of *gonfaloniers*, and finally of *kings*. Nor should I here omit an observation, the truth of which appears to me incontestible — the English constitution seems to be the fruit of the experience of all anterior time, in which monarchy is so tempered that the monarch finds himself checked in his efforts to seize absolute power; and the authority of the people is so regulated that anarchy is not to be feared. But for us it is to be apprehended that, when the counterpoise of monarchy shall no longer exist, the democratic power may carry all before it and involve the whole state in confusion and ruin. Then an ambitious citizen may arise, seize the reins of power, and annihilate liberty forever; for such is the ordinary career of ill-balanced democracies, they fall into anarchy, and thence under despotism.

Such are the opinions which might have been offered you with more eloquence, but assuredly not with more zeal or sincerity. May heaven grant that such sinister forebodings be not one day accomplished! May it not permit that, in this solemn concourse of the friends of country, the impassioned language of presumptuous and ardent men should have more influence than the pacific exhortations of good and sober citizens; prudence and moderation found and preserve empires; temerity and presumption occasion their downfall.

The discourse of Dickinson was heard with attention; but the current flowed irresistibly strong in a contrary direction, and, fear acting upon many more powerfully even than their opinion, the majority pronounced in favor of independence. The deputies of Pennsylvania were accordingly authorized to return to Congress, and to consent that the Confederate Colonies should declare themselves free and independent states.

106.

Thomas Jefferson: Debate on Independence

During the debate on R. H. Lee's resolution for independence in June 1776, many of the old arguments for and against independence were restated. Thomas Jefferson recorded the views of both sides in notes that he made during the proceedings of the Continental Congress. These notes were later included in Jefferson's Autobiography.

Source: H. A. Washington, VIII, pp. 12-26.

Friday, June 7, 1776. The delegates from Virginia moved, in obedience to instructions from their constituents, that the Congress should declare that these United Colonies are and of right ought to be free and independent states; that they are absolved from all allegiance to the British Crown, and that all political connection between them and the state of Great Britain is and ought to be totally dissolved; that measures should be immediately taken for procuring the as-

sistance of foreign powers, and a confederation be formed to bind the colonies more closely together.

The House being obliged to attend at that time to some other business, the proposition was referred to the next day, when the members were ordered to attend punctually at 10 o'clock.

Saturday, June 8. They proceeded to take it into consideration and referred it to a committee of the whole, into which they immediately resolved themselves, and passed that day and Monday, the 10th, in debating on the subject.

It was argued by Wilson, Robert R. Livingston, E. Rutledge, Dickinson, and others:

That, though they were friends to the measures themselves and saw the impossibility that we should ever again be united with Great Britain, yet they were against adopting them at this time;

That the conduct we had formerly observed was wise and proper now, of deferring to take any capital step till the voice of the people drove us into it;

That they were our power, and without them our declarations could not be carried into effect;

That the people of the middle colonies (Maryland, Delaware, Pennsylvania, the Jerseys, and New York) were not yet ripe for bidding adieu to British connection, but that they were fast ripening and in a short time would join in the general voice of America;

That the resolution entered into by this House on the 15th of May for suppressing the exercise of all powers derived from the Crown had shown, by the ferment into which it had thrown these middle colonies, that they had not yet accommodated their minds to a separation from the mother country;

That some of them had expressly forbidden their delegates to consent to such a declaration, and others had given no instructions and, consequently, no powers to give such consent;

That if the delegates of any particular colony had no power to declare such colony independent, certain they were the others could not declare it for them, the colonies being as yet perfectly independent of each other;

That the Assembly of Pennsylvania was now sitting abovestairs, their convention would sit within a few days, the convention of New York was now sitting, and those of the Jerseys and Delaware counties would meet on the Monday following; and it was probable these bodies would take up the question of independence and would declare to their delegates the voice of their state;

That if such a declaration should now be agreed to, these delegates must retire, and possibly their colonies might secede from the Union;

That such a secession would weaken us more than could be compensated by any foreign alliance;

That in the event of such a division, foreign powers would either refuse to join themselves to our fortunes, or, having us so much in their power as that desperate declaration would place us, they would insist on terms proportionably more hard and prejudicial;

That we had little reason to expect an alliance with those to whom alone, as yet, we had cast our eyes;

That France and Spain had reason to be jealous of that rising power which would one day certainly strip them of all their American possessions;

That it was more likely they should form a connection with the British court, who, if they should find themselves unable otherwise to extricate themselves from their difficulties, would agree to a partition of our territories, restoring Canada to France and the Floridas to Spain, to accomplish for themselves a recovery of these colonies;

That it would not be long before we should receive certain information of the disposition of the French court from the agent whom we had sent to Paris for that purpose;

That if this disposition should be favorable, by waiting the event of the present campaign, which we all hoped would be successful, we should have reason to expect an alliance on better terms;

That this would in fact work no delay of any effectual aid from such ally, as, from the advance of the season and distance of

Charles Thomson, secretary of the Continental Congress

our situation, it was impossible we could receive any assistance during this campaign;

That it was prudent to fix among ourselves the terms on which we should form alliance before we declared we would form one at all events;

And that if these were agreed on and our Declaration of Independence ready by the time our ambassador should be prepared to sail, it would be as well as to go into that Declaration at this day.

On the other side it was urged by J. Adams, Lee, Wythe, and others:

That no gentleman had argued against the policy or the right of separation from Britain, nor had supposed it possible we should ever renew our connection; that they had only opposed its being now declared;

That the question was not whether, by a Declaration of Independence, we should make ourselves what we are not, but whether we should declare a fact which already exists;

That, as to the people or Parliament of England, we had always been independent of them, their restraints on our trade deriving efficacy from our acquiescence only and

not from any rights they possessed of imposing them, and that so far our connection had been federal only and was now dissolved by the commencement of hostilities;

That, as to the King, we had been bound to him by allegiance, but that this bond was now dissolved by his assent to the last act of Parliament, by which he declares us out of his protection, and by his levying war on us, a fact which had long ago proved us out of his protection, it being a certain position in law that allegiance and protection are reciprocal, the one ceasing when the other is withdrawn;

That James II never declared the people of England out of his protection, yet his actions proved it and the Parliament declared it;

No delegates then can be denied, or ever want, a power of declaring an existing truth;

That the delegates from the Delaware counties having declared their constituents ready to join, there are only two colonies, Pennsylvania and Maryland, whose delegates are absolutely tied up, and that these had, by their instructions, only reserved a right of confirming or rejecting the measure;

That the instructions from Pennsylvania might be accounted for from the times in which they were drawn, near a twelvemonth ago, since which the face of affairs has totally changed;

That within that time it had become apparent that Britain was determined to accept nothing less than a *carte blanche,* and that the King's answer to the lord mayor, aldermen, and Common Council of London, which had come to hand four days ago, must have satisfied everyone of this point;

That the people wait for us to lead the way;

That *they* are in favor of the measure, though the instructions given by some of their *representatives* are not;

That the voice of the representatives is

not always consonant with the voice of the people, and that this is remarkably the case in these middle colonies;

That the effect of the resolution of the 15th of May has proved this, which, raising the murmurs of some in the colonies of Pennsylvania and Maryland, called forth the opposing voice of the freer part of the people and proved them to be the majority, even in these colonies;

That the backwardness of these two colonies might be ascribed partly to the influence of proprietary power and connections, and partly to their having not yet been attacked by the enemy;

That these causes were not likely to be soon removed, as there seemed no probability that the enemy would make either of these the seat of this summer's war;

That it would be vain to wait either weeks or months for perfect unanimity, since it was impossible that all men should ever become of one sentiment on any question;

That the conduct of some colonies, from the beginning of this contest, had given reason to suspect it was their settled policy to keep in the rear of the Confederacy, that their particular prospect might be better even in the worst event;

That, therefore, it was necessary for those colonies who had thrown themselves forward and hazarded all from the beginning to come forward now also, and put all again to their own hazard;

That the history of the Dutch revolution, of whom three states only confederated at first, proved that a secession of some colonies would not be so dangerous as some apprehended;

That a Declaration of Independence alone could render it consistent with European delicacy for European powers to treat with us, or even to receive an ambassador from us;

That till this they would not receive our vessels into their ports, nor acknowledge the adjudications of our Courts of Admiralty to be legitimate in cases of capture of British vessels;

That, though France and Spain may be jealous of our rising power, they must think it will be much more formidable with the addition of Great Britain, and will therefore see it their interest to prevent a coalition; but should they refuse, we shall be but where we are; whereas, without trying, we shall never know whether they will aid us or not;

That the present campaign may be unsuccessful, and therefore we had better propose an alliance while our affairs wear a hopeful aspect;

That to wait the event of this campaign will certainly work delay, because, during this summer, France may assist us effectually by cutting off those supplies of provisions from England and Ireland on which the enemy's armies here are to depend; or by setting in motion the great power they have collected in the West Indies, and calling our enemy to the defense of the possessions they have there;

That it would be idle to lose time in settling the terms of alliance till we had first determined we would enter into alliance;

That it is necessary to lose no time in opening a trade for our people, who will want clothes and will want money, too, for the payment of taxes;

And that the only misfortune is that we did not enter into alliance with France six months sooner, as, besides opening her ports for the vent [sale] of our last year's produce, she might have marched an army into Germany and prevented the petty princes there from selling their unhappy subjects to subdue us.

It appearing in the course of these debates that the colonies of New York, New Jersey, Pennsylvania, Delaware, Maryland, and South Carolina were not yet matured for falling from the parent stem, but that they were fast advancing to that state, it was thought most prudent to wait a while for them, and to postpone the final decision to July 1; but, that this might occasion as little delay as possible, a committee was appointed to prepare a Declaration of Independence. The committee were John Adams, Dr. Franklin, Roger Sherman, Robert R. Livingston, and myself. Committees were also appointed at the same time to prepare a plan of confederation for the colonies, and to state the terms proper to be proposed for foreign alliance. The committee for drawing the Declaration of Independence desired me to do it. It was accordingly done, and, being approved by them, I reported it to the House on Friday, the 28th of June, when it was read and ordered to lie on the table.

On Monday, the 1st of July, the House resolved itself into a committee of the whole and resumed the consideration of the original motion made by the delegates of Virginia, which, being again debated through the day, was carried in the affirmative by the votes of New Hampshire, Connecticut, Massachusetts, Rhode Island, New Jersey, Maryland, Virginia, North Carolina, and Georgia. South Carolina and Pennsylvania voted against it. Delaware had but two members present, and they were divided. The delegates from New York declared they were for it themselves, and were assured their constituents were for it, but that their instructions having been drawn near a twelvemonth before, when reconciliation was still the general object, they were enjoined by them to do nothing which should impede that object. They therefore thought themselves not justifiable in voting on either side and asked leave to withdraw from the question, which was given them. The committee rose and reported their resolution to the House.

Mr. Edward Rutledge of South Carolina then requested the determination might be put off to the next day, as he believed his colleagues, though they disapproved of the resolution, would then join in it for the sake of unanimity. The ultimate question, whether the House would agree to the resolution of the committee, was accordingly postponed to the next day, when it was again moved and South Carolina concurred in voting for it. In the meantime, a third member had come post from the Delaware counties and turned the vote of that colony in favor of the resolution. Members of a different sentiment attending that morning from Pennsylvania also, her vote was changed, so that the whole twelve colonies who were authorized to vote at all gave their voices for it; and within a few days the convention of New York approved of it and thus supplied the void occasioned by the withdrawing of her delegates from the vote.

Congress proceeded the same day to consider the Declaration of Independence, which had been reported and lain on the table the Friday preceding, and on Monday referred to a committee of the whole. The pusillanimous idea that we had friends in England worth keeping terms with still haunted the minds of many. For this reason, those passages which conveyed censures on the people of England were struck out, lest they should give them offense. The clause, too, reprobating the enslaving the inhabitants of Africa was struck out in complaisance to South Carolina and Georgia, who had never attempted to restrain the importation of slaves, and who, on the contrary, still wished to continue it. Our Northern brethren, also, I believe, felt a little tender under those censures; for though their people had very few slaves themselves, yet they had been pretty considerable carriers of them to others.

The debates, having taken up the greater parts of the 2nd, 3rd, and 4th days of July, were, on the evening of the last, closed. The Declaration was reported by the committee, agreed to by the House, and signed by every member present, except Mr. Dickinson.

107.

The Declaration of Independence

The Declaration of Independence was formally adopted by the delegates to the Second Continental Congress, meeting in Philadelphia, on July 4, 1776. Two days earlier, a resolution had been passed which said "that these United Colonies are, and of right ought to be, free and independent States, that they are absolved from all allegiance to the British Crown, and that all political connection between them and the state of Great Britain is and ought to be totally dissolved." The introduction on June 7 of this resolution, by Richard Henry Lee of Virginia, had been followed by the appointment of a committee to draft a statement declaring the reasons for the impending separation. Of the members of this committee, which included Thomas Jefferson, John Adams, Benjamin Franklin, Roger Sherman, and Robert Livingston, it was Jefferson who prepared the draft, submitting it to the others for consideration. Minor changes in Jefferson's draft were suggested by Adams and Franklin. Some further alterations were made after it was presented to the Congress on June 28. The final words, however, were still largely those of Jefferson. At its passage it was signed only by John Hancock, the presiding officer. Four days later the Declaration of Independence was read aloud in the city of Philadelphia at what later became Independence Square. Copies were made, sent to the legislatures of the colonies, and published throughout the country. The Declaration was not signed by the other members of the Congress until August 2, when a copy engrossed on parchment was witnessed with their names.

Source: *Journals*, I: "Thursday, July 4, 1776."

WHEN, IN THE COURSE OF HUMAN EVENTS, it becomes necessary for one people to dissolve the political bands which have connected them with another, and to assume, among the powers of the earth, the separate and equal station to which the laws of nature and of nature's God entitle them, a decent respect to the opinions of mankind requires that they should declare the causes which impel them to the separation.

We hold these truths to be self-evident, that all men are created equal, that they are endowed by their Creator with certain unalienable rights, that among these are life, liberty, and the pursuit of happiness. That, to secure these rights, governments are instituted among men, deriving their just powers from the consent of the governed. That, whenever any form of government becomes destructive of these ends, it is the right of the people to alter or to abolish it, and to institute new government, laying its foundation on such principles, and organizing its powers in such form, as to them shall seem most likely to effect their safety and happiness.

Prudence, indeed, will dictate that governments long established should not be changed for light and transient causes; and, accordingly, all experience has shown, that mankind are more disposed to suffer, while evils are sufferable, than to right themselves by abolishing the forms to which they are accustomed.

But, when a long train of abuses and usurpations, pursuing invariably the same object, evinces a design to reduce them under absolute despotism, it is their right, it is their duty, to throw off such government, and to provide new guards for their future security. Such has been the patient sufferance of these colonies; and such is now the necessity which constrains them to alter their former systems of government. The history of the present King of Great Britain is a history of repeated injuries and usurpations, all having in direct object the establishment of an absolute tyranny over these states. To prove this, let facts be submitted to a candid world.

He has refused his assent to laws the most wholesome and necessary for the public good.

He has forbidden his governors to pass laws of immediate and pressing importance, unless suspended in their operation till his assent should be obtained; and when so suspended, he has utterly neglected to attend to them.

He has refused to pass other laws for the accommodation of large districts of people, unless those people would relinquish the right of representation in the legislature; a right inestimable to them and formidable to tyrants only.

He has called together legislative bodies at places unusual, uncomfortable, and distant from the depository of their public records, for the sole purpose of fatiguing them into compliance with his measures.

He has dissolved representative houses repeatedly, for opposing, with manly firmness, his invasions on the rights of the people.

He has refused for a long time, after such dissolutions, to cause others to be elected; whereby the legislative powers, incapable of annihilation, have returned to the people at large for their exercise; the state remaining in the meantime exposed to all the dangers of invasion from without, and convulsions within.

He has endeavored to prevent the population of these states; for that purpose obstructing the laws for naturalization of foreigners; refusing to pass others to encourage their migrations hither, and raising the conditions of new appropriations of lands.

He has obstructed the administration of justice, by refusing his assent to laws for establishing judiciary powers.

He has made judges dependent on his will alone, for the tenure of their offices, and the amount and payment of their salaries.

He has erected a multitude of new offices, and sent hither swarms of officers to harass our people, and eat out their substance.

He has kept among us, in times of peace, standing armies, without the consent of our legislatures.

He has affected to render the military independent of and superior to the civil power.

He has combined with others to subject us to a jurisdiction foreign to our constitution, and unacknowledged by our laws; giving his assent to their acts of pretended legislation:

For quartering large bodies of armed troops among us;

For protecting them, by a mock trial, from punishment for any murders which they should commit on the inhabitants of these states;

For cutting off our trade with all parts of the world;

For imposing taxes on us without our consent;

For depriving us, in many cases, of the benefits of trial by jury;

For transporting us beyond seas to be tried for pretended offenses;

For abolishing the free system of English laws in a neighboring province, establishing therein an arbitrary government, and enlarging its boundaries, so as to render it at once an example and fit instrument for introducing the same absolute rule into these colonies;

For taking away our charters, abolishing our most valuable laws, and altering fundamentally the forms of our governments;

For suspending our own legislatures, and declaring themselves invested with power to legislate for us in all cases whatsoever.

He has abdicated government here, by declaring us out of his protection, and waging war against us.

He has plundered our seas, ravaged our coasts, burnt our towns, and destroyed the lives of our people.

He is at this time transporting large armies of foreign mercenaries to complete the works of death, desolation, and tyranny, already begun with circumstances of cruelty and perfidy scarcely paralleled in the most barbarous ages, and totally unworthy the head of a civilized nation.

He has constrained our fellow citizens, taken captive on the high seas, to bear arms against their country, to become the executioners of their friends and brethren, or to fall themselves by their hands.

He has excited domestic insurrections amongst us, and has endeavored to bring on the inhabitants of our frontiers, the merciless Indian savages, whose known rule of warfare is an undistinguished destruction of all ages, sexes, and conditions.

In every stage of these oppressions, we have petitioned for redress, in the most humble terms. Our repeated petitions have been answered only by repeated injury. A prince, whose character is thus marked by every act which may define a tyrant, is unfit to be the ruler of a free people.

Nor have we been wanting in attentions to our British brethren. We have warned them from time to time of attempts by their legislature to extend an unwarrantable jurisdiction over us. We have reminded them of the circumstances of our emigration and settlement here. We have appealed to their native justice and magnanimity, and we have conjured them by the ties of our common kindred, to disavow these usurpations, which would inevitably interrupt our connections and correspondence. They too have been deaf to the voice of justice and of consanguinity. We must, therefore, acquiesce in the necessity, which denounces our separation, and hold them, as we hold the rest of mankind, enemies in war, in peace friends.

We, therefore, the representatives of the United States of America, in General Congress assembled, appealing to the Supreme Judge of the world for the rectitude of our intentions, do, in the name, and by authority of the good people of these colonies, solemnly publish and declare, that these United Colonies are, and of right ought to be free and independent states; that they are absolved from all allegiance to the British Crown, and that all political connection between them and the state of Great Britain is and ought to be totally dissolved; and that, as free and independent states, they have full power to levy war, conclude peace, contract alliances, establish commerce, and to do all other acts and things which independent states may of right do. And for the support of this declaration, with a firm reliance on the protection of Divine Providence, we mutually pledge to each other our lives, our fortunes, and our sacred honor.

There, I guess King George will be able to read that.
JOHN HANCOCK, affixing a bold signature to the Declaration of Independence, July 4, 1776

108.

Samuel Hopkins: The Inconsistency of Slavery

In 1776, Samuel Hopkins published A Dialogue Concerning the Slavery of
the Africans *which he directed at the Continental Congress, urging it to abolish the
institution of slavery. The act required some courage on Hopkins' part, for at the
time Newport, Rhode Island, was one of the centers of the slaveholding interest, and
many of his congregation were either slaveholders themselves or at least financially
involved in the slave trade. A portion of his* Dialogue, *one of the earliest antislavery
protests from the Congregational ministry, is reprinted here.*

Source: *The Works of Samuel Hopkins,* Boston, 1854, Vol. II, pp. 551-588.

THE SLAVERY THAT NOW TAKES PLACE is in a
Christian land, and without the express
sanction of civil government; and it is all of
the same kind and from one original, which
is most notoriously unjust. And if it be unrighteous in one instance, it is so in almost
every instance; and the unrighteousness of it
is most apparent, and most masters have no
color of claim to hold their servants in
bondage. And this is become a general and
crying sin for which we are under the awful
frowns of heaven. These things . . . make it
duty to oppose and bear testimony, both in
public and more privately, against this evil
practice, which is so evidently injurious to
individuals, and threatens our ruin as a
people. . . .

It has always been the way of tyrants to
take great pains to keep their vassals in ignorance, especially to hide from them the
tyranny and oppression of which they are
the subjects; and for this reason they are
enemies to the liberty of the press, and are
greatly provoked when their conduct is set
in a true light before the public and the unrighteousness they practise properly ex-

posed. The complaint we are now considering seems to be of the same kind with
this, and well becomes all those petty tyrants who have slaves in their possession,
which they are conscious they cannot vindicate, but the unrighteousness will be detect-
ed if free inquiry and freedom of speech
cannot be suppressed. And this complaint is
of the same kind with the conduct of the
masters of slaves in the West Indies in opposing their being taught anything of Christianity, because they know every gleam of
this light carries a discovery of the unrighteousness of the treatment they receive.

The present situation of our public affairs
and our struggle for liberty, and the abundant conversation this occasions in all companies — while the poor Negroes look on
and hear what an aversion we have to slavery and how much liberty is prized, they
often hearing it declared publicly and in private, as the voice of all, that slavery is more
to be dreaded than death, and we are resolved to live free or die, etc. — this, I say,
necessarily leads them to attend to their
own wretched situation more than other-

wise they could. They see themselves deprived of all liberty and property, and their children after them, to the latest posterity, subject to the will of those who appear to have no feeling for their misery, and are guilty of many instances of hardheartedness and cruelty toward them, while they think themselves very kind; and, therefore, to make the least complaint, would be deemed the height of arrogance and abuse; and often if they have a comparatively good master now, with constant dread they see a young one growing up, who bids fair to rule over them, or their children, with rigor. . . .

No wonder there are many and great difficulties in reforming an evil practice of this kind, which has got such deep root by length of time and is become so common. But it does not yet appear that they cannot be removed by the united wisdom and strength of the American colonies, without any injury to the slaves or disadvantage to the public. Yea, the contrary is most certain, as the slaves cannot be put into a more wretched situation, ourselves being judges, and the community cannot take a more likely step to escape ruin and obtain the smiles and protection of Heaven. This matter ought, doubtless, to be attended to by the general assemblies, and continental and provincial congresses; and if they were as much united and engaged in devising ways and means to set at liberty these injured slaves as they are to defend themselves from tyranny, it would soon be effected. . . . Surely we have no reason to conclude it cannot be done till we see a suitable zeal and resolution among all orders of men, and answerable attempts are thoroughly made.

Let this iniquity be viewed in its true magnitude and in the shocking light in which it has been set in this conversation; let the wretched case of the poor blacks be considered with proper pity and benevolence, together with the probably dreadful

Engraving of Samuel Hopkins

consequence to this land of retaining them in bondage, and all objections against liberating them would vanish. . . .

If parents have a son pressed on board a king's ship, how greatly are they affected with it! They are filled with grief and distress, and will cheerfully be at almost any cost and pains to procure his liberty; and we wonder not at it, but think their exercises and engagedness for his deliverance very just, and stand ready to condemn him who has no feeling for them and their son, and is not ready to afford all the assistance in his power in order to recover him. At the same time, we behold vast numbers of blacks among us, torn from their native country and all their relations, not to serve on board a man-of-war for a few years but to be abject, despised slaves for life, and their children after them, and yet have not the least feelings for them or desire of their freedom. These very parents, perhaps, have a number of Negro slaves on whom they have not the least pity, and stand ready highly to resent it if anyone espouses their cause so much as to propose they should be set at liberty. What reason for this partiality? Ought this so to be? An impartial person, who is not under the prejudices of interest, education, and custom, is shocked with it beyond all expression. The poor Negroes have sense enough to see and feel it, but have no friend to speak a word for them, none to whom they may complain. . . .

The slaves who are become unprofitable to their masters by the present calamitous state of our country will be with the less reluctance set at liberty, it is hoped; and if no public provision be made for them that they may be transported to Africa, where they might probably live better than in any other country, or be removed into those places in this land where they may have profitable business and are wanted, now so many are called from their farms to defend our country; I say, if this be not done, the masters, by freeing them, would lose nothing by it, even though they continue to support them, till some way shall be open for them to help themselves. I must here again desire every owner of slaves to make their case his own, and consider, if he or his children were unjustly in a state of slavery, whether he should think such an objection against their being set at liberty of any weight.

Would he not rather think it reasonable that the masters who had held them in bondage against all right and reason would consider their being, by an extraordinary Providence, rendered unprofitable to them, as an admonition to break off their sins by righteousness and their iniquity by showing mercy to these poor; and that it ought to be a greater satisfaction to them thus to do justice without delay and relieve these oppressed poor than to possess all the riches,

honors, and pleasures of this world? And if these masters should disregard such an admonition and neglect this opportunity to set them at liberty, putting it off to a more convenient season, would it not be very grievous to him and overwhelm him in despair of their ever doing it? Is it not very certain that they who make this objection against freeing their slaves without delay would not free them if the times should change and they again become profitable? If they must maintain them, can they not do it as well when they are free as while they are slaves, and ought they not to do it with much more satisfaction? . . .

But if we obstinately refuse to reform what we have implicitly declared to be wrong, and engaged to put away the holding the Africans in slavery, which is so particularly pointed out by the evil with which we are threatened and is such a glaring contradiction to our professed aversion to slavery and struggle for civil liberty, and improve the favor God is showing us as an argument in favor of this iniquity and encouragement to persist in it . . . have we not the greatest reason to fear, yea, may we not with great certainty conclude, God will yet withdraw His kind protection from us and punish us yet seven times more? This has been God's usual way of dealing with His professing people; and who can say it is not most reasonable and wise?

He, then, acts the most friendly part to these colonies and to the masters of slaves, as well as to the slaves themselves, who does his utmost to effect a general emancipation of the Africans among us. And, in this view, I could wish the conversation we have now had on this subject, if nothing better is like to be done, were published and spread through all the colonies, and had the attentive perusal of every American.

109.

Declaration on the Free Exercise of Religion

The Church of England was the American religious establishment in the colonies for whose support all were taxed regardless of individual affiliation. It was not surprising that the demand for religious liberty paralleled the acquisition of political independence. When the General Assembly of Virginia met for the first time under its new constitution on October 7, 1776, it was besieged by petitions protesting religious discrimination. On October 24, the Presbytery of Hanover presented a memorial arguing for religious freedom in the familiar language of natural rights. On this occasion, the impetus for the memorial came from the frontier areas of the states where the establishment was very weak.

Source: William Henry Foote, *Sketches of Virginia, Historical and Biographical,* Philadelphia, 1850, pp. 323-324.

THE MEMORIAL of the Presbytery of Hanover humbly represents that your memorialists are governed by the same sentiments which have inspired the United States of America; and are determined that nothing in our power and influence shall be wanting to give success to their common cause. We would also represent that dissenters from the Church of England in this country have ever been desirous to conduct themselves as peaceable members of the civil government, for which reason they have hitherto submitted to several ecclesiastical burdens and restrictions that are inconsistent with equal liberty. But now when the many and grievous oppressions of our mother country have laid this continent under the necessity of casting off the yoke of tyranny and of forming independent governments upon equitable and liberal foundations, we flatter ourselves that we shall be free from all the encumbrances which a spirit of domination, prejudice, or bigotry has interwoven with most other political systems. This we are the more strongly encouraged to expect by the Declaration of Rights, so universally applauded for that dignity, firmness, and precision with which it delineates and asserts the privileges of society and the prerogatives of human nature, and which we embrace as the Magna Charta of our commonwealth that can never be violated without endangering the grand superstructure it was destined to sustain. Therefore, we rely upon this Declaration, as well as the justice of our honorable legislature, to secure us the free exercise of religion according to the dictates of our consciences; and we should fall short in our duty to ourselves, and the many and numerous congregations under our care, were we, upon this occasion, to neglect laying before you a state of the religious grievances under which we have hitherto labored that they no longer may be continued in our present form of government.

It is well known that in the frontier counties, which are justly supposed to contain a fifth part of the inhabitants of Virginia, the dissenters have borne the heavy burdens of purchasing glebes [lands], building churches, and supporting the established clergy where there are very few Episcopalians either to assist in bearing the expense or to reap the advantage; and that throughout the other parts of the country, there are also many thousands of zealous friends and defenders of our state who, besides the invidious and disadvantageous restrictions to which they have been subjected, annually pay large taxes to support an establishment from which their consciences and principles oblige them to dissent — all which are confessedly so many violations of their natural rights, and, in their consequences, a restraint upon freedom of inquiry and private judgment.

In this enlightened age and in a land where all of every denomination are united in the most strenuous efforts to be free, we hope and expect that our representatives will cheerfully concur in removing every species of religious, as well as civil, bondage. Certain it is that every argument for civil liberty gains additional strength when applied to liberty in the concerns of religion; and there is no argument in favor of establishing the Christian religion but what may be pleaded, with equal propriety, for establishing the tenets of Mohammed by those who believe the Alcoran; or if this be not true, it is at least impossible for the magistrate to adjudge the right of preference among the various sects that profess the Christian faith, without erecting a chair of infallibility, which would lead us back to the Church of Rome.

We beg leave farther to represent that religious establishments are highly injurious to the temporal interests of any community. Without insisting upon the ambition and the arbitrary practices of those who are favored by government, or the intriguing seditious spirit which is commonly excited by this as well as every other kind of oppression, such establishments greatly retard population, and consequently the progress of arts, sciences, and manufactories. Witness the rapid growth and improvements of the northern provinces compared with this. No one can deny that the more early settlement and the many superior advantages of our country would have invited multitudes of artificers, mechanics, and other useful members of society to fix their habitation among us, who have either remained in their place of nativity, or preferred worse civil governments and a more barren soil where they might enjoy the rights of conscience more fully than they had a prospect of doing it in this. From which we infer that Virginia might have now been the capital of America and a match for the British arms without depending on others for the necessaries of war, had it not been prevented by her religious establishment.

Neither can it be made to appear that the gospel needs any such civil aid. We rather conceive that when our blessed Savior declares His kingdom is not of this world, He renounces all dependence upon state power, and as His weapons are spiritual and were only designed to have influence on the judgment and heart of man, we are persuaded that if mankind were left in the quiet possession of their inalienable rights and privileges, Christianity, as in the days of the apostles, would continue to prevail and flourish in the greatest purity by its own native excellence and under the all-disposing providence of God.

We would humbly represent that the only proper objects of civil government are the happiness and protection of men in the present state of existence; the security of the life, liberty, and property of the citizens; and to restrain the vicious and encourage the virtuous by wholesome laws, equally extending to every individual. But that the duty which we owe our Creator, and the manner of discharging it, can only be directed by reason and conviction, and is nowhere cognizable but at the tribunal of the universal Judge.

Therefore, we ask no ecclesiastical establishments for ourselves; neither can we approve of them when granted to others. This indeed would be giving exclusive or separate emoluments or privileges to one set (or sect) of men, without any special public services to the common reproach and injury of every other denomination. And for the reasons recited, we are induced earnestly to entreat that all laws now in force in this commonwealth which countenance religious domination may be speedily repealed, that all of every religious sect may be protected in the full exercise of their several modes of worship and exempted from all taxes for the support of any church whatsoever further than what may be agreeable to their own private choice or voluntary obligation. This being done, all partial and invidious distinctions will be abolished, to the great honor and interest of the state; and everyone be left to stand or fall according to merit, which can never be the case so long as any one denomination is established in preference to others.

That the great Sovereign of the universe may inspire you with unanimity, wisdom, and resolution, and bring you to a just determination on all the important concerns before you, is the fervent prayer of your memorialists.

110.

Concord's Call for a State Constitutional Convention

In creating new state governments, the mechanics of constitution making was probably the heart of the problem. The great question was: Who possessed the rightful authority to make a constitution? The Concord town meeting felt that the authority rested only with the people of the state. In their proposals of October 22, 1776, they urged the suggestion of a state-wide constitutional convention which has since become the traditional American practice. In Massachusetts, the suggestions of the Concord meeting were not heeded until 1779.

Source: *Bulletins for the Constitutional Convention 1917-1918*, Boston, 1919, Vol. II, Bulletin No. 35: "The Proceedings of the Town of Concord, Massachusetts, October 22, 1776."

A MEETING OF THE INHABITANTS (free men and twenty-one years of age and older) of the town of Concord met by adjournment on October 21, 1776, to take into consideration a resolve of the honorable House of Representatives of this state made on September 17. The town resolved as follows:

Resolve 1. This state being presently destitute of a properly established form of government, it is absolutely necessary that a government should be immediately formed and established.

Resolve 2. The supreme legislative, either in its proper capacity or in a joint committee, is by no means a body proper to form and establish a constitution or form a government, for the following reasons:

First, because we conceive that a constitution in its proper idea intends a system of principles established to secure the subject in the possession and enjoyment of their rights and privileges against any encroachments of the governing part.

Second, because the same body that forms a constitution has a power to alter it.

Third, because a constitution alterable by the supreme legislature is no security at all to the subject against any encroachment of the governing part on any or on all of their rights and privileges.

Resolve 3. It appears highly necessary and expedient to this town that a convention or congress be immediately chosen to form and establish a constitution by the inhabitants of the respective towns in this state, who are free and twenty-one years of age and older, in proportion as the representa-

tives of this state formerly were chosen. The convention or congress is not to consist of a greater number than the House of Assembly of this state might consist of, except that each town and district shall have liberty to send one representative, or otherwise as shall appear meet to the inhabitants of this state in general.

Resolve 4. When the convention or congress has formed a constitution, they are to adjourn for a short time and publish their proposed constitution for the inspection of the inhabitants of this state.

Resolve 5. The honorable House of Assembly of this state desires to recommend to the inhabitants of the state to proceed to choose a convention or congress for the purpose abovesaid as soon as possible.

111.

Tom Paine: The American Crisis

Tom Paine was the author of a series of patriotic tracts called The Crisis *papers, which appeared in print from 1776 to 1783. The first of these so stirred General Washington that he ordered it read to his troops late in December 1776 at a time when the American cause seemed to be faltering. This paper, combined with the subsequent victory of his army at Trenton, New Jersey, later in the month, had the probable effect of inspiring many soldiers, whose term of service would expire January 1, to reenlist. The first* Crisis *paper appeared in the* Pennsylvania Journal, *December 19, 1776, and within a week was reissued as a pamphlet.*

Source: *The Political Writings of Thomas Paine,* New York, 1830, Vol. I, pp. 75-82.

THESE ARE THE TIMES that try men's souls. The summer soldier and the sunshine patriot will, in this crisis, shrink from the service of his country; but he that stands it now deserves the love and thanks of man and woman. Tyranny, like hell, is not easily conquered; yet we have this consolation with us — that the harder the conflict, the more glorious the triumph. What we obtain too cheap, we esteem too lightly: It is dear-ness only that gives everything its value. Heaven knows how to put a proper price upon its goods; and it would be strange indeed if so celestial an article as freedom should not be highly rated. Britain, with an army to enforce her tyranny, has declared that she has a right not only to tax but "to bind us in all cases whatsoever," and if being bound in that manner is not slavery, then is there not such a thing as slavery upon earth. Even the expression is impious, for so unlimited a power can belong only to God.

Whether the independence of the continent was declared too soon or delayed too long, I will not now enter into as an argument; my own simple opinion is, that had it been eight months earlier, it would have been much better. We did not make a proper use of last winter; neither could we, while we were in a dependent state. However, the fault, if it were one, was all our own; we have none to blame but ourselves. But no great deal is lost yet; all that Howe has been doing for this month past is rather a ravage than a conquest, which the spirit of the Jerseys a year ago would have quickly repulsed, and which time and a little resolution will soon recover.

I have as little superstition in me as any man living, but my secret opinion has ever been, and still is, that God Almighty will not give up a people to military destruction, or leave them unsupportedly to perish, who have so earnestly and so repeatedly sought to avoid the calamities of war by every decent method which wisdom could invent. Neither have I so much of the infidel in me as to suppose that He has relinquished the government of the world and given us up to the care of devils; and as I do not, I cannot see on what grounds the king of Britain can look up to Heaven for help against us — a common murderer, a highwayman, or a housebreaker has as good a pretense as he.

It is surprising to see how rapidly a panic will sometimes run through a country. All nations and ages have been subject to them: Britain has trembled like an ague at the report of a French fleet of flat-bottomed boats; and in the 14th century the whole English Army, after ravaging the kingdom of France, was driven back like men petrified with fear; and this brave exploit was performed by a few broken forces collected and headed by a woman, Joan of Arc. Would that Heaven might inspire some Jersey maid to spirit up her countrymen and save her fair fellow sufferers from ravage and ravishment! Yet panics, in some cases, have their uses; they produce as much good as hurt. Their duration is always short; the mind soon grows through them and acquires a firmer habit than before. But their peculiar advantage is that they are the touchstones of sincerity and hypocrisy, and bring things and men to light which might otherwise have lain forever undiscovered. In fact, they have the same effect on secret traitors which an imaginary apparition would have upon a private murderer. They sift out the hidden thoughts of man and hold them up in public to the world. Many a disguised Tory has lately shown his head, that shall penitentially solemnize with curses the day on which Howe arrived upon the Delaware.

As I was with the troops at Fort Lee, and marched with them to the edge of Pennsylvania, I am well acquainted with many circumstances which those who live at a distance know but little or nothing of. Our situation there was exceedingly cramped, the place being a narrow neck of land between the North River and the Hackensack. Our force was inconsiderable, being not onefourth so great as Howe could bring against us. We had no army at hand to have relieved the garrison, had we shut ourselves up and stood on our defense. Our ammunition, light artillery, and the best part of our stores had been removed on the apprehension that Howe would endeavor to penetrate the Jerseys, in which case Fort Lee could be of no use to us; for it must occur to every thinking man, whether in the army or not, that these kind of field forts are only for temporary purposes, and last in use no longer than the enemy directs his force against the particular object, which such forts are raised to defend.

Such was our situation and condition at Fort Lee on the morning of the 20th of November, when an officer arrived with information that the enemy with 200 boats had landed about seven miles above. Major General Green, who commanded the garrison, immediately ordered them under arms, and sent express to General Washington at the town of Hackensack, distant, by the way of the ferry, six miles. Our first object was to secure the bridge over the Hackensack, which laid up the river between the enemy and us, about six miles from us, three from them. General Washington arrived in about three-quarters of an hour, and marched at the head of the troops toward the bridge, which place I expected we should have a brush for; however, they did not choose to dispute it with us, and the greatest part of our troops went over the bridge, the rest over the ferry, except some which passed at a mill on a small creek, between the bridge and the ferry, and made their way through some marshy grounds up to the town of Hackensack, and there passed the river. We brought off as much baggage as the wagons could contain; the rest was lost. The simple object was to bring off the garrison and march them on till they could be strengthened by the Jersey or Pennsylvania militia, so as to be enabled to make a stand.

We stayed four days at Newark, collected our outposts with some of the Jersey militia, and marched out twice to meet the enemy, on being informed that they were advancing, though our numbers were greatly inferior to theirs. Howe, in my little opinion, committed a great error in generalship in not throwing a body of forces off from Staten Island through Amboy, by which means he might have seized all our stores at Brunswick and intercepted our march into Pennsylvania. But if we believe the power of hell to be limited, we must likewise believe that their agents are under some providential control.

I shall not now attempt to give all the particulars of our retreat to the Delaware; suffice it for the present to say that both officers and men, though greatly harassed and fatigued, frequently without rest, covering, or provision — the inevitable consequences of a long retreat — bore it with a manly and martial spirit. All their wishes centered in one, which was, that the country would turn out and help them to drive the enemy back. Voltaire has remarked that King William never appeared to full advantage but in difficulties and in action; the same remark may be made on General Washington, for the character fits him. There is a natural firmness in some minds which cannot be unlocked by trifles, but which, when unlocked, discovers a cabinet of fortitude; and I reckon it among those kind of public blessings which we do not immediately see, that God has blessed him with uninterrupted health, and given him a mind that can even flourish upon care.

I shall conclude this paper with some miscellaneous remarks on the state of our affairs; and shall begin with asking the following question: Why is it that the enemy have left the New England provinces and made these middle ones the seat of war? The answer is easy: New England is not infested with Tories, and we are. I have been tender in raising the cry against these men, and used numberless arguments to show them their danger, but it will not do to sacrifice a world either to their folly or their baseness. The period is now arrived in which either they or we must change our sentiments, or one or both must fall. And what is a Tory? Good God! What is he? I should not be afraid to go with a hundred Whigs against a thousand Tories, were they to attempt to get into arms. Every Tory is a coward, for servile, slavish, self-interested fear is the foundation of Toryism; and a man under such influence, though he may be cruel, never can be brave.

But, before the line of irrecoverable separation be drawn between us, let us reason the matter together. Your conduct is an invitation to the enemy, yet not one in a thousand of you has heart enough to join him. Howe is as much deceived by you as the American cause is injured by you. He expects you will all take up arms and flock to his standard, with muskets on your shoulders. Your opinions are of no use to him, unless you support him personally, for it is soldiers, and not Tories, that he wants.

I once felt all that kind of anger which a man ought to feel against the mean principles that are held by the Tories. A noted one, who kept a tavern at Amboy, was standing at his door with as pretty a child in his hand, about eight or nine years old, as I ever saw, and after speaking his mind as freely as he thought was prudent, finished with this unfatherly expression. "Well! give me peace in my day." Not a man lives on the continent but fully believes that a separation must some time or other finally take place; and a generous parent should have said, "If there must be trouble, let it be in my day, that my child may have peace." And this single reflection, well applied, is sufficient to awaken every man to duty.

Not a place upon earth might be so happy as America. Her situation is remote from all the wrangling world, and she has nothing to do but to trade with them. A man can distinguish himself between temper and principle, and I am as confident, as I am that God governs the world, that America will never be happy till she gets clear of foreign dominion. Wars, without ceasing, will break out till that period arrives, and

the continent must in the end be conqueror; for though the flame of liberty may sometimes cease to shine, the coal can never expire.

America did not, nor does not want force; but she wanted a proper application of that force. Wisdom is not the purchase of a day, and it is no wonder that we should err at the first setting off. From an excess of tenderness, we were unwilling to raise an army, and trusted our cause to the temporary defense of a well-meaning militia. A summer's experience has now taught us better; yet with those troops, while they were collected, we were able to set bounds to the progress of the enemy, and, thank God! they are again assembling. I always considered militia as the best troops in the world for a sudden exertion, but they will not do for a long campaign.

Howe, it is probable, will make an attempt on this city. Should he fail on this side the Delaware, he is ruined; if he succeeds, our cause is not ruined. He stakes all on his side against a part on ours; admitting he succeeds, the consequences will be that armies from both ends of the continent will march to assist their suffering friends in the middle states; for he cannot go everywhere, it is impossible. I consider Howe as the greatest enemy the Tories have; he is bringing war into their country, which, had it not been for him and partly for themselves, they had been clear of. Should he now be expelled, I wish, with all the devotion of a Christian, that the names of Whig and Tory may never more be mentioned; but should the Tories give him encouragement to come, or assistance if he come, I as sincerely wish that our next year's arms may expel them from the continent, and the Congress appropriate their possessions to the relief of those who have suffered in well-doing. A single successful battle next year will settle the whole.

America could carry on a two years' war by the confiscation of the property of disaffected persons, and be made happy by their expulsion. Say not that this is revenge, call it rather the soft resentment of a suffering people, who, having no object in view but the good of all, have staked their own all upon a seemingly doubtful event. Yet it is folly to argue against determined hardness; eloquence may strike the ear, and the language of sorrow draw forth the tear of compassion, but nothing can reach the heart that is steeled with prejudice.

Quitting this class of men, I turn with the warm ardor of a friend to those who have nobly stood and are yet determined to stand the matter out. I call not upon a few, but upon all; not in this state or that state, but on every state. Up and help us; lay your shoulders to the wheel; better have too much force than too little, when so great an object is at stake. Let it be told to the future world that in the depth of winter, when nothing but hope and virtue could survive, that the city and country, alarmed at one common danger, came forth to meet and to repulse it. Say not that thousands are gone, turn out your tens of thousands; throw not the burden of the day upon Providence, but "show your faith by your works," that God may bless you. It matters not where you live, or what rank of life you hold, the evil or the blessing will reach you all. The far and the near, the home counties and the back, the rich and the poor will suffer or rejoice alike. The heart that feels not now is dead; the blood of his children will curse his cowardice who shrinks back at a time when a little might have saved the whole, and made *them* happy. I love the man that can smile in trouble, that can gather strength from distress, and grow brave by reflection. It is the business of little minds to shrink; but he whose heart is firm, and whose conscience approves his conduct, will pursue his principles unto death.

My own line of reasoning is to myself as straight and clear as a ray of light. Not all the treasures of the world, so far as I believe, could have induced me to support an offensive war, for I think it murder; but if a thief breaks into my house, burns and destroys my property, and kills or threatens to kill me, or those that are in it, and to "bind me in all cases whatsoever" to his absolute will, am I to suffer it? What signifies it to me whether he who does it is a king or a common man; my countryman or not my countryman; whether it be done by an individual villain or an army of them? If we reason to the root of things we shall find no difference; neither can any just cause be assigned why we should punish in the one case and pardon in the other. Let them call me rebel and welcome, I feel no concern from it; but I should suffer the misery of devils were I to make a whore of my soul by swearing allegiance to one whose character is that of a sottish, stupid, stubborn, worthless, brutish man. I conceive likewise a horrid idea in receiving mercy from a being who at the last day shall be shrieking to the rocks and mountains to cover him, and fleeing with terror from the orphan, the widow, and the slain of America.

There are cases which cannot be overdone by language, and this is one. There are persons, too, who see not the full extent of the evil which threatens them; they solace themselves with hopes that the enemy, if he succeed, will be merciful. It is the madness of folly to expect mercy from those who have refused to do justice; and even mercy, where conquest is the object, is only a trick of war. The cunning of the fox is as murderous as the violence of the wolf, and we ought to guard equally against both. Howe's first object is, partly by threats and partly by promises, to terrify or seduce the people to deliver up their arms and receive mercy. The Ministry recommended the same plan to Gage, and this is what the Tories call making their peace, "a peace which passeth all understanding," indeed! — a peace which would be the immediate forerunner of a worse ruin than any we have yet thought of.

Ye men of Pennsylvania, do reason upon these things! Were the back counties to give up their arms, they would fall an easy prey to the Indians, who are all armed; this perhaps is what some Tories would not be sorry for. Were the home counties to deliver up their arms, they would be exposed to the resentment of the back counties, who would then have it in their power to chastise their defection at pleasure. And were any one state to give up its arms, that state must be garrisoned by all Howe's army of Britons and Hessians to preserve it from the anger of the rest. Mutual fear is the principal link in the chain of mutual love, and woe be to that state that breaks the compact. Howe is mercifully inviting you to barbarous destruction, and men must be either rogues or fools that will not see it. I dwell not upon the vapors of imagination; I bring reason to your ears, and, in language as plain as A, B, C, hold up truth to your eyes.

I thank God that I fear not. I see no real cause for fear. I know our situation well, and can see the way out of it. While our army was collected, Howe dared not risk a battle; and it is no credit to him that he decamped from the White Plains and waited a mean opportunity to ravage the defenseless Jerseys. But it is great credit to us

that, with a handful of men, we sustained an orderly retreat for near a hundred miles, brought off our ammunition, all our field-pieces, the greatest part of our stores, and had four rivers to pass. None can say that our retreat was precipitate, for we were near three weeks in performing it, that the country might have time to come in. Twice we marched back to meet the enemy, and remained out till dark. The sign of fear was not seen in our camp, and had not some of the cowardly and disaffected inhabitants spread false alarms through the country, the Jerseys had never been ravaged. Once more we are again collected and collecting, our new army at both ends of the continent is recruiting fast, and we shall be able to open the next campaign with sixty thousand men, well armed and clothed.

This is our situation, and who will may know it. By perseverance and fortitude we have the prospect of a glorious issue; by cowardice and submission, the sad choice of a variety of evils — a ravaged country — a depopulated city — habitations without safety and slavery without hope — our homes turned into barracks and bawdy houses for Hessians, and a future race to provide for, whose fathers we shall doubt of. Look on this picture and weep over it! And if there yet remains one thoughtless wretch who believes it not, let him suffer it unlamented.

I only regret that I have but one life to lose for my country.
NATHAN HALE, last words before being hanged as a spy by the British, New York, Sept. 22, 1776

112.

BENJAMIN RUSH: On the Progress of the War

Dr. Benjamin Rush was a member of the Second Continental Congress and a signer of the Declaration of Independence. He made the following cautious appraisal of the war's progress in a letter to Richard Henry Lee, who was serving in Congress at the time. The letter was written on December 30, 1776, while Rush was stationed with the American Army in New Jersey.

Source: Richard H. Lee, *Memoir of the Life of Richard Henry Lee, etc., etc.,* Philadelphia, 1825, Vol. II, pp. 161-163.

THERE IS NO SOIL so dear to a soldier as that which is marked with the footsteps of a flying enemy — everything looks well. Our army increases daily, and our troops are impatient to avenge the injuries done to the state of New Jersey; the Tories fly with the precipitation of guilty fear to General Howe. A detachment from our body yesterday took four of them, and killed one; two of the former were officers of Howe's new militia establishment.

We suffer much for the want of intelligence, which can only be procured by money that will pass in both camps. Howe owes the superiority and regularity of his intelligence above ours, not so much to the voluntary information of the Tories as to the influence of his gold. Pray send £ 2,000 or £ 3,000 in hard money immediately to General Washington; it will do you more service than twenty new regiments. Let not this matter be debated and postponed in the usual way for two or three weeks; the salvation of America, under God, depends upon its being done in an *instant.*

I beg leave for a moment to call off your attention from the affairs of the public to inform you that I have heard from good authority that my much honored father-in-law, who is now a prisoner with General Howe, suffers many indignities and hardships from the enemy, from which not only his rank but his being a man ought to exempt him. I wish you would propose to Congress to pass a resolution in his favor similar to that they have passed in favor of General Lee; they owe it to their own honor as well as to a member of their body. I did not want this intelligence to rouse my resentment against the enemy, but it has increased it. Every particle of my blood is electrified with revenge, and if justice cannot be done to him in any other way, I declare I will, in defiance of the authority of the Congress and the power of the army, drive the first rascally Tory I meet with a hundred miles barefooted through the first deep snow that falls in our country.

Two small brigades of New England troops have consented to serve a month after the time of their enlistments expire. There is reason to believe all the New England troops in their predicament will follow their example. We have just learned that the enemy are preparing to retreat from Princeton. Adieu. General Washington must be invested with dictatorial power for a few months, or we are undone. The *vis inertiae* of the Congress has almost ruined this country.

THE HORSE AMERICA, throwing his Master.

Pub.'as the Act directs Aug.t 1st 1779, by W.m White, Angel Court, Westminster

THE REVOLUTIONARY WAR

The struggle for the control of North America, which had seemed decisively ended by Britain's victory over France in 1763, was renewed when the rebellion of the American colonies became in 1776 a war for independence. In this conflict the British had many material advantages, including a large population and a regular army. But they overestimated the support that Loyalists in America would give, for Loyalists were not well organized and their enthusiasm seldom matched that of the revolutionaries. Indeed, unlike the earlier wars, in which the colonies had supplied many British needs, practically everything the Redcoats required had to be shipped 3,000 miles across the Atlantic. The American Army, on the other hand, was seldom better provisioned than the British since Congress had little power to requisition supplies, and much of the fighting was by state militias, whose numbers depended on the nearness of the enemy. Most important in raising American strength was the aid of the French, especially the French Navy, whose king wished to see Britain's empire weakened and her armies defeated. Thus the longest American war became an international war whose outcome, so familiar today, remained long in doubt.

Officers and Men

Congress chose George Washington as commander in chief of the Army. His character and ability as a leader of men made up for any lack of training or experience. Against Washington the British first placed William Howe, an experienced officer of high reputation. Richard Howe, the general's brother, was admiral of the fleet. They were authorized to seek peace as well as to wage war and this confusion of purpose may account for what seemed to be a lack of aggressiveness on their part.

New York Public Library

"English recruits for America," engraving dated 1780

Sir William Howe, 1778

Library of Congress

George Washington, by C. W. Peale, 1772

Washington and Lee University

National Gallery of Art

Richard, Earl Howe, by Joseph Wright

Letter to British troops en route to America

Addreſs to the Soldiers.

GENTLEMEN,

YOU are about to embark ____ to commit your Fellow Subjects there to ____ to POPERY and SLAVERY.

It is the Glory of the Britiſh Soldier, that he is the *Defender*, not the *Deſtroyer*, of the Civil and Religious Rights of the People. The *Engliſh* Soldiery are immortalized in Hiſtory, for their Attachment to the Religion and Liberties of their Country.

When King JAMES the Second endeavoured to introduce the Roman-catholic Religion and arbitrary Power into ____ Britain, he had an Army encamped on *Hounſlow* ____ , to terrify the People. Seven Biſhops were ſeized upon, and ſent to the Tower. But they appealed to the Laws of their Country, and were ſet at Liberty. When this News reached the Camp, the Shouts of Joy were ſo great, that they re-echoed in the Royal Palace. This, however, did not quite convince the King, of the Averſion of the Soldiers to be the Inſtruments of Oppreſſion againſt their Fellow Subjects. He therefore made another Trial. He ordered the Guards to be drawn up, and the Word was given, that thoſe who did not chuſe to ſupport the King's Meaſures, ſhould ground their Arms. When, behold, to his utter Confuſion, and their eternal Honour—the whole Body grounded their Arms.

You, Gentlemen, will ſoon have an Opportunity of ſhewing equal Virtue. You will be called upon to imbrue your Hands in the Blood of your Fellow Subjects in *America*, becauſe they will not admit to be Slaves, and are alarmed at the Eſtabliſhment of Popery and Arbitrary Power in one Half of their Country.

Whether you will draw thoſe Swords which have defended them againſt their Enemies, to butcher them into a Reſignation of their Rights, which they hold as the Sons of *Engliſhmen*, is in your Breaſts. That you will not ſtain the Laurels you have gained from *France*, by dipping them in Civil Blood, is every good Man's Hope. Art will no doubt be uſed to perſuade you, that it is your Duty to obey Orders; and that you are ſent upon the juſt and righteous Errand of cruſhing Rebellion. But your own Hearts will tell you, that the People may be ſo ill treated, as to make Reſiſtance neceſſary. You know, that Violence and Injury offered from one Man to ____ , has always ſome Pretence of Right or Reaſon ____ it. So it is between the People and their Rule ____

____ , whatever hard Names and heavy Accuſa ____ be beſtowed upon your Fellow Subjects, in ____ red they have not deſerved them; but ____ the moſt cruel ____ into Deſpair. In this Deſpair they are compelled to defend their Liberties, after having tried, in Vain, every peaceable Means of obtaining Redreſs of their manifold Grievances.

Before God and Man they are right.

Your Honour then, Gentlemen, as Soldiers, and your Humanity as Men, forbid you to be the Inſtruments of forcing Chains upon your injured and oppreſſed Fellow Subjects. Remember that your firſt Obedience is due to God, and that whoever bids you ſhed innocent Blood, bids you act contrary to his Commandments.

I am, GENTLEMEN,

your ſincere Well-wiſher,

AN OLD SOLDIER.

Isaac Royall, portrait by Copley

Loyalists

Loyalists, or "Tories," were of many kinds: conservative people of all classes tended to be Loyalists, as did Anglican clergymen and crown officials. Some were Tories after analysis of the issues, some simply because personal enemies were rebels. There was no freedom of speech for Loyalists in the colonies, many of whom had their property confiscated or burned. During and after the war, many Loyalists fled north to Canada, where they made an important contribution to that country's growth.

Rivington James, Tory who later aided the patriots

The TORY'S Day of JUDGMENT.

Two engravings showing the American treatment of Loyalists from "M'Fingal" by John Trumbull

The PROCESSION.

1776

Hessian troops captured at Trenton by Washington

With the Declaration of Independence fresh in their minds, the colonists were confident of victory. In July the Howe brothers landed at Staten Island, bringing a pardon from the British crown as an effort to halt hostilities. When this was rejected, there ensued the Battle of Long Island in which Washington and his unskilled militia were badly beaten by the British regulars. The Americans retreated to New Jersey and with winter approaching, Howe did not pursue. This gave Washington a chance to regroup his forces, enabling them to muster strength to attack and capture Trenton in December, restoring the colonists' confidence in their military leader.

Americans defeat British forces at Princeton

Burning of New York City

British and Hessian forces attack the Americans at Fort Washington

Negotiations with the French

Although the French had fought the Americans in the colonial wars before 1763, they were eager to give aid against their real enemy, Great Britain. The French secretly supplied cannons and gunpowder from almost the beginning of the Revolution. Much of this aid was arranged by Pierre de Beaumarchais. Meanwhile, American agents in France were attempting to secure open and increased aid from Louis XVI. But since the colonies had won no major battles, the French hesitated as long as there was the possibility that the Americans would accept peace without independence.

Bibliotheque Nationale

King Louis XVI of France

Conn. Historical Society

Silas Deane, portrait by Peale

Virginia Historical Society

Arthur Lee, portrait by Peale

City Art Museum of St. Louis

Benjamin Franklin, America's chief negotiator with France

Beaumarchais

New York Public Library

Franklin's home in Passy, France, sketched by Hugo

New York Public Library

Dissent in Parliament

Lord North's ministry was anxious to bring the war to a conclusion in 1777. After a long and costly conflict with France, the British could ill afford the expense of the war in America. In addition, the possibility of an alliance between France and America demanded that the war be ended quickly. Meanwhile, a few members of Parliament, including such eloquent and controversial figures as John Wilkes, Isaac Barre, and Charles Fox, were openly critical of the war and urged conciliation. For these reasons, Burgoyne's advance south from Canada was planned as the decisive blow to bring the colonists to their knees.

National Portrait Gallery, London

Frederick, Lord North; portrait by N. Dance

Historical Society of Pennsylvania

George III; portrait by Benjamin West

National Portrait Gallery, London

Charles Fox, portrait by Hickel

The Brooklyn Museum

Isaac Barre

Library of Congress

Cartoon reflecting English view that Fox belonged in America

Howe Takes Philadelphia

General Howe's main effort for 1777 was the capture in September of the American capital city, Philadelphia. A few days later he repelled a poorly executed American attack at Germantown, a Philadelphia suburb. But in taking the capital, Howe had gained little more than some real estate, for the Congress escaped with their records to York, and Washington's Army remained intact.

The Building in which the American Congress sat during the gloomiest period of the Revolution.

Library of Congress

The American Congress retreated to York after the British captured Philadelphia

Independence National Historical Park

Henry Laurens, president of Congress

Battle of Germantown in which British troops withstood the American attack

Library of Congress

Saratoga

The British plan was to divide and conquer: Burgoyne was instructed to lead an army down the Champlain-Hudson River route to New York and split the colonies in two. But as he moved south, Burgoyne's supply lines became dangerously extended, casualties and desertions depleted his ranks, and most of his Indians disappeared. Meanwhile, the American forces daily grew larger as reinforcements arrived. On September 19 and again on October 7, 1777, British efforts to move south from encampment at Saratoga were halted in fierce battles. The American forces, by now three times those of Burgoyne, held an impregnable position at Bemis Heights, which had been fortified on the advice of Tadeusz Kosciuszko. Attempting to retreat from Saratoga, Burgoyne was surrounded and surrendered his entire army to General Gates on October 17.

Saratoga was a significant turning point in the war. Not only were British hopes for an early victory smashed and American morale boosted, but more importantly, France was convinced that the Americans were worthy of open support. Negotiations to that end were soon underway in Paris.

Library of Congress

The Frick Collection

(**Above left**) French engraving showing the surrender of Burgoyne; (**above right**) portrait of Burgoyne by Joshua Reynolds; (**below**) Burgoyne's army encamped on the left bank of the Hudson

Library of Congress

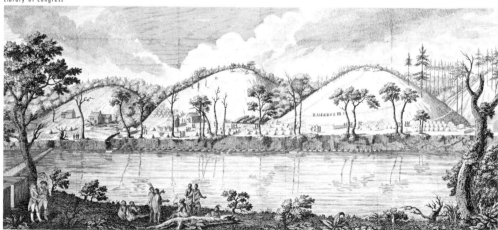

Tadeusz Kosciuszko

Gen. Horatio Gates

Daniel Morgan

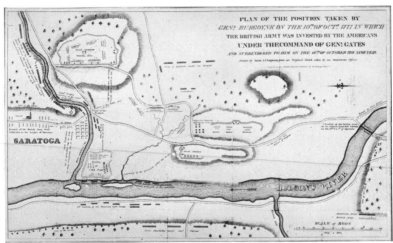

Plan showing positions of the two armies during the battle at Saratoga

Prison camp for Burgoyne's army at Charlotte, Va.

Dr. Franklin erhält, als Gesandter des Americanischen Frey Staats, seine rste Audienz in Frankreich, zu Versailles. am 20ten März, 1778.

(Left) Franklin's first audience with Louis XVI; (above) English cartoon shows Lord North's peace commission scorned by three members of Congress in Tartar dress

The French Alliance

Armed with news of the victory at Saratoga, Benjamin Franklin, America's commissioner to France, feigned interest in conciliation with the British. French foreign minister Vergennes wanted the war to continue and persuaded the king to offer the Americans an alliance. Lord North tardily dispatched a peace commission to America to keep Congress from ratifying the French treaty. But the English did not offer the colonies independence, and Congress would not receive them. The alliance was ratified on May 4, 1778, and the French Navy was soon on its way.

Freedom, Peace, Plenty, all in vain advance,
Spurned by Brittannia's Children, dupes to France:
Aspiring Chiefs in congress scourge the land,
All Laws subverting to usurp command.

Tyrants they prove, while Patriots they appear;
And Popish Leagues mark their absurd career.
May Heav'n in timely mercy make them wise,
Ere French and Spanish Chains their crimes chastize.

Drawing at left pities America for her "Popish Leagues"; (below) "The Curious Zebra" is examined by English and French statesmen

L'Escadre françoise sortant de la Mediterranée le 16. mai 1778.

A Le Mont Gibraltar. | C Corvette Angloise mettant en panne dans la baye | D Batiments hollandois
B Le Mont aux Singes. | de Gibraltar en essuyant son canon a terre. | sortant de la Mediterranée.

(Above) D'Estaing's fleet sails out of the Mediterranean Sea, bound for America

(Right) The Angel of France depicted as driving the English from Philadelphia while Americans rejoice in the background

Cow representing English commerce is milked and de-horned by France, Spain, Holland, and America while the British lion sleeps

dre francoise entrant dans Newport sous le feu des Batteries et forcant le passage le 8 Aoust 1778. Jour que les Ameri
passerent sur l'Isle de Rode Island par le chemin d'bowland's Ferry.

le de Newport.	D Isle de Conanicut.	H Batterie qui fut abandonnée apres avoir tiré sur le premier Vaisseau francois qui tourn
ies sur Rode Island faisant feu	E Vaisseaux francois forcant le passage.	Conanicut.
r Vaisseaux.	F Vaisseaux Francois tournant ou qui on tourné	I Fregate francoise restant mouillée en debors avec une prise tandis que les deux autre
us sur Goat Island faisant feu sur	l'Isle de Conanicut.	sont dans le Canal de l'Est ou elles assurent le passage d'bowland's ferry apr
Vaisseaux.	G Batiments Anglois en feu.	fait brulée les deux Batimens Gardes côtes Anglois qui deffendoient ce Canal.
N.a Les Anglois brulerent ou coulerent a Rode Island, les Fregates l'Orphée, la Junon, le Lark en la flore de 32 Canons le Cerbere en le Faucon de 28. sans pa		
grand nombre de Batimens Marchands.		

(Above) The French fleet sails into Newport; (below) Comte d'Estaing, commander of the fleet

The French Arrive

Seventeen French warships arrived in America in July 1778, and promptly disappointed the patriots. Comte d'Estaing, an army officer for most of his career, proved cautious as a naval commander, and the Americans thought he was too reluctant to fight. Later, under Admiral de Grasse, the French fleet was important in forcing Cornwallis' surrender at Yorktown.

Siege of Rhode Island at Newport, August 1778

Foreign Officers

Many European officers volunteered to serve in the American forces, but since Americans would rarely agree to serve under foreign officers, most of the volunteers served as special advisors in artillery, military engineering, and battlefield tactics where their professional training was most useful. Some of those not pictured elsewhere, who made significant contributions to the American cause, are shown here.

Massachusetts Historical Society

Marquis de Lafayette, outstanding soldier and invaluable liason between the French and American governments; portrait by Joseph Boze

Giraudon

Comte Rochambeau, leader of the French forces in America, who donated several thousand dollars to the Continental Army

Baron von Steuben, who supervised the military drilling of the troops at Valley Forge; portrait by C. W. Peale

Independence National Historical Park

Johann, baron de Kalb, who came to America with Lafayette, was killed at the battle of Camden, 1780; portrait by C. W. Peale

Independence National Historical Park

Southern Campaigns

The defeat at Saratoga and continued failure to draw Washington into battle caused the British to turn south, where they expected wide Loyalist support. The British won major victories in Georgia and in South Carolina. However, these initial successes were followed by the brilliant victory of the colonials under General Daniel Morgan at Cowpens, near the Carolinas' border, and by guerilla action that destroyed the outposts left behind by the main British advance. Loyalist support had been overestimated, and by 1781 only Savannah and Charleston in the South were held by British forces.

Benjamin Lincoln (below left) was forced to surrender Charleston (above) to the British, May 1780. General Gates (below right) was relieved of his command after surrendering at Camden, S.C., in August 1780

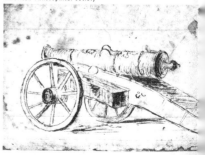

(Above) The victory at Cowpens, led by Daniel Morgan (bottom); Thomas Sumter (below left) excelled in guerilla warfare; Nathanael Greene (below right) directed operations in the South

Fogg Art Museum, Harvard

Yorktown

Cornwallis, the British commander in the South, was trying to concentrate his strength in Virginia in October 1781, when he found himself surrounded at Yorktown by the armies of Washington and Rochambeau. Meanwhile, De Grasse's fleet had arrived off the Yorktown peninsula to prevent Cornwallis from escaping by sea. After a long siege the British surrendered. Although few on the battlefield realized its significance, Yorktown was the last major battle of the war. When news of the defeat reached London, the government resolved to end the protracted and costly war.

National Portrait Gallery,
London

(Above) George Washington, painted in 1784 by C. W. Peale; Charles Cornwallis, first marquis of Cornwallis, by Gainsborough, 1783; plan of the siege of Yorktown, with the British surrounded on three sides and backed up against the river

New York Historical Society

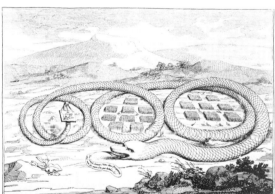

(**Top**) Painting of the allied armies at the siege, by a French eyewitness; (above left) the snake has "Burgoyn'd" two armies and has "room for more"; (above right and below) fanciful versions of the landing of British forces at Yorktown and of the surrender of Cornwallis

Peace

In accordance with the terms of the alliance with France, Congress instructed the peace commissioners not to negotiate without French cooperation. But Franklin and his colleagues found that American and French interests were not parallel. France sup-

ported independence, but sought terms that would keep America dependent on France. But, in order to end the war and weaken Franco-American ties, Great Britain offered the Americans very generous peace terms. In light of this, the commissioners ignored French objections and their instructions from Congress by signing a separate treaty with Great Britain; it was quickly approved by Congress.

(Above) Spain and France try to keep America and Britain apart, while the Dutch await a victor; West's painting, showing Jay, Adams, Franklin, Laurens and William Franklin, is unfinished because the British commissioners refused to sit with their American counterparts

Ende der Feindseeligkeiten. Die Eng=
länder räumen den Americanern
Neu=Yorck ein: ——— 1783.

(Above left) an engraving celebrating independence; (right) New Yorkers watch the Redcoats leave;
(below) inaccuracies in this map used by the commissioners led to later boundary disputes

1777

113.

Black Voices Raised for Freedom

Blacks in America took the words of the Declaration of Independence seriously. It seemed to many of them to verge on hypocrisy that 700,000 people should be held in bondage while the nation fought a war under the banner of liberty and equality. The following petition against slavery was presented to the Massachusetts House of Representatives on January 13, 1777.

Source: MHSC, 5th series, III.

THE PETITION OF A GREAT NUMBER of blacks detained in a state of slavery in the bowels of a free and Christian country humbly shows that your petitioners apprehend that they have in common with all other men a natural and unalienable right to that freedom which the Great Parent of the universe has bestowed equally on all mankind and which they have never forfeited by any compact or agreement whatever. But they were unjustly dragged by the hand of cruel power from their dearest friends and some of them even torn from the embraces of their tender parents, from a populous, pleasant, and plentiful country and in violation of laws of nature and of nations and in defiance of all the tender feelings of humanity, brought here either to be sold like beasts of burden and, like them, condemned to slavery for life — among a people professing the mild religion of Jesus; a people not insensible of the secrets of rational being, nor without spirit to resent the unjust endeavors

of others to reduce them to a state of bondage and subjection. Your Honor need not be informed that a life of slavery like that of your petitioners, deprived of every social privilege of everything requisite to render life tolerable, is far worse then nonexistence.

In imitation of the laudable example of the good people of these states, your petitioners have long and patiently awaited the event of petition after petition presented by them to the legislative body of this state, and cannot but with grief reflect that their success has been but too similar. They cannot but express their astonishment that it has never been considered that every principle from which America has acted in the course of their unhappy difficulties with Great Britain pleads stronger than a thousand arguments in favor of your petitioners.

They therefore humbly beseech Your Honors to give this petition its due weight and consideration, and cause an act of legislation to be passed whereby they may be restored to the enjoyments of that which is the natural right of all men, and that their children, who were born in this land of liberty, may not be held as slaves after they arrive at the age of twenty-one years. So may the inhabitants of this state, no longer chargeable with the inconsistency of acting themselves the part which they condemn and oppose in others, be prospered in their present glorious struggle for liberty and have those blessings for themselves.

114.

The Constitution of Vermont

The work of state constitution making progressed rapidly in the midst of the war. By July of 1777, all the states but three had constitutions of their own devising. Vermont's first constitution, adopted July 8, 1777, was a copy of the democratic constitution of Pennsylvania. Vermont was not at this time recognized as a separate state by the rest of the colonies; its territory was claimed by both New Hampshire and New York. Thus the preamble is a declaration of independence from New York. The body of the constitution also contained provisions regarding civil liberties and expressly forbade the importation of slaves.

Source: Poore, II, pp. 1857-1860.

Whereas all government ought to be instituted and supported for the security and protection of the community, as such, and to enable the individuals who compose it to enjoy their natural rights, and other blessings which the Author of existence has bestowed upon man; and whenever those great ends of government are not obtained, the people have a right, by common consent, to change it, and take such measures as to them may appear necessary to promote their safety and happiness;

And whereas the inhabitants of this state have (in consideration of protection only) heretofore acknowledged allegiance to the King of Great Britain, and the said King has not only withdrawn that protection, but commenced, and still continues to carry on, with unabated vengeance, a most cruel and unjust war against them; employing therein not only the troops of Great Britain, but foreign mercenaries, savages and slaves, for the avowed purpose of reducing them to a total and abject submission to the despotic domination of the British Parliament, with many other acts of tyranny (more fully set forth in the declaration of Congress) whereby all allegiance and fealty to the said King and his successors are dissolved and at an end, and all power and authority derived from him ceased in the American colonies.

And whereas the territory which now comprehends the State of Vermont did antecedently, of right, belong to the government of New Hampshire; and the former governor thereof, viz., His Excellency Benning Wentworth, Esq., granted many charters of lands and corporations, within this state, to the present inhabitants and others;

And whereas the late Lieutenant Governor Colden, of New York, with others, did, in violation of the tenth command, covet those very lands; and by a false representation made to the court of Great Britain (in the year 1764, that for the convenience of trade and administration of justice, the inhabitants were desirous of being annexed to that government) obtained jurisdiction of those very identical lands *ex parte;* which ever was, and is, disagreeable to the inhabitants; *And whereas* the legislature of New York ever have, and still continue to disown the good people of this state, in their landed property, which will appear in the complaints hereafter inserted, and in the 36th Section of their present constitution, in which is established the grants of land made by that government:

They have refused to make regrants of our lands to the original proprietors and occupants, unless at the exorbitant rate of $2,300 fees for each township; and did enhance the quitrent threefold, and demanded an immediate delivery of the title derived before, from New Hampshire.

The judges of their Supreme Court have made a solemn declaration that the charters, conveyances, etc. of the lands included in the before described premises, were utterly null and void, on which said title was founded: in consequence of which declaration, writs of possession have been by them issued, and the sheriff of the county of Albany sent, at the head of 600 or 700 men, to enforce the execution thereof.

They have passed an act, annexing a penalty thereto, of £30 fine and six months imprisonment, on any person who should refuse assisting the sheriff, after being requested, for the purpose of executing writs of possession.

The governors, Dunmore, Tyron, and Colden, have made regrants of several tracts of land included in the premises to certain favorite land jobbers in the government of New York, in direct violation of His Britannic Majesty's express prohibition in the year 1767.

They have issued proclamations, wherein they have offered large sums of money, for the purpose of apprehending those very persons who have dared boldly and publicly to appear in defense of their just rights.

They did pass twelve acts of outlawry, on the 9th day of March, A.D. 1774, empowering the respective judges of their Supreme Court to award execution of death against those inhabitants in said district that they should judge to be offenders, without trial.

They have, and still continue, an unjust claim to those lands, which greatly retards emigration into, and the settlement of, this state.

They have hired foreign troops, emigrants from Scotland, at two different times, and armed them to drive us out of possession.

They have sent the savages on our frontiers to distress us.

They have proceeded to erect the counties of Cumberland and Gloucester, and establish courts of justice there, after they were discountenanced by the authority of Great Britain.

The free convention of the State of New York, at Harlem, in the year 1776, unanimously voted, "That all quitrents, formerly due to the king of Great Britain, are now due and owing to this convention, or such future government as shall be hereafter established in this state."

In the several stages of the aforesaid oppressions, we have petitioned His Britannic Majesty, in the most humble manner, for redress and have, at very great expense, received several reports in our favor; and, in other instances, wherein we have petitioned the late legislative authority of New York, those petitions have been treated with neglect.

And whereas the local situation of this state, from New York, at the extreme part, is upward of 450 miles from the seat of that government, which renders it extreme difficult to continue under the jurisdiction of said state.

Therefore, it is absolutely necessary, for the welfare and safety of the inhabitants of this state, that it should be, henceforth, a free and independent state; and that a just, permanent, and proper form of government should exist in it, derived from, and founded on, the authority of the people only, agreeable to the direction of the honorable American Congress.

We, the representatives of the freemen of Vermont, in general convention met, for the express purpose of forming such a government — confessing the goodness of the Great Governor of the universe (who alone knows to what degree of earthly happiness mankind may attain, by perfecting the arts of government) in permitting the people of this state, by common consent, and without violence, deliberately to form for themselves such just rules as they shall think best for governing their future society; and being fully convinced that it is our indispensable duty to establish such original principles of government as will best promote the general happiness of the people of this state, and their posterity, and provide for future improvements, without partiality for, or prejudice against, any particular class, sect, or denomination of men whatever do, by virtue of authority vested in us by our constituents, ordain, declare, and establish the following declaration of rights and frame of government to be the constitution of this Commonwealth, and to remain in force therein, forever unaltered, except in such articles as shall hereafter, on experience, be found to require improvement, and which shall, by the same authority of the people, fairly delegated, as this frame of government directs, be amended or improved, for the more effectual obtaining and securing the great end and design of all government, herein before mentioned.

A DECLARATION OF THE RIGHTS OF THE INHABITANTS OF THE STATE OF VERMONT

1. That all men are born equally free and independent, and have certain natural, inherent, and unalienable rights, amongst which are the enjoying and defending life and liberty; acquiring, possessing, and protecting property, and pursuing and obtaining happiness and safety. Therefore, no male person, born in this country or brought from over sea, ought to be holden by law to serve any person as a servant, slave, or apprentice after he arrives to the age of twenty-one years, nor female, in like manner, after she arrives to the age of eighteen years, unless they are bound by their own consent, after they arrive to such age or bound by law, for the payment of debts, damages, fines, costs, or the like.

2. That private property ought to be subservient to public uses, when necessity requires it; nevertheless, whenever any particular man's property is taken for the use of the public, the owner ought to receive an equivalent in money.

3. That all men have a natural and unalienable right to worship Almighty God according to the dictates of their own consciences and understanding, regulated by the word of God; and that no man ought or of right can be compelled to attend any religious worship, or erect or support any place of worship, or maintain any minister, contrary to the dictates of his conscience; nor can any man who professes the Protestant religion be justly deprived or abridged of any civil right as a citizen on account of his religious sentiment or peculiar mode of religious worship, and that no authority can or ought to be vested in, or assumed by, any power whatsoever, that shall, in any case, interfere with, or in any manner control, the rights of conscience in the free exercise of religious worship; nevertheless, every sect or denomination of people ought to observe the Sabbath, or the Lord's day, and keep up and support some sort of religious worship, which to them shall seem most agreeable to the revealed will of God.

4. That the people of this state have the sole, exclusive, and inherent right of governing and regulating the internal police of the same.

5. That all power being originally inherent in, and consequently derived from, the people, therefore all officers of government, whether legislative or executive, are their trustees and servants, and at all times accountable to them.

6. That government is, or ought to be, instituted for the common benefit, protection, and security of the people, nation or community, and not for the particular emolument or advantage of any single man, family, or set of men who are a part only of that community; and that the community has an indubitable, unalienable, and indefeasible right to reform, alter, or abolish government, in such manner as shall be by that community judged most conducive to the public weal.

7. That those who are employed in the legislative and executive business of the state may be restrained from oppression, the people have a right, at such periods as they may think proper, to reduce their public officers to a private station, and supply the vacancies by certain and regular elections.

8. That all elections ought to be free; and that all freemen, having a sufficient, evident, common interest with, and attachment to, the community, have a right to elect officers or be elected into office.

9. That every member of society has a right to be protected in the enjoyment of life, liberty, and property, and therefore is bound to contribute his proportion toward the expense of that protection, and yield his personal service, when necessary, or an equivalent thereto; but no part of a man's property can be justly taken from him, or applied to public uses, without his own consent or that of his legal representatives; nor can any man who is conscientiously scrupulous of bearing arms be justly compelled thereto, if he will pay such equivalent; nor are the people bound by any law, but such as they have, in like manner, assented to for their common good.

10. That in all prosecutions for criminal offenses a man has a right to be heard by himself and his counsel; to demand the cause and nature of his accusation; to be confronted with the witnesses — to call for evidence in his favor, and a speedy public trial by an impartial jury of the country; without the unanimous consent of which jury, he cannot be found guilty; nor can he be compelled to give evidence against himself; nor can any man be' justly deprived of his liberty, except by the laws of the land or the judgment of his peers.

11. That the people have a right to hold themselves, their houses, papers, and possessions free from search or seizure; and therefore warrants, without oaths or affirmations first made, affording a sufficient foundation for them, and whereby any officer or messenger may be commanded or required to search suspected places, or to seize any person or persons, his, her, or their property, not particularly described, are contrary to that right, and ought not to be granted.

12. That no warrant or writ to attach the person or estate of any freeholder within this state shall be issued in civil action without the person or persons who may request such warrant or attachment first make oath, or affirm, before the authority who may be requested to issue the same, that he, or they, are in danger of losing his, her, or their debts.

13. That in controversies respecting property, and in suits between man and man, the parties have a right to a trial by jury; which ought to be held sacred.

14. That the people have a right to freedom of speech, and of writing and publishing their sentiments; therefore, the freedom of the press ought not be restrained.

15. That the people have a right to bear arms for the defense of themselves and the state; and as standing armies, in the time of peace, are dangerous to liberty, they ought not to be kept up; and that the military should be kept under strict subordination to, and governed by, the civil power.

16. That frequent recurrence to fundamental principles, and a firm adherence to justice, moderation, temperance, industry, and frugality are absolutely necessary to preserve the blessings of liberty, and keep government free. The people ought, therefore, to pay particular attention to these points, in the choice of officers and representatives, and have a right to exact a due and constant regard to them, from their legislators and magistrates, in the making and executing such laws as are necessary for the good government of the state.

17. That all people have a natural and inherent right to emigrate from one state to another that will receive them; or to form a new state in vacant countries, or in such countries as they can purchase, whenever they think that thereby they can promote their own happiness.

18. That the people have a right to assemble together; to consult for their common good; to instruct their representatives; and to apply to the legislature for redress of grievances, by address, petition, or remonstrance.

19. That no person shall be liable to be transported out of this state for trial for any offense committed within this state.

115.

NICHOLAS CRESSWELL: On General Washington

Nicholas Cresswell came to America from England in 1774 at the age of twenty-four. It is likely that he hoped to stay in the colonies and establish a new life for himself, but the growing enmity with the mother country made it difficult for him to remain. He felt he was regarded as a Tory and a spy by the rebelling Americans and so returned home three years later. During these years he kept a diary from which the following entry of July 13, 1777, is taken.

Source: *The Journal of Nicholas Cresswell,* New York, 1924.

Sunday, July 13th, 1777: News that our army has surprised Washington and taken him prisoner. Afraid it is too good to be authentic. His great caution will always prevent him being made a prisoner to our inactive general. Washington is certainly a most surprising man, one of nature's geniuses, a heaven-born general, if there is any of that sort. That a Negro-driver should, with a ragged banditti of undisciplined people, the scum and refuse of all nations on earth, so long keep a British general at bay, nay, even oblige him, with as fine an army of veteran soldiers as ever England had on the American continent, to retreat — it is astonishing. It is too much. By Heavens, there must be double-dealing somewhere. General Howe, a man brought up to war from his youth, to be puzzled and plagued for two years together, with a Virginia tobacco planter. O! Britain, how thy laurels tarnish in the hands of such a lubber! The life of General Washington will be a most copious subject for some able biographer to exercise his pen upon. Nature did not make me one of the biographic order. However, I will make some remarks concerning this great and wonderful man.

George Washington, the American hero, was second son of a creditable Virginia tobacco planter (which I suppose may, in point of rank, be equal to the better sort of yeomanry in England). I believe his mother is still living and two of his brothers. One of them lives in Berkley County in Virginia, the other in Faquire County in Virginia. Both able planters and men of good character. In the early part of his life he was surveyor of Fairfax County in Virginia. It was then a frontier county and his office was attended with much trouble but not any considerable profit. This business accustomed him to the woods and gained him the character of the best woodsman in the colony. His older brother, Mr. Augustine Washington, was a captain in the American troops raised for the expedition against Cartagena, but afterward incorporated with the regulars. He died in the service, and our hero George came to the patrimonial estate.

In the year 1755 he was chosen by the Assembly of Virginia to go to the French forts on the Ohio to know the reason why they made encroachments on the back parts of Virginia, which office he performed to the entire satisfaction of his employers. On his return he published his journal which did him great credit and first made him popular amongst his countrymen.

In the year 1754 the governor of Virginia gave him the command of about 1,000 troops (all Virginians), with orders to drive the French from their encroachments in the back settlements. In this expedition he proved unsuccessful. On the 3rd of July, 1754, he suffered himself to be surrounded by the French and Indians at the Big Meadows in the Allegheny Mountain and was obliged to capitulate, but upon what

terms I do not recollect. He by some means or other got from the French very soon and had the command of a regiment of Virginians, and was with the unfortunate General Braddock when he was defeated by the French and Indians on the banks of the Monongahela River, July 9, 1755, prior to which he, with a part of his regiment, fell in with a scouting party of his own in the woods, an engagement began, and a number of men were killed before the mistake was discovered. He continued in the Army most of the war, but never performed any action to render himself conspicuous.

Before the expiration of the war he married a Mrs. Custis, a widow lady, with whom he had a very good fortune. By her entreaties he left the Army, in which he never gained any great esteem by his own country officers or men. By all accounts it was his frugality that lost him the goodwill of his officers, and the strict discipline he always observed, the love of his men. Indeed, any kind of order or subordination ill agrees with his countrymen in general. After he quitted the Army, he was made a member of the Virginia House of Burgesses, in which he was much respected for his good private character, but always looked upon as too bashful and timid for an orator. He lived as a country gentleman, much noted for his hospitality, great knowledge in agriculture, and industry in carrying his various manufactories of linen and woolen to greater perfection than any man in the colony.

On the breaking out of these troubles he was chosen, in company with Messrs. Peyton Randolph, Richard Henry Lee, Patrick Henry, Richard Bland, Benjamin Harrison, and Edmund Pendleton, Esqs., to act as deputies or delegates for the colony of Virginia in the first Congress or Sanhedrin held at Philadelphia, September 5, 1774, and appointed general and commander in chief of all the rebel forces (by Congress) June 17, 1775. I believe he accepted this post with reluctance, but the great and almost unexpected success he has had may now soothe and become agreeable to his natural ambitious temper. He undoubtedly pants for military fame, and, considering the little military knowledge and experience he had before he was made a general, he has performed wonders. He was generally unfortunate (indeed I may with propriety say always) in every action where he was immediately concerned until the affair at Trenton in the Jerseys. Since that unlucky period (for us) he has only been too successful.

His education is not very great nor his parts shining, his disposition is rather heavy than volatile, much given to silence. In short, he is but a poor speaker and but shines in the epistolary way. His person is tall and genteel, age between forty and fifty, his behavior and deportment is easy, genteel, and obliging, with a certain something about him which pleases everyone who has anything to do with him. There cannot be a greater proof of his particular address and good conduct than his keeping such a number of refractory, headstrong people together in any tolerable degree of decorum.

His house is at a place called Mount Vernon, about twelve miles below Alexandria on the banks of the Potomac River in Virginia, where he has a very fine plantation and farm, but, by the best accounts I could get, his estate, altogether, before these troubles did not amount to more than £300 a year in Virginia currency. But estates in this country are seldom valued by the year; it is some difficulty to know exactly what they are worth where they keep great numbers of Negroes and make large crops of tobacco. His friends and acquaintances reckon him a just man, exceedingly honest, but not very generous. Perhaps they may give him this character because he manages his estate with industry and economy, and very seldom enters into those foolish, giddy, and expensive frolics natural to a Virginian.

He keeps an excellent table, and a stranger, let him be of what country or nation, he will always meet with a most hospitable reception at it. His entertainments were always conducted with the most regularity and in the genteelest manner of any I ever was at on the continent (and I have been at several of them, that is, before he was made a general). Temperance he always observed, was always cool-headed and exceedingly cautious himself, but took great pleasure in seeing his friends entertained in the way most agreeable to themselves. His lady is of a hospitable disposition, always good-humored and cheerful, and seems to be actuated by the same motives with himself, but she is rather of a more lively disposition. They are to all appearances a happy pair.

He has no children by his wife, but she had two by her first husband, a son and daughter. The daughter died unmarried; the son, Mr. John Custis, a very worthy young gentleman, is lately married and lives with his mother at Mount Vernon. He lives entirely as a country gentleman; has no post, civil or military.

The general seems by nature calculated for the post he is in; he has a manner and behavior peculiar to himself and particularly adapted to his present station and rank in life. It is said (and I believe with great truth) that he never had an intimate, particular bosom friend, or an open professed enemy in his life. By this method of behavior he in a great measure prevents all parties and factions, and raises a spirit of emulation among his officers and men. As there is no favorite to pay their court to and pave their way to preferment, and the general, I believe, is proof against bribery, they have no way to advance themselves but by merit alone. His private character is amiable; he is much beloved and respected by all his acquaintances.

From my personal acquaintance with him, and from everything that I have been able to learn of him, I believe him to be a worthy, honest man, guilty of no bad vice, except we reckon ambition among the number, and here we ought to judge charitably. The temptation was very great to a mind naturally ambitious. Nature made him too weak to resist it.

As an officer, he is quite popular, almost idolized by the southern provinces, but I think he is not so great a favorite with the northern ones. The ignorant and deluded part of the people look up to him as the savior and protector of their country, and have implicit confidence in everything he does. The artful and designing part of the people, that is, the Congress and those at the head of affairs, look upon him as a necessary tool to compass their diabolical purposes.

He certainly deserves some merit as a general, that he, with his banditti, can keep General Howe dancing from one town to another for two years together, with such an army as he has. Confound the great chucklehead, he will not unmuzzle the mastiffs, or they would eat him and his ragged crew in a little time were they properly conducted with a man of resolution and spirit. Washington, my enemy as he is, I should be sorry if he should be brought to an ignominious death.

116.

Benjamin Rush: On the Care of the Wounded

In April 1777, Dr. Benjamin Rush was appointed surgeon general of the Continental Army. He found the medical service in a deplorable condition and protested to General Washington in a letter dated December 26, 1777. Rush accused Dr. William Shippen, the director general of the medical service, of maladministration. When Washington referred the matter to Congress, Shippen was cleared of the charges, whereupon Rush resigned his post of surgeon general.

Source: Butterfield, I.

I HAVE DELAYED troubling Your Excellency with the state of our hospitals in hopes you would hear it from the director general, whose business it is to correspond with Your Excellency upon this subject. . . . I beg leave therefore at last to look up to you, and through you to the Congress, as the only powers that can redress our grievances or do us justice.

I need not inform Your Excellency that we have now upward of 5,000 sick in our hospitals. This number would cease to be alarming if our hospitals could afford such accommodations to the poor fellows as would ensure them a speedy recovery. But this is far from being the case. There cannot be a greater calamity for a sick man than to come into our hospital at this season of the year. Old disorders are prolonged, and new ones contracted among us. This last is so much the case that I am safe when I assert that a great majority of those who die under our hands perish with diseases caught in our hospitals. When I consider the present army under Your Excellency's command as the last hope of America, I am more alarmed and distressed at these facts than I have words to express. I can see nothing to prevent the same mortality this winter among our troops that prevailed last year. Every day deprives us of 4 or 5 patients out of 500 in the hospital under my care in this place. The same complaints are heard from every quarter. The surgeons have been blamed for these things, but without reason. I shall briefly point out to Your Excellency the real causes of them.

1. Too many sick are crowded together in one house. I have seen twenty sick men in one room, ill with fevers and fluxes, large enough to contain only six or eight well men without danger to their health. Six of our surgeons have died since the 1st of last May from attending the sick under these circumstances, and almost every surgeon in the department has been ill in a greater or lesser degree with fevers caught in our hospitals. It should be the business (as it is certainly the interest) of the surgeons to prevent the sick being thus crowded. But unfortunately the Congress have given the sole power of judging of these things to the director general and his deputies, who from the nature of their business are never obliged to go inside a hospital.

2. The hospitals are provided in the most scanty manner with the stores necessary for sick people, and these are too often withheld from them from the want of checks upon the officers of the hospital whose business it is to provide and administer them. Beef and bread are by no means suitable diet for men in fevers.

3. There is a want of hospital shirts, sheets, and blankets to be worn by the sick. Nothing but a miracle can save the life of a soldier who lies in a shirt and blanket which he has worn for four or five months before he came into the hospital.

4. There is a want of guards and an officer to command at every hospital. It is foreign to my purpose to take notice of the inconveniences which attend a soldier living any time at a hospital without being subject to military government. All the discipline and sense of subordination he acquires at camp are generally lost as soon as he enters the door of our hospitals. But it is my business to mention other inconveniences which arise from our want of guards. The men, by going out when they please, catch colds, they sell their arms, blankets, and clothes to buy rum or provisions that are unsuitable for them, they plunder and insult the inhabitants; while within doors they quarrel and fight with each other, disobey their surgeons, matrons, and nurses, and thus defeat the most salutary plans that can be contrived for their recovery. An officer with a suitable guard at every hospital I am sure would save many hundred lives and many thousand pounds to the continent every year.

5. The medical establishment is a bad one. It gives the director general the most incompatible offices. The offices held by him are held by no less than three physicians in the British hospitals, who are all independent of each other and who, by checking each other, perfectly secure to the sick all the good offices and medical stores that are intended for them by government.

Before any material change can be made in our system, it will be in Your Excellency's power to stop in some measure the ravages our hospitals are making upon the army by ordering the surgeons immediately to billet such of the sick as are able to help themselves in farmhouses. The air and diet of a farmer's kitchen are the best physic in the world for a soldier worn down with the fatigues of a campaign. I have prescribed them with great success in this neighborhood, but my influence is not great enough to make the practice universal through the department. I have found the farmers volunteer in taking the poor fellows into their houses, especially when they were indulged with the soldiers' rations of beef and bread in exchange for the milk and vegetables they gave them. If this most necessary measure can be immediately carried into execution, I am sure it will add 3,000 men to your army in the spring who must otherwise perish in our hospitals. Perhaps the authority of Congress may be necessary, or the state of Pennsylvania, to facilitate the execution of the measure. If Your Excellency will only recommend it, I am sure it will immediately take place.

117.

"Johnny Has Gone for a Soldier"

In one form or another the feelings expressed by the following song must have been shared by thousands during wars throughout history. "Johnny Has Gone for a Soldier," a lament of one girl a soldier left behind, is said to date from the American Revolution.

❧ JOHNNY HAS GONE FOR A SOLDIER

Here I sit on Buttermilk Hill,
Who could blame me cry me fill?
And every tear would turn a mill;
Johnny has gone for a soldier.

Shool, shool, shool a-roo,
Shool a-sac-a-rac-ca bib-ba-lib-ba-boo.
If I should die for Sally Bobolink
Come bib-ba-lib-ba-boo so rare-o.

I'd sell my clock, I'd sell my reel,
Likewise I'd sell my spinning wheel
To buy my love a sword of steel;
Johnny has gone for a soldier.

Shool, shool, shool a-roo,
Shool a-sac-a-rac-ca bib-ba-lib-ba-boo.
If I should die for Sally Bobolink
Come bib-ba-lib-ba-boo so rare-o.

1778

118.

Benjamin Rush: On the Need for a General in the South

Benjamin Rush's military career came to an end early in 1778. He became discouraged with the progress of the war and began to doubt Washington's competence as commander in chief. Rush conveyed his feelings in an anonymous letter to Patrick Henry on January 12, suggesting possible replacements for Washington. Henry sent the letter on to Washington who recognized its authorship and accused Rush of being disloyal to him. Finding it impossible to continue in service, Rush retired to medical practice in Philadelphia.

Source: *The Writings of George Washington*, Jared Sparks, ed., Vol. V, Boston, 1855, pp. 495-497.

THE COMMON DANGER of our country first brought you and me together. I recollect with pleasure the influence of your conversation and eloquence upon the opinions of this country in the beginning of the present controversy. You first taught us to shake off our idolatrous attachment to royalty, and to oppose its encroachments upon our liberties with our very lives. By these means you saved us from ruin. The independence of America is the offspring of that liberal spirit of thinking and acting which followed the destruction of the specters of kings and the mighty power of Great Britain.

But, sir, we have only passed the Red Sea. A dreary wilderness is still before us, and unless a Moses or a Joshua are raised up in our behalf, we must perish before we reach the Promised Land. We have nothing to fear from our enemies on the way. General Howe, it is true, has taken Philadelphia; but he has only changed his prison. His dominions are bounded on all sides by his outsentries. America can only be undone by herself. She looks up to her councils and arms for protection; but alas! what are they? Her representation in Congress dwindled to only twenty-one members; her Adams, her Wilson, her Henry are no more among them; her councils weak, and partial remedies applied constantly for universal diseases.

Nathanael Greene was given command of the Army of the South in 1780. Portrait by C. W. Peale.

Her Army — what is it? A major general belonging to it called it a few days ago, in my hearing, a mob. Discipline unknown or wholly neglected; the quartermaster's and commissary's departments filled with idleness, ignorance, and peculation; our hospitals crowded with 6,000 sick but half-provided with necessaries or accommodations, and more dying in them in one month than perished in the field during the whole of the last campaign; the money depreciating without any effectual measures being taken to raise it; the country distracted with the Don Quixote attempts to regulate the price of provisions; an artificial famine created by it and a real one dreaded from it; the spirit of the people failing through a more intimate acquaintance with the causes of our misfortunes — many submitting daily to General Howe, and more wishing to do it only to avoid the calamities which threaten our country.

But is our case desperate? By no means. We have wisdom, virtue, and strength enough to save us if they could be called into action. The Northern Army has shown us what Americans are capable of doing with a general at their head. The spirit of the Southern Army is no way inferior to the spirit of the Northern. A Gates, a Lee, or a Conway would in a few weeks render them an irresistible body of men. The last of the above officers has accepted of the new office of inspector general of our Army in order to reform abuses. But the remedy is only a palliative one. In one of his letters to a friend he says, "A great and good God hath decreed America to be free, or the [General] and weak counselors would have ruined her long ago."

You may rest assured of each of the facts related in this letter. The author of it is one of your Philadelphia friends. A hint of his name, if found out by the handwriting, must not be mentioned to your most intimate friend. Even the letter must be thrown in the fire. But some of its contents ought to be made public in order to awaken, enlighten, and alarm our country. I rely upon your prudence.

———————◆———————

That the flag of the thirteen United States be thirteen stripes, alternate red and white; that the union be thirteen stars, white in a blue field, representing a new constellation.

Resolution of Continental Congress, June 14, 1777

119.

George Washington: On the Organization of the Army

After the Battle of Bunker Hill, General George Washington was put in command of the Continental Army in Massachusetts. His task was to transform a disorganized mob of patriotic recruits into a disciplined army, all the while fighting a war. By early 1778, several deficiencies in the military establishment had become apparent. Discipline, officer status, and short-term enlistments were among the problems that caused Washington to appeal to Congress for a reorganization of the army. The following communication was addressed to a committee of Congress on January 28, 1778, while the army was in camp at Valley Forge. It was issued under Washington's name, but it was written by Alexander Hamilton, who was Washington's confidential aide from 1777 to 1781.

Source: J. C. Hamilton, II, pp. 139-152: "Reorganization of the Army."

THE NUMEROUS DEFECTS in our present military establishment, rendering many reformations and many new arrangements absolutely necessary, and Congress having been pleased to appoint you a committee, in concert with me, to make and recommend such as shall appear eligible, in pursuance of the various objects expressed in the resolution, for that purpose; I have, in the following sheets, briefly delivered my sentiments upon such of them as appeared to me most essential, so far as observation has suggested and leisure permitted. These are submitted to consideration, and I shall be happy, if they are found conducive to remedying the evils and inconveniences we are now subject to, and putting the army upon a more respectable footing. Something must be done; important alterations must be made; necessity requires that our resources should be enlarged and our system improved, for without it, if the dissolution of the army should not be the consequence, at least its operations must be feeble, languid, and ineffectual.

As I consider a proper and satisfactory provision for officers as the basis of every other arrangement and regulation necessary to be made (since without officers no army can exist) and unless some measures be devised to place those officers in a more desirable condition, few of them would be able, if willing, to continue in it. . . .

A HALF-PAY AND PENSIONARY ESTABLISHMENT

A SMALL KNOWLEDGE of human nature will convince us that, with far the greatest part of mankind, interest is the governing principle, and that almost every man is more or less under its influence. Motives of public virtue may, for a time, or in particular instances, actuate men to the observance of a conduct purely disinterested, but they are not sufficient of themselves to produce a persevering conformity to the refined dictates of social duty. Few men are capable of making a continual sacrifice of all views of private interest or advantage, to the common good. It is in vain to exclaim against the depravity of human nature on this account; the fact is so, the experience of every age and nation has proved it, and we must in a great measure change the constitution of man before we can make it otherwise. No institution not built on the presumptive truth of these maxims can succeed.

We find them exemplified in the American officers as well as in all other men. At the commencement of the dispute, in the first effusions of their zeal, and looking upon the service to be only temporary, they entered into it without paying any regard to pecuniary or selfish considerations. But, finding its duration to be much longer than they at first expected, and that instead of deriving any advantage from the hardships and dangers to which they were exposed, they, on the contrary, were losers by their patriotism, and fell far short even of a competency to supply their wants; they have gradually abated in their ardor, and, with many, an entire disinclination to the service, under its present circumstances, has taken place. To this, in an eminent degree, must be ascribed the frequent resignations daily happening, and the more frequent importunities for permission to resign, and from some officers of the greatest merit. To this also may we ascribe the apathy, inattention, and neglect of duty which pervade all ranks, and which will necessarily continue and increase while an officer, instead of gaining, is impoverished by his commission, and conceives he is conferring, not receiving, a favor in holding it. There can be no tie upon men possessing such sentiments, nor can we adopt any method to oblige those to a punctual discharge of their duty who are indifferent about their continuance in the service, and are often seeking a pretext to disengage themselves from it. Punishment, in this case, will be unavailing; but when an officer's commission is made valuable to him, and he fears to lose it, then may you exact obedience from him.

It is not indeed consistent with reason or justice to expect that one set of men should make a sacrifice of property, domestic ease and happiness, encounter the rigors of the field, the perils and vicissitudes of war to obtain those blessings which every citizen will enjoy in common with them, without some adequate compensation.

It must also be a comfortless reflection to any man that, after he may have contributed to the securing the rights of his country at the risk of his life and the ruin of his fortune, there would be no provision to prevent himself and family from sinking into indigence and wretchedness. I urge these sentiments with the greater freedom because I cannot, and shall not, receive the smallest benefit from the establishment, and have no other inducement for proposing it, than a full conviction of its utility and propriety. . . .

OF COMPLETING THE REGIMENTS AND ALTERING THEIR ESTABLISHMENT

THE NECESSITY OF THE FIRST, in the most expeditious manner possible, is too self-evident to need illustrations or proof; and I shall, therefore, only beg leave to offer some reflections on the mode. Voluntary enlistments seem to be totally out of the question; all the allurements of the most exorbitant bounties, and every other inducement that could be thought of, have been tried in vain, and seem to have had little other effect than to increase rapacity and raise the demands of those to whom they were held out. We may fairly infer that the country has been already pretty well drained of that class of men whose tempers, attachments, and circumstances disposed them to enter permanently, or for a length of time, into the army; and that the residue of such men who, from different motives, have kept out of the army, if collected, would not augment our general strength in any proportion to what they require. If experience has demonstrated that little more can be done by voluntary enlistments, some other mode must be concerted, and no other presents itself than that of filling the regiments by drafts from the militia. This is a disagreeable alternative but it is an unavoidable one.

As drafting for the war, or for a term of years, would probably be disgusting and dangerous, perhaps impracticable, I would propose an annual draft of men, without officers, to serve till the 1st day of January in each year. That on or before the 1st day of October preceding, these drafted men should be called upon to reenlist for the succeeding year; and as an incitement to doing it, those being much better and less expensive than raw recruits, a bounty of $25 should be offered. That upon ascertaining at this period the number of men willing to reengage, exact returns should be made to Congress of the deficiency in each regiment and transmitted by them to the respective states, in order that they may have their several quotas immediately furnished and sent on to camp, for the service of the ensuing year, so as to arrive by or before the 1st day of January.

This method, though not so good as that of obtaining men for the war, is perhaps the best our circumstances will allow; and, as we shall always have an established corps of experienced officers, may answer tolerably well. It is the only mode I can think of for completing our battalions in time that promises the least prospect of success; the accomplishment of which is an object of the last importance; and it has this advantage, that the minds of the people being once reconciled to the experiment, it would prove a source of continual supplies hereafter.

Men drafted in this manner should not, in the first instance, receive any bounty from the public; which being solemnly enjoined upon each state, and a stop put to the militia substitution laws, would probably be attended with very happy consequences.

A number of idle mercenary fellows would be thrown out of employment, precluded from their excessive wages as substitutes for a few weeks or months, and constrained to enlist in the Continental Army. In speaking of abolishing the militia substitution laws, it is not meant to hinder a person who might be drafted in the annual allotments from procuring a substitute in his stead, himself in consequence being excused. This indulgence would be admissible, and, considering all things, necessary, as there are many individuals whose dispositions and private affairs would make them irreconcilably averse from giving their personal services for so long a duration, and with whom it would be impolitic to use compulsion. The allowance of substitution upon a smaller scale, in the occasional coming out of the militia for a few weeks, a month or two, is the thing meant to be reprobated. It is highly productive of the double disadvantage of preventing the growth of the army and depreciating our currency. . . .

OF THE ARRANGEMENT OF THE ARMY

Virginia, I understand, though not from any direct authority, has resolved to draft toward the completion of her battalions; and as this mode seems to be the only one calculated to answer the end, it is to be hoped she will be able to furnish her full complement of fifteen, including the state regiment. What plan Maryland has fallen upon, or may adopt, to fill her battalions I know not, but as the powers of government are with her in full vigor, and the abilities of the state entirely adequate, I think her original quota ought to be depended upon. Delaware must, undoubtedly, contribute one battalion; no change having happened since that portion was assigned her sufficient to afford a plea for reducing it. In behalf of Pennsylvania, much may be said; the exhausted state of her regiments; loss of her capital, and intestine divisions, ever destructive to the energy of government, may perhaps incapacitate her from completing her thirteen regiments now on foot. I suppose the number should be, for the present, diminished to eight, and the state should exert herself to fill them in the first place. When this shall be accomplished, if her resources appear equal to any further efforts, she may proceed to raising the remaining five. Jersey, New York, Connecticut, Rhode Island, Massachusetts, and New Hampshire are fully competent to the quotas respectively required of them, and no abatement seems necessary with respect to either. We have reason to hope their exertions will keep pace with their abilities, and that they will take decisive measures to send their several proportions into the field.

I am at a loss what to propose concerning the German battalion, Hazen's regiment, and the sixteen additionals. Appertaining to no particular state or states, they will have no chance of being filled by drafts, and as little by any other means. They must either remain weak and imperfect corps, be adopted by the states, or incorporated into each other, and then, if possible, be recruited. The first, upon every principle, ought not to be the case, and as the second would not be altogether eligible, from the difficulty of apportioning them without dividing and subdividing the regiments, the third seems to be the expedient to which we must have recourse. Let Maryland take the German battalion, wholly, as one of her eight, for she already claims a part of it; and then let the sixteen additionals, none of which are strong, some extremely weak, and others only partly organized, be thrown into nine. There is this number of them, which, comparatively speaking, are tolerably respectable, and have undergone a good deal of hard service in the course of the campaign. These, after having received the men out of the reduced corps, licensed, though a barren experiment, ought to try what can be done by voluntary enlistments throughout the continent at large. Hazen's regiment might be added to them, and united in the same privilege.

If these propositions are approved, the whole number of battalions on the establishment will be eighty, and, if complete, the total amount of them 40,320 rank and file. Upon this number of battalions, I shall make my arrangements. Whether full or not they will require to be thrown into brigades. . . .

PAYMASTER GENERAL

THIS DEPARTMENT is well conducted, so far as depends upon the gentleman at the head of it, but the want of money, which too frequently happens, is extremely injurious to our affairs. It is unnecessary to observe that besides feeding and clothing a soldier well, nothing is of greater importance than paying him punctually; and it is perhaps more essential in our army than any other, because our men are worse supplied and more necessitous; and the notions of implicit subordination not being as yet sufficiently ingrafted among them, they are more apt to reason upon their rights, and rendered readier to manifest their sensibility of anything that has the appearance of injustice to them, in which light they consider their being kept out of their pay after it is due. Nor does the evil end here. The inhabitants who through choice, accident, or necessity have any pecuniary concerns with the army, finding themselves frequently disappointed in the payments they have a right to expect, grow dissatisfied and clamorous; the credit of the army, and, which is nearly the same thing, the credit of the continent, is impaired, our supplies of course are impeded, and the price of every article we want raised. This circumstance is not among the least causes of the depreciation of the currency.

A question has arisen whether officers, prisoners with the enemy, who come out on parole, and are not provided for by any actual appointments, are entitled to pay during their imprisonment.

A resolve of Congress of the 19th instant provides that all continental officers, prisoners with the enemy, either while in confinement or on parole, so long as they continue officers of the United States, shall be entitled to their pay and rations, liable to a deduction for what they may have received in confinement; and that all flying camp and militia officers should be entitled to the same while in confinement only. This resolve excludes from pay all officers liberated on parole who have not actual appointments in the Continental Army. Will it not be deemed a hardship and injustice to such officers, especially to those who merely from their absence have been neglected in arrangements posterior to their capture, as has been too much the case?

While they continue prisoners, whether in possession of the enemy or out on parole, they can have little opportunity of prosecuting any business for a livelihood, and must be in a distressful situation, unless they have a private fortune sufficient to maintain them. It has in many instances happened that officers in captivity have been omitted in promotions made in their absence, upon which a question has arisen whether there should not be a restoration of rank with respect to those who are men of merit. It seems but reasonable there should.

Several new regulations will, I imagine, be found useful in the articles of war, which the judge advocate, from his official experience of the deficiency, can more accurately indicate. One thing we have suffered much from is the want of a proper gradation of punishments. The interval between a hundred lashes and death is too great, and requires to be filled up by some intermediate stages. Capital crimes in the army are frequently commuted, particularly in the instance of desertion. Actually to inflict capital punishment or death upon every deserter, or other heinous offender, would incur the imputation of cruelty, and by the too common exhibition of the example, destroy its efficacy. On the other hand, to give only a hundred lashes to such criminals is rather a burlesque on the crime than a serious correction, and affords encouragement to obstinacy and to imitation. The courts are often in a manner compelled, by the enormity of the facts, to pass sentences of death. I am as often obliged to remit, on account of the number in the same circumstances, and let the offenders pass wholly unpunished. This would be avoided if there were other punishments short of the destruction of life in some degree adequate to the crime. These the courts would ordain, and I should have executed. . . .

THE POSITION

THE REGIMENTAL SURGEONS complain that for want of medicines and other necessaries they are disabled from giving that assistance in slight cases, and in the first stages of dangerous complaints, which would serve to check their progress to maturity and save the lives of the soldiery. The hospital surgeons reply that their stores are incapable of bearing the excessive drafts which the profusion and carelessness of the regimental surgeons would make upon them if indulged in their demands.

I shall not attempt to decide the merits of this dispute, nor can I conceive any adequate mode of adjusting the difference. But one would imagine it might not be impossible to fix some general rule of allowance by which the supplies to the regimental surgeons might be regulated, and to make them accountable for the right and economical application of what they received.

At all events, as the accommodation of the sick and the preservation of men's lives are the first and great objects to be consulted, the regimental surgeons ought not to be destitute of a reasonable quantity of medicines and other conveniences of which the sick stand in need. The ill effects resulting from it are many and glaring.

Either men, at every slight indication of disease, must be sent away to distant hospitals, and the army unnecessarily deprived of the services of numbers who, if the means were at hand, might in a day or two be restored; or they must remain without proper assistance till their disorders confirm themselves, and with many get beyond the power of cure.

Other ill consequences that have attended the sending so many men away to a distance from the army are desertions and the waste of arms and clothing, for which reason it ought to be avoided as much as possible. To prevent these evils, as far as can be done, a field officer is stationed at each hospital to see the arms of the soldiers carefully deposited at their admission into it, take care of them in their convalescent state, and send them on to join their regiments under proper officers, as soon as they are fit for duty. . . .

Upon the whole, gentlemen, I doubt not you are fully impressed with the defects of our present military system, and of the absolute necessity of speedy and decisive measures to put it upon a satisfactory footing. The disagreeable picture I have given you of the wants and sufferings of the army and the discontents reigning among the officers is a just representation of evils equally melancholy and important; and unless effectual remedies be applied without loss of time, the most alarming and ruinous consequences are to be apprehended.

———————◆———————

Put none but Americans on guard tonight.

GEORGE WASHINGTON, based on his "Circular Letter" to regimental commanders regarding recruits for his bodyguard: "You will therefore send me none but natives," April 30, 1777

120.

George Washington: Against the Appointment of Foreign Officers

Unemployed professional soldiers were plentiful in Europe, and when war broke out in America they were eager to serve in the Continental Army. Securing passage money and letters of recommendation from Benjamin Franklin, the American representative in France, they came to America and offered their services to the army. Congress appointed these mercenaries to ranks as high as major general, leaving it to General Washington to find something for them to do. Most of them were given positions on Washington's staff because some Americans disliked serving under foreigners. With this situation in view, Washington addressed a letter to Gouverneur Morris, from White Plains, New York, on July 24, 1778.

Source: John P. Sanderson, *The Views and Opinions of American Statesmen on Foreign Immigration,* Philadelphia, 1856, pp. 108-109.

THE DESIGN OF THIS is to touch cursorily upon a subject of very great importance to the being of these states; much more so than will appear at first view, I mean the appointment of so many foreigners to offices of high rank and trust in our service.

The lavish manner in which rank has hitherto been bestowed on these gentlemen will certainly be productive of one or the other of these two evils, either to make us despicable in the eyes of Europe, or become a means of pouring them in upon us like a torrent, and adding to our present burden.

But it is neither the expense nor the trouble of them I most dread; there is an evil more extensive in its nature and fatal in its consequence to be apprehended, and that is the driving of all our officers out of the service, and throwing not only our own Army, but our military councils entirely into the hands of foreigners.

The officers, my dear sir, on whom you must depend for the defense of the cause, distinguished by length of service and military merit, will not submit much, if any, longer to the unnatural promotion of men over them who have nothing more than a little plausibility, unbounded pride and ambition, and a perseverance in the application to support their pretensions, not to be resisted but by uncommon firmness; men who, in the first instance, say they wish for nothing more than the honor of serving so glorious a cause as volunteers, the next day solicit rank without pay; the day following want money advanced to them; and in the course of a week, want further promotion. The expediency and policy of the measure remain to be considered, and whether it is consistent with justice or prudence to promote these military fortune hunters at the hazard of our Army.

Baron Steuben, I now find, is also wanting to quit his inspectorship for a command in the line. This will be productive of much discontent. In a word, although I think the Baron an excellent officer, I do most devoutly wish that we had not a single foreigner among us except the Marquis de Lafayette, who acts upon very different principles from those which govern the rest. Adieu.

121.

THOMAS JEFFERSON: On the Superiority of Science to Politics

The caliber of scientific attainment in eighteenth-century America is attested to by such names as John Bartram, Cadwallader Colden, Benjamin Rush, and of course the illustrious Franklin. One of the most highly respected scholars of his time was David Rittenhouse, an astronomer and mathematician from Philadelphia. The quality of his many accomplishments was assessed by Jefferson in the Notes on the State of Virginia: *"We have supposed Mr. Rittenhouse second to no astronomer living; that in genius he must be the first because he is self-taught. As an artist he has exhibited as great a proof of mechanical genius as the world has ever produced." The increasing involvement of Rittenhouse in the war effort against Britain prompted Jefferson to make the following remarks in a letter to the scientist on July 19, 1778.*

Source: Ford, II, pp. 162-164.

WRITING TO A PHILOSOPHER, I may hope to be pardoned for intruding some thoughts of my own, though they relate to him personally. Your time for two years past has, I believe, been principally employed in the civil government of your country. Though I have been aware of the authority our cause would acquire with the world from its being known that yourself and Dr. Franklin were zealous friends to it, and am myself duly impressed with a sense of the arduousness of government, and the obligation those are under who are able to conduct it, yet I am also satisfied there is an order of geniuses above that obligation, and therefore exempted from it. Nobody can conceive that nature ever intended to throw away a Newton upon the occupations of a crown. It would have been a prodigality for which even the conduct of Providence might have been arraigned, had he been by birth annexed to what was so far below him. Cooperating with nature in her ordinary economy, we should dispose of and employ the geniuses of men according to their several orders and degrees.

I doubt not there are in your country many persons equal to the task of conducting government: but you should consider that the world has but one Rittenhouse, and that it never had one before. The amazing mechanical representation of the solar system which you conceived and executed has never been surpassed by any but the work of which it is a copy. Are those powers then, which being intended for the erudition of the world are, like air and light, the world's common property, to be taken from their proper pursuit to do the commonplace drudgery of governing a single state, a work which may be executed by men of an ordinary stature, such as are always and everywhere to be found?

Without having ascended Mount Sinai for inspiration, I can pronounce that the precept, in the decalogue of the vulgar, that they shall not make to themselves "the likeness of anything that is in the heavens above" is reversed for you, and that you will fulfill the highest purposes of your creation by employing yourself in the perpetual breach of that inhibition.

122.

John Adams: On an Alliance with France

France had been giving aid secretly to the American cause for at least two years. However, the country was unwilling to enter into an open alliance until it became certain that there would be no reconciliation between America and Britain. Washington's conduct of the war in the winter of 1777-1778 convinced France of the practicability of a treaty. On February 6, 1778, two agreements were signed with France: a treaty of alliance and a treaty of amity and commerce. On July 28, John Adams, then commissioner to France, discussed the merits of the alliance in a letter to Sam Adams.

Source: *The Revolutionary Diplomatic Correspondence of the United States,* Francis Wharton, ed., Washington, 1889, Vol. II, pp. 667-668.

THE SOVEREIGN OF BRITAIN and his Council have determined to instruct their commissioners to offer you independence, provided you will disconnect yourselves from France. The question arises, how came the King and Council by authority to offer this? It is certain that they have it not.

In the next place, is the treaty of alliance between us and France now binding upon us? I think there is not room to doubt it; for declarations and manifestos do not make the state of war — they are only publications of the reasons of war. Yet the message of the King of Great Britain to both houses of Parliament, and their answers to that message, were as full a declaration of war as ever was made, and, accordingly, hostilities have been frequent ever since. This proposal, then, is a modest invitation to a gross act of infidelity and breach of faith. It is an observation that I have often heard you make that "France is the natural ally of the United States." This observation is, in my opinion, both just and important. The reasons are plain. As long as Great Britain shall have Canada, Nova Scotia, and the Floridas, or any of them, so long will Great Britain be the enemy of the United States, let her disguise it as much as she will.

It is not much to the honor of human nature, but the fact is certain that neighboring nations are never friends in reality. In the times of the most perfect peace between them their hearts and their passions are hostile, and this will certainly be the case forever between the thirteen United States and the English colonies. France and England, as neighbors and rivals, never have been and never will be friends. The hatred and jealousy between the nations are eternal and irradicable. As we, therefore, on the one hand, have the surest ground to expect the jealousy and hatred of Great Britain, so on the other we have the strongest reasons to depend upon the friendship and alliance of France, and no one reason in the world to expect her enmity or her jealousy, as she has given up every pretension to any spot of ground on the continent.

The United States, therefore, will be for ages the natural bulwark of France against the hostile designs of England against her, and France is the natural defense of the United States against the rapacious spirit of Great Britain against them. France is a nation so vastly eminent, having been for so many centuries what they call the dominant power of Europe, being incomparably the most powerful at land, that united in a close alliance with our states, and enjoying the benefit of our trade, there is not the smallest reason to doubt but both will be a sufficient curb upon the naval power of Great Britain.

This connection, therefore, will forever secure a respect for our states in Spain, Portugal, and Holland too, who will always choose to be upon friendly terms with powers who have numerous cruisers at sea, and indeed, in all the rest of Europe. I presume, therefore, that sound policy as well as good faith will induce us never to renounce our alliance with France, even although it should continue us for some time in war. The French are as sensible of the benefits of this alliance to them as we are, and they are determined as much as we to cultivate it.

In order to continue the war, or at least that we may do any good in the common cause, the credit of our currency must be supported. But how? Taxes, my dear sir, taxes! Pray let our countrymen consider and be wise; every farthing they pay in taxes is a farthing's worth of wealth and good policy. If it were possible to hire money in Europe to discharge the bills, it would be a dreadful drain to the country to pay the interest of it. But I fear it will not be. The house of Austria has sent orders to Amsterdam to hire a very great sum, England is borrowing great sums, and France is borrowing largely. Amidst such demands for money, and by powers who offer better terms, I fear we shall not be able to succeed.

123.

Count d'Estaing: Appeal to French Canadians to Aid America

In the early part of 1778, a treaty of military alliance had been signed between America and France against England. Count d'Estaing, a French admiral, commanded the first French naval expedition in support of the colonies. He arrived in July 1778 and remained in American waters for fifteen months without, however, having any great effect on the course of the war. On October 28, 1778, while the fleet was in Boston Harbor, the count wrote the following open letter in which he exhorted the Frenchmen in North America to aid the colonies.

Source: Niles: "A Declaration Addressed in the Name of the King of France, to All the Ancient French in North America, by the Count d'Estaing, Commander of the French Squadron at Boston, Mass., October 28, 1778."

The undersigned, authorized by His Majesty, and thence clothed with the noblest of titles, with that which effaces all others; charged, in the name of the father of his country, and the beneficent protector of his subjects, to offer a support to those who were born to enjoy the blessings of his government:

To all his countrymen in North America.

You were born French: you never could cease to be French. The late war, which was not declared but by the captivity of nearly all our seamen, and the principal advantages of which our common enemies entirely owed to the courage, the talents, and the numbers of the brave Americans, who are now fighting against them, has wrested from you that which is most dear to all men, even the name of your country.

To compel you to bear the arms of parricides against it, must be the completion of misfortunes. With this you are now threatened. A new war may justly make you dread being obliged to submit to this most intolerable law of slavery. It has commenced like the last, by depredations upon the most valuable part of our trade. Too long already have a great number of unfortunate Frenchmen been confined in American prisons. You hear their groans. The present war was declared by a message in March last from the king of Great Britain to both houses of Parliament; a most authentic act of the British sovereignty, announcing to all orders of the state that to trade (with America), though without excluding others from the same right, was to offend; that frankly to avow such intention was to defy this sovereignty; that she would revenge it, and deferred this only to a more advantageous opportunity, when she might do it with more appearance of legality than in the last war. For she declared that she had a right, the will, and the ability to revenge; and, accordingly, she demanded of Parliament the supplies.

The calamities of war thus proclaimed have been restrained and retarded, as much as was possible, by a monarch whose pacific and disinterested views now reclaim the marks of your former attachment, only for your own happiness. . . .

Can the Canadians, who saw the brave Montcalm fall in their defense, can they become the enemies of his nephews? Can they fight against their former leaders, and arm themselves against their kinsmen? At the bare mention of their names, the weapons would fall out of their hands.

I shall not observe to the ministers of the altars, that their evangelic efforts will require the special protection of Providence, to prevent faith being diminished by example, by worldly interest, and by sovereigns whom force has imposed upon them, and whose political indulgence will be lessened proportionably as those sovereigns shall have less to fear. I shall not observe that it is necessary for religion that those who preach it should form a body in the state; and that in Canada no other body would be more considered, or have more power to do good than that of the priests taking a part in the government, since their respectable conduct has merited the confidence of the people.

I shall not represent to that people, nor to all my countrymen in general, that a vast monarchy, having the same religion, the same manners, the same language, where they find kinsmen, old friends, and brethren, must be an inexhaustible source of commerce and wealth, more easily acquired, and better secured, by their union with powerful neighbors, than with strangers of another hemisphere, among whom everything is different, and who, jealous and despotic sovereigns, would sooner or later treat them as a conquered people, and doubtless much worse than their late countrymen, the Americans, who made them victorious. I shall not urge to a whole people that to join with the United States is to secure their own happiness; since a whole people, when they acquire the right of thinking and acting for themselves, must know their own interest. But I will declare, and I now formally declare, in the name of His Majesty, who has authorized and commanded me to do it, that all his former subjects in North America, who shall no more acknowledge the supremacy of Great Britain, may depend upon his protection and support.

Done on board His Majesty's ship the *Languedoc*, in the harbor of Boston, the 28th day of October, in the year 1778.

124.

George Washington: Against War with Canada

The French would have been pleased to regain Canada in the course of their alliance with the United States during the Revolution, but they did not dare attempt it lest they drive the Americans to make common cause with the British. Neither did France wish the Americans to invade Canada themselves, since if they were successful the Americans might see no further reason to make common cause with France against the British. The French policy, therefore, or at least the policy of the foreign minister, the Comte de Vergennes, was to let well enough alone. But Vergennes reckoned without the young Marquis de Lafayette, who passionately wanted to have a command by which he could demonstrate his support of American liberty, and who in 1778 proposed a joint French and American expedition against Canada. Vergennes did not commit himself, but he was willing to see what would happen, and the proposal was laid before the Continental Congress at Philadelphia. The Congress consulted General Washington, who disapproved Lafayette's scheme on strategic grounds, and who also wrote a private letter to Henry Laurens, dated November 14, objecting to it as politically unwise. As an expression of his view of the relationship between alliances and the national interest, the letter prefigures Washington's Farewell Address.

Source: *The Writings of George Washington*, Jared Sparks, ed., Vol. VI, Boston, 1834, pp. 106-110.

This will be accompanied by an official letter on the subject of the proposed expedition against Canada. You will perceive I have only considered it in a military light; indeed, I was not authorized to consider it in any other; and I am not without apprehensions that I may be thought, in what I have done, to have exceeded the limits intended by Congress. But my solicitude for the public welfare which I think deeply interested in this affair will, I hope, justify me in the eyes of all those who view things through that just medium.

I do not know, sir, what may be your sentiments in the present case; but, whatever they are, I am sure I can confide in your honor and friendship and shall not hesitate to unbosom myself to you on a point of the most delicate and important nature.

The question of the Canadian expedition in the form in which it now stands appears to me one of the most interesting that has hitherto agitated our national deliberations. I have one objection to it, untouched in my public letter, which is, in my estimation, insurmountable and alarms all my feelings for the true and permanent interests of my country. This is the introduction of a large body of French troops into Canada, and putting them in possession of the capital of that province, attached to them by all the ties of blood, habits, manners, religion, and former connection of government. I fear this would be too great a temptation to be resisted by any power actuated by the common maxims of national policy.

Let us realize for a moment the striking advantages France would derive from the possession of Canada; the acquisition of an extensive territory abounding in supplies for the use of her islands; the opening a vast source of the most beneficial commerce with the Indian nations, which she might then monopolize; the having ports of her own on this continent independent of the precarious goodwill of an ally; the engrossing of the whole trade of Newfoundland whenever she pleased, the finest nursery of seamen in the world; the security afforded to her islands; and, finally, the facility of awing and controlling these states, the natural and most formidable rival of every maritime power in Europe. Canada would be a solid acquisition to France on all these accounts and because of the numerous inhabitants, subjects to her by inclination, who would aid in preserving it under her power against the attempt of every other.

France, acknowledged for some time past the most powerful monarchy in Europe by land, able now to dispute the empire of the sea with Great Britain, and if joined with Spain, I may say certainly superior, possessed of New Orleans on our right, Canada on our left, and seconded by the numerous tribes of Indians on our rear from one extremity to the other, a people so generally friendly to her and whom she knows so well how to conciliate, would, it is much to be apprehended, have it in her power to give law to these states.

Let us suppose that, when the 5,000 French troops (and under the idea of that number twice as many might be introduced) had entered the city of Quebec, they should declare an intention to hold Canada as a pledge and surety for the debts due to France from the United States, or, under other specious pretenses, hold the place till

Fogg Art Museum, Harvard

Marquis de Lafayette by Duplessis

they can find a bone for contention; and, in the meanwhile, should excite the Canadians to engage in supporting their pretenses and claims — what should we be able to say with only 4,000 or 5,000 men to carry on the dispute? It may be supposed that France would not choose to renounce our friendship by a step of this kind, as the consequence would probably be a reunion with England on some terms or other; and the loss of what she had acquired, in so violent and unjustifiable a manner, with all the advantages of an alliance with us. This in my opinion is too slender a security against the measure to be relied on. The truth of the position will entirely depend on naval events. If France and Spain should unite and obtain a decided superiority by sea, a reunion with England would avail very little and might be set at defiance. France, with a numerous army at command, might throw in what number of land forces she thought proper to support her pretensions; and England, without men, without money, and inferior on her favorite element, could give no effectual aid to oppose them. Resentment, reproaches, and submission seem to be all that would be left to us. Men are very apt to run into extremes; hatred to England may carry some into an excess of confidence in France, especially when motives of gratitude are thrown into the scale. Men of this description would be unwilling to suppose France capable of acting so ungenerous a part. I am heartily disposed to entertain the most favorable sentiments of our new ally and to cherish them in others to a reasonable degree; but it is a maxim founded on the universal experience of mankind that no nation is to be trusted farther than it is bound by its interest; and no prudent statesman or politician will venture to depart from it. In our circumstances we ought to be particularly cautious, for we have not yet attained sufficient vigor and maturity to recover from the shock of any false step into which we may unwarily fall.

If France should even engage in the scheme, in the first instance with the purest intentions, there is the greatest danger that, in the progress of the business, invited to it by circumstances and, perhaps, urged on by the solicitations and wishes of the Canadians, she would alter her views.

As the marquis clothed his proposition when he spoke of it to me, it would seem to originate wholly with himself; but it is far from impossible that it had its birth in the cabinet of France and was put into this artful dress to give it the readier currency. I fancy that I read in the countenance of some people on this occasion more than the disinterested zeal of allies. I hope I am mistaken and that my fears of mischief make me refine too much and awaken jealousies that have no sufficient foundation.

But upon the whole, sir, to waive every other consideration, I do not like to add to the number of our national obligations. I would wish as much as possible to avoid giving a foreign power new claims of merit for services performed to the United States and would ask no assistance that is not indispensable.

———◆———

My men, yonder are the Hessians. They were bought for seven pounds and ten pence a man. Are you worth more? Prove it. Tonight, the American flag floats from yonder hill or Molly Stark sleeps a widow!
GENERAL JOHN STARK, before the Battle of Bennington, Aug. 16, 1777

125.

ALEXANDER HAMILTON: War Profiteering

As a soldier, Alexander Hamilton shared Washington's disgust with civilians who would turn the opportunity offered by the war to their own economic benefit. One case of such profiteering came to light in the person of Congressman Samuel Chase of Maryland, who took advantage of his position in the government to make extensive grain purchases that he knew would be needed by the French fleet when it arrived. It was this occurrence that set Hamilton to writing the letters signed "Publius" to the New-York Journal *in the fall of 1778. The letter of October 19 is reprinted here.*

Source: J. C. Hamilton, II, pp. 156-157.

WHILE EVERY METHOD IS TAKEN to bring to justice those men whose principles and practices have been hostile to the present revolution, it is to be lamented that the conduct of another class, equally criminal, and if possible more mischievous, has hitherto passed with impunity, and almost without notice. I mean that tribe who, taking advantage of the times, have carried the spirit of monopoly and extortion to an excess, which scarcely admits of a parallel. Emboldened by the success of progressive impositions, it has extended to all the necessaries of life. The exorbitant price of every article, and the depreciation upon our currency, are evils derived essentially from this source. When avarice takes the lead in a state, it is commonly the forerunner of its fall. How shocking is it to discover among ourselves, even at this early period, the strongest symptoms of this fatal disease.

There are men in all countries, the business of whose lives it is to raise themselves above indigence by every little art in their power. When these men are observed to be influenced by the spirit I have mentioned, it is nothing more than might be expected, and can only excite contempt. When others, who have characters to support, and credit enough in the world to satisfy a moderate appetite for wealth in an honorable way, are found to be actuated by the same spirit, our contempt is mixed with indignation. But when a man, appointed to be the guardian of the state, and the depositary of the happiness and morals of the people, forgetful of the solemn relation in which he stands, descends to the dishonest artifices of a mercantile projector, and sacrifices his conscience and his trust to pecuniary motives, there is no strain of abhorrence of which the human mind is capable, no punishment the vengeance of the people can inflict, which may not be applied to him with justice.

If it should have happened that a member of Congress has been this degenerate character, and has been known to turn the knowledge of secrets, to which his office gave him access, to the purposes of private profit by employing emissaries to engross an article of immediate necessity to the public service, he ought to feel the utmost rigor of public resentment, and be detested as a traitor of the worst and most dangerous kind.

126.

George Washington: On the Lack of a National Spirit

At no time during the Revolution was there unity of public mind or purpose in America. Even many of those who generally accepted independence were reluctant to give wholehearted support with taxes or military service. General Washington's unequivocal devotion to the American cause made him unwilling, perhaps unable, to accept anything less from the public. He could not help censuring the men whose sense of duty did not equal his own and whose private interest normally came before the common cause. In the following letter of December 30, 1778, to Benjamin Harrison, Speaker of the Virginia House of Delegates, Washington expressed himself in no uncertain terms.

Source: *The Writings of George Washington*, John C. Fitzpatrick, ed., Vol. XIII, Washington, 1936, pp. 466-468.

I HAVE SEEN NOTHING since I came here to change my opinion . . . but abundant reason to be convinced that our affairs are in a more distressed, ruinous, and deplorable condition than they have been in since the commencement of the war. By a faithful laborer then in the cause; by a man who is daily injuring his private estate without even the smallest earthly advantage not common to all in case of a favorable issue to the dispute; by one who wishes the prosperity of America most devoutly and sees or thinks he sees it on the brink of ruin, you are beseeched, most earnestly, my dear Colonel Harrison, to exert yourself in endeavoring to rescue your country by (let me add) sending your ablest and best men to Congress. These characters must not slumber nor sleep at home in such times of pressing danger; they must not content themselves in the enjoyment of places of honor or profit in their own country while the common interests of America are moldering and sinking into irretrievable (if a remedy is not soon applied) ruin, in which theirs also must ultimately be involved.

If I was to be called upon to draw a picture of the times and of men from what I have seen, heard, and in part know, I should in one word say that idleness, dissipation, and extravagance seems to have laid fast hold of most of them; that speculation, peculation, and an insatiable thirst for riches seems to have got the better of every other consideration and almost of every order of men; that party disputes and personal quarrels are the great business of the day, while the momentous concerns of an empire — a great and accumulated debt, ruined finances, depreciated money, and want of credit (which in their consequences is the want of everything) — are but secondary considerations and postponed from day to day, from week to week, as if our affairs wear the most promising aspect. After drawing this picture, which from my soul I believe to be a true one, I need not repeat to you that I am alarmed and wish to see my countrymen roused.

I have no resentments, nor do I mean to point at any particular characters; this I can declare upon my honor, for I have every attention paid me by Congress than I can possibly expect and have reason to think that I stand well in their estimation. But in the present situation of things I cannot help asking — Where is Mason, Wythe, Jefferson, Nicholas, Pendleton, Nelson, and another I could name? And why, if you are sufficiently impressed with your danger, do you not (as New York has done in the case of Mr. Jay) send an extra member or two for at least a certain limited time till the great business of the nation is put upon a more respectable and happy establishment?

Your money is now sinking 5 percent a day in this city; and I shall not be surprised if in the course of a few months a total stop is put to the currency of it. And yet an assembly, a concert, a dinner or supper (that will cost £300 or £400) will not only take men off from acting in, but even from thinking of, this business, while a great part of the officers of your Army, from absolute necessity, are quitting the service; and the more virtuous few, rather than do this, are sinking by sure degrees into beggary and want.

I again repeat to you that this is not an exaggerated account. That it is an alarming one I do not deny, and confess to you that I feel more real distress on account of the present appearances of things than I have done at any one time since the commencement of the dispute. But it is time to bid you once more adieu. Providence has heretofore taken us up when all other means and hope seemed to be departing from us.

127.

Two Patriotic Songs

In the minds of patriots, George Washington inevitably became the living embodiment of the American cause and the natural subject for many songs. Several rousing (if not very graceful) songs about Washington were written by his friend Francis Hopkinson, an author and musician and father of the composer of "Hail Columbia!" The "Toast to Washington" reprinted here is a good example of the elder Hopkinson's work. William Billings was a singing master and composer of hymns; after about 1775 his productions took on a decidedly patriotic tenor. "Let Tyrants Shake" (also known as "Chester") was the most popular of his patriotic hymns; it followed the soldiers to camp and became a favorite of the fife and drum corps.

Source: "A Favorite New Patriotic Song in Honor of Washington, To Which Is Added A Toast Written and Composed by F. Hopkinson, Esq.," Philadelphia, 1799.

[William Billings] *The Singing Master's Assistant or Key to Practical Music, etc., etc.*, Boston, 1778.

 A TOAST

'Tis Washington's health fill a bumper all round,
    For he is our glory and pride;
Our arms shall in battle with conquest be crowned
    Whilst virtue and he's on our side;
Our arms shall in battle with conquest be crowned
    Whilst virtue and he's on our side
        And he's on our side.

'Tis Washington's health loud cannons should roar,
 And trumpets the truth should proclaim;
There cannot be found, search all the world o'er,
 His equal in virtue and fame;
There cannot be found, search all the world o'er,
 His equal in virtue in fame
  In virtue and fame.

'Tis Washington's health our hero to bless,
 May heaven look graciously down;
Oh! long may he live, our hearts to possess,
 And freedom still call him her own;
Oh! long may he live, our hearts to possess,
 And freedom still call him her own
  Still call him her own.

Francis Hopkinson

LET TYRANTS SHAKE (CHESTER)

Let tyrants shake their iron rod,
And slavery-clank her galling chains,
We fear them not, we trust in God,
New England's God forever reigns.

Howe and Burgoyne and Clinton too,
With Prescott and Cornwallis joined,
Together plot our overthrow
In one infernal league combined.

When God inspired us for the fight,
Their ranks were broke, their lines were forced,
Their ships were shattered in our sight,
Or swiftly driven from our coast.

The foe comes on with haughty stride,
Our troops advance with martial noise,
Their veterans flee before our youth,
And generals yield to beardless boys.

What grateful offering shall we bring,
What shall we render to the Lord?
Loud Hallelujahs let us sing,
And praise His name on every chord.

William Billings

While Commerce spreads her canvass o'er the main,
And Agriculture ploughs the grateful plain
Minerva aids Columbia's rising race
With arms to triumph and with arts to grace

THE INGREDIENTS
FOR A NEW NATION

By the 1770s an American culture was emerging in the heterogeneous colonies strung out along the coast. The English heritage was adapted to the varying locales, incorporating rather than smothering the customs of other European settlers. As cities grew, they acquired distinctive characters, reflecting new colonial interest in architecture and in enjoying the comforts common-

place in England. Having provided for basic needs, the colonists devoted more energy to education, invention, and scientific inquiry. Expanded newspaper circulation kept colonists aware of the political ideas and activities in Europe. Because traveling between the colonies was difficult, the newspapers also served as a major link in communications and as a forum for debate.

Boston

Boston, the second largest town in the colonies, was one of a dozen prosperous seaports in New England. The inhabitants reflected the homogeneity of New England with fewer extremes in wealth and no dominant landed aristocracy. Suffrage was extended to almost all adult white males. The church and the town meeting exposed Bostonians to democratic principles, making the city highly antagonistic to England's hard line tactics.

(Right) View from Beacon Hill in Boston drawn by a British officer during the Battle of Charlestown, 1775; (below) woodcut from a broadside distributed in Boston following the execution of Levi Ames and intended to instruct "thoughtless Youth"

(Below) Plan of Boston, 1769; (right and below right) the opposing sides in the conflict with Britain are represented in Copley's portraits of Nathaniel Hurd, a silversmith and patriot and Joseph Green, a Loyalist merchant

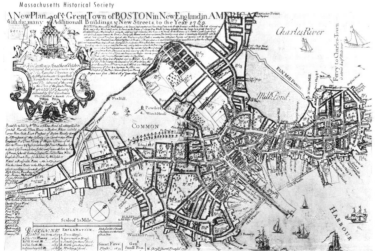

(Above) Freelove Ol-
ney by J. S. Copley;
(above right) Boston
state house

Boston Common with
British troops in drill
formation

New York

The cosmopolitan nature of New York was already in evidence by the 1770s. Stately homes of the merchants lined the river while nearby were slums occupied by day laborers, dockhands, and free Negroes. Up the river lived the landed gentry. Because the franchise was restricted to property owners, this group controlled the colony's politics.

(Top) New York from Brooklyn Heights, by Archibald Robertson, 1778; (bottom) view to the southeast on Manhattan Island, 1768

(Top) New York along the Battery; (left) Hudson River at Ft. Montgomery, showing chain which the Americans stretched across the river to stop British vessels; (above) Philipse Manor, Yonkers; (bottom) French vessels blocking English ships from New York harbor

L'Escadre françoise mouillée devant New york, bloquant l'Escadre Angloise et interceptant les Batimens qui vouloient y entrer. Le 12 juillet. 1778.

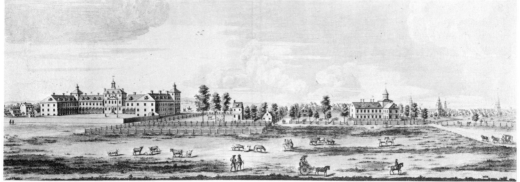

Philadelphia

(Top) The Pennsylvania Hospital, almshouse, and the house of employment, located on the outskirts of the city; (center) the Quaker meetinghouse and the almshouse run by the Friends

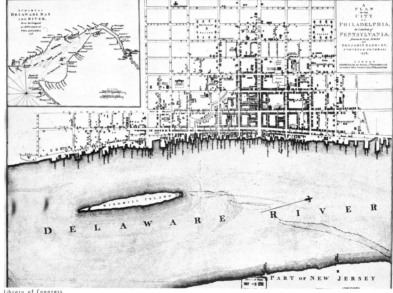

By the 1770s Philadelphia had become a highly cultured and prosperous city, the largest in America. It possessed many fine public buildings, semi-public librar-. ies, a college, and the only hospital and medical school in the colonies. Many of the neatly laid out streets were paved, lined with sidewalks, and lighted and policed at night. The city also possessed the only Catholic church outside Maryland. Its central position in the colonies made it an ideal location for the political gatherings that preceded the war for independence.

Library of Congress

ree Library of Philadelphia

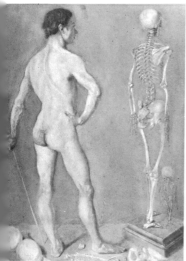

nnsylvania Hospital

Pennsylvania Hospital

(Top left) Old Swedes' Church (Gloria Dei); (top right) Christ Church; (left) drawing by Dr. Fothergill, one of 18 donated to Pennsylvania Hospital (above) for use in anatomy class at the medical school in the 1760s

David Rittenhouse, by C. W. Peale

Science

Rittenhouse's orrery, built in 1767, traced the relative positions and motions of bodies in the solar system

The Franklin stove, adapted from a German model, provided better ventilation and more heat than a fireplace

The general prosperity of the colonies brought increasing interest in and support for scientific and educational endeavors. In addition to the medical research at the Pennsylvania Hospital and the activities of the American Philosophical Society, David Rittenhouse, an astronomer and mathematician, and the botanist John Bartram gained international reputations.

John Bartram, the American botanist, produced many improved hybrids by crossing native and imported plants

Map of the Gulf Stream drawn by Benjamin Franklin

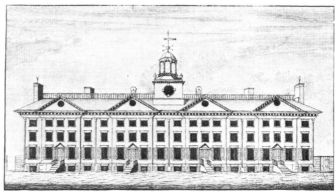

Samuel Johnson, first president of King's College (right), a nonsectarian school founded in New York City in 1754. It was renamed Columbia College in 1784. Portrait by Smibert

(Left) Samuel Davies, a Presbyterian minister, was president of the College of New Jersey 1759-61; (below) Nassau Hall, built in 1756, was the college's first and largest building

Education

Among the academies and colleges founded before the Revolution were several that later grew to major importance. Education of the clergy was still a primary motive for the colleges, but there was increasing pressure for secular instruction, particularly in law.

(Above) Rhode Island College (Baptist), founded in 1764, and renamed Brown University in 1804; (left) Ezra Stiles, president of Yale University in 1777 and a founder of Brown

Cartoon emphasizing the folly of ruining the country's wealth and trade in war, 1779

THE NEW *MASSACHUSETTS*
LIBERTY SONG,

[*To the Tune of the* Britiſh Grenadier.]

I.

THAT Seat of Science ATHENS, and Earth's great Miſtreſs ROME,
Where now are all their Glories, we ſcarce can find their Tomb :
Then guard your Rights, AMERICANS ! nor ſtoop to lawleſs Sway,
Oppoſe, oppoſe, oppoſe, oppoſe,——thy brave AMERICA.

II.

Proud ALBION bow'd to *Cæſar*, and num'rous *Lords* before,
To *Picts*, to *Danes*, to *Normans*, and many Maſters more :
But we can boaſt AMERICANS ! we never fell a Prey ;
Huzza, huzza, huzza, huzza, for brave AMERICA.

Patriotic "Liberty Song" composed in 1770

Politics

In innumerable meetings and congresses and a flood of pamphlets and broadsides, political opinion in the colonies gradually polarized around the issue of independence. Many who eventually supported independence had earlier advocated less radical means and the war's economic disruptions led even some who were not Loyalists to argue for early settlement. In addition to a basic conflict between Loyalists and radicals, disagreement over the form and structure of the new government was revealed in the Articles of Confederation and its rejection of central authority.

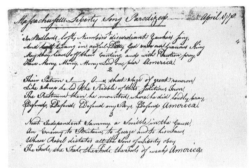

Parody of the "Liberty Song" which satirizes the activities of James Otis and Samuel Adams

Conflicting viewpoints at a town meeting

Dickinson draft of the Articles of Confederation

View of Portsmouth, N.H., from "Atlantic Neptune"

Town and Country

In spite of the growth of several cities in the colonies, the vast majority of the population at the time of the Revolution (perhaps as much as 90 percent) lived in small towns or in the country and earned their living from the land or the sea. Particularly in New England, the numerous villages came to exemplify an ideal of local self-government, where an enterprising man could parlay the fruits of his labors into a position of respect.

"Moses Marcey of Sturbridge," painting by an unknown artist

"Village Common," watercolor by an anonymous artist, 1780

By the Revolution most of the coastal areas and river valleys from New Hampshire to Virginia were dotted with towns, but even with designated local responsibility for maintaining roads, travel was difficult. Tolls for private roads and ferries, where they existed, were an added burden.

The town of Concord in 1776 from "Massachusetts Magazine"

View from Bushongo Tavern near Yorktown on the Baltimore Road from "Columbian Magazine"

Ferry three miles below Bristol, Pa.

Map of Fairfield County, Connecticut, c. 1775

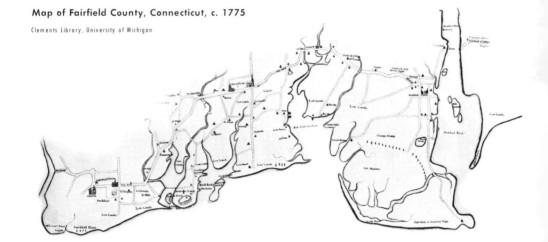

Plan of a granary drawn for "Columbian Magazine," 1779

View of a frontier sawmill and blockhouse

Generally, farming outside the South was a subsistence enterprise, little improved by experiments with new tools or methods. Large landowners, however, profited by demands for such basics as timber. The war increased the need for salt and other products formerly imported.

VENERATE THE PLOUGH

Salt works in Salisbury, Massachusetts, 1776

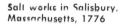

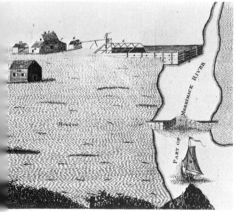

Various steps in the manufacture of woolens

New method of reaping as illustrated in "Columbian Magazine" in 1780

A Bird in the Hand is worth two in the Bush

(Above left) Two woodcuts from "A New Guide to the English Tongue," 1770; (top right) plate from "The Frugal Housewife," 1772; (center) contents page for Dilworth's "New Guide"; (center right) poem dedicated to his patrons by a newsboy; (bottom) covers of two almanacs published in the colonies

Popular Reading

In addition to political tracts and the Bible, colonial presses put forth a variety of material of general interest, from an array of popular almanacs containing weather information and helpful hints to "primers" filled with aphorisms and moral lessons for the younger generation to learn.

Folk Art

In matters of artistic patronage even the cities could barely sustain the few trained portraitists available. A small-town patron bought plain likenesses by itinerant limners or the local sign painter. In the German settlements there was a genuine and vibrant decorative folk art, derived from native styles.

(Above) "The Domino Girl," artist unknown; (right) "Capt. Samuel Chandler" by Winthrop Chandler, most accomplished of the primitives; (below) "Lady Washingdon - Exselence George General Washingdon" by an unknown artist; fraktur of a parrot by Heinrich Otto, 1785

Furniture

The decorative arts flourished in America from early in the 17th century with the arrival of immigrant European craftsmen. Furniture designs reflected familiar Renaissance and Baroque styles, learned before emigration. The two room settings recreate a large hall used for cooking, eating, and sleeping, as in the medieval tradition, and a formal dining room later in the century.

(Top left) 17th-century room from a house at Essex, Mass.; (top right) oak armchair attributed to Thomas Dennis, Ipswich, 1660-75; (left) Queen Anne style dining room with paneling from New Hampshire and chairs from New York; (below, left to right) slat-back armchair, probably New York, about 1700; tip-top table, Philadelphia; easy chair, New England, 1700-25

Glass and Metalwork

(Left) Loving cup by John Coney, 1701; (center) sugar bowl by Jacob Ten Eyck, about 1720; (right) pewter chalice, mid-18th century

(Both) Winterthur Museum

The designs of colonial silversmiths were distinguished for their simplicity and grace. Of these craftsmen, John Coney and Paul Revere of Boston were most famous.

"Baron" Stiegel established an "industrial plantation" on the Delaware River where he produced ironware and glassware of high quality.

(Right) Silver tea service by Paul Revere; (below, left to right) glass sugar bowl and "Valentine" tumbler, both c. 1764-74, and cast iron stove plate, c. 1760, all by Henry William Stiegel

Minneapolis Institute of Arts

Corning Museum of Glass

Corning Museum of Glass

Philadelphia Museum of Art

1779

128.

ALEXANDER HAMILTON: A Proposal to Arm and Then Free Slaves

The success of the British in Georgia and South Carolina in early 1779 threatened to sever the southern states from the Union. The Continental Army could spare few troops for the southern theater of war. In a letter of March 14, 1779, to John Jay, Alexander Hamilton proposed the arming of slaves to make up for the shortage.

Source: Johnston, I, pp. 191-193.

COLONEL LAURENS, who will have the honor of delivering you this letter, is on his way to South Carolina, on a project which I think, in the present situation of affairs there, is a very good one and deserves every kind of support and encouragement. This is to raise two, three, or four battalions of Negroes, with the assistance of the government of that state, by contributions from the owners in proportion to the number they possess. If you should think proper to enter upon the subject with him, he will give you a detail of his plan. He wishes to have it recommended by Congress to the state; and, as an inducement, that they would engage to take those battalions into continental pay.

It appears to me that an expedient of this kind, in the present state of Southern affairs, is the most rational that can be adopted, and promises very important advantages. Indeed, I hardly see how a sufficient force can be collected in that quarter without it; and the enemy's operations there are growing infinitely serious and formidable. I have not the least doubt that the Negroes will make very excellent soldiers, with proper management; and I will venture to pronounce that they cannot be put into better hands than those of Mr. Laurens. He has all the zeal, intelligence, enterprise, and every other qualification necessary to succeed in such an undertaking. It is a maxim with some great military judges that with sensible officers soldiers can hardly be too stupid; and on this principle it is thought that the Russians would make the best troops in the world if they were under other officers than their own. The king of Prussia is among the number who maintain this doctrine and has a very emphatical saying on the occasion, which I do not exactly recollect. I mention this because I frequently hear it objected to the scheme of embodying Negroes that they are too stupid to make soldiers. This is so far from appearing to me a valid objection that I think their want of cultivation (for their natural faculties are probably as good as ours), joined to that habit of subordination which they acquire from a life of servitude, will make them sooner become soldiers than our white inhabitants. Let officers be men of sense and sentiment, and the nearer the soldiers approach to machines perhaps the better.

I foresee that this project will have to combat much opposition from prejudice and self-interest. The contempt we have been taught to entertain for the blacks makes us fancy many things that are founded neither in reason nor experience; and an unwillingness to part with property of so valuable a kind will furnish a thousand arguments to show the impracticability or pernicious tendency of a scheme which requires such a sacrifice. But it should be considered that if we do not make use of them in this way, the enemy probably will; and that the best way to counteract the temptations they will hold out will be to offer them ourselves. An essential part of the plan is to give them their freedom with their muskets. This will secure their fidelity, animate their courage, and I believe will have a good influence upon those who remain, by opening a door to their emancipation. This circumstance, I confess, has no small weight in inducing me to wish the success of the project; for the dictates of humanity and true policy equally interest me in favor of this unfortunate class of men.

1780

129.

Massachusetts Bill of Rights

The new American states knew that their political survival depended on having workable systems of government under law. During the years in which the Revolution was fought, nearly all the states created new constitutions. Sensitive to the lack of provisions in the colonial charters to safeguard life, liberty, and property, the citizens of the states were determined to limit their governments by means of "bills of rights." Among the reasons for the defeat of the Massachusetts Constitution of 1778 was its lack of any such safeguards. A second constitution containing the following declaration of rights was drafted by John Adams and ratified on June 15, 1780.

Source: Poore, 2nd edition, I, pp. 956-960.

PREAMBLE

THE END OF THE INSTITUTION, maintenance, and administration of government is to secure the existence of the body politic, to protect it, and to furnish the individuals who compose it with the power of enjoying in safety and tranquillity their natural rights and the blessings of life. And whenever these great objects are not obtained, the people have a right to alter the government, and to take measures necessary for their safety, prosperity, and happiness.

The body politic is formed by a voluntary association of individuals; it is a social compact by which the whole people covenants with each citizen and each citizen with the whole people that all shall be governed by certain laws for the common good. It is the duty of the people, therefore, in framing a constitution of government to provide for an equitable mode of making laws as well as for an impartial interpretation and a faithful execution of them, that every man may, at all times, find his security in them.

We, therefore, the people of Massachusetts, acknowledging with grateful hearts the goodness of the great Legislator of the universe in affording us in the course of His Providence an opportunity, deliberately and peaceably, without fraud, violence, or surprise, of entering into an original, explicit, and solemn compact with each other; and of forming a new constitution of civil government, for ourselves and posterity; and devoutly imploring His direction in so interesting a design, do agree upon, ordain, and establish the following Declaration of Rights, and frame of government, as the Constitution of the Commonwealth of Massachusetts.

A DECLARATION OF THE RIGHTS OF THE INHABITANTS OF THE COMMONWEALTH OF MASSACHUSETTS

I. All men are born free and equal, and have certain natural, essential, and unalienable rights; among which may be reckoned the right of enjoying and defending their lives and liberties; that of acquiring, possessing, and protecting property; in fine, that of seeking and obtaining their safety and happiness.

II. It is the right as well as the duty of all men in society publicly, and at stated seasons, to worship the Supreme Being, the great Creator and Preserver of the universe. And no subject shall be hurt, molested, or restrained in his person, liberty, or estate for worshiping God in the manner and season most agreeable to the dictates of his own conscience; or for his religious profession or sentiments; provided he does not disturb the public peace, or obstruct others in their religious worship.

III. As the happiness of a people and the good order and preservation of civil government essentially depend upon piety, religion, and morality; and as these cannot be generally diffused through a community but by the institution of the public worship of God and of public instruction in piety, religion, and morality. Therefore, to promote their happiness and to secure the good order and preservation of their government, the people of this Commonwealth have a right to invest their legislature with power to authorize and require, and the legislature shall from time to time, authorize and require, the several towns, parishes, precincts, and other bodies politic or religious societies to make suitable provision, at their own expense, for the institution of the public worship of God and for the support and maintenance of public Protestant teachers of piety, religion, and morality in all cases where such provision shall not be made voluntarily.

And the people of this Commonwealth have also a right to, and do, invest their legislature with authority to enjoin upon all the subjects an attendance upon the instructions of the public teachers aforesaid, at stated times and seasons, if there be any on whose instructions they can conscientiously and conveniently attend.

Provided, notwithstanding, that the several towns, parishes, precincts, and other bodies politic, or religious societies, shall at all times have the exclusive right of electing their public teachers and of contracting with them for their support and maintenance.

And all moneys paid by the subject to the support of public worship and of the public teachers aforesaid shall, if he require it, be uniformly applied to the support of the public teacher or teachers of his own religious sect or denomination, provided there be any on whose instructions he attends; otherwise it may be paid toward the support of the teacher or teachers of the parish or precinct in which the said moneys are raised.

And every denomination of Christians, demeaning themselves peaceably and as good subjects of the Commonwealth, shall be equally under the protection of the law; and no subordination of any one sect or denomination to another shall ever be established by law.

IV. The people of this Commonwealth have the sole and exclusive right of governing themselves as a free, sovereign, and independent state, and do, and forever hereafter shall, exercise and enjoy every power, jurisdiction, and right which is not, or may not hereafter be, by them expressly delegated to the United States of America, in Congress assembled.

V. All power residing originally in the people, and being derived from them, the several magistrates and officers of government, vested with authority, whether legislative, executive, or judicial, are the substitutes and agents, and are at all times accountable to them.

VI. No man, nor corporation, or association of men have any other title to obtain advantages, or particular and exclusive privileges distinct from those of the community than what rises from the consideration of services rendered to the public; and this title being in nature neither hereditary, nor transmissible to children, or descendants, or relations by blood; the idea of a man born a magistrate, lawgiver, or judge is absurd and unnatural.

VII. Government is instituted for the common good, for the protection, safety, prosperity, and happiness of the people and not for the profit, honor, or private interest of any one man, family, or class of men; therefore the people alone have an incontestable, unalienable, and indefeasible right to institute government; and to reform, alter, or totally change the same when their protection, safety, prosperity, and happiness require it.

VIII. In order to prevent those who are vested with authority from becoming oppressors, the people have a right, at such periods and in such manner as they shall establish by their frame of government, to cause their public officers to return to private life, and to fill up vacant places by certain and regular elections and appointments.

IX. All elections ought to be free; and all the inhabitants of this Commonwealth, having such qualifications as they shall establish by their frame of government, have an equal right to elect officers, and to be elected, for public employments.

X. Each individual of the society has a right to be protected by it in the enjoyment of his life, liberty, and property, according to standing laws. He is obliged, consequently, to contribute his share to the expense of this protection; to give his personal service, or an equivalent, when necessary; but no part of the property of any individual can, with justice, be taken from him, or applied to public uses, without his own consent, or that of the representative body of the people. In fine, the people of this Common-wealth are not controllable by any other laws than those to which their constitutional representative body have given their consent. And whenever the public exigencies require that the property of any individual should be appropriated to public uses, he shall receive a reasonable compensation therefor.

XI. Every subject of the Commonwealth ought to find a certain remedy, by having recourse to the laws, for all injuries or wrongs which he may receive in his person, property, or character. He ought to obtain right and justice freely, and without being obliged to purchase it; completely, and without any denial; promptly, and without delay, conformably to the laws.

XII. No subject shall be held to answer for any crimes or no offense until the same is fully and plainly, substantially and formally, described to him; or be compelled to accuse or furnish evidence against himself; and every subject shall have a right to produce all proofs that may be favorable to him; to meet the witnesses against him face to face; and to be fully heard in his defense by himself, or his counsel at his election. And no subject shall be arrested, imprisoned, despoiled, or deprived of his property, immunities, or privileges, put out of the protection of the law, exiled, or deprived of his life, liberty, or estate, but by the judgment of his peers, or the law of the land.

And the legislature shall not make any law that shall subject any person to a capital or infamous punishment, excepting for the government of the Army and Navy, without trial by jury.

XIII. In criminal prosecutions, the verification of facts, in the vicinity where they happen, is one of the greatest securities of the life, liberty, and property of the citizen.

XIV. Every subject has a right to be secure from all unreasonable searches and seizures of his person, his houses, his papers, and all his possessions. All warrants, therefore, are contrary to this right, if the cause or foundation of them be not previously supported by oath or affirmation, and if the order in the warrant to a civil officer to make search in suspected places, or to arrest one or more suspected persons, or to seize their property, be not accompanied with a special designation of the persons or objects of search, arrest, or seizure; and no warrant ought to be issued but in cases, and with the formalities, prescribed by the laws.

XV. In all controversies concerning property, and in all suits between two or more persons, except in cases in which it has heretofore been otherways used and practised, the parties have a right to a trial by jury; and this method of procedure shall be held sacred, unless, in causes arising on the high seas, and such as relate to mariners' wages, the legislature shall hereafter find it necessary to alter it.

XVI. The liberty of the press is essential to the security of freedom in a state; it ought not, therefore, to be restrained in this Commonwealth.

XVII. The people have a right to keep and to bear arms for the common defense. And as, in time of peace, armies are dangerous to liberty, they ought not to be maintained without the consent of the legislature; and the military power shall always be held in an exact subordination to the civil authority, and be governed by it.

XVIII. A frequent recurrence to the fundamental principles of the constitution, and a constant adherence to those of piety, justice, moderation, temperance, industry, and frugality, are absolutely necessary to preserve the advantages of liberty, and to maintain a free government. The people ought, consequently, to have a particular attention to all those principles in the choice of their officers and representatives. And they have a right to require of their lawgivers and magistrates an exact and constant observance of them in the formation and execution of the laws necessary for the good administration of the Commonwealth.

XIX. The people have a right in an orderly and peaceable manner to assemble to consult upon the common good, give instructions to their representatives, and to request of the legislative body, by the way of addresses, petitions, or remonstrances, redress of the wrongs done them, and of the grievances they suffer.

XX. The power of suspending the laws, or the execution of the laws, ought never to be exercised but by the legislature, or by authority derived from it, to be exercised in such particular cases only as the legislature shall expressly provide for.

XXI. The freedom of deliberation, speech, and debate, in either house of the legislature, is so essential to the rights of the people that it cannot be the foundation of any accusation or prosecution, action or complaint, in any other court or place whatsoever.

XXII. The legislature ought frequently to assemble for the redress of grievances, for correcting, strengthening, and confirming the laws, and for making new laws, as the common good may require.

XXIII. No subsidy, charge, tax, impost, or duties ought to be established, fixed, laid, or levied, under any pretext whatsoever, without the consent of the people or their representatives in the legislature.

XXIV. Laws made to punish for actions done before the existence of such laws, and which have not been declared crimes by preceding laws, are unjust, oppressive, and inconsistent with the fundamental principles of a free government.

XXV. No subject ought, in any case or in any time, to be declared guilty of treason or felony by the legislature.

XXVI. No magistrate or court of law shall demand excessive bail or sureties, impose excessive fines, or inflict cruel or unusual punishments.

XXVII. In time of peace, no soldier ought to be quartered in any house without the consent of the owner; and in time of war, such quarters ought not to be made but by the civil magistrate, in a manner ordained by the legislature.

XXVIII. No person can in any case be subject to law-martial, or to any penalties or pains by virtue of that law, except those employed in the Army or Navy, and except the militia in actual service, but by authority of the legislature.

XXIX. It is essential to the preservation of the rights of every individual, his life, liberty, property, and character, that there be an impartial interpretation of the laws, and administration of justice. It is the right of every citizen to be tried by judges as free, impartial, and independent as the lot of humanity will admit. It is, therefore, not only the best policy, but for the security of the rights of the people, and of every citizen, that the judges of the Supreme Judicial Court should hold their offices as long as they behave themselves well; and that they should have honorable salaries ascertained and established by standing laws.

XXX. In the government of this Commonwealth, the legislative department shall never exercise the executive and judicial powers, or either of them; the executive shall never exercise the legislative and judicial powers, or either of them; the judicial shall never exercise the legislative and executive powers, or either of them; to the end it may be a government of laws and not of men.

130.

The Cumberland Compact

A large portion of land along the Cumberland River and south of it was acquired from the Cherokees in 1775 by the associates known as the Transylvania Company. Several forts and settlements were established in the area, which at this time was the western edge of the frontier. The original thirteen seaboard states claimed all the land directly west of them as a part of their territory, hindering the formation of any new states on the frontier. Whatever political forms existed in the West had to operate at the local level, since there could be no definite allegiance to any state authority. The frontiersman was as intent as any other citizen on securing for himself the protection of a government under law. The Cumberland County Compact of 1780, drawn up by Richard Henderson, leader of the Transylvania Company, is an instance of community self-government.

Source: *History of Tennessee*, Nashville, 1886, pp. 184-188.

LANDS SHALL BE RESERVED for the particular person in whose name they shall be entered, or their heirs, provided such persons shall remove to this country and take possession of the respective place or piece of land so chosen or entered, or shall send a laborer or laborers and a white person in his or her stead to perform the same on or before the 1st day of May, 1781; and also provided such land so chosen and entered for is not entered and claimed by some person who is an inhabitant and shall raise a crop of corn the present year at some station or place convenient to the general settlement in this country. But it is fully to be understood that those who are actually at this time inhabitants of this country shall not be debarred of their choice or claim on account of the right of any such absent or returning person or persons.

It is further proposed and agreed that no claim or title to any lands whatsoever shall be set up by any person in consequence of any mark, or former improvement, unless the same be entered with the entry taker within twenty days from the date of this association and agreement. And that when any person hereafter shall mark or improve land or lands for himself, such mark or improvement shall not avail him, or be deemed an evidence of prior right, unless the same be entered with the entry taker in thirty days from the time of such mark or improvement. No other person shall be entitled to such land so as aforesaid to be reserved in consequence of any purchase, gift, or otherwise.

If the entry taker to be appointed shall neglect or refuse to perform his duty, or be found by the said judges or a majority of them to have acted fraudulently to the prejudice of any person whatsoever, such entry taker shall be immediately removed from his office and the book taken out of his possession by the said judges, until another shall be appointed to act in his room.

As often as the people in general are dissatisfied with the doings of the judges or triers, so to be chosen, they may call a new election at any of the said stations and elect others to act in their stead, having due respect to the number now agreed to be elected at each station, which persons so to be chosen shall have the same power with those in whose room or place they are or may be chosen to act.

As no consideration money for the lands on Cumberland River within the claim of the said Richard Henderson and Company, which is the subject of this association, is demanded or expected by the said company until a satisfactory and indisputable title can be made, we think it reasonable and just that the £26 13s. 4d., current money, per hundred acres, the price proposed by the said Richard Henderson, shall be paid according to the value of money on the 1st day of January last, being the time when the price was made public, and settlement was encouraged thereon by said Henderson. Richard Henderson on his part does hereby agree that, in case of the rise or appreciation of money, an abatement shall be made in the sum according to its raised or appreciated value.

When any person shall remove to this country with intent to become an inhabitant and shall depart this life, either by violence or in the natural way, before he shall have performed the requisites necessary to obtain lands, the child or children of such deceased person shall be entitled in his or her room to such quantity of land as such person would have been entitled to in case he or she had lived to obtain a grant in their own name. And if such death be occasioned by the Indians, the said Henderson does promise and agree that the child or children shall have as much as amounts to their headrights gratis, surveyors' and other incidental fees excepted.

Whereas from our remote situation and want of proper offices for the administration of justice, no regular proceedings at law can be had for the punishment of offenses and attainment of right, it is therefore agreed that until we can be relieved by government from the many evils and inconveniences arising therefrom, the judges or triers to be appointed as before directed, when qualified, shall be and are hereby declared a proper court or jurisdiction for the recovery of any debt or damages; or where the cause of action or complaint has arisen or hereafter shall commence for anything done or to be done among ourselves within this, our settlement on Cumberland aforesaid or in our passage hither; where the laws of our country could not be executed or damages repaired in any other way, that is to say, in all cases where the debt or damages or demand does or shall not exceed $100. Any three of the said judges or triers shall be competent to make a court and finally decide the matter in controversy. But if for a larger sum, and either party shall be dissatisfied with the judgement or decision of such court, they may have an appeal to the whole twelve judges or triers. In which case, nine members shall be deemed a full court whose decision, if seven agree in one opinion upon the matter in dispute, shall be final and their judgment carried into execution in such manner and by such person or persons as they may appoint. The said courts respectively shall have full power to tax such costs as they may think just and reasonable, to be levied or collected with the debt or damages so to be awarded.

It is further agreed that a majority of the said judges, triers, or general arbitrators shall have power to punish in their discretion, having respect to the laws of our country, all offenses against the peace, misdemeanors, and those criminal or of a capital nature, provided such court does not proceed with execution so far as to effect life or member. In case any should be brought before them whose crime is or shall be dangerous to the state or for which the benefit of clergy is taken away by law, and sufficient evidence or proof of the fact or facts can probably be made, such courts or a majority of the members shall and may order and direct him, her, or them to be safely bound and sent under a strong guard to the place where the offense was or shall be committed or where legal trial of such offense can be had. This shall accordingly be done and the reasonable expense attending the discharge of this duty ascertained by the court and paid by the inhabitants in such proportion as shall be hereafter agreed on for that purpose.

As this settlement is in its infancy, unknown to government and not included within any county in North Carolina, the state to which it belongs, so as to derive the advantages of those wholesome and salutary laws for the protection and benefits of its citizens, we find ourselves constrained from necessity to adopt this temporary method of restraining the licentious and supplying, by unanimous consent, the blessings flowing from a just and equitable government, we declare and promise that no action or complaint shall be hereafter instituted or lodged in any court of record within this state or elsewhere for anything done, or to be done, in consequence of the proceedings of the said judges or general arbitrators, to be chosen and established by this our Association.

As the well-being of this country entirely depends, under Divine Providence, on unanimity of sentiment and concurrence in measures, and as clashing interests and opinions without being under some restraint will most certainly produce confusion, discord, and almost certain ruin, we think it our duty to associate and hereby form ourselves into one society for the benefit of present and future settlers. Until the full and proper exercise of the laws of our country can be in use and the powers of government exerted among us, we do most solemnly and sacredly declare and promise to each other that we will faithfully and punctually adhere to, perform, and abide by this our Association, and will at all times, if need be, compel by our united force a due obedience to these our rules and regulations. In testimony whereof we have hereunto subscribed our names in token of our entire approbation of the measures adopted.

The following additional resolutions were adopted and entered into at Nashborough, May 13, 1780:

All young men over the age of sixteen years and able to perform militia duty shall be considered as having a full right to enter for and obtain lands in their own names as if they were of full age, and in that case not be reckoned in the family of their father, mother, or master, so as to avail them of any land on their account.

When any person shall mark or improve land or lands with intent to set up a claim thereto, such person shall write or mark in legible characters the initial letters of his name, at least, together with the day of the month and year on which he marked or improved the same at the spring or most notorious part of the land on some convenient tree, or other durable substance, in order to notify his intention to all such as may inquire or examine. In case of dispute with respect to priority of right, proof of such transaction shall be made by the oath of some indifferent witness or no advantage or benefit shall be derived from such mark or improvement. In all cases where priority of mark or occupancy cannot be ascertained according to the regulations and prescriptions herein proposed and agreed to, the oldest or first entry in the office to be opened in consequence of this Association shall have the preference and the lands granted accordingly.

It is further proposed and agreed that the entry office shall be opened at Nashborough on Friday, May 19 instant, and kept from thenceforward at the same place unless otherwise directed by any future convention of the people in general or their representatives.

The entry taker shall and may demand and receive $12 for each entry to be made in his book in manner before directed, and shall give a certificate thereof if required. He also may take the same fee for every caveat or counterclaim to any lands before entered, and in all cases where a caveat is to be tried in manner before directed, the entry book shall be laid before the said committee of judges, triers, or general arbitrators for their inspection and information. Their judgment upon the matter in dispute is to be fairly entered as before directed. The said court or committee is also to keep a fair and distinct journal or minutes of all their proceedings as well with respect to lands as to other matters which may come before them in consequence of these our resolutions.

It is also firmly agreed and resolved that no person shall be admitted to make an entry for any lands with the said entry taker or permitted to hold the same unless such person shall subscribe his name and conform to this our Association, confederacy, and general agreement, unless it be for persons who have returned home and are permitted to have lands reserved for their use until May 1 next. In which case, entries may be made for such absent persons according to the true meaning of this writing without their personal presence, but shall become utterly void if the particular person or persons for whom such entry shall be made should refuse or neglect to perform the same as soon as conveniently may be after their return and before the said May 1, 1781.

Whereas, the frequent and dangerous incursions of the Indians and almost daily massacre of some of our inhabitants renders it absolutely necessary for our safety and defense that due obedience be paid to our respective officers elected and to be elected, at the several stations or settlements, to take command of the men or militia at such fort or station.

It is further agreed and resolved that when it shall be adjudged necessary and expedient by such commanding officer to draw out the militia of any fort or station to pursue or repulse the enemy, the said officer shall have power to call out such and so many of his men as he may judge necessary. In case of disobedience he may inflict such fine as he, in his discretion, shall think just and reasonable. He also may impress the horse or horses of any person or persons whomsoever, which if lost or damaged in such service shall be paid for by the inhabitants of such fort or station in such manner and such proportion as the committee hereby appointed or a majority of them shall direct and order. But if any person shall be aggrieved or think himself unjustly used and injured by the fine or fines so imposed by his official, such person may appeal to the said judges or committee of general arbitrators who, or a majority of them, shall have power to examine the matter fully and make such order thereon as they may think just and reasonable, which decision shall be conclusive on the party complaining as well as the officer or officers inflicting such fine. The money arising from such fines shall be carefully applied for the benefit of such fort or station in such manner as the said arbitrators shall hereafter direct.

It is lastly agreed and firmly resolved that a dutiful and humble address or petition be presented by some person or persons, to be chosen by the inhabitants, to the General Assembly, giving the fullest assurance of the fidelity and attachment to the interest of our country and obedience to the laws and constitution thereof. It shall set forth that we are confident that our settlement is not within the bounds of any nation or tribe of Indians, as some of us know and all believe that they have fairly sold and received satisfaction for the lands or territories whereon we reside, and we therefore hope we may not be considered as acting against the laws of our country or the mandates of government: That we do not desire to be exempt from the ratable share of the public expense of the present war or other contingent charges of government; that we are, from our remote situation, utterly destitute of the benefit of the laws of our country, and exposed to the depredations of the Indians without any justifiable or effectual means of embodying our militia or defending ourselves against the hostile attempts of our enemy.

We pray and implore the immediate aid and protection of government by erecting a county to include our settlements and appointing proper officers for the discharge of public duty; taking into consideration our distressed situation with respect to the Indians, and granting such relief and assistance as in wisdom, justice, and humanity may be thought reasonable.

131.

James Bowdoin: The Encouragement of Knowledge

James Bowdoin of Massachusetts played as much of a part in the political life of his state as his health would allow. As a member of the General Court, president of the constitutional convention of 1779, and governor during the period of Shays's Rebellion, he helped guide Massachusetts through the revolutionary ferment to the stability of statehood under the federal Constitution. Apart from his business and political activities, Bowdoin maintained an interest in astronomy and physics. His reputation in science gained him the presidency of the American Academy of Arts and Sciences, which was founded in Boston in 1780 by a group of Harvard graduates. In this capacity he delivered the following address on November 8, 1780.

Source: *A Philosophical Discourse, Addressed to the American Academy, of Arts and Sciences, etc., etc.,* Boston, 1780.

When I consider that among the members of the Academy there are gentlemen of abilities superior to my own, especially in the walks of philosophy, I feel a consciousness that its honors might in one instance have been better placed. But if a defect of abilities could be compensated by a good will to serve its interest and promote the end of its institution, I should have the satisfaction to think myself not wholly unqualified for the station with which your suffrages have honored me.

It is in discharge of the duties of it that I appear in this place: and in the discharge of them, both at present and on future occasions, as I greatly need it, so I doubt not I shall always experience your candor — the candor which ever accompanies generous minds and is the result of the due exercise of the social affections.

The social affections in man are the principal source of his happiness; and the operation of them, as directed by his wants and other circumstances, forms his connections in society. Their first objects in the order of nature are our relations and near friends; next to these our neighbors and countrymen succeed; then the people of other countries in political connection with us; and in the last place, mankind in general. In proportion however as these objects are more remote, those affections are the less powerful.

After operating on their first objects in our family connections and carrying us to the vicinity, they are drawn forth more particularly to such individuals as discover a likeness to ourselves in genius and disposition and appear to have interests coincident with our own. The acquaintance thus begun strengthens and improves by time; and the pleasure and mutual benefits resulting from it prompt us to continue and enlarge it. These social circles increase with population and at length occasion the establishment of societies, more effectually to secure those benefits and render them permanent. But the social principle is of a nature so active and comprehensive that it leads mankind to associate in larger bodies, and to establish great communities in which, the strength and abilities of individuals being united and consolidated, each individual personally, as well as the community at large, may enjoy the security and advantages resulting from that union.

Hence have originated government and the various political connections subservient and necessary to it. Hence, amidst a variety of others of different kinds, have sprung the numerous institutions for promoting philosophical knowledge and investigating the works of nature: among which some in Europe, and in particular the Royal Academy of Sciences at Paris, and the Royal Society of London, bear a distinguished character.

Hence too the societies of a similar nature which begin to adorn America; particularly the Philosophical Society at Philadelphia, whose first essays, so ingeniously executed, are received by us as a pledge for still nobler productions. It is hoped they will excite in this new-formed society a generous ardor and emulation in the same laudable pursuits; and that, as optic glasses by collecting the solar rays do assist and strengthen the corporeal sight, so the two societies, by concentering in a proper focus the scattered rays of science, may aid and invigorate the intellectual: benefiting by their productions not only the communities in which they are respectively instituted but America and the world in general; both together resembling some copious river whose branches, after refreshing the neighboring region, unite their waters for the fertilizing a more extensive country.

The end and design of instituting this society are fully declared in the act of the legislature for its incorporation, namely,

> To promote and encourage the knowledge of the antiquities of America, and of the natural history of the country; and to determine the uses to which its various natural productions may be applied; to promote and encourage medical discoveries; mathematical disquisitions; philosophical inquiries and experiments; astronomical, meteorological, and geographical observations; and improvements in agriculture, arts, manufactures and commerce; and, in fine, to cultivate every art and science which may tend to advance the interest, honor, dignity, and happiness of a free, independent, and virtuous people.

Here is opened a wide and extensive field, which the sons of literature are invited to cultivate and improve: a field richly watered by the fountain of science, and so varied in its soils as to be adapted to every mode of cultivation. Here they will find abundant matter for the employment of their industry; and the most ample room for the exercise of their genius in its utmost power of expansion.

At that fountain they may recreate themselves, and drink of its delicious waters without the danger of intoxication; or in case of danger, contrary to the effect of some other waters, it diminishes in proportion to the largeness of the draught, as intimated in the elegant lines of a well-known poet:

A little learning is a dangerous thing:
Drink deep, or taste not the Pierian
    spring
There shallow draughts intoxicate the
    brain
And drinking largely sobers us again.

We shall now take a cursory view of some of the subjects which are to employ the inquiries and researches of this society, and which we shall notice in the order observed in the act for incorporating it, making, in our progress, a few observations that naturally result from them.

The antiquities of America are the first mentioned. A knowledge in the antiquities of a country necessarily implies a knowledge of its ancient history; and the researches into them lead directly to the sources and original of things. . . .

With respect to America, there may be many things of European extraction that come under the name and description of antiquities. So far as they relate to general laws, customs, and religion, they are, for the most part, homogeneous with what took place in the same age, and in the countries from which the first European colonists emigrated; and it is probable they may be learned, or explained, by the general or antiquarian history of those countries. These things, together with what was peculiar to those emigrants and worthy of notice, if not already recorded in American history, will, with other remains of ancient times, be proper subjects of our inquiry.

Whatever relates to the aboriginal natives of America not already noticed in history may be comprised in a very narrow compass. Their want of civilization and improvement, and in particular their total want of literature, by which the small degree of knowledge they acquired by experience might have been transmitted to succeeding generations, will justify the opinion that the present race of them, in manners and conduct, differ very little from their ancestors who lived centuries ago, excepting in some few particulars occasioned by their intercourse with foreigners. It may naturally be conjectured, therefore, that the ancient and modern history of these people, with the exception of what might regard their wars, would appear but little more than a transcript of each other; and that it would be in vain to search among them for antiquities.

It is not improbable however [that] there may be many ancient historical records and other valuable remains of antiquity, both American and European, in the possession of descendants from families which first settled America; and of other persons upon this continent. It were to be wished that gentlemen possessed, or knowing, of such remains, or of any kind of collections likely to contain such, would cause them to be examined; and if they tend to elucidate, enlarge, or correct history, or in any other way can be beneficial to the public, that they would have the goodness to communicate to this society some account of them: which, at the same time it will characterize them benefactors to the public, will entitle them to the thanks of the society.

The subject next mentioned in the act is natural history. The society are to encourage the knowledge of the natural history of the country, and to determine the uses to which its various natural productions may be applied.

Natural history is a copious subject, or rather it includes a very great variety of subjects. The several classes of animals, vegetables, minerals, and fossils — in short, everything produced by nature, whether in the earth, the sea, or air, inclusive of these, is within its department.

The knowledge of it is so necessary to the good of mankind that it has been cultivated in its several branches, perhaps more than any other part of science; and in proportion to that cultivation, the properties and qualities of things and their fitness for certain uses have been discovered. This discovery has occasioned the application of them to those uses; and those have led to others, according as the wants or the inventive faculties of man have directed him. Hence have been derived the conveniences and ornaments of life, and every improvement in the arts of living.

At first, however, at the origination of man, when it was indispensably necessary he should be supplied with the means of subsistence, before he had acquired sufficient knowledge and ability to provide for himself, his beneficent Creator, the first and the supremely great naturalist, made known to him the nature and qualities of things, and the uses to which they might be applied, so far as man's well-being required; and having provided for that, and endowed him with sufficient faculties, he was pleased to leave him and his posterity to the exercise of those faculties for the gaining a further degree in natural knowledge, in proportion to which, and to their improving it to the purposes for which it was adapted, he intended their future accommodations should be. Accordingly, in different nations, from a greater or less exertion of equal faculties, or from a happier application of them, we find a greater or less degree of natural knowledge and improvement, and a proportionable difference in their respective conveniences and accommodations. Hence, with regard to these latter, the difference between Europe and Africa; between the most improved and best accommodated of mankind and the Hottentots. But if their natural faculties are unequal, collectively taken, as probably is the case, the reason of that difference will strike us the more forcibly.

On the supposition of such inequality, it may in a great measure be accounted for by the operation of natural causes: for although before the dispersion of mankind over the earth, which their increased numbers made necessary, the human faculties, by reason of a sameness in situation and other circumstances, might in general be equal, yet in process of time an inequality would probably take place from a change of climate.

Different climates differ greatly in their degrees of heat and cold, as well as in their natural productions. The tendency of immoderate heat is to relax, unbrace, and debilitate the human frame, and thereby diminish the powers of the mind as well as body, and indispose them to exercise and application: which indisposition strengthened by the force of habit, at length becomes insurmountable. On the other hand, immoderate cold too much contracts, and gives too great a degree of rigidity to, the fibres and nervous system; and thereby making them less susceptible of quick and lively sensations, must proportionably affect the mind. Hence in both cases an inferiority of intellects. But in climates duly tempered with heat and cold, where the organs of sense and motion are in due tone, it may be expected, if this theory be true, that mankind will be capable of greater exertions both of mind and body.

It will not from hence follow that the exertions of different nations dwelling in the same latitudes and climates should be equal. For on the supposition of equality of capacity, there may be a variety of things on

James Bowdoin III, portrait by Gilbert Stuart

which their exerting it may depend — such as education, religion, government, and other circumstances, or the appearance of some happy genius to instruct and direct them; and as these should happen to differ and influence them, their exertions would be proportionably different.

By way of illustration, we may instance in what has taken place among ourselves and ask whether the people of these United States whose natural capacity, without doubt, equals that of Europeans in the same temperate climates, would in certain different circumstances have opposed the unreasonable claims of Britain upon them? Would they, if at all, have exerted themselves so vigorously against her enslaving domination, if they had not been educated in the principles of liberty; if their religion, like that of some sectaries among them, had not allowed them to make use of carnal weapons in the defense of their liberty; or if they had lived under a despotic government and believed in the doctrine of passive obedience and nonresistance? Or, lastly, if some

among them, well situated to observe the course and tendency of British policy, had not alarmed them of their danger?

If all or any of these circumstances had been different from, or contrary to, what have in fact taken place, the advantages derived from climate in reference to natural capacity had probably been lost; and the world had not been astonished at the noble and unexpected exertions we so happily made against the power of Britain: a power distinguished for its magnitude, and with which we had to contend under the pressure of the greatest difficulties and discouragements; but which, very fortunately, was not directed by the most consummate wisdom.

One ardent wish will be indulged to me on this occasion: that we may ever deserve to be possessed of freedom and independence; and by deserving them, convince our enemies that the Supreme Arbiter of the fate of nations will not suffer Britain to wrest them from us. The first of them — freedom — in a constitutional sense, while we remained connected with Britain, and until she spurned our repeated prayers to her for its restoration, was the only object of our exertions; and the latter — independence — wholly alien at that time from our inclinations, but now radicated in them, was the necessary effect of her obstinate injustice.

With respect to the Indian tribes of America and the blacks of Africa, if they descended from the same original stock, and are alike affected with the rest of mankind, they will partake of the advantages and disadvantages of climate in common with them (unless it be supposed that the unexplored cause of the difference of color may, in any measure, alter the effects of climate). If it does not alter them, and if all nations in the same latitudes, considered in the gross, have equal capacities, the difference that on comparison appears between them must be casual; arising from certain adventitious circumstances which take place in some of them and not in others; and which, as they arise, call those capacities into action and thereby occasion the difference.

If by public encouragement, or by any other means, knowledge in general, and particularly natural knowledge, be supposed equal in any two or more nations, their different modes of applying it will produce very different effects; which, taken together in each, may be equally valuable and useful. And if those effects come under the name of manufactures, they may be exchanged for each other to mutual benefit, even where the natural materials are the same in kind and quality; but where the materials differ in these respects, the greater must be the difference in those artificial productions, and the greater the benefit arising from the exchange.

The various productions, natural and artificial, of different countries, and the benefit resulting from a mutual exchange of them give rise to commerce, navigation, and their attendants; in regard of which, the balance of advantage will always be in favor of that people whose skill, industry, and cheapness of labor enable them to manufacture and export the greatest quantity of commodities, whether manufactured from the rough products of their own or of other countries. And that balance, if the government of such a people be wisely administered, will give them a national superiority in riches, influence, and prosperity, which are principal objects with the honest and well-informed politician.

The foregoing general observations and particularly those concerning man and the effects of climate, with the exception of some few of them incidentally made, come under the head and are included in the idea of natural history.

What has been said of the influence of climate agrees in part with the doctrine of the celebrated Montesquieu. So far as it differs from him, it may need apology; but it is submitted to your candor, just as it stood written before I had consulted him on that subject.

The natural productions of this country are perhaps as numerous as those of any other; but it does not appear by any publications on the subject that they have been examined to any great extent, so that our natural history is very imperfect not only in relation to such productions as we have in common with other countries but such as are peculiar to our own. It is apprehended, however, that gentlemen of ingenuity and observation have noticed and described many of them, and that their several descriptions and collections, brought into one stock, properly methodized and classed, would make a respectable figure and encourage further examinations and researches, in order to our obtaining an extensive and well-digested body of American natural history. For a purpose so beneficial in itself, and so honorary to our country, it is hoped such gentlemen will favor the academy with their descriptions and collections, and also with the result of their future researches relative to the same subject.

To these cursory observations on the subject of antiquities and natural history I must here put an end, as I shall stand in need of the remains of your patience and candor while I make a few observations of a different kind which, though not necessarily connected with the subjects that fall under the consideration of the Academy, will not be deemed impertinent or unsuitable to this occasion.

The instituting of this society, and the necessity there was that it should be preceded by such an institution as Harvard's, naturally carry us back to the early times of this country, when Harvard College was first founded.

Our worthy ancestors, knowing from their own experience the advantages of a good education, very early after their coming hither provided the means of it for their children and posterity; and that excellent man Mr. Harvard made a large and generous bequest for that purpose, in consequence of which, the college was founded; and in honor of him, and to perpetuate the remembrance of his generosity, his name was given to it. From that time to the present, it has been productive of the happiest effects; and the influence and benefit of its instruction have been widely felt. Learning and the principles of good morals have been disseminated; the arts and sciences cultivated; and a spirit of freedom and inquiry promoted and encouraged — in virtue of which the best foundations have been laid for excellence in the learned professions.

All these have operated in so forcible and extensive a manner that they have produced the other seminaries in America, established for the like noble purposes, so that our alma mater may be justly considered as the remote parent of them all. I say *our* alma mater, not merely in relation to the members of this society, individually considered, most of whom from her breasts drew the nectareous milk of science, but in relation also to the complex body, the society itself; for, by her discipline and unremitted inculcations, the way has been prepared for philosophical disquisitions, and an examen into the works of nature; without which, or some such preparative discipline, this society could not have been formed; or being formed, could not have answered the end of its institution.

At the same time we are acknowledging our obligations to our alma mater, justice demands the tribute of gratitude to her benefactors.

Foremost among these stands the Reverend Harvard; reverend by his profession, but much more so by real worth and true dignity of character. By his generous bequest and the spirit it inspired, the government was enabled to establish the college — which, by reason of the low state of the finances of the country, could not have been done without such assistance — so that he may justly be considered as the father and founder of the university; and in that character his memory may be transmitted to posterity.

In the same catalogue also, the names of Stoughton, Hollis, Holden, Hancock, Boylston, and Hearsey, whose vital part is disencumbered of its earthborn cottage, hold a distinguished place. Their noble and public-spirited benefactions, with those of other friends and encouragers of science, are at large recorded in the archives of the university; and therefore need not here be specifically enumerated.

Ye disembodied spirits, now "joined to the great majority," if ye are conscious of what is transacting in this place, and will deign to regard it, permit us to express our gratitude to you arising from a sense of the benefits already derived, and which are deriving, to individuals and the public from your institutions and benefactions.

If divinity and morality; if the knowledge of the Hebrew Scriptures, and of the Oriental and other languages; if mathematics and natural and experimental philosophy; if the medical art, the belles lettres, and literature in general are beneficial to mankind, ye have not lived in vain. Since to promote the knowledge of these has been the object of your aim in those institutions; and your aim has been crowned with the most happy and extensive success. This has insured to you, at least in this country, universal approbation; and your names will be remembered with honor so long as literature shall be esteemed or any vestige of it remain here.

Though wrapped in the shroud of death be your mortal part, ye still live, and through successive generations may ye continue to live in the grateful breasts of your lettered sons. Consecrated to fame, and borne on its strongest pinions, may your memory reach to the remotest ages, expanding as it flies. And when ages cease to roll; when all things shall be engulfed in vast eternity; when eternity itself shall be absorbed in the self-existence of the Deity, may ye be blessed, as we humbly trust ye now are supremely blessed, with the approbation of Him who gave you the means and the will to do good. In fine, may your virtues and excellent example, by inspiring imitation procure such benefactions to Harvard College as to make it, in the most proper and extensive sense, a university.

With respect to its surviving benefactors, I shall not attempt to name or characterize them, as the doing it might offend their delicacy, or savor of adulation. They will, however, have the pleasing satisfaction to reflect that the eulogium on the similar virtues of others is a eulogium on their own, and a consciousness of merit will compel them, without hazarding the charge of a vainglorious appropriation, to apply it to themselves.

To have said thus much on the subject of the college will not on this occasion be deemed impertinent, as the instituting of it was not merely consistent with the forming such a society as ours, but necessary to precede it; and as the old institution may with propriety be reputed the genuine parent of the new one. Such is the connection between them, and such the dependence of this upon the other, that as most of its present members are sons of Harvard, so its future vernacular members will probably, for the most part, be supplied from the same stock; at least so long as Harvard's sons shall continue to be distinguished for scientific accomplishments, which, it is fervently hoped, will be as long as science, or any trait of it, remains in the world, or as long as nature, the great subject of it, endures.

Derived from such a parentage, and animated by the noble example of other philosophical institutions, may this society contribute its full share to the common stock of knowledge, and endeavor by the most generous exertions to answer the valuable purposes of its institution.

"Rapt into future time," and anticipating the history of our country, methinks I read in the admired pages of some American Livy or Thucydides to the following effect:

A century is now elapsed since the commencement of American independence. What led to it, and the remarkable events of the war which preceded and followed it, have been already related in the course of this history.

It was not to be expected that our ancestors, involved as they were in a civil war made peculiarly calamitous by British humanity, could give any attention to literature and the sciences; but, superior to their distresses and animated by the generous principles which liberty and independence inspire, they instituted the excellent society called the American Academy of Arts and Sciences.

This society formed itself on the plan of the philosophical societies in Europe, adopting such rules and principles of conduct as were best suited to answer the end of its institution. Among others, they laid it down as a fundamental principle that, as true physics must be founded on experiments, so all their inquiries should, as far as possible, be carried on and directed by them. This method was strongly recommended by Sir Francis Bacon, "a genius born to embrace the whole compass of science, and justly styled the first great reformer of philosophy." It was adopted by succeeding philosophers, and particularly by the immortal Newton, whose system of philosophy, founded on the laws of nature, will for that reason be as durable as nature itself.

Taking these great characters for their guide, and influenced by their illustrious example, they proceeded on fact and observation, and did not admit of any reasonings or deductions but such as clearly resulted from them. This has been the uniform practice of the society whose members, from time to time, having been chosen from men of every country, from every class and profession, without any other distinction than was dictated by the dignity of their characters, by their morality, good sense, and professional abilities. We find in the printed transactions of the society the best compositions on every subject within the line of their department. We find in those transactions new facts, new observations and discoveries (or old ones placed in a new light and new deductions made from them).

They have particularly attended to such subjects as respected the growth, population, and improvement of their country, in which they have so happily succeeded that we now see agriculture, manufactures, navigation, and commerce in a high degree of cultivation, and all of them making swift advances in improvement as population increases. In short, they have, agreeably to the declared end of their institution, "cultivated every art and science which might tend to advance the interest and honor of their country, the dignity and happiness of a free, independent, and virtuous people."

This is demonstrably evident from the numerous volumes the society have published of their transactions. These volumes are a noble collection of useful knowledge; and considered together in their miscellaneous state, strike the mind with a splendor resembling the galaxy in the heavens, derived from the combined light of countless myriads of constellations; and like that too, when the several corresponding parts are viewed in their proper connection they appear to be parts of a whole, and to constitute the most useful systems — systems distinguished by their beauty, regularity, and proportion.

Thus far our historian.

May this prophetic history be realized by fact, and may the transactions of this society justify the future historian in giving it a character like the one just delineated; or rather, a character deservedly more exalted.

In the meantime, as the society is formed on the most liberal principles, and is of no sect or party in philosophy, it wide extends its arms to embrace the sons of science of every denomination and wheresoever found; and with the warmth of fraternal affection invites them to a philosophical correspondence. And they may be assured, their communications will be esteemed a favor, and duly acknowledged by the society.

I shall close this discourse with a short reflection resulting from one of the subjects we have been considering.

When we contemplate the works of nature, animate and inanimate, connected with our earth [and] observe the immense number and variety of them; their exquisite beauty and contrivance, and the uses to which they are adapted; when we raise our view to the heavens and behold the beauteous and astonishing scenes they present to us — unnumbered worlds revolving in the immeasurable expanse, systems beyond systems composing one boundless universe, and all of them, if we may argue from analogy, peopled with an endless variety of inhabitants; when we contemplate these works of nature, which no human eloquence can adequately describe, they force upon us the idea of a Supreme Mind, the consummately perfect author of them.

That universal spirit, which informs,
Pervades, and actuates the wondrous
    whole.

In compare with whom his works, great and stupendous as they are, are nothing, less than nothing, and vanity. But — though annihilated by the comparison, yet — viewed in themselves, they powerfully persuade us to exclaim, in the rapturous and sublime language of inspiration, "Great and marvellous are Thy works, Lord God Almighty, in wisdom hast Thou made them all."

132.

On the Formation of New States

The original Crown charters by which the colonies were created failed in many cases to set western boundaries to their territories, which in theory thus extended indefinitely toward the Mississippi River, and even beyond it. The potential of these western regions was early apparent to provincial entrepreneurs, so the Proclamation of 1763 that closed the country west of the Appalachians to colonial settlement was greatly resented, and had much to do with creating the movement toward independence. After independence was achieved, or at least announced, the states had to clarify their western claims, which overlapped and were otherwise conflicting. There was general sentiment, particularly among those states without such claims, that they should all be ceded to the central government, which could then decide how to administer the vast expanse of land involved. As a result, and in anticipation of this cession, the Continental Congress on October 10, 1780, passed the following resolution indicating the policy it would follow toward any territory placed in its charge.

Source; *Journals*, III: "Tuesday, October 10, 1780."

Resolved, that the unappropriated lands that may be ceded or relinquished to the United States by any particular states, pursuant to the recommendation of Congress on the 6th day of September last, shall be disposed of for the common benefit of the United States and be settled and formed into distinct republican states which shall become members of the federal Union, and shall have the same rights of sovereignty, freedom, and independence as the other states.

That each state which shall be so formed shall contain a suitable extent of territory, not less than 100 nor more than 150 miles square, or as near thereto as circumstances will admit.

That the necessary and reasonable expenses which any particular state shall have incurred since the commencement of the present war, in subduing any of the British posts or in maintaining forts or garrisons within and for the defense, or in acquiring any part of the territory that may be ceded or relinquished to the United States, shall be reimbursed.

That the said lands shall be granted and settled at such times and under such regulations as shall hereafter be agreed on by the United States in Congress assembled, or any nine or more of them.

133.

Thomas Pownall: The New Relation Between the Old and the New World

Thomas Pownall, former governor of Massachusetts and member of Parliament since 1767, had considerable experience in administering colonial affairs. The Revolutionary War led him to survey the policy that he felt the European powers should adopt in their commercial and political relations with the new nation. Pownall wrote a tract in July of 1780, entitled A Memorial Most Humbly Addressed to the Sovereigns of Europe. *Pownall did not permit his name to appear on the title page, but he used so many quotations from his earlier work,* The Administration of the Colonies, *that its authorship was easily recognized. The editor of the* Monthly Review *lauded the work as a scholarly presentation by a competent authority, even though the authorship was not known at the time.*

Source: *A Memorial Most Humbly Addressed to the Sovereigns of Europe on the Present State of Affairs, Between the Old and New World,* 2nd edition, London, 1780, pp. 4-71.

North America is *de facto* an independent power which has taken its equal station with other powers, and must be so *de jure.* The politicians of the governments of Europe may reason or negotiate upon this idea, as a matter *sub lite* [under consideration]. The powers of those governments may fight about it as a new power coming into establishment; such negotiations and such wars are of no consequence either to the right or the fact. It would be just as wise, and just as effectual, if they were to go to war to decide or set on foot negotiations to settle to whom for the future the sovereignty of the moon should belong. The moon has been long common to them all, and they may all in their turns profit of her reflected light.

The independence of America is fixed as fate; she is mistress of her own fortune, knows that she is so, and will actuate that power which she feels she has so as to establish her own system and to change the system of Europe.

I will not lose time, in a useless waste of words, by attempting to prove the existence of this fact. The rapid progress of events at this crisis will not wait for such trifling. The only thing which can be useful to the world is to examine what the precise change of system is; what will be the general consequence of such change; and with what spirit and by what conduct the advancing state of things should be met.

If the powers of Europe will view the state of things *as they do really exist,* and will treat them *as being what they are,* the lives of thousands may be spared; the happiness of millions may be secured; and the peace of the whole world preserved. If they will not, they will be plunged into a sea of troubles, a sea of blood, fathomless and boundless. The war that has begun to rage between Britain, France, and Spain, which is almost gorged between Britain and America, will extend itself to all the maritime, and most likely, afterwards, to all the inland powers of Europe; and like the Thirty Years' War of the 16th and 17th centuries, will not end but as that did — by a new and general resettlement of powers and interests, according to the new spirit of the new system which has taken place.

Why may not all this be done by a congress of all the powers before as well as after war? If the powers of the present world fought for dominion by extirpation, then war is the proper engine; but if they war in order to treat for settlements of power, as has been long the system of Europe, then is war a wanton, clumsy, useless cruelty. . . .

There is nowhere in the European part of the Old World such a greatness of interwoven and combined interest, communicating through such largeness of territory, as that in North America, possessed and actuated by the English nation. The northern and southern parts of Europe are possessed by different nations, actuated by different spirits, and conducted under very different systems. Instead of actuating an intercommunion by an attractive [system], their intercourse is at perpetual variance under a repellent principle; their communion also is obstructed by the difficulties of intercourse, both over land and through the seas. They are, moreover, cut off, as it were, in the middle by other intervening nations, whose principles and systems are alike repellent and obstructive of free communion.

On the contrary, when the site and circumstances of the large extended territories of North America are examined, one finds everything united in it which forms greatness of dominions, *amplitude and growth of state.*

The nature of the coast and of the winds upon that coast is such as renders marine navigation, from one end of its extent to the other, a perpetually moving intercourse of communion; and the nature of the rivers, which open (where marine navigation ends) an inland navigation which, with short interruptions, carries on a circulation throughout the whole, renders such inland navigation but a further process of that communion — all which becomes, as it were, a one vital principle of life, extended through a one organized being.

While the country, by the *capability* of this natural communion, becomes thus united at its root, its largeness of territory, expanded through such a variety of climates, produces, upon this communion, everything that nature requires, that luxury loves to abound in, or that power can use as an instrument of its activity. All those things which the different nations in Europe (under every difficulty that a defect of natural communion, under every obstruction that an artificial and perverted system threw in their way) barter for in the Old World are here in the New World possessed, under an uninterrupted natural communion, by an unobstructed navigation, under a universal freedom of commerce, by one nation.

The naval stores, the timber, the hemp, the fisheries, the salted provisions of the North; the tobacco, rice, cotton, silk, indigo, finer fruits, and perhaps, in no very distant period, the wines, the resin and tar of the South, form the reciprocation of wants and supplies of each respectively. The bread-corn, the flour, the produce of agriculture in every form of farming, and the several increasing articles of manufactures which the middle colonies produce, not only fill up the communion but complete its system. They unite those parts which were before connected, and organize (as I have said) the several parts into a one whole. . . .

In this New World we see all the inhabitants not only free but allowing a universal naturalization to all who wish to be so; and an uncontrolled liberty of using any mode of life they choose, or any means of getting a livelihood that their talents lead them to. Free of all restraints which take the property of themselves out of their own hands, their souls are their own, and their reason; they are their own masters, and they act; their labor is employed on their own property, and what they produce is their own. In a country like this, where every man has the full and free exertion of his powers, where every man may acquire any share of the good things thereof, or of interest and power which his spirit can work him up to — there, an unabated application of the powers of individuals and a perpetual struggle of their spirits sharpens their wits and gives constant training to the mind.

The acquirement of information in things and business which becomes necessary to this mode of life gives the mind, thus sharpened and thus exercised, a turn of inquiry and investigation which forms a *character peculiar to these people*, which is not to be met with, nor ever did exist in any other to the same degree, unless in some of the ancient republics, where the people were under the same predicament. This turn of character, which in the ordinary occurrences of life is called "inquisitiveness," and which, when exerted about trifles, goes even to a degree of ridicule in many instances, is yet, in matters of business and commerce, a most useful and efficient talent. Whoever knows these people and has viewed them in this light will consider them as *animated in this New World* (if I may so express myself) *with the spirit of the new philosophy*. Their system of life is a course of experiments; and, standing on that high ground of improvement up to which the most enlightened parts of Europe have advanced, like eaglets they commence the first efforts of their pinions from a towering advantage.

Nothing in the Old World is less regarded than a poor man's wisdom; and yet a rich man's wisdom is generally naught but the impression of what others teach him.

On the other hand, the poor man's wisdom is not learning but knowledge of his own acquiring and picking up, and founded upon fact and nature by simple experience. In America, the wisdom and not the man is attended to; and *America is peculiarly a poor man's country.* Everything in this wilderness of woods being totally different from an Old World, almost worn out; and every person here far removed from the habits, example, and perversion, or obstruction, of those who assume the power of directing them — the settlers reason not from what they hear but from what they see and feel. They move not but as nature calls forth their activity, nor fix a step but where use marks the ground, and take the direction of their courses by that line only, where truth and nature lead hand in hand. They find themselves at liberty to follow what mode they like; they feel that they can venture to try experiments, and that the advantages of their discoveries are their own. They, therefore, try what the soil claims, what the climate permits, and what both will produce and sustain to the greatest advantage. Advancing in this line of labor *by such a spirit of induction*, they have brought forward into culture an abundant produce, more than any other nation of the Old World ever did or could. . . .

When the field of agriculture shall be filled with husbandmen, and the classes of handicrafts fully stocked — as there are here no laws that frame conditions on which a man is to become entitled to exercise this or that trade, or by which he is excluded from exercising the one or the other, in this or that place; as there are here no laws that prescribe the manner in which, and the prices at which, he is to work, or that lock him up in that trade which it has been his misfortune to have attached himself to, although, while he is starving in that, he could, in some other line of business which his circumstances point out and his talents lead him to be useful to the public, and maintain himself; as there are none of those oppressing, obstructing, dead-doing laws here, the moment that the progress of civilization, carried thus on in its natural course, is ripe for it — the branch of manufactures will take its shoot and will grow and increase with an astonishing exuberancy.

Although the civilizing activity of America does not, by artificial and false helps contrary to the natural course of things, inconsistent with, and checking the first applications of, its natural labor, and before the community is ripe for such endeavor, attempt to force the establishment of manufactures; yet following, as use and experience lead, the natural progress of improvement, it is every year producing a surplus profit; which surplus, as it enters again into the circulation of productive employment, creates an accumulating, accelerated, progressive series of surpluses. *With these accumulated surpluses* of the produce of the earth and seas, *and not with manufactures*, the Americans carry on their *commercial* exertions. Their fish, wheat, flour, rice, tobacco, indigo, livestock, barrel pork and beef (some of these articles being peculiar to the country and staple commodities) form the exports of their commerce. This has given them a direct trade to Europe; and, with some additional articles, a circuitous trade to Africa and the West Indies.

The same ingenuity of mechanic handicraft, which arises concomitant with agriculture, does here also rise concomitant with commerce and is exerted in shipbuilding. It is carried on not only to serve all the purposes of their own carriage, and that of the West Indies in part, but to an extent of sale, so as to supply a great part of the shipping of Britain. And, further, if it continues to advance with the same progress, it will supply a great part of the trade of Europe, also, with shipping, at cheaper rates than they can anywhere, or by any means, supply themselves.

Thus, their commerce, although subsisting (while they were subordinate provinces) under various restrictions, by its advancing progress in shipbuilding has been striking deep root, and is now shot forth an *active commerce*, growing into *amplitude of state* and great power.

Stating the ground on which an objection is made to this description of the improving commerce of America will open to view another extraordinary source of *amplitude and growth of state*. It will be said that the fact of the balance of trade being at all times, and in every channel, finally against America, so as to draw all the gold and silver it can collect from it, is but a damning circumstance of its progressive advance in commerce and opulence. . . .

North America has advanced, and is every day advancing, to growth of state, with a steady and continually accelerating motion, of which there has never yet been any example in Europe. . . .

When one looks to the progressive *population* which this fostering happiness does, of course, produce, one cannot but see, in North America, that God's first blessing, "Be fruitful and multiply; replenish the earth and subdue it," has operated in full manifestation of His will. In Europe, on the contrary, where a wretched, selfish, self-obstructing policy has rendered barren not only fruitful countries but even the womb itself; one may say, in melancholy truth, that the first curse, "I will greatly multiply thy sorrow in procreation; in sorrow shalt thou bring forth children," seems to have been executed in judgment. . . . In North America, children are a blessing, are riches and strength to the parents; and *happy is every man that has his quiver full of them.* . . .

Let us here view this world . . . now separated and fallen off from that vital union by which it was once an organized member of the English Empire. Let us view it *as it now is* — AN INDEPENDENT STATE *that has taken its equal station amid the nations of the earth* — as an empire, the spirit of whose government extends from the center to its extreme parts, exactly in proportion as the will of those parts does reciprocally unite in that center. Here we shall find (as has always been found) "That universal participation of council creates reciprocation of universal obedience. The seat of government will be well informed of the state and condition of the remote and extreme parts; and the remote and extreme parts, by participation in the legislature, will from self-consciousness, be informed and satisfied in the reasons and necessity of the measures of government. These parts will consider themselves as acting in every grant that is made and in every tax which is imposed. This consideration alone will give efficacy to government, and will create that *consensus obedientium* on which only the permanent power of the imperium of a state can be founded. This will give extension and stability of empire as far as it can extend its dominions."

This might have been, indeed, the spirit of the British Empire, America being a part of it. *This is the spirit* of the government of the new empire of America, Great Britain being no part of it. It is a vitality liable, indeed, to many disorders, many dangerous diseases; but it is young and strong, and will struggle, by the vigor of internal healing principles of life, against those evils and surmount them. Like the infant Hercules, it will strangle these serpents in its cradle. Its strength will grow with its years, and it will establish its constitution, and perfect adultness in growth of state.

To this greatness of empire it will certainly arise. That it is removed 3,000 miles distant from its enemy; that it lies on another side of the globe where it has no enemy; that it is earthborn and like a giant ready to run its course are not alone the grounds and reasons on which a speculatist may pronounce this. The fostering care with which the rival powers of Europe will nurse it, ensures its establishment beyond all doubt or danger.

Where a state is founded on such amplitude of base as the union of territory in this New World forms, whose communion is actuated by such a spirit of civilization; where all is enterprise and experiment; where agriculture, led by this spirit, has made discoveries in so many new and peculiar articles of culture, and has carried the ordinary produce of bread-corn to a degree that has wrought it to a staple export for the supply of the Old World; whose fisheries are mines producing more solid riches to those who work them than all the silver of Potosi; where experimental application of the understanding as well as labor to the several branches of the mechanics has invented so many new and ingenious improvements; where the arts and sciences, legislation and politics are soaring, with a strong and extended pinion, to such heights of philosophic induction; where, under this blessedness, population has multiplied like the seeds of the harvest; where the strength of these numbers, taking a military form, "shall lift up itself as a young lion"; where trade, of a most extensive orbit circulated in its own shipping, has wrought up this effort of the community to an *active commerce;* where all these powers unite and take the form of establishment of empire — I may suppose that I cannot err, nor give offense to the greatest power in Europe, when, upon a comparison of the state of mankind and of the states of those powers in Europe with that of America, I venture to suggest to their contemplation that America is growing too large for any government in Europe to govern as subordinate; that the government of North America is too firmly fixed in the hands of its own community to be either directed by other hands or taken out of the hands in which it is; and that the power in men and arms (be they contemned or contemptible, as the wisdom of Europe may suppose) is too much to be forced at the distance of 3,000 miles.

1781

134.

The Articles of Confederation

On June 7, 1776, Richard Henry Lee moved that Congress appoint a committee to draw up articles of confederation among the several states — as they would soon be if his resolution for independence was adopted. One member of each state was chosen for this committee, which on July 12 presented a plan of union drafted by John Dickinson of Pennsylvania. Dickinson's plan was much debated, and not until November 1777 was it adopted in greatly revised form. It did not go into effect until 1781, since the ratification of all the states was required for its adoption. It has become as common to defend the Articles as formerly it was to malign them. Certainly they did not create, nor could any form of government have easily cured, the postwar economic depression that beset the former colonies. The trouble was that the Confederation which the Articles established was not a federation, though it was a good deal more, at least on paper, than a mere league between the states. It had no control over taxation and trade, it lacked both a federal executive and a federal judiciary, and it was entirely without sanctions by which the Congress could enforce its will. The result was that relations within the Confederation were essentially international, while at the same time the states were without the resources to function as independent sovereignties. Such an arrangement could not last indefinitely; in fact, it was superseded within eight years by the government set up by the Constitution.

Source: Poore, 2nd edition, I, pp. 7-12.

Articles of Confederation and Perpetual Union Between the States of New Hampshire, Massachusetts Bay, Rhode Island and Providence Plantations, Connecticut, New York, New Jersey, Pennsylvania, Delaware, Maryland, Virginia, North Carolina, South Carolina, and Georgia.

Article I. The style of this confederacy shall be "The United States of America."

Article II. Each state retains its sovereignty, freedom, and independence, and every power, jurisdiction, and right which is not by this confederation expressly delegated to the United States in Congress assembled.

Article III. The said states hereby severally enter into a firm league of friendship with each other, for their common defense, the security of their liberties, and their mutual and general welfare, binding themselves to assist each other against all force offered to, or attacks made upon them, or any of them, on account of religion, sovereignty, trade, or any other pretense whatever.

Article IV. The better to secure and perpetuate mutual friendship and intercourse among the people of the different states in this union, the free inhabitants of each of these states, paupers, vagabonds, and fugitives from justice excepted, shall be entitled to all privileges and immunities of free citizens in the several states; and the people of each state shall have free ingress and regress to and from any other state and shall enjoy therein all the privileges of trade and commerce, subject to the same duties, impositions, and restrictions as the inhabitants thereof respectively, provided that such restrictions shall not extend so far as to prevent the removal of property imported into any state, to any other state of which the owner is an inhabitant; provided also that no imposition, duties, or restriction shall be laid by any state on the property of the United States, or either of them.

If any person guilty of or charged with treason, felony, or other high misdemeanor in any state shall flee from justice, and be found in any of the United States, he shall, upon demand of the governor or executive power of the state from which he fled, be delivered up and removed to the state having jurisdiction of his offense.

Full faith and credit shall be given in each of these states to the records, acts, and judicial proceedings of the courts and magistrates of every other state.

Article V. For the more convenient management of the general interests of the United States, delegates shall be annually appointed in such manner as the legislature of each state shall direct, to meet in Congress on the first Monday in November, in every year, with a power reserved to each state to recall its delegates, or any of them, at any time within the year and to send others in their stead for the remainder of the year.

No state shall be represented in Congress by less than two nor by more than seven members; and no person shall be capable of being a delegate for more than three years in any term of six years; nor shall any person, being a delegate, be capable of holding any office under the United States for which he, or another for his benefit, receives any salary, fees, or emolument of any kind.

Each state shall maintain its own delegates in a meeting of the states and while they act as members of the Committee of the States.

In determining questions in the United States in Congress assembled, each state shall have one vote.

Freedom of speech and debate in Congress shall not be impeached or questioned in any court or place out of Congress, and the members of Congress shall be protected in their persons from arrests and imprisonments during the time of their going to and from, and attendance on, Congress, except for treason, felony, or breach of the peace.

Article VI. No state, without the consent of the United States in Congress assembled, shall send any embassy to, or receive any embassy from, or enter into any conference, agreement, alliance, or treaty with any king, prince, or state; nor shall any person holding any office of profit or trust under the United States, or any of them, accept of any present, emolument, office, or title of any kind whatever from any king, prince, or foreign state; nor shall the United States in Congress assembled, or any of them, grant any title of nobility.

No two or more states shall enter into any treaty, confederation, or alliance whatever between them without the consent of the United States in Congress assembled, specifying accurately the purposes for which the same is to be entered into and how long it shall continue.

No state shall lay any imposts or duties which may interfere with any stipulations in treaties entered into by the United States in Congress assembled with any king, prince, or state, in pursuance of any treaties already proposed by Congress, to the courts of France and Spain.

No vessels of war shall be kept up in time of peace by any state except such number only as shall be deemed necessary by the United States in Congress assembled for the defense of such state or its trade; nor shall any body of forces be kept up by any state in time of peace except such number only as in the judgment of the United States in Congress assembled shall be deemed requisite to garrison the forts necessary for the defense of such state; but every state shall always keep up a well-regulated and disciplined militia, sufficiently armed and accoutered, and shall provide and constantly have ready for use, in public stores, a due number of field pieces and tents and a proper quantity of arms, ammunition, and camp equipage.

No state shall engage in any war without the consent of the United States in Congress assembled unless such state be actually invaded by enemies, or shall have received certain advice of a resolution being formed by some nation of Indians to invade such state, and the danger is so imminent as not to admit of a delay till the United States in Congress assembled can be consulted; nor shall any state grant commissions to any ships or vessels of war, nor letters of marque or reprisal, except it be after a declaration of war by the United States in Congress assembled, and then only against the kingdom or state and the subjects thereof against which war has been so declared and under such regulations as shall be established by the United States in Congress

assembled, unless such state be infested by pirates, in which case vessels of war may be fitted out for that occasion and kept so long as the danger shall continue or until the United States in Congress assembled shall determine otherwise.

Article VII. When land forces are raised by any state for the common defense, all officers of or under the rank of colonel shall be appointed by the legislature of each state respectively, by whom such forces shall be raised, or in such manner as such state shall direct, and all vacancies shall be filled up by the state which first made the appointment.

Article VIII. All charges of war and all other expenses that shall be incurred for the common defense or general welfare, and allowed by the United States in Congress assembled, shall be defrayed out of a common treasury, which shall be supplied by the several states in proportion to the value of all land within each state, granted to or surveyed for any person, as such land the buildings and improvements thereon shall be estimated according to such mode as the United States in Congress assembled shall from time to time direct and appoint. The taxes for paying that proportion shall be laid and levied by the authority and direction of the legislatures of the several states within the time agreed upon by the United States in Congress assembled.

Article IX. The United States in Congress assembled shall have the sole and exclusive right and power of determining on peace and war, except in the cases mentioned in the sixth article — of sending and receiving ambassadors — entering into treaties and alliances, provided that no treaty of commerce shall be made whereby the legislative power of the respective states shall be restrained from imposing such imposts and duties on foreigners as their own people are subjected to or from prohibiting the exportation or importation of any species of goods or commodities whatsoever — of establishing rules for deciding in all cases what captures on land or water shall be legal, and in what manner prizes taken by land or naval forces in the service of the United States shall be divided or appropriated — of granting letters of marque and reprisal in times of peace — appointing courts for the trial of piracies and felonies committed on the high seas and establishing courts for receiving and determining finally appeals in all cases of captures, provided that no member of Congress shall be appointed a judge of any of the said courts.

The United States in Congress assembled shall also be the last resort on appeal in all disputes and difference now subsisting or that hereafter may arise between two or more states concerning boundary, jurisdiction, or any other cause whatever, which authority shall always be exercised in the manner following: Whenever the legislative or executive authority or lawful agent of any state in controversy with another shall present a petition to Congress stating the matter in question and praying for a hearing, notice thereof shall be given by order of Congress to the legislative or executive authority of the other state in controversy, and a day assigned for the appearance of the parties by their lawful agents, who shall then be directed to appoint, by joint consent, commissioners or judges to constitute a court for hearing and determining the matter in question. But if they cannot agree, Congress shall name three persons out of each of the United States, and from the list of such persons each party shall alternately strike out one, the petitioners beginning, until the number shall be reduced to thirteen. And from that number not less than seven nor more than nine names, as Congress shall direct, shall in the presence of Congress be drawn out by lot, and the persons whose names shall be so drawn, or any five of them, shall be commissioners or judges to hear and finally determine the controversy, so always as a major part of the judges who shall hear the cause shall

agree in the determination. . . .

If either party shall neglect to attend at the day appointed, without showing reasons, which Congress shall judge sufficient, or being present shall refuse to strike, the Congress shall proceed to nominate three persons out of each state, and the secretary of Congress shall strike in behalf of such party absent or refusing. . . . The judgment and sentence of the court to be appointed, in the manner before prescribed, shall be final and conclusive. . . . If any of the parties shall refuse to submit to the authority of such court, or to appear or defend their claim or cause, the court shall nevertheless proceed to pronounce sentence or judgment, which shall in like manner be final and decisive, the judgment or sentence and other proceedings being in either case transmitted to Congress and lodged among the acts of Congress for the security of the parties concerned. Provided that every commissioner, before he sits in judgment, shall take an oath to be administered by one of the judges of the supreme or superior court of the state where the cause shall be tried, "well and truly to hear and determine the matter in question, according to the best of his judgment, without favor, affection, or hope of reward": provided, also, that no state shall be deprived of territory for the benefit of the United States.

All controversies concerning the private right of soil claimed under different grants of two or more states, whose jurisdictions as they may respect such lands, and the states which passed such grants are adjusted, the said grants or either of them being at the same time claimed to have originated antecedent to such settlement of jurisdiction shall, on the petition of either party to the Congress of the United States, be finally determined as near as may be in the same manner as is before prescribed for deciding disputes respecting territorial jurisdiction between different states.

The United States in Congress assembled

shall also have the sole and exclusive right and power of regulating the alloy and value of coin struck by their own authority or by that of the respective states — fixing the standard of weights and measures throughout the United States — regulating the trade and managing all affairs with the Indians not members of any of the states, provided that the legislative right of any state within its own limits be not infringed or violated — establishing or regulating post offices from one state to another, throughout all the United States, and exacting such postage on the papers passing through the same as may be requisite to defray the expenses of the said office — appointing all officers of the land forces in the service of the United States excepting regimental officers — appointing all the officers of the naval forces, and commissioning all officers whatever in the service of the United States — making rules for the government and regulation of the said land and naval forces, and directing their operations

The United States in Congress assembled shall have authority to appoint a committee, to sit in the recess of Congress, to be denominated "A Committee of the States," and to consist of one delegate from each state; and to appoint such other committees and civil officers as may be necessary for managing the general affairs of the United States under their direction — to appoint one of their number to preside, provided that no person be allowed to serve in the office of President more than one year in any term of three years; to ascertain the necessary sums of money to be raised for the service of the United States, and to appropriate and apply the same for defraying the public expenses — to borrow money or emit bills on the credit of the United States, transmitting every half-year to the respective states an account of the sums of money so borrowed or emitted — to build and equip a navy — to agree upon the number of land forces, and to make requisitions from each state for its quota, in proportion to the number of white inhabitants in such state, which requisition shall be binding. . . .

Thereupon the legislature of each state shall appoint the regimental officers, raise the men and clothe, arm, and equip them in a soldier-like manner, at the expense of the United States; and the officers and men so clothed, armed, and equipped shall march to the place appointed and within the time agreed on by the United States in Congress assembled. But if the United States in Congress assembled shall, on consideration of circumstances, judge proper that any state should not raise men or should raise a smaller number than its quota and that any other state should raise a greater number of men than the quota thereof, such extra number shall be raised, officered, clothed, armed, and equipped in the same manner as the quota of such state, unless the legislature of such state shall judge that such extra number cannot be safely spared out of the same, in which case they shall raise, officer, clothe, arm, and equip as many of such extra number as they judge can be safely spared. And the officers and men so clothed, armed, and equipped shall march to the place appointed and within the time agreed on by the United States in Congress assembled.

The United States in Congress assembled shall never engage in a war, nor grant letters of marque and reprisal in time of peace, nor enter into any treaties or alliances, nor coin money, nor regulate the value thereof, nor ascertain the sums and expenses necessary for the defense and welfare of the United States, or any of them, nor emit bills, nor borrow money on the credit of the United States, nor appropriate money, nor agree upon the number of vessels of war to be built or purchased or the number of land or sea forces to be raised, nor appoint a commander in chief of the Army or Navy, unless nine states assent to the same;

nor shall a question on any other point, except for adjourning from day to day, be determined unless by the votes of a majority of the United States in Congress assembled.

The Congress of the United States shall have power to adjourn to any time within the year, and to any place within the United States, so that no period of adjournment be for a longer duration than the space of six months, and shall publish the journal of their proceedings monthly, except such parts thereof relating to treaties, alliances, or military operations as in their judgment require secrecy; and the yeas and nays of the delegates of each state on any question shall be entered on the journal when it is desired by any delegate; and the delegates of a state, or any of them, at his or their request, shall be furnished with a transcript of the said journal, except such parts as are above excepted, to lay before the legislatures of the several states.

Article X. The Committee of the States, or any nine of them, shall be authorized to execute, in the recess of Congress, such of the powers of Congress as the United States in Congress assembled, by the consent of nine states, shall from time to time think expedient to vest them with; provided that no power be delegated to the said committee, for the exercise of which, by the Articles of Confederation, the voice of nine states in the Congress of the United States assembled is requisite.

Article XI. Canada acceding to this Confederation, and joining in the measures of the United States, shall be admitted into and entitled to all the advantages of this union; but no other colony shall be admitted into the same unless such admission be agreed to by nine states.

Article XII. All bills of credit emitted, moneys borrowed, and debts contracted by or under the authority of Congress, before the assembling of the United States, in pursuance of the present Confederation, shall be deemed and considered as a charge against the United States, for payment and satisfaction whereof the said United States and the public faith are hereby solemnly pledged.

Article XIII. Every state shall abide by the determinations of the United States in Congress assembled on all questions which by this Confederation are submitted to them. And the Articles of this Confederation shall be inviolably observed by every state, and the union shall be perpetual; nor shall any alteration at any time hereafter be made in any of them; unless such alteration be agreed to in a Congress of the United States and be afterward confirmed by the legislatures of every state.

And whereas it has pleased the Great Governor of the world to incline the hearts of the legislatures we respectively represent in Congress to approve of, and to authorize us to ratify the said Articles of Confederation and Perpetual Union. Know ye that we the undersigned delegates, by virtue of the power and authority to us given for that purpose, do by these presents, in the name and in behalf of our respective constituents, fully and entirely ratify and confirm each and every of the said Articles of Confederation and Perpetual Union and all and singular the matters and things therein contained. And we do further solemnly plight and engage the faith of our respective constituents that they shall abide by the determinations of the United States in Congress assembled on all questions which by the said Confederation are submitted to them. And that the articles thereof shall be inviolably observed by the states we respectively represent and that the union shall be perpetual. In witness whereof we have hereunto set our hands in Congress.

135.

Thomas Rodney: First Steps Toward Peace

Between 1781 and 1788 Thomas Rodney was five times elected by the General Assembly of Delaware to membership in the Confederation Congress. On June 14, 1781, Rodney wrote a letter from Philadelphia to his brother Caesar, at that time president of Delaware. In the letter, Thomas Rodney described European attempts to negotiate a peace between America and Britain.

Source: Niles: "Thos. Rodney to C. Rodney."

You will find by the contents of this that it is a confidential letter, conveying you very important and pleasing intelligence.

Congress has received a letter from the king of France, and also otherwise officially informed by his minister here, that the empress of Russia threw out an invitation for the belligerent powers to apply for her mediation, at which the court of London eagerly caught, and mentioned the emperor of Germany as another mediator — and a congress was proposed to be opened at Vienna for the purpose of settling a general peace. The answer of the court of France was that they could send no plenipotentiaries to said congress till they had consulted their allies; but, in [that] the mediators are such respectable powers, and may be so fully relied on for justice, the king presses the United States to submit to the mediation — and that the first preliminary he will insist on, previous to any other negotiation, shall be the independence of the United States in full — and upon obtaining this, request that the states may be as moderate in all other demands as possible, that the mediating powers may thereby receive favorably impressions of our equity and justice.

The same mediating application was made to the court of Spain, and their answer was that they could not do anything but in conjunction with their ally, the king of France — so that the congress of mediation is likely to be delayed till our despatches reach France. However, the king says that if he is so pressed that he cannot decently delay sending a plenipotentiary till that time, he shall insist on the preliminary before mentioned, and then only proceed in the negotiation so as to have it in such forwardness as will not injure America against their plenipotentiaries and instructions arrived.

The king of France thinks that very equitable terms of peace may be obtained through this mediation, but urges us strongly to exert ourselves this campaign — as the wresting of the southern states out of the hands of the British will contribute greatly to lessen their demands and make them more readily incline to equitable terms of peace. . . . Our exertions ought to be quick and vigorous, lest a truce should take place. . . . To ensure the success of this mediation we ought to make the most ample and vigorous preparations for carrying on the war.

Britain made an attempt, through a Mr. Cumberland, to negotiate a separate treaty with Spain; but this has failed, though Mr. Cumberland is still at Madrid. Spain would not treat but in conjunction with France, and France cannot treat but in conjunction with America. Thus are we linked together, so that the independence of America now stands on prosperous ground, and no further doubt need to remain about it. For this much is certain — all the powers of Europe (Britain excepted) wish us to be independent.

Thus far in confidence, with this addition, that Congress have appointed Dr. Franklin, J. Adams, J. Jay, H. Laurens and Governor Jefferson plenipotentiaries for settling the peace. They first agreed to appoint but one, and Adams was appointed before I came up; they then agreed to add two more, then Jay was appointed — then Jefferson had five votes, Franklin four, and Laurens one. The states voted the same way three times.

Then I proposed to the members of Virginia and Pennsylvania that we should appoint them both, which being generally agreed to, this day was appointed for the purpose, and then Laurens was included — so the appointment now consists of five; New Hampshire, Pennsylvania, Delaware and Maryland were for Franklin, South Carolina for Laurens, and Massachusetts, Connecticut, Jersey, Virginia and North Carolina for Jefferson, Rhode Island and New York unrepresented; Georgia absent. Mr. M'Kean wanted to alter in favor of Jefferson and leave Franklin out, which, upon Georgia's coming in, would have carried him; but I would not give up Franklin, and by the manner of proposing to appoint them both, got him appointed — though this was exceedingly against the grain of several members. He will not be put at the head of the commission. His abilities, character, and influence are what will be of most use to us in Europe.

He defeated the Americans with great slaughter.
>   Inscription on the tomb of Lord Cornwallis, in Westminster Abbey. The surrender of Cornwallis at Yorktown, Oct. 17, 1781, virtually ended the Revolutionary War.

1781 -1782

136.

THOMAS JEFFERSON: Notes on the State of Virginia

In reply to a series of questions about Virginia by the Marquis de Barbé-Marbois,
secretary of the French legation in Philadelphia, Jefferson wrote Notes on the State
of Virginia *during 1781 and 1782. It contains informal essays on scientific, social,*
and political topics. Fearing a public reaction to some of its contents, Jefferson was
unwilling to publish the manuscript in America and took it with him to France in 1784.
The first edition was a French translation published anonymously in Paris in 1785.
The English edition, published in London in 1786, was the first edition to carry the
author's name.

Source: H. A. Washington, VIII, pp. 358-406

THE CONSTITUTION OF THE STATE AND ITS SEVERAL CHARTERS

IN EACH STATE SEPARATELY a new form of government was established. Of ours particularly the following are the outlines. The executive powers are lodged in the hands of a governor, chosen annually, and incapable of acting more than three years in seven. He is assisted by a council of eight members. The judiciary powers are divided among several courts, as will be hereafter explained. Legislation is exercised by two houses of assembly, the one called the House of Delegates, composed of two members from each county, chosen annually by the citizens possessing an estate for life in 100 acres of uninhabited land, or 25 acres with a house on it, or in a house or lot in some town; the other called the Senate, consisting of twenty-four members, chosen quadrennially by the same electors, who for this purpose are distributed into twenty-four districts. The concurrence of both houses is necessary to the passage of a law. They have the appointment of the governor and council, the judges of the superior courts, auditors, attorney general, treasurer, register of the land office, and delegates to Congress. As the dismemberment of the state had never had its confirmation but, on the contrary, had always been the subject of protestation and complaint, that it might never be in our own power to raise scruples on that subject or to disturb the harmony of our new Confederacy, the grants to Maryland, Pennsylvania, and the two Carolinas were ratified.

This constitution was formed when we were new and unexperienced in the science of government. It was the first, too, which was formed in the whole United States. No wonder then that time and trial have discovered very capital defects in it.

1. The majority of the men in the state who pay and fight for its support are unrepresented in the legislature, the roll of freeholders entitled to vote not including generally the half of those on the roll of the militia, or of the tax gatherers.

2. Among those who share the representation the shares are very unequal. Thus the county of Warwick, with only 100 fighting men, has an equal representation with the county of Loudon, which has 1,746. So that every man in Warwick has as much influence in the government as 17 men in Loudon. But lest it should be thought that an equal interspersion of small among large counties, through the whole state, may prevent any danger of injury to particular parts of it, we will divide it into districts, and show the proportions of land, of fighting men, and of representation in each. . . .

	Square Miles	Fighting Men	Delegates	Senators
Between the seacoast and falls of the rivers . . . . ,	11,205	19,012	71	12
Between the falls of the rivers and the Blue Ridge Mountains	18,759	18,828	46	8
Between the Blue Ridge and the Allegheny	11,911	7,673	16	2
Between the Allegheny and Ohio	79,650	4,458	16	2
Total	121,525	49,971	149	24

3. The Senate is, by its constitution, too homogenous with the House of Delegates. Being chosen by the same electors, at the same time, and out of the same subjects, the choice falls, of course, on men of the same description. The purpose of establishing different houses of legislation is to introduce the influence of different interests or different principles. Thus in Great Britain it is said their constitution relies on the House of Commons for honesty, and the Lords for wisdom; which would be a rational reliance if honesty were to be bought with money, and if wisdom were hereditary. In some of the American states the delegates and senators are so chosen, as that the first represent the persons, and the second the property, of the state. But with us, wealth and wisdom have equal chance for admission into both houses. We do not therefore derive from the separation of our legislature into two houses those benefits which a proper complication of principles is capable of producing, and those which alone can compensate the evils which may be produced by their dissensions.

4. All the powers of government, legislative, executive, and judiciary, result to the legislative body. The concentrating these in the same hands is precisely the definition of despotic government. It will be no alleviation that these powers will be exercised by a plurality of hands, and not by a single one. One hundred and seventy-three despots would surely be as oppressive as one. Let those who doubt it turn their eyes on the republic of Venice. As little will it avail us that they are chosen by ourselves. An *elective despotism* was not the government we fought for; but one which should not only be founded on free principles, but in which the powers of government should be so divided and balanced among several bodies of magistracy, as that no one could transcend their legal limits without being effectually checked and restrained by the others.

For this reason that convention, which passed the ordinance of government, laid its foundation on this basis: that the legislative, executive, and judiciary departments should be separate and distinct, so that no person should exercise the powers of more than one of them at the same time. But no barrier was provided between these several powers. The judiciary and executive members were left dependent on the legislative for their subsistence in office, and some of them for their continuance in it. If therefore the legislature assumes executive and judiciary powers, no opposition is likely to be made; nor, if made, can it be effectual; because in that case they may put their proceedings into the form of an act of assembly, which will render them obligatory on the other branches. They have accordingly, in many instances, decided rights which should have been left to judiciary controversy; and the direction of the executive, during the whole time of their session, is becoming habitual and familiar. . . .

To render these considerations the more cogent, we must observe in addition:

5. That the ordinary legislature may alter the constitution itself. On the discontinuance of assemblies, it became necessary to substitute in their place some other body, competent to the ordinary business of government, and to the calling forth the powers of the state for the maintenance of our opposition to Great Britain. Conventions were therefore introduced, consisting of two delegates from each country, meeting together and forming one house, on the plan of the former House of Burgesses, to whose places they succeeded. These were at first chosen anew for every particular session. But in March 1775, they recommended to the people to choose a convention, which should continue in office a year. This was done accordingly in April 1775, and in the July following that convention passed an ordinance for the election of delegates in the month of April annually.

It is well known that in July 1775 a separation from Great Britain and establishment of republican government had never

yet entered into any person's mind. A convention, therefore, chosen under that ordinance cannot be said to have been chosen for purposes which certainly did not exist in the minds of those who passed it. Under this ordinance, at the annual election in April 1776, a convention for the year was chosen. Independence and the establishment of a new form of government were not even yet the objects of the people at large. One extract from the pamphlet called *Common Sense* had appeared in the Virginia papers in February, and copies of the pamphlet itself had got in a few hands. But the idea had not been opened to the mass of the people in April, much less can it be said that they had made up their minds in its favor.

So that the electors of April 1776, no more than the legislators of July 1775, not thinking of independence and a permanent republic, could not mean to vest in these delegates powers of establishing them, or any authorities other than those of the ordinary legislature. So far as a temporary organization of government was necessary to render our opposition energetic, so far their organization was valid. But they received in their creation no powers but what were given to every legislature before and since. They could not therefore pass an act transcendent to the powers of other legislatures. If the present assembly pass any act, and declare it shall be irrevocable by subsequent assemblies, the declaration is merely void, and the act repealable, as other acts are.

So far, and no farther authorized, they organized the government by the ordinance entitled a constitution or form of government. It pretends to no higher authority than the other ordinances of the same session; it does not say that it shall be perpetual; that it shall be unalterable by other legislatures; that it shall be transcendent above the powers of those who they knew would have equal power with themselves. Not only the silence of the instrument is a proof they thought it would be alterable, but their own practice also; for this very convention, meeting as a House of Delegates in general assembly with the Senate in the autumn of that year, passed acts of assembly in contradiction to their ordinance of government; and every assembly from that time to this has done the same.

I am safe therefore in the position that the constitution itself is alterable by the ordinary legislature. Though this opinion seems founded on the first elements of common sense, yet is the contrary maintained by some persons.

1. Because, say they, the conventions were vested with every power necessary to make effectual opposition to Great Britain. But, to complete this argument, they must go on and say further that effectual opposition could not be made to Great Britain without establishing a form of government perpetual and unalterable by the legislature, which is not true. An opposition which at some time or other was to come to an end could not need a perpetual institution to carry it on; and a government, amendable as its defects should be discovered, was as likely to make effectual resistance as one which should be unalterably wrong. Besides, the assemblies were as much vested with all powers requisite for resistance as the conventions were. If therefore these powers included that of modeling the form of government in the one case, they did so in the other. The assemblies then as well as the conventions may model the government; that is, they may alter the ordinance of government.

2. They urge that if the convention had meant that this instrument should be alterable, as their other ordinances were, they would have called it an ordinance; but they have called it a constitution, which *ex vi termini* [by force of the term] means "an act above the power of the ordinary legislature." I answer that *constitutio, constitutum, statutum, lex* [constitution, covenant, statute, law] are convertible terms. . . . To get rid of the magic supposed to be in the word *constitution*, let us translate it into its definition as given by those who think it above the power of the law; and let us suppose the convention, instead of saying, "We, the ordinary legislature, establish a *constitution*," had said, "We, the ordinary legislature, establish an act *above the power of the ordinary legislature*." Does not this expose the absurdity of the attempt?

3. But, say they, the people have acquiesced, and this has given it an authority superior to the laws. It is true that the people did not rebel against it; and was that a time for the people to rise in rebellion? Should a prudent acquiescence, at a critical time, be construed into a confirmation of every illegal thing done during that period? Besides, why should they rebel? At an annual election they had chosen delegates for the year, to exercise the ordinary powers of legislation, and to manage the great contest in which they were engaged. These delegates thought the contest would be best managed by an organized government. They therefore, among others, passed an ordinance of government. They did not presume to call it perpetual and unalterable. They well knew they had no power to make it so; that our choice of them had been for no such purpose, and at a time when we could have no such purpose in contemplation. Had an unalterable form of government been meditated, perhaps we should have chosen a different set of people. There was no cause then for the people to rise in rebellion. But to what dangerous lengths will this argument lead?

Did the acquiescence of the colonies under the various acts of power exercised by Great Britain in our infant state confirm these acts, and so far invest them with the authority of the people as to render them unalterable, and our present resistance wrong? On every unauthoritative exercise of power by the legislature must the people rise in rebellion, or their silence be construed into a surrender of that power to them? If so, how many rebellions should we have had already? One, certainly, for every session of assembly. The other states in the Union have been of opinion that, to render a form of government unalterable by ordinary acts of assembly, the people must delegate persons with special powers. They have accordingly chosen special conventions to form and fix their governments.

The individuals then who maintained the contrary opinion in this country should have the modesty to suppose it possible that they may be wrong and the rest of America right. But if there be only a possibility of their being wrong, if only a plausible doubt remains of the validity of the ordinance of government, is it not better to remove that doubt by placing it on a bottom which none will dispute? If they be right, we shall only have the unnecessary trouble of meeting once in convention. If they be wrong, they expose us to the hazard of having no fundamental rights at all. True it is, this is no time for deliberating on forms of government. While an enemy is within our bowels, the first object is to expel him. But when this shall be done, when peace shall be established, and leisure given us for entrenching within good forms the rights for which we have bled, let no man be found indolent enough to decline a little more trouble for placing them beyond the reach of question. If anything more be requisite to produce a conviction of the expediency of calling a convention at a proper season to fix our form of government, let it be the reflection:

That the assembly exercises a power of determining the quorum of their own body which may legislate for us. . . . When, therefore, it is considered that there is no legal obstacle to the assumption by the assembly of all the powers, legislative, executive, and judiciary, and that these may come to the hands of the smallest rag of delegation, surely the people will say — and their representatives, while yet they have honest representatives, will advise them to say — that they will not acknowledge as laws any acts not considered and assented to by the major part of their delegates.

In enumerating the defects of the constitution, it would be wrong to count among them what is only the error of particular persons. In December 1776, our circumstances being much distressed, it was proposed in the House of Delegates to create a *dictator*, invested with every power legislative, executive, and judiciary, civil and military, of life and of death, over our persons and over our properties: and in June 1781, again under calamity, the same proposition was repeated and wanted a few votes only of being passed.

One who entered into this contest from a pure love of liberty and a sense of injured rights, who determined to make every sacrifice and to meet every danger, for the reestablishment of those rights on a firm basis, who did not mean to expend his blood and substance for the wretched purpose of changing this master for that, but to place the powers of governing him in a plurality of hands of his own choice, so that the corrupt will of no one man might in future oppress him, must stand confounded and dismayed when he is told that a considerable portion of that plurality had mediated the surrender of them into a single hand, and, in lieu of a limited monarch, to deliver him over to a despotic one! How must we find his efforts and sacrifices abused and baffled, if he may still by a single vote be laid prostrate at the feet of one man!

In God's name from whence have they derived this power? . . . Is it from any principle in our new constitution, expressed or implied? Every lineament of that, expressed or implied, is in full opposition to it. Its fundamental principle is that the state shall be governed as a commonwealth. It provides a republican organization, proscribes under the name of *prerogative* the exercise of all powers undefined by the laws; places on this basis the whole system of our laws; and, by consolidating them together, chooses that they shall be left to stand or fall together, never providing for any circumstances, nor admitting that such could arise, wherein either should be suspended, no, not for a moment.

Our ancient laws expressly declare that those who are but delegates themselves shall not delegate to others powers which require judgment and integrity in their exercise. Or was this proposition moved on a supposed right in the movers of abandoning their posts in a moment of distress? The same laws forbid the abandonment of that post, even on ordinary occasions; and much more a transfer of their powers into other hands and other forms without consulting the people. They never admit the idea that these, like sheep or cattle, may be given from hand to hand without an appeal to their own will. Was it from the necessity of the case? Necessities which dissolve a government do not convey its authority to an oligarchy or a monarchy. They throw back into the hands of the people the powers they had delegated, and leave them as individuals to shift for themselves. A leader may offer, but not impose himself, nor be imposed on them. Much less can their necks be submitted to his sword, their breath to be held at his will or caprice. The necessity which should operate these tremendous effects should at least be palpable and irresistible. Yet in both instances, where it was feared, or pretended with us, it was belied by the event. It was belied, too, by the preceding experience of our sister-states, several of whom had grappled through greater difficulties without abandoning their forms of government.

When the proposition was first made, Massachusetts had found even the government of committees sufficient to carry them through an invasion. But we at the time of that proposition were under no invasion. When the second was made, there had been added to this example those of Rhode Island, New York, New Jersey, and Pennsylvania, in all of which the republican form had been found equal to the task of carrying them through the severest trials. In this state alone did there exist so little virtue that fear was to be fixed in the hearts of the people, and to become the motive of their exertions and principle of their government? The very thought alone was treason against the people; was treason against mankind in general, as riveting forever the chains which bow down their necks, by giving to their oppressors a proof, which they would have trumpeted through the universe, of the imbecility of republican government, in times of pressing danger, to shield them from harm.

Those who assume the right of giving away the reins of government, in any case, must be sure that the herd, whom they hand on to the rods and hatchet of the dictator, will lay their necks on the block when he shall nod to them. But if our assemblies supposed such a resignation in the people, I hope they mistook their character. I am of opinion that the government, instead of being braced and invigorated for greater exertions under their difficulties, would have been thrown back upon the bungling machinery of county committees for administration, till a convention could have been called, and its wheels again set into regular motion. What a cruel moment was this for creating such an embarrassment, for putting to the proof the attachment of our countrymen to republican government!

Those who meant well, of the advocates for this measure (and most of them meant well, for I know them personally, had been their fellow laborer in the common cause, and had often proved the purity of their principles) had been seduced in their judgment by the example of an ancient republic whose constitution and circumstances were fundamentally different. They had sought this precedent in the history of Rome, where alone it was to be found, and where at length, too, it had proved fatal. They had taken it from a republic rent by the most bitter factions and tumults, where the government was of a heavy-handed unfeeling aristocracy, over a people ferocious and rendered desperate by poverty and wretchedness; tumults which could not be allayed under the most trying circumstances, but by the omnipotent hand of a single despot.

Their constitution therefore allowed a temporary tyrant to be erected, under the name of a dictator; and that temporary tyrant, after a few examples, became perpetual. They misapplied this precedent to a people, mild in their dispositions, patient under their trial, united for the public liberty, and affectionate to their leaders. But if from the constitution of the Roman government there resulted to their Senate a power of submitting all their rights to the will of one man, does it follow that the assembly of Virginia have the same authority? What clause in our constitution has substituted that of Rome, by way of residuary provision, for all cases not otherwise provided for? Or if they may step *ad libitum* into any other form of government for precedents to rule us by, for what oppression may not a precedent be found in this world of the *bellum omnium in omnia* [war of all against all]?

Searching for the foundations of this proposition, I can find none which may pretend a color of right or season, but the defect before developed, that there being no barrier between the legislative, executive, and judiciary departments, the legislature may seize the whole; that having seized it, and possessing a right to fix their own quorum, they may reduce that quorum to one, whom they may call a chairman, speaker, dictator, or by any other name they please. Our situation is indeed perilous, and I hope my countrymen will be sensible of it and will apply, at a proper season, the proper remedy; which is a convention to fix the constitution, to amend its defects, to bind up the several branches of government by certain laws, which when they transgress their acts shall become nullities; to render unnecessary an appeal to the people, or in other words a rebellion, on every infraction of their rights, on the peril that their acquiescence shall be construed into an intention to surrender those rights.

THE ADMINISTRATION OF JUSTICE AND THE DESCRIPTION OF THE LAWS

ANOTHER OBJECT OF THE REVISAL is to diffuse knowledge more generally through the mass of the people. This bill proposes to lay off every county into small districts of five or six miles square, called hundreds, and in each of them to establish a school for teaching reading, writing, and arithmetic. The tutor to be supported by the hundred, and every person in it entitled to send their children three years gratis, and as much longer as they please, paying for it. These schools to be under a visitor, who is annually to choose the boy of best genius in the school, of those whose parents are too poor to give them further education, and to send him forward to one of the grammar schools, of which twenty are proposed to be erected in different parts of the country for teaching Greek, Latin, geography, and the higher branches of numerical arithmetic. Of the boys thus sent in any one year, trial is to be made at the grammar schools one or two years, and the best genius of the whole selected, and continued six years, and the residue dismissed. By this means twenty of the best geniuses will be raked from the rubbish annually, and be instructed, at the public expense, so far as the grammar schools go.

At the end of six years' instruction, one-half are to be discontinued (from among whom the grammar schools will probably be supplied with future masters); and the other half, who are to be chosen for the superiority of their parts and disposition, are to be sent and continued three years in the study of such sciences as they shall choose, at William and Mary College, the plan of which is proposed to be enlarged, as will be hereafter explained, and extended to all the useful sciences. The ultimate result of the whole scheme of education would be the teaching all the children of the state reading, writing, and common arithmetic; turning out ten annually, of superior genius, well taught in Greek, Latin, geography, and the higher branches of arithmetic; turning out ten others annually, of still superior parts, who to those branches of learning shall have added such of the sciences as their genius shall have led them to; the furnishing to the wealthier part of the people convenient schools at which their children may be educated at their own expense.

The general objects of this law are to provide an education adapted to the years, to the capacity, and the condition of every one, and directed to their freedom and happiness. Specific details were not proper for the law. These must be the business of the visitors entrusted with its execution. The first stage of this education being the schools of the hundreds wherein the great mass of the people will receive their instruction, the principal foundations of future order will be laid here. Instead, therefore, of putting the Bible and Testament into the hands of the children at an age when their judgments are not sufficiently matured for religious inquiries, their memories may here be stored with the most useful facts from Grecian, Roman, European, and American history. The first elements of morality, too, may be instilled into their minds; such as, when further developed as their judgments advance in strength, may teach them how to work out their own greatest happiness, by showing them that it does not depend on the condition of life in which chance has placed them but is always the result of a good conscience, good health, occupation and freedom in all just pursuits.

Those whom either the wealth of their parents or the adoption of the state shall destine to higher degrees of learning will go on to the grammar schools . . . there to be instructed in the languages. . . .

By that part of our plan which prescribes the selection of the youths of genius from among the classes of the poor, we hope to avail the state of those talents which nature has sown as liberally among the poor as the rich but which perish without use if not sought for and cultivated.

But of all the views of this law none is more important, none more legitimate, than that of rendering the people the safe, as they are the ultimate, guardians of their own liberty. For this purpose the reading in the first stage, where they will receive their whole education, is proposed, as has been said, to be chiefly historical. History, by apprising them of the past, will enable them to judge of the future; it will avail them of the experience of other times and other nations; it will qualify them as judges of the actions and designs of men; it will enable them to know ambition under every disguise it may assume and, knowing it, to defeat its views. In every government on earth is some trace of human weakness, some germ of corruption and degeneracy, which cunning will discover and wickedness insensibly open, cultivate, and improve.

Every government degenerates when trusted to the rulers of the people alone. The people themselves, therefore, are its only safe depositories; and, to render even them safe, their minds must be improved to a certain degree. This indeed is not all that is necessary, though it be essentially necessary. An amendment of our constitution must here come in aid of the public education. The influence over government must be shared among all the people. If every individual which composes their mass participates of the ultimate authority, the government will be safe, because the corrupting the whole mass will exceed any private resources of wealth, and public ones cannot be provided but by levies on the people. In this case every man would have to pay his own price. The government of Great Britain has been corrupted because but one man in ten has a right to vote for members

136. Thomas Jefferson

of Parliament. The sellers of the government therefore get nine-tenths of their price clear. It has been thought that corruption is restrained by confining the right of suffrage to a few of the wealthier of the people; but it would be more effectually restrained by an extension of that right to such numbers as would bid defiance to the means of corruption.

Lastly, it is proposed by a bill in this revisal, to begin a public library and gallery by laying out a certain sum annually in books, paintings, and statues. . . .

THE DIFFERENT RELIGIONS RECEIVED INTO THAT STATE

THE PRESENT STATE OF OUR LAWS on the subject of religion is this. The convention of May 1776, in their declaration of rights, declared it to be a truth, and a natural right, that the exercise of religion should be free; but when they proceeded to form on that declaration the ordinance of government, instead of taking up every principle declared in the Bill of Rights, and guarding it by legislative sanction, they passed over that which asserted our religious rights, leaving them as they found them. The same convention, however, when they met as a member of the General Assembly in October 1776, repealed all acts of Parliament which had rendered criminal the maintaining of any opinions in matters of religion, the forbearing to repair to church, and the exercising any mode of worship; and suspended the laws giving salaries to the clergy, which suspension was made perpetual in October 1779. Statutory oppressions in religion being thus wiped away, we remain at present under those only imposed by the common law or by our own acts of assembly. . . .

By our own act of assembly of 1705, c. 30, if a person brought up in the Christian religion denies the being of a God, or the Trinity, or asserts there are more gods than one, or denies the Christian religion to be true, or the Scriptures to be of divine authority, he is punishable on the first offense by incapacity to hold any office or employment, ecclesiastical, civil, or military; on the second, by disability to sue, to take any gift or legacy, to be guardian, executor, or administrator, and by three years' imprisonment without bail. A father's right to the custody of his own children being founded in law on his right of guardianship, this being taken away, they may of course be severed from him, and put by the authority of a court into more orthodox hands. This is a summary view of that religious slavery under which a people have been willing to remain, who have lavished their lives and fortunes for the establishment of their civil freedom. The error seems not sufficiently eradicated, that the operations of the mind, as well as the acts of the body, are subject to the coercion of the laws. But our rulers can have no authority over such natural rights, only as we have submitted to them. The rights of conscience we never submitted, we could not submit. We are answerable for them to our God. The legitimate powers of government extend to such acts only as are injurious to others. But it does me no injury for my neighbor to say there are twenty gods or no god. It neither picks my pocket nor breaks my leg. If it be said, his testimony in a court of justice cannot be relied on, reject it then, and be the stigma on him. Constraint may make him worse by making him a hypocrite, but it will never make him a truer man. It may fix him obstinately in his errors but will not cure them. Reason and free inquiry are the only effectual agents against error. Give a loose to them, they will support the true religion by bringing every false one to their tribunal, to the test of their investigation. They are the natural enemies of error and of error only. Had not the Roman government permitted free inquiry, Christianity could never have been introduced. Had not free inquiry been indulged, at the era of the Reformation, the corruptions of Christianity could not have been purged away. If it be restrained now, the present corruptions will be protected, and new ones encouraged. Was the government to prescribe to us our medicine and diet, our bodies would be in such keeping as our souls are now. . . .

Reason and experiment have been indulged, and error has fled before them. It is error alone which needs the support of government. Truth can stand by itself. Subject opinion to coercion; whom will you make your inquisitors? Fallible men: men governed by bad passions, by private as well as public reasons. And why subject it to coercion? To produce uniformity. But is uniformity of opinion desirable? No more than of face and stature. Introduce the bed of Procrustes then, and, as there is danger that the large men may beat the small, make us all of a size by lopping the former and stretching the latter.

Difference of opinion is advantageous in religion. The several sects perform the office of a *Censor morum* [censor of morals] over each other. Is uniformity attainable? Millions of innocent men, women, and children, since the introduction of Christianity, have been burned, tortured, fined, imprisoned; yet we have not advanced one inch toward uniformity. What has been the effect of coercion? To make one half the world fools, and the other half hypocrites. To support roguery and error all over the earth. Let us reflect that it is inhabited by a thousand millions of people. That these profess probably a thousand different systems of religion. That ours is but one of that thousand. That if there be but one right, and ours that one, we should wish to see the 999 wandering sects gathered into the fold of truth. But against such a majority we cannot effect this by force. Reason and persuasion are the only practicable instruments. To make way for these, free inquiry must be indulged; and how can we wish others to indulge it while we refuse it ourselves. But every state, says an inquisitor, has established some religion. No two,

say I, have established the same. Is this a proof of the infallibility of establishments?

Our sister-states of Pennsylvania and New York, however, have long subsisted without any establishment at all. The experiment was new and doubtful when they made it. It has answered beyond conception. They flourish infinitely. Religion is well supported; of various kinds, indeed, but all good enough; all sufficient to preserve peace and order; or if a sect arises whose tenets would subvert morals, good sense has fair play and reasons and laughs it out of doors without suffering the state to be troubled with it. They do not hang more malefactors than we do. They are not more disturbed with religious dissensions. On the contrary, their harmony is unparalleled and can be ascribed to nothing but their unbounded tolerance, because there is no other circumstance in which they differ from every nation on earth. They have made the happy discovery that the way to silence religious disputes is to take no notice of them.

Let us too give this experiment fair play and get rid, while we may, of those tyrannical laws. It is true, we are as yet secured against them by the spirit of the times. I doubt whether the people of this country would suffer an execution for heresy or a three years' imprisonment for not comprehending the mysteries of the Trinity. But is the spirit of the people an infallible, a permanent reliance? Is it government? Is this the kind of protection we receive in return for the rights we give up? Besides, the spirit of the times may alter, will alter. Our rulers will become corrupt, our people careless. A single zealot may commence persecutor, and better men be his victims. It can never be too often repeated that the time for fixing every essential right on a legal basis is while our rulers are honest and ourselves united. From the conclusion of this war we shall be going downhill. It will not then be necessary to resort every moment to the people for support. They will be forgotten, therefore, and their rights disregarded. They will forget themselves, but in the sole faculty of making money, and will never think of uniting to effect a due respect for their rights. The shackles, therefore, which shall not be knocked off at the conclusion of this war will remain on us long, will be made heavier and heavier, till our rights shall revive or expire in a convulsion. . . .

THE PRESENT STATE OF MANUFACTURES, COMMERCE, INTERIOR AND EXTERIOR TRADE

WE NEVER HAD HAD AN INTERIOR TRADE of any importance. Our exterior commerce has suffered very much from the beginning of the present contest. During this time we have manufactured within our families the most necessary articles of clothing. Those of cotton will bear some comparison with the same kinds of manufacture in Europe; but those of wool, flax, and hemp are very coarse, unsightly, and unpleasant; and such is our attachment to agriculture and such our preference for foreign manufactures that, be it wise or unwise, our people will certainly return as soon as they can to the raising of raw materials and exchanging them for finer manufactures than they are able to execute themselves.

The political economists of Europe have established it as a principle that every state should endeavor to manufacture for itself; and this principle, like many others, we transfer to America, without calculating the difference of circumstance which should often produce a difference of result. In Europe the lands are either cultivated or locked up against the cultivator. Manufacture must therefore be resorted to of necessity, not of choice, to support the surplus of their people. But we have an immensity of land courting the industry of the husbandman. Is it best then that all our citizens should be employed in its improvement, or that one half should be called off from that

to exercise manufactures and handicraft arts for the other? Those who labor in the earth are the chosen people of God, if He ever had a chosen people, whose breasts He has made His peculiar deposit for substantial and genuine virtue. It is the focus in which He keeps alive that sacred fire, which otherwise might escape from the face of the earth. Corruption of morals in the mass of cultivators is a phenomenon of which no age nor nation has furnished an example. It is the mark set on those who, not looking up to heaven, to their own soil and industry, as does the husbandman, for their subsistence, depend for it on the casualties and caprice of customers. Dependence begets subservience and venality, suffocates the germ of virtue, and prepares fit tools for the designs of ambition. This, the natural progress and consequence of the arts, has sometimes perhaps been retarded by accidental circumstances; but, generally speaking, the proportion which the aggregate of the other classes of citizens bears in any state to that of its husbandmen is the proportion of its unsound to its healthy parts, and is a good enough barometer whereby to measure its degree of corruption.

While we have land to labor then, let us never wish to see our citizens occupied at a workbench, or twirling a distaff. Carpenters, masons, smiths, are wanting in husbandry; but for the general operations of manufacture, let our workshops remain in Europe. It is better to carry provisions and materials to workmen there than bring them to the provisions and materials, and with them their manners and principles. The loss by the transportation of commodities across the Atlantic will be made up in happiness and permanence of government. The mobs of great cities add just so much to the support of pure government, as sores do to the strength of the human body. It is the manners and spirit of a people which preserve a republic in vigor. A degeneracy in these is a canker which soon eats to the heart of its laws and constitution.

1782

137.

ROBERT MORRIS: The Incorporation of the Bank of North America

The financial needs of the colonies toward the end of the Revolution reached crisis proportions. To meet these needs the Bank of North America was chartered in 1782. Because of doubts over the authority of Congress to charter a bank, it was incorporated in the state of Pennsylvania. This was the first private commercial bank in the United States, as well as the first government-incorporated bank. Largely through the ability of Robert Morris, who headed the bank, foreign loans were secured and Washington's army fed and clothed for the remainder of the war. The following letter of January 8, 1782, was a circular to the governors of the states.

Source: *The Diplomatic Correspondence of the American Revolution,*
Jared Sparks, ed., Vol. XII, Boston, 1830, pp. 76-77.

I HAVE THE HONOR TO TRANSMIT herewith an ordinance passed by the United States in Congress assembled the 31st day of December, 1781, incorporating the subscribers of the Bank of North America, together with sundry resolutions recommending to the several states to pass such laws as they may judge necessary for giving the said ordinance its full operation. The resolutions of the 26th of May last speak so clearly to the points necessary to be established by those laws that I need not enlarge on them. Should anything more be found necessary upon experience, the president and directors will no doubt make suitable applications to Congress, or to the states respectively, as the case may require.

It affords me great satisfaction to inform you that this bank commenced its operations yesterday, and I am confident that with proper management it will answer the most sanguine expectations of those who befriend the institution. It will facilitate the management of the finances of the United States. The several states may, when their respective necessities require, and the abilities of the bank will permit, derive occasional advantages and accommodations from it. It will afford to the individuals of all the states a medium for their intercourse with each other, and for the payment of taxes more convenient than the precious metals, and equally safe. It will have a tendency to increase both the internal and external commerce of North America, and undoubtedly will be infinitely useful to all the traders of every state in the Union, provided, as I have already said, it is conducted on principles of equity, justice, prudence, and economy. The present directors bear characters which cannot fail to inspire confidence, and as the corporation is amenable to the laws, power can neither sanctify any improper conduct nor protect the guilty.

Under a full conviction of these things, I flatter myself that I shall stand excused for recommending in the strongest manner this well-meant plan, to all the encouragement and protection which your state can give, consistently with wisdom and justice.

138.

ALEXANDER HAMILTON: Arguments for Increasing the Power of the Federal Government

Hardly had the new government begun to function, under the Articles of Confederation, when voices began calling for a stronger central authority. One such critic was Alexander Hamilton, who published a series of articles under the pseudonym, "The Continentalist." The last of these, which is reprinted here, appeared on July 4, 1782. By this time Hamilton had resigned his position on Washington's staff and was taking steps to implement his proposals in Congress.

Source: J. C. Hamilton, II, pp. 194-201: "The Continentalist, No. VI."

LET US SEE what will be the consequences of not authorizing the federal government to regulate the trade of these states. Besides the want of revenue and of power; besides the immediate risk to our independence, the dangers of all the future evils of a precarious Union; besides the deficiency of a wholesome concert and provident superintendence to advance the general prosperity of trade — the direct consequence will be that the landed interest and the laboring poor will, in the first place, fall a sacrifice to the trading interest, and the whole eventually to a bad system of policy made necessary by the want of such regulating power.

Each state will be afraid to impose duties on its commerce lest the other states, not doing the same, should enjoy greater advantages than itself by being able to afford native commodities cheaper abroad and foreign commodities cheaper at home.

A part of the evils resulting from this would be a loss to the revenue of those moderate duties, which, without being injurious to commerce are allowed to be the most agreeable species of taxes to the people. Articles of foreign luxury, while they would contribute nothing to the income of the state being less dear by an exemption from duties, would have a more extensive consumption.

Many branches of trade, hurtful to the

common interest, would be continued for want of proper checks and discouragements. As revenues must be found to satisfy the public exigencies in peace and in war, too great a proportion of taxes will fall directly upon land and upon the necessaries of life — the produce of that land. The influence of these evils will be to render landed property fluctuating and less valuable — to oppress the poor by raising the prices of necessaries; to injure commerce by encouraging the consumption of foreign luxuries; by increasing the value of labor; by lessening the quantity of home productions, enhancing their prices at foreign markets, of course obstructing their sale, and enabling other nations to supplant us.

Particular caution ought at present to be observed in this country not to burden the soil itself and its productions with heavy impositions, because the quantity of unimproved land will invite the husbandmen to abandon old settlements for new, and the disproportion of our population for some time to come will necessarily make labor dear — to reduce which, and not to increase it, ought to be a capital object of our policy.

Easy duties, therefore, on commerce, especially on imports, ought to lighten the burdens which will unavoidably fall upon land. Though it may be said that, on the principle of a reciprocal influence of prices whereon the taxes are laid in the first instance, they will in the end be borne by all classes, yet it is of the greatest importance that no one should sink under the immediate pressure. The great art is to distribute the public burdens well, and not suffer them, either first or last, to fall too heavily on parts of the community; else, distress and disorder must ensue — a shock given to any part of the political machine vibrates through the whole.

As a sufficient revenue could not be raised from trade to answer the public purposes, other articles have been proposed. A moderate land and poll tax being of easy and unexpensive collection, and leaving nothing to discretion, are the simplest and best that could be devised.

It is to be feared the avarice of many of the landholders will be opposed to a perpetual tax upon land, however moderate. They will ignorantly hope to shift the burdens of the national expense from themselves to others — a disposition as iniquitous as it is fruitless — the public necessities must be satisfied; this can only be done by the contributions of the whole society. Particular classes are neither able nor will be willing to pay for the protection and security of the others; and where so selfish a spirit discovers itself in any member, the rest of the community will unite to compel it to do its duty.

Indeed, many theorists in political economy have held that all taxes, wherever they originate, fall upon land, and have therefore been of opinion that it would be best to draw the whole revenue of the state immediately from that source to avoid the expense of a more diversified collection, and the accumulations which will be heaped in their several stages upon the primitive sums advanced in those stages which are imposed on our trade. But though it has been demonstrated that this theory has been carried to an extreme, impracticable in fact, yet it is evident, in tracing the matter, that a large part of all taxes, however remotely laid, will, by an insensible circulation, come at last to settle upon land — the source of most of the materials employed in commerce.

It appears from calculation made by the ablest master of political arithmetic about sixty years ago that the yearly product of all the lands in England amounted to £42 million sterling, and the whole annual consumption at that period, of foreign as well as domestic commodities, did not exceed £49 million, and the surplus of the exportation above the importation, £2 million, on which sums arise all the revenues in whatever shape which go into the treasury. It is easy to infer from this, how large a part of them must, directly or indirectly, be derived from land.

Nothing can be more mistaken than the collision and rivalship which almost always subsist between the landed and trading interests; for the truth is, they are so inseparably interwoven that one cannot be injured without injury nor benefited without benefit to the other. Oppress trade, lands sink in value; make it flourish, their value rises — incumber husbandry, trade declines; encourage agriculture, commerce revives. The progress of this mutual reaction might be easily delineated, but it is too obvious to every man who turns his thoughts, however superficially, upon the subject to require it. It is only to be regretted that it is too often lost sight of, when the seductions of some immediate advantage or exemption tempt us to sacrifice the future to the present.

But perhaps the class is more numerous of those who, not unwilling to bear their share of public burdens, are yet averse to the idea of perpetuity, as if there ever would arrive a period when the state would cease to want revenues, and taxes become unnecessary. It is of importance to unmask this delusion and open the eyes of the people to the truth. It is paying too great a tribute to the idol of popularity to flatter so injurious and so visionary an expectation. The error is too gross to be tolerated anywhere but in the cottage of the peasant. Should we meet with it in the Senate house, we must lament the ignorance or despise the hypocrisy, on which it is ingrafted.

Expense is, in the present state of things, entailed upon all governments; though, if we continue united, we shall be hereafter less exposed to wars by land than most other countries; yet, while we have powerful neighbors on either extremity, and our frontier is embraced by savages whose alliance they may without difficulty command,

we cannot, in prudence, dispense with the usual precautions for our interior security. As a commercial people, maritime power must be a primary object of our attention, and a navy cannot be created or maintained without ample revenues. The nature of our popular institutions requires a numerous magistracy, for whom competent provision must be made; or we may be certain our affairs will always be committed to improper hands, and experience will teach us that no government costs so much as a bad one.

We may preach, till we are tired of the theme, the necessity of disinterestedness in republics without making a single proselyte. The virtuous declaimer will neither persuade himself nor any other person to be content with a double mess of pottage instead of a reasonable stipend for his services. We might as soon reconcile ourselves to the Spartan community of goods and wives, to their iron coin, their long beards, or their black broth. There is a total dissimilarity in the circumstances, as well as the manners of society among us, and it is as ridiculous to seek for models in the small ages of Greece and Rome as it would be to go in quest of them among the Hottentots and Laplanders.

The public, for the different purposes that have been mentioned, must always have large demands upon its constituents, and the only question is, whether these shall be satisfied by annual grants, perpetually renewed by a perpetual grant, once for all, or by a compound of permanent and occasional supplies. The last is the wisest course. The federal government should neither be independent nor too much dependent. It should neither be raised above responsibility or control, nor should it want the means of maintaining its own weight, authority, dignity and credit. To this end, permanent funds are indispensable, but they ought to be of such a nature and so moderate in their amount as never to be inconvenient. Extraordinary supplies can be the objects of extraordinary emergencies, and in that salutary medium will consist our true wisdom.

It would seem as if no mode of taxation could be relished but the worst of all modes, which now prevails by assessment. Every proposal for a specific tax is sure to meet with opposition. It has been objected to a poll tax at a fixed rate that it will be unequal, and the rich will pay no more than the poor. In the form in which it has been offered in these papers, the poor, properly speaking, are not comprehended, though it is true that beyond the exclusion of the indigent the tax has no reference to the proportion of property; but it should be remembered that it is impossible to devise any specific tax that will operate equally on the whole community. It must be the province of the legislature to hold the scales with a judicious hand and balance one by another. The rich must be made to pay for their luxuries, which is the only proper way of taxing their superior wealth.

Do we imagine that our assessments operate equally? Nothing can be more contrary to the fact. Wherever a discretionary power is lodged in any set of men over the property of their neighbors, they will abuse it; their passions, prejudices, partialities, dislikes will have the principal lead in measuring the abilities of those over whom their power extends; and assessors will ever be a set of petty tyrants, too unskillful, if honest, to be possessed of so delicate a trust, and too seldom honest to give them the excuse of want of skill.

The genius of liberty reprobates everything arbitrary or discretionary in taxation. It exacts that every man, by a definite and general rule, should know what proportion of his property the state demands; whatever liberty we may boast in theory, it cannot exist in fact while assessments continue. The admission of them among us is a new proof how often human conduct reconciles the most glaring opposites; in the present case, the most vicious practice of despotic governments with the freest constitutions and the greatest love of liberty.

The establishment of permanent funds would not only answer the public purposes infinitely better than temporary supplies but it would be the most effectual way of easing the people.

With this basis for procuring credit, the amount of present taxes might be greatly diminished. Large sums of money might be borrowed abroad, at a low interest, and introduced into the country to defray the current expenses and pay the public debts; which would not only lessen the demand for immediate supplies but would throw more money into circulation, and furnish the people with greater means of paying the taxes.

Though it be a just rule that we ought not to run in debt to avoid present expense, so far as our faculties extend, yet the propriety of doing it cannot be disputed when it is apparent that these are incompetent to the public necessities. Efforts beyond our abilities can only tend to individual distress and national disappointment. The product of the three foregoing articles will be as little as can be required to enable Congress to pay their debts and restore order into their finances. In addition to them:

The disposal of the unlocated lands will hereafter be a valuable source of revenue, and an immediate one of credit. As it may be liable to the same condition with the duties on trade, that is, the product of the sales within each state to be credited to that state, and as the rights of jurisdiction are not infringed, it seems to be susceptible of no reasonable objection.

Mines in every country constitute a branch of the revenue. In this, where nature has so richly impregnated the bowels of the earth, they may in time become a valuable one; and as they require the care and attention of government to bring them to perfection, this care and a share in the profits of it will very properly devolve upon Congress.

All the precious metals should absolutely be the property of the federal government, and with respect to the others, it should have a discretionary power of reserving, in the nature of a tax, such part as it may judge not inconsistent with the encouragement due to so important an object. This is rather a future than a present resource.

The reason of allowing Congress to appoint its own officers of the customs, collectors of the taxes, and military officers of every rank is to create in the interior of each state a mass of influence in favor of the federal government. The great danger has been shown to be that it will not have power enough to defend itself and preserve the Union, not that it will ever become formidable to the general liberty; a mere regard to the interests of the confederacy will never be a principle sufficiently active to crush the ambition and intrigues of different members.

Force cannot effect it. A contest of arms will seldom be between the common sovereign and a single refractory member, but between distinct combinations of the several parts against each other. A sympathy of situations will be apt to produce associates to the disobedient. The application of force is always disagreeable — the issue uncertain. It will be wise to obviate the necessity of it by interesting such a number of individuals in each state, in support of the federal government, as will be counterpoised to the ambition of others, and will make it difficult for them to unite the people in opposition to the first and necessary measures of the Union.

There is something noble and magnificent in the perspective of a great federal republic, closely linked in the pursuit of a common interest — tranquil and prosperous at home, respectable abroad. But there is something proportionably diminutive and contemptible in the prospect of a number of petty states, with the appearance only of union, jarring, jealous, and perverse, without any determined direction, fluctuating and unhappy at home, weak and insignificant by their dissensions in the eyes of other nations.

Happy America, if those to whom thou has entrusted the guardianship of thy infancy know how to provide for thy future repose, but miserable and undone if their negligence or ignorance permits the spirit of discord to erect her banner on the ruins of thy tranquillity!

139.

HUGH H. BRACKENRIDGE: A Negative View of Indian Rights

In the eighteenth century, many white men did not look upon Native Americans as human beings, but viewed them as an obstacle to westward expansion. Brackenridge, presenting himself as the spokesman of his fellow Westerners, wrote a letter to the editor of the Freeman's Journal or the North American Intelligencer, *describing the sufferings of a physician and a frontiersman who had been captured by Native Americans in 1782. Brackenridge expressed his sentiments regarding Indian rights in the following excerpt taken from the letter.*

Source: *Indian Atrocities: Narratives of the Perils and Sufferings of Dr. Knight and John Slover, Among the Indians, During the Revolutionary War,* Cincinnati, 1867, pp. 62-72.

WITH THE NARRATIVE ENCLOSED, I subjoin some observations with regard to the animals vulgarly called Indians. It is not my intention to write any labored essay; for at so great a distance from the city, and so long unaccustomed to write, I have scarcely resolution to put pen to paper. Having an opportunity to know something of the character of this race of men, from the deeds they perpetrate daily round me, I think proper to say something on the subject. Indeed, several years ago, and before I left your city, I had thought different from some others with respect to the right of soil and the propriety of forming treaties and making peace with them.

In the *United States Magazine* in the year 1777, I published a dissertation denying them to have a right in the soil. I perceive a writer in your very elegant and useful paper has taken up the same subject, under the signature of "Caractacus," and unanswerably shown that their claim to the extensive countries of America is wild and inadmissible. I will take the liberty in this place to pursue this subject a little.

On what is their claim founded? Occupancy. A wild Indian with his skin painted red and a feather through his nose has set his foot on the broad continent of North and South America; a second wild Indian with his ears cut in ringlets, or his nose slit like a swine or a malefactor, also sets his foot on the same extensive tract of soil. Let the first Indian make a talk to his brother and bid him take his foot off the continent, for he being first upon it had occupied the whole to kill buffaloes and tall elks with long horns. This claim in the reasoning of some men would be just, and the second savage ought to depart in his canoe and seek a continent where no prior occupant claimed the soil.

Is this claim of occupancy of a very early date? When Noah's three sons, Shem, Ham, and Japhet, went out to the three quarters of the Old World — Ham to Africa, Shem to Asia, Japhet to Europe — did each claim a quarter of the world for his residence? Suppose Ham to have spent his time fishing or gathering oysters in the Red Sea, never once stretching his leg in a long walk to see his vast dominions from the mouth of the Nile, across the mountains of Ethiopia and the River Niger, to the Cape of Good Hope, where the Hottentots, a cleanly people, now stay; or supposing him, like a Scots peddler, to have traveled over many thousand leagues of that country — would this give him a right to the soil? In the opinion of some men it would establish an exclusive right. Let a man in more modern times take a journey or voyage like Patrick Kennedy and others to the heads of the Mississippi or Missouri rivers — would he gain a right ever after to exclude all persons from drinking the waters of these streams? Might not a second Adam make a talk to them and say — Is the whole of this water necessary to allay your thirst, and may I also drink of it?

The whole of this earth was given to man, and all descendants of Adam have a right to share it equally. There is no right of primogeniture in the laws of nature and of nations. There is reason that a tall man, such as the chaplain in the American Army we call the High Priest, should have a large spot of ground to stretch himself upon; or that a man with a big belly, like a goodly alderman of London, should have a larger garden to produce beans and cabbage for his appetite; but that an agile, nimble runner, like an Indian called the Big Cat, at Fort Pitt, should have more than his neighbors because he has traveled a great space, I can see no reason.

I have conversed with some persons and found their mistakes on this subject to arise from a view of claims by individuals in a state of society from holding a greater proportion of the soil than others; but this is according to the laws to which they have

consented. An individual holding one acre cannot encroach on him who has a thousand, because he is bound by the law which secures property in this unequal manner. This is the municipal law of the state under which he lives. The member of a distant society is not excluded by the laws from a right to the soil. He claims under the general law of nature, which gives a right, equally to all, to so much of the soil as is necessary for subsistence. Should a German from the closely peopled country of the Rhine come into Pennsylvania, more thinly peopled, he would be justifiable in demanding a settlement, though his personal force would not be sufficient to effect it. It may be said that the cultivation or melioration of the earth gives a property in it. No — if an individual has engrossed more than is necessary to produce grain for him to live upon, his useless gardens, fields, and pleasure walks may be seized upon by the person who, not finding convenient ground elsewhere, chooses to till them for his support.

It is a usual way of destroying an opinion by pursuing it to its consequence. In the present case we may say that if the visiting [of] one acre of ground could give a right to it, the visiting of a million would give a right on the same principle; and thus a few surly, ill-natured men might in the earlier ages have excluded half the human race from a settlement; or should any have fixed themselves on a territory, visited before they had set a foot on it, they must be considered as invaders of the rights of others.

It is said that an individual building a house or fabricating a machine has an exclusive right to it, and why not those who improve the earth? I would say, should man build houses on a greater part of the soil than falls to his share, I would, in a state of nature, take away a proportion of the soil and the houses from him. But a machine or any work of art does not lessen the means of subsistence to the human race, which an extensive occupation of the soil does.

Claims founded on the first discovery of soil are futile. When gold, jewels, manufactures, or any work of men's hands is lost, the finder is entitled to some reward; that is, he has some claims on the thing found, for a share of it.

When, by industry or the exercise of genius, something unusual is invented in medicine or in other matters, the author doubtless has a claim to an exclusive profit by it; but who will say the soil is lost, or that anyone can found a claim by discovering it. The earth with its woods and rivers still exists, and the only advantage I would allow to any individual for having cast his eye first on any particular part of it is the privilege of making the first choice of situation. I would think the man a fool and unjust who would exclude me from drinking the waters of the Mississippi River because he had first seen it. He would be equally so who would exclude me from settling in the country west of the Ohio because in chasing a buffalo he had been first over it.

The idea of an exclusive right to the soil in the natives had its origin in the policy of the first discoverers, the kings of Europe. Should they deny the right of the natives from their first treading on the continent, they would take away the right of discovery in themselves by sailing on the coast. As the vestige of the moccasin in one case gave a right, so the cruise in the other was the foundation of a claim.

Those who, under these kings, derived grants were led to countenance the idea; for, otherwise, why should kings grant or they hold extensive tracts of country? Men become enslaved to an opinion that has been long entertained. Hence it is that many wise and good men will talk of the right of savages to immense tracts of soil.

What use do these ringed, streaked, spotted, and speckled cattle make of the soil? Do they till it? Revelation said to man, "Thou shalt till the ground." This alone is human life. It is favorable to population, to science, to the information of a human mind in the worship of God. Warburton has well said that before you can make an Indian a Christian you must teach him agriculture and reduce him to a civilized life. To live by tilling is *more humano* [the way of humans], by hunting is *more bestiarum* [the way of the beasts]. I would as soon admit a right in the buffalo to grant lands, as in Killbuck, the Big Cat, the Big Dog, or any of the ragged wretches that are called chiefs and sachems. What would you think of going to a big lick or place where the beasts collect to lick saline nitrous earth and water, and addressing yourself to a great buffalo to grant you land? It is true he could not make the mark of the stone or the mountain reindeer, but he could set his cloven foot to the instrument like the great Ottoman, the father of the Turks; when he put his signature to an instrument, he put his large hand and spreading fingers in the ink and set his mark to the parchment. To see how far the folly of some would go, I had once a thought of supplicating some of the great elks or buffaloes that run through the woods to make me a grant of a hundred thousand acres of land and prove he had brushed the weeds with his tail and run fifty miles.

I wonder if Congress or the different states would recognize the claim? I am so far from thinking the Indians have a right to the soil that, not having made a better use of it for many hundred years, I conceive they have forfeited all pretense to claim and ought to be driven from it.

With regard to forming treaties or making peace with this race, there are many ideas:

They have the shapes of men and may be of the human species, but certainly in their present state they approach nearer the character of devils. Take an Indian, is there any faith in him? Can you bind him by favors? Can you trust his word or confide in his promise? When he makes war upon you, when he takes you prisoner and has you in his power, will he spare you? In this he departs from the law of nature, by which, according to Baron Montesquieu and every other man who thinks on the subject, it is unjustifiable to take away the life of him who submits; the conqueror in doing otherwise becomes a murderer who ought to be put to death. On this principle are not the whole Indian nations murderers?

Many of them may have not had an opportunity of putting prisoners to death, but the sentiment which they entertain leads them invariably to this when they have it in their power or judge it expedient; these principles constitute them murderers, and they ought to be prevented from carrying them into execution, as we would prevent a common homicide who should be mad enough to conceive himself justifiable in killing men.

The tortures which they exercise on the bodies of their prisoners justify extermination. Gelo of Syria made war on the Carthaginians because they oftentimes burned human victims, and made peace with them on conditions they would cease from this unnatural and cruel practice. If we could have any faith in the promises they make we could suffer them to live, provided they would only make war amongst themselves, and abandon their hiding or lurking on the pathways of our citizens, emigrating unarmed and defenseless inhabitants; and murdering men, women, and children in a defenseless situation; and on their ceasing in the meantime to raise arms no more among the American citizens.

140.

MICHEL GUILLAUME JEAN DE CRÈVECOEUR: What Is an American?

Crèvecoeur came to the British-American colonies in 1759, and by 1765 had become a naturalized citizen. From 1769 to 1780 he owned a farm in New York. A Loyalist in the Revolution, Crèvecoeur refused to accept the excesses of those who, in his words, were "perpetually bawling about liberty without knowing what it was." In 1780, he left America for France until the war in America was over. It was during his years as a New York farmer that he wrote his best-known collection of essays, Letters from an American Farmer, *from which the following selection is taken. They were originally published in London, in 1782, under the pen name of "J. Hector St. John."*

Source: *Letters from an American Farmer*, London, 1782, pp. 45-86.

I WISH I COULD BE ACQUAINTED with the feelings and thoughts which must agitate the heart and present themselves to the mind of an enlightened Englishman when he first lands on this continent. He must greatly rejoice that he lived at a time to see this fair country discovered and settled; he must necessarily feel a share of national pride when he views the chain of settlements which embellishes these extended shores. When he says to himself, this is the work of my countrymen, who, when convulsed by factions, afflicted by a variety of miseries and wants, restless and impatient, took refuge here. They brought along with them their national genius, to which they principally owe what liberty they enjoy and what substance they possess. Here he sees the industry of his native country displayed in a new manner, and traces in their works the embryos of all the arts, sciences, and ingenuity which flourish in Europe. Here he beholds fair cities, substantial villages, extensive fields, an immense country filled with decent houses, good roads, orchards, meadows, and bridges, where a hundred years ago all was wild, woody, and uncultivated!

What a train of pleasing ideas this fair spectacle must suggest! It is a prospect which must inspire a good citizen with the most heartfelt pleasure. The difficulty consists in the manner of viewing so extensive a scene. He is arrived on a new continent; a modern society offers itself to his contemplation, different from what he had hitherto seen. It is not composed, as in Europe, of great lords who possess everything, and of a herd of people who have nothing. Here are no aristocratical families, no courts, no kings, no bishops, no ecclesiastical dominion, no invisible power giving to a few a very visible one, no great manufacturers employing thousands, no great refinements of luxury. The rich and the poor are not so far removed from each other as they are in Europe.

Some few towns excepted, we are all tillers of the earth, from Nova Scotia to West Florida. We are a people of cultivators, scattered over an immense territory, communicating with each other by means of good roads and navigable rivers, united by the silken bands of mild government, all respecting the laws without dreading their power, because they are equitable. We are all animated with the spirit of industry, which is unfettered and unrestrained, because each person works for himself. If he travels through our rural districts, he views

not the hostile castle and the haughty mansion, contrasted with the clay-built hut and miserable cabin, where cattle and men help to keep each other warm, and dwell in meanness, smoke, and indigence. A pleasing uniformity of decent competence appears throughout our habitations. The meanest of our log houses is a dry and comfortable habitation.

Lawyer or merchant are the fairest titles our towns afford; that of a farmer is the only appellation of the rural inhabitants of our country. It must take some time before he can reconcile himself to our dictionary, which is but short in words of dignity and names of honor. There, on a Sunday, he sees a congregation of respectable farmers and their wives, all clad in neat homespun, well mounted, or riding in their own humble wagons. There is not among them an esquire, saving the unlettered magistrate. There he sees a parson as simple as his flock, a farmer who does not riot on the labor of others. We have no princes for whom we toil, starve, and bleed; we are the most perfect society now existing in the world. Here man is free as he ought to be; nor is this pleasing equality so transitory as many others are. Many ages will not see the shores of our great lakes replenished with inland nations, nor the unknown bounds of North America entirely peopled. Who can tell how far it extends? Who can tell the millions of men whom it will feed and contain? For no European foot has as yet traveled half the extent of this mighty continent!

The next wish of this traveler will be to know whence came all these people. They are a mixture of English, Scotch, Irish, French, Dutch, Germans, and Swedes. From this promiscuous breed that race now called Americans have arisen. The eastern provinces must indeed be excepted as being the unmixed descendants of Englishmen. I have heard many wish they had been more intermixed also; for my part, I am no wisher; and think it much better as it has happened. They exhibit a most conspicuous figure in this great and variegated picture; they too enter for a great share in the pleasing perspective displayed in these thirteen provinces. I know it is fashionable to reflect on them, but I respect them for what they have done; for the accuracy and wisdom with which they have settled their territory; for the decency of their manners: for their early love of letters; their ancient college, the first in this hemisphere; for their industry, which to me, who am but a farmer, is the criterion of everything. There never was a people, situated as they are, who, with so ungrateful a soil, have done more in so short a time. Do you think that the monarchial ingredients which are more prevalent in other governments have purged them from all foul stains? Their histories assert the contrary.

In this great American asylum, the poor of Europe have by some means met together, and in consequence of various causes; to what purpose should they ask one another, what countrymen they are? Alas, two-thirds of them had no country. Can a wretch who wanders about, who works and starves, whose life is a continual scene of sore affliction or pinching penury — can that man call England or any other kingdom his country? A country that had no bread for him, whose fields procured him no harvest, who met with nothing but the frowns of the rich, the severity of the laws, with jails and punishments, who owned not a single foot of the extensive surface of this planet? No! urged by a variety of motives, here they came. Everything has tended to regenerate them: new laws, a new mode of living, a new social system. Here they are become men; in Europe they were as so many useless plants, wanting vegetative mold and refreshing showers; they withered and were mowed down by want, hunger, and war — But now, by the power of transplantation, like all other plants, they have taken root

and flourished! Formerly they were not numbered in any civil list of their country, except in those of the poor; here they rank as citizens. By what invisible power has this surprising metamorphosis been performed? By that of the laws and that of their industry.

The laws, the indulgent laws, protect them as they arrive, stamping on them the symbol of adoption; they receive ample rewards for their labors; these accumulated rewards procure them lands; those lands confer on them the title of freemen; and to that title every benefit is affixed which men can possibly require. This is the great operation daily performed by our laws. From whence proceed these laws? From our government. Whence that government? It is derived from the original genius and strong desire of the people, ratified and confirmed by the Crown. This is the great chain which links us all; this is the picture which every province exhibits, Nova Scotia excepted. There the Crown has done all; either there were no people who had genius, or it was not much attended to. The consequence is that the province is very thinly inhabited indeed; the power of the Crown, in conjunction with the mosquitos, has prevented men from settling there. Yet some part of it flourished once, and it contained a mild, harmless set of people. But for the fault of a few leaders the whole were banished. The greatest political error the Crown ever committed in America was to cut off men from a country which wanted nothing but men.

What attachment can a poor European emigrant have for a country where he had nothing? The knowledge of the language, the love of a few kindred as poor as himself were the only cords that tied him. His country is now that which gives him land, bread, protection, and consequence. *Ubi panis ibi patria* [where my bread is earned, there is my country] is the motto of all emigrants. What then is the American, this new man? He is either a European or the descendant of a European; hence that strange mixture of blood which you will find in no other country. I could point out to you a man whose grandfather was an Englishman whose wife was Dutch, whose son married a French woman, and whose present four sons have now four wives of different nations. *He* is an American who, leaving behind him all his ancient prejudices and manners, receives new ones from the new mode of life he has embraced, the new government he obeys, and the new rank he holds. He becomes an American by being received in the broad lap of our great alma mater.

Here individuals of all nations are melted into a new race of men, whose labors and posterity will one day cause great change in the world. Americans are the western pilgrims who are carrying along with them that great mass of arts, sciences, vigor, and industry which began long since in the east; they will finish the great circle. The Americans were once scattered all over Europe; here they are incorporated into one of the finest systems of population which has ever appeared, and which will hereafter become distinct by the power of the different climates they inhabit. The American ought, therefore, to love this country much better than that wherein either he or his forefathers were born. Here the rewards of his industry follow with equal steps the progress of his labor; his labor is founded on the basis of nature, self-interest. Can it want a stronger allurement? Wives and children, who before in vain demanded of him a morsel of bread, now, fat and frolicsome, gladly help their father to clear those fields whence exuberant crops are to arise to feed and to clothe them all, without any part being claimed, either by a despotic prince, a rich abbot, or a mighty lord. Here, religion demands but little of him; a small voluntary salary to the minister, and gratitude to God. Can he refuse these?

The American is a new man, who acts upon new principles; he must, therefore, entertain new ideas and form new opinions. From involuntary idleness, servile dependence, penury, and useless labor he has passed to toils of a very different nature, rewarded by ample subsistence. This is an American.

North America is divided into many provinces, forming a large association, scattered along a coast 1,500 miles extent and about 200 wide. This society I would fain examine, at least such as it appears in the middle provinces. If it does not afford that variety of tinges and gradations which may be observed in Europe, we have colors peculiar to ourselves. For instance, it is natural to conceive that those who live near the sea must be very different from those who live in the woods; the intermediate space will afford a separate and distinct class.

Men are like plants; the goodness and flavor of the fruit proceed from the peculiar soil and exposition in which they grow. We are nothing but what we derive from the air we breathe, the climate we inhabit, the government we obey, the system of religion we profess, and the nature of our employment. Here you will find but few crimes; these have acquired as yet no root among us. I wish I were able to trace all my ideas. If my ignorance prevents me from describing them properly, I hope I shall be able to delineate a few of the outlines, which are all I propose.

Those who live near the sea feed more on fish than on flesh, and often encounter that boisterous element. This renders them more bold and enterprising; this leads them to neglect the confined occupations of the land. They see and converse with a variety of people; their intercourse with mankind becomes extensive. The sea inspires them with a love of traffic, a desire of transporting produce from one place to another; leads them to a variety of resources, which supply the place of labor. Those who inhabit the middle settlements, by far the most numerous, must be very different. The simple cultivation of the earth purifies them; but the indulgences of the government, the soft remonstrances of religion, the rank of independent freeholders must necessarily inspire them with sentiments very little known in Europe among people of the same class.

What do I say? Europe has no such class of man. The early knowledge they acquire, the early bargains they make, give them a great degree of sagacity. As freemen, they will be litigious; pride and obstinacy are often the cause of lawsuits; the nature of our laws and governments may be another. As citizens, it is easy to imagine that they will carefully read the newspapers, enter into every political disquisition, freely blame or censure governors and others. As farmers, they will be careful and anxious to get as much as they can, because what they get is their own. As northern men, they will love the cheerful cup. As Christians, religion curbs them not in their opinions. The general indulgence leaves everyone to think for himself in spiritual matters; the laws inspect our actions; our thoughts are left to God. Industry, good living, selfishness, litigiousness, country politics, the pride of freemen, religious indifference are their characteristics. If you recede still farther from the sea, you will come into more modern settlements; they exhibit the same strong lineaments in a ruder appearance. Religion seems to have still less influence, and their manners are less improved.

Now we arrive near the great woods, near the last inhabited districts. There men seem to be placed still farther beyond the reach of government, which in some measure leaves them to themselves. How can it pervade every corner? As they were driven there by misfortunes, necessity of beginnings, desire of acquiring large tracts of land, idleness, frequent want of economy, ancient debts — the reunion of such people does not afford a very pleasing spectacle. When discord, want of unity and friendship — when either drunkenness or idleness prevail in such remote districts — contention, inactivity, and wretchedness must ensue. There are not the same remedies to these evils as in a long-established community. The few magistrates they have are in general little better than the rest. They are often in a perfect state of war; that of man against man, sometimes decided by blows, sometimes by means of the law; that of man against every wild inhabitant of these venerable woods, of which they are come to dispossess them. There men appear to be no better than carnivorous animals of a superior rank, living on the flesh of wild animals when they can catch them; and when they are not able, they subsist on grain.

He who would wish to see America in its proper light and have a true idea of its feeble beginnings and barbarous rudiments must visit our extended line of frontiers where the last settlers dwell, and where he may see the first labors of settlement, the mode of clearing the earth, in all their different appearances; where men are wholly left dependent on their native tempers and on the spur of uncertain industry, which often fails when not sanctified by the efficacy of a few moral rules. There, remote from the power of example and check of shame, many families exhibit the most hideous parts of our society. They are a kind of forlorn hope, preceding by ten or twelve years the most respectable army of veterans which come after them. In that space, prosperity will polish some; vice and the law will drive off the rest, who, uniting again with others like themselves, will recede still farther, making room for more industrious people, who will finish their improvements, convert the log house into a convenient habitation, and, rejoicing that the first heavy labors are finished, will change in a few years that hitherto barbarous country into a fine, fertile, well-regulated district.

Such is our progress, such is the march of the Europeans toward the interior parts of this continent. In all societies there are off-casts; this unpure part serves as our precursors or pioneers. My father himself was one of that class; but he came upon honest principles and was therefore one of the few who held fast. By good conduct and temperance, he transmitted to me his fair inheritance when not above one in fourteen of his contemporaries had the same good fortune.

Forty years ago this smiling country was thus inhabited; it is now purged, a general decency of manners prevails throughout; and such has been the fate of our best countries.

Exclusive of those general characteristics, each province has its own, founded on the government, climate, mode of husbandry, customs, and peculiarity of circumstances. Europeans submit insensibly to these great powers, and become in the course of a few generations not only Americans in general but either Pennsylvanians, Virginians, or provincials under some other name. Whoever traverses the continent must easily observe those strong differences, which will grow more evident in time. The inhabitants of Canada, Massachusetts, the middle provinces, the southern ones will be as different as their climates; their only points of unity will be those of religion and language. . . .

Europe contains hardly any other distinctions but lords and tenants. This fair country alone is settled by freeholders, the possessors of the soil they cultivate, members of the government they obey, and the framers of their own laws by means of their representatives. This is a thought which you have taught me to cherish; our distance from Europe, far from diminishing, rather adds to our usefulness and consequence as men and subjects. Had our forefathers remained there, they would only have crowded it, and perhaps prolonged those convulsions which had shaken it so long. Every industrious European who transports himself here may be compared to a sprout growing at the foot of a great tree; it enjoys and draws but a little portion of sap. Wrench it from the parent roots, transplant it, and it will become a tree bearing fruit also. Colonists are therefore entitled to the consideration due to the most useful subjects. A hundred families barely existing in some parts of Scotland will here in six years cause an annual exportation of 10,000 bushels of wheat, 100 bushels being but a common quantity for an industrious family to sell if they cultivate good land. It is here, then, that the idle may be employed, the useless become useful, and the poor become rich. But by riches I do not mean gold and silver; we have but little of those metals. I mean a better sort of wealth· cleared lands, cattle, good houses, good clothes, and an increase of people to enjoy them.

There is no wonder that this country has so many charms and presents to Europeans so many temptations to remain in it. A traveler in Europe becomes a stranger as soon as he quits his own kingdom; but it is otherwise here. We know, properly speaking, no strangers; this is every person's country; the variety of our soils, situations, climates, governments, and produce has something which must please everybody. No sooner does a European arrive, no matter of what condition, than his eyes are opened upon the fair prospects. He hears his language spoken; he retraces many of his own country manners; he perpetually hears the names of families and towns with which he is acquainted; he sees happiness and prosperity in all places disseminated; he meets with hospitality, kindness, and plenty everywhere. He beholds hardly any poor; he seldom hears of punishments and executions; and he wonders at the elegance of our towns, those miracles of industry and freedom. He cannot admire enough our rural districts, our convenient roads, good taverns, and our many accommodations; he involuntarily loves a country where everything is so lovely.

When in England, he was a mere Englishman; here he stands on a larger portion of the globe, not less than its fourth part, and may see the productions of the north in iron and naval stores; the provisions of Ireland, the grain of Egypt, the indigo, the rice of China. He does not find, as in Europe, a crowded society, where every place is overstocked; he does not feel that perpetual collision of parties, that difficulty of beginning, that contention which oversets so many.

There is room for everybody in America. Has he any particular talent or industry? He exerts it in order to procure a livelihood, and it succeeds. Is he a merchant? The avenues of trade are infinite. Is he eminent in any respect? He will be employed and respected. Does he love a country life? Pleasant farms present themselves; he may purchase what he wants, and thereby become an American farmer. Is he a laborer, sober and industrious? He need not go many miles nor receive many informations before he will be hired, well-fed at the table of his employer, and paid four or five times more than he can get in Europe. Does he want uncultivated lands? Thousands of acres present themselves, which he may purchase cheap. Whatever be his talents or inclinations, if they are moderate, he may satisfy them.

I do not mean that everyone who comes will grow rich in a little time; no, but he may procure an easy, decent maintenance by his industry. Instead of starving, he will be fed; instead of being idle, he will have employment; and these are riches enough for such men as come over here. The rich stay in Europe; it is only the middling and poor that emigrate. Would you wish to travel in independent idleness, from north to south, you will find easy access and the most cheerful reception at every house; society without ostentation, good cheer without pride, and every decent diversion which the country affords, with little expense. It is no wonder that the European who has lived here a few years is desirous to remain. Europe with all its pomp is not to be compared to this continent for men of middle stations or laborers.

A European, when he first arrives, seems limited in his intentions as well as in his views; but he very suddenly alters his scale; 200 miles formerly appeared a very great distance; it is now but a trifle. He no sooner breathes our air than he forms schemes and embarks in designs he never would have thought of in his own country. There the plenitude of society confines many useful ideas, and often extinguishes the most laudable schemes which here ripen into maturity. Thus Europeans become Americans.

But how is this accomplished in that crowd of low, indigent people who flock here every year from all parts of Europe? I will tell you: they no sooner arrive than they immediately feel the good effects of that plenty of provisions we possess; they fare on our best food and are kindly entertained; their talents, character, and peculiar industry are immediately inquired into; they find countrymen everywhere disseminated, let them come from whatever part of Europe.

Let me select one as an epitome of the rest. He is hired, he goes to work and works moderately. Instead of being employed by a haughty person, he finds himself with his equal, placed at the substantial table of the farmer, or else at an inferior one as good. His wages are high, his bed is not like that bed of sorrow on which he used to lie. If he behaves with propriety and is faithful, he is caressed and becomes, as it were, a member of the family. He begins to feel the effects of a sort of resurrection; hitherto he had not lived but simply vegetated; he now feels himself a man, because he is treated as such. The laws of his own country had overlooked him in his insignificancy; the laws of this cover him with their mantle.

Judge what an alteration there must arise in the mind and thoughts of this man; he begins to forget his former servitude and dependence; his heart involuntarily swells and glows, this first swell inspires him with those new thoughts which constitute an American. What love can he entertain for a country where his existence was a burden to him! if he is a generous, good man, the love of his new adoptive parent will sink deep into his heart. He looks around and sees many a prosperous person who but a few years before was as poor as himself. This encourages him much; he begins to form some little scheme, the first, alas, he ever formed in his life. If he is wise, he thus spends two or three years, in which time he acquires knowledge, the use of tools, the modes of working the lands, felling trees, etc. This prepares the foundation of a good name, the most useful acquisition he can make. He is encouraged; he has gained friends; he is advised and directed; he feels bold; he purchases some land; he gives all the money he has brought over, as well as what he has earned, and trusts to the God of harvests for the discharge of the rest. His good name procures him credit; he is now possessed of the deed conveying to him and his posterity the fee simple and absolute property of 200 acres of land, situated on such a river.

What an epoch in this man's life! He has become a freeholder, from perhaps a German boor — he is now an American, a Pennsylvanian, an English subject. He is naturalized; his name is enrolled with those of the other citizens of the province. Instead of being a vagrant, he has a place of residence; he is called the inhabitant of such a county, or of such a district, and for the first time in his life counts for something; for hitherto he had been a cipher. I only repeat what I have heard many say, and no wonder their hearts should glow and be agitated with a multitude of feelings not easy to describe. From nothing to start into being; from a servant to the rank of master; from being the slave of some despotic prince to become a free man, invested with

lands, to which every municipal blessing is annexed! What a change indeed! It is in consequence of that change that he becomes an American.

This great metamorphosis has a double effect; it extinguishes all his European prejudices; he forgets that mechanism of subordination, that servility of disposition which poverty had taught him, and sometimes he is apt to forget it too much, often passing from one extreme to the other. If he is a good man, he forms schemes of future prosperity; he proposes to educate his children better than he has been educated himself; he thinks of future modes of conduct, feels an ardor to labor he never felt before. Pride steps in and leads him to everything that the laws do not forbid; he respects them; with a heartfelt gratitude he looks toward that government from whose wisdom all his new felicity is derived and under whose wings and protection he now lives. These reflections constitute him the good man and the good subject.

Ye poor Europeans; ye who sweat and work for the great — ye, who are obliged to give so many sheaves to the church, so many to your lords, so many to your government, and have hardly any left for yourselves — ye, who are held in less estimation than favorite hunters or useless lapdogs — ye, who only breathe the air of nature because it cannot be withheld from you; it is here that ye can conceive the possibility of those feelings I have been describing; it is here the laws of naturalization invite everyone to partake of our great labors and felicity, to till unrented, untaxed lands!

Many, corrupted beyond the power of amendment, have brought with them all their vices and, disregarding the advantages held out to them, have gone on in their former career of iniquity until they have been overtaken and punished by our laws. It is not every emigrant who succeeds; no, it is only the sober, the honest, and industrious. Happy those to whom this transition has served as a powerful spur to labor, to prosperity, and to the good establishment of children, born in the days of their poverty; and who had no other portion to expect but the rags of their parents, had it not been for their happy emigration. Others again have been led astray by this enchanting scene; their new pride, instead of leading them to the fields, has kept them in idleness; the idea of possessing lands is all that satisfies them; though surrounded with fertility, they have moldered away their time in inactivity, misinformed husbandry, and ineffectual endeavors.

How much wiser, in general, the honest Germans than almost all other Europeans. They hire themselves to some of their wealthy landsmen, and in that apprenticeship learn everything that is necessary. They attentively consider the prosperous industry of others, which imprints on their minds a strong desire of possessing the same advantages. This forcible idea never quits them; they launch forth, and by dint of sobriety, rigid parsimony, and the most persevering industry, they commonly succeed. Their astonishment at their first arrival from Germany is very great; it is to them a dream. The contrast must be very powerful indeed. They observe their countrymen flourishing in every place; they travel through whole counties where not a word of English is spoken; and in the names and the language of the people they retrace Germany. They have been a useful acquisition to this continent, and to Pennsylvania in particular — to them it owes some share of its prosperity; to their mechanical knowledge and patience, it owes the finest mills in all America, the best teams of horses, and many other advantages. The recollection of their former poverty and slavery never quits them as long as they live.

The Scotch and the Irish might have lived in their own country perhaps as poor, but enjoying more civil advantages. The effects of their new situation do not strike them so forcibly, nor has it so lasting an effect. From whence the difference arises, I know not; but out of twelve families of emigrants of each country, generally, seven Scotch will succeed; nine German, and four Irish. The Scotch are frugal and laborious; but their wives cannot work so hard as the German women, who, on the contrary, vie with their husbands and often share with them the most severe toils of the field, which they understand better. They have therefore nothing to struggle against but the common casualties of nature. The Irish do not prosper so well; they love to drink and to quarrel, they are litigious, and soon take to the gun, which is the ruin of everything. They seem, besides, to labor under a greater degree of ignorance in husbandry than the others; perhaps it is that their industry had less scope and was less exercised at home. I have heard many relate how the land was parceled out in that kingdom. Their ancient conquest has been a great detriment to them, by oversetting their landed property. The lands, possessed by a few, are leased down *ad infinitum*; and the occupiers often pay five guineas an acre. The poor are worse lodged there than anywhere else in Europe. Their potatoes, which are easily raised, are perhaps an inducement to laziness. Their wages are too low and their whiskey too cheap.

There is no tracing observations of this kind without making at the same time very great allowances, as there are everywhere to be found a great many exceptions. The Irish themselves, from different parts of that kingdom, are very different. It is difficult to account for this surprising locality. One would think on so small an island all Irishmen must be alike, yet it is not so; they are different in their aptitude to and in their love of labor.

The Scotch, on the contrary, are all industrious and saving. They want nothing more than a field to exert themselves in; and they are commonly sure of succeeding.

The only difficulty they labor under is, that technical American knowledge, which requires some time to obtain. It is not easy for those who seldom saw a tree to conceive how it is to be felled, cut up, and split into rails and posts. . . .

After a foreigner from any part of Europe has arrived and become a citizen, let him devoutly listen to the voice of our great parent, which says to him, "Welcome to my shores, distressed European; bless the hour in which thou didst see my verdant fields, my fair navigable rivers, and my green mountains! If thou wilt work, I have bread for thee; if thou wilt be honest, sober, and industrious, I have greater rewards to confer on thee — ease and independence. I will give thee fields to feed and clothe thee; a comfortable fireside to sit by, and tell thy children by what means thou hast prospered; and a decent bed to repose on. I shall endow thee, besides, with the immunities of a freeman. If thou wilt carefully educate thy children, teach them gratitude to God, and reverence to that government, that philanthropic government which has collected here so many men and made them happy, I will also provide for thy progeny. And to every good man this ought to be the most holy, the most powerful, the most earnest wish he can possibly form, as well as the most consolatory prospect when he dies. Go thou, and work and till; thou shalt prosper, provided thou be just, grateful, and industrious."

———————◆———————

I cannot conclude without mentioning how sensibly I feel the dismemberment of America from this empire, and that I should be miserable indeed if I did not feel that no blame on that account can be laid at my door, and did I not also know that knavery seems to be so much the striking feature of its inhabitants that it may not in the end be an evil that they will become aliens to this kingdom.
GEORGE III, letter to Shelburne, Nov. 10, 1782

COLONIAL ARCHITECTURE

Wayne Andrews

Mission of San Esteban, Acoma, New Mexico, probably completed by 1642

French and Spanish

Spanish colonists built in the baroque style of their homeland, and their massive and ornate architecture was a means of propagating faith in church and state. Relatively little French colonial architecture has survived, but the distinctive method of construction (wood posts with a stone or brick filling), and the preference for a porch overhung by a steep-pitched roof, can be seen below.

Wayne Andrews

(Above right) Church of San Xavier del Bac, Tucson, Ariz., 1784-97; (below left) Cahokia courthouse, Illinois, c. 1737; (below right) "Madame John's Legacy" house, New Orleans, La., c. 1727

Library of Congress

Louisiana State Museum

New England and the South

During the 17th century the houses and churches of the Atlantic seaboard faithfully reflected the medieval buildings of rural England. The tall, clustered chimneys, steep gables, and the square, Norman-looking church tower seen on this page are some typically English features. By the 18th century an evolution in taste and expanding economic means led to the adoption of the formal and elaborate Georgian styles, illustrated on the facing page. The designs reflect the work of such English architects as James Gibbs and Sir John Vanbrugh.

(Left) St. Michael's Church, Charleston, S.C., 1752-61; (below) Old Colony House, Newport, R.I., by Richard Munday, 1739-41; (bottom left) Tulip Hill, Maryland, built by Samuel Galloway about 1756; (bottom right) ''Stratford,'' Westmoreland County, Va., about 1725-30

OPPOSITE PAGE: (Top left) House of Seven Gables, Salem, Mass., 1668; (top right) Bacon's Castle, Surry County, Va., about 1655; (bottom left) St. Luke's Church near Smithfield, Va., 17th century; (bottom right) Parson Capen House, Topsfield, Mass., 1683

(Left) Sleepy Hollow Church, Tarrytown, N.Y., Dutch, 1699. OPPOSITE PAGE: (Top) Old Swedes' Church (Gloria Dei), Philadelphia, 1700; (bottom left) the "Saron" or Sisters' House, Ephrata, Pa., German, 1743; (bottom right) Bertolet-Herbein cabin, near Limekiln, Pa., 1737-45

Middle Colonies

The Dutch and Flemings, like the Swedes and Germans, looked back to the medieval architectural traditions of their native lands and reproduced these in a simple and unpretentious manner. They built houses of brick, stone, or wood crowned by steep gabled roofs, and churches whose plain walls were topped by flared gambrels or peaked gables surmounted by a belfry.

(Left) Ackerman house, Hackensack, N.J., Flemish, 1704; (below) two houses built by the Bronck family in West Coxsackie, N.Y., Dutch, 1663 (left) and 1738

American Museum of Photography

Library of Congress

1783

141.

GEORGE WASHINGTON: Address to the Officers of the Army

By the end of the Revolutionary War, the financial resources of the Americans were exhausted. Soldiers who had fought for independence had to be sent home without pay. Some members of the army hoped to be able to take by force what they felt entitled to. One officer, Major John Armstrong, in what is known as the "Newburgh Address," urged the army to override civilian authority and disown a government that was unable to fulfill its obligations. General Washington met and defeated this suggestion in his address to the officers of the army on March 15, 1783. Promising that Congress would do them justice, Washington rebuked all those who would use the military to coerce the civilian authority.

Source: John Marshall, *The Life of George Washington, etc., etc.*, 2nd edition, Philadelphia, 1848, Vol. II, pp. 46-52.

Gentlemen:

By an anonymous summons, an attempt has been made to convene you together. How inconsistent with the rules of propriety! How unmilitary! And how subversive of all order and discipline, let the good sense of the Army decide.

In the moment of this summons, another anonymous production was sent into circulation, addressed more to the feelings and passions than to the reason and judgment of the Army. The author of the piece is entitled to much credit for the goodness of his pen, and I could wish he had as much credit for the rectitude of his heart; for, as men see through different optics and are induced by the reflecting faculties of the mind to use different means to attain the same end, the author of the address should have had more charity than to mark for suspicion the man who should recommend moderation and longer forbearance — or, in other words, who should not think as he thinks and acts as he advises. But he had another plan in view, in which candor and liberality of sentiment, regard to justice, and love of country have no part; and he was right to insinuate the darkest suspicion to effect the blackest design.

That the address is drawn with great art and is designed to answer the most insidious purposes; that it is calculated to impress the mind with an idea of premeditated injustice in the sovereign power of the United States, and rouse all those resentments which must unavoidably flow from such a belief; that the secret mover of this scheme (whoever he may be) intended to take advantage of the passions while they were warmed by the recollection of past distresses, without giving time for cool, deliberative thinking, and that composure of mind which is so necessary to give dignity and stability to measures is rendered too obvious, by the mode of conducting the business, to need other proof than a reference to the proceedings.

Thus much, gentlemen, I have thought it incumbent on me to observe to you, to show upon what principles I opposed the irregular and hasty meeting which was proposed to have been held on Tuesday last, and not because I wanted a disposition to give you every opportunity consistent with your own honor and the dignity of the Army to make known your grievances. If my conduct heretofore has not evinced to you that I have been a faithful friend to the Army, my declaration of it at this time would be equally unavailing and improper. But as I was among the first who embarked in the cause of our common country; as I have never left your side one moment but when called from you on public duty; as I have been the constant companion and witness of your distresses, and not among the last to feel and acknowledge your merits; as I have ever considered my own military reputation as inseparably connected with that of the Army; as my heart has ever expanded with joy when I have heard its praises, and my indignation has arisen when the mouth of detraction has been opened against it, it can *scarcely be supposed*, at this late stage of the war, that I am indifferent to its interests. But how are they to be promoted? The way is plain, says the anonymous addresser.

If war continues, remove into the unset-tled country; there establish yourselves and leave an ungrateful country to defend itself. But who are they to defend? Our wives, our children, our farms, and other property which we leave behind us, or, in this state of hostile separation, are we to take the two first (the latter cannot be removed) to perish in a wilderness, with hunger, cold, and nakedness?

If peace takes place, never sheath your swords, says he, until you have obtained full and ample justice. This dreadful alternative, of either deserting our country in the extremest hour of her distress or turning our arms against it (which is the apparent object, unless Congress can be compelled into instant compliance), has something so shocking in it that humanity revolts at the idea. My God! What can this writer have in view, by recommending such measures? Can he be a friend to the Army? Can he be a friend to this country? Rather, is he not an insidious foe? Some emissary, perhaps, from New York, plotting the ruin of both by sowing the seeds of discord and separation between the civil and military powers of the continent? And what a compliment does he pay to our understandings when he recommends measures in either alternative, impracticable in their nature?

But here, gentlemen, I will drop the curtain, because it would be as imprudent in me to assign my reasons for this opinion as it would be insulting to your conception to suppose you stood in need of them. A moment's reflection will convince every dispassionate mind of the physical impossibility of carrying either proposal into execution.

There might, gentlemen, be an impropriety in my taking notice, in this address to you, of an anonymous production; but the manner in which that performance has been introduced to the Army, the effect it was intended to have, together with some other circumstances, will amply justify my observations on the tendency of that writing.

With respect to the advice given by the

author, to suspect the man who shall recommend moderate measures and longer forbearance, I spurn it, as every man who regards that liberty and reveres that justice for which we contend undoubtedly must; for if men are to be precluded from offering their sentiments on a matter which may involve the most serious and alarming consequences that can invite the consideration of mankind, reason is of no use to us — the freedom of speech may be taken away and, dumb and silent, we may be led, like sheep, to the slaughter.

I cannot, in justice to my own belief and what I have great reason to conceive is the intention of Congress, conclude this address without giving it as my decided opinion that that honorable body entertains exalted sentiments of the services of the Army; and, from a full conviction of its merits and sufferings, will do it complete justice. That their endeavors to discover and establish funds for this purpose have been unwearied, and will not cease till they have succeeded, I have not a doubt.

But like all other large bodies where there is a variety of different interests to reconcile, their deliberations are slow. Why then should we distrust them, and, in consequence of that distrust, adopt measures which may cast a shade over that glory which has been so justly acquired, and tarnish the reputation of an Army which is celebrated through all Europe for its fortitude and patriotism? And for what is this done? To bring the object we seek nearer? No! Most certainly, in my opinion, it will cast it at a greater distance.

For myself (and I take no merit in giving the assurance, being induced to it from principles of gratitude, veracity, and justice), a grateful sense of the confidence you have ever placed in me, a recollection of the cheerful assistance and prompt obedience I have experienced from you, under every vicissitude of fortune, and the sincere affection I feel for an Army I have so long had

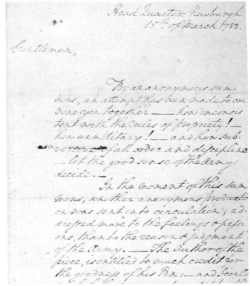

Massachusetts Historical Society

Manuscript of Washington's address to the Army, March 15, 1783

the honor to command, will oblige me to declare in this public and solemn manner that, in the attainment of complete justice for all your toils and dangers, and in the gratification of every wish, so far as may be done consistently with the great duty I owe my country and those powers we are bound to respect, you may freely command my services to the utmost of my abilities.

While I give you these assurances and pledge myself in the most unequivocal manner to exert whatever ability I am possessed of, in your favor, let me entreat you, gentlemen, on your part, not to take any measures which, viewed in the calm light of reason, will lessen the dignity and sully the glory you have hitherto maintained. Let me request you to rely on the plighted faith of your country, and place a full confidence in the purity of the intentions of Congress; that, previous to your dissolution as an Army they will cause all your accounts to be fairly liquidated, as directed in their resolutions, which were published to you two days ago, and that they will adopt the most effectual measures in their power to render ample justice to you for your faithful and meritorious services. And let me conjure you, in the name of our common country, as you value your own sacred honor, as you respect the rights of humanity, and as you regard the military and national character of America, to express your utmost horror and detestation of the man who wishes, under any specious pretenses, to overturn the liberties of our country, and who wickedly attempts to open the floodgates of civil discord and deluge our rising empire in blood.

By thus determining, and thus acting, you will pursue the plain and direct road to the attainment of your wishes. You will defeat the insidious designs of our enemies, who are compelled to resort from open force to secret artifice. You will give one more distinguished proof of unexampled patriotism and patient virtue, rising superior to the pressure of the most complicated sufferings; and you will, by the dignity of your conduct, afford occasion for posterity to say, when speaking of the glorious example you have exhibited to mankind, "had this day been wanting, the world had never seen the last stage of perfection to which human nature is capable of attaining."

142.

GEORGE WASHINGTON: On Disbanding the Army

After the Revolution was over and while he waited for the British to evacuate New York, George Washington wrote a circular letter to the state governors, expressing his hopes for the future of the United States. Claiming that the basic requirement for future happiness and security was "an indissoluble union," Washington asserted that the honor of the country required that the public debt and the nation's defenders be paid. His letter is a forthright statement of the problems facing the Confederation.

Source: *The Writings of George Washington*, John C. Fitzpatrick, ed., Vol. XXVI, Washington, 1938, pp. 483-496.

THE GREAT OBJECT for which I had the honor to hold an appointment in the service of my country being accomplished, I am now preparing to resign it into the hands of Congress, and to return to that domestic retirement which, it is well known, I left with the greatest reluctance; a retirement for which I have never ceased to sigh, through a long and painful absence, and in which (remote from the noise and trouble of the world) I meditate to pass the remainder of my life in a state of undisturbed repose. But before I carry this resolution into effect, I think it a duty incumbent on me to make this my last official communication; to congratulate you on the glorious events which heaven has been pleased to produce in our favor; to offer my sentiments respecting some important subjects which appear to me to be intimately connected with the tranquility of the United States; to take my leave of Your Excellency as a public character; and to give my final blessing to that country in whose service I have spent the prime of my life, for whose sake I have consumed so many anxious days and watchful nights, and whose happiness, being extremely dear to me, will always constitute no inconsiderable part of my own.

Impressed with the liveliest sensibility on this pleasing occasion, I will claim the indulgence of dilating the more copiously on the subjects of our mutual felicitation. When we consider the magnitude of the prize we contended for, the doubtful nature of the contest, and the favorable manner in which it has terminated, we shall find the greatest possible reason for gratitude and rejoicing. This is a theme that will afford infinite delight to every benevolent and liberal mind, whether the event in contemplation be considered as the source of present enjoyment or the parent of future happiness; and we shall have equal occasion to felicitate ourselves on the lot which Providence has assigned us, whether we view it in a natural, a political, or moral point of light.

The citizens of America, placed in the most enviable condition as the sole lords and proprietors of a vast tract of continent, comprehending all the various soils and climates of the world and abounding with all the necessaries and conveniences of life, are now, by the late satisfactory pacification, acknowledged to be possessed of absolute freedom and independency. They are, from this period, to be considered as the actors on a most conspicuous theater, which seems to be peculiarly designated by Providence for the display of human greatness and felicity. Here they are not only surrounded with everything which can contribute to the completion of private and domestic enjoyment, but Heaven has crowned all its other blessings by giving a fairer opportunity for political happiness than any other nation has ever been favored with. Nothing can illustrate these observations more forcibly than a recollection of the happy conjuncture of times and circumstances under which our republic assumed its rank among the nations.

The foundation of our empire was not laid in the gloomy age of ignorance and superstition but at an epoch when the rights of mankind were better understood and more clearly defined than at any former period. The researches of the human mind, after social happiness, have been carried to a great extent; the treasures of knowledge, acquired by the labors of philosophers, sages, and legislators through a long succession of years, are laid open for our use; and their collected wisdom may be happily applied in the establishment of our forms of government. The free cultivation of letters, the unbounded extension of commerce, the progressive refinement of manners, the growing liberality of sentiment, and, above all, the pure and benign light of revelation have had a meliorating influence on mankind and increased the blessings of society. At this auspicious period, the United States came into existence as a nation; and, if their citizens should not be completely free and happy, the fault will be entirely their own.

Such is our situation, and such are our prospects; but notwithstanding the cup of blessing is thus reached out to us; notwithstanding happiness is ours, if we have a disposition to seize the occasion and make it our own; yet it appears to me there is an option still left to the United States of America, that it is in their choice, and depends upon their conduct, whether they will be respectable and prosperous, or contemptible and miserable, as a nation. This is the time of their political probation; this is the moment when the eyes of the whole world are turned upon them; this is the moment to establish or ruin their national character forever; this is the favorable moment to give such a tone to our federal government as will enable it to answer the ends of its institution; or this may be the ill-fated moment for relaxing the powers of the Union, annihilating the cement of the Confederation, and exposing us to become the sport of European politics, which may play one state against another, to prevent their growing importance and to serve their own interested purposes. For, according to the system of policy the states shall adopt at this moment, they will stand or fall; and by their confirmation or lapse, it is yet to be decided whether the Revolution must ultimately be considered as a blessing or a curse — a blessing or a curse not to the present age alone, for with our fate will the destiny of unborn millions be involved.

With this conviction of the importance of the present crisis, silence in me would be a crime. I will therefore speak to Your Excellency the language of freedom and of sincerity without disguise. I am aware, however, that those who differ from me in political sentiment may perhaps remark I am stepping out of the proper line of my duty, and may possibly ascribe to arrogance or ostentation what I know is alone the result of the purest intention. But the rectitude of my own heart, which disdains such unworthy motives; the part I have hitherto acted in life; the determination I have formed of not taking any share in public business hereafter, the ardent desire I feel, and shall continue to manifest, of quietly enjoying in private life, after all the toils of war, the benefits of a wise and liberal government will, I flatter myself, sooner or later convince my countrymen that I could have no sinister views in delivering, with so little reserve, the opinions contained in this address.

There are four things which, I humbly conceive, are essential to the well-being, I may even venture to say to the existence, of the United States as an independent power.

First, an indissoluble union of the states under one federal head.

Second, a sacred regard to public justice.

Third, the adoption of a proper peace establishment; and,

Fourth, the prevalence of that pacific and friendly disposition among the people of the United States which will induce them to forget their local prejudices and policies; to make those mutual concessions which are requisite to the general prosperity; and, in some instances, to sacrifice their individual advantages to the interest of the community.

These are the pillars on which the glorious fabric of our independency and national character must be supported. Liberty is the basis; and whoever would dare to sap the foundation, or overturn the structure, under whatever specious pretext he may attempt it, will merit the bitterest execration and the severest punishment which can be inflicted by his injured country.

On the three first articles I will make a few observations, leaving the last to the good sense and serious consideration of those immediately concerned.

Under the first head, although it may not be necessary or proper for me, in this place, to enter into a particular disquisition on the principles of the Union, and to take up the great question which has been frequently agitated — whether it be expedient and requisite for the states to delegate a larger proportion of power to Congress or not — yet it will be a part of my duty, and that of every true patriot, to assert without reserve, and to insist upon, the following positions: That, unless the states will suffer Congress to exercise those prerogatives they are undoubtedly invested with by the constitution, everything must very rapidly tend to anarchy and confusion. That it is indispensable to the happiness of the individual states that there should be lodged somewhere a supreme power to regulate and govern the general concerns of the confederated republic, without which the Union cannot be of long duration. That there must be a faithful and pointed compliance, on the part of every state, with the late proposals and demands of Congress, or the most fatal consequences will ensue. That whatever measures have a tendency to dissolve the Union, or contribute to violate or lessen the sovereign authority, ought to be considered as hostile to the liberty and independency of America, and the authors of them treated accordingly. And lastly, that unless we can be enabled, by the concurrence of the states, to participate of the fruits of the Revolution and enjoy the essential benefits of civil society, under a form of government so free and uncorrupted, so happily guarded against the danger of oppression as has been devised and adopted by the Articles of Confederation, it will be a subject of regret that so much blood and treasure have been lavished for no purpose, that so many sufferings have been encountered without a compensation, and that so many sacrifices have been made in vain.

Many other considerations might here be adduced to prove that, without an entire conformity to the spirit of the Union, we cannot exist as an independent power. It will be sufficient for my purpose to mention but one or two which seem to me of the greatest importance.

It is only in our united character, as an empire, that our independence is acknowledged, that our power can be regarded, or our credit supported, among foreign nations. The treaties of the European powers with the United States of America will have no validity on a dissolution of the Union. We shall be left nearly in a state of nature; or we may find, by our own unhappy experience, that there is a natural and necessary progression from the extreme of anarchy to the extreme of tyranny, and that arbitrary power is most easily established on the ruins of liberty abused to licentiousness.

As to the second article, which respects the performance of public justice, Congress have, in their late address to the United States, almost exhausted the subject. They have explained their ideas so fully, and have enforced the obligations the states are under to render complete justice to all the public creditors with so much dignity and energy that, in my opinion, no real friend to the honor or independency of America can hesitate a single moment respecting the propriety of complying with the just and honorable measures proposed. If their arguments do

not produce conviction, I know of nothing that will have greater influence, especially when we recollect that the system referred to, being the result of the collected wisdom of the continent, must be esteemed, if not perfect, certainly the least objectionable of any that could be devised; and that, if it shall not be carried into immediate execution, a national bankruptcy, with all its deplorable consequences, will take place before any different plan can possibly be proposed and adopted. So pressing are the present circumstances, and such is the alternative now offered to the states.

The ability of the country to discharge the debts which have been incurred in its defense is not to be doubted; an inclination, I flatter myself, will not be wanting. The path of our duty is plain before us; honesty will be found, on every experiment, to be the best and only true policy. Let us then, as a nation, be just; let us fulfill the public contracts, which Congress had undoubtedly a right to make for the purpose of carrying on the war, with the same good faith we suppose ourselves bound to perform our private engagements. In the meantime, let an attention to the cheerful performance of their proper business, as individuals and as members of society, be earnestly inculcated on the citizens of America; then will they strengthen the hands of government and be happy under its protection. Everyone will reap the fruit of his labors, everyone will enjoy his own acquisitions, without molestation and without danger.

In this state of absolute freedom and perfect security, who will grudge to yield a very little of his property to support the common interest of society and ensure the protection of government? Who does not remember the frequent declarations, at the commencement of the war, that we should be completely satisfied if, at the expense of one-half, we could defend the remainder of our possessions? Where is the man to be found who wishes to remain indebted for the defense of his own person and property to the exertions, the bravery, and the blood of others without making one generous effort to repay the debt of honor and gratitude? In what part of the continent shall we find any man, or body of men, who would not blush to stand up and propose measures purposely calculated to rob the soldier of his stipend and the public creditor of his due? And were it possible that such a flagrant instance of injustice could ever happen, would it not excite the general indignation, and tend to bring down upon the authors of such measures the aggravated vengeance of heaven?

If, after all, a spirit of disunion, or a temper of obstinacy and perverseness, should manifest itself in any of the states; if such an ungracious disposition should attempt to frustrate all the happy effects that might be expected to flow from the Union; if there should be a refusal to comply with the requisition for funds to discharge the annual interest of the public debts; and if that refusal should revive again all those jealousies and produce all those evils which are now happily removed, Congress, who have, in all their transactions, shown a great degree of magnanimity and justice, will stand justified in the sight of God and man. And the state alone which puts itself in opposition to the aggregate wisdom of the continent, and follows such mistaken and pernicious counsels, will be responsible for all the consequences.

For my own part, conscious of having acted, while a servant of the public, in the manner I conceived best suited to promote the real interests of my country; having, in consequence of my fixed belief, in some measure pledged myself to the Army that their country would finally do them complete and ample justice; and not wishing to conceal any instance of my official conduct from the eyes of the world, I have thought proper to transmit to Your Excellency the enclosed collection of papers, relative to the half pay and commutation granted by Congress to the officers of the Army.

From these communications, my decided sentiments will be clearly comprehended, together with the conclusive reasons which induced me, at an early period, to recommend the adoption of this measure, in the most earnest and serious manner. As the proceedings of Congress, the Army, and myself are open to all, and contain, in my opinion, sufficient information to remove the prejudices and errors which may have been entertained by any, I think it unnecessary to say anything more than just to observe that the resolutions of Congress now alluded to are undoubtedly as absolutely binding upon the United States as the most solemn acts of confederation or legislation.

As to the idea, which, I am informed, has in some instances prevailed, that the half pay and commutation are to be regarded merely in the odious light of a pension, it ought to be exploded forever. That provision should be viewed as it really was — a reasonable compensation offered by Congress at a time when they had nothing else to give to the officers of the Army for services then to be performed. It was the only means to prevent a total dereliction of the service. It was a part of their hire. I may be allowed to say, it was the price of their blood, and of your independency. It is therefore more than a common debt; it is a debt of honor; it can never be considered as a pension or gratuity, nor be canceled until it is fairly discharged.

With regard to a distinction between officers and soldiers, it is sufficient that the uniform experience of every nation of the world, combined with our own, proves the utility and propriety of the discrimination. Rewards, in proportion to the aids the public derives from them, are unquestionably due to all its servants. In some lines, the soldiers have perhaps generally had as ample a compensation for their services by the large bounties which have been paid to them as their officers will receive in the proposed commutation; in others if, besides the donation of lands, the payment of arrearages of clothing and wages (in which articles all the component parts of the Army must be put upon the same footing), we take into the estimate the *douceurs* [presents] many of the soldiers have received, and the gratuity of one year's full pay, which is promised to all, possibly their situation (every circumstance being duly considered) will not be deemed less eligible than that of the officers. Should a further reward, however, be judged equitable, I will venture to assert no one will enjoy greater satisfaction than myself on seeing an exemption from taxes for a limited time (which has been petitioned for in some instances) or any other adequate immunity or compensation granted to the brave defenders of their country's cause; but neither the adoption nor rejection of this proposition will in any manner affect, much less militate against, the act of Congress by which they have offered five years' full pay, in lieu of the half pay for life, which had been before promised to the officers of the Army.

Before I conclude the subject of public justice, I cannot omit to mention the obligations this country is under to that meritorious class of veteran noncommissioned officers and privates who have been discharged for inability, in consequence of the resolution of Congress of April 23, 1782, on an annual pension for life. Their peculiar sufferings, their singular merits, and claims to that provision need only be known to interest all the feelings of humanity in their behalf. Nothing but a punctual payment of their annual allowance can rescue them from the most complicated misery; and nothing could be a more melancholy and distressing sight than to behold those who have shed their blood or lost their limbs in the service of their country without a shelter, without a friend, and without the means of obtaining any of the necessaries or comforts of life, compelled to beg their daily bread from door to door. Suffer me to recommend those of this description belonging to your state to the warmest patronage of Your Excellency and your legislature.

It is necessary to say but a few words on the third topic which was proposed, and which regards particularly the defense of the republic, as there can be little doubt but Congress will recommend a proper peace establishment for the United States, in which a due attention will be paid to the importance of placing the militia of the Union upon a regular and respectable footing. If this should be the case, I would beg leave to urge the great advantage of it in the strongest terms. The militia of this country must be considered as the palladium of our security, and the first effectual resort in case of hostility. It is essential, therefore, that the same system should pervade the whole; that the formation and discipline of the militia of the continent should be absolutely uniform; and that the same species of arms, accouterments, and military apparatus should be introduced in every part of the United States. No one who has not learned it from experience can conceive the difficulty, expense, and confusion which result from a contrary system, or the vague arrangements which have hitherto prevailed.

If, in treating of political points, a greater latitude than usual has been taken in the course of this address, the importance of the crisis and the magnitude of the objects in discussion must be my apology. It is, however, neither my wish nor expectation that the preceding observations should claim any regard, except so far as they shall appear to be dictated by a good intention, consonant to the immutable rules of justice, calculated to produce a liberal system of policy, and founded on whatever experience may have been acquired by a long and close attention to public business.

Here I might speak with the more confidence from my actual observations; and if it would not swell this letter (already too prolix) beyond the bounds I had prescribed to myself, I could demonstrate to every mind open to conviction that in less time, and with much less expense than has been incurred the war might have been brought to the same happy conclusion if the resources of the continent could have been properly drawn forth; that the distresses and disappointments which have very often occurred have, in too many instances, resulted more from a want of energy in the continental government than a deficiency of means in the particular states; that the inefficacy of measures arising from the want of an adequate authority in the supreme power, from a partial compliance with the requisitions of Congress in some of the states, and from a failure of punctuality in others, while it tended to damp the zeal of those which were more willing to exert themselves, served also to accumulate the expenses of the war and to frustrate the best concerted plans; and that the discouragement occasioned by the complicated difficulties and embarrassments in which our affairs were by this means involved would have long ago produced the dissolution of any army less patient, less virtuous, and less persevering than that which I have had the honor to command. But, while I mention these things, which are notorious facts, as the defects of our federal constitution, particularly in the prosecution of a war, I beg it may be understood that, as I have ever taken a pleasure in gratefully acknowledging the assistance and support I have derived from every class of citizens, so shall I always be happy to do justice to the unparalleled exertions of the individual states on many interesting occasions.

I have thus freely disclosed what I wished to make known before I surrendered up my public trust to those who committed it to me. The task is now accomplished. I now bid adieu to Your Excellency as the chief magistrate of your state, at the same time I bid a last farewell to the cares of office and all the employments of public life.

It remains, then, to be my final and only request that Your Excellency will communicate these sentiments to your legislature at their next meeting, and that they may be considered as the legacy of one who has ardently wished, on all occasions, to be useful to his country, and who, even in the shade of retirement, will not fail to implore the divine benediction upon it.

I now make it my earnest prayer that God would have you, and the state over which you preside, in His holy protection; that He would incline the hearts of the citizens to cultivate a spirit of subordination and obedience to government; to entertain a brotherly affection and love for one another, for their fellow citizens of the United States at large, and particularly for their brethren who have served in the field; and finally, that He would most graciously be pleased to dispose us all to do justice, to love mercy, and to demean ourselves with that charity, humility, and pacific temper of mind which were the characteristics of the Divine Author of our blessed religion, and without a humble imitation of whose example in these things we can never hope to be a happy nation.

May we never see another war! For in my opinion there never was a good war or a bad peace.
BENJAMIN FRANKLIN, letter to Josiah Quincy, Sept. 1783

143.

GEORGE WASHINGTON: Public Lands for Veterans

Washington's army throughout the Revolution had suffered from official neglect and meager pay. Washington repeatedly urged Congress to meet its obligations to the soldiers of the Continental Army. "If, retiring from the field, they [the officers] are to grow old in poverty, wretchedness and contempt," he wrote in 1782; "if they are to wade thro' the vile mire of dependency, and owe the miserable remnant of that life to charity, which has hitherto been spent in honor; then shall I have learned what ingratitude is, then shall I have realized a tale, which will embitter every moment of my future life." On June 17, 1783, Washington requested, in a letter to Congress, that it set aside public lands for the veterans of the war.

Source: William Parker Cutler and Julia Perkins Cutler, *Life, Journals, and Correspondence of Rev. Manasseh Cutler*, Cincinnati, 1888, Vol. I, pp. 172-174.

I HAVE THE HONOR of transmitting to Your Excellency, for the consideration of Congress, a petition from a large number of officers of the army in behalf of themselves and such other officers and soldiers of the Continental Army as are entitled to rewards in lands, and may choose to avail themselves of any privileges and grants which may be obtained in consequence of the present solicitation. I enclose also the copy of a letter from Brigadier General Putnam, in which the sentiments and expectations of the petitioners are more fully explained, and in which the ideas of occupying the posts in the western country will be found to correspond very nearly with those I have some time since communicated to a committee of Congress, in treating of the subject of a peace establishment. I will beg leave to make a few more observations on the general benefits of the location and settlement now proposed, and then submit the justice and policy of the measure to the wisdom of Congress.

Although I pretend not myself to determine how far the district of unsettled country, which is described in the petition, is free from the claim of every state, or how far this disposal of it may interfere with the views of Congress, yet it appears to me this is the tract which, from local position and peculiar advantages, ought to be first settled in preference to any other whatever; and I am perfectly convinced that it can not be so advantageously settled by any other class of men as by disbanded officers and soldiers of the Army to whom the faith of government has long since been pledged, that lands should be granted at the expiration of the war in certain proportions, agreeably to their respective grades.

I am induced to give my sentiments thus freely on the advantages to be expected from this plan of colonization, because it would connect our governments with the frontiers, extend our settlements progressively, and plant a brave, a hardy, and respectable race of people as our advanced post, who would be always ready and willing (in case of hostility) to combat the savages and check their incursions. A settlement formed by such men would give security to our frontiers; the very name of it would awe the Indians, and more than probably prevent the murder of many innocent families, who frequently, in the usual mode of extending our settlements and encroachments on the hunting grounds of the natives, fall the hapless victims to savage barbarity. Besides the emoluments which might be derived from the peltry trade at our factories, if such should be established, the appearance of so formidable a settlement in the vicinity of their towns (to say nothing of the barrier it would form against our other neighbors) would be the most likely means to enable us to purchase, upon equitable terms, of the aborigines, their right of preoccupancy, and to induce them to relinquish our territories and to remove into the illimitable regions of the West.

Much more might be said of the public utility of such a location, as well as of the private felicity it would afford to the individuals concerned in it. I will venture to say it is the most rational and practicable scheme which can be adopted by a great proportion of the officers and soldiers of our Army, and promises them more happiness than they can expect in any other way. The settlers being in the prime of life, inur-

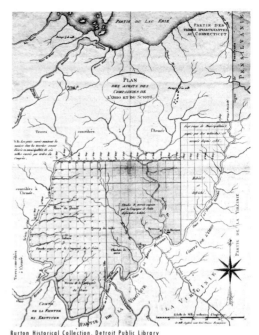

Tardieu map of Ohio, showing lands designated for veterans in the northern part of the territory

ed to hardship, and taught by experience to accommodate themselves in every situation, going in a considerable body, and under the patronage of government, would enjoy in the first instance advantages in procuring subsistence, and all the necessaries for a comfortable beginning, superior to any common class of emigrants, and quite unknown to those who have heretofore extended themselves beyond the Appalachian Mountains. They may expect, after a little perseverance, competence and independence for themselves, a pleasant retreat in old age, and the fairest prospects for their children.

144.

Virginia's Opposition to the Federal Congress

The Articles of Confederation were not given the chance to provide more than a weak government, because the states feared a strong central authority after their recent experience with British imperial domination. The weakness of the Confederation was especially manifest in its inability to raise revenue; since a unanimous vote of all states was needed to amend the Articles, even the attempt to give Congress a limited power to procure an independent income failed. The attempt was accompanied by an aggressive campaign on the part of some members of Congress to augment the central authority; this was met, in turn, by intensified opposition on the part of some of the states. The nature of such resistance is indicated by the instructions of Fairfax County, Virginia, to the state legislature on May 30, 1783. Mainly authored by George Mason, the instructions urged Virginia's representatives in Congress to oppose all encroachments on the "sovereignty and jurisdiction of the separate states."

Source: Kate Mason Rowland, *The Life of George Mason,* New York, 1892, Vol. II, pp. 48-52.

WE DESIRE AND INSTRUCT you that you give not your assent to, and that you firmly oppose, granting any exclusive privileges or advantages in our trade to any particular kingdom or nation, other than what may be stipulated in the commercial treaties concluded by the authority of Congress, it being the true and permanent interest of America to admit the trade of all nations, upon equal terms, without preference to any, further than the goodness and cheapness of their commodities may entitle them to. . . .

We desire and instruct you to oppose all future emissions of paper money; all interference of the legislature in private contracts, they being properly cognizable in the judiciary departments of the state; all *ex post facto* laws, except such only as are warranted by the greatest emergencies and the plain principles of justice; and that you endeavor to procure a revisal or repeal of all laws which may have been heretofore made contrary to such principles. . . .

We desire and instruct you to promote a strict inquiry into the expenditure of public money, and the bringing to speedy account and punishment all public delinquents and defaulters.

We desire and instruct you to endeavor to procure ample justice to the officers and soldiers of the American Army, who, though constantly surrounded with uncommon distress and difficulties, have so bravely defended the rights and liberties of their country. . . .

We desire and instruct you strenuously to oppose all encroachments of the American Congress upon the sovereignty and jurisdiction of the separate states, and every assumption of power not expressly vested in them by the Articles of Confederation. If experience shall prove that further powers are necessary and safe, they can be granted only by additional articles to the Confederation, duly acceded to by all the states; for if Congress, upon the plea of necessity, or upon any pretense whatever, can arrogate powers not warranted by the Articles of Confederation, in one instance, they may in another, or in an hundred; every repetition will be strengthened and confirmed by precedents.

And in particular we desire and instruct you to oppose any attempts which may be made by Congress to obtain a perpetual revenue, or the appointment of revenue officers. Were these powers superadded to those they already possess, the Articles of Confederation and the constitutions of government in the different states would prove mere parchment bulwarks to American liberty.

We like not the language of the late address from Congress to the different states, and of the report of their committee upon the subject of revenue published in the same pamphlet. If they are carefully and impartially examined, they will be found to exhibit strong proofs of lust of power. They contain the same kind of arguments which were formerly used in the business of ship money and to justify the arbitrary measures of the race of Stuarts in England. And the present King and Council of Great Britain might not improperly adopt great part of them to prove the expediency of levying money without consent of Parliament. After having reluctantly given up part of what they found they could not maintain, they still insist that the several states shall invest *the United States in Congress assembled with a power to levy*, for the use of the United States, the following duties, etc., and that the revenue officers shall be amenable to Congress. The very style is alarming. The proposed duties may be proper but the separate states only can safely have *the power of levying taxes*. Congress should not have even the appearance of such a power. Forms generally imply substance, and such a precedent may be applied to dangerous purposes hereafter. When the same man, or set of men, holds both the sword and the purse, there is an end of liberty.

As little are we satisfied with the resolution of Congress of the 10th of October, 1780, lately renewed, engaging that *the unappropriated lands* "that may be ceded or relinquished to the United States by any particular states, shall be disposed of for the common benefit of the United States." Who is to judge of the quality and legality of pretended appropriations? And will this vague resolution be a sufficient bar to Congress against confirming the claims under Indian purchases, or pretended grants from the Crown of Great Britain, in which many of their own members are interested as partners, and by which great part of the ceded lands may be converted to private instead of public purposes? The intrigues of the great land companies, and the methods by which they have strengthened their interest, are no secret to the public. We are also at a loss to know whence Congress derives the powers of demanding cessions of lands and of erecting new states before such powers have been granted them by their constituents.

And, finally, we recommend it to you (for in this we will not presume to give positive instructions) to endeavor to obtain an instruction from the General Assembly to the Virginia delegates in Congress against sending ambassadors to the courts of Europe; it being an expense which (in our present circumstances) these United States are unable to support. Such appointments can hardly fail of producing dangerous combinations, factions, and cabals in the great council of America. And from the great distance and the difficulty of knowing and examining their conduct, there is danger, too, that some of the persons so sent may be corrupted and pensioned by the courts where they reside. We are of opinion that consuls to superintend our trade (at less than a tenth part of the charge of ambassadors) will be sufficient to answer every good purpose. And nature having separated us by an immense ocean from the European nations, the less we have to do with their quarrels or politics, the better.

Having thus, gentlemen, given you our opinions and instructions upon such subjects as we deem at this time most important, we remain, with sentiments of great respect and esteem, your friends and fellow citizens.

145.

ALEXANDER HAMILTON: Arguments for a Strong Federal Government

Hamilton's ideas on the need for a strong central government were more advanced than those entertained by most of his colleagues in the Congress. Certainly they went far beyond what was acceptable to the states making up the federation. Thus the following resolutions, which he drew up in 1783, had no popular appeal and in fact were never even presented for discussion. It was only after the Constitution was adopted in 1788 that he was able to put his ideas to work.

Source: J. C. Hamilton, II, pp. 269-275: "Resolutions for a General Convention."

Whereas, in the opinion of this Congress, the Confederation of the United States is defective in the following essential points. . . .

First, and generally, in confining the power of the federal government within too narrow limits; withholding from it that efficacious authority and influence in all matters of general concern, which are indispensable to the harmony and welfare of the whole; embarrassing general provisions by unnecessary details and inconvenient exceptions incompatible with their nature, tending only to create jealousies and disputes respecting the proper bounds of the authority of the United States, and of that of the particular states, and a mutual interference of the one with the other.

Second, in confounding legislative and executive powers in a single body, as, that of determining on the number and quantity of force, land and naval, to be employed for the common defense, and of directing their operations when raised and equipped, with that of ascertaining and making requisitions for the necessary sums or quantities of money to be paid by the respective states into the common treasury — contrary to the most approved and well-founded maxims of free government, which require that the legislative, executive, and judicial authorities should be deposited in distinct and separate hands.

Third, in want of a federal judicature, having cognizance of all matters of general concern in the last resort, especially those in which foreign nations and their subjects are interested; from which defect, by the interference of the local regulations of particular states militating, directly or indirectly, against the powers vested in the Union, the national treaties will be liable to be infringed, the national faith to be violated, and the public tranquillity to be disturbed.

Fourth, in vesting the United States, in Congress assembled, with the power of general taxation, comprehended in that of "ascertaining the necessary sums of money to be raised for the common defense, and of appropriating and applying the same for defraying the public expenses"; and yet rendering that power, so essential to the existence of the Union, nugatory, by withholding from them all control over either the imposition or the collection of the taxes for raising the sums required, whence it happens that the inclinations, not the abilities, of the respective states are, in fact, the criterion of their contributions to the common expense, and the public burden has fallen, and will continue to fall, with very unequal weight.

Fifth, in fixing a rule for determining the proportion of each state toward the common expense, which, if practicable at all, must in the execution be attended with great expense, inequality, uncertainty, and difficulty.

Sixth, in authorizing Congress "to borrow money, or emit bills, on the credit of the United States," without the power of establishing funds to secure the repayment of the money borrowed or the redemption of the bills emitted, from which must result one of these evils — either a want of sufficient credit, in the first instance, to borrow, or to circulate the bills emitted, whereby in great national exigencies the public safety may be endangered, or, in the second instance, frequent infractions of the public engagements, disappointments to lenders, repetitions of the calamities of depreciating paper, a continuance of the injustice and mis-

chiefs of an unfunded debt, and, first or last, the annihilation of public credit. Indeed, in authorizing Congress at all to emit an unfunded paper as the sign of value: a resource, which, though useful in the infancy of this country, indispensable in the commencement of the Revolution, ought not to continue a formal part of the constitution, nor ever hereafter to be employed, being in its nature pregnant with abuses, and liable to be made the engine of imposition and fraud, holding out temptations equally pernicious to the integrity of government and to the morals of the people.

Seventh, in not making proper or competent provisions for interior or exterior defense: for interior defense, by leaving it to the individual states to appoint all regimental officers of the land forces, to raise the men in their own way, to clothe, arm, and equip them, at the expense of the United States; from which circumstances have resulted, and will hereafter result, great confusion in the military department, continual disputes of rank, languid and disproportionate levies of men, an enormous increase of expense for want of system and uniformity in the manner of conducting them, and from the competitions of state bounties; — by an ambiguity in the fourth clause of the Sixth Article, susceptible of a construction which would devolve upon the particular states in time of peace the care of their own defense both by sea and land, and would preclude the United States from raising a single regiment or building a single ship before a declaration of war, or an actual commencement of hostilities; a principle dangerous to the Confederacy in different respects, by leaving the United States at all times unprepared for the defense of their common rights, obliging them to begin to raise an army and to build and equip a navy at the moment they would have occasion to employ them, and by putting into the hands of a few states, who from their local situations are more immediately exposed, all the standing forces of the country, thereby not only leaving the care of the safety of the whole to a part, which will naturally be both unwilling and unable to make effectual provision at its particular expense but also furnishing grounds of jealousy and distrust between the states, unjust in its operation to those states in whose hands they are, by throwing the exclusive burden of maintaining those forces upon them, while their neighbors immediately, and all the states ultimately, would share the benefits of their services; for exterior defense, in authorizing Congress "to build and equip a navy," without providing any means of manning it, either by requisitions of the states, by the power of registering and drafting the seamen in rotation, or by embargoes in cases of emergency, to induce them to accept employment on board the ships of war; the omission of all which leaves no other resource than voluntary enlistment; a resource which has been found ineffectual in every country, and for reasons of peculiar force, in this.

Eighth, in not vesting in the United States a general superintendence of trade, equally necessary in the view of revenue and regulation: of revenue, because duties on commerce, when moderate, are one of the most agreeable and productive species of it, which cannot without great disadvantages be imposed by particular states, while others refrain from doing it, but must be imposed in concert, and by laws operating upon the same principles, at the same moment, in all the states; otherwise those states which should not impose them would engross the commerce of such of their neighbors as did: of regulation, because by general prohibitions of particular articles, by a judicious arrangement of duties, sometimes by bounties on the manufacture or exportation of certain commodities, injurious branches of commerce might be discouraged, favorable branches encouraged, useful products and manufactures promoted;

none of which advantages can be effectually attained by separate regulations without a general superintending power; because, also, it is essential to the due observance of the commercial stipulations of the United States with foreign powers, an interference with which will be unavoidable if the different states have the exclusive regulation of their own trade, and of course the construction of the treaties entered into.

Ninth, in defeating essential powers by provisos and limitations inconsistent with their nature, as the power of making treaties with foreign nations, "provided that no treaty of commerce shall be made whereby the legislative power of the respective states shall be restrained from imposing such imposts and duties on foreigners as their own people are subjected to, or from prohibiting the importation or exportation of any species of goods or commodities whatever"; a proviso susceptible of an interpretation which includes a constitutional possibility of defeating the treaties of commerce entered into by the United States. As also the power "of regulating the trade, and managing all affairs with the Indians, not members of any of the states; provided, that the legislative right of any state within its own limits be not infringed or violated," and others of a similar nature.

Tenth, in granting the United States the sole power "of regulating the alloy and value of coin struck by their own authority, or by that of the respective states," without the power of regulating foreign coin in circulation, though the one is essential to the due exercise of the other, as there ought to be such proportions maintained between the national and foreign coin, as will give the former a preference in all internal negotiations; and without the latter power, the operations of government, in a matter of primary importance to the commerce and finances of the United States, will be exposed to numberless obstructions.

Eleventh, in requiring the assent of nine

states to matters of principal importance, and of seven to all others, except adjournments from day to day, a rule destructive of vigor, consistency, or expedition in the administration of affairs, tending to subject the sense of the majority to that of the minority, by putting it in the power of a small combination to retard and even to frustrate the most necessary measures, and to oblige the greater number, in cases which require speedy determinations, as happens in the most interesting concerns of the community, to come into the views of the smaller; the evils of which have been felt in critical conjunctures, and must always make the spirit of government a spirit of compromise and expedience, rather than of system and energy.

Twelfth, in vesting in the federal government the sole direction of the interests of the United States in their intercourse with foreign nations, without empowering it to pass all general laws in aid and support of the laws of nations; for the want of which authority the faith of the United States may be broken, their reputation sullied, and their peace interrupted by the negligence or misconception of any particular state.

And whereas experience has clearly manifested that the powers reserved to the Union in the Confederation are unequal to the purpose of effectually drawing forth the resources of the respective members for the common welfare and defense; whereby the United States have, upon several occasions, been exposed to the most critical and alarming situations; have wanted an army adequate to their defense and proportioned to the abilities of the country; have on account of that deficiency seen essential posts reduced — others imminently endangered — whole states, and large parts of others, overrun and ravaged by small bodies of the enemy's forces; have been destitute of sufficient means of feeding, clothing, paying, and appointing that army, by which the troops, rendered less efficient for military

Courtesy, The New York Historical Society

Alexander Hamilton, portrait by Trumbull

operations, have been exposed to sufferings, which nothing but unparalleled patience, perseverance, and patriotism could have endured.

Whereby, also, the United States have been too often compelled to make the administration of their affairs a succession of temporary expedients, inconsistent with order, economy, energy, or a scrupulous adherence to the public engagements, and now find themselves, at the close of a glorious struggle for independence, without any certain means of doing justice to those who have been its principal supporters — to an army which has bravely fought and patiently suffered — to citizens who have cheerfully lent their money — and to others who have in different ways contributed their property and their personal service to the common cause; obliged to rely for the only effectual mode of doing that justice, by funding the debt on solid securities, on the precarious concurrence of thirteen distinct deliberatives, the dissent of either of which may defeat the plan, and leave these states, at this early period of their existence, involved in all the disgrace and mischiefs of violated faith and national bankruptcy.

And whereas, notwithstanding we have, by the blessing of Providence, so far happily escaped the complicated dangers of such a situation, and now see the object of our wishes secured by an honorable peace, it would be unwise to hazard a repetition of the same dangers and embarrassments in any future war in which these states may be engaged, or to continue this extensive empire under a government unequal to its protection and prosperity.

And whereas, it is essential to the happiness and security of these states that their Union should be established on the most solid foundations, and it is manifest that this desirable object cannot be effected but by a government capable, both in peace and war, of making every member of the Union contribute in just proportion to the common necessities, and of combining and directing the forces and wills of the several parts to a general end; to which purposes, in the opinion of Congress, the present confederation is altogether inadequate.

And whereas, on the spirit which may direct the councils and measures of these states, at the present juncture, may depend their future safety and welfare, Congress conceive it to be their duty freely to state to their constituents the defects which, by experience, have been discovered in the present plan of the federal Union, and solemnly to call their attention to a revisal and amendment of the same.

Therefore resolved, that it be earnestly recommended to the several states to appoint a convention, to meet at —— on the —— day of ——, with full powers to revise the Confederation, and to adopt and propose such alterations as to them shall appear necessary, to be finally approved or rejected by the states respectively — and that a committee of —— be appointed to prepare an address upon the subject.

Monarchy is like a splendid ship, with all sails set; it moves majestically on, then it hits a rock and sinks forever. Democracy is like a raft. It never sinks, but, damn it, your feet are always in the water.

FISHER AMES

146.

WILLIAM CUSHING: The Quock Walker Case — Slavery Unconstitutional in Massachusetts

Slavery was not expressly forbidden by the constitution of Massachusetts. However, its first article was patterned after the Virginia Declaration of Rights and copied the language of the Declaration of Independence. Accordingly, when in 1783 one Nathaniel Jennison, indicted for assault on Quock Walker, an African American, defended the assault on the grounds that Walker was his slave, his defense was rejected by the Superior Court on the ground that slavery was by inference unconstitutional in the Commonwealth of Massachusetts. While the case was never reported officially, the opinion of Chief Justice Cushing, part of which is reprinted here, was preserved in his private notebook.

Source: MHSP, XIII, p. 294.

AS TO THE DOCTRINE OF SLAVERY and the right of Christians to hold Africans in perpetual servitude, and sell and treat them as we do our horses and cattle, that (it is true) has been heretofore countenanced by the province laws formerly, but nowhere is it expressly enacted or established. It has been a usage — a usage which took its origin from the practice of some of the European nations, and the regulations of British government respecting the then colonies, for the benefit of trade and wealth. But whatever sentiments have formerly prevailed in this particular or slid in upon us by the example of others, a different idea has taken place with the people of America, more favorable to the natural rights of mankind, and to that natural, innate desire of liberty, which with heaven (without regard to color, complexion, or shape of noses) . . . has inspired all the human race. And upon this ground our constitution of government, by which the people of this commonwealth have solemnly bound themselves, sets out with declaring that all men are born free and equal — and that every subject is entitled to liberty, and to have it guarded by the laws, as well as life and property — and in short is totally repugnant to the idea of being born slaves. This being the case, I think the idea of slavery is inconsistent with our own conduct and constitution; and there can be no such thing as perpetual servitude of a rational creature, unless his liberty is forfeited by some criminal conduct or given up by personal consent or contract.

Verdict: Guilty.

147.

Virginia's Cession of Western Lands

Ratification of the Articles of Confederation had been long delayed, primarily because of conflicting claims to land on the frontier by several states. It was only Virginia's offer to cede all land claims north of the Ohio River to Congress that finally induced Maryland to ratify the Articles in March 1781. This land cession was burdened with too many conditions for Congress to accept it. But Virginia's offer of December 20, 1783, was approved, and the deed for the land was signed on March 1, 1784.

Source: Poore, 2nd edition, I, pp. 427-428.

Section 1. *Whereas* the Congress of the United States did, by their act of the 6th day of September, in the year 1780, recommend to the several states in the Union, having claims to waste and unappropriated lands in the western country, a liberal cession to the United States of a portion of their respective claims for the common benefit of the Union:

Section 2. *And whereas* this Commonwealth did, on the 2nd day of January, in the year 1781, yield to the Congress of the United States, for the benefit of the said states, all right, title, and claim which the said Commonwealth had to the territory northwest of the River Ohio, subject to the conditions annexed to the said act of cession:

Section 3. *And whereas* the United States in Congress assembled have, by their act of the 13th of September last, stipulated the terms on which they agreed to accept the cession of this state, should the legislature approve thereof, which terms, although they do not come fully up to the propositions of this Commonwealth, are conceived, on the whole, to approach so nearly to them as to induce this state to accept thereof, in full confidence that Congress will, in justice to this state for the liberal cession she has made, earnestly press upon the other states claiming large tracts of waste and uncultivated territory the propriety of making cessions equally liberal for the common benefit and support of the Union:

Be it enacted by the General Assembly that it shall and may be lawful for the delegates of this state to the Congress of the United States, or such of them as shall be assembled in Congress, and the said delegates, or such of them so assembled, are hereby fully authorized and empowered, for and on behalf of this state, by proper deeds or instrument in writing, under their hands and seals, to convey, transfer, assign, and make over unto the United States in Congress assembled, for the benefit of the said states, all right, title, and claim, as well of soil as jurisdiction, which this Commonwealth has to the territory or tract of country within the limits of the Virginia charter, situated, lying, and being to the northwest of the River Ohio, subject to the terms and conditions contained in the before-recited act of

Congress of the 13th day of September last, that is to say:

Upon condition that the territory so ceded shall be laid out and formed into states, containing a suitable extent of territory, not less than 100 nor more than 150 miles square, or as near thereto as circumstances will admit; and that the states so formed shall be distinct republican states, and admitted members of the federal Union, having the same rights of sovereignty, freedom, and independence as the other states; that the necessary and reasonable expenses incurred by this state in subduing any British posts, or in maintaining forts or garrisons within and for the defense, or in acquiring any part of the territory so ceded or relinquished, shall be fully reimbursed by the United States; and that one commissioner shall be appointed by Congress, one by this Commonwealth, and another by those two commissioners, who, or a majority of them, shall be authorized and empowered to adjust and liquidate the account of the necessary and reasonable expenses incurred by this state, which they shall judge to be comprised within the intent and meaning of the act of Congress of the 10th of October, 1780, respecting such expenses.

That the French and Canadian inhabitants, and other settlers of the Kaskaskies [Kaskaskia], Saint Vincents [Vincennes], and the neighboring villages, who have professed themselves citizens of Virginia, shall have their possessions and titles confirmed to them, and be protected in the enjoyment of their rights and liberties. That a quantity, not exceeding 150,000 acres of land, promised by this state, shall be allowed and granted to the then Colonel, now General, George Rogers Clark, and to the officers and soldiers of his regiment who marched with him when the posts of Kaskaskies and Saint Vincents were reduced, and to the officers and soldiers that have been since incorporated into the said regiment, to be laid off in one tract, the length of which not to exceed double the breadth, in such place on the northwest side of the Ohio as a majority of the officers shall choose, and to be afterward divided among the said officers and soldiers in due proportion according to the laws of Virginia.

That in case the quantity of good lands on the southeast side of the Ohio, upon the waters of Cumberland River, and between the Green River and Tennessee River, which have been reserved by law for the Virginia troops upon continental establishment, should, from the North Carolina line bearing in farther upon the Cumberland lands than was expected, prove insufficient for their legal bounties, the deficiency should be made up to the said troops in good lands, to be laid off between the Rivers Scioto and Little Miami, on the northwest side of the River Ohio, in such proportions as have been engaged to them by the laws of Virginia.

That all the lands within the territory so ceded to the United States, and not reserved for or appropriated to any of the before-mentioned purposes, or disposed of in bounties to the officers and soldiers of the American Army, shall be considered as a common fund for the use and benefit of such of the United States as have become, or shall become, members of the Confederation or federal alliance of the said states, Virginia inclusive, according to their usual respective proportions in the general charge and expenditure, and shall be faithfully and bona fide disposed of for that purpose, and for no other use or purpose whatsoever.

Provided, that the trust hereby reposed in the delegates of this state shall not be executed unless three of them, at least, are present in Congress.

Index of Authors

The numbers in brackets
indicate selection numbers
in this volume

ADAMS, ABIGAIL (Nov. 22, 1744-Oct. 28, 1818), wife of John Adams and mother of John Quincy Adams. [86] See also Author Index, Vols. 3, 4.

ADAMS, JOHN (Oct. 30, 1735-July 4, 1826), lawyer and journalist. Second President of the United States (1797-1801); representative (1770-71) to the Massachusetts General Court; member (1774-78) of the Continental Congress; signed the Declaration of Independence; commissioner to France (1778); helped draft the Massachusetts state constitution (1780); foreign minister to England (1785-88); Vice-President of the United States under Washington. [28, 70, 76, 89, 97, 99, 122] See also Author Index, Vols. 3, 4.

ADAMS, SAMUEL (Sept. 27, 1722-Oct. 2, 1803), Revolutionary leader. Signed the Declaration of Independence; representative (1766-74) to the Massachusetts General Court; second cousin of John Adams. [48]

ALISON, FRANCIS (1705-Nov. 28, 1779), educator and Presbyterian clergyman. [10]

AMES, NATHANIEL (July 22, 1708-July 11, 1764), physician and producer of almanacs. [7]

BACKUS, ISAAC (Jan. 9, 1724-Nov. 20, 1806), Baptist clergyman, advocate of religious freedom, historian. [88]

BERNARD, FRANCIS (c. July 12, 1712-June 16, 1779), colonial governor of New Jersey and Massachusetts. His policies were bitterly opposed by the colonists. [27, 34]

BILLINGS, WILLIAM (Oct. 7, 1746-Sept. 26, 1800), singer and composer of hymns. [127]

BOUCHER, JONATHAN (March 12, 1738-April 27, 1804), Anglican clergyman and Loyalist in the Revolution. [80]

BOWDOIN, JAMES (Aug. 7, 1726-Nov. 6, 1790), public official, merchant, and scientist. Revolutionary leader; governor of Massachusetts. [131]

BRACKENRIDGE, HUGH H. (1748-June 25, 1816), author, jurist, and public official. Friend of Philip Freneau and James Madison; wrote *The Battle of Bunker's Hill* (1776), *The Death of General Montgomery* (1777), *Modern Chivalry* (1792-1815). [139] See also Author Index, Vols. 3, 4.

BRUCE, R. G. (fl. 1766), soldier (?) and art connoisseur. [35]

BURKE, EDMUND (Jan. 12, 1729-July 9, 1797), British statesman, political theorist, and parliamentary orator. Advocated liberality and consistency in dealing with the American colonies; wrote *On American Taxation* (1774), *On Conciliation with America* (1775), *Reflections on the Revolution in France* (1790). [71]

COPLEY, JOHN SINGLETON (July 3, 1738-Sept. 9, 1815), portrait painter. Painter of many prominent figures in Boston and London. [35]

CORBIN, RICHARD (fl. 1759), Virginia plantation owner. [9]

CRESSWELL, NICHOLAS (Dec. 1750-July 14, 1804), English diarist. Lived in America during Revolutionary years. [115]

CRÈVECOEUR, MICHEL GUILLAUME JEAN DE (Jan. 31, 1735-Nov. 12, 1813), author and farmer. Born in Caen, Normandy; officer in Canada; settled in Orange County, New York; wrote *Letters From an American Farmer* (1782). [140]

CROGHAN, GEORGE (?1720-Aug. 31, 1782), Indian agent and trader. Helped establish working relations with many Indian tribes; envisioned greatness of western lands; land speculator in Pennsylvania. [24]

CUSHING, WILLIAM (March 1, 1732-Sept. 13, 1810), jurist. Chief justice of the Massachusetts Supreme Court; associate justice (1789-1810) of the U.S. Supreme Court; member of the first Massachusetts state constitutional convention (1779); member of the Massachusetts Ratifying Convention of 1788. [146]

DARTMOUTH, WILLIAM LEGGE, 2nd Earl of (June 20, 1731-July 15, 1801), secretary of state for the colonies (1772-75). Advocated suppression of colonial uprisings; lord privy seal (1775-82); Dartmouth College was named for him. [53]

DAVIES, SAMUEL (Nov. 3, 1723-Feb. 4, 1761), Presbyterian clergyman. President (1759-61) of the College of New Jersey (Princeton). [6] See also Author Index, Vol. 1.

DICKINSON, JOHN (Nov. 8, 1732-Feb. 14, 1808), lawyer and statesman. "The penman of the Revolution"; member (1774-76) of the Continental Congress and (1782-83) of the Congress of the Confederation; helped write the first draft (1776) of the Articles of Confederation; at first opposed signing the Declaration of Independence; president of the Annapolis Convention (1786); member of the Constitutional Convention (1787). [38, 105]

DULANY, DANIEL (June 28, 1722-March 17, 1797), lawyer and public official for the province of Maryland. Member of the

Governor's Council, commissary general, and province secretary; Loyalist in the Revolution. [29]

DUNMORE, JOHN MURRAY, 4th Earl of (1732-March 5, 1809), colonial governor of New York (1770) and Virginia (1771-75), Scottish peer in the English Parliament, and governor of the Bahamas. [84]

ESTAING, CHARLES HECTOR, Count d' (Nov. 24, 1729-April 28, 1794), French admiral. Commander of the first expedition during the Revolution in support of the colonies; guillotined in Paris during the Reign of Terror. [123]

FITCH, THOMAS (c. 1700-July 18, 1774), lawyer and governor of colonial Connecticut. Directed the revision of Connecticut's legal code; opposed the Stamp Act (1765). [18]

FONTAINE, PETER (fl. 1757), clergyman in Virginia. [4]

FRANKLIN, BENJAMIN (Jan. 17, 1706-April 17, 1790), printer, author, philanthropist, inventor, scientist, diplomat, and statesman. Born Boston; published *Poor Richard's Almanack* (1732-57); signed the Declaration of Independence; in France, 1776-85; member of the Constitutional Convention (1787); author of *Autobiography*. [8, 12, 23, 49, 90] See also Author Index, Vols. 1, 3.

GAGE, THOMAS (1721-April 2, 1787), last colonial governor of Massachusetts and commander in chief of the British forces in North America. [41, 45, 46, 83]

GALLOWAY, JOSEPH (c. 1731-Aug. 29, 1803), lawyer and statesman. Member of the legislature in colonial Pennsylvania; member (1774-75) of the Continental Congress; colonial patriot who opposed separation from England but advocated greater self-government for the colonies; exiled for his beliefs after the Revolution. [13, 60]

GALT, JOHN (May 2, 1779-April 11, 1839), Scottish novelist. Wrote about country life; biographer of Byron; secretary of the Canada Land Company; founded Guelph, Ontario. [14]

GATES, HORATIO (c. 1727-April 10, 1806), Revolutionary general in the Continental

Army. Some unsuccessfully sought to have him replace the commander in chief, George Washington; participated in the two battles of Saratoga. [79]

HAMILTON, ALEXANDER (?Jan. 11, 1755-July 12, 1804), soldier, lawyer, and statesman. Member (1782-83) of the Congress of the Confederation; New York delegate to the Constitutional Convention (1787); author with James Madison and John Jay of *The Federalist* (1787-88); secretary of the treasury (1789-95) under Washington and creator of the first Bank of the United States. Mortally wounded in a duel with Aaron Burr. [125, 128, 138, 145] See also Author Index, Vols. 3, 4.

HENRY, PATRICK (May 29, 1736-June 6, 1799), lawyer, orator, and statesman. Member (1765-73) of the Virginia House of Burgesses; member (1774-75) of the Continental Congress; governor (1776-79, 1784-86); a principal advocate of the Bill of Rights. [72] See also Author Index, Vol. 3.

HOPKINS, SAMUEL (Sept. 17, 1721-Dec. 20, 1803), Congregational theologian, missionary, and philanthropist. Disciple of Jonathan Edwards; one of the earliest opponents of slavery. [108]

HOPKINSON, FRANCIS (Sept. 21, 1737-May 9, 1791), statesman, political satirist, lawyer, and musician. Member (1776) of the Continental Congress; signed the Declaration of Independence; helped design the American flag. [127]

INGLIS, CHARLES (1734-Feb. 24, 1816), first colonial Anglican bishop, missionary to the Mohawk Indians, and Loyalist during the Revolution. [96]

JAY, JOHN (Dec. 12, 1745-May 17, 1829), jurist, diplomat, and statesman. Member (1774) and' president (1778) of the Continental Congress; commissioner to Great Britain (1782); author with James Madison and Alexander Hamilton of *The Federalist* (1787-88); first chief justice (1789-95) of the U.S. Supreme Court. [63] See also Author Index, Vol. 3.

JEFFERSON, THOMAS (April 13, 1743-July 4, 1826), lawyer, architect, agriculturalist, educator, political philosopher, diplomat, and statesman. Third President of the United States (1801-09); member (1775-76) of the Continental Congress; author of the Declaration of Independence; governor of Virginia (1779-81); minister to France (1785-89); secretary of state (1790-93) under Washington; Vice-President of the United States under John Adams; founder of the University of Virginia. [58, 106, 121, 136] See also Author Index, Vols. 3, 4, 5.

JENYNS, SOAME (Jan. 1, 1704-Dec. 18, 1787), English poet and essayist, member of Parliament, and commissioner of the Board of Trade. [31]

LEONARD, DANIEL (May 18, 1740-June 27, 1829), lawyer. Loyalist in the Revolution; chief justice of Bermuda; member of a prominent Massachusetts family. [69]

MITTLEBERGER, GOTTLIEB (fl. 1756), German minister. Traveled to Pennsylvania to observe conditions of German immigrants. [2]

MOORE, HENRY (Feb. 7, 1713-Sept. 11, 1769), colonial governor of Jamaica (1756-62) and of New York (1765-69). [36]

MORRIS, GOUVERNEUR (Jan. 31, 1752-Nov. 6, 1816), lawyer, diplomat, and statesman. Member of the Revolutionary provincial congress of New York (1776-77); signed the Articles of Confederation (1781); member (1777-79) of the Continental Congress and (1787) of the Constitutional Convention; commissioner to England (1790-91); minister to France (1792-94); U.S. senator (1800-03). [54] See also Author Index, Vol. 4.

MORRIS, ROBERT (Jan. 31, 1734-May 7, 1806), merchant and banker. Signed the Declaration of Independence; financier of the Revolution; superintendent of finance under the Articles of Confederation; established (1781) the Bank of North America; member of the Constitutional Convention (1787). [137]

NILES, NATHANIEL (April 3, 1741-Oct. 31, 1828), theologian, politician, inventor, author of "The American Hero." [77]

NOYES, JOSEPH (fl. 1757), clergyman and member of the Corporation of Yale College. [5]

OTIS, JAMES (Feb. 5, 1725-May 23, 1783), lawyer and Revolutionary statesman. Representative to the Massachusetts General Court; influential spokesman for the colonial cause; wrote *The Rights of the British Colonies Asserted and Proved.* [15, 20]

PAINE, THOMAS (Jan. 29, 1737-June 8, 1809), political philosopher, journalist, and pamphleteer. One of the most influential advocates of colonial independence; editor of the *Pennsylvania Magazine;* published *The Crisis* (1776-83); advocated republicanism in France and England; wrote *Common Sense* (1776), *The Rights of Man* (1791-92), *The Age of Reason* (1794, 1796). [94, 95, 111]

POWNALL, THOMAS (1722-Feb. 25, 1805), colonial administrator. Secretary to the governor of New York (1753); lieutenant governor of New Jersey (1755); governor of Massachusetts (1757-60). [19, 133]

RODNEY, THOMAS (June 4, 1744-Jan. 2, 1811), jurist, soldier, and farmer. Delaware delegate (1781-88) to the Congress of the Confederation. [135]

RUSH, BENJAMIN (1745-April 19, 1813), physician, medical educator, and public official. Signed the Declaration of Independence; member (1776-77) of the Continental Congress; treasurer of the United States (1797-1813); his *Medical Inquiries and Observations Upon the Disease of the Mind* (1812) was the first systematic American work on that subject. [40, 112, 116, 118] See also Author Index, Vols. 3, 4.

SEABURY, SAMUEL (Nov. 30, 1729-Feb. 25, 1796), clergyman. First bishop of the Protestant Episcopal Church in U.S.; Loyalist in the Revolution. [67]

SMITH, WILLIAM (Sept. 7, 1727-May 14, 1803), Anglican clergyman and educator. Teacher at and first provost of the Academy and Charitable School of Philadelphia (University of Pennsylvania); established (1757) *The American Magazine and Monthly Chronicle of the British Colonies.* [96]

TRUMBULL, JOHN (June 6, 1756-Nov. 10, 1843), artist, architect, and author. Aide and cartographer to George Washington in the Revolutionary War; president (1817-36) of the American Academy of Fine Arts; painter of four of the eight large pictures in the rotunda of the Capitol at Washington, D.C. [68] See also Author Index, Vol. 3.

WARREN, JOSEPH (June 10, 1741-June 14, 1775), Revolutionary officer and physician. President pro tempore (1775) of the Massachusetts Provincial Congress; killed in the Battle of Bunker Hill. [47, 74]

WASHINGTON, GEORGE (Feb. 22, 1732-Dec. 14, 1799), surveyor, planter, soldier, and statesman. First President of the United States (1789-97); member (1759-74) of the Virginia House of Burgesses; delegate (1774-75) to the Continental Congress; commander (1775-83) of all Continental armies; president of the Constitutional Convention (1787); commander in chief (1798-99) of U.S. Army. [1, 119, 120, 124, 126, 141, 142, 143] See also Author Index, Vols. 3, 4.

WEST, BENJAMIN (Oct. 10, 1738-March 11, 1820), artist. Charter member and president of the Royal Academy; patronized by George III. [35]

WILSON, JAMES (Sept. 14, 1742-Aug. 21, 1798), lawyer and political philosopher. Member (1775-77) of the Continental Congress; signed the Declaration of Independence; advocate general for France (1779); Pennsylvania delegate to the Constitutional Convention (1787); associate justice (1789-98) of the U.S. Supreme Court. [98] See also Author Index, Vol. 3.

WOODMASON, CHARLES (fl. 1767), Anglican clergyman, missionary in South Carolina, and Loyalist in the Revolution. [39]

WOOLMAN, JOHN (Oct. 19, 1720-Oct. 7, 1772), Quaker leader, Abolitionist, and author. His *Journal* (1756-72) is considered a classic record of religious experience. [3, 16]